MASSACRES OF THE MOUNTAINS

AN INDIAN VILLAGE.

MASSACRES OF THE MOUNTAINS

➤—┤◆➤•⊙•◄➤┤—◄

A History of The Indian Wars of the Far West

➤—┤◆➤•⊙•◄➤┤—◄

J. P. DUNN, JR.

With a new introduction by David Dary

STACKPOLE
BOOKS

New introduction copyright © 2002 by Stackpole Books

Published by
STACKPOLE BOOKS
5067 Ritter Road
Mechanicsburg, PA 17055
www.stackpolebooks.com

Cover design by Tracy Patterson
Cover illustration: "Joseph's Last Battle," from Chapter 19

Printed in the United States of America

10 9 8 7 6 5 4 3 2 1

FIRST EDITION

Library of Congress Cataloging-in-Publication Data

Dunn, Jacob Piatt, 1855–1924.
    Massacres of the mountains : a history of the Indian wars of the Far West, 1815–1875 / Jacob P. Dunn ; with a new introduction by David Dary.— 1st ed.
        p. cm. — (Frontier Classics)
    Originally published: New York : Harper, 1886.
    Includes bibliographical references and index.
    ISBN 0-8117-2813-7
        1. Indians of North America—Wars—1815–1875. 2. Indians of North America—Wars—1866–1895. 3. Indians of North America—Wars—West (U.S.) I. Title.
    II. Series.

E81 .D92 2002
973'.0497—dc21   2002018730

CONTENTS.

CHAPTER I.

PAGE

INTRODUCTORY 1

CHAPTER II.

THE ACQUISITION OF THE MOUNTAINS 27

CHAPTER III.

THE ONE OFFENCE OF THE PUEBLOS 49

CHAPTER IV.

THE MURDER OF THE MISSIONARIES 80

CHAPTER V.

THE CURSE OF GOLD 118

CHAPTER VI.

OATMAN FLAT 151

CHAPTER VII.

THE ROGUE RIVER, YAKIMA, AND KLICKITAT WARS 189

CHAPTER VIII.

ASH HOLLOW AND THE CHEYENNE EXPEDITION 219

CHAPTER IX.

LOS NABAJOS 244

CHAPTER X.

MOUNTAIN MEADOWS 273

CHAPTER XI.

THE WAR WITH THE SPOKANES, CŒUR D'ALÊNES, AND PELOUSES . . 324

CHAPTER XII.   PAGE
DEATH TO THE APACHE!.. 356

CHAPTER XIII.
SAND CREEK... 396

CHAPTER XIV.
CAÑON DE CHELLY AND BOSQUE REDONDO....................... 447

CHAPTER XV.
FORT PHIL KEARNEY... 477

CHAPTER XVI.
PUNISHING THE PIEGANS..................................... 509

CHAPTER XVII.
THE TRAGEDY OF THE LAVA BEDS.............................. 543

CHAPTER XVIII.
THE LITTLE BIG HORN....................................... 584

CHAPTER XIX.
JOSEPH'S NEZ PERCÉS....................................... 629

CHAPTER XX.
WHITE RIVER AGENCY.. 675

CHAPTER XXI.
CRUELTY, PITY, AND JUSTICE................................ 716

LIST OF AUTHORITIES....................................... 757

INDEX... 765

ILLUSTRATIONS.

An Indian Village .... *Frontispiece*

Map of the Indian Reservations within the United States.... *faces page* 1

The Northwest in 1841.................................. " " 84

	PAGE		PAGE
Santa Anna...................	28	Piute Squaw and Papoose.....	126
Traders Approaching Santa Fé.	30	The Yosemite	130
Colonel Zebulon Pike	31	Yosemite from the Mariposa	
A Trail in the Sierra San Juan.	39	Trail......................	134
John C. Fremont..............	48	Beach Fishing at Cape Mendo-	
Kearny's Soldiers Crossing the		cino.......................	136
Mountains..................	50	How the Diggers Fought......	139
Restoration of Pueblo Hungo		A Group of Diggers..........	141
Pavie...............	53	The Ruins of San Carlos de	
Casas Grandas — Ruins in Ari-		Monterey..................	146
zona	55	View near the Gila...........	153
Ruins of Pueblo Pintado......	57	Pima Girls	156
Council in the Estufa at Zuñi..	59	Pima Village	160
Pueblo of Taos—South Pueblo.	63	Antonio Azul.................	161
Sterling Price	70	Scene of Oatman Massacre....	169
Pueblo of Taos—North Pueblo	71	Irataba, Mohave Chief	175
Plan of Storming Pueblo de		Pasqual, Yuma Chief	179
Taos......................	75	A Mohave Dwelling..........	182
Chinook Woman and Child....	82	Old Fort Yuma..............	185
Indian Sweat-house..........	84	Charles D. Poston	187
Chemakane Mission..........	91	General Joe Lane.............	189
Old Fort Walla-Walla........	97	Philip Kearny...............	192
Medicine-man Destroying Girl		Mount Shasta from Valley of	
by Necromancy............	103	Sacramento.................	197
Fort Vancouver in 1850.......	111	The Dalles	205
John A. Sutter	120	Seattle	209
Valley of the American River at		Spearing Salmon at the Cascades	213
Time of Discovery of Gold..	123	The Cascades................	215

PAGE

Cheyenne Village............. 220
Indian Village on the Move... 222
Squaws Curing Robes......... 228
Sioux Hunting Buffalo........ 230
On the Oregon Trail.......... 233
Before the Days of Stage Sta-
    tions....................... 237
Bound for Pike's Peak........ 241
Cañons in the Navajo Country. 247
Navaho Squaws Weaving a
    Blanket.................... 251
Chapitone.................... 257
Fort Defiance................. 259
Mesa of Chusca Mountains.... 264
Navajo in War Costume...... 266
Group of Navahos............ 269
Washakie.................... 276
Ute Squaws of Utah.......... 278
Snake Indians of Utah........ 280
President John Taylor........ 284
Brigham Young.............. 288
Cactus in Desert.............. 292
John D. Lee.................. 296
Scene of Massacre............ 303
Kanosh...................... 307
George Q. Cannon............ 315
Execution of John D. Lee.... 321
The Jesuit Missionary........ 326
Pend d'Oreille Mission........ 329
General Isaac I. Stevens...... 332
View of the Columbia above the
    Dalles..................... 337
Charge of Cavalry at Four Lakes 339
Falls of the Spokane.......... 345
Cœur d'Alêne Mission........ 349
An Apache Warrior.......... 360
Black Knife.................. 363
Silver Mines of Santa Rita.... 375
A Record of Mangas Colorado. 382
Papago Chief................. 384

PAGE

Apache Crucified by Papagos.. 387
Apaches Watching a Train.... 390
Tubac....................... 393
Apache Boot, Head-dress, etc.. 395
Texan Rangers............... 399
Old Fort Union............... 405
Standing off the Cheyennes.... 409
Which Tribe Did It?......... 413
Little Raven.................. 418
Friday—a Good Arapahoe..... 421
George Bent.................. 425
On the Little Blue........... 428
Indians Attacking Stage....... 432
Indian Scouts Celebrating..... 435
The Charge on Black Kettle's
    Camp...................... 441
Giant's Arm-chair............. 449
Cañon de Chelly.............. 454
Cliff House in Cañon de Chelly. 459
Colonel Kit Carson........... 463
Near the Head-waters of the
    Navaho.................... 469
Moqui Pueblo................. 473
Prospectors in the Mountains.. 478
Spotted Tail.............faces 482
On the Bozeman Trail........ 485
Torture by Prairie Indians.... 489
Fort Phil Kearney and Vicinity. 493
The Last Stand............... 497
Red Cloud................... 501
Sioux Village in Winter...... 505
Blackfeet and Trappers....... 512
Trader's Camp............... 515
"No Horses to Spare"....... 519
Edmonton House............. 525
Fort Benton.................. 529
Lieut.-general P. H. Sheridan.. 533
Summer Camp on Marias River 539
Map of the Modoc Country... 544
Modoc Squaws............... 547

	PAGE
Major-general E. R. S. Canby	551
A View of the Caves	555
View of Camp and Lake	557
The Rev. Dr. Thomas	560
General Alvin Gillem	566
Donald McKay, Leader of the Scouts	572
General Jefferson C. Davis	575
Captain Jack and Companions	579
The Bad Lands	586
Sitting Bull's First Adventure	592
Sitting Bull Storms a Crow Encampment and Takes Thirty Scalps	593
Sitting Bull Scalps a Teamster	594
Sitting Bull Steals a Drove of Horses	595
Old Fort Reno—Crook's Supply Camp	599
Rosebud River	605
Plan of Custer's Fight on the Little Big Horn	613
Massacre Monument	619
Major-general George A. Custer	622
Sitting Bull	625
Young Joseph	630
Ollacut	635
General O. O. Howard	638
Lapwai	643
Plain of the Geysers	653
The Stinking Water	656
General S. D. Sturgis	657
Joseph's Last Battle	661
General N. A. Miles	669
The Snowy Range	677
Ouray	683
Henry M. Teller	686
Captain Billy	689
Southern Utes	693
Jack	696
Colorow	700
Antelope	703
Plan of White River Agency	707
Douglas	710
Major T. T. Thornburgh	713
Haunts of the Apaches	718
Effect of Extermination Policy on Arizona Settler	720
General George Crook	728
General Pope	741
San Xavier del Bac	745
Crook's Battle-field in the Sierra Madre	751
Alcatraz Island	753

INTRODUCTION

by David Dary

A half century ago the dean of Chicago antiquarian booksellers, Wright Howes, compiled what is considered to be the "bible" of Americana bibliographies, *U.S.IANA: A Selective Bibliography in Which are Described 11,620 Uncommon and Significant Books Relating to the Continental Portion of the United States*. Howes listed Jacob P. Dunn's *Massacres of the Mountains: A History of the Indian Wars of the Far West* and described the book as the "best single volume covering the subject."

That was more than sixty years after Dunn's book was first published in 1886 by Harper and Brothers on Franklin Square in New York. The first edition of Dunn's 784-page work was published in olive green cloth with line drawings of Indian teepees across the bottom front cover and red Indian pictographs over a field of gold across the top. In between are the title and the author's name printed in gilt letters outlined in black. Between the book's two covers are twenty-one chapters, a chapter by chapter listing of his sources, a fold-out map showing Indian reservations in the United States in 1884, another map of the Pacific Northwest in 1841, more than 160 illustrations, and a comprehensive index. In 1886 Dunn's book sold for $3.75 a copy.

Exactly how many copies of the first edition were printed is not known, but today copies in very good condition sell for several hundred dollars and are much sought after by collectors of Western Americana. Dunn's book is valuable not only because of its scarcity on the antiquarian book trade, but also because of the fact that Dunn was the first historian to use government documents as his primary source to chronicle the Indian Wars. Dunn's scholarly treatment outlined where and why the Indian Wars occurred, the difficulties behind them, who started them, and how they ended.

When *Massacres of the Mountains* was first published in 1886, the book was quickly recognized as a minor classic and Dunn gained national recognition. Custer's defeat in the Battle of the Little Big Horn had occurred only ten years earlier, and the Indian Wars in the West were not yet over.

The battles between whites and Indians that occurred following the Civil War were still fresh in the minds of most Americans. There were strong sentiments on both sides of what many called "the Indian issue."

Between May and August 1886, Dunn's book was widely reviewed by newspapers and magazines in New York; Boston; St. Louis; Chicago; Hartford, Connecticut; Williamstown, Massachusetts; and Providence, Rhode Island. The May 8 issue of *The Keynote* in New York City devoted nearly a full page to the book and included an illustration from the book depicting an Indian fishing with a spear. The paper's unidentified reviewer wrote, in part:

> Mr. Dunn gives an unbiased opinion of the Indian character, he does not allow the admiration he may feel for aboriginals carry him away. He is keenly alive to their many faults, their laziness and dissipation, and if he finds much good in them as a race, he also finds much that is bad. Very few American writers discuss the subject calmly; they either err on one side or the other. One author is rabid in his desire to have the Indians exterminated; another sentimentalizes over their decay as a nation, and places all of the blame at the doors of the government. The perfect fairness with which Mr. Dunn has described the causes and results of the Indian Wars, makes his book an invaluable addition to American History. It is for the reader to decide who deserves the blame and who the praise.
>
> The author possesses a scholarly style and fluent powers of expression. Of the many descriptions of "The Mountain Meadows Massacre," none have been so complete as his, nor so finely written. He has drawn largely from the best authorities and State documents for proof of every occurrence, and the result is a volume which, in completeness of detail and historical value, has no equal in American literature.

Another reviewer wrote in *The Critic,* published in New York City on May 15:

> Despite the somewhat sensational cast of its leading title, it may be characterized as a thoroughly sensible book. Of the many volumes which have been written on our Indian wars, this of Mr. Dunn is entitled to rank among the best,

if not as the very best. The admirable work of the lamented Helen Jackson—her *Century of Dishonor*—is in some respects more comprehensive, and is wonderfully touching and effective; but it is rather a series of pleadings than a history. Mr. Dunn is not an advocate, nor yet is he, on the other hand, a mere analyst. He writes impartially, but with spirit and feeling, weighing the merits and faults of both parties, and distributing praise and blame judicially, according to their respective deserts. He delivers his judgments without fear or favor, and strikes without hesitation at the highest crests. Cabinet ministers, federal generals, Roman Catholic bishops, are dealt with as severely as thievish Indian agents and Mormon murderers.

George Parsons Lathrope, reviewing Dunn's book in the New York *Star*, June 6, also remarked on the book's "sensational" title but that it was "fully justified by the contents, which are drawn from the unexaggerated facts of our movement westward and our relation to the Indians." Lathrope adds:

> The trend of evidence in this book is very strong toward proving that we have dealt with the Indians atrociously, savagely. The mere array of facts is a most potent argument for some more intelligent and human policy. Not impossibly historians ages hence, inferring to such records as these, will conclude that the white men of the United States were merely a more enlightened species of barbarians who swept across the continent displacing the feebler red barbarians and the relics of old. . . . We have much to do in perfecting our civilization.

Reviews in the New York *Telegram* (April 17, 1886), *Graphic* (May 1), and *Evening Post* (July 1) were similarly positive, as was Estes & Lauriat's review in the Boston *Transcript* on August 25. The reviewers noted: "The author believes that, if treated with justice and fairness, the Indians may in the course of time be brought to a self-reliant, honorable manhood."

The reviewer for another Boston newspaper, the *Congregationalist*, August 5, wrote:

> Of course the narrative is one of terrible and repeated outrages upon the different Indian tribes. These can be

neither denied nor palliated. The worse treacheries and brutalities of which any Indians have been guilty towards the whites have been only the natural result of the behavior of the whites, and of the United States government, towards the tribes. The most peaceable and orderly Indians appear to have been treated with as little consideration as the most vicious and hostile. Mr. Dunn makes this plain, yet he shows no sentimental regard for the Indian, but rather a dislike. He means to deal fairly with both sides, and we think he generally succeeds. But in the cases of individuals he sometimes goes too far. For example, the contemptuous tone of his criticism of Colonel (now General) Carrington in regard to the Fort Phil Kearney affair is unworthy of such a book, and the severity of it is wholly unjustifiable in view of the fact, which he has to admit, that 'the commission which investigated the affair exonerated Carrington altogether.' This illustrates one defect of the work, a tendency to impassioned language which is not quite in order in historical writing of this sort.

Of sixteen known reviews of Dunn's book published during the spring and summer of 1886, the one in the *Congregationalist* contained the most criticism. Still, it had a positive tone. All of the reviews undoubtedly attracted attention to Dunn's book and helped its sales. One person who purchased a copy was twenty-eight-year-old Theodore Roosevelt, then at work researching and writing *The Winning of the West*, a four-volume series. He read and was impressed by Dunn's book. Less than two years later, Roosevelt again read the book and was moved to send Dunn a letter from his Oyster Bay Home on Long Island. Dated April 22, 1888, Roosevelt wrote:

Dear Sir:
Being obliged, in the course of some studies I have recently made, to re-read your admirable book, I have been so struck with its absolute fairness and incisive truthfulness that I can not forbear writing to express my appreciation. I only regret that you did not include all the Indian wars west of the Mississippi. My own experience with Indians has been very limited, yet I could substantiate ever therefrom statement after statement you make. I could give fifty instances of white wrong doing that would

please even "H.H." [Helen Hunt Jackson] and fifty more that would make the average citizen take the ultra-border view of an Indian. The average writer gives merely one set of cases; and I am glad that there is as fair a history as yours to serve—as I have no doubt it will—as one of our standards. I also like Colonel Dodge's book.

I was particularly pleased with your accounts of the Oregon and Mormon massacres, the Sand Creek affair and Chief Joseph's campaign.

Very truly yours
Theodore Roosevelt

Not surprisingly, when the first volume of Roosevelt's *The Winning of the West* was published a year later in 1889, he wrote that Dunn's book and two earlier works by Col. Richard Irving Dodge—*The Hunting Grounds of the Great West* (1877) and *Our Wild Indians: Thirty-Three Years' Personal Experience Among the Red Men of the Great West* (1882)—provided readers with a "fair idea of the Indians of the present day [1889] and of our dealings with them."

Reflecting the controversy of the time, Roosevelt criticized others who had written about Indians, including Helen Hunt Jackson and George W. Manypenny. He called them "zealous reformers" and "foolish sentimentalists." Manypenny wrote *Our Indian Wards* (1880) and Jackson produced *A Century of Dishonor: A Sketch of the United States Government's Dealing With Some of the Indian Tribes* (1881). Roosevelt wrote that Jackson's work was,

a mere spiteful diatribe against various Army officers, and neither its manner nor its matter warrants more than an allusion. Mrs. Jackson's book is capable of doing more harm because it is written in good English, and because the author, who had lived a pure and noble life, was intensely in earnest in what she wrote, and had the most praiseworthy purpose—to prevent our committing any more injustice to the Indians. This was all most proper, every good man or woman should do whatever is possible to make the government treat the Indians of the present time in the fairest and most generous spirit, and to provide against any repetition of such outrages as were inflicted upon the Nez Perces and upon part of the Cheyennes, or the wrongs with which the civilized nations of the Indian territory are sometimes threatened. The purpose of the book is excellent, but the spirit in which it is written cannot be called even technically honest. . . . It is not too much to say that the book is thoroughly untrustworthy from cover to cover, and that not a single statement it contains should be accepted without independent proof, for even those that are not absolutely false are often as bad on account of so much of the truth having been suppressed.

Roosevelt asked his readers to compare Jackson's accounts of the Sioux and the Plains tribes to those in Colonel Dodge's works, "or her recital of the Sandy Creek massacre with the facts as stated by Mr. Dunn, who is apt, if anything, to lean to the Indian's side." Dunn, however, was not as negative toward Jackson as was Roosevelt. Helen Hunt Jackson died in August 1885, about a year before Dunn's book was published by the same publisher who produced Hunt's book, and he used a footnote in *Massacres of the Mountains* to tell of her death, adding, "the Indians of America lost one of the most active and intelligent friends they ever had." Later in his book, after describing how Indians in California had been treated, Dunn writes: "It is hardly possible, if we are to retain any faith whatever in a common humanity, that these wrongs can be pushed any farther. The reports of B. C. Whiting, in 1871, of John G. Ames, in 1873, and of Helen Hunt Jackson, with various unofficial publications, have brought these things home keenly to people who are capable of shame over a national disgrace."

Dunn argued against the government's concentration of the Indians on reservations mainly on the grounds that the policy hindered their being "civilized." Roosevelt favored a national and equitable Indian policy, but he firmly believed that the Indian nations had no claim to the land they inhabited and were in fact nomadic people whose temperament lacked a desire to hold property.

After reading *Massacres of the Mountains*, Roosevelt might have wondered what motivated a Hoosier to write such a book. Whether or not Roosevelt looked into Dunn's background is not known. If he had, Roosevelt would have found insights in Dunn's background and education. Dunn's father, Jacob Piatt Dunn, Sr., was born at Lawrenceburg, Indiana, on June 24, 1811, where his parents had settled in 1806. Lawrenceburg was a small town located in Dearborn County, Indiana, on the Ohio River just across the border from Cincinnati. At the age of eighteen Jacob P. Dunn, Sr., made his living in the mercantile business. In 1849, at the age of 38, he joined thirteen other Lawrenceburg men and started with ox teams for the gold fields of California. Led by his brother, George Dunn, the company left Lawrenceburg by boat on May 6, 1849, traveled to St. Louis and then to St. Joseph, Missouri, where they crossed the Missouri River on June 3. From there their company traveled overland via South Pass, the Humboldt River, and Lassen Cutoff to Long's Bar, California, and into the gold fields.

Whether Jacob P. Dunn, Sr., struck it rich in California is not known, but six pages of his recollections of the overland journey may be found today in the files of the Indiana Historical Society. He relates how his company passed perhaps a thousand fresh graves on the plains, the remains of people traveling ahead of Dunn's party who had died of cholera. He also relates how the Sioux, demoralized by the disease, would come to his company's wagons to beg for medicine and would abandon their sick in their teepees.

Soon after Jacob P. Dunn, Sr., returned to Lawrenceburg in 1854, his wife became pregnant and on April 12, 1855, Jacob P. Dunn, Jr., was born in Lawrenceburg. Not long after his son was born, Jacob P. Dunn, Sr., moved his family to a farm formerly owned by Gen. Joseph Lane along the Ohio River in Vanderburg County, Indiana. There the family remained until 1859, when they moved back to Lawrenceburg. In 1861, about the time the Civil War began, Dunn moved his family to Indianapolis. It was then that Jacob P. Dunn, Jr., began his schooling in the city's public schools.

One can imagine that after Jacob P. Dunn, Jr., was old enough to understand, his father related stories about his adventures crossing the plains and mountains of the West. Those stories probably made a deep impression in the young boy's mind. Young Jacob Dunn is described as showing much maturity for a boy of his age. After his public schooling, Dunn entered Earlham College at Richmond, Indiana, operated by the Religious Society of Friends (Quakers). At the age of nineteen, Dunn received his bachelor of science degree from Earlham College.

First established as a boarding school in 1847, Earlham added a collegiate department and became a college in 1859. Then, as today, Earlham College prepared students for life. Its mission statement emphasizes "the pursuit of truth, wherever that pursuit leads; lack of coercion, letting the evidence lead that search; respect for the consciences of others; openness to new truth and the willingness to search; veracity, rigorous integrity in dealing with the facts; application of what is known to improving our world."

Dunn followed this creed in his work and throughout much of his life. Two years before he was graduated from Earlham College, he made a temperance pledge in 1874 which he apparently kept. After Earlham College, Dunn enrolled in the University of Michigan and in 1876 received his bachelor of laws degree. Returning to Indiana, Dunn practiced law at

Indianapolis until 1879, when his father sent him and two brothers to Colorado to look after their father's stake in silver mines and to prospect themselves. Failing to find any riches, Jacob became a journalist and served as a reporter for newspapers in Denver and Leadville. During this time he became seriously interested in the history of the American Indians. Five years later, in 1884, Dunn returned to Indianapolis to practice law and continue to research Indian history for *Massacres of the Mountains.*

Dunn's book is for the most part an even-handed work. Although he uses government documents for sources in chronicling the Indian battles, the reformer in Dunn comes through as he argues against the government's concentration of the Indians on reservations, principally on the grounds that the policy hindered their being "civilized." Dunn seeks to educate by asking his readers not to stereotype Indians. (Dunn, of course, does not use the word "stereotype," which in 1886 had yet to be coined.) In Dunn's words, "Just here let me caution the reader that if he wishes to understand Indian history, he must not be deluded by that false truth, so popular in America, that 'an Indian is an Indian.' There are tribes now existing that have never raised a hostile hand against us, though they have been sorely tried. There are Indians that, so far as race characteristics and race prejudices are concerned, have no identity with the typical Indian, except in the fact that they have been maltreated by the whites."

Toward the end of his introduction, Dunn writes,

> The Indian problem is not solved. It will require years of patient effort to bring these people to a self-reliant, honorable, civilized manhood. It is extremely impolitic to do anything needlessly that will increase the difficulties in the way. If not impeded, humanity and charity will solve the problem, but the "peace policy" of the past eighteen years [1868–1886] will not do it. It is no humanity to offer a man a theoretically better home, and kill him because he will not accept it.
>
> It is no charity to give a man a nickel with one hand, and rob him of five dollars' worth of property with the other. It is no Christianity to starve a man, and offer him a Sunday-school by way of extreme unction. Let us be honest and fair with the Indian, and temper our justice with religion and education.

While Dunn's *Massacres of the Mountains* provides readers with background information on Indians and their relations with whites beginning in 1815, the bulk of his work focuses on their place in the history of the westward movement beyond the Great Plains. He documents atrocities on both white and Indian sides and seeks to show why and how they occurred. This is especially true in his accounts of both the Modoc War and the Sand Creek massacre, in the latter of which he defends the actions of Colonel Chivington and brands the Cheyenne as fiends. Dunn's account of the Modoc Indians is accurate but brief. He does not record the end of the Apache wars because *Massacres of the Mountains* was published the same year Geronimo surrendered to Gen. Nelson A. Miles in Arizona. The last of twenty-one chapters in Dunn's book titled "Cruelty, Pity, and Justice" concerns the Apaches in Arizona up to about 1883. Dunn writes: "There has been much talk of removing the Apaches from Arizona, which, if it were attempted, would produce war; it would be a terrible war too. The Apaches cannot be driven about like cattle. On the other hand, if the policy of the last three years is followed to its proper limits—if the Apaches are treated fairly, and all disturbing causes are removed, as far as possible— there is no reason why these demons of the past should not continue to develop into a quiet, self-sustaining people."

While the serious reader of *Massacres of the Mountains* can sense Dunn's desire for political reform, twenty-five years passed after the book's publication before he set down in writing his philosophy about the blending of history and politics. In the December 1910 issue of *Indiana Magazine of History*, Dunn agreed with the Roman historian Tacitus that the "chief use of history is to promote good government." He noted that the democracy of his own day was a far cry from the absolute monarch of Tacitus's time. Dunn then theorized:

> History in our times is the record of progress in civilization and government. It is the record of experience of the state, and a state should profit by its experiences just as an individual does. But there is this difference: An individual carries the memory of his experience with him, while the governing powers of a state are frequently changed, and the experience of one generation is lost to following ones, unless it be recorded in some permanent way.

Dunn abandoned his profession as a lawyer in 1888 to join the staff of the Indianapolis *Journal.* That same year his *Indiana, a Redemption from Slavery,* a state history of more than five hundred pages was published. Late that year, at the annual meeting of the Indiana Historical Society, Dunn sponsored a resolution calling for women to be admitted as members. His effort failed. It was not until 1907 that women were given membership. Meanwhile, Dunn's newspaper editorial work gained him prominence in Indiana politics. Dunn became head of the Indiana Democratic State Central Committee's literary bureau in 1888, and, for his support of the Democratic party, was elected state librarian in 1889 and 1891, working to modernize the State Library and serving on the Indiana Public Library Commission for twenty years.

In the early 1890s Dunn joined the editorial staff of the Indianapolis *Sentinel* and for a time served as editor. In his spare time he completed another book, *Documents Relating to the French Settlements on the Wabash*, published in 1894. While Dunn later wrote for three additional Indianapolis newspapers—the *Star*, *News*, and the *Times*—he continued his historical research on Indians, and in 1908 published *True Indian Stories with Glossary of Indiana Indian Names* at Indianapolis. The book contains factual Indian tales that Dunn had collected.

By then Dunn was trying to preserve the language of the Miami Indians. For a time the U.S. Bureau of American Ethnology funded his linguistic work, but he failed to find financial backers for his proposed Society for the Preservation of Indian Languages. He did not live to see his dictionary of the Miami Indian language published, but Charles Frederick Voegelin included it in *Shawnee Stems and the Jacob P. Dunn Miami Dictionary*, which was published in five volumes by the Indiana Historical Society beginning in 1938. A year before the first volume appeared, the society published his daughter's 59-page work *Jacob Piatt Dunn: His Miami Language Studies and Indian Manuscript Collection*. Caroline Dunn (1903–1994), who later became librarian at the Indiana Historical Society, wrote that her father regarded the American Indian "as neither 'savage' nor 'noble,' but as another human being. He had a sympathetic attitude toward them and an understanding of their point of view in the treatment accorded them by the whites and by the United States government."

In 1902, Dunn ran for a seat in Indiana's Seventh Congressional District but lost. He then served as Indianapolis city comptroller for two terms (1904–1906 and 1914–16). Between his two terms, Dunn produced in 1910 *Greater Indianapolis*, a two-volume work that has been the city's standard history for nearly a century. As he ended his second term as Indianapolis city comptroller, Dunn was working to reverse Indiana's poor national reputation and to inspire Hoosiers to take a genuine sense of pride in their state. Although Dunn mainly blamed Indiana's political corruption for giving his state its sordid national standing, he pointed out that part of the blame also rested on "ignorance on the part of ourselves and of the world at large of what Indiana has to be proud of. We put in our time reading Eastern periodicals, studying European politics, and striving in general to keep up with what we call the progress of the century, instead of noting the real progress that is being made on all sides of us."

In the midst of his efforts to improve Indiana's reputation and at the same time to give Hoosiers a sense of pride in their state, Dunn produced a surprisingly objective five-volume state history, *Indiana and Indianans* in 1919. Like most of his books, it is still useful today. Although Dunn never became a giant in Indiana's political history, he is credited with having done more than any other person in working behind the scenes and in public to reduce fraud and ensure honest elections in Indiana. He once said, "The corruption of the ballot destroys the very foundation of popular government, and if that be not guarded, the rest is not worth guarding."

In 1921, when Dunn was sixty-six years old, his interest in mining was rekindled and he joined a group of prominent Indianapolis men in organizing the Hispaniola Mining Company to search for mineral deposits in Haiti. Appointed the company's field agent, he traveled to the Caribbean island to explore possible mining sites. After three months of searching without success, he returned to Indianapolis.

In 1924, at the age of sixty-nine, Jacob P. Dunn, Jr., died. His books on Indiana remain prominent among the literature of his native state, but Dunn's national reputation rests on *Massacres of the Mountains*. John A. Hawgood, an Englishman who wrote about the history of the American West, considered it a classic, as did Nebraskan John G. Neihardt, who relied heavily on Dunn in writing both *A Cycle of the West*, and his most widely known prose work, *Black Elk Speaks*. The late historian Ray Allen Billington drew on Dunn's work in writing several editions of his book *Westward Expansion: A History of the American Frontier*, first published in 1949.

In the area of bibliography, Dunn's book is cited in Josephus Nelson Larned's five-volume *History for Ready Reference, from the Best Historians, Biographers, and Specialists*, first published by the C. A. Nichols Co. in Springfield, Massachusetts, 1894–95. T. N. Luther, an authority on George Armstrong Custer, described Dunn's work in his *Custer High Spots* (1972) as "one of the more thoughtful, carefully researched books appearing on this phase of Western history up to that time [1886]." It is also listed as a reliable source in the *Harvard Guide to American History* (1974), and included in Chad J. Flake's *Mormon Bibliography, 1830–1930: Books, Pamphlets, Periodicals, and Broadsides Relating to the First Century of Mormonism* published in Salt Lake City by the University of Utah Press in 1978. More recently (1977), Dunn's place in history was recognized by the Indiana Historical Society's publication of Ray E. Boomhower's biography, *Jacob Piatt Dunn, Jr.: A Life in History and Politics, 1855–1924.*

Jacob P. Dunn's *Massacres of the Mountains* is indeed a classic on the American Indian wars. His pioneering use of using government documents as source material led the way for other historians who followed. It is good to see the work reprinted in Stackpole's Frontier Classics series, where it is again available to a wide audience. Ultimately, it may help to attract new attention to the Indian Wars, an era too often overshadowed by other periods of American history.

MASSACRES OF THE MOUNTAINS.

CHAPTER I.

INTRODUCTORY.

" Two hundred years ago it required millions to express in
numbers the Indian population, while at the present time
less than half the number of thousands will suffice for the
purpose." This quotation from General Custer is a concise
expression of the most common and, perhaps, most remarkable delusion concerning the American Indians. There are
at present in the United States, exclusive of Alaska, about
270,000 Indians. Doubling this number and increasing it
to millions would give a population of 540,000,000 for two
hundred years ago. It may possibly occur to the reader that
an estimate for that period of from nine to ten times our
present total population is somewhat exaggerated. It is exaggerated. There were never 500,000,000 Indians within
the present bounds of the United States, nor 50,000,000, nor
5,000,000; at the time of the discovery of America by Columbus there were possibly 1,000,000, but more probably
there were only about one-half of that number. Some
modern authorities of the highest rank maintain that there
has been no decrease at all since the close of the fifteenth century. What the number may have been at that time is a
matter of conjecture, but there are certain rules of population, and some more or less reliable statistical data, that give
a solution of the problem within limits. The most important
of these is the estimate by the amount of land necessary to
support one man in the pure hunter state, $i.e.$, when subsisting wholly by the chase. This is an indeterminate quantity,
estimates having ranged all the way from 6000 to 50,000

1

acres, but the most plausible estimate is that of Mr. School-craft, whose extensive acquaintance with Indian life and history, coupled with a discerning and logical mind, made him an authority of great weight on such a question. He says, "Estimates were made by me, while residing in the West, that it required 8000 acres of land, to be kept in a wilderness state, in order to support a single Indian by the chase. Consequently a family of five persons would need 40,000 acres." Applying this estimate to our territory of 3,010,000 square miles, or 1,926,600,000 acres (still excluding Alaska), we should have a population of 240,000; but there are two reasons why an estimate of this kind cannot be considered accurate.

Primarily, the Indians can hardly be said to have been in the pure hunter state. Almost every tribe cultivated maize, and some cultivated other edible plants. Notably agricultural were the Pueblo and Pima Indians, of New Mexico and Arizona, and, in the opinion of the writer, the Navahos devoted far less attention to agriculture fifty years ago than they did three centuries before, for they had not, at the earlier date, the flocks which subsequently furnished their chief support. Inasmuch as the rudest agriculture will materially decrease the number of acres required for support, the number of inhabitants must reasonably be supposed to have been in excess of the result attained by the method mentioned. As a second consideration, by the number of acres required for support in the pure hunter state is meant the number of acres that will afford a continuing support; in other words, the hunter must be supported by the natural increase of the game, so that his preserves will not become less capable of supporting him. There is evidence tending to show that a state of evenly balanced supply and demand did not exist in America, but that the game was slowly decreasing under the slowly increasing demands of the aboriginal inhabitants.

This is certainly true of the buffalo, the best food animal of the country, for it formerly existed as far east as the Atlantic; and it disappeared east of the Mississippi River before the whites had fairly come in contact with it. Purchas relates that the early Virginia colonists, prior to 1613, had discovered, "a slow kinde of cattell, as bigge as kine, which were good meate;" and Hakluyt published, in 1589, of some animals then existing in Newfoundland, "I did see them farre off, not able to discerne them perfectly, but their steps showed that their feete were cloven, and bigger than the feete of camels. I suppose them to be a kind of buffes, which I read to be in the countreys adjacent, and very many in the firme land." The supposition has been advanced that these were musk-oxen, which may possibly be correct. A more certain testimony is found in the "New English Canaan," by Thomas Morton, one of the first settlers of New England, published in 1637. He says, "The Indians have also made description of great heards of well-growne beasts that live about the parts of this lake (Erocoise,) now Lake Champlain, such as the Christian world (until this discovery) hath not bin made acquainted with. These beasts are of the bigness of a cowe, their flesh being very good foode, their hides good leather; their fleeces very useful, being a kind of woole, as fine almost as the woole of the beaver; and the salvages do make garments thereof. It is tenne yeares since first the relation of these things came to the eares of the English." Colonel Croghan in his journal (1765) mentions buffalo as being very numerous at different points in Ohio and Indiana, and says that at the Big Lick on the Great Miami they "came into a large road which the Buffaloes have beaten, spacious enough for two waggons to go abreast, and leading straight into the Lick." Still these animals were so nearly extinct east of the Mississippi, when the white emigration began moving over the Alleghanies, that even their former existence there is not a matter of universal cognizance. In the histories of forty and fifty years ago mention is sometimes made of old hunters who remember to have killed buffalo in Ohio, Indiana, or Kentucky, but seldom is anything recorded to indicate that there were ever large numbers of them in these sections. It is an historical truth that the white man had little to do with the extinction of the buffalo east of the Mississippi, though he may claim a large share in the more recent work of extermination on the plains and in the Rocky

Mountains.* This excess of demand for food above the supply indicates an excess of population over that which has been estimated from the basis of the pure hunter state.

On the other hand, as one of the largest estimates by any person whose opinions are entitled to serious consideration, may be taken the statement of Mr. Jefferson of the number of the Virginia tribes. On the authority of Captain Smith and other early colonists he estimates the Powhatan confederacy, which occupied about 8000 square miles, to have consisted of 8000 souls—one to a square mile. If this were correct, and similar conditions existed elsewhere, it would indicate a population of 3,000,000 for the United States; but in addition to the consideration that the opinions of the early settlers were probably exaggerated, there are others which show this estimate to be neither correct nor a proper basis for a general estimate. In 1669 the census taken by order of the Assembly of Virginia showed the Powhatan confederacy to number only about one-third of the earlier estimate. If the natives of Virginia had decreased at the rate of sixty-six per cent. in sixty years, the Indians would have been extinct long ago; for the natives of the entire country elsewhere have suffered from more wars, more disease, and more whiskey, proportionately, since then, than they did in Virginia in those years. The more reasonable inference is that the original estimate was two or three times too large.

The country occupied by the Powhatan confederacy was one of the most fertile and salubrious regions within our boundaries. The Indians there subsisted largely on cultivated plants and vegetable food of natural growth, besides having the fish and oysters of their numerous streams and inlets, which, if we may credit the early chroniclers, existed in astonishing abundance, and were taken by the natives in many ingenious ways. Fully one-third of the United States afforded no such adventitious supplies to the hunter, and in many

---

* The bison, formerly found in nearly all parts of the Rocky Mountains, is considered by some a distinct variety, as it has shorter legs, finer fur, and quicker motion than the bison of the plains. I have found their skulls at an elevation of 10,000 feet above the sea. There are probably a few still to be found, but, like those of the plains, they are practically extinct.

localities no game was found upon which man could rely for subsistence. The country of the " Root-Diggers," for example, is known to have been very sparsely inhabited for these reasons. Furthermore, there were extensive tracts of habitable country which are known to have been entirely uninhabited, the best authenticated instance being that of the present State of Kentucky. The Indian town of Lulgebrud, in Clarke County, the oldest Indian settlement in the State, was established by some Shawnee refugees about the year 1730.

A native population of 1,000,000, or one to every three square miles, may be reasonably assumed as a maximum limit, and 240,000 would appear to be a just minimum. Between these bounds conjecture becomes more vague, but there are still facts tending towards a convergence between these extremes. It is almost beyond doubt that the Indians have decreased somewhat. In the pure hunter state the relation of births to deaths is such that a slight increase of population is to be expected under ordinary circumstances, but when to the ordinary ills of that state are added those of an encroaching civilization, a decrease becomes almost a matter of certainty. The known ravages of war, disease, and whiskey, the white man's most potent allies, justify the common belief that the American race has been fading away; but, on the other hand, those agencies have not been nearly so destructive as is ordinarily supposed. The methods of Indian warfare prevent any great loss to them in fighting—a fact which has often been expressed of late years in the statement that it costs the government a million dollars to kill an Indian. The bitter campaign of 1864, against the Arizona Apaches, when the regular, citizen, and friendly Indian forces of the United States and Mexico joined in a war of extermination against the hostiles, resulted only in the death of two hundred and sixteen Apaches. Even when surprised, and apparently helpless, the Indians have usually lost but small numbers. The four most damaging attacks on the Indians of modern times— Sand Creek, Camp Grant, Custer's fight on the Washita, and Baker's surprise of the Piegans on the Marias—averaged only about one hundred and seventy-five victims each. Small-

pox, measles, syphilis, malaria, consumption, and whiskey have
been far more destructive than our arms, but even these
have not caused the loss of life that has generally been attributed to them.   Counteracting these destroying agencies
have been the superior sanitary measures of civilization.
Tribes that have adopted wholly or in part protective clothing, residence in houses, and the use of medicines, have shown
a great decrease in infant mortality, and often an increase
in numbers.   Even among what are still called the wild
tribes, small-pox has been robbed of its terrors by the introduction of vaccination.   The tendency of late statistics
is to show a slight increase at present in the Indian tribes.
The returns for 1884 (not including the civilized or taxed Indians) show an excess of 300 births over deaths; in 1883 the
excess was 250; in 1882 the excess was 520, but the report
was incomplete.   The natural presumption is that the relation of births to deaths among the civilized Indians would
add to these numbers.

It is not probable that more than one-half of the total
decrease in the tribes occurred prior to 1829.   At that time
there had been no material contact between the whites and
the Indians in at least one-half of our present territory, and
large numbers of the tribes with whom we had been in contact still existed.   The white population of the country was
then 12,866,000.   Our great increase in numbers in the fifty-
five years since that time, and the enormous extension of our
settlements, have produced a contact that is fully equal to all
that of the three hundred and thirty-five years preceding.
Our population during the greater part of that time was inconsiderable; in 1790 it had reached only 3,929,000, of which
ninety-seven per cent. was east of the Alleghanies.   In 1829
Generals Cass and Clarke made an elaborate estimate of the
Indians within our borders, placing the number at 313,130.
The additional territory acquired by the annexation of Texas
and the cession from Mexico was estimated to contain 145,000,
by subsequent statisticians of merit, making a total for our
present territory of 458,000.   If these figures were correct
we should have a decrease of 188,000 in fifty-five years, which
would, on our hypothesis, indicate an original population of

646,000 ; but the estimates of Cass and Clarke, as well as the later ones, are almost certainly above the reality. Their figures on the tribes in proximity to the settlements may be accepted as trustworthy, but they accounted 80,000 west of the Rockies, between parallels 44 and 49, which was more than twice their probable number; and having allowed 20,000 for those within the Rockies, between those parallels, they estimated 94,300 to be between the Rockies and the Mississippi, exclusive of Louisiana, Arkansas, and Missouri, which was also too large a figure. There is scarcely a doubt that the Indians at that time did not number over 400,000, which, on the hypothesis mentioned, would denote an original population of 530,000. There are other considerations, which cannot be elaborated here, tending to show that this estimate is approximately correct.

Beginning with these bases of an existing increase, and a past decrease of only fifty per cent. through nearly four centuries of war, disease, and debauchery, we may eliminate the possibility of extermination from the discussion of the Indian question at the outset. The people who are lamenting "the vanishing spectre on the horizon," and those who rejoice over the prospect of extermination, in the belief that "the only good Indians are dead ones," have very little cause for their emotions. The probability is that there will be more of the race a century hence than there are now; there will be, certainly, if they receive such treatment as they are usually supposed to receive under "the humane policy." The only problems that are worth considering are how these people are to be brought to a fit condition for citizenship, and how we are to live peaceably with them until that end is accomplished. In this connection the reader is asked to remember that it has not been the object of the following pages to solve or even to discuss these problems. The writer has had no theory to support. He has conscientiously endeavored to search out the true causes, the actual occurrences, and the exact results of the leading Indian troubles of modern years, leaving the credit or the blame to fall to whatever individual or whatever policy it may belong. From the facts collected certain principles are deducible, and in this introductory, which might with equal propriety be made a conclusion, these will be briefly summed up.

In all consideration of the Indian question it must be remembered that the Indian stands in a relation to our government different from that of any other human being, and that whatever the results of this distinction may have been, its object was one of benefit and kindness to the red man. All the nations that colonized in America recognized in the Indians the right of possession of the soil, but claimed for themselves the fee-simple, or actual ownership. The United States followed the same theory with all its consequences, the most important of which is that no valid transfer of land can be made by the Indian, except to our government, without the government's consent. The settlers in each of the thirteen colonies paid the Indians something for their possessory right, though all of them claimed the fee-simple under their charters. The tradition that William Penn alone bought land of the Indians is wholly erroneous; each colony has records of similar purchases. The United States has always done the same, except in the case of the cessions from Mexico (in which the Indian title was considered to have been extinguished by the Mexican Government), and under its system the Indian title never rises any higher than a possessory right, unless there is an express treaty confirmation of ownership in fee or an issue of patents. By the customary provisions of organic acts, the Indian reservations are excluded from State and territorial boundaries. They cannot be taxed; they are not subject to the jurisdiction of courts, except as specially provided; legal process of courts of the adjoining territory cannot be served within them. Still the provisions of treaties, that the lands are reserved to particular tribes and their descendants forever, mean merely that the possession of them is so guaranteed; the ownership still remains in the United States, in contemplation of law. From respect for their desire for self-government, we have treated the tribes as independent powers, but we have never conceded the actual title to any portion of land to be in any tribe, for such land thus ceded to an independent power would then cease to be a part of the United States.

The theory of their relation to us, which has always been adhered to by our courts, was thus stated by Marshall, C. J., in the case of the Cherokee Nation *vs.* Georgia, 5 Peters, 1: "The condition of the Indians in relation to the United States is, perhaps, unlike that of any other two people in existence. In general, nations not owing a common allegiance are foreign to each other . . . yet it may well be doubted whether these tribes which reside within the acknowledged boundaries of the United States can, with strict accuracy, be denominated foreign nations. They may, more correctly, perhaps, be denominated domestic dependent nations. They occupy a territory to which we assert a title independent of their will, which must take effect in point of possession, when their right of possession ceases. Meanwhile they are in a state of pupilage; their relation to the United States resembles that of a ward to his guardian. They look to our government for protection, rely upon its kindness and its power, appeal to it for relief to their wants, and address the President as their great father." The reader will observe that here is outlined by our highest court the only policy that our government can justly follow. By our own laws we, who have assumed control over these tribes, are bound to protect them, to be kind to them, to relieve their wants. The relation of guardian to ward under our laws is not consistent with the neglect, oppression, mistreatment, or robbery of the weaker party. Whenever our treatment of a tribe is such as our own courts would not allow in a guardian, we are self-condemned. We must be honest, we must not oppress the Indians, we must not take their property without just compensation, or we are law-breakers.

In accordance with this theory, and in accordance with the wishes of the tribes, it has been customary to allow them to make and enforce their own laws for the punishment of Indians for injuries to the person or property of other Indians. We have had laws to punish white men for wronging Indians, and laws to punish Indians for wronging white men, but the natives have been left at liberty to prey upon one another as their customs might allow. Some of the tribes have reasonably good laws for their own government, but others have such inadequate ones that the feelings of humane men have often been shocked by crimes for which there was no earthly punishment.   Says Bishop Hare, "Women are brutally beaten and outraged, men are murdered in cold blood, the Indians who are friendly to schools and churches are intimidated and preyed upon by the evil-disposed, children are molested on their way to school, and schools are dispersed by bands of vagabonds, but there is no redress. This accursed condition of things is an outrage upon the One Law-giver.   It is a disgrace to our land.   It should make every man who sits in the national halls of legislation blush."   One of the most aggravating of these offences of recent times was the murder of Spotted Tail, the Sioux chief, who had stood by us in many troubled times, by Crow Dog. The murderer was tried, convicted, and sentenced to be hanged, but was released by the Supreme Court (*Ex parte* Crow Dog, 109 U. S., p. 556) for the reason that our courts had no jurisdiction of the offence.   He returned to Rosebud Agency in 1884, and his release has been the cause of the death of several men since then, especially of White Thunder and Thunder Hawk, on May 29th of that year.

The evil of this system is evident.   It has undoubtedly been the greatest stumbling-block in the way of the Indian's advancement to civilization and citizenship.   The worst element necessarily controls so long as there is no power to restrain the work of intimidation.   The system was adopted at a time when our government was physically unable to enforce laws in the Indian country, except for the protection of its own subjects, but there is no reason for a longer continuance of it.   The only obstacle is the fact that a change will be an infraction of treaty rights; but the treaties have been broken for bad purposes so often, that breaking them for a good purpose would almost be an apology for our former bad faith.   This is one of the few evils that may be remedied without creating a new evil.   At present a large part of the law administered on agencies is simply the will of the agent in charge, if he has power to enforce it.   Some agents prohibit polygamy and other Indian customs; others permit them.   The "laws" are liable to be changed whenever there

is a change of agents. A quite recent instance of the ab-
surdities which this results in was an attempt of the agent of
the Navahos to force that tribe to observe the Sabbath. He
had almost got them into a state of war, when General Pope
interfered and removed the over-zealous law-maker. The
evil has been remedied partially by the establishment of
"courts of Indian offences" on some of the reservations by
the Indian Bureau, but they are probably beyond the authority of the department, and would hardly be sustained
by our judiciary. The only remedy at all adequate is for
Congress to adopt a code for the government of the tribes,
but in so doing it ought not to interfere with the tribes
that have adopted and enforced adequate laws of their own.

A treaty with an Indian tribe has the same rank and effect
in law as a treaty with a foreign nation. "They are treaties
within the meaning of the Constitution, and, as such, are the
supreme laws of the land" (5 McLean, C. C., p. 344). The
effect of all treaties has been necessarily to nationalize the
tribe treated with, and put its members farther away from
citizenship and allegiance to our government. From this
consideration Congress, on March 3, 1871, passed a law prohibiting future treaties with Indian tribes, though recognizing
those already made. There is among many intelligent men,
whose friendship for the Indians cannot be questioned, a desire for still further movement towards the disintegration of
the tribes, and a faster advance towards the citizenship which
must sooner or later be reached. This is a step which to the
white man appears advantageous, but it may at least be said
that no action of that kind should be forced on the Indians.
Aside from their reluctance to abandon the ties that make
them a people and endear to them a related ancestry, there
are matters of a more practical nature which may well cause
us to consider the proposed change maturely. The case of
the Pueblos will serve as an illustration of the fact that important benefits do not always result from citizenship. In
the recent case of the United States vs. Joseph, 94 U. S.,
p. 614, an action for the statutory penalty for settling on the
lands of the Pueblo of Taos, the Supreme Court held that
the Pueblo Indians of New Mexico were not "Indian tribes"

under our laws; that they have a perfect title in fee to their lands through Spanish grants and United States patents; and a broad intimation is given that whenever the question shall be presented they will be held to be citizens of the United States. They have the right to vote, which is of no especial use to them, as they have always elected their village officers and have no great interest in others; they have the right to be taxed; they have the right to be sued in the local courts, which will probably give them justice so long as their interests do not conflict too seriously with those of their white neighbors. A number of the Pueblo land grants have been intersected by railways within the past few years, and on one of them the Denver and Rio Grande Company has established a station named Wallace. The Indians refused to sell land for a station or a town site at this point, but, in spite of their protests, white men went there and settled, and the only chance for relief is by tedious litigation. The government cannot interpose as it could if the intruders were upon the lands of "Indian tribes." Its hands are tied by the citizenship of the Pueblos. They have gained a questionable benefit and lost a powerful protector.

The policy of the government heretofore has been to lead the tribes into the adoption of civilized pursuits as far as possible, and then make treaty arrangements by which the members may become citizens on showing a good character and a stated ability to support themselves. Under this system some forty thousand Indians have come into citizenship. The number of taxed Indians, who are in fact citizens, was found by the census of 1880 to be 66,407, but this includes the Pueblos and the Mission Indians of California, who have their right by the treaty of Guadalupe Hidalgo, with Mexico. A majority of the taxed Indians are not qualified for citizenship, in the sense that they are able to cope with the white man in the pursuits of civilized life. The Indian Bureau has had agents at work for over a year past investigating the property rights of these Indians, and it has been found in very many instances that they have been defrauded of their lands either by tax-sales, when their land was not taxable, or by other devices. On the other hand, there is much plausibility in the theory that the ballot is the best weapon that can be given to a man for the defence of his rights, and the experience of the country with the negro certainly shows that the consciousness of manhood and equality is a strong incentive to self-improvement. An enactment of June 18, 1881, that will probably have a decided influence in bringing the Indian to citizenship, provides that any adult Indian who abandons tribal relations may take up land under the homestead law, and still be entitled to his distributive share in all tribal annuities, funds, lands, and other property. The loss of tribal property rights by one who left the tribe, formerly acted as a premium for remaining in tribal relations. On the whole, as to citizenship, it is safe to say that a general naturalization law should be passed by which any Indian who desires to abandon tribal relations may become a citizen on manifesting a certain degree of fitness. The requirement of fitness is no reflection on the Indian; it will operate for his benefit. The alien in this country is simply a visitor, and has only the rights of a visitor until he takes steps towards naturalization. The Indian, theoretically, receives as much protection as the citizen, and is supposed to have his temporal wants, at least, provided for. If the government be true to its guardianship, the Indian has nothing to gain by the transition but the simple freedom of citizenship.

As the law stands at present, an Indian who leaves his tribe, except under treaty provisions, becomes a man without a country. It was declared in the celebrated Ponca case—U. S. *ex rel.* Standing Bear *vs.* George Crook (5 Dillon, C. C., p. 454)—that an Indian had a clear right of expatriation, or abandonment of his tribe; but in Elk *vs.* Wilkins (112 U. S., p. 94) the Supreme Court held that, while a person might abandon one country, he could not force himself upon another as a citizen without its consent, and that the laws of the United States had not made it possible for an Indian to become a citizen by simply leaving his tribe. This being the law, and there being no general provision for the naturalization of Indians, an Indian who leaves his tribe remains in the condition of an alien who has taken no steps towards naturalization, unless he comes within some treaty provision. He may hold and transfer property, sue and be sued, and be indicted for crime. If illegally deprived of his liberty, he may be released on writ of habeas corpus. This right was granted on the application of Standing Bear, above referred to, but the intimation in that case that a similar rule had not obtained in England is incorrect. In 1810 a negro woman, named Saartje Baartman, known as the Hottentot Venus, who was being exhibited in England on account of her beauty and physical perfection, was brought before the Court of King's Bench on a rule for her custodians to show cause why the writ should not issue for her release. The affidavit on which the court granted the rule alleged that she had been clandestinely inveigled away from the Cape of Good Hope without the knowledge of the British governor, " who extends his peculiar protection in nature of a guardian over the Hottentot nation under his government, by reason of their general imbecile state." In other words, she was in the same state of pupilage as the American Indians. The rule was discharged on it being shown that she was with the showmen of her free-will.

The right of Indians in tribal relations to appear in State, territorial, or United States courts for any purpose, except as provided by the national statutes, rests on a very uncertain foundation, for neither the common-law nor any statutes for the enforcement of ordinary rights extend over the reservations. Still, Indians have been allowed in several cases to sue on contracts made on reservations, for assaults committed on reservations, and for trespasses on reservation lands. Various tribes or nations, as independent governments, have exercised the privilege of appearing as parties in the courts for the enforcement of treaty rights.

While theoretically our provisions for the control and advancement of the Indians show good intentions, they have not received the practical application that would have made them useful; and the laws themselves are fatally defective in that there is no adequate provision for their enforcement. It is much as though we had passed a law against murder or larceny and prescribed no penalty for the crime. We agree that white men shall not go on reservations, and pass a law giving a penalty of $1000 against each intruder. A white man enters the reservation; the military removes him; the government sues him, and has judgment for $1000; he owns no property, and goes scot-free. We agree to educate a tribe; money is appropriated for schools, and expended for no one knows what; at the end of ten or twenty years it is discovered that the Indians have learned nothing. How did it happen? Because the law did not provide for any one to see that the money was applied to the purpose for which it was designed. We agree to give the Indians a certain amount of food, clothing, and other property, and appropriate money for the purpose, without taking the precautions for its proper application that any business man would use in his ordinary affairs. That the Indians get but little of it, as a rule, is so notorious that it is a standing joke in this country. Do Indian agents steal? The reports of dozens of investigating committees say they do. Did you ever hear of one being punished? Some of them come out of office without materially increasing their wealth, but not many. The general result is as Medicine Cow said of Dr. Burleigh, "When he came here he had only a trunk, but now he is high up—rich." Dr. Burleigh's services were dispensed with, and the good people of Dakota, in recognition of his distinguished ability, sent him to Congress. There have been tried various checks for this malfeasance, but none adequate to the evil. Every investigation reveals the continuing wrong. If there is a single report of a Congressional or department committee on Indian frauds that does not find a shameful state of robbery and corruption in existence, I have never discovered it.

The most sensible remedy ever adopted was the appointment of the Board of Indian Commissioners, as quasi supervisors of the Indian Bureau, but it has barely checked the progress of wrong. Let us notice a few revelations made since the organization of that body. In 1873 a House committee made a report, in a volume of eight hundred pages, headed in large type, "By this investigation and report the committee hope to do something to rid the Indians and the Indian service of those heartless scoundrels who infest it, and who do so much damage to the Indian, the settler, and the government." It is hardly necessary to say that the hopes of the committee were not realized. In 1874 Prof. O. C. Marsh, of Yale College, happened at Red Cloud Agency on a geological expedition, and was detained there for several days by Indian hostilities. He took some observations of the management of the agency, and obtained samples of the provisions given to the Indians. On his return he printed charges in the newspapers and in pamphlet form, besides writing to and interviewing the authorities. There was an attempt to ignore the charges, the agent stating that he considered it "one of the usual effervescences of the moment," but Professor Marsh pushed the matter, and a commission was sent to investigate. It reported eight hundred and forty pages of damaging testimony, recommended the removal of the agent and inspector, and urged the exclusion of all the contractors from future contracts. Reference will be made hereafter to other frauds, but it is worthy of note here that in the month of July, 1885, there was developed incontrovertible evidence of still existing rascality. In the count of the Cheyenne and Arapahoe Indians, it was found that there were 1300 Arapahoes instead of 2366 reported last fall, and 2077 Cheyennes instead of 3905 reported last fall. A mistake of 3000 Indians out of a reported total of 6271 is impossible. It is simply another illustration of a game that has been played by the Indian rings for years: the more Indians reported, the greater allowance made for their support; and the fewer Indians to issue to, the more goods left for the agent. No casual visit of an inspector will disclose a fraud of that kind. The agent perpetrates it with impunity.

The money loss is the least objectionable part of this thieving. If we may believe either of the great political parties, a few millions stolen, more or less, will make but little difference in the aggregate. The greatest evil is that the Indians are poorly clothed and badly fed or starved, and unless they are so degraded as to have lost all spirit they make trouble. It is amusing to hear some people talk of "fed savages" and "Uncle Sam's pets," in connection with the reservation system. I doubt if there is a reservation in the country on which the average white laboring man would be content to live and subsist on Indian rations, though the food is generally better now than it used to be. Take this description of the fare at Crow Creek Agency in 1863–64: "Some time about the middle of the winter a large vat was constructed of cotton-wood lumber, about six feet square and six feet deep, in connection with the steam saw-mill, with a pipe leading from the boiler into the vat. Into this vat was thrown beef, beef heads, entrails of beeves, some beans, flour, and pork. I think there was put into the vat two barrels of flour each time, which was not oftener than once in twenty-four hours. This mass was then cooked by the steam from the boiler passing through the vat. When that was done, all the Indians were ordered to come there with their pails and get it. It was dipped out to the Indians with a long-handled dipper made for the purpose. I cannot say the quantity given to each. It was of about the consistency of very thin gruel. The Indians would pour off the thinner portion and eat that which settled to the bottom. . . . The Santees and Winnebagos were fed from this vat; some of the Indians refused to eat it, saying they could not eat it, it made them sick . . . they told the agent that it was only fit for hogs, and they were not hogs, they said. . . . The Indians reported several deaths from starvation; they were constantly begging for something to eat, and I visited the lodges frequently while they were sick, and found them destitute of food. . . . From what I saw and know, I am satisfied that the representations of Indians as to some of the Indians dying of starvation were true." This was the testimony of S. C. Haynes, assistant-surgeon of the Sixth Iowa Cavalry. It was fully sustained by the testimony of other white men, and even worse was proven, for it was shown that beeves were used that had died natural deaths, and that meat was issued which stank and was full of maggots. But, it may be said, that sort of thing is all over with now. Is it, indeed? Just last year the Piegans lived for two months on the bark of trees, and about two hundred of them starved to death. It is a glorious privilege to be a " fed savage!"

No one need be surprised at these things. Since the

2

world has existed, men put in absolute power over other men
have often been cruel and wicked, and the race has not out-
grown the quality. You need not go to foreign countries
nor back to the Dark Ages for instances. Tewkesbury alms-
house, the Georgia penitentiary, the contract labor convicts
of Louisiana, or the Soldiers' Orphans' Home of Indiana will
do well enough. Guard as well as you can institutions where
men rule men absolutely, and you cannot escape some wrong.
But what safeguards have we given the Indians? An agent
is put over them who is at once their master and representative, besides representing the government. Isolated from
civilized mankind, he does much as he pleases, and his own
reports are the chief information of his doings that reach the
Indian Bureau and the world at large. Once a year or oftener an inspector visits the agency and is entertained by
the agent; sometimes there are other visitors; sometimes
there is a missionary. If the agent and inspector should accidentally happen to be in a "ring," where do the government and the Indian appear? We put better safeguards than
these around our county jails. There is a very simple way
in which all this might be much improved. For years a
strong party has advocated turning the Indians over to the
War Department, on the plea, which all reasonable men will
concede, that the officers who would have charge of the Indians are more honest than the class of men who are accustomed to receive appointments; they have been educated by
the government as gentlemen, and taught that no gentleman
can be dishonest; and they are under constant liability to
court-martial for conduct unbecoming officers and gentlemen.
This has been met by the plea that a transfer to the War
Department would involve stationing soldiers on the reservations who would demoralize the Indians, and that while
under charge of the War Department, which they were until
1849, the Indian affairs were no better managed than since
then by the Interior Department. Admitting a large amount
of truth in both propositions, why not combine the good
features of both departments? To insure morality, let the
Indian Bureau continue in control; but to insure honesty
—to be certain that the morality of the agent is not hypocrisy

—detail an officer once a month from the nearest post, to audit the agent's accounts, inspect the management of the agency, and report. He need not interfere with the duties of the agent at all. It would add practically nothing to government expenses. There are only sixty-two agencies. The officers are close to most of them, and have plenty of leisure time. But the two departments would be hostile! So much the better. That would insure a knowledge of the truth, beyond question. It is a wrong both to the government and the Indians not to put some impartial supervising power back of the agents.

Admitting the full disturbing force of broken treaties, dishonest agents, inadequate supplies, lawless white men, and intractable Indians, the following pages will show that the large majority of our modern Indian wars have been occasioned by a wholly different cause. That cause has been made a part of the "peace policy," and is commonly known as the concentration or consolidation policy. The peace policy, as defined by Secretary Delano in an open letter to L. L. Crounse, on April 15, 1873, has five leading features: (1) "To place the Indians upon reservations as rapidly as possible, where they can be provided for in such manner as the dictates of humanity and Christian civilization require;" (2) when Indians refuse to go upon reservations, and continue their nomadic habits, "accompanied with depredations and outrages upon our frontier settlements," to punish them until they are willing to go on reservations and remain in peace; (3) to see that all goods and supplies shall be furnished at fair and reasonable prices to the Indians; (4) by every means, to secure "competent, upright, moral, and religious agents;" (5) to establish schools, Sabbath-schools, etc., that the Indians may "be prepared ultimately to become citizens of this great nation."* To the first and second feat-

---

* The principal means by which these ends were hoped to be compassed was permitting the various churches to nominate the Indian agents for the tribes assigned to them. Nearly all the agents were thus nominated for about fifteen years, but this feature of the policy was discontinued by Secretary Teller during Mr. Arthur's administration, and the churches have now no voice in the appointments.

ures has since been added, practically, the policy of bringing
the smaller bands upon the larger reservations, and sometimes
of changing the location of the larger tribes.   This concentration was not a leading feature of the original peace policy,
as may be inferred from its omission by Mr. Delano.   In
1874 Commissioner E. P. Smith said, "Experience, however,
shows that no effort is more unsuccessful with an Indian
than that which proposes to remove him from the place of
his birth and the graves of his fathers.   Though a barren
plain, without wood or water, he will not voluntarily exchange it for any prairie or woodland, however inviting."

The views of Commissioner J. Q. Smith, who next held
the office, were totally different, and in 1876 he announced
as the principal feature of his policy, "Concentration of all
Indians on a few reservations."   His successor, E. A. Hayt,
was of the same opinion, his doctrine being, "A steady concentration of the smaller bands of Indians upon the larger
reservations."   This policy was followed by him through his
long term of office, and has been adopted, though to a somewhat less extent, by his successors.   By act of March 1, 1883,
the President was empowered, in his discretion, to consolidate
either agencies or tribes, "with the consent of the tribes to
be affected thereby, expressed in the usual manner."   There
is nothing objectionable in the appearance of this act; it reads
like a rather benevolent design; but the words do not express
what it really means in its practical application.   To express
it properly, the act should read, "The President is authorized and empowered to drive the Indians from their native
homes, and place them on uncongenial and unhealthy reservations, whenever sufficient political influence has been brought
to bear upon the Commissioner of Indian Affairs or the Secretary of the Interior, by men who desire the lands of any
tribe, to induce a recommendation for their removal; *Provided*, that before any tribe shall be removed, the members
shall be bullied, cajoled, or defrauded into consenting to the
removal."

It may be said that this is an exaggeration.   Let us see.
The Modoc war was caused by attempting to keep them on
a reservation with the Klamaths, who maltreated them so

much that they could not live peacefully or raise food for themselves; they asked a small reservation of their own, but the Indian Bureau would not give it to them. The great Sioux war of 1876 was simply the enforcement of an order for that nation to abandon the Powder River country, which we had guaranteed them as a hunting-ground, and to keep within the bounds of their established reservation, where there was little or no game. The Nez Percé war of 1877 was caused by an attempt to force the Lower Nez Percés, whose nomadic habits were not "accompanied with depredations and outrages upon our frontier settlements," to go upon the Lapwai reservation instead of giving them their old home in the Wallowa Valley, which had never been bought from them, and with which they would have been satisfied. All the troubles with the Chiricahua Apaches, since 1876, resulted from an attempt to remove them from their native mountains to San Carlos Agency, an unhealthy and intolerable place for mountain Indians, and occupied by bands that were unfriendly to the Chiricahuas. The wars with Victorio's Mimbreños Apaches resulted from the discontinuance of his reservation at Ojo Caliente, in his native country, where he had expressed willingness to live in peace, and an order for the removal of his band to San Carlos. The war with the Northern Cheyennes resulted from an attempt to make them stay in Indian Territory, which had proved a very unhealthy place for them, instead of leaving them with their old allies the Sioux, where they wished to remain. The disgraceful affair of the Ponca removal—so repugnant to all sense of fairness and justice that Judge Dundy, who released the fugitive Poncas on writ of habeas corpus, condemned it from the bench, and expressed his pleasure that General Crook had " no sort of sympathy in the business in which he is forced by his position to bear a part so conspicuous"—was only a concentration and removal to Indian Territory. The Hualapais were removed in 1874 from their old country to La Paz reservation, on the Colorado River, a place so terribly unhealthy that they were saved from extermination only by fleeing in a body. The White Mountain Coyoteros, always our friends, were removed from their farms to the hot, unhealthy valley of the Gila, to save the expense of an agency, and throw the tribal trade from New Mexico to Arizona, "where it properly belonged." The tribe became demoralized; their advance in agriculture was stopped; a part of them became wanderers.

All these facts and others will appear more fully hereafter, and they show that the translation made above is not exaggerated. An examination of the arguments of those who favor concentration will show that the advantages claimed for it are purely theoretical. There is not a single instance of benefit resulting from an enforced removal—not one in which the fair presumption is not that the Indians would have done as well or better in their native homes. In a majority of cases the results have been very bad, and in many of them the discontent resulting from removal has been so lasting that the Indian Bureau has been obliged to give up its project, and return them to the place whence they were removed. If there were ever a penny-wise and pound-foolish idea, it is that concentration cheapens the Indian service. The wars alone that have resulted from it, leaving out of consideration life and property destroyed, have cost more money than all that the tribes affected by removals have cost the government otherwise. In addition to that, several tribes that were previously self-supporting were made utterly destitute and helpless by removal, and some became hopelessly demoralized. There is, in reason, no cause why Indians may not be taught and civilized in one state or territory as well as in another, and if the presence of Indians be considered objectionable, there is no justice in moving them from contiguity with one lot of white neighbors to put them near others. The concentration policy has not a single foundation, either in fact or in logical argument, to support it. It is almost beyond comprehension how it could have been adopted by reasoning men.

The objections to it from principle are quite as great as those derived from its expensiveness and inexpediency. Is it a light thing to drive a people from their native land? There was never an exile of any other race to whom the American heart did not warm. There was never even a foreign nation struggling for the peaceful possession of its fatherland with which we did not sympathize. The patriots of Ireland, Poland, Switzerland, and Greece have always had our veneration and love. Our school-children are instructed in their histories, and taught to repeat their inspiring words. We have proclaimed to the world by our Monroe doctrine that no foreign government shall interfere with American liberty on American soil. We profess to place highest in the category of human virtues the love of native land. How comes it, then, that Americans can favor forcing our " wards " to leave the " rocks and rills," the "woods and templed hills " that they love? Can we not respect Joseph when he says, " A man who would not love his father's grave is worse than a wild animal"? Can we not even understand poor, worthless, old Homily when he says, "The gravel stones and sand of Wallula make me happy—my tilicums [adult companions] are there"? The American Indians do love their country. They have taught us that in a hundred bloody wars. If any American will but cast aside the prejudice of race, he must feel the truth of Wendell Phillips's words, " From Massachusetts Bay back to their own hunting-grounds, every few miles is written down in imperishable record as a spot where the scanty, scattered tribes made a stand for justice and their own rights. Neither Greece, nor Germany, nor the French, nor the Scotch, can show a prouder record. And instead of searing it over with infamy and illustrated epithets, the future will recognize it as a glorious record of a race that never melted out and never died away, but stood up manfully, man by man, foot by foot, and fought it out for the land God gave him against the world, which seemed to be poured out over him. I love the Indian because there is something in the soil and climate that made him that is fated, in the thousand years that are coming, to mould us."

I would not carry the feeling of admiration for aboriginal virtues too far, lest the recollection of the vices of barbarism cause an undue recoil from the point we should reach. That many Indians are lazy, drunken, and vicious is undeniable; that some of their habits are revolting to us is true. But there is much to extenuate all this. Why should we be hor-

rified at their eating snakes, lizards, grasshoppers, dogs, and
the intestines of larger animals, when we swallow snails, oysters, frogs' legs, sardines, and tripe? Your epicure has his
woodcock cooked without cleaning, and smacks his lips over
calves' brains. This is but custom. An Apache or Navaho
would not touch bear meat or taste of pork. The white man
looks on the Indian of to-day and laughs at the idea of a
"noble red man," but the Indian of Cooper is not wholly
mythical. One might as well seek a Roman Senator in an
Italian pea-nut vender, or a Knight of the Round Table in
an English swell. Take the proudest crusader that ever bore
a lance, strip off his armor, clothe him in rags, and feed him
on slop; where would be the glamour of his chivalry? There
are plenty of well-authenticated instances of Indian chivalry.
The romance of war and the chase has always been theirs.
If you want the romance of love, a thousand elopements in the
face of deadly peril will supply you with Lochinvars. If you
want the romance of friendship, you may find, in the "companion warriors" of the prairie tribes, rivals for Damon and
Pythias. If you want the romance of grief take that magnificent Mandan, Mah-to-to-pa (Four Bears), who starved himself
to death because of the ravages of small-pox in his tribe, or
Ha-won-je-tah (One Horn), the Minneconjou chief, who was
so maddened by the death of his son that he swore to kill the
first living thing that crossed his path; armed only with a
knife he attacked a buffalo bull, and perished on the horns
of the furious animal. If you seek pure knight-errantry, I
commend you to the young Pawnee Loup brave, Petalesharro, who at the risk of his life freed a Comanche girl from
the stake and returned her unharmed to her people—who
afterwards saved a Spanish boy from a similar fate by offering a ransom for him, and interposing his own life to force
the release. If you desire the grander chivalry of strength
of mind and nobility of soul, I will pit Chief Joseph against
any barbarian that ever lived.

Just here let me caution the reader that if he wishes to
understand Indian history, he must not be deluded by that
false truth, so popular in America, that "an Indian is an
Indian." There are tribes now existing that have never

raised a hostile hand against us, though they have been sorely tried. There are Indians that, so far as race characteristics and race prejudices are concerned, have no identity with the typical Indian, except in the fact that they have been maltreated by the whites. Mr. McCormick, of Arizona, well said in the House of Representatives, "We have Indians there [in Arizona] of every style and character. We have Indians that differ as much from each other as Americans do from Japanese or Chinese. We have a class of Indians whose tendency is to civilization. We have a large class whose tendency is to barbarism, who are as wild as the birds of the air or the beasts of the mountains. We have therefore to pursue a varying course towards the Indians in that territory and in all our frontier country." This is simple truth. There is as much difference between a Pueblo and an Apache, or a Nez Percé and an Arapahoe, as there is between a Broadway merchant and a Bowery rough. When the Nez Percé captives were brought down the Missouri River, the people along the stream, who had been used to Indians all their lives, were constantly remarking, "What fine-looking men!" "How clean they are!" "How dignified they appear!" These are extremes, and there are all gradations between them.

But we have wandered from the subject of concentration. The worst result of a forced removal is its hinderance to civilization. If the Indian is to be civilized, he must first be brought into a complacent state of mind. You may force a man to do right, but you cannot force him to think right. You cannot compel him to be contented. Apparently, then, it is absurd to begin the work of improving and making gentle a mind, by an act of harshness that will be felt longer and more keenly than anything else imaginable. The Indian problem is not solved. It will require years of patient effort to bring these people to a self-reliant, honorable, civilized manhood. It is extremely impolitic to do anything needlessly that will increase the difficulties in the way. If not impeded, humanity and charity will solve the problem, but the "peace policy" of the past eighteen years will not do it. It is no humanity to offer a man a theoretically better home, and kill him because he will not accept it. It is no charity to give a man a nickel with one hand, and rob him of five dollars' worth of property with the other. It is no Christianity to starve a man, and offer him a Sunday-school by way of extreme unction. Let us be honest and fair with the Indian, and temper our justice with religion and education. The missionary and teacher are working nobly, though the fields are white with the harvest and the harvesters are but few. Religion is within the reach of most of the tribes. The schools at Carlisle, Hampton, Forest Grove, Chilocco, Genoa, and Albuquerque are doing much towards the education of the rising generation. If the government and the people will supplement these efforts by the observance of common honesty and good faith, if an intelligent effort is made to prevent wrong and remove disturbing causes, by the close of the century the Indian will be almost lost in the American.

CHAPTER II.

THE ACQUISITION OF THE MOUNTAINS.

ABOUT half a century has elapsed since the idea of possessing and settling the Rocky Mountain region began to develop in the minds of the American people. Before that time it existed only as a speculative belief of far-sighted men, or a daring hope of adventurous ones. We then owned but little of our present western territory. On the south and west our boundary was the present eastern border of Texas, with the line of the "Panhandle" carried north to the Arkansas River, thence up the Arkansas and the continental divide to parallel forty-two of north latitude, and west on it to the Pacific. We have since acquired on that side all of Texas, New Mexico, Arizona, California, Nevada, and Utah, the greater portion of Colorado, and parts of Wyoming, Kansas, and Indian Territory. On the north our line was wholly unsettled west of the summit of the Rockies—we claiming as far north as the Russian possessions, and England claiming as far south as California, but both offering to take less. Meantime the disputed territory was under a joint occupancy by the traders of both countries.

The causes which operated on the public mind in regard to occupying this mountain region were various, though they afterwards blended to a certain extent. First may be mentioned the Texas agitation. Large numbers of Americans had settled in Texas, under grants of the various Mexican governments, but they did not revolutionize with the facility of the natives, and the two races did not harmonize. In 1833 the Americans, who numbered over 20,000, determined to separate from the State of Coahuila, of which they formed a part, and seek admission as a separate State into the Mexican republic. This did not meet with favor when submitted to Santa Anna, then President, and he managed to put the Texans off until he had an opportunity, between insurrections, to throw his troops into their country. Open hostilities followed in 1835 and 1836, and in the latter year Texas declared and virtually established her independence. The State became a bone of contention in our politics at the first, and remained one until the dissolution of the Whig party. There was a feeling of friendliness to the struggling Texans

SANTA ANNA.

which was naturally strongest in the South and West, whence chiefly they had emigrated, but when the real political motives in the controversy are reached, all feelings and all interests are found to be subordinated to one consideration—the extension of slave territory. The South wanted "the Lone Star admitted to the galaxy of her sister States," and broadly threatened secession if the desire were not gratified. It was claimed that Texas was needed to preserve the equilibrium north and south of Mason and Dixon's line. With the South this consideration outweighed every other. Martin Van Buren, who had until then been the popular candidate for nomination, ventured, shortly before the Democratic convention, to write a public letter in which he took a position against annexation. The South abandoned him at once, and was strong enough to defeat him in the convention. The Whigs took the position that any intervention on our part against Mexico was an outrage on a sister republic; that Houston and his followers had gone to Texas to stir up a rebellion; and that the whole affair was "the consummation of the perfidious treason of Aaron Burr." It is true that Tyler extended the offer of annexation to Texas, which was accepted, but it was after his veto of the bank bill had caused the desertion of his party and the resignation of his cabinet, excepting Webster. The position of the Whigs was unfortunate for them, as it forced them to oppose the brilliantly successful Mexican war, to object to the occupation of New Mexico and California, and to advocate compromise with England in the Oregon matter. The Democratic party, on the other hand, having no legitimate reason to offer for the acquisition of slave territory only, drifted into the advocacy of the acquisition of territory in general, a position naturally attractive to the American people, and which soon became very popular.

A second instrumentality in moulding public sentiment was the Santa Fé trade. This had been carried on for a number of years in a desultory and generally unsuccessful way. There had even been one or two traders, though of small importance, who reached Santa Fé before the expedition of Lieutenant Pike. This officer was sent up the Arkansas River in 1806 with instructions to penetrate to the sources of the Red River, for which those of the Canadian fork were then mistaken. He missed both but reached the Rio Grande and prepared to winter there, supposing it to be the Red River. Being only seventy or eighty miles from the northern Mexican settlements, his presence was soon discovered and a force was sent to remove him. On being informed that he was in Mexican territory, and that an escort had been sent to convoy his men and baggage out of the country, he consented

to leave, it being agreed that they should go by way of
Santa Fé. Arrived there, however, the governor sent Pike
and his men to the commandant-general at Chihuahua, who
seized most of his papers and returned the party to the
United States by way of San Antonio de Bexar. Their glowing reports of the country excited general attention, and in
1812 a considerable party of traders started across the plains,
following the directions given by Lieutenant Pike. They

TRADERS APPROACHING SANTA FÉ.

reached Santa Fé just in time to get the benefit of a revolution in favor of the royalists. Their goods were confiscated;
they were seized as spies, and imprisoned in the *calabozos* of
Chihuahua. At the end of nine years the Mexican repub-
licans, under Iturbide, regained the ascendancy, and the luck-
less traders were released. Two of them returned home in
1821, and two small expeditions were sent out in the same
year, both of which were successful. The trade was a very

profitable one, as all other New Mexican supplies were brought in by way of Vera Cruz, at such enormous expense that common calicoes sold for two and three dollars per yard. These expeditions were therefore kept up from year to year, notwithstanding the hardship and peril, though on a rather small scale and with varying success, until the year 1831. In that year Independence, Mo., became the starting - place for the Santa Fé trains, and the trade began to assume greater proportions. In 1822 the goods sent out amounted to $15,000, and the men employed were fifteen, besides the sixty proprietors. In 1831 the goods exported were valued at $250,000. There were eighty owners and three hundred men employed. In 1843 the trade had come under the control of thirty proprietors, who sent out half a million dollars' worth of goods and employed four hundred men. These caravans moved across the plains in military order, usually four wagons abreast. They were escorted by troops on only two occasions prior to 1843.

COL. ZEBULON PIKE.

The published narratives of the traders afforded the principal information concerning the regions traversed, and their prosperity demonstrated that the mountain country was by no means worthless.

The fur trade of the North-west was a large factor in the determination of our boundaries. The fur-traders, French, English, and American, were ever the pioneers in the North. In British America Frobisher established a trading-post on Lake Athabasca in 1778. In 1789 Mackenzie followed down the river bearing his name to the Arctic, and in 1793 he gained the Pacific overland. On his recommendation there followed a union of the North-west and Hudson's Bay companies in the occupancy of the explored country, which continued until their consolidation in 1821. In 1805 the Northwest Company sent one Laroque with an expedition to occupy the Columbia country, but he did not cross the mountains. After the Louisiana purchase, in 1803, the United States sent out the Lewis and Clarke expedition to explore the new territory, which was then almost unknown. They returned in 1806, and their reports quickly begot an active interest in the fur trade with this region. In 1808 the American Fur Company was organized, with head-quarters at St. Louis. They established posts on the sources of the Mississippi and Missouri, and Major Henry, one of their agents, established Post Henry on the Lewis River, the first trading-post located by white men in the Columbia basin. In 1810 Astor started his overland expedition from St. Louis to Oregon. The establishment of Astoria, its terrible misfortunes and final disgraceful sale and surrender by Mr. Astor's Canadian associates, need only be referred to here. Their publication in Irving's "Astoria" in 1836 had a wide-spread effect in the formation of public opinion, not so much by acquainting the people with the country as by arousing the national prejudice against England. This last has always been a potent factor in our affairs, and was never more so than at this time. It was known that England desired to have Texas remain independent and without slavery. It was currently believed that she was planning to obtain California. A Southern congressman did not much misrepresent the American feeling when he said, "It were worth twenty years' war to prevent California falling into the hands of the English."

The British flag floated over Astoria, then called St. George, until 1818. In that year there was a nominal surrender of the country, and the American flag was once more raised, but Astoria remained in the possession of the consolidated "Honorable Hudson's Bay Fur Company" until 1845. At the time of its final surrender by the British it had become a formidable stockade fort, 250 feet by 150, with two bastions, and walls twelve feet high. It was garrisoned by sixty-five men, and by way of armament had two 18-pounders, six 6-pounders, four 4-pound carronades, two 6-pound coehorns, and seven swivels. By the agreement of 1818 there was to be a joint occupation for ten years of "any country that may be claimed by either party on the North - western coast of America, westward of the Stony Mountains;" and this agreement was extended indefinitely in 1827, with the privilege of termination at any time by either party on one year's notice. The occupation that resulted was practically the occupation of the British fur companies, for the Americans did not succeed in permanently establishing a trading - post in the whole Columbia country. When one was set up, the British companies quickly ruined its trade by setting up a rival and underselling. They were even successful in causing the failure of trading expeditions such as Pilcher's and Capt. Bonneville's.

In 1832 a novel expedition for Oregon left Cambridge, under N. J. Wyeth. There were twenty-two of them, all equipped for an ideal frontier life. They wore uniforms, and had prepared themselves for the hardships of Western life by camping out for ten days on an island in Boston Harbor. In company with a party of experienced trappers, led by William Sublette, they reached the head-waters of the Snake River and established Fort Hall. The Hudson's Bay Company soon after established Fort Boisée and ruined their trade. In 1839 Mr. Wyeth, who had returned home a less romantic but wiser person, announced the truth that "the United States as a nation are unknown west of the mountains." But while the British companies succeeded in monopolizing the fur trade of the Columbia country, the Americans were pushing up to its borders. In 1823 Ashley had his men on Green River and the Sweetwater. In 1824 he established a trading - post in the Great Salt Lake basin, to which he conveyed a six-pound cannon in 1826, and wagons two years later. The return of $180,000 worth of furs by Ashley's company in a single year aroused great interest in the trade, and caused the organization of the Rocky Mountain Fur Company, which carried its trade through all California. Private enterprise reached out into every corner of the wilderness. Posts were established all along the foot-hills—Bent's Fort on the Arkansas, St. Vrain's on the South Platte, Laramie on the North Platte, Union, Clark, Berthold, and others on the Missouri. In 1834 John Jacob Astor sold his interest in the American Fur Company to Pierre Chouteau, Jr., of St. Louis, and his associates. The company known as P. Chouteau, Jr., & Co., was organized soon afterwards, and eventually secured the control of both the fur trade and the Santa Fé trade. The information concerning the western mountains and plains which reached the people through the fur-traders was of course considerable. It would be impossible to estimate it with accuracy as to quantity, but its value will be easily appreciated by those who remember the "Great American Desert" of earlier days, as portrayed in the geographies of Morse, Cummings, and others, indicated by those little dots which are the geographical symbols of sterility and starvation, and comparable in size only to the Great Sahara. Lieutenant Pike, in his account of his explorations, had reported the great plains as a providential desert barrier which would restrain the American people from thin diffusion and ruin. He said, " Our citizens being so prone to rambling and extending themselves on the frontiers will, through necessity, be constrained to limit their extent on the west to the borders of the Missouri and Mississippi, while they leave the prairies incapable of cultivation to the wandering and uncivilized aborigines of the country." Lieutenant Long, in 1818, improved on Pike's account only by placing the beginning of the desert some two hundred miles farther westward. Even so lately as 1843 George McDuffie, of Georgia, announced in the Senate of the United States his understanding that the country for "seven hundred miles this side of the Rocky Mountains is uninhabitable."

A fourth agency in the occupation and settlement of the mountain country, and the last one I shall consider, was missionary work in Oregon. Away back in 1817, Hall J. Kelly, a Boston teacher, became impressed with the idea of colonizing Oregon, converting the Indians, and establishing a new republic on the Pacific coast. For this end he worked ardently, memorializing Congress for co-operation repeatedly, and issuing several pamphlets treating of his project. In 1829 he formed a society to carry out his views, which had then become definite in a plan for an overland expedition. In 1831 he induced the Legislature of Massachusetts to incorporate "The American Society for Encouraging the Settlement of Oregon Territory." Several hundred names were enrolled on the emigration books, among others, Captain Bonneville and N. J. Wyeth, when opposition sprung up. It seems to have been customary in those days to suspect every pioneer leader of being another Aaron Burr. Kelly's motives were assailed, the press misrepresented the difficulties of the undertaking, and the expedition was broken up. But several of the members went out, of whom Bonneville and Wyeth have already been mentioned. John Ball, Calvin Tibbitts, and others went also in 1832. They reached Oregon, established the first school among the Indians, under the auspices of the Hudson's Bay Company, and did the first farming in that region in 1833. The Methodist Board of Missions was to have sent two missionaries with this party, but on its being broken up the ministers selected were sent to Liberia instead. Kelly tried vainly to reconstruct his company, and finally, in desperation, started for Oregon himself, by way of Mexico. At Vera Cruz the revenue officials appropriated most of his goods, although they were not subject to duty, and though he was travelling under a passport from our department of State, endorsed by the Mexican Government. At Monterey, Cal., he induced Ewing Young and a small party to accompany him, and sailing thence arrived at Fort Vancouver in 1834. The Monterey party settled permanently, and formed the nucleus of the subsequent settlement. The estate of Ewing Young, which escheated in default of heirs, gave the provisional government of Oregon its first and, for some time, only funds. Kelly's health was impaired and his spirits depressed by misfortune. He soon returned to the East, and went down to death in poverty, worn out by exposure, and in premature decay.

There were others besides Kelly who were advocating a settlement in Oregon at an early day. The idea of a seaport on the Pacific coast, which should be the western terminus on

our continent of a line of trade with Asia, had originated
with Thomas Jefferson. He foresaw a vast Oriental traffic
across America, and tried to have the country explored long
before he sent out Lewis and Clarke. Some of his worshippers followed up the thought, particularly Colonel Benton,
who wrote newspaper articles favoring the settlement of the
North-west as early as 1819. In 1820 Dr. Floyd, of Virginia,
endeavored to get action towards that end in the House of
Representatives. In 1825 Benton introduced in the Senate
a bill for the occupation of the Columbia, which received
fourteen votes. While philosophers were still speculating
and enthusiasts arguing, a romantic event occurred which
brought about the desired end. In 1832 a deputation of four
Nez Percé Indians visited St. Louis. They were no usual
visitors there, and they had come on a strange errand. Some
trapper had told their tribe of a wonderful Book that the
white men had—a Book which told all about the Great Spirit,
the happy hunting-grounds, and the trail that led to them—
and they had come after it. From away in their mountain-
girt valleys beyond the Columbia they had searched out a
pathway, over mountains and plains, through the fierce tribes
of their deadly enemies, until they reached the great village
of the white man. They found there, as Indian Superintendent, Gen. William Clarke, who had visited their country
twenty-seven years before. He received them kindly. They
were feasted, and loaded with presents, but they failed to obtain the Book. It was not printed in a language which they
could understand, and no missionary volunteered to return
with them. The two older Indians died at St. Louis, and
the younger ones returned to their homes, ascending the Missouri to the mouth of the Yellowstone by the first steamboat
that traversed those waters. It was sent up by the American
Fur Company, and bore also the celebrated George Catlin,
whose work among the Indians is known to the world.
When the Nez Percés bade farewell to General Clarke they
were full of sadness at the failure of their mission, and por-
trayed, in their graceful imagery, the disappointment which
their tribe would feel. A young clerk overheard the conversation. It was one of those happenings which seem to be

the work of some great guiding hand. He wrote an account
of the entire circumstance to friends in Pittsburg, who
showed the letter to Catlin on his return. Catlin felt sure
there was some mistake about it, for he had become acquainted with the Nez Percés on the boat, and they had not
spoken of their mission to him, but on corresponding with
General Clarke he found it to be true. They had come solely
to obtain the Book, and they had failed. The young clerk's
letter was then published. It touched the hearts of Christian America. The Methodist Board of Missions at once
sent out Jason and Daniel Lee and others. The American
Board of Commissioners of Foreign Missions sent Samuel
Parker and Marcus Whitman, M.D., who were to have gone
with the Lees but missed the convoy of the American Fur
Company, and did not reach the American rendezvous on
Green River until 1835. Here they luckily met a party of
Nez Percés whom Mr. Parker accompanied to their home.
He remained with them until 1836, and then returned home
by way of the Sandwich Islands. Whitman saw a great duty
placed before him, and he undertook it without hesitation.
Having persuaded two of the Nez Percé boys to accompany
him, he returned to the East to prepare for his life-work. In
the following spring he married Miss Narcissa Prentiss, and
having secured as colleagues Rev. H. H. Spalding and wife,
a newly-married couple who were about going as missionaries
to the Osages, they started on their bridal tour to Oregon.
But taking women among the Indians was a new project,
and was looked on as foolhardy by experienced frontiersmen.
They had to turn a deaf ear to warnings of danger from the
time they started until they left the settlements. The American Fur Company at first refused to convoy them, but finally
consented. At Council Bluffs they found that the company's
party had started six days before them, but accompanied by
W. H. Gray, who had joined them as agent for the proposed
mission, they followed on and overtook it at Loup Fork.
They crossed the South Pass six years before Fremont "discovered it," and in July reached the place of the annual fair
of the Indians and traders, midway between South Pass and
Fort Hall. Here they met their Nez Percé friends, and ac-

companied by them and some Hudson's Bay Company men, they proceeded on their journey. They reached Fort Walla-Walla in September; the missions at Wailatpu and Lapwai were soon established, and the Book was given to the Nez Percés and their neighbors.

It had been usual for these trading parties to leave their wagons at Fort Laramie, but Dr. Whitman insisted on taking his through. He succeeded in getting it as far as Fort Hall, then under British control, and there, after many objections and representations of the impassability of the trail by the Hudson's Bay men, he compromised by making a cart of it. At Fort Boisée the convoy rebelled. They said that if he wanted to take the wagon farther he must take it apart and pack it on horses, as the road was absolutely impassable. The cart was accordingly left till a future time. It appeared to be a part of the policy of the British companies to prevent wagons passing beyond Fort Hall, thus building up the impression that there could be no overland route to Oregon. They succeeded with party after party following Whitman, and in 1842, when one hundred and twenty-seven emigrants had reached Oregon, of whom thirty-four were white women, thirty-two white children, and twenty-four ministers, no wagon had passed Fort Hall except the doctor's cart.

In October, 1842, Dr. Whitman was at Fort Walla-Walla, attending a patient, when word was brought of the arrival of a party of British settlers at Fort Colville. Prior to that time the representatives of England were trappers and attachés of the fur companies only. The people of the fort were at dinner when the news was announced. General joy prevailed, and a young priest, in the excess of his enthusiasm, tossed up his cap and cried, "Hurrah for Oregon! America is too late, and we have got the country." Dr. Whitman was the only American present. To him that cry was an expression of the British policy. They were planning an actual occupation of the country as a basis of future action. A few moments' talk confirmed this opinion, and he was taunted with his inability to prevent it. On the instant he determined to defeat the scheme. Winter was at hand, but he must act at once. The latest information he had was that Lord Ashbur-

A TRAIL IN THE SIERRA SAN JUAN.

ton, on the part of the English, and Daniel Webster, on the part of the Americans, were negotiating a treaty for the settlement of the disputed boundary. Any delay might prevent his reaching Washington before a treaty was signed. In two hours he was at Wailatpu, twenty-five miles away ; in twenty-four hours he was started for Washington; in eleven days he was at Fort Hall, six hundred and forty miles on his journey. Here he made a mistake. Deterred from the usual South Pass route by anticipations of severe weather, he and his companion, Mr. Lovejoy, undertook a long détour to Bent's Fort by way of Fort Uintah, Fort Uncompahgre, Taos, and Santa Fé. Instead of being a better route, it took them into the desert of Eastern Utah and Western Colorado, and forced them to cross the lofty San Juan Mountains, where Fremont's fourth expedition narrowly escaped destruction afterwards. They succeeded in reaching Bent's Fort on January 3, 1843, after appalling perils and exposure, and, pressing on alone, Dr. Whitman reached St. Louis, clad in furs, with fingers, ears, nose, and feet frost-bitten, after four months in the saddle. From there he took the stage to Washington, and reached his destination on March 3d. He found that the Ashburton treaty had been signed before he left Oregon, but Oregon had been left out. The line had been determined only to the Rocky Mountains. He was too late for that treaty, but in good time for the next one. He furnished the government with explicit and reliable information concerning the country, and in the summer led back an emigrant train of two hundred wagons.

As soon as Whitman reached the settlements he had spread broadcast his report of the country, by word and in printed circulars, and notified the people that an emigrant company would leave Westport, Missouri, in the June following. Eight hundred and seventy-five emigrants met him there and accompanied him, while others followed in their trail. In 1846 the American population of Oregon was fully 10,000, and of other nationalities not to exceed one tenth of that number, living under a local government which was established in 1843. It was this emigration that decided public sentiment on the Oregon question. It settled the mooted questions of the agri-

cultural value of Oregon and the feasibility of overland emigration, besides binding the Mississippi Valley to the Columbia by ties of blood and friendship. The government had
understood well enough that emigration would settle the
Oregon question, beforehand, but how to get the emigration
was another matter. Congress had been discussing the bill
"for the occupation and settlement of Oregon" while Whitman was making his long ride, and the plan of inducing "fifty
thousand rifles" to settle on the Columbia, by giving each settler 640 acres of land and 160 additional for his wife and
each child, had met with favor, until Mr. Choate pointed out
its infringement on the joint-occupation agreement, and told
the Senate that America could not afford to sully her honor,
however much she advanced her interests. Congress had no
other inducement to offer. Dr. Whitman got the emigration.
It is true that Linn, Benton, and others had shown Oregon to
be much more desirable than it had been believed to be, a
few years back, but other congressmen had controverted their
propositions, and the matter was left in doubt. Whitman
solved the doubt. He accomplished what the statesmen, without him, had been unable even to plan for. That is the measure of his work and the just measure of his praise.

Meantime, the Democratic party had asserted the right of
the United States to the whole of Oregon, in their platform
of 1844, and the campaign in which "Fifty-four, Forty, or
Fight" was a rallying-cry had resulted in the election of Mr.
Polk by a majority of sixty-five of the two hundred and
seventy-five electoral votes. Mr. Polk, in his message, advised
giving the agreed one year's notice of the termination of joint
occupation, and an armed occupation of the country. The
question received a long consideration in Congress, during
which it was made manifest that the only land really in
controversy was that between parallel 49 and the Columbia
River, for the United States had repeatedly offered to compromise on 49, and England had as often offered to compromise on 49 to the Columbia and by it to the ocean. A
bill ordering notice finally passed in April, 1846, bearing, by
amendment, a pacificatory preamble and a provision leaving
the time of serving the notice at the discretion of the Presi-

dent. It was served at once, and England came to terms forthwith. Mr. Pakenham offered to compromise on 49. Here was a dilemma. England offered all America had asked, but could Mr. Polk, after the declarations of the late campaign and subsequent debate, consistently accept it? He did so secretly, and threw the responsibility of a public acceptance on the Senate. The Senate accepted it by a full vote of the Whigs and the compromise faction of the Democrats. The treaty establishing the present line was signed on June 15, and proclaimed as a law of the land on August 5, 1846. The meaning of the treaty as to what was "the channel separating Vancouver's Island from the mainland" was not finally settled until 1872, and then under arbitration, by Emperor William of Germany.

It should be borne in mind that although the Democratic platform of 1844 declared in favor of "the reoccupation of Oregon and the reannexation of Texas at the earliest practicable period," the great political parties were not thoroughly united either for or against these propositions. The Whig platform did not mention either subject, and many Whigs insisted that they were not in issue between the parties. The fact is that there was serious question in the minds of many thoughtful men as to the policy of extending our territory to so great an extent. To some it appeared that the occupation of these vast regions would create a detrimental diffusion of our population, for they could not foresee the wonderful increase our population was destined to have. Others feared the extension of slavery, for they could not foresee that slavery was to be blotted out forever. Others feared the union of distant sections with no means of ready communication, for they could not foresee the rails and wires of to-day. Others thought the country impracticable of settlement and worthless, for they could not foresee the discovery of the enormous mineral wealth which now makes the mountains to resound with the hum of labor. The two objections last mentioned were the more serious. When we remember that the first railroad reached the Mississippi in 1854, we are not so much surprised that ten years earlier a railroad to the Pacific was viewed by many as chimerical. At that time it took months to get letters across the continent by the swiftest couriers, and the transportation of supplies was proportionately slower. The difficulty of transporting armies, with their subsistence, to the frontier of such domains, might well appal a statesman. The feasibility of even a wagon-road to the Pacific was not yet settled. Who then could foresee that in forty years three lines of railroad should cross the Rocky Mountains, and half a dozen span the great plains? It is true that at that time a transcontinental railroad was widely discussed, but it was from a wholly speculative standpoint. With the information then had, I doubt if a more sensible statement of the situation was made than the following in the *New York Evening Post*, in 1846: "I apprehend it would require the whole white population west of Independence, Missouri, to act as mere servants of the line, allowing it was now built and in operation; and to prevent the Indians and storms from destroying the road would require an army of 10,000 soldiers, laborers besides. It will be time enough for the Government of the United States to make railroads beyond St. Louis when the people shall have completed roads from New York to St. Louis or the Mississippi River. . . . Such a railroad will be, but not within forty years." There was just one thing that prevented the accomplishment of this prediction, and of it no one dreamed then. It was the mineral wealth of the Rocky Mountains. Without it there had not been a rail laid in the mountains to-day. Nevertheless, John Plumbe had begun his survey of a road from Lake Michigan to the Pacific in 1836, fifteen years before a road reached Chicago, had received aid from Congress in 1838, and was still appealing to the people to buy stock long after the above extract was written.

As to the value of the territory to be acquired or held, the popular notion of the country east of the mountains has been mentioned. In regard to Texas, it was contended by those who opposed the annexation that the country was not worth enough to compensate us for her debt of $10,000,000, which we were to assume. The country west of the mountains was generally estimated a desert. In the year 1839 Robert Greenhow, translator and librarian to the Department of State, prepared an exhaustive memoir on this question, for the use of

Congress. He had all the information in the country at his disposal, and he favored our claim to Oregon. His statements may therefore be taken as at least not underestimating the country as it was then known. He says of the California coast: "The soil and climate appear to be favorable to the growth of every vegetable substance necessary for the subsistence and enjoyment of man ; but no large portion of the territory will probably be found fruitful without artificial irrigation. Of the interior of California little is known." Oregon he divides into three parts; the first reaching from the coast to the Cascade Mountains; the second, from the Cascade range to the Blue Mountains; the third, the remaining country, to the Rockies. Of the first he says: "The climate of this region is more favorable to agriculture than those of the other parts of Oregon, although it is certainly adverse to great productiveness." Of the second he quotes Wyeth, that "the agriculture of this territory must always be limited to the wants of a pastoral people." Of the third he says that the climate is "sufficient to render any attempts at cultivation in this region entirely fruitless." He continues: "The country east of the Rocky Mountains, for more than two hundred miles, is almost as dry and barren as that immediately on the western side." The whole matter is summed up as follows: "In what other pursuits besides the fur trade British capitalists may advantageously employ their funds in Northwest America, is, therefore, an interesting question at present. From what has been hitherto learned of those countries, they do not offer prospects of a speedy return for the investment of capital in any other way. They contain lands in detached portions which will immediately yield to the industrious cultivator the means of subsistence, and enable him, perhaps, to purchase some foreign articles of luxury or necessity. But this is all; they produce no precious metals or commodities, no gold, nor silver, nor coffee, nor cotton, nor opium, nor are they, like India, inhabited by a numerous population, who may be easily forced to labor for the benefit of a few." With such information before them, and lacking the gift of prophecy, our statesmen certainly had little reason to desire the territory on account of its intrinsic value.

But back of all these questions was a more serious question with many patriots. Was our form of government adequate for the wants of so great domains, with their conflicting interests, and might not the undue extension disrupt the whole union ? Washington thought there was danger of losing our territory west of the Alleghanies when we extended only to the Mississippi. Jefferson always favored more than one government within our present boundaries. In a letter to Mr. Astor, expressing his regret at the failure of the Astoria venture, he tells how it had been his hope to see the Pacific coast covered with "free and independent Americans, unconnected with us but by the ties of blood and interest, and enjoying, like us, the right of self-government." Jackson early advised the limitation of our boundaries until our territory was more densely populated. Benton wrote the first newspaper article calling attention to the importance of occupying Oregon, but at the first he wanted it occupied as Jefferson had. In fact, he says he took his idea from Jefferson. In this vein he said, on March 1, 1825 : "The ridge of the Rocky Mountains may be named without offence as presenting a convenient, natural, and everlasting boundary. Along the back of this ridge the western limits of the republic should be drawn, and the statue of the fabled god Terminus should be raised upon its highest peak, never to be thrown down. In planting the seed of a new power on the coast of the Pacific Ocean, it should be well understood that, when strong enough to take care of itself, the new government should separate from the mother empire as the child separates from the parent at the age of manhood." Mr. Winthrop, of Massachusetts, referred to this sentiment with approval, in 1844, when Benton had changed his mind, and when he saw in the Pacific Ocean a more satisfactory boundary. Of Oregon, McDuffie, of Georgia, said in the Senate, in 1843 : "If there was an embankment of five feet to be removed, I would not consent to expend five dollars to remove that embankment to enable our population to go there. I thank God for his mercy in placing the Rocky Mountains there." Mr. Webster said, in 1845, when opposing the admission of Texas : "The government is very likely to be endangered, in my opinion, by a further enlargement of the ter-

ritorial surface, already so vast, over which it is extended."
In 1847, in a speech at Springfield, after disclaiming any sympathy with Mexico, he said: "Mexico had no ground of complaint in the annexation of Texas; we are the party to complain—we did not want Texas." This feeling was not caused
by any want of sympathy on the part of the citizens of the
United States for those of other parts of America. The announcement of the Monroe doctrine, in 1823, and the popular
favor which it received, preclude such a supposition. It was
a doubt of the elasticity of the Union, which was well for-
mulated by the venerable Genevan, Albert Gallatin, thus:
"Viewed as an abstract proposition, Mr. Jefferson's opinion
appears correct, that it will be best for both the Atlantic and
the Pacific American nations, while entertaining the most
friendly relations, to remain independent, rather than to be
united under the same government." The statesmen were
not yet ready for the bold position of Stephen A. Douglas—
"I would make this an ocean-bound republic, and have no
more disputes about boundaries, or 'red lines' upon the
maps."

The people were less timorous, perhaps because less
thoughtful. When the question was submitted to them they
warmly supported the extensions. The defeat of Mr. Van
Buren, as a candidate for nomination, and of Mr. Clay, as a
candidate for election, by Mr. Polk, who was then a comparatively unknown man, showed how strongly the people were
attached to the principle. Mr. Polk had therefore no occasion for hesitancy in his policy after the Mexican war was
begun, and he acted promptly and wisely. One of the first
steps of the war was to despatch an army under General
Kearny to occupy New Mexico and California, in order
that if the war should close with a treaty on a *uti pos-
sidetis* basis we should hold those states. New Mexico was
taken without opposition. California had been partially conquered by Commodore Stockton and Lieutenant Fremont
when Kearny reached it. Insurrection broke out afterwards,
but their united forces soon disposed of it; and when
the Mexican war ended, with the treaty of Guadalupe
Hidalgo, in consideration of $15,000,000, we were left

JOHN C. FREMONT.

in possession of all of our present western territory except the strip south of the Gila River in Arizona known as " the Gadsden Purchase." This we bought of Mexico in 1853, for $10,000,000. There was an insurrection in New Mexico after General Kearny left it, but it was, in its nature, rather an Indian massacre than a war movement by a military force. An account of it forms the chapter following.

CHAPTER III.

THE ONE OFFENCE OF THE PUEBLOS.

On the 30th of June, 1846, the advance of the "Army of the West," under Colonel Stephen W. Kearny, marched from Fort Leavenworth for New Mexico. Two troops of dragoons followed in July, and overtook the first division at Bent's Fort. The remainder of the army, consisting of a regiment of mounted volunteers from Missouri, under Colonel Price, and the Mormon battalion of 500 men, did not march until early autumn. None of the troops followed the regular Santa Fé trail, which led in an almost direct line from Independence to the Mexican settlements, but left it at the Arkansas, and followed up the river to Bent's Fort. The first division, as it invaded New Mexico, numbered 1658 men, including six companies of dragoons, two batteries of light artillery with sixteen pieces, two companies of infantry, and a regiment of cavalry. The dragoons were regulars and the rest raw recruits. They straggled across the plains very much at will, and took possession of New Mexico without a struggle. The Mexican general, also governor and despot, Armijo, had collected something over 5000 men, and partly completed fortifications at Apache Cañon, the natural approach to Santa Fé. His position there was almost impregnable—a breastwork, thrown across the road where it hangs in mid-air, with a solid rock wall on one side and a precipice on the other, that could be taken only by a direct assault, under a flanking fire from both sides of the cañon—but he and his army retired as the Americans advanced. This has been usually mentioned as an instance of Mexican cowardice, but there is a bit of secret history back of it. There accompanied the expedition a Mr. James Magoffin, an old Santa Fé trader, well acquainted all through the Mexicos, who went, with Lieutenant-colonel Cooke, in ad-

4

KEARNY'S SOLDIERS CROSSING THE MOUNTAINS.

vance of the army, from Bent's Fort, on a little mission to Santa Fé. He "operated upon Governor Armijo," and secured from him a promise to make no stand at the cañon. Armijo's second in command, Colonel Diego Archuleta, was determined to fight, but Magoffin got rid of him by informing him that Kearny's mission was only to occupy the country east of the Rio del Norte, and that the country west of the river might easily be seized by him, Archuleta, and held under an independent government. The original intention had been as Magoffin stated, and as he still believed it to be, but Kearny had subsequently received different orders. Kearny was notified that the coast was clear; he made a hurried march, and passed the point of danger in safety. Magoffin, for his services, received $30,000 from the government, which, he said, barely covered his "expenses" in this and a similar move attempted in behalf of Colonel Doniphan, in Chihuahua. The conquest of New Mexico might otherwise have been stopped at Apache Cañon, a place which was destined to be the scene of a decisive battle, but not yet—not until 1862, when the Southern Confederacy was stretching out a brawny arm to seize the mountains.

Armijo's army was disbanded at Santa Fé, and he fled to the south, leaving the invaders to enter the New Mexican capital, the oldest city in the United States, in peaceful triumph, on August 18. Five weeks later, General Kearny (he had received his commission *en route*) marched with 300 dragoons to conquer California. On October 12 the Mormon battalion reached Santa Fé. They were undisciplined, poorly equipped, and much worn. They had received permission to bring their families with them, and were badly encumbered with women and children. About one hundred of the more inefficient men, with all of the women except five of the officers' wives, were sent to the pueblo on the Arkansas (present Pueblo, Colorado), where they remained all winter. The remainder, under Lieutenant-colonel Cooke, marched for California on October 19, taking a route south of the Gila River. Cooke was instructed to report on the practicability of this route for a railroad. His report was favorable, so far as natural obstacles were concerned, and was largely the cause of the Gadsden purchase. Southern interests prevailed in the administration of 1853, and a Southern Pacific railroad would, of course, have been a desirable institution, when slavery should be carried across the continent under the Southern theory of the Missouri Compromise. On December 14 and 16 Colonel Doniphan's command, of 856 men, started on the conquest of Chihuahua. The advance, 500 strong, met and routed a force of 1220 Mexicans at Bracito, and this was the only battle fought on New Mexican soil during the conquest. The remainder of the army left in New Mexico, after these detachments had marched, was under command of Colonel Sterling Price, subsequently a noted leader of the Confederacy.

From a military standpoint, the expedition into New Mexico was in many respects remarkable. An "army" of less than 1700 men was sent to reduce, reorganize, and occupy a territory large enough for an empire—a long-settled territory, protected by regular troops. It marched across a waste country, peopled only by hostile savages, hundreds of miles beyond

its base of supplies, leaving no force to protect its communication.   It was so poorly supplied that its rations from Bent's
Fort to Santa Fé were calculated barely to hold out by rapid
and uninterrupted marches.   Having reached its destination,
the entire territory was "annexed," and its people declared
citizens of the conquering nation, thus taking from the invaders the conqueror's right to levy supplies, although at that
time the army was completely destitute of means.   Having
brushed away these trifling obstacles, the army divides into
bands, each of which moves on to conquer equal empires beyond.

Before leaving Sante Fé, General Kearny, under authority
of the Secretary of War, organized a provisional government,
with Charles Bent as governor.   This appointment was probably the best that could have been made.   Mr. Bent was one
of the pioneers of the Santa Fé trade, and had wide experience
all along the frontier.   He and his brothers had afforded a hospitable shelter to hundreds of weary wayfarers at their fort on
the Arkansas.   This structure, built in 1829, was one hundred
feet square, with adobe walls thirty feet high.   It had bastions
at the northeast and southwest corners, armed with cannon.
On the inside the apartments were built against the walls, in
the Mexican fashion, and in the centre was the robe-press or
storehouse for furs.   In 1846 it justified Colonel Cooke's as-
sertion that it was " in reality the only *fort* at the West."   In
1880 it was "a rude and wild corral, deserted and decaying."
It may also be mentioned, in this connection, that Charles
Bent introduced the custom of furnishing the draught-oxen
of the plains with iron shoes.   Besides being a man of practical knowledge, Bent was a man of talent, energy, and patriotism.   He had married a Spanish lady, and established his
residence at Don Fernandez de Taos, where Kit Carson, Judge
Beaubien, the St. Vrains, and other pioneers had also settled.*
The community over which Bent was called to rule was complex.   The Americans were trifling in number, outside the
military.   The people generally may be classed as Mexicans,

* This town is now plain Taos, as Santa Fé de San Francisco has become
only Santa Fé, and San Francisco de Asis is known to us simply as San
Francisco.

Pueblos, and wild Indians, though there existed in abundance every imaginable gradation in blood and habits between these classes. The wild Indians were treated with, to some extent, but were not under control. They were at first very friendly to the Americans because of their enmity to the Mexicans; but when the country passed under American rule, and the government was put under obligations to protect its Mexican citizens, their friendship went with the cause of it. The large majority of the Mexicans were then, as now, in the state of peonage, a sort of cross between slavery and service, owned and controlled by a few grandees, or *ricos*, as they are called. They were avaricious, revengeful, fickle, and treacherous. The Pueblos were the most interesting and, indeed, the most reliable class of the three.

RESTORATION OF PUEBLO HUNGO PAVIE.

They are not a nation or tribe, as is the too common impression, but include a number of tribes, speaking six distinct languages. They are, as the name signifies, Indians who live in permanent towns. Most of them were Christianized, after a fashion, at an early date, and they are sometimes, accordingly, spoken of as the Christian or Catholic Indians. The term is misleading, for a Catholic New Mexican Indian is not necessarily a Pueblo, nor is a Pueblo necessarily a convert. At the time of our conquest they inhabited the twenty-six villages which they still occupy. Of these the seven villages of the Moquis are separated from the rest, being situated in that northeastern portion of Arizona which is cut off by the Little

4*

Colorado River. The original name of the Moquis was Hapeka.
They received the name Moqui, which means "death," many
years ago, at a time when smallpox was ravaging their villages.
Zuñi is also within the bounds of Arizona, just on the edge of
the Pacific slope. It is a well-built town, covering some ten
acres of land, and having a population of about 3000. The
other villages are situated in the valley of the Rio Grande,
extending over two hundred miles, interspersed with Mexican
towns, from Taos, on the north, to Ysleta, on the south. Of
the origin of these Indians nothing certain is known. They
were there, and living in their pueblos, when Alvar Nuñez and
his three companions, the sorry remnant of the Floridan expedition of Pamfilio Narvaez, passed through the land, from
the Gulf of Mexico, seeking their way to the Spanish settlements. This was prior to 1538, and was the first time that
white men had reached their country. They were then, as
now, an agricultural people, raising grain and vegetables.
They also manufactured pottery and cotton fabrics, but this
latter art they now appear to have lost. There is no trace of
even the rudest forms of poetry or music among them. Some
have thought the Pueblos to be of the same stock as the Incas
of Peru, a theory whose only support is that they are sun-
worshippers, and communicate to some extent by knotted
cords. The opinion that they are the remains of a former
Aztec settlement of the country has received much support.
They have traditions of an early government by the Monte-
zumas, and are said still to preserve the sacred fires instituted
by them. On the other hand, these people were utterly unknown in Mexico at the time of the Spanish conquest, and
many of the best authorities doubt that the Aztecs came from
the North at all.

There is a general tendency to believe that they are a distinct people, having no connection with any of the other
civilized aborigines of America. The best evidence of this
is found in the hundreds of ruins, lying principally to the
southwest of the present villages, similar to them in structure, and which cannot be identified with any other architecture. These ruins extend over a territory more than four
hundred miles in length, from northeast to southwest, and

CASAS GRANDAS—RUINS IN ARIZONA.

RUINS OF PUEBLO PINTADO.

varying in width from fifty to one hundred miles, besides some scattered ones outside these limits. They are usually collected in groups, some of the cities having evidently contained thousands of inhabitants. The largest building yet discovered is three hundred and fifty feet by one hundred and fifty, surrounded with embankments, moats, outer walls, and reservoirs. It stands in the centre of a city near Salt River, some twenty miles above the town of Phœnix, Arizona. There are also buildings which appear to have been joined, surrounding courts of such magnitude that no roof could have covered them. All through this country are the ruins of immense *acequias* (irrigating canals—sometimes written *zequia*), some of which can yet be traced through lengths of fifty miles or more. Their grade is so perfect that modern engineers have been unable to gain an inch of fall to the mile over theirs. Another fact showing a knowledge of engineering is that many of their towns and works are laid out with regard to the points of the compass. The ledges of rock in this country abound in hieroglyphs. Pottery and stone implements are found in quantities, but no implements of iron and no bones of large domestic animals have been discovered in these ruins. The people who built these towns must have had all this land under cultivation, and must have been more advanced in the arts and sciences than the Pueblos. This, however, does not show that the Pueblos are not their descendants, for they may have retro-graded. As I have already mentioned, they have lost the art of manufacturing cotton fabrics since the whites knew them, and this is an art which the prehistoric race had, for cotton cloth has been found in the cliff dwellings, six feet below the present surface of the floors. It is also quite probable that they have had and lost the art of writing. In the Pueblo of Zuñi is said to be preserved a book of dressed skins, the pages of which are covered with figures and characters of all shapes, in red, blue, and green. They say it is a history of their tribe, which has moved fourteen times, this being their fif-teenth settlement. The last man who could read it died many years ago, and it is now kept as a sacred relic. A more enticing field for some American Champollion could hardly be imagined.

The common characteristic of the ancient and modern races is the pueblo itself, which is a large building, of many rooms, capable of accommodating numerous families. Some of them are built of stone, some of adobes, and some are caves cut in the cliffs, with artificial structure added where neces-sary. They range from two to eight stories in height; the walls of each succeeding story set back from those of the one below, making a succession of terraces to the top of the build-ing. There are no entrances through the lower walls. The interior is reached by mounting from terrace to terrace on ladders, and then descending through trap-doors. At night the ladders are pulled up, and the inmates rest out of reach of their enemies. Each story is divided into tiers of rooms, the outer ones lighted by narrow windows; the inner ones, which are used chiefly as store-rooms, being dark. In each pueblo is a large room called the *estufa*, which serves as a council-chamber, a place of worship, and a public hall. Some of these pueblos have furnished a habitation for hundreds of people for centuries. In general, the religion of this people is an odd mixture of Catholicism and paganism, but the dif-ferent villages vary widely in their tenets. In government and laws the villages are entirely independent. They hold yearly elections of their officers, who are a governor or ca-cique, a judge or alcalde, a constable, and a war captain, the

COUNCIL IN THE ESTUFA AT ZUÑI.

last having no authority in time of peace. They have also a council of wise men in each village, who act as advisers to the governor.

The Pueblos are ignorant and superstitious, as compared with modern civilized peoples, but they are industrious, honest, sober, frugal, brave, and peaceable. When first conquered by the Spanish they were reduced to a grievous state of slavery, which they endured restlessly till 1680. In that year, roused by persistent attempts to force Catholicism on them, they rebelled and drove the Spanish out. They held their country for thirteen years before they could be reconquered. Though then forced to accept the Spanish faith, they were treated more liberally, but several revolts occurred afterwards. At the time of the American conquest they were practically in harmony with the Mexican population, and accepted the new government with equal resignation.

Notwithstanding the good grace with which the people had submitted, many of them were sore over the cowardly manner in which the country had been surrendered, and were ready for the machinations of designing men. Such men were there, and, as the various bodies of troops left for other points, they began to plot. This was only natural. When a Mexican has nothing else to busy him he gets up an insurrection. Indeed, some of them would neglect a profitable business for this purpose. The leaders in this project were the disappointed Colonel Diego Archuleta and his friend Tomas Ortiz, men of talent and enterprise, made doubly desperate by intemperance and unlucky gambling. They were supported by a number of prominent *ricos* and priests, and had enlisted the aid of the Taosan Indians, as well as the Mexicans. The rising was to have been on the 19th of December, but, owing to defective organization, it was postponed to Christmas Eve. At dead of night the church bells were to be rung, and, at that signal, the conspirators were to sally forth, seize the artillery, and murder every American and friendly native in the province. Three days before the time of attack the plot was revealed to the Americans. An ex-officer of the Mexican army was arrested, and a list of the disbanded soldiers of Armijo was found on him. Several others supposed to be implicated were arrested, but Ortiz and Archuleta escaped to the south and reached Mexico. Early in January Governor Bent issued a proclamation calculated to quiet the people. The insurrection was believed to have been suppressed by these measures, but the leaderless organization remained like a giant blast in the midst of the social fabric, ready to explode at the touch of any spark. The explosion came on January 19, 1847.

Early in the morning of that day a large number of Pueblos assembled at Don Fernandez and insisted on the release of three of their tribe, notorious thieves, who were confined in the *calabozo*. The sheriff, Stephen Lee, seeing no means of resistance at hand, was about to comply with their demand, when the Mexican prefect, Cornelio Vigil, appeared and forbade him, at the same time denouncing all the Indians as thieves and scoundrels. This was the needed spark. The Indians sprang on him with the fury of devils, killed him, cut off his limbs, cut him to pieces, and then released the prisoners. Lee escaped in the confusion, but was followed and killed. The blood of the Indians was now at fever heat, and the slumbering impulses of savagery came into control again, as they were incited to further action by the Padre Martinez and others of the original conspirators. They hastened to the house of Governor Bent, who had been in Fernandez for several days. He was yet in bed, but was aroused by his wife and warned of the imminent peril. He quickly realized the situation. Telling his wife it was useless to attempt fighting such a mob single-handed, he sprang to a window which opened into an adjoining house and asked for assistance. The Mexicans there told him it was useless to hope for aid — that he must die. At the same time he was wounded by two arrows from Indians who had mounted the housetops. He withdrew into his room and the Indians began tearing up the roof. With all the calmness of a nòble soul he stood awaiting his doom. His wife brought him his pistols and told him to fight, to avenge himself, even if he must die. The Indians were exposed to his aim, but he replied: "No; I will not kill any one of them; for the sake of you, my wife, and you, my children. At present, my

PUEBLO OF TAOS—SOUTH PUEBLO.

death is all these people wish." As the savages poured into the room he appealed to their manhood and honor, but in vain. They laughed at his plea. They told him they were about to kill every American in New Mexico and would begin with him. An arrow followed the word—another, and another—but the mode was not swift enough. One, more impatient, sent a bullet through his heart. As he fell, Tomas, a chief, stepped forward, snatched one of his pistols, and shot him in the face. They took his scalp, stretched it on a board with brass nails, and carried it through the streets in triumph.

James W. Leal, a private in the La Clede Rangers, fared even worse. He was on furlough, and had been appointed prosecuting attorney for the northern district. They seized him at his house, stripped him naked, and marched him about the streets, pushing arrows into his flesh, inch by inch, as they dragged him along. They conducted him again to his house, where they made a target of him, and amused themselves by shooting at his eyes, his nose, and his mouth. They tore away his bleeding scalp, and left him writhing in agony while they went in search of other victims. Several hours after they began their fiendish work they returned and finished it by shooting him to death with arrows. His body was thrown out, and the hogs had eaten part of it, when Mrs. Beaubien, the Spanish wife of Judge Beaubien, learned of it, and had some men bury the remains. Meanwhile the Beaubiens were in deep affliction. There had been at their house another member of the La Clede Rangers, Robert Cary by name, but he had gone to Santa Fé on the day previous with Judge Beaubien. The Indians, supposing him to be there still, went to the house, where they were met by Narcissus Beaubien, the judge's son, a promising youth of twenty, who had just finished his education in the States. They murdered him, probably mistaking him for Cary. They also murdered Pablo Harvimeah, a friendly Mexican. General Elliott Lee, of St. Louis, was in Fernandez at the time. He fled to the house of a friendly priest, who concealed him under some sacks of wheat. The Indians searched for him some time before they discovered his hiding-place. They were then about to drag him

5

forth and kill him, but the priest interceded and persuaded them to go away. They returned several times, with renewed determination to have his life, but the padre succeeded in saving him. The only other American who escaped from the place was Charles Towne. His father-in-law, a Mexican, mounted him on a swift mule, and he brought the news of the massacre to Santa Fé.

The insurrection was now under full headway. Messengers were sent in every direction to urge the people to rise against the Americans. The Rio Abajo (the lower river country, as distinguished from the Rio Arriba, or upper river country) was especially called on for aid. On the evening of the same day eight Americans were captured, robbed, and shot, by the insurgents, on the road near Mora, a town of some 2000 inhabitants, situated about seventy-five miles east of Santa Fé, near the road to the States. They were Romulus Culver, L. L. Waldo, Benjamin Praett, Louis Cabano, Mr. Noyes, and three others in company. On the same day also two Americans were killed on the Colorado, and shortly afterwards several grazing camps were attacked, the guards killed, and the cattle run off. These outrages were by Mexicans, and are not properly within our province. I will mention, however, that Captain Hendley, who was stationed near Mora, attacked the Mexicans there on January 24. He was killed and his force repulsed. On February 1, Captain Morin, with 200 men, attacked and destroyed the town, with everything in it; but Cortez, the Mexican leader there, escaped. Let us now return to our Indians.

Twelve miles above Don Fernandez the road through the *Valle de Taos* crosses the Arroyo Hondo (Deep Creek. Arroyo means a small river, but is commonly used in the West to indicate any land subject to overflow, from a dry gulch to a river bottom). At this place Simeon Turley, an American, had established a mill and a distillery. These buildings, with the stables and outhouses, were enclosed in a square corral. On one side, at a distance of about twenty yards, ran the stream; on the other the ground was broken, and rose abruptly, at a short distance, forming the bank of the ravine. At the rear was a little garden, to which a small gate opened from the corral. Turley was not apprehensive of danger, and, indeed, had personally little cause to be. He had married a Mexican woman. He was well known and generally liked. He was celebrated for his generosity and humanity; no needy man was turned unaided from his door. He had even been warned of the intended revolt, but had paid no attention to the warning. On the morning of the 19th one of his employés, named Otterbees, who had been to Santa Fé on an errand, rode up to the mill at full speed. He reined his panting horse only long enough to tell them that the Indians had risen and massacred Governor Bent and others, and then galloped on. Even then Turley did not anticipate any molestation, but there were eight white men, mostly American trappers, at the mill, and on their solicitation the gates of the corral were closed and preparations made for defence. In a few hours a large crowd of Pueblos and Mexicans, armed with guns, bows, and lances, made their appearance, and, advancing under a white flag, demanded the surrender of the place and the men. They told Turley that they would spare his life, but that the other Americans must die; that they had killed the governor and all the Americans at Fernandez, and not one was to be left alive in New Mexico. It was a hard choice for Turley. On one side was his life, his family, and his property. On the other were the lives of eight of his countrymen. He did not hesitate for an instant. His answer was: " I will never surrender my house or my men. If you want them you must take them." The enemy drew off, consulted for a few minutes, scattered, and began their attack. Under cover of the rocks and cedar bushes, which were abundant on all sides, they surrounded the corral and kept up an incessant but ineffectual fire on the mill. The defenders did better. They had blocked the windows, leaving only loopholes, and from one of these there sped a ball with unerring aim at every assailant who showed himself. During the day several were killed, and parties were kept busy bearing the wounded out of the cañon. Nightfall brought no material change in the condition of the besieged. They wasted no ammunition in the dark, but passed the night in running bullets, cutting patches, and completing the defenses of the place. It was the last night on earth for all but two of them.

The attacking party originally numbered about five hundred, and was constantly growing. They kept up a continual fire during the night at the upper part of the buildings, while a part of them effected a lodgment in the stables and outbuildings. One squad reached a shed which joined the main building and attempted to secure an entrance by breaking through the wall, but its combined strength of logs and adobes resisted all their efforts. When morning broke, this party still remained in the shed, which proved unavailable, however, as a point of attack. Finding that they could not injure the besieged from that position, they began running across the open space to the stables beyond, and several had done so in safety before the men in the mill noticed them. The next who attempted to cross was a Pueblo chief. He dropped dead in his tracks near the centre of the open space. An Indian at once dashed out and attempted to drag his body in. A rifle cracked, the Indian leaped into the air, and fell across the body of his chief, shot through the heart. A second followed, and a third, only to meet the same fate. Then three Indians rushed to the place together. They had laid hold of the chief's corpse by the head and legs and lifted it up, when three puffs of blue smoke came from the loopholes, three rifles rang out, and three more bodies were added to the ghastly pile. Then a great shout of rage went up from the besiegers, and a rattling volley was poured into the mill. Until then no one in the mill had been injured, but from this volley two men fell mortally wounded. One was shot through the loins and suffered great agony. He was removed to the still-house and placed on a pile of grain, which was the softest bed at hand. The conflict then lulled a little.

In the middle of the day the assailants, growing more furious at their baffled attempts, renewed the attack more fiercely than ever. The little garrison stood to their defence as coolly and bravely as before, and their rifles spoke death to every Indian or Mexican who exposed himself. But their ammunition was failing, and, what was worse, the enemy had succeeded in firing the mill. It blazed up fiercely and threatened destruction, but the inmates succeeded in quenching the flames. While they were thus occupied the assailants entered the corral and vented their rage by spearing the hogs and sheep, which had been gathered there for protection. As fast as the flames were extinguished in one place they broke out in another. The assailants were constantly increasing in numbers. It was evident that a successful defence was hopeless. The besieged therefore determined to fight until night, and then each one make his escape as best he could. Just at dusk two of the men ran to the wicket-gate that opened into the garden, in which were a number of armed Mexicans. They rushed out at the same time and discharged their rifles full in the faces of the crowd. In the confusion that ensued one of them threw himself under the fence, and from there he saw his companion shot down and heard his cries for mercy, mingled with shrieks of pain, as the assassins pierced him with their knives and lances. He lay motionless under the fence until it was quite dark, and then escaped to the mountains. After travelling day and night, with scarcely an hour's rest, he finally succeeded in reaching a trader's fort, half dead with hunger and fatigue. Turley also succeeded in reaching the mountains unseen. There he met a Mexican with whom he had been on intimate terms for years. He was mounted. Turley offered him his watch for the use of the horse, the animal itself not being worth one third as much, but was refused. Still the inhuman hypocrite affected compassion for him and promised to bring him assistance if he would remain at a certain rendezvous. He then proceeded to the mill and informed the Indians of Turley's whereabouts. A large party of them hurried to the place and shot him to death. One other man made his escape and reached Santa Fé in safety. The others, Albert Turbush, William Hatfield, Louis Tolque, Peter Roberts, Joseph Marshall, and William Austin, perished at the mill. Everything about the place that the victorious party desired they carried off, and the rest was burned. On the morning of the 21st all that remained of Turley's mill was a smouldering ruin — the smoking ashes of a bloody funeral pyre.

The news of the murders at Don Fernandez was brought to Colonel Price on the 20th, and on the same day he intercepted some of the messengers sent by the insurgents to the

Rio Abajo, on whom were found letters which showed their plans in full.   All the Americans in Santa Fé were thrown

STERLING PRICE.

into a fury of excitement and indignation when they heard of the horrible treatment of their universally beloved governor. Colonel Price reviewed the troops, and announced to them that he would inflict summary punishment on the guilty.   He at once sent orders to Major Edmonson to come up from Albuquerque with his regiment of mounted Missouri volunteers and garrison Santa Fé.   Captain Burgwin, who was at the same place with two companies of dragoons, was instructed to leave one company at Santa Fé and join Price in the field with the other.   Felix St. Vrain, Bent's partner, organized a company of mounted volunteer "avengers," which was joined by merchants, clerks, teamsters, and mountaineers, to the number of fifty.   Without waiting for the troops from Albuquerque, Price marched for Taos on the 23d, with 353 infantry, four 12-pound howitzers, and St. Vrain's company.   On the next day they met the insurgents near La Cañada, about 1500 strong, seemingly anxious for a fight, but a brief cannonade and a gallant charge put them to flight.   A detachment of them undertook to destroy the wagon-train, but Captain St. Vrain's force beat them off.   Our loss was two killed and seven wounded; the insurgents left thirty-six dead on the field.   On the 28th the command reached Luceros, and was there joined by Captain Burgwin with two companies, one mounted, and Lieutenant Wilson of the 1st dragoons, with a 6-pounder, increasing the command, rank and file, to 479 men.

The succeeding day it was learned that the enemy, 650 strong, were posted in the cañon leading to the town of Embudo.   As the road through the cañon was impassable for artillery and wagons, a detachment of 180 men, under Captain

PUEBLO OF TAOS—NORTH PUEBLO.

Burgwin, including St. Vrain's volunteers, was sent to dislodge them. This detachment reached the enemy's position and found them posted on both sides of the narrow gorge, screened by forests and masses of rock. The Americans dismounted and charged up both sides of the cañon, in open order, firing rapidly. The enemy broke at once and fled towards Embudo, with a speed which made pursuit vain. The detachment occupied Embudo that night, and rejoined the main body at Trampas on the 31st. Their loss at Embudo was one killed and one—Dick, the colored servant of the late governor—severely wounded; the insurgents lost twenty killed and sixty wounded. The march from Trampas was one of great hardship, the road being up Taos mountain and down into the valley beyond. The troops had to wade through deep snow, two and three feet of it at the summit, and break a road for the wagons. They had no tents, and their blankets were carried on their backs. They bore their trials with the uncomplaining patience of veterans, although many were frost-bitten, and all were jaded. The exposure of this march proved to be as fatal as the arms of the enemy, for numbers contracted fevers which resulted in death; among these were Lieutenants Lackland and Mansfield.

The command marched up the valley, passing through Don Fernandez de Taos without any opposition, until, on the afternoon of February 3, they reached the pueblo where the enemy were strongly fortified. The village was entirely surrounded by adobe walls and strong pickets, the enclosure being almost a rectangle in shape, about 250 yards long and 200 yards wide. In the northeast and southeast corners were the two large houses, or pueblos proper, rising like pyramids to heights of seven and eight stories, and capable of sheltering 800 men each. In the northwestern corner was the large adobe church, opening to the south in a corral. Between each of these buildings and the walls was an open passage-way. There were also a number of small buildings within the enclosure, mostly to the north of the small stream which enters near the southwest corner and passes out on the east side. The exterior wall and those of the buildings were pierced for rifles, and every point of the exterior wall was flanked by projecting buildings at the angles.

The little army halted before this stronghold of the ancient time. Its inhabitants hurled their jeering defiance from their housetops, or peered with curious eyes through their narrow windows at the deluded foe who had expected to injure them. They were face to face; the oldest civilization of the United States and its newest; the one confident in its numbers and its massy walls, the other in its engines of war, its discipline, and its valor. There they fought their battle out, and settled their differences forever. The artillery was unlimbered, and played on the west side of the church for two hours and a half, but with no perceptible effect. At the end of that time, as the men were suffering from the cold, and the ammunition-wagon had not come up, the Americans retired to Fernandez for the night. Colonel Price, in the meantime, had thoroughly reconnoitred the village, and decided on his plan of attack. The Indians on the housetops mistook the withdrawal for a retreat, and, with insulting gestures and epithets, told the Americans to come on if they wanted to be killed. The invitation was accepted early on the following morning, the village being surrounded and work begun in earnest. Captain Burgwin, with the dragoons and two howitzers, was stationed on the west side, opposite the church. Captains Slack and St. Vrain, with the mounted men, were placed on the east side, to prevent the escape of fugitives to the mountains. The balance of the command was on the north side, with the remaining two howitzers and the 6-pounder. The batteries opened upon the village at nine o'clock, and continued firing till eleven. Finding it impossible to breach the walls with the cannon, the troops charged on the north and west sides. They gained the shelter of the church walls, and some began their attack on the thick clay barrier, while others mounted a rude ladder and fired the roof. The artillery meanwhile plied the village with grape and shell. The battle was becoming more exciting. The soldiers cut holes through the church walls and threw in lighted shells with their hands. The Indians and their allies maintained a rambling fire on them from the church and the bastions. Captain Burgwin, with Lieutenants McIlvaine, Royall, and Lackland, climbed over into the corral at the front of the church, and tried to force the door.

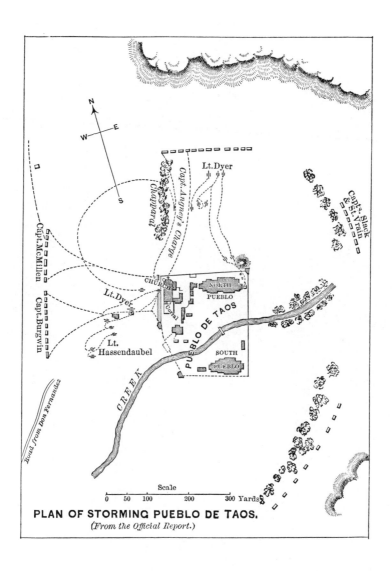

PLAN OF STORMING PUEBLO DE TAOS.

(From the Official Report.)

In this exposed position the gallant captain received a bullet wound which disabled him, and from which he died on the 9th. The fatal shot is supposed to have been fired by a Delaware Indian desperado, well known on the frontier as " Big Negro," who had joined the insurgents, and afterwards made his escape to the Cheyennes and Comanches. He claimed to have killed five Americans at the pueblo. The officers who followed Burgwin found their efforts fruitless, and retired behind the wall. At half - past three in the afternoon the 6-pounder was run up within sixty yards of the church, and in ten rounds made a practicable breach of one of the holes cut by the axe-men. The gun was brought within ten yards, and three charges of grape and a shell were thrown in. Then the storming party poured in, under cover of the dense smoke which filled the church. They occupied it without opposition, no Indians being seen except a few who were hurrying out of the gallery, where an open door admitted the air. Another charge was made at once on the north side, and the enemy then abandoned the western part of the town altogether. Some took refuge in the two large houses, while others tried to escape to the mountains on the east. They might better have tried any other place, for here were the " avengers," who were only desirous of an opportunity to earn their title. Fifty-one of the fugitives fell by their hands, and only two or three escaped. Among those killed was Jesus de Tafoya, one of the leaders, who was wearing Governor Bent's coat and shirt. He was shot by Captain St. Vrain. When night fell, the troops moved quietly forward and occupied the deserted buildings of the Indians. In the morning the Indians, men and women, bearing white flags, crucifixes, and images, came to Colonel Price, and on their knees begged for mercy. They had lost about 150 killed, besides the wounded, out of a force of some 650, and the colonel thought that their punishment was almost enough. He granted their prayer, on condition that they surrendered a number of the leading offenders, especially their chief Tomas, who has been mentioned in connection with Governor Bent's murder, and who had taken an active part throughout.

The principal Mexican leaders of the insurrection were Ta-

foya, Pablo Chaves, Pablo Montoya, and Cortez, the leader at
Mora.   Chaves was killed at Embudo, and Tafoya at the
pueblo.   Montoya, a man of considerable influence, who styled
himself the Santa Anna of the North, was tried by court-
martial and hanged in the presence of the army, at Fernandez,
on February 7.   Tomas was shot by a sentinel while trying to
escape from the guard-house at the same place.   Fourteen of
the insurrectionists were indicted for the murder of Governor
Bent, and tried at Taos.   They were all convicted and executed.   Antonio Trujillo and several others were sentenced to
be hanged on convictions of treason, but were pardoned by the
President on the ground that Mexican citizens could not commit treason against the United States while actual war existed
between the two countries.   The army returned to Santa Fé,
and there, on the 13th, the bodies of Governor Bent and Prose-
cuting-attorney Leal were buried with civic, masonic, and
military honors.   After a third interment, the remains of
Governor Bent now lie in the Masonic Cemetery at the
New Mexican capital, beneath a handsome monument and
honorable epitaph.

On no other occasion have the Pueblos proven hostile to
the Americans, and in this instance the Taosans only were
guilty.   Even in the insurrectionary troubles of the succeeding summer the Pueblos took no part.   For what they did
they were not really very blameworthy, except for their savage
cruelty.   What feelings of patriotism they had attached them
to the Mexicans, and their Mexican leaders had persuaded
them that they could easily drive out the Americans, capture
Santa Fé, and repossess the country.   Insurrection was an
every-day affair with the entire community, and assassination
was the popular method of warfare.   Fiendish as their crime
was, it was little worse than was perpetrated on soldiers of
our army by Mexicans in the course of the war; and the recollection of it, even as an historical fact, has been almost blotted
out by their faithful and trustworthy conduct in the years
that followed.   At the time of our conquest the number of
the Pueblos was between ten and eleven thousand, but they
have now declined to about nine thousand, besides having degenerated somewhat physically.   The cause of their decadence

is probably their continuous intermarriage in the same pueblo, the young men very rarely seeking wives from other villages. They have been judicially recognized as citizens of the United States, but they have not exercised the right of suffrage, under the laws of New Mexico.* The old Spanish grants were confirmed to them in 1858 by Congress, and on these they pursue in peace their quiet agricultural life. The only troubles that have ruffled their quietude in late years were some slight religious dissensions, for which they were not much to be blamed. In 1868 a new policy was inaugurated for the control of the Indians, and under it the various tribes were assigned to the different churches for missionary work. This was done with the best of intentions, but the military impartiality with which the allotment was made seemed to indicate a desire to give each denomination a fair show at the heathen, rather than to gratify any sectarian preferences of the Indians themselves. In the distribution the Pueblos fell to the Campbellites, and afterwards, on their failure to act, to the Presbyterians. Calvinism would not hinge with even the crude Catholicism of the Pueblos, and a period of " rum, Romanism, and rebellion " ensued. In 1872 the caciques of fifteen pueblos protested against their established church, and in 1874 appealed to the government. The matter was satisfactorily adjusted and peace has since reigned supreme.

---

* An attempt has recently been made to tax them, and a delegation of their leading men visited Washington a short time since to protest against this privilege of citizenship.

CHAPTER IV.

THE MURDER OF THE MISSIONARIES.

We will now leave New Mexico for a time and see what is being done in Oregon. As we make this change of position let us examine the country and its inhabitants, in a general way. Suppose we can rise in the air to a convenient height and take a bird's-eye view of the entire region. We are now over the southeastern corner of the mountain country. Directly north from us runs the great continental divide, until it reaches about the 41st parallel of latitude, just west of the site of the future city of Cheyenne; there it turns to the left and trends northwest to our boundary. The foothills, which occupy only a narrow strip of country between the main range and the plains as far north as parallel 41, bear gradually to the east above that point, thus leaving a great triangular body of comparatively low mountain land, east of the continental divide, for the northeastern corner of our region. It will eventually form Western Dakota and nearly all of Wyoming and Montana. West of the divide the country is separated into four great natural divisions. The farthest from us is the immediate slope of the Pacific, cut off from the great central basins by the Sierra Nevada and Cascade mountain ranges, which follow the general contour of the coast-line. This division will hereafter make California and the western parts of Oregon and Washington Territory. At about parallel 42 of north latitude we see an immense, transverse water-shed crossing the central mountain region from the Rockies to the Sierra Nevada. To the north of it the country is drained by the tributaries of the Columbia, a noble stream, which breaks its way through the Cascade Mountains and flows to the Pacific. Idaho, with the eastern parts of Oregon and Washington Territory, will be carved from this section. On the south side of the transverse

water-shed lie the great Utah basin and the valleys of the
head-waters of the Rio Colorado, separated by the Wahsatch
Mountains at about longitude 111° west of Greenwich (the
western line of Wyoming) as far south as $37\frac{1}{2}$° of north latitude, where this water-shed turns to the west at a right angle
and continues to the Sierra Nevada.   The Utah basin includes
the future state of Nevada and western Utah.   The land drained
by the Colorado system will be known after some years as
Eastern Utah, Western Colorado, and Arizona.   The artificial
divisions of the mountain country, as we look at it, are very
simple.   All the country east of the divide is embraced in
Missouri Territory and New Mexico, which are separated by
the Arkansas River.   West of the divide likewise there are
two sections, Oregon and Upper California, separated by parallel 42 of north latitude.

There are few whites in the country as yet.   There is a
little settlement at Pueblo, on the Arkansas, a considerable
colony of Mormons southeast of the Great Salt Lake, and a
few ranches in California.   Aside from the scattered forts and
trading-posts, we see no more establishments of white men except in Oregon, where they are almost wholly west of the Cascade range.   The natives find their tribal boundaries to a
large extent in the natural ones mentioned above.   On the
neighboring plains to the east of us are the Kiowas and
Comanches.   North of them, on the plains near the mountains, are the Cheyennes and Arapahoes, ranging from the
Arkansas to the Platte.   To the north again, along the border
of the foothills, is the numerous Sioux or Dakota family, extending to our northern boundary and far to the east.   Parts
of the great northeastern triangle are inhabited by the Crows
and the Assinaboines, who are of the Dakota family; the Blackfeet, who, like the Cheyennes, are a branch of the great Algonquin family of the East; and the confederated Minnetarees or
Hidatsa, Ricarees (Arikaras, Rees) or Black Pawnees, and
Mandans, the latter a strange tribe, believed by many to be
descendants of Madoc's Welsh colony of the twelfth century.
The southeastern part of the triangle is a common battle-
ground for the surrounding tribes, who, though nearly all
related, are hostile — a veritable dark and bloody ground,

6

over which the besom of destruction swept again and again
both before and after the whites entered it. On the Pacific
coast the principal families are the Chinooks and Nasquallas, of Oregon, and the California Indians. From the Rio
Colorado to our point of observation, the Pima nation
dwells, and the tribes of Apaches and Navahos, whose lan-

CHINOOK WOMAN AND CHILD.

guage identifies them with the extensive Athabascan family
of British America. In the lapse of years they, as well as
the Umpquas of western Oregon, have been separated from
their northern brethren, and are also much changed in character, our New Mexican neighbors being very demons in their
daring and fierceness, while the Tinné, or northern Athabas-

cans, are mild and timid. Nearly all the remainder of the mountains is held by the great Shoshonee stock, which includes many tribes. Of these the Shoshonees proper, or Snakes, live on the Snake River, south of the Salmon Mountains; the Bannocks (Bonacks, Panocks) south of the Snakes, on the same stream; and the various tribes of the Utahs (Youtas, Ewtaws, or Utes) hold the Utah basin and the headwaters of the Colorado. The Modocs of Southwestern Oregon are related to them, as are also the Kiowas and Comanches. These latter tribes have separated from their relatives over the most natural roadway across the mountains, southeast from the Dalles of the Columbia to the South Pass. (It now forms the route of a proposed railway to connect Oregon with the Gulf of Mexico, the building of which is only a question of time.) It is the same road that Dr. Whitman followed with his emigrants. We will follow it into his missionary field of Eastern Oregon, the only part of the central region not occupied by the Shoshonees.

We find Eastern Oregon subdivided in two parts by the Blue and the Salmon Mountains, really one range, which is cut by the Lewis or Snake River. These mountains form the northern limits of the Shoshonees, except that the lower Nez Percés own the country as far south as the Powder River. At present, however, they are across the mountains, with their brethren, receiving "The Book" from Mr. Spalding. North and west of these mountains is the mission field, in which there are three principal Indian families. Nearest the British possessions is the Selish (Salish, Saalis) or Flathead family, including the Flatheads proper (to whom belong the Spokanes), the Cœur d'Alênes (Pointed Hearts or Skitsnish), the Kalispels (Pend d'Oreilles), and some small tribes grouped about forts Colville and Okanogan. None of these Indians practice flattening the head, as their name would imply; that is a custom confined to the tribes of the Lower Columbia and the coast, and by them allowed only to the higher classes.*

---

* This habit has been discontinued, old settlers stating that they have not known of a case in the last thirty years; a reform unquestionably due to the precept and example of white mothers who settled among them. The Nez Percés had formerly a custom of piercing the cartilage of the nose, and

To the south of the Selish is the Sahaptin or Saptin family, including the Nez Percés and the Walla-Wallas, the latter embracing the Klickitats (Tlickitacks), Des Chutes, Yakimas, and Pelouse (Palus, Paloose). Still south, below the Columbia, is the Wailatpu family, including the Cayuses (Kayouse, Cailloux, Caaguas, Skyuse *) and the Moleles (Mollallas), a proud and insolent people, quite wealthy, especially in horses.†

We follow the emigrants' road through the Grande Ronde, over the Blue Mountains and down Walla-Walla Creek. The

INDIAN SWEAT-HOUSE.

first white settlement we find is the mission at Wailatpu (the Place of Wild Rye), the home of Dr. Whitman, close by the village of the Cayuse chief Tilokaikt (Crawfish that Walks Forward). The establishment and its surroundings indicate peace and prosperity. It covers a triangular piece of ground of about four hundred feet to the side, in a bit of bottom-land between Mill Creek and Walla-Walla Creek. The wooden building at the southern apex is the mill. The rest of the buildings, along the northern line, are in order, at the east a story and

---

putting a bone through the puncture until it healed. This was abandoned so long since that many modern writers have been puzzled to know the origin of their name.

* The word is probably Cailloux, the French for flints.

† An Indian pony is called a cayuse throughout the western country north of parallel 42. South of that it is a bronco.

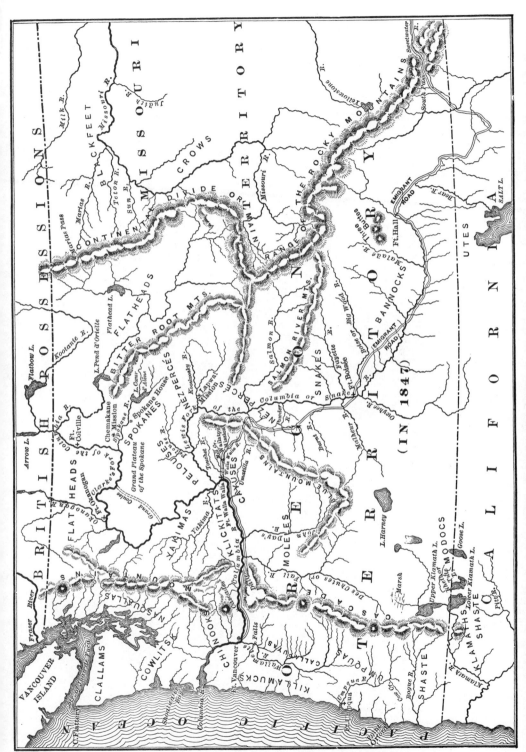

THE NORTHWEST IN 1841.

a half house, called the mansion; eighty yards west, the black-smith-shop; at the end of the line, the doctor's house, fronting west. This last is quite commodious. The main building is 18 × 62 feet, with adobe walls. At the south end is the library and bedroom; in the middle the dining and sitting room, 18 × 24; on the north end the Indian room, 18 × 26. Joining the house on the east is the kitchen, 18 × 26, with fireplace in the centre and bedroom in the rear. Joining the kitchen on the east is the schoolroom, 18 × 30. On the southeastern side of the mission are the mill-pond and Walla-Walla Creek. Along the north side runs the waste-water ditch from the mill, which also serves for irrigating.

The mission has no immediate white neighbors. Twenty-five miles west, at the mouth of the creek, is Fort Walla-Walla, a Hudson's Bay Company's post (present village of Wallula). It is a strong-looking stockade, built of driftwood taken from the Columbia, with log bastions at the northeast and southwest corners, each provided with two light cannon and small arms. Down the Columbia, at the Dalles, is the nearest of the original Methodist missions, lately transferred to the American Board, and others are west of the Cascade range, especially in the Willamette or Wallamet Valley, where most of the pioneer settlers have established themselves. On the north side of the Columbia, just above the mouth of the Wallamet, is Fort Vancouver, headquarters of the Hudson's Bay Company, a substantial stockade enclosing two acres of land, with hewn-timber houses, well armed and manned. One hundred and twenty miles northeast of Wailatpu, where Lapwai Creek debouches into the Kooskoosky or Clear-water River, Mr. Spalding and wife are laboring successfully with the Nez Percés. Away to the north, near the Spokane River, sixty-five miles south of Fort Colville, is Cimiakin (Chemakane, Ishimikane), another mission of the American Board, where Messrs. Walker and Eells, with their helpers, are making lasting conversions.

In order to understand the real condition of affairs which exists under the seeming peaceful exterior of the country, we must go back a little. Whitman's missionary party had been kindly received by the officials of the Hudson's Bay Company, and, having been put on their guard as to its designs, they remained on friendly terms for some years. But a time came at length when they were forced to go in opposition to it, or throw away all patriotism, and they took the former course, as we have seen. The company realized that its control of the fur trade, and of the country in general, depended on England's retaining its sovereignty. It desired England to retain control, simply because it would make more money in that event. To maintain the immense profits which they reaped from the trade, its managers used every means, fair and foul. They gave the Indians rum, because it was a profitable commodity. They countenanced and maintained Indian slavery, because it gave control over the natives. They strenuously opposed agriculture, even by British missionaries, because agriculture spoiled good hunting-grounds, and, if learned by the Indians, would give them an easier mode of support than hunting. They paid the Indians very little for furs, and allowed no one to pay more than their established " tariff." They sold the Indians guns and ammunition, because it made their hunting more successful. When it became evident that the Americans were forcing the settlement of the country, the company fought every step of their progress, and yet reaped the advantages of civilization as well as savagery. At first it owned nearly all the cattle in the country, and would let the settlers have them only on terms that they and all their increase should belong to the company, subject to its recall at any time; and, if they died, to be paid for by the borrower. In order to obtain cattle of their own, the Methodist missionaries, with Mr. Ewing Young (one of the party brought into Oregon by Hall J. Kelly), organized the Wallamet Cattle Company, and brought in stock from California. As soon as they got their cattle in, the Hudson's Bay Company organized the Puget Sound Agricultural Company, which was maintained out of the fund established by the corporation for the purpose of fighting hostile interests, and began selling cattle lower than the other company could. In 1842 the American settlers, with great difficulty, succeeded in getting a mill started at the falls of the Wallamet. The company at once put up an opposition saw and grist mill at the same place. Some parties settled at those falls, and forthwith Dr. McLaughlin, chief factor of the company, claimed the land as his, warned the trespassers off, and laid off the town site of Oregon City.

Dr. McLaughlin, however, had too much conscience for the company. He had, indeed, carried out their instructions up to this point, but they desired him to go further. They insisted that he must no longer furnish supplies on credit to needy American settlers, and he, after explaining to them that he could not, in common humanity, obey them, told the directors: "If such is your order, gentlemen, I will serve you no longer." He served them no longer, and his place was filled by James Douglass (afterwards Sir James), who was more complaisant. About the same time McKinley, their factor at Fort Walla-Walla, who was a little friendly with the Americans, was removed, and his place filled by one McBean, who proved thoroughly reliable, from a company standpoint. By misrepresentations American immigrants were prevented from bringing their wagons farther than Fort Hall, until Dr. Whitman broke their blockade in 1843, and after that Captain Grant, the factor at that place, and others, used all their powers of persuasion to turn the immigration into California. Among those, it is claimed, whom they succeeded in turning into those then unknown deserts was the Donner party, whose frightful sufferings and enforced cannibalism have since furnished a theme of horror to many writers. At the same time Sir George Simpson, at Washington, and other emissaries elsewhere, were representing to our government the desert nature of the country and slandering our settlers. In short, they tried to do in Oregon what they had done in British America, where, by an English authority, they "hold a monopoly in commerce and exercise a despotism in government; and have so used that monopoly and wielded that power as to shut up the earth from the knowledge of man, and man from the knowledge of God." From these facts it is only a fair inference that the Jesuit priests, who came into Oregon in 1838, were brought there by the Hudson's Bay Company to counteract the effect of the Protestant missions. Certain it is that the Jesuits came under their convoy, and, from first to last, received such sympathy and assistance as no Protestant missionary, British or American, ever received at their hands.

The motives of the Jesuits need not be questioned. Father De Smet probably states them truly in a letter written to their Belgian friends for further assistance. He says: "Time passes; already the sectaries of various shades are preparing to penetrate more deeply into the desert, and will wrest from those degraded and unhappy tribes their last hope —that of knowing and practising the sole and true faith." Aside from this apprehension of heresy, there was no need of their concentrating on Oregon. If they were merely solicitous for the eternal welfare of Indians, there were thousands of them elsewhere to whom no missionary had yet spoken. The fact cannot be evaded that they made their war on Protestantism, not heathenism. The results of their labors might reasonably have been anticipated. In a short time the simple natives were involved in the same sectarian controversy that had deluged all Europe in blood. The priests told the Indians that if they followed the teachings of the Protestants they would go to hell. The Protestants extended the same cheering information in regard to Catholicism. The priests used, in teaching, a colored design of a tree surmounted by a cross, and called "the Catholic tree." It showed the Protestants continually going out on the limbs and falling from their ends into fires, which were fed with Protestant books by the priests, while the Catholics were safely climbing the trunk to the emblem of salvation above. Mr. Spalding was equal to the emergency. He had his wife paint a series of Bible pictures in water-colors, the last and crowning one of which showed the "broad way that leadeth to destruction," crowded with priests, who were tumbling into hell at the terminus, while the Protestants ascended the narrow path to glory. The Indians became divided among themselves, and bitter controversies became common. The priests gained steadily. Churches, nunneries, and schools sprang up at French Prairie, Oregon City, Vancouver, the Dalles, Umatilla, Pend d'Oreille, Colville, and Ste. Marie. They had potent allies in the French - Canadian interpreters and other em-

CHEMAKANE MISSION. (FROM THE PAINTING BY STANLEY.)

ployés of the company. When the Indians appealed to these
to know which was the true religion, they were informed that
the priests had the genuine article. So it went on until the
Indians were in a fit state of mind for the crime which followed. They became restless and turbulent. Some of the
Protestant missionaries left the country. Even the indomita-
ble Dr. Whitman called his Cayuses together several times,
and told them he would leave whenever a majority of them
said he should, but the majority remained with him.

In the summer of 1847 the newly-appointed Jesuit Bishop
of Oregon, F. N. Blanchet, returned with a reinforcement of
thirteen clergymen, of different ranks, and seven nuns; eight
priests and two nuns also arrived overland the same season.
The bishop proceeded up the river, and on September 5
reached Fort Walla-Walla, accompanied by the superior of
Oblates and two other clergymen. On September 23 he was
met there by Dr. Whitman, who, according to Father Brouillet, showed that he was agitated and wounded by the bishops'
arrival. He said: " I know very well for what purpose you
have come." The bishop replied: " All is known. I come
to labor for the conversion of the Indians, and even of the
Americans, if they are willing to listen to me." The bishop
and his party remained at the fort enjoying the hospitality of
the company. On October 26, Ta-wai-tau (Young Chief), a
Catholic Cayuse chief, arrived and held a conference with the
bishop. On November 4 a general council was held, at which
Tilokaikt, who owned the land on which Whitman's mission
stood, was present. The Protestants say the Indians were
given to understand that the priests would like to have Whitman's place; the Jesuits say it was offered to them and they
refused to take it. On November 27 the bishop and party
left for the Umatilla, a few miles below, to occupy a house
offered them by Young Chief at his and Five Crows' village,
which was twenty-five miles southwest of Wailatpu.

Two days have passed. It is half-past one o'clock of
Monday, November 29. Nothing appears to mar the usual
quiet which prevails at the Wailatpu mission. The only
sounds distinguishable are the rumbling of the mill, where
Mr. Marsh is grinding, and the tapping of a hammer in

one of the rooms of the doctor's house, where Mr. Hall is lay-
ing a floor.   There is, too, the low hum of the school, which
Mr. Sanders has just called for the afternoon.   Between the
buildings, near the ditch, Kimball, Hoffman, and Canfield are
dressing an ox.   Gillan, the tailor, is on his bench in the mansion.   Mr. Rogers is in the garden.   In the blacksmith's
shop, where Canfield's family lives, young Amos Sales is lying sick.   Crockett Bewley, another young man, is sick at
the doctor's house.   The Sager boys, orphans of some unfortunate emigrants, who with their younger sisters had been
adopted by the doctor, are scattered about the place.   John,
who is just recovering from the measles, is in the kitchen,
Francis in the school-room, and Edward outside.   In the
dining-room are Dr. Whitman, Mrs. Whitman, three of the
little Sager girls—all sick—Mrs. Osborne, and her sick child.
As the doctor reads from the Bible several Indians open the
door from the kitchen and ask him to come out.   He goes,
Bible in hand, closes the door after him, sits down, and Tilokaikt begins talking to him.   As they converse, Tamsaky
(Tumsuckee) steps carelessly behind the doctor, and the other
Indians gather about, seeming much interested.   Suddenly
Tamsaky draws a pipe-tomahawk from beneath his blanket,
and strikes the doctor on the head.   His head sinks on his
breast, and another blow, quickly following, stretches him
senseless on the floor.   John Sager jumps up and draws a
pistol.   The Indians in front of him crowd back in terror
to the door, crying, "He will shoot us," but those behind
seize him and throw him to the floor.   At the same time
knives, tomahawks, pistols, and short Hudson's Bay Company
muskets flash from beneath their blankets, and John is shot
and gashed until he is senseless.   His throat is cut, and a
woollen tippet is stuffed in the wound.   With demoniac yells
the Indians rush outside to join in the work there.   The
sounds of the deadly struggle are heard in the dining-room.
Mrs. Whitman starts up and wrings her hands in agony, crying, "Oh, the Indians, the Indians!   That Joe [meaning Joe
Lewis] has done it all."   Mrs. Osborne runs into the Indian
room with her child, and they, with Mr. Osborne, are soon
secreted under the floor.   Mrs. Hall comes screaming into

the dining-room, from the mansion. With her help, Mrs. Whitman draws the doctor into that room, places his head on a pillow, and tries to revive him. In vain! he is unconscious, and past all help. To every loving word and sympathetic question he faintly whispers, " No."

Outside is a scene of wild confusion. At the agreed signal all the members of the mission had been attacked. Gillan was shot on his bench; Marsh was shot at the mill; he ran a few yards towards the house and fell. Sanders had hurried to the door of the schoolroom, where he was seized by a crowd of Indians, thrown to the ground, shot, and wounded with tomahawks. Being a powerful man, he threw off his assailants, regained his feet, and tried to run away, but was overtaken and cut down. Hall snatched a loaded gun from an Indian and escaped to the bushes. The men working at the ox received a volley from pistols and guns, which wounded them all, but not mortally. Kimball fled to the doctor's house, with a broken arm. Canfield escaped to the mansion, where he hid until night. Hoffman lunged desperately among the Indians with his butcher-knife, but was soon cut down ; his body was ripped open and his vitals torn out. Rogers was shot in the arm, and wounded on the head with a tomahawk, but managed to get into the doctor's house. Several women and children have fled in the same direction. To this place, the Indians, who have been running to and fro, howling wildly as they pursued their prey, now assemble, led by Joe Lewis and Nicholas Finlay, French half-breeds, Tamsaky and his son Waiecat, Tilokaikt and his sons Edward and Clark. Joe Lewis enters the schoolroom and brings into the kitchen the children, who had hid in the loft. Among them is Francis Sager, who, as he passes his brother John, kneels and takes the bloody tippet from his throat. John attempts to speak, but in the effort only gasps and dies. The trembling children remain huddled together, surrounded by the savages, who point their guns at them and constantly cry, "Shall we shoot?" On the other side of the house an Indian approaches the window, and shoots Mrs. Whitman in the breast. She falls, but creeps to the sofa, and her voice rises in prayer for her adopted children and her aged father and

mother. The fugitives up-stairs hear her and help her up to
them. There are now gathered in that upper chamber Mrs.
Hays, Mrs. Whitman, Miss Bewley, Catharine Sager and her
three sick sisters, three half-breed girls, also sick, Mr. Kimball,
and Mr. Rogers. Hardly have they closed and fastened the
doors, when the war-whoop sounds below; the Indians break
in the lower doors and windows and begin plundering, while
Tilokaikt goes to the doctor, who still breathes, and chops his
face to shreds with his tomahawk.

The people up-stairs have found an old gun, and the Indians, as they start to go up, find it pointed in their faces.
They retire in great alarm. A parley is held, and Tamsaky
goes up. He assures the fugitives that he is sorry for what
has been done, and advises them to come down, as the young
men are about to burn the house. He promises them safety.
They do not know of his part in the tragedy, and follow him.
As they enter the dining-room Mrs. Whitman catches sight
of the doctor's mangled face. She becomes faint, and is
placed on the sofa. They pass on through the kitchen, Mrs.
Whitman being carried on the sofa by Joe Lewis and Mr.
Rogers. As they reach the outside Lewis drops his end of
the sofa and the Indians fire their guns. Mr. Rogers throws
up his hands, cries, " Oh, my God, save me !" and falls groaning to the earth. Mrs. Whitman receives two balls and ex-
pires. The Indians spring forward, strike her in the face,
and roll her body into the mud. They heighten the terror
of the wretched survivors by their terrible yelling, and the
brandishing of their weapons. Miss Bewley runs away, but
is overtaken and led over to the mansion. Mr. Kimball and
the Sager girls run back through the house and regain the
chamber, where they remain all night. Darkness has now
come on, and the Indians, having finished their plundering,
and perpetrated their customary indignities on the dead, retire to Finlay's and Tilokaikt's lodges to consult on their
future action. The first and great day of blood is ended.

It may easily be imagined that the night was one of gloom
and horror to the unfortunate captives, and yet it afforded
security to some of those who were in peril. Under its
friendly cover Mr. Canfield escaped and made some progress

OLD FORT WALLA-WALLA. (FROM THE PAINTING BY STANLEY.)

towards Lapwai, which he eventually reached in safety. Mr. Osborne, with his family, stole forth from their place of concealment under the doctor's house, and reached Fort Walla-Walla on the following day. Mr. Hall reached the same place early in the morning, nearly naked, wounded, and exhausted. He was put across the river by McBean, the factor, and was never heard of afterwards. It is probable that information of the massacre was sent that night to the other Cayuse villages, Camaspelo's and the one on the Umatilla. The other chiefs were consulted before the affair occurred, and Five Crows (called by the whites Hezekiah, which Brouillet mistakes for Achekaia) was then head chief of the tribe. On the next day Mr. Kimball was shot as he went from his concealment in the chamber for water for himself and the sick children. The young Indian who shot him afterwards claimed his eldest daughter for a wife, as a recompense for this murder. On the same day they killed Mr. Young, a young man who had come up from the saw-mill, twenty miles away. In the evening Vicar-general Brouillet arrived. On Wednesday Brouillet and Joseph Stanfield buried the victims. This Stanfield was a French Catholic who had been employed at the mission, and was without doubt deeply implicated in the massacre, though he escaped conviction. Later in the day, Brouillet, having made a sympathetic call on the widows and orphans, returned to the Umatilla. On the way he met Mr. Spalding and notified him of the massacre. Spalding struck off into the woods and reached Lapwai, after six days of terrible exposure and suffering, without shoes, blanket, or horse. On Saturday night, and repeatedly afterwards, the three oldest of the girls were dragged out and outraged. On the Monday following, young Bewley and Sales were murdered. On Thursday Miss Bewley was taken to the Umatilla and turned over to the tender mercies of Five Crows. At the same time the other two of the older girls were taken as wives by the sons of Tilokaikt (called Edward and Clark Tilokaikt by the whites), in pursuance of an agreement which had been made at the Umatilla. One of these young braves, whose Indian name was Shumahiccie (Painted Shirt), became very much

7

attached to his enforced bride, a beautiful girl of fourteen, and wanted her to remain with him when the other captives were surrendered. He said he was a great brave and owned many cattle and horses; he would give them all to her, or, if she did not like his people, he would forsake them and live with the pale faces. But he pleaded in a hopeless cause. His hands were stained with the blood of her elder brother, and she had lived with him until that time only because he had threatened to kill her younger sisters if she did not.

The news of the massacre reached the settlements west of the mountains on December 7, by a messenger of the Hudson's Bay Company. Mr. Ogden, of the company, at once started for Fort Walla-Walla, and on December 23, by his efforts, an arrangement was effected for the surrender of all the captives, in exchange for a considerable amount of goods, including guns and ammunition. On December 29 the captives at Wailatpu, forty-six in number, arrived at the fort. On January 1, Mr. Spalding and wife, with the other whites from Lapwai, came in. The Nez Percés offered to protect them and the mission, if they would remain, but affairs were so unsettled, and Mr. and Mrs. Spalding were in such anxiety for their daughter, that they decided to leave. All of these, together with the five fugitives already at the fort, started down the river on January 2, and arrived in safety below.

On December 8, Governor Abernethy had convened the provisional legislature at Oregon City and prepared at once for a levy of troops. A company of forty-two men was organized, and started within twenty-four hours, and Captain Lee with ten of the men reached the Dalles on the 21st. This being the last settlement on the river, below the missions, and the families having gone below, the volunteers remained for a time to protect the houses. When the captives were brought down the river there was no further call for their immediate presence above, so they remained there until the last of the reinforcements, under Colonel Gilliam, arrived, on February 23. Captain Lee was then sent on a scouting expedition among the Des Chutes, who were the nearest hostiles. He found them on the 28th, and a skirmish ensued in which half a dozen Indians were killed, with no loss to the whites. The main

body, 160 men, then moved towards Wailatpu. On the
30th they were attacked by an equal number of Indians,
who were driven back with a loss of twenty men, forty
horses, and a large amount of goods. A few days later an
attempt was made, under pretence of treating for peace, to
entrap them on the prairie between Mud Spring and Umatilla, by about 500 Indians, under Nicholas Finlay, the Wailatpu murderer, but the troops formed a hollow square and
continued their march, very little damage being done on either
side. They reached Wailatpu, established Fort Waters at that
point, and held a talk with the friendly Indians who came in,
mostly Nez Percés, including Camaspelo, of the Cayuses.
Their words were all to the effect that they were not implicated in the massacre and would not protect the murderers.
One of the speeches was by Joseph, chief of the lower Nez
Percés and half-brother to Five Crows. We shall have occasion to speak of him hereafter. He said: " Now I show my
heart. When I left my home I took the Book (a Testament
given him by Mr. Spalding) in my hand and brought it with
me; it is my light. I heard the Americans were coming to
kill me. Still I held my Book before me and came on. I
have heard the words of your chief. I speak for all the Cayuses present and all my people. I do not wish my children
engaged in this war, although my brother (Five Crows) is
wounded. You speak of the murderers; I shall not meddle
with them; I bow my head; this much I speak."

As the troops advanced into their country, part of the hostile Cayuses retired into the neighboring mountains; the remainder fell back on the country of the Nez Percés. The
troops, after several skirmishes, succeeded in driving them
across the divide, and capturing their horses and cattle to the
number of 500 or more, but the Indians escaped. Small gar-
risons were kept at Fort Waters and the Dalles until September, 1848, and the tribes of the murderers, not daring to
return to their old homes, were forced to pursue a wandering
life among the mountains. In the spring of 1850 they purchased peace by surrendering five of the leading offenders,
including Tilokaikt and Tamsaky, all of whom were tried,
convicted, and, on June 3 of the same year, hung at Oregon

City. They all embraced the Catholic faith, and were baptized by Bishop Blanchet a few hours before their death.

The buildings at Wailatpu were all burned by the Indians, and to-day their places are marked by mounds of earth, into which the adobe walls sank as the elements wore upon them, except that on the site of the doctor's house a residence was afterwards erected by an old friend and co-laborer of his. A few rods away, on a hillside, is the common grave of the victims. The visitor who runs over to the site of the mission, from the little town of Walla-Walla, finds still, as living remembrancers of those Christian pioneers, two or three weather-beaten apple-trees and a rank growth of scarlet poppies, which have run wild from the old garden.

During the massacre at Wailatpu and the succeeding troubles, no employé of the Hudson's Bay Company, no relative of such employés, no Catholic, and no one who professed friendship for Catholicism, was in any way injured. A heated dispute arose afterwards as to the relation of the company and the Jesuits to the murderers. Preliminary to a view of this question, it may be remarked that very little instigation would have been necessary to induce the Indians to act as they did. Sickness, from ills which were new to the Indians, was very prevalent and unusually fatal. Mr. Spalding says: "It was most distressing to go into a lodge of some ten fires and count twenty or twenty-five, some in the midst of measles, others in the last stage of dysentery, in the midst of every kind of filth, of itself sufficient to cause sickness, with no suitable means to alleviate their inconceivable sufferings, with, perhaps, one well person to look after the wants of two sick ones. They were dying every day, one, two, and sometimes five in a day, with dysentery, which very generally followed the measles. Everywhere the sick and dying were pointed to Jesus, and the well were urged to prepare for death." Although sickness was equally prevalent among the Americans—"Suapies" or "Bostons," as the Indians called them—the Indians professed to believe that they were being poisoned, and, in view of their peculiar superstitions, it is probably true that they did. Dr. Whitman was treating many of them, and his treatment was generally made useless by their failure to follow his directions.

MEDICINE-MAN DESTROYING GIRL BY NECROMANCY. (FROM A SKETCH BY CAPTAIN EASTMAN.)

The idea prevails with many Indian tribes that the recovery or death of a patient depends on the good or bad will of the doctor, and it is not unusual, therefore, for Indians to murder unsuccessful practitioners, as, for instance, Tamouche, an old war-chief of the Utes, is remembered by early settlers of New Mexico to have killed two medicine-men, "under whose able treatment," respectively, his first and second wives had died. Among the Oregon Indians this was a common practice, and, as this point has been controverted and left unsettled by previous writers, the following testimony is cited in confirmation of the statement. In 1843, Mr. Ogden, of the Hudson's Bay Company, related the following event as occurring at a meeting for worship at the Dalles: "There was in the outskirts of the congregation an Indian woman who had been for many years a doctress in the tribe, and who had just expended all her skill upon a patient, the only son of a man whose wigwam was not far distant, and for whose recovery she had become responsible by consenting to become his physician. All her efforts to remove the disease were unavailing; the father was doomed to see his son expire. Believing that the doctress had the power of preserving life or inflicting death according to her will, and that instead of curing she had killed his boy, he resolved upon the most summary revenge. Leaving his dead son in the lodge, he broke into the congregation with a large butcher-knife in his hand, and, rushing upon the now terrified doctress, seized her by the hair, and with one blow across her throat laid her dead at his feet."

Major Alvord, who had enjoyed the fullest opportunities for investigation, reported thus to the government in 1853: "A universal belief prevails among all the tribes (of Oregon) that the medicine-man possesses wonderful faculties of conjuration, and a god-like power of killing those against whom he shall hurl his direful charms or glances. His mere look, if inimical to the victim, can kill. They will hide or avert their heads in his presence to escape his glances. Such is the fixed faith of these poor Indians, and I have had occasion to witness frequent instances among the Waskows, in my immediate vicinity. If once possessed with the idea that they are subjected to the dire frown of their medicine-man, they droop and pine away, often refuse to eat, and die of starvation and melancholy, if not of necromancy—thus confirming and verifying, with their neighbors, a belief that this portentous power is actually possessed. The natural consequences of such deep-rooted faith in these powers is that when a death occurs it is often attributed to the doctor, who is murdered by the relations of the deceased to avenge the fate of the victim. All the murders which I can hear of among them occur in this manner, and three doctors have been killed, in the last four months, in different tribes, within the distance of forty miles of this post (the Dalles). . . . The doctors are often killed for the mere failure to cure a patient, though it is always attended with a belief, on the part of the bloody avengers, in his having exercised a malign or necromantic power. In a recent case, a doctor of the Wishrams, when the smallpox was raging, was foolish enough to threaten openly what havoc he would spread among them, making use of the pestilence to magnify his office; and, to surround his person with greater elements of power, boasting that he held the fearful quiver in his own hands, ready to hurl the arrows of death in any direction. The people rose in a body and hung him in the most barbarous mode. Tying his hands and feet, they put a rope around his neck, threw it over the pommel of a saddle, and, starting the horse, his life was taken in this shocking manner. . . . It will be asked if these murders of the doctors are sanctioned among the Indians. The answer must be that the punishments inflicted are very inadequate and inefficient. A council of the head men is called by the chief, and he decides that a certain number of horses and blankets will be turned over by the murderers to the family or the relations of the deceased. It is remarkable that the murderer never attempts to run away, and, indeed, generally comes forward and confesses his crime. . . . Strenuous exertions have been made by the missionaries, and the commanding officer of this post (Alvord himself), to induce the chief to cause punishment for murder to be made by hanging. As yet no such punishment has been inflicted. On the contrary, the effect of our advice has, it would seem, fallen thus far upon one of the doctors, instead of being used for their protection. . . . I am informed that but two murders in twelve years have occurred among the Nez Percés, but they were doctors."

In 1857, Special Agent Browne reported of the Indians on the Grande Ronde reservation (between the Willamette and the coast) as follows: "They are unable to account for it, why they should die off more rapidly here than at their old homes, and whenever death occurs they attribute it to 'bad medicine,' or an evil influence put upon them by the government or its agents. Their own medicine-men are called upon to counteract this bad influence, and if the patient dies it is considered that the operator is in league with other bad spirits, and they kill him. Sometimes they put to death the medicine-men of other tribes. This gives rise to frequent and bloody quarrels, in which many are wounded or killed. It is almost impossible for the agent to preserve order among them. They tell him he has nothing to do with their customs, and insist upon it that he shall take no part in their quarrels."

In 1881, Mr. Nash, an English settler in Oregon, relates the following as occurring on the Siletz reservation (on the Oregon coast) and coming to his notice: "Some mistiness on the moral law yet remains. For instance, a murder was committed by three of them a month or two ago. It took place on the northern and remote part of the reserve, far away from the agency itself. Here lived one who, being a quack doctor, claimed the character of a mighty medicine-man, having power to prescribe for both the bodies and souls of his patients. To him resorted many of his neighbors, whose faith in his charms and spells was boundless. He undertook the cure of the wife of one Charlie, and the poor thing endured his remedies patiently. But the woman grew worse and worse. Charlie and his friends debated the case, and at last concluded that if the medicine-man could not cure the woman, according to his contract, and that she died, it would prove to them that the doctor was a humbug, and deserved to die the death. The catastrophe arrived, for the woman died. A council was held and due inquiry made. The decision was fatal to the doctor, and Charlie and two friends undertook to secure that no one else should be misled and defrauded by the quack. Proceeding to his house, away up north by Salmon River, near the sea-coast, the three fell on the medicine-man with clubs, and, despite threats, prayers, and entreaties, they beat him to death." This instance, for which, by the way, the Indians were arrested and punished, is the more satisfactory evidence of the custom from the very evident fact that the writer who recorded it did not know such a custom to exist. Some further instances will be found in subsequent chapters.

With such superstitions, and in the midst of general sickness, it was constantly reported among the Indians that Whitman was poisoning them to get their land for the Bostons. It is conceded that Joseph Lewis, Nicholas Finlay, and others were circulating, confirming, and magnifying these reports. The question still remains whether the employés of the Hudson's Bay Company and the Jesuits were doing the same thing. This is the definitive point in controversy, and it bids fair to take rank with other noted questions of sectarian persecution. It has been formally investigated and reported on by the Congregational Association of Oregon, the Old School Presbytery, the Cumberland Presbytery, the U. P. Presbytery, the Methodist Conference of Oregon, and other denominational bodies. They agree in holding the Hudson's Bay Company and the Jesuits to some extent responsible. Newspaper articles, pamphlets, and volumes have been written on this subject, which is far too extensive for full consideration in the space we can give it. As to the Hudson's Bay Company, it can only be added here, to what has already been said, that the messenger who carried the news of the massacre down the river gave the Indians at the Dalles a magnified report of the outbreak, and, under the instructions of McBean, the factor at Walla-Walla, gave the whites no intimation of it; on the contrary, he told them that four French employés of the company had died, and that he was going below to get others to take their places. Also, on August 21, 1848, during the operations against the Cayuses and other hostiles, by the provisional government, the troops seized at Wascopum 1080 pounds of powder, 1900 pounds of balls, 300 pounds of buckshot, and three cases of guns, consigned by the Hudson's Bay Company to the Jesuits, and at the same time the friendly Indians there sent away their women and children, and hid in the mountains, giving as their reason for so doing that the Cayuses had told them the French priests were going to furnish them plenty of ammunition, and they were going to kill all the Bostons and friendly Indians.

As to the Jesuits, the evidence is partly circumstantial and partly statements by the Indians. The consideration of the former would consume an undue amount of space; the latter is objected to by Father Brouillet. He says: "If, in most parts of the States of the Union, the testimony of Indians is never admitted as proof against the whites in any court of justice, it would be here inconsistent to make it the base of public opinion." It is sufficient for present purposes to say that the Protestants have made a case on which most unprejudiced persons would respond "guilty," though some might add "but not proven." While passing this question, it may safely be affirmed, however, that the proven action of the Jesuit priests at the time was certainly not prompted by any motives of humanity. In proof of this I will quote but two witnesses. The first is Father Brouillet himself. He says: "I left [Umatilla] on Tuesday the 30th of November, late in the afternoon, for Tilokaikt's camp, where I arrived between seven and eight o'clock in the evening. It is impossible to conceive my surprise and consternation, when, upon my arrival, I learned that the Indians the day before had massacred the doctor and his wife, with the greater part of the Americans at the mission. I passed the night [in Tilokaikt's camp] without scarcely closing my eyes. Early the next morning I baptized three sick children [Indians], two of whom died soon after, and then hastened to the scene of death, to offer to the widows and orphans all the assistance in my power. I found five or six women and over thirty children in a situation deplorable beyond description. Some had just lost their husbands, and others their fathers, whom they had seen massacred before their eyes, and were expecting every moment to share the same fate. The sight of those persons caused me to shed tears, which, however, I was obliged to conceal, for I was the greater part of the day in the presence of the murderers, and closely watched by them, and, if I had shown too marked an interest on behalf of the sufferers, it would only have endangered their lives and mine. . . . [He then goes to assist in burying the victims.] I assure you, sir, that during the time I was occupied in burying the victims of this disaster I was far from feeling safe, being obliged to go here and there gathering up the dead bodies, in the midst of assassins, whose hands were still stained with blood, and who, by their manners, their countenances, and the arms which they still carried, sufficiently announced that their thirst for blood was yet unsatiated. Assuming as composed a manner as possible, I cast more than one glance aside and behind at the knives, pistols, and guns, in order to assure myself whether there were not some of them directed towards me. Having buried the dead, I hastened to prepare for my return to my mission, in order to acquaint Mr. Spalding of the danger which threatened him; because on Monday evening [the 29th], when he supped with us, he said that it was his intention to return to Dr. Whitman's on the following Wednesday or Thursday; and I wished to meet him in time to give him a chance to escape. . . . [He then pays another visit to the captives and starts for the Umatilla, followed by his interpreter and one of Tilokaikt's sons. On the way Tilokaikt's son "fortunately" empties his pistol and forgets to reload it. About three miles out they meet Mr. Spalding, who at once begins talking.] While Mr. Spalding was asking me those different questions, I had spoken to my interpreter, telling him to entreat the Indian, in my name, not to kill Mr. Spalding; which I begged of him as a special favor, and hoped that he would not refuse it to me. I was waiting for his answer, and did not wish to relate the disaster to Mr. Spalding before getting it, for fear he might, by his manner, discover to the Indian what I had told him; for the least motion like flight would have cost him his life, and probably exposed mine also. [To the empty pistol? The Indian goes back to the village. Spalding is informed of the massacre and takes to the woods. Shortly afterwards a party of Cayuses come up in pursuit. Brouillet returns to the Umatilla mission and all the priests remain there till the 19th, not daring to leave Young Chief's camp for fear of the Indians.] On the 11th of December we had the affliction to hear that one of the captives had been carried off from the doctor's house by the orders of Five Crows and brought to him, and

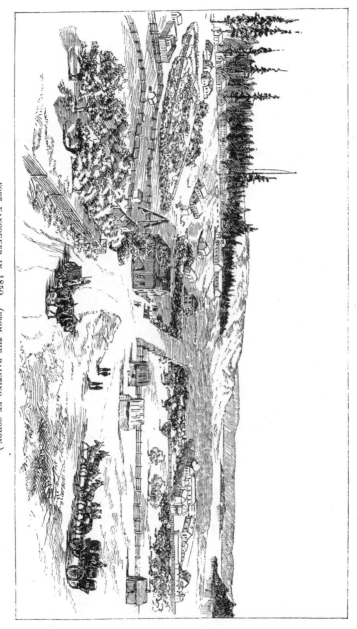

FORT VANCOUVER IN 1850. (FROM THE PAINTING BY SOHON.)

we learned that two others had been violated at the doctor's house."

From this it appears that this very cautious man was restrained from doing anything in behalf of the captives solely by personal timidity; that, although so frightened, he remained in the Indian village over-night and about the mission in the morning, doing what under the circumstances was of no benefit to any one, when he might have left the savages he so feared at any time; that during nearly twenty-four hours after he learned of the massacre he sent no word of warning to any one, although he might have gone himself or sent his interpreter—a peculiarly significant fact, in connection with his constant fear for the safety of Mr. Spalding, whom he had left at the Umatilla, and who was expected at Wailatpu at any moment; that before giving Spalding any warning he begged the Indian with the "fortunately" unloaded weapon not to kill him, and the Indian at once went for assistance. Let us now look at a companion to this picture of cowardice, hypocrisy, or want of sense, as you may choose to call it. I quote from the deposition of Miss Lorinda Bewley.

"Q. When did the priest [Brouillet] arrive [at Wailatpu]?

"A. Wednesday, while the bodies were being prepared for the grave. The bodies were collected into the house on Tuesday evening.

"Q. Did the Indians bury a vial or bottle of the doctor's medicine?

"A. They said they did. Joe Stanfield made the box to bury it in, and the Indians said they buried it.

"Q. Why did they bury it?

"A. They said the priests said it was poison. Stanfield and Nicholas were their interpreters to us.

"Q. How did they obtain this vial?

"A. The Indians said the priests found it among the doctor's medicines, and showed it to them, and told them that if it broke it would poison the whole nation.

＊   ＊   ＊   ＊   ＊   ＊   ＊

"Q. Where did you spend your time when at the Umatilla?

"A. Most of the time at the house of the bishop; but the

Five Crows, most of the nights, compelled me to go to his lodge and be subject to him during the night. I obtained the privilege of going to the bishop's house before violation on the Umatilla, and begged and cried to the bishop for protection either at his house or to be sent to Walla-Walla. I told him I would do any work by night and day for him if he would protect me. He said he would do all he could. Although I was taken to the lodge, I escaped violation the first four nights. There were the bishop, three priests, and two Frenchmen at the bishop's house. The first night the Five Crows came, I refused to go, and he went away, apparently mad, and the bishop told me I had better go, as he might do us all an injury, and the bishop sent an Indian with me. He took me to the Five Crows' lodge. The Five Crows showed me the door and told me I might go back, and take my clothes, which I did. Three nights after this the Five Crows came for me again. The bishop finally ordered me to go; my answer was, 'I had rather die.' After this, he still insisted on my going, as the best thing I could do. I was then in the bishop's room; the three priests were there. I found I could get no help, and had to go, as he told me, out of his room. The Five Crows seized me by the arm and jerked me away to his lodge.

"Q. How long were you at the Umatilla?

"A. Two weeks, and from Friday till Monday. I would return early in the morning to the bishop's house, and be violently taken away at night. The bishop provided kindly for me while at his house. On my return one morning, one of the young priests asked me, in a good deal of glee, how I liked my companion. I felt that this would break my heart, and cried much during the day. . . . When the tall priest [Brouillet], that was at the doctor's at the first, was going to Walla-Walla, after hearing of Mr. Ogden's arrival, he called me out of the door and told me if I went to the lodge any more I must not come back to his house. I asked him what I should do. He said I must insist or beg of the Indian to let me stop at his house; if he would not let me, then I must stay at his lodge. I did not feel well, and towards night I took advantage of this and went to bed, determined I would die there before

I would be taken away. The Indian came, and, on my refusing to go, hauled me from my bed and threw my bonnet and shawl at me, and told me to go. I would not, and at a time when his eyes were off I threw them under the table and he could not find them. I sat down, determined not to go, and he pushed me nearly into the fire. The Frenchmen were in the room, and the bishop and priests were passing back and forth to their rooms. When the Indian was smoking, I went to bed again, and when he was through smoking he dragged me from my bed with more violence than the first time. I told the Frenchman to go into the bishop's room and ask him what I should do; he came out and told me that the bishop said it was best for me to go. I told him the tall priest said, if I went, I must not come back again to this house; he said, the priests dared not keep women about their house, but if the Five Crows sent me back again, why come. I still would not go. The Indian then pulled me away violently without bonnet or shawl. Next morning I came back and was in much anguish, and cried much. The bishop asked me if I was in much trouble. I told him I was. He said it was not my fault, that I could not help myself; that I must pray to God and Mary. He asked me if I did not believe in God; I told him I did."

This deposition was taken December 12, 1848, and Miss Bewley's statements are neither denied nor explained in Brouillet's defence, which was published more than four years afterwards, although he was fully aware of the story she had told of her wrongs. He refers to it only in the extract quoted above, but his excuse for all other actions is fear. The Protestants say, the action in regard to Miss Bewley was part of an attempt to implicate Five Crows, the head chief, and force him to join the hostiles. Let us accept fear, then, as the true cause, it being more favorable to the Jesuits, and what a defence it is! Think of it! Six white men—four of them priests of the God of the widow and the orphan—to stand by thus and see a defenceless girl so treated by her brutal ravisher; to counsel and command her to submit, even after the savage had desisted; to say to her: "How did you like your companion?" "If you go to the lodge any more you must not

8

return here." "Are you in much trouble?" What a contrast is this with the noble pioneers of their order, who carried
the cross through the Mississippi valley! What a contrast
with the New Mexican padre of our last chapter, who saved
an American soldier under surroundings of far greater danger
to himself than these! What a contrast with hundreds of
heroic deeds by the Christian fathers, all through the history
of the frontier! And how deplorable that, in the minds of
many, a foul blot has thus been put on the fair fame of an
entire Church!

And what was the sequel of all this? The Indians, as we
have seen, were made wanderers, until five of the most blameworthy expiated the crime of all. The Jesuits succeeded to
the missions of the Northwest. Mr. Spalding, indeed, returned,
some time afterwards, to the Nez Percés, on their invitation,
but he was not sustained by the American Board, and, through
various influences, abandoned the field in despair. He is remembered by their old people with the kindliest regard, even
to this day. The Hudson's Bay Company, in the course of
the adjustment of damages under the treaty, filed its claims
for itself and the Puget Sound Agricultural Company, against
the United States, for £1,025,350, of which £200,000 was for
the right of trade in Oregon; £300,000 for the right of free
navigation of the Columbia River; and the remainder for
losses, improvements, and 160,000 acres of land which they
claimed to have pre-empted! They were allowed $650,000, or
about thirteen per cent. of their claim, at the final adjustment
in 1864, and that is quite as much as they were entitled to.
Considering their action in Oregon, some have said they
should have had nothing; but why not? Their action only
adds another chapter to the history of frontier troubles for
which England was responsible, and which Americans have
patiently endured. On the bank of the Ohio River, eight
miles below old Fort Henry (now the city of Wheeling) was
erected, many years ago, a little monument with this inscription: "This humble stone is erected to the memory of Captain Foreman and twenty-seven of his men, who were slain
by a band of ruthless savages—the allies of a civilized nation
of Europe—on the 25th of September, 1777." There are

hundreds of graves, all through our territory, over which similar legends might most appropriately be written.*

---

* A movement has been inaugurated in Oregon for erecting a monument to the memory of Dr. Whitman. Mr. W. H. Gray, of Olney, Corresponding Secretary of the Pioneer and Historical Society of Oregon, has been designated as the custodian of subscriptions. The Presbyterian Church, as is generally known, re-established its missions some years later, and, with other Protestant denominations, is now working successfully in this region.

CHAPTER V.

THE CURSE OF GOLD.

Two months had passed after the tragedy at Wailatpu, and the volunteers were still at the Dalles, when an event occurred that revolutionized the Pacific coast, changed the course of affairs throughout the United States, and visibly affected the entire world. It was the discovery of gold in California, or rather the discovery that it existed in quantity. The Spaniards had long known that there was gold in the country, and Mr. Dana, with Wilkes's exploring expedition, had picked up auriferous rock in Oregon and on the Sacramento, but no one thought it to be in paying quantity, and no attention was paid to it. The Mormons claim to have worked the placers before Marshall made his discovery, but their story is either untrue, or so adulterated with untruth as to deserve no credence, besides being contrary to other evidence. The account of their discovery, as published in September, 1854, by George M. Evans, the professed discoverer, is, in substance, as follows: "During the month of October or November, 1845, in a house or groggery on Pacific Street, San Francisco (as it is now called), a Mexican, who was called 'Salvador,' was shot because he had a bag of gold dust, described as about one thousand to two thousand dollars, and would not tell where he got it. At last, when dying, he pointed in the direction of San José Mountains, and said, '*Lejos, lejos*' ('beyond, beyond'). [Evans then relates how, in consequence of this event, he looked casually for gold at a sand point of a small island opposite the entrance to Stockton, then called Lindsley's Lake, and found some particles. This was in 1846, and the gold found was sent with other specimens to Peale's Museum. Also, in August, 1847, Evans, with Major Reading and T. W. Perkins, found gold in more abundance in the mountains between San Diego and the Gila River, but were driven away by hostile Indians.] When the Mormon battalion was disbanded in 1847, a number of the Mormons came to San Francisco, and among them was one Henderson Cox and one Beardsley, who boarded in the same house with me. They having worked in the Georgia mines, told me, in conversation on the subject, that they were about prospecting for a road (since called the Mormon Pass) for the Mormons to return to Salt Lake, and in so doing would prospect the streams in their route (this was in the end of August or first of September, 1847). I then described the death of Salvador, and where I found the gold, and gave them a chart of the country from memory. In the following January I returned to San Francisco from the journey above referred to, when I received an invitation to go to Mormon Island, so named afterwards by Henderson Cox. On the 19th of January, 1848, I went there, and with the bounty they gave me and what I worked out myself I had $19,000 on the 8th of February, 1848. On the 9th of February, I, with Henderson Cox, Beardsley, Beers, two shepherds, and a number more were in the lower end of the mill-race, when Marshall, the overseer, and his little girl came in, and the child picked up a pretty stone, as she called it, and showed it to her father, who pronounced it gold. He was so excited about it that he saddled his horse and that day rode to Sutter's Fort to tell Captain Sutter—but he did not believe it worth notice, and for a while the idea died away. The Mormons wishing to keep their discoveries a secret from people not Mormons, worked out the gold and said nothing more. On the 1st of April, 1848, the first mail from San Francisco to Salt Lake was started, and a number of the California *Star* was printed purposely for that mail containing a special article, written by Dr. Fourgend and myself, concerning the minerals and metals of California, and among other mentioned metals was gold—but as the printer and publishers were [not] Mormons, the full facts were not stated. It was not until the 12th of May, 1848, that the existence of gold in quantity in California was publicly made known in San Francisco by Samuel Brannan, High Bishop of the Mormons, and of Vigilance Committee notoriety. Beardsley and

JOHN A. SUTTER.

Henderson Cox were killed at the foot of the Sierra Nevada in September, 1848. Marshall died either four days before he arrived home in the Eastern States with a barrel of gold, or four days from the coast." It would hardly be anticipated that any person could be found so silly as to believe this story of earning a thousand dollars a day at Mormon Island on February 8th, and, on February 9th, being in the mill-race at Sutter's saw-mill, twenty-five miles away, working for wages, except he had first educated his faith by swallowing the revelations of the angel Moroni and other Mormon supernaturals. Yet some have believed it, and a cloud has been thrown on the just claims of Mr. Marshall, the discoverer.

The story of Marshall's discovery in the race at Sutter's saw-mill has been told too often to need repetition. Sutter and Marshall agreed to keep the matter quiet until the grist-mill near Sutter's Fort was finished, but soon after the discovery Sutter sent down to Colonel Mason, military governor of California, at Monterey, and desired to preempt the land on which the saw-mill and the race were situated, near the future town of Coloma. He was informed that the country was held by conquest, and that there were no laws for pre-emption, but that there was no probability that he would be disturbed in possession. The messengers who brought his letter also brought some of the newly-discovered metal with them, to ask if it was gold. Lieutenant Sherman, now familiarly known as "Old Tecumseh," who was acting as adjutant-general for Mason, bit the metal, and gave his opinion that it was. They went back, and it was soon known among the Mormon hands that there was gold in the river. They wanted to dig for it at the saw-mill, but Marshall threatened to shoot them if they attempted it, so they prospected down the river and discovered the rich placer known as Mormon Island. They informed their fellow Mormons at Sutter's grist-mill, nineteen miles below, and they struck for higher wages. Sutter conceded their price, and they struck again, and so on till they wanted ten dollars a day. Then he stopped, and the mills were left to decay, while the Mormons went to work at the island, where they made from forty to one hundred dollars per day. Their accumulations soon began to circulate as far as San Francisco. Brannan & Co., the principal merchants at Sutter's Fort, reported to Governor Mason that they had taken twenty-six thousand dollars' worth of gold, between May 1st and July 10th, in exchange for goods. At that time "High Bishop Brannan" had nothing to say about Mormon discoveries previous to January 28th. On June 1st, Mr. T. O. Larkin, of San Francisco, wrote the Secretary of State: "It is now two or three weeks since the men employed in these washings have appeared in this town with gold, to exchange

for merchandise and provisions.   I presume near twenty
thousand dollars ($20,000) of this gold has, as yet, been so
exchanged."   The excitement grew intense.   Half of the
houses in San Francisco were locked up.   Merchants and pro-
fessional men went with the mechanics and laborers.   Soldiers deserted their posts, and sailors their ships.   One ship-
captain, seeing his men were bound to go, went with them,
furnished the tools, and took a percentage.   Travellers arrived
on the coast, jocosely wrote home that the Californians had
gone stark mad, and the next day were hurrying to the mines
themselves.   The news reached the East, and the adventurous
and far-seeing began to come.   The reports, startling at the
first, grew constantly in magnitude, and were soon fully confirmed by a long despatch from Governor Mason, which was
made a special message to Congress by the President.   The
messenger brought with him two hundred and thirty ounces
of the gold.   Doubt was removed, and the emigration overland and by sea became a great flood.

The event was looked at in strangely different ways.
Some thought it a good thing; others very bad.   The question of the effect of the extraordinary increase of gold in circulation was gravely canvassed by thoughtful men.   Some
thought it would alter the relative worth of gold and silver
and unsettle all values; others said there were channels already opened into which it would naturally flow, without
affecting the existing circulation.   Even the local effect was
variously speculated upon.   Benton, the gifted and erudite,
the friend and champion of the West, said in the Senate:
" I am a friend to a gold currency, but not to gold mining.
That is a pursuit which the experience of nations shows to
be both impoverishing and demoralizing to a nation.   I regret that we have these mines in California; but they are
there, and I am for getting rid of them as soon as possible.
Make the working as free as possible. . . . If you want revenue, raise it from the permits—a small sum for each—and
upon the coinage.   In that way it would be practicable to raise
as much as ought to be raised.   But revenue is no object compared to the great object of clearing the ground of this attraction, which puts an end to all regular industry, and com-

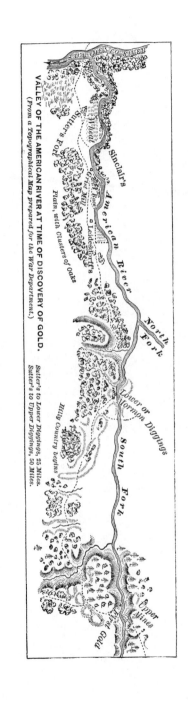

VALLEY OF THE AMERICAN RIVER AT TIME OF DISCOVERY OF GOLD.

(From a Topographical Map prepared for the War Department.)

Sutter's to Lower Diggings, 25 Miles.
Sutter's to Upper Diggings, 50 Miles.

pared to the object of putting the gold into circulation. I care not who digs it up. I want it dug up. I want the fever to be over. I want the mining finished. Let all work that will. Let them ravage the earth—extirpate and exterminate the mines. Then the sober industry will begin which enriches and ennobles a nation." Mr. Benton said this because he had just demonstrated to the Senate that placers were transient things. He neglected to include this speech in his "Abridgment of the Debates," or to refer to it in his "Thirty Years' View."

But this is not a history of the gold discoveries of California, and we must leave the subject, enticing though it be. What effect did this discovery have on the Indians? It was fraught with greater evil for them than any other one event in the history of America, except the discovery of America itself. Gold is a magnet that draws with irresistible force. No power has yet been found able to counteract its attraction. Cold, hunger, and every imaginable peril will not keep men from seeking it. No government has been able to hold its subjects from the spot where it could be found. The United States has repeatedly found itself helpless, and early adopted the policy, when gold was found on Indian reservations, of treating for the lands as quickly as possible, and moving the Indians away. As General Carleton put it, "The miners *will* go to their country, and the question which comes up is, shall the miners be protected and the country be developed, or shall the Indians be suffered to kill them and the nation be deprived of its immense wealth?" Through every nook and corner of the mountains the intrepid prospector has pursued his search, hiding from the Indians if he could, fighting if he must; dying, perhaps, but never giving up the search till he did die. When his search was successful, a new mining excitement broke out, a new district was populated, new roads were opened, and the Indians fell back. Indians seldom trouble a mining camp. They attack the stage, the emigrant-wagon, and the supply-train, and thus indirectly harass the miners; but the camp itself is not interfered with. Miners are usually "bad medicine" for Indians.

In "make-up" the early California population, as to its

effect on the Indians, may be divided into three classes, and it is a fair type of all new mining regions of the West. First, there was a large number of mountain men, *i.e.*, trappers and restless spirits who had adopted wild life from choice. Many of them had lived with Indians, imbibed Indian superstitions, and adopted Indian customs. With them the killing of a hostile Indian, or one who from his tribal connection ought to be hostile, was an honor. They would

PIUTE SQUAW AND PAPOOSE.

steal the horses of unfriendly Indians, carry off their women, and scalp their dead without the least qualms of conscience. And why not? Their adopted brethren, the Indians, did the same things themselves. Second, there was a still larger percentage of desperadoes — villainous wretches whose sole redeeming feature was their bravery, and some lacking even that — to whom robbery was a business and murder a virtue. Does the reader think the statement a strong one? He may read the proof of it in the proceedings of a thousand vigilance committees, and if justice had been done he might have read it in ten thousand more. These men have made life a hell for the timid in every frontier settlement in the West. White men they oppressed as far as they dared, and Indians they treated as they found convenient. The very best of them committed crimes which were legally punishable with death, perpetrated indignities on persons they disliked, terrorized whole communities, and obtained a halo of romantic glory simply because people dared not talk about them. The third class, and it included the majority of the people, were men of decent character and sentiment, but they had little sympathy for the Indians in general. It was but a short time since the great removal of the tribes to the Indian territory, and the sentiment against the red man was still strong in the Mississippi Valley. Many had seen instances of the frightful cruelty of the Indians, and many had been attacked on their overland journey when they had given no cause for it. Besides, they had absolutely no time to consider abstract questions of right and wrong. If white men became too troublesome they favored lynching, and if Indians were troublesome they favored the speediest and most effectual way of stopping them. To know who was to blame was of minor importance; the point was that the community could not and would not be kept from the pursuit of wealth by anybody. It was on the same principle that a great railroad magnate once set fire to a wrecked freight train. He destroyed much valuable property, but he cleared the track. He had to take one of two evils, and so did they. Men of the first and second classes wronged the Indians; the Indians retaliated, usually on the innocent, because they were more convenient and less dangerous; the entire community was involved, and frequently innocent Indians suffered. Such is the oft-repeated history of the mining regions of the West.

There was less of this in California than in other mining localities. The reason was that a part of the Indians submitted to the indignities put upon them, and the rest got out of the way. A few resisted and were killed. The reader of California story sometimes wonders that he does not find any

record of the events of Indian wars. The reason is that there
were none in the gold fields. There was one exception. In
extreme northern California, above and on both sides of
Yreka, there were Indians who would and did fight, but the
troubles with them are properly a part of the Oregon wars,
and will be considered in a subsequent chapter. South of
these, throughout the State, was the great body of California
Indians. In these there was no fight, and the so-called wars
with them were pure farces. They were degraded and brutal
sensualists. There were probably never a dozen warriors
among them who would not rather have eaten a substantial
meal than killed an enemy. They had no arms but bows
and arrows, which were not dangerous at over fifty yards.
They were divided into numerous small tribes, of dissimilar
languages, and with no faculty for union. They were most
arrant cowards. Even in their battles among themselves they
displayed no bravery. They usually began war by challenge;
heralds then met and arranged the time and place of the
conflict; the armies advanced against each other, jumping
about, with shouts and gestures, to distract the aim of the
foe. Frequently, by agreement, armistices occurred, during
which children from the opposing armies ran to the ranks of
the other side and picked up arrows for use again. The battle generally terminated with the first blood drawn. They
seldom scalped the dead, but occasionally ate pieces of their
flesh, or cut off the head, hands, or feet for trophies. Their
prisoners were exchanged or killed, they being almost the
only Western Indians who did not practise slavery. With all
his childish timidity, the California warrior could meet death
with stoical fortitude, if it were inevitable, and he had one
habit which was always aggravating, and often as dangerous
to the white man as open war. He would steal—steal anything, at any time, and under almost any circumstances.

It has often been a subject for jest that the people of
the frontier punished horse-stealing more severely than murder, but the people of settled countries do not realize that
horse-stealing may mean death, and a cruel, lingering death
at that. The emigrant who lost his stock on the plains was
hopelessly stranded. If no one came along to help him, he

and his family were almost certainly doomed to die. If other emigrants did find him, he still, usually, lost his wagon and goods, for those prairie ships could add but little to their cargoes. Other losses might be equally serious. Provisions ran short on that long overland trip, and on the latter part of it, through what is now Nevada, money, often, would not buy food from other emigrants. There are men yet living who managed to get through that last stretch, only because they were Masons or Odd Fellows, and were given aid as Brethren after money had been refused. Even in the mines, stealing provisions was a grievous injury. At times any kind of meat cost one dollar per pound, and flour, sugar, coffee, and other supplies the same. Occasionally they got as low as twenty-five cents the pound, but not often. Theft might almost be equivalent to murder there. Indeed, Indian theft was frequently accompanied by murder, when the latter could be accomplished by stealth, or was thought necessary. It is not at all surprising that California miners had no love for Indians. It was a very natural thing.

The first trouble with Indians in California began on Mormon Island. A miner took some liberties with the squaw of an Indian chief; the chief objected, and was promptly killed. There were a few hostilities. A few whites were killed and some Indians. It was represented that troops were necessary, and a militia regiment was organized under "Col. William Rogers." He took what supplies he wanted from Ringgold merchants and others, and began his campaign. His command had no engagements with the Indians, but succeeded in "protecting the settlers," and piling up an immense bill of expenses which the State paid. By the winter of 1850–51 a remarkable misunderstanding of the situation had been brought about by men who were charged with scheming to bring on a war, and many citizens of California believed there was serious danger on the frontier. A local author stated that "thousands of miners were hemmed within narrow and unproductive limits during the whole of last winter (1850–51), because of the peril of explorations beyond populous settlements." On March 1, 1851, Governor McDougal wrote the President: "The valley of Los Angeles, of the

San Joaquin, of the tributaries of the Sacramento, and the country around the main sources of that river, and the northern coast, contain an Indian force estimated at not less than one hundred thousand warriors, all animated by a spirit of bitter hostility, and whom a pacific and forbearing policy encourages into renewed acts of outrage. Rendered bold by impunity and encouraged by success, they are now everywhere rising in arms, and every day brings the report of

THE YOSEMITE.   [BY HILL.]

some new outbreak." Unfortunately for the success of his appeal for authority to call out the militia, for service as United States troops, the governor neglected to tell what the outbreaks referred to were.

His estimate of "one hundred thousand warriors" is the most preposterous statement made in connection with California Indian wars that has come to my notice. Superintendent Beale comes next with his anticipations of trouble, in 1853, in changing the hereditary mode of life of "one hundred thousand persons." In 1856 Superintendent Henley succeeded in getting the number of California Indians down to 61,600. He professed to give a statement by reservations and counties, and in proof of his accuracy it is noteworthy that he dealt only in round numbers. Every number he gives, even of the residents at the reservations, ends in at least two ciphers. In reality the number of Indians, men, women, and children, in California, at any time after the discovery of gold, did not exceed 20,000. Don Antonio de Alcedo, the best Spanish authority, based his estimate on the returns of the Spanish missionaries in 1802, and stated the mission Indians at 14,931, the mustees and mulattoes at 1300, and the wild Indians at 16,000, making a total of 32,231. Mr. Schoolcraft adopted these figures in his census of 1850, but he neglected to take into consideration the ravages of small-pox in the year 1839, and their general rapid decline during the past decade. Forbes, in his "History of Upper and Lower California" (London, 1839), estimated the converted Indians at 18,683, and others 4342. Duflot de Mofras, an attaché of the French legation in Mexico, estimated the mission Indians in 1834 at 30,620, but he made his estimate in 1842, when he visited California. This was after the missions had been taken away from the priests, and the mission Indians reduced to 4450, and Mofras's sympathies were probably excited by exaggerated stories. He is not a very reliable statistician in other matters. He estimated the population of the Antilles at 3,500,000, for instance. As a fair offset to Mofras, we have Captain Wilkes, U. S. N., who travelled through California in 1841. He says, "The number of Indians is variously stated at from twelve to fifteen thousand; but it is believed by some of the best informed, that their number, since the small-pox made its ravages among them, is not much more than one-half of this number, or eight or nine thousand. The principal part of these are the tribes on the Sacramento." He estimated the entire population of Alta California, whites, Indians, and mixed, to be about 15,000. The war department, in its estimate of 1848, put the number of wild Indians at 3000, and made the total for California,

9

16,930, but in this estimate the mission of La Purissima Concepcion is omitted, apparently by mistake. Under the priests, it was said to have 1000 Indians. With this correction the war department's aggregate harmonizes reasonably with Alcedo's estimate, for it is agreed by all testimony that the number of Indians decreased very rapidly during the latter part of the Mexican occupation (1822–47), especially in the country about San Francisco, which was almost wholly depopulated. Said a decrepit Indian of Dolores to agent Johnston, in 1849, "I am very old; my people were once around me as the sands of the shore—many—many. They have all passed away—they have died like the grass—they have gone to the mountains. I do not complain—the antelope falls by the arrow. I had a son—I loved him—when the pale-faces came he went away—I know not where he is. I am a Christian Indian—I am all that is left of my people— I am alone." By the census of 1860, in which, by mistake, the officials returned all the Indians in the State, instead of those subject to taxation, the number of California Indians was 17,798. In 1870 the census return was 7241, and the latest returns of the Indian Bureau at that date fixed the remaining Indians at 12,414; but it is quite probable that these two sums would give an over-estimate of the whole number, as some Indians were probably counted in both. By the census of 1880, the taxed Indians of California were returned at 16,277, but by the statistics of the Indian Bureau, for the same year, the total of the Indians for that State was only 10,666, of whom 4648 were on reservations and 6018 not under agents. In 1884 the Indian Bureau returned 11,317 Indians in California, of whom 6759 were not under agents, and 4738 were on reservations. The character of the Indians was as much misrepresented by Governor McDougal as their number. The valley tribes, it is true, always represented the mountain tribes to be extremely fierce and warlike. They were so only in comparison with the valley tribes. They made some forays, ran off some cattle, and now and then killed a settler, but their most violent crimes were really crimes of stealth. Their murders were the murders of the Thug, not of the bravo. There were then in California, at the time Governor McDougal wrote, 3000 to 4000 "warriors," mission and wild, poorly armed, disunited, and of little or no spirit.

The national government did not furnish any more troops for California, but did send its quota of arms for 100,000 militia. Militia regiments had been raised and were about to take the field, when the general government altered its plans. Three commissioners were appointed to treat with the California tribes, and the militia were ordered to be held subject to their orders. The treaties they made were simply agreements for the Indians to go on reservations. The Indian titles were never extinguished in California as they were in the other States. Most of the tribes made the agreement gladly, but some of the mountain tribes feared to come in, on account of anticipated punishment, or because they preferred their mountain lairs, and these were treated as hostiles. Catching these Indians and bringing them in constituted the "war of '51 and '52." The Mariposa battalion did this work in the country bordering the San Joaquin Valley. Captain Kuykendall's company brought in the Chowchillas, a tribe of the Kaweah family, who had been among the most active hostiles. Their chief, José Rey, had openly declared for war, and the tribe had committed several outrages. Before the organization of the militia a party of volunteers had marched against them, surprised their camp, killed twenty-three of them and mortally wounded José Rey, after which the Chowchillas had wisely kept out of the way of the whites. Captain Kuykendall succeeded in surprising their camp again, and killing a number of them, his loss being one man wounded by an arrow. After that the Chowchillas kept hid until they were nearly starved, and then came in and accepted the terms of the commissioners.

Captain Boling's company brought in the Yosemites (Yosemitys, Oosamites), the dreaded "Grizzly Bears," the terrible tribe that made their home in the wonderful cañon valley that perpetuates their name, the warriors whom the lowland tribes warned the whites especially to shun. Dr. Bunnell, a member of the company, has given a minutely detailed account of their work, and the sole hostility offered by these

YOSEMITE FROM THE MARIPOSA TRAIL.

dangerous Indians, during several weeks that the company
passed in searching the valley and neighboring country in
parties of two and three, consisted in rolling down some
rocks at two soldiers, by which one of them was knocked
down a declivity and badly bruised.   At no time did they
offer to use a weapon, but kept their village concealed near

the border of Lake Tenieya until they were finally discovered and captured. At their capture there was not an offer of resistance, the miserable wretches throwing up their hands and crying "pace! pace!" (peace! peace!). The war in and around the Sacramento Valley was of substantially the same character. Said Commissioner McKee, whose opportunities for knowing were unsurpassed, "The late war in that section was, I am told, a greater piece of tomfoolery and humbug than even the former on the Fresno and the San Joaquin. The State has been involved for some eighty or one hundred thousand dollars more without the slightest necessity, or accomplishing the least good." The stores of the Indians (cachés of acorns) were destroyed whenever found, and the Indians were obliged to come in or starve. The militia were disgusted. Says Dr. Bunnell, "We had discussed the matter in camp, and contrasted the lack of spirit exhibited by these people with what we knew of the warlike character of the Indians of Texas and of the North-western plains. In these comparisons, respect for our captives was lost in contempt. 'The noble red man' was not here represented. The only ones of the Pacific slope, excepting the Navahos, Pimas, and Maricopahs, that bear any comparison with the Eastern tribes for intelligence and bravery, are the Youmahs of the Colorado River, the Modocs, and some of the Rogue and Columbia river tribes, but none of these really equal the Sioux and some other Eastern tribes."

When these fierce savages were all subdued, an improved reservation system was put in force by the government, in 1853. There were five reservations. Klamath reservation, on the river of that name, was occupied by the extreme northern tribes, not the ones of whom we have been treating; it cost about sixteen thousand dollars a year, was fairly well managed, and quite successful. The largest of the reservations of our Californians was Nome Lackee, west of the Sacramento, in the foot-hills of Tehama County. It had no game, no acorns, no fishery, and no rain, and hence, being useful for nothing else, was eminently fitted for a reservation. Adjunct to Nome Lackee was Nome Cult, a pretty valley of about 20,000 acres, about sixty miles south-west of the for-

mer, and across the Coast Range. The Indians did very well
at this place, till the agent and employés got their relatives,
friends, and partners to come in and settle there. Before
long that place became too good for Indians, as we shall see
presently. Mendocino reservation, below the cape of that
name, on the Noyo River, was an excellent place. There were

BEACH FISHING AT CAPE MENDOCINO.

fish and mussels enough there for all the Indians located
there, if it had not been that some white friends of the agency started a saw-mill and filled the river with logs, so that a
fish could not get through. Tejon reservation, near the base
of the Sierra Nevada, where it joins the Coast Range, in
Southern California, was a nice, dry place, where the Indians were never bothered by rain or crops. There were also

farms at Tule River and Mattole Valley, and finally, as public land was very scarce in California, the United States rented the farms of Mr. Vinsonhaller and Mr. Campbell, which were called respectively Fresno reservation and King's River farm. Farming was supposed to be begun on a broad and liberal scale at these places, which were fitted up, on paper, regardless of cost. Tejon absorbed about $30,000 per year; Fresno the same; Nome Lackee nearly $50,000; Nome Cult about $10,000; and Mendocino $48,000. About $50,000 more went annually for the other reserves and general purposes, and by November, 1858, the sum of $1,173,000 had been invested in the California reservations.

The management of these reservations was under one of the ablest Indian rings ever known in America. Not a reliable report went in to the Commissioner of Indian Affairs for five years, but their work was so well done that they received compliments for their able accounts of their labors. The total number of Indians was scandalously exaggerated, as we have seen, and the number at the reservations in like manner. So far as can be learned, not more than 2000 Indians were subsisted at the reservations at any time, and they drew principally on the oak-trees, the manzanita bushes, and the clover fields for their rations. The great majority of the Indians were quietly earning their living as vaqueros and farmhands, or picking it up in the mountains, as they had before the government began civilizing them. Fabulous numbers of acres were reported to be under cultivation, and magnificent crops were always just about to be harvested when blight or mildew or smut or drought intervened and ruined them. A small army of employés was on hand to instruct the Indians and defend the agency in case of outbreak, and the agent or employé who failed to get a claim of his own, and have it fenced and improved by Indian labor, was a man of no enterprise.

In 1858, in consequence of repeated charges and protestations by army officers and citizens, special agent Bailey was sent out to investigate affairs in California. He did not seem to grasp the whole truth, but he was not in the ring, and he told the truth as he saw it. He showed that the salaries

alone of the employés amounted to $81,889.48, besides sub-
sistence for themselves and families, which would bring the
amount to over $100,000; that there was no such number of
Indians on the reservations as reported; that the value of the
crops was much less than a quarter of the salaries of the employés; that the only contented Indians were off the reservations; that friends and relatives of the agent and employés
had been allowed to settle in the Nome Cult and create disturbance there; and that the Indians were neither being
taught anything nor civilized in any respect. The Commissioner of Indian affairs reported that the California reservations were a failure. He gave among other reasons of the
failure, the statement that the Indians had not been "sufficiently thrown on their own resources." It is difficult to see
how they could have been thrown on their own resources
more fully, unless the acorn, berry, and grass crops could have
been destroyed. After a year or such a matter a change was
made. A new superintendent was appointed; the appropriation was cut down to $50,000 a year; and Tejon, Fresno,
King's Valley, Nome Lackee, and Mattole, with all their improvements, were abandoned in the course of a few years.

There was more "Indian war" in California in 1858, and
several years succeeding. At Nome Cult over one hundred
and fifty Indians were cruelly murdered by the whites, who
had been allowed to settle on the reservation. No charge of
aggression, except cattle-stealing, was given as an excuse, and
this proved, on investigation, to be false. The real cause was
that the Indians drove away from the reservation the cattle
of the settlers, which had been roaming the reservation and
consuming the acorns, on which the Indians depended mainly
for subsistence. Armed parties went to the rancherias in the
open day and shot down the wretched "Diggers," without
regard to age or sex. Then they called on the State government for aid, and, organized as militia, roamed the country
round, killing every Indian they could find. At King's River
the settlers drove the Indians away because the government
did not support them, and they were an annoyance to the
community. The Indians fled to Fresno, where there was not
food sufficient for those already there. Then these kind-

HOW THE DIGGERS FOUGHT.

hearted people of King's River hauled over the acorns which
the Indians had collected there, and sold them to the government for food for its protégés.   At Mattole Station the settlers killed a number of Indians because they considered them
a burden.   In the neighborhood of Humboldt Bay the settlers made the same complaint; the State sent out militia, who
took those that would consent to go to Mendocino, and killed
the refractory.   Life at Mendocino was not appreciated as

A GROUP OF DIGGERS.

highly by them as it should have been, and some of them returned to their old haunts.   Highly indignant at this outrage,
a party of settlers attacked their camp at night, using fire-
arms at first, and knives when the battue grew more exciting.
In the morning sixty corpses of men, women, boys, girls, and
infants, ornamented with bullet wounds, stabs, and gaping
throats, showed that justice had been done.   There were other
wars, but these samples will suffice.   It is perhaps better to

call them wars, because the word massacre has come by usage
to mean such a murder as Indians would commit, and an Indian who was not wholly lost to self-respect would not do
such things as these.

There is another chapter in the history of California
that is as disgraceful as the treatment of the so-called "wild
tribes." It is the story of the Mission Indians. This does
not include accounts of assassination under the name of war,
of midnight surprises and noonday butcheries, of women cut
to pieces and children brained. It is the record of a slow advance of a superior race, driving the natives from their ancient homes with remorseless power, and crushing them back
into the mountains and the desert. There is no need of going fully into the story of their wrongs here—it has been recorded ably in various publications that are within the reach
of almost every reader; neither is it properly within the
province of this work, except as an illustration of some of the
most serious flaws in our Indian system. Under the old
treaty system the Indians lost their rights easily enough, but
they were still recognized to have rights. That they were
often deceived, defrauded, and intimidated into making treaties against their interest is unquestionable, but still a treaty
was necessary, and their consent must be obtained in some
way before their lands could be taken. Since the abrogation
of the treaty-making power, there has been a constant tendency towards the concentration of absolute power over the
Indians in the Executive Department. This is bad policy, in
the abstract, for the fewer steps that are required to get Indian lands, the more easily it will be accomplished. When
all the obstacles are centred in one man it will be most easy
to overcome them. If from good or bad intent, in weakness
or in ignorance, he abolish a reservation and return the land
to the public domain, the evil is undone with the utmost difficulty. White men become vested with rights and cling to
them tenaciously. In some instances the courts might remedy
the wrong, but courts give relief only to suitors whose claims
are properly presented. As a rule, Congress is the only source
of relief, unless the Executive sees the mistake and endeavors
to retrace its steps, a move not often easily accomplished.

In the country obtained by cession from Mexico, the tribes are in a far more helpless situation than those of other sections, for they have not been recognized as having even a possessory title to the lands on which they lived. From these, however, are to be excepted those to whom specific grants had been made by the Spanish and Mexican governments for their settlement and support. The policy of Spain was theoretically the same as our own. The Indians were in a state of pupilage, and were to be redeemed to Christian civilization by the government. The close connection of the Catholic Church with the government, and its well-known missionary proclivities, made this a more hopeful task for Spain than it has proven for Protestant countries. A devoted agent for the work in Alta California was found in Father Junipero Serra, a Franciscan monk, who was sent into that unknown region in 1769 by the Spanish authorities, their colonization previous to that time having been confined to the peninsula. Beginning with the Mission of San Diego, in 1769, Serra and his co-laborers established the missions of San Carlos de Monterey, San Antonio de Padua, San Gabriel, San Luis Obispo, San Francisco (Dolores), San Juan Capistrano, Santa Clara, and San Buena Ventura, in the order named, by 1782. After Serra's death, in 1784, the work was continued by the order, and the missions of Santa Barbara, La Purissima Concepcion, Santa Cruz, Soledad, San José, San Juan Bautista, San Miguel, San Fernando Rey, and San Luis de Francia, were founded within the century. Santa Inez was established in 1804, San Rafael in 1819, and San Francisco de Solano in 1823; the latter two never attained any great importance. Under the care of the Franciscans the missions grew strong and rich. There was no starvation then. Great herds and flocks supplied meat and clothing, while the wonderful vines and other vegetable growth of California added luxuries to their subsistence. The Indians were happy, contented, religious, and growing steadily into the ways of the civilized world. The priests had instructed them in the mechanical arts until there were skilled workmen at all the missions capable of doing almost any kind of work.

The intentions of Spain towards the Indians must be

gathered chiefly from the laws concerning them, of which it has been well said, "All of them manifest the great anxiety which the rulers of Mexico have felt, to collect the natives together in communities and subject them to municipal regulations, to secure to them the ability to pay the tribute imposed upon them for the supply of the national treasury, to induce them to forget their ancient religious rites and embrace the Catholic faith, to reform their idle and roving propensities and make them industrious and useful subjects." The chief purpose of the colonization was to make the country valuable to Spain. It was the object of every European power, that established colonies anywhere, to secure from them a money return to the mother-country. The natives especially were assets of the State, which it was desirable to make available as speedily as possible. The Church did not receive the treatment at the hands of Spain that might have been expected. At the suppression of the Jesuits, just prior to the entry of the Franciscans into California, the government took control of the "Pious Fund" belonging to that order, in trust for Church purposes, but it was swallowed up eventually by the State. The disadvantages to the Church of an alliance with the State were similar to those in England, under Henry VIII., though the property was not taken in the same forcible way. That a secularization of the Missions was early contemplated was shown by the establishment of the pueblos of Los Angeles and San José, and the presidios of San Diego, Monterey, Santa Barbara, and San Francisco. It is also reasonably certain that Spain contemplated granting the ownership of the Mission lands to the Indians of the respective Missions, but this was not done until after Mexico had asserted her independence, and then in such a way that the title has not held good, except in case of some of the San Juan Capistrano lands.

Both Spain and Mexico taxed the Missions heavily, and in carrying out the secularization policy, by the edict of 1834, Mexico appropriated the greater part of the property. Each Indian head of a family was given a small tract of land; one-half of the movable property was ordered to be divided among the emancipated people; and everything else was taken by the government. Some of the Franciscans left the country; others remained, and lived among their beggared and helpless flocks; one, at least, starved to death. The affairs of the Missions went from bad to worse until they were financial ruins. Many of the Indians scattered, and resumed their old mode of life. The greater part of the Missions themselves were sold by the State, but in an irregular and illegal way. Under our control there was a very slight improvement. By a decision of the land commission in 1856, the Mission buildings and a few acres of land about them, such as were considered to be devoted to the immediate use of the priesthood, were set off to the Catholic Church, on the ground that they were sacred property, which was inalienable under the Spanish law. The remainder of the Mission lands were treated as belonging to the government, but this decision was not a final one, although it has been followed through all its consequences.

There was never a grimmer satire on justice than this. The Indians, whose labor had made the buildings, tilled the lands, and created the orchards and vineyards, were left with absolutely nothing. The Church obtained the buildings, already well advanced towards ruin, but was left with a beggared laity, and with no mode of recuperation except the purchase of additional lands for a renewal of the Mission work. This was not resorted to, and time, with neglect, has since almost completed the work of destruction that the Mexican Government began. Many of the Indians remained in their former homes, considering, with the stupid, unresisting nature that has always characterized them, that they were appendages to the land. They had worked for the priests for no compensation but support, and they did the same for the holders of the ranchos. Adam Johnston wrote, in 1850, " They think themselves the property of the owners of the respective ranchos where they reside, as much as does the negro of the South to the owner of his cotton plantation. Indeed, the owner of a rancho looks upon them as his property, and in estimating the value of his lands, he always counts upon the services of his fifty or one hundred Indians, as the case may be, to enhance its value." Mr. Johnston

called the attention of the government to the fact that the
Mexican authorities held the Mission lands in trust for the
Indians, and suggested that our government should do the
same, but the suggestion was not adopted. They could have
been provided for at that time easily and with little cost, but
the government neglected to do it. It always moves slowly
to the relief of friendly Indians, and the Indians understand

THE RUINS OF SAN CARLOS DE MONTEREY.

it well. It is no wonder that Indian agents have had cause
to complain again and again of hostile tribes advising peaceable ones to go to war if they wished to get presents from
us. Our "wards" have had to fight very frequently before
the "guardian" paid any attention to their wants.

In 1852 B. D. Wilson, of Los Angeles, reported the condition of these Indians to the Interior Department, but still

nothing was done for them. They lived as best they could among the white settlers, or retired into the mountains. If they had any rights no one regarded them. White men pre-empted lands that they had held for years, and even their villages, which had been in their actual occupancy long enough to give them a title by prescription against any one but the government, were swallowed up by these cormorants. It is a fact that since the war of the rebellion, whole villages of these people have been driven from their homes by officers of the law, under proceedings to quiet title to land, and forced to seek new homes where they could find them. They did not know enough to defend the rights which they might possibly have sustained, and there was no one to do it for them. It was not until 1883, and then on the recommendation of a woman,* that the government even employed attorneys to defend the rights they did have. There is not much doubt that the valleys of Pala and San Pasqual might have been held by the Indians there, if any attention had been given to the defence of their claims. The pueblos there had been established under the Mexican secularization law of 1834, and the lands had been parcelled out to the Indians, under the law, by the prefects and priests. They had lived there continuously afterwards, but unfortunately had failed to have their rights passed upon by the land commission, appointed under the act of 1851 to adjust private land claims in California.

In 1869 Superintendent Whiting recommended that these valleys be reserved to the Indians, and an Executive order to that effect was made in 1870. This caused general indignation among the white people who wanted those lands, and a remonstrance against it was forwarded to Washington. It is said that most of the signatures to this paper were appended by a monte-dealer named McCan and two confederates. Even the dead protested against the reservation of these lands; at least the names of people who had been bur-

---

* Mrs. Helen Hunt Jackson, by whose death, on August 12, 1885, the Indians of America lost one of the most active and intelligent friends they ever had.

ied for years were signed to the remonstrance. The obnoxious order was revoked; the whites preempted the lands that Mexico had given to these Indians; and our "wards" were made wanderers. Congress refused to do anything for the Mission Indians because they were citizens, and the people of California would let them have nothing because they were not citizens. The agent at the land office in Los Angeles informed them that they could not preempt land because they were not citizens. In 1873 three of them applied for registration as voters, but the Clerk of Los Angeles County refused them, on the ground that they were not citizens. They appealed to the United States Commissioner at that point, and he transmitted their affidavits to the District Attorney at San Francisco, in whose office they probably still repose. Yet the Supreme Court of California held, in 1865 (People vs. Antonio, 27 Cal. 404), that the statute of that State for the punishment and protection of Indians did not apply to Indians who had "been living for years among white men," or, in other words, to the Mission Indians. They were subject to punishment under the same laws as white men, and yet by the statutes of California they could testify neither for nor against a white man. They had all the disadvantages of both the state of pupilage and the state of citizenship, and none of the advantages of either. Theoretically this was an impossibility; practically it was true. It is doubtful if even under the fourteenth and fifteenth amendments they have any enforcible rights. That many of them were citizens of Mexico at the time of the treaty of Guadalupe Hidalgo is unquestionable, and under that treaty they became citizens of the United States; but prior to the amendments each State could prescribe the qualifications of its electors, and the Supreme Court has held that the amendments do not apply to Indian tribes, so that the benefit of the amendments to Indians debarred of citizenship by State laws is very uncertain. Moreover, the Executive Department has virtually declared them in a state of pupilage again, by various orders establishing reservations for them, from 1875 to 1883.

The attention of the government was called to these people many times. In 1865 J. Q. A. Stanley, of Los Angeles, offered to act as distributing agent to them, without compensation, and the government graciously accepted his offer. He reported, several times, the constant and shameful encroachments of white men, and begged the authorities to do something for the protection of the Indians; especially to secure them lands for homes. Mr. Whiting, Superintendent of California in 1869, urged not only the provision for the future but also a remedy for the recent past. He said, "It seems to me that while the government assumes to act as guardian for the Indians, and the latter are treated as minors, the settlers should never be allowed to acquire title (from the guardian) to lands conceded to have been donated to the neophytes by a former government. If these Indians are recognized as minors in law, and incapable of transacting business of a complicated nature, no laches of theirs can deprive them of their legal rights. . . . It is quite certain that since my last annual report, and since it was known that I contemplated establishing a reservation for the Mission Indians, all of the best lands claimed by the Indians at Pala and San Pasqual, and especially the watering-places, have been taken up and occupied by settlers. The immigration has crowded off the Indians, and left thousands without a home. By sharp practice, and under various pretences, they have also been deprived of their horses, their working-oxen, their cows and stock cattle. Illicit traffic in ardent spirits unquestionably aided in the accomplishment of these wicked robberies." And yet such people as these settlers profane words, in some sense sacred, by talking of entering Indian lands "in good faith," and establishing "happy homes." The Pala and San Pasqual reservations were thrown open by fraud. The white robbers dwell in Pala, San Pasqual, and Temecuela to-day, some of them in houses that the Indians built. The Indians have no title to bar entrance even to their present lairs in the mountains, except the thin covering of an Executive order, revokable at will.

It is hardly possible, if we are to retain any faith whatever in a common humanity, that these wrongs can be pushed any farther. The reports of B. C. Whiting, in 1871, of John G. Ames, in 1873, and of Helen Hunt Jackson, in 1883, with various unofficial publications, have brought these things home keenly to people who are capable of shame over a national disgrace. The national authorities have shown a disposition to do something. Under Mrs. Jackson's recommendation, attorneys have been employed to defend their remaining interests, and possibly a long-deferred justice may still rescue something from the chaos of their rights. One thing is certain. Our laws should not be left so that any one man, or dozen men, can take away from these, or any other Indians, their homes, and permit white men to acquire vested rights therein. There is a Winnebago reservation case on the nation's hands to-day, and a possibility of others. It is not the probability of wrong that makes the laws bad; it is the possibility. If the privilege of the writ of habeas corpus were suspended for a week, or a day, it would cause intense indignation throughout the land, not because extensive wrong would probably be done, but because possibly it might. Under the Constitution no white man's property can be taken from him without due process of law. In parity of justice, before any rights could possibly be taken from our " wards," the legislative, executive, and judicial departments should all pass on the expediency and fairness of the act. It has ever been, and now is, too easy to do a wrong to these people, and too difficult to right one. If the former had always been as difficult as the latter, we should not, as a nation, have had to apologize for half of the injustice that has been done.

CHAPTER VI.

OATMAN FLAT.

IF an American who was not acquainted with the country might be seized by some supernal power and suddenly placed in Southwestern Arizona, he would never suspect that he was within the boundaries of the United States. Its soil, its vegetation, its sierra outlines, its dry, phantasmagoric atmosphere, its animal life, and its inhabitants, are all strange. Towards the Gulf of California the country for many miles is dry, barren, and desert, with no plant life but the cactuses, and even these seem depressed and hopeless, except when an angel's visit of rain brightens them. A little farther back come ranges of granite mountains, still more desert than the plains, for on their sides no vegetation appears, nor any soil to support vegetation. White and glistening, they rear their crests like the skeletons of mountains whose flesh had dropped away. Still farther back more vegetation shows, but it is strange to the average American. There is a broken carpet of grass in many places, brown and dead in appearance. Here and there is a mezquite, a palo verde, or a patch of sage. The Spanish bayonet thrusts out its sharp leaves. The century plant rears its lance-like stem and floats its graceful flowers. The prickly pear spreads its flat, jointed limbs in the heated air. Most striking of all, the saguarra, or pitahaya (petahyah), the giant cereus of the naturalists, sometimes solitary and sometimes in small forests, raises its fluted column from thirty to sixty feet, and lifts its stove-pipe arms above the other plants. Its color is green; the surface is smooth, and armed with clusters of thorns, as in the other cactuses. This plant is of great value to the natives. Its flowers form a bright-colored circle around its top, and give place to a ring of fruit, each as large as a hen's egg and much resembling a fig. From the juice of this they make a syrup of which they are very fond ; the pulp is pressed in cakes for winter use. Within the dead trunks are found rod-like threads of wood fibre, which, bound together, serve to reach the fruit. Water is scarce in this land. There can hardly be said to be any streams except the Colorado and the Gila, and the latter is dry at times in some parts. Their valleys, with fringes of willow, cottonwood, and mezquite, form a pleasant contrast to the table-lands. The chief reliance of the natives for water is on the natural tanks, which occur at well-known places in the rocks, or in beds of clay. There are also a few springs, which form pools ordinarily, but in very dry seasons these fail, and the Indians are forced to dig to the underlying rock, and gather the water drop by drop. Since the whites have made a thoroughfare of the country they have sunk wells at many points.

This region was inhabited by two classes of natives. South of the Gila were the Pimas, Maricopas, and Papagos. They are all of good disposition and have long been friendly to their Mexican neighbors, whose settlements join them on the southeast. The Pimas and Maricopas live in the Gila valley, occupying a strip of country about twenty miles long and four miles wide. These two tribes are on terms of the closest friendship and intercourse, but speak different languages and maintain entire independence in government and religion. They live in villages and support themselves by agriculture. Their fields, which are watered by irrigating ditches from the Gila, produce good crops of wheat, corn, melons, pumpkins, and cotton. The cotton they weave into excellent blankets, an art which they had when the Spaniards invaded their country. While of a quiet nature, these people are brave warriors, and have beaten the Apaches so often that those scourges of the desert retain a salutary dread of them. In the tribes of both nations there are legends of their wars, in which the Pimas and their allies obtained all the victories and celebrated them right royally. On one occasion, it is said, the Pimas spread flour on the ground for three miles, as a carpet for their victorious chief. The Papagos live to the south of these, and are, in fact, merely converted Pimas, their name being an adaption of *bapconia*, the Pima word for baptized.

VIEW NEAR THE GILA.

They say they originally lived still farther south, but were driven back by the Spaniards into their desert home, commonly called Papagueria or Papagoria. They are on friendly terms with the Mexicans, and have long assisted them in fighting their common enemies, the Apaches. Their principal settlement is at San Xavier del Bac, an old mission, established by the Jesuits in 1668. The stately old cathedral there was preserved by them after the Jesuit power passed away in Mexico, and it remains to-day, a splendid monument of Saracenic architecture, that would be an ornament to any city in the country.

In customs the Cocopahs resembled these tribes. They were a small band, numbering some three hundred warriors, who lived along the Colorado, next above the Gulf of California. They are agricultural, and raise excellent crops in the valley of the Colorado, which overflows nearly every year, usually in July. Their pumpkins and melons are especially large and fine. The previously mentioned tribes are quite decently clothed, but the Cocopahs make no pretensions to dress. Their men wear a light breech-cloth, and the women two little aprons of bark, one before and one behind. The Cocopahs and Maricopas were both originally parts of the Yuma nation, but seceded from it. The secession of the Cocopahs was not opposed; that of the Maricopas was, and a bitter war followed, in which the Yumas were aided by the Cocopahs. The Maricopas fled to the Pimas, who agreed to let them settle in their country, if they would adopt an agricultural life, and make no war except in defence, or to revenge aggressions. To this the Maricopas agreed, and have since kept their agreement. All these tribes were enemies of the Colorado River tribes above the Gila, and of the Apaches, and all remained so except the Cocopahs, who, in 1854, made a treaty of peace with the tribe next above them, known as the Yumas. The Cocopahs also differed from the others in the loose virtue of their women. They, like the Yumas, were well-made and handsome, but the comeliness of their women served only to attract the passion of their white neighbors, and bring upon themselves the diseases that have well nigh destroyed them. They spend half their time in the Colorado, swimming, or sitting immersed near the banks, their heads plastered over with fresh mud.

PIMA GIRLS.

The nation of the Yumas (Sons of the River), according to their statement, includes five tribes: the Cuchans, the Mahaos, the Mohaves, the Hah-wal-coes or Hualapais, and the Yampais or Yavipais. The Cuchans, who are commonly known as the Yumas, lived next above the Cocopahs, to whom they were very similar in habits. In 1850 they numbered about four hundred and fifty warriors. Above them on the Colorado were the

Chem-e-hue-ves (Chim-me-wah-wahs, Kem-ah-wi-vis) a branch
of the Pi-Utes, who are found in large numbers west of the Colorado in California. Above the Chem-e-hue-ves, and north of
Bill Williams Fork, were the Mo-ha-ves. Their name is from
two Yuma words: *hamook*, three, and *habi*, mountains, referring to the third mountain range, at which their territory
begins. The name is written Hamockhaves, Yamockhaves,
Yamajabs, Tamatabs, Jamajabs, Amochaves, and Mojaves.
They are a large tribe, closely related to the Yumas, and very
friendly with them. These two tribes intermarry, and both
are related, by numerous marriages, with the Coahuillas of the
Colorado desert, and the Diegenos (Indians of San Diego) of
Southern California, with whom they are on terms of intimate
friendship. The habits of the Mohaves are generally similar
to those of the lower tribes, but they make much better
houses, and appear rather more intelligent. Above the Mohaves, occupying the country in the great bend of the Colorado
to the south, were the Yampais. The Tonto Apaches lived
east of these, in the neighborhood of Bill Williams Mountain.
The Yampais and Tontos have been called the same by some
authorities, and both are generally considered mongrels—connecting links between the Apaches and the river tribes. The
Tontos were not of the bold, roaming disposition that characterized the other Apaches. They are small, not well-formed,
and in their manner of life degraded. All of the tribes mentioned were foot soldiers when they came under our rule.
They had some horses and mules, but not many, and they
were prone to use them for food in times of scarcity. The
lance was a weapon little used by them. Their arms were
bows, arrows, and clubs. The last named is a weapon seldom
used by other Indians, but those of the Colorado River were
never without it. It is simply a stick cut from a kind of live-
oak that grows in the mountains—one of the few species of
American woods that will sink in water after it has been sea-
soned.

It is to this section of Arizona that we must next transfer ourselves, but in 1850–51 there was no Arizona. The
country south of the Gila belonged to Mexico until the Gadsden purchase of December 30, 1853, and that north of the

Gila was a part of the Territory of New Mexico. The land south of the Gila, after its purchase, was sometimes called the Gadsden Purchase and sometimes Arizuna. The Territory of Arizona was set off from New Mexico in 1863, and the northwest corner of the tract, then included in its bounds, was afterwards ceded to Nevada. In 1850–51 the region was still in the condition in which it had been for the past century. The tribes north of the Gila were in what appears to have been their aboriginal condition. They had not acquired guns, nor had they contracted the vices and diseases of civilization. They had not even become expert horsemen and learned the use of the lance, as had their relatives a little farther east, from contact with the cavaliers of Spain. They still revelled in the independence and filth of absolute savagery. The country was almost wholly unknown. Kearny and Cooke had gone across it on their marches to California, and mail-carriers had made their way through by the same routes or by the northern road, which circled two hundred miles above its starting-point, through Southern Utah. At this time Captain Sitgreaves was on his exploring expedition down the Colorado, and Bartlett, with the Mexican Boundary Commission, was locating the eastern portion of the line. The few emigrants who pushed through to California by the southern road had to rely chiefly on the Mexicans and friendly Indians for information, assistance, and protection. There was a small force stationed on the Colorado, at the mouth of the Gila, called Camp Yuma. Fort Yuma was afterwards established in the same locality.

In the year 1849 a project was originated in the western part of Illinois for a settlement in the neighborhood of the mouth of the Gila River. Among those who determined to join this party was Royse Oatman, a man forty years of age, who had lived in the West since childhood. For a long time he was a successful merchant at La Harpe, Illinois, but, like many others, was brought to ruin by holding a large amount of wild-cat-bank paper when the collapse of 1842 came. After his failure he went to Pennsylvania, expecting to settle among relatives who lived in the Cumberland Valley, but the East had lost its charms for him, and he returned to Illinois. Here he began farming, near Fulton, but, in the course of his work, so injured himself by overlifting that his health failed. In consequence of the seeming hopelessness of recovering, or even being relieved from suffering, in a northern region, owing to his extreme sensitiveness to cold and damp, he joined the projected colony, hoping to find the climate a balm for his ailment. He was accompanied by his family, consisting of a wife and seven children. The colony, numbering some eighty souls, rendezvoused at Independence, Missouri, and on August 10, 1850, started on their long overland journey. One week's travel revealed the fact that the members were uncongenial, owing to differences of religious opinions. A part threatened to turn back, but the differences were smoothed over by the commendable diplomacy of some of the better-balanced heads. By the time the colony reached the junction of the north and south roads, at Santa Fé pass, the quarrels had become so acrimonious that the company divided. The larger party took the northern road. The smaller, consisting of twenty persons, with eight wagons, moved on to the Rio Grande and took Colonel Cooke's route to the south.

Slowly the little train crawled along, over mountain and plain, through cañons and across valleys, down into Mexico, across to the sources of the Santa Cruz, up through the old Spanish towns of Santa Cruz and Tubac, and, as the year closed, filed into Tucson, the city that disputes with Santa Fé the honor of being the first permanent white settlement within the borders of the United States. There they halted for a month. The Mexicans received them kindly and begged them to remain, as had also the inhabitants of the lower towns. The repute of American arms was so great, and the conflict of the Mexicans with the Apaches was so continuous, that American settlers were desirable. Part of the train concluded to stop for a year, at least, and rest. The Oatman, Wilder, and Kelly families decided to go on. Their cattle were in poor condition, and there was no opportunity to improve them much at Tucson. The Apaches had destroyed all the crops, and supplies were scarce at any price. The three families moved on into the "ninety-mile desert," the stretch of dry, hard, gravelly land, with its scant growth of mezquite and

cactus, that separates Tucson from the Pima villages. Dreary
and tiresome as it is now, it was far more so then, for there
were then no wells in it, and the traveller had no chance to
obtain water, except that during some seasons there were pools
at the Picacho, a peak midway of the desert. In this desolate region the Coyotero Apaches began to threaten them,
and each night they had to place a guard, who frequently
wakened the others to resist attacks. On the 16th of February, discouraged, destitute, and almost worn out, they reached
the lands of the Pimas. To add to the gloominess of their
prospects their provisions were now so reduced that it appeared impossible for them to hold out through the one hundred and ninety miles yet to be traversed before reaching
Camp Yuma.

They remained at the Pima and Maricopa villages until
March 11, and then the Oatmans started on alone. The motives that actuated the party to this division have never been

PIMA VILLAGE.

satisfactorily explained. It is stated by Lorenzo Oatman that Wilder and Kelly determined to remain, and risk obtaining support by trade with the Indians, while his father believed that starvation, or death at the hands of the Indians, would result from tarrying. On the other hand, it has been said that there was no good reason for the Oatmans going on alone, and it is certain that Wilder and Kelly started after them about ten days later. While in a state of indecision as to their course, Dr. Le Conte, the scientist, accompanied by a Mexican guide, arrived at the villages. He reported that he had passed

ANTONIO AZUL.

through the country between there and Camp Yuma twice, within the past few months, and that he had seen no signs of Indians anywhere. This information decided Oatman to go on. The road continues down the river to the Maricopa Wells, and then leaves it. The river bends to the north, and after a long detour of one hundred and twenty miles, around two ranges of granite hills, comes back to the same general course about fifty miles to the west. The road cuts across the country between these two points, which is known as the Desert of the Gila Bend. For seven days the Oatmans plodded along across this and down the Gila beyond. Their cattle, which were now reduced to one yoke of oxen and two yokes of cows, were almost exhausted. The roads had been made very bad by a recent rain. When they came to one of the numerous hills on the road, they were obliged to unload the two wagons and carry the goods, piece by piece, to the top. The cattle were frequently unable to pull up even the empty wagons without assistance.

On the seventh day, Dr. Le Conte overtook and passed them. He was touched by their sad condition, and promised to send assistance to them as soon as he reached Camp Yuma, then about one hundred and thirty miles distant. He pushed on rapidly, and that night camped thirty miles ahead of them. At daybreak, while preparing for the day's ride, Le Conte was surprised to see twelve Indians stalk into his camp. He and the guide seized their weapons and stood on their guard. The Indians professed friendship, and tried to divert their attention in order to gain an advantage. After some time their visitors went on their way, and soon after the two men discovered that their animals, which had been left in the valley below, had been driven off, probably during the visit of the Indians. The doctor ordered his guide to go on to Camp Yuma for horses, while he remained and guarded the packs, but the guide had not gone long before the doctor remembered the Oatmans and his promise. He placed a card conspicuously on a tree near the road, informing them of his misfortune at the hands of the Apaches, and promising to proceed at once to the fort for help. The Oatmans never reached this point.

On the evening of the 18th they came to the Gila, at the head of what is now called Oatman's Flat, one hundred and eighteen miles east of Fort Yuma. They attempted to cross, but the stream was swollen and rapid. After a hard struggle they succeeded in reaching a little sand island that still raised its crest above the waters. Darkness had fallen. The animals were mired. They determined to camp for the night on the island. The surroundings were depressing. The night was cold, and the wind blew in fitful blasts, at times driving the waters of the river almost over the island. The hour was late before a fire was started and the little allowance of food to which they were reduced was doled out. None of them could sleep. The parents sat apart and conversed in low tones. The children grouped around the little fire and considered the situation in their childish way. The rush of the river and the moan of the wind, as it whirled through the gullies and swept over the distant hills, turned their thoughts to the dangers that might be lurking in the wilds about them. They talked of the Indians, although they had seen none and no indications of any since they started. Each had his crude idea of the course he would pursue, and Olive, the second girl, a child of twelve years, said that she, at least, would not be taken by those miserable brutes. "I will fight as long as I can, and if I see that I am about to be taken I will kill myself," she said, defiantly. The dreary night passed away. With the first rays of the morning they made ready to leave their dismal camp. They gained the opposite bank and made preparations to ascend the hill of the mesa, which is elevated about two hundred feet above the flat. The ascent is over a hill formation, caused by the wash of water that is common all through the West. The upper strata, to a thickness of twenty feet, are harder than those beneath. As the ground has washed from below, the upper part has broken and fallen, making a perpendicular wall, from the base of which the detritus forms a sloping descent to the plain below. The mesa is covered with a growth of saguarras, which appear from below to stand as sentinels along its border.

Up this hill the Oatmans were obliged to carry all their goods, the teams being unable to pull the empty wagons without assistance. The day was spent thus and in resting, with the intention of moving on at night. The full moon afforded ample light, and they hoped to make the journey easier for their cattle by resting in the heat of the day. One of the wagons was taken up the hill and drawn about a mile beyond, to the summit of a swell in the mesa, beyond which one yoke of the cattle could pull it. As the sun set Oatman turned back for the other wagon, which, with the unloaded goods, remained at the top of the hill. Here the family gathered to eat a few morsels of dry bread and a cup of bean soup before starting. The depression of the night before had scarcely abated. Oatman, especially, was weighed down by gloomy apprehensions. For an hour on the preceding night he had wept bitterly, and during the afternoon he had sunk down by the wagon and groaned out: "Mother, mother, in the name

11

of God, I know that something dreadful is about to happen!"
His manhood appeared to have failed him completely. As they
packed the wagons, he moved about listlessly, buried in his
gloomy thoughts. Lorenzo, who was assisting his father,
glanced down the road through the flat, and, to his horror,
saw a number of Indians leisurely approaching them. He
spoke to his father, who turned hastily. As his eyes fell on
the Indians the climax of his terror was reached. His face
flushed deeply, and then paled to a ghastly hue. His form
stiffened, and the muscles of his mouth twitched convulsively.
Several minutes passed before he regained any command of
himself. Even then his every movement betrayed his fears.
Doubtless it was the result of his presentiment, for he had
been known before as a man of coolness and courage. He
had also often met and dealt with Indians, and was deeply
impressed with the belief that if treated kindly and firmly
they would seldom do any injury. Although this theory has
often been successfully tested, it must be remembered that
the firmness is more important than the kindness. An Indian despises a man who fears him, and will often mistreat
such a one, when he would not annoy a man that put on a
bold front.

The Indians, nineteen in number, came up to them. They
were naked, except their small breech-clouts. Repulsive in
features, filthy of person, and with dishevelled hair, they
formed a wild and barbarous group. Each carried a bow and
arrows and a club. Oatman motioned them to sit down, and
spoke to them in Spanish. Some of them understood that
language, and replied to him with vehement protestations of
friendship. They asked for tobacco and a pipe, to smoke in
token of amity. Oatman prepared one, took a whiff, and
passed it to them. They then asked for something to eat.
Oatman told them that he had scarcely anything; that if he
gave them food he would be robbing his children. By this
time they had gauged the party with whom they were dealing,
and knew that they would meet no serious resistance. They
ignored his excuses, and increased the vehemence of their demands until their clamors became furious. Oatman took
some bread from the wagon and gave it to them, telling them

that he was bringing his family to starvation by doing so. They devoured it and demanded more, but he refused. They then gathered on one side and consulted in their own tongue, while the family hurried on with their packing. Mr. Oatman and Lorenzo were handing in the goods at the back of the wagon. Mrs. Oatman was inside arranging them. Olive and Lucy, her older sister, were on the side nearest the Indians, arranging some of the property. Mary Ann, a child of seven, sat on a stone in front, holding the halter of the foremost yoke. The remainder of the children were on the opposite side of the wagon. They were almost ready to start. A few minutes more, and they would leave their disagreeable visitors forever, they hoped.

The Indians came closer to them. They scanned the horizon and looked carefully up and down the road, as though in expectation of some one. Then, with wild yells, they leaped upon the hapless group before them. Of all weapons known to man, the club is most fitting to the brutal nature. It was the first weapon to which man laid his hand in the primordial dawn. It is the weapon of some of the higher apes to-day. The ragged hole left by the rifle-ball, the gaping cut of the stiletto, and the broad gash of the lance or the sabre are shocking to the sight, but they have nothing of the horror and repulsiveness of the crush of the war-club, that distorts the features till they lose the semblance of humanity. This was the weapon of the Tontos, for such these Indians were, and they plied it with the ferocity of devils and the excitement of madmen. Oatman was beaten to the ground and his skull crushed by repeated blows, as he writhed and groaned in his torment. Lorenzo received a blow on the back of his head that brought him to his knees, and another that tumbled him over, dazed and helpless. Mrs. Oatman leaped from the wagon and clasped to her bosom her youngest child, a boy of two years. The savages dashed upon her with tiger bounds, pounding out the life of mother and child at once, while her screams for help startled the desert echoes and were mockingly thrown back from the bleak hills. Lucy had been seized by the hair at the first, and beaten until she was not only dead, but almost unrecognizable. The smallest girl, less than four years old, was despatched at one blow. Royse, her next older brother, was the last to fall of those that died. He had stood farthest away. He saw the others killed and stood nerveless, overcome with horror. As the savages came upon him he gave one piercing shriek, and a moment later was struggling in unconscious convulsion, under the stroke of the club. The other two children, Olive and Mary, were spared. This was the predetermined intention of the Indians, for Olive was drawn to one side by one of them, and Mary was seized by another, at the outset.

The work of plunder began. They tore the canvas cover from the wagon, broke open boxes, and rifled the clothing of the dead, taking what they wanted and strewing the rest over the ground. As they came to Lorenzo he showed some signs of life. They removed his hat and shoes. Two of them seized him by the feet, dragged him to the edge of the bluff, and hurled him over. Down, twenty feet, to the slope, he fell. Down, over the ragged rocks, he rolled. During part of this time he had a dim consciousness of his surroundings, but no power of motion. He heard the shrieks of his brothers and sisters, and the despairing cry of his mother. He felt the Indians searching him, and knew that they were dragging him over the ground. Then came the weird feeling of a wandering consciousness. At one moment he seemed to move between great rows of pictures hung in the distant air. At another his senses were shocked by the din of unearthly and discordant noises. Again, he was lulled by strains of heavenly music that soothed him into ecstatic rest. At the same time he was conscious that he lay on the rocky slope, in the bright moonlight, with the blood flowing from his ears and nose. Then darkness came.

When he next gained consciousness the mid-day sun was beating upon his face. His head throbbed with a maddening pain. He tried to open his eyes, but could not. As his mind cleared, he rubbed away the clotted blood that locked his eyelids, and looked about him. His clothing was in shreds. He put his hand to his head, and felt his scalp torn from his skull and stiffened like parchment. Up the slope he saw the stains of blood that had marked his fall, and realized how he had reached his present place. His thoughts wandered back to the tragedy enacted on the mesa above. An uncontrollable impulse came upon him to look again on the faces of the kindred who lay there. It was so short a distance, and yet how great. Faint and dizzy, he crawled up the rocky slope. His strength failed—he fainted ; his consciousness returned—he crept on ; up—up—up, full fifty feet he struggled, and then, looking across a gully that broke the edge of the mesa, he saw the wagon lifting its bare ribs in the parched air. It brought the full horror of the place back to him. His desire to look on the features of the dead was gone. His only thought was to get away from the horrible spot. He crawled along the slope to the road, and down the road to the river, every muscle aching, every nerve strained, and his head pulsating with pain and delirium. The Gila, muddy and warm, how he drank of it and bathed his bruised body ! It brought relief. He slept. When he awoke it was night. With the aid of a stick that he found by the riverside, he gained his feet and began to walk. The road crosses the Gila twice at this bend, to avoid the bluff that juts out from the south side. Lorenzo avoided crossing by making his way over the bluff. He walked all through the night and the following morning. Near mid-day he reached a pool of warm, muddy water, of which he drank deeply, and fell asleep in the glowing sunshine. After a short sleep he awoke, partially delirious, and continued his journey. In the middle of the afternoon, as he was crossing a high, barren table-land, his strength suddenly vanished and he fell in a faint.

When he recovered, near evening, his ears were filled with a strange noise that seemed to be approaching him. Before he could rise to his feet he was surrounded by a pack of coyotes, growling, snarling, and licking their lank jaws in anticipation of the feast before them. Here was a new danger, for the coyote, though cowardly to an active enemy, is fierce and desperate as its congener the gray wolf to the helpless. Lorenzo started to his feet with a yell, the first utterance he had made since the massacre, striking one of them as he rose. At this they fell back a little and he started on his

march again.   They followed him.   Twilight came, and
darkness.   They pressed upon him, surrounding him on all
sides with a circle of glistening fangs and glaring eye-balls,
but fear brought him a new strength.   He gathered stones
and threw at them till they fell back again.   He hurried on,
tormented by the horrible thought that he might faint and
be devoured.   For hours they dogged his footsteps, but at
length they abandoned the pursuit, and by midnight he had
the satisfaction of hearing their howls die away in the distant hills.   Towards morning he had another season of
troubled sleep, after which he started on once more.   About
noon, as he was passing through a dark cañon, he came in
sight of two Pima Indians.   They hastily drew their bows at
sight of this strange being, but when he raised his hand and
spoke to them, they rode up to him.   One of them was an
Indian with whom the Oatmans had been acquainted in the
village.   Quickly as they saw who was before them they dismounted and embraced him, with expressions of pity and
sympathy.   They spread their blankets under a tree, for a
couch, and brought him a gourd of water and a piece of their
ash-baked bread — all that they had.   They rode on to the
scene of the massacre, telling him to remain until they returned and they would convey him to their villages.

He slept till evening.   On awakening he became fearful
that the two Indians might prove treacherous.   The awful
tragedy of a few hours back made him distrust a dark face.
He left the cañon and continued his march through the night
and to the middle of the morning.   On the crest of a hill,
overlooking a long, winding valley, he crept under a bush
and slept for two or three hours.   When he awoke he felt
completely exhausted from hunger and pain.   He had a
desire to sleep longer, but fought it off.   As he lay there,
thinking over his hopeless situation, he looked down across
the valley, and saw objects moving on the road.   He was
sure they were Indians.   For an hour, in the tortures of suspense, he watched the specks moving towards him, straining
his aching eyes to their utmost, and at length, as they crossed
a little hill, he saw that they were wagons.   A great flood of
gladness came over him, and he swooned away.   When he

SCENE OF OATMAN MASSACRE.

recovered the wagons of the Wilders and Kellys were standing near him, and Robert Kelly was approaching him. In a few minutes he was surrounded by friends, and breaking his weary fast on a bowl of bread and milk. On hearing his story the two families turned back to the Pima villages, to stay until they should be reinforced by others travelling in the same direction. The two men, with a number of Pimas, went on to the scene of the murder, and covered the remains of the victims with stones to protect them from the wolves. Two weeks later six white men who were going to Camp Yuma arrived, and the two families journeyed on with them. Lorenzo, who had already recovered somewhat from his sufferings, was cared for at Yuma by Dr. Hewitt, the post-surgeon, until his health was restored.

While Lorenzo was making his weary way along the road, his sisters, Olive and Mary, were being driven across the desert north of the Gila by the Indians. As soon as the work of plunder was completed the savages moved away a short distance, made a fire, and prepared a supper of bean soup and ash-baked bread. The girls could not eat. After the meal the Indians diverted themselves by terrifying little Mary. They would threaten and scowl at her until, in an agony of nervous fear, she would run to her sister's arms, sobbing wildly. Then they would brandish their clubs and frighten her into silence. For an hour they remained at this place, from which the children could see the bows of the wagon, in the moonlight, marking the spot of the massacre. They were oppressed with grief and suspense. The events of the past hour were so horrible that older persons might well have been overwhelmed by them. All their kindred—father, mother, sisters, and brothers—they had seen fall beneath the clubs of their captors. For themselves was absolute uncertainty as to their future fate, with all the apprehensions of torture that their childish knowledge of Indian customs could bring them. Another element of torture was soon to be added — it was bodily suffering. The Indians took from them their hats and shoes, and started on their march. An Indian led; the two captives followed; the other Indians formed the rear-guard. Across the desert they hurried, the tender feet of the captives being bruised at every step. Sharp stones gashed them, and cactus thorns pierced them cruelly. After several hours Mary sank down and refused to go farther. Blows and threats had no effect upon her. She said she had rather die than live. At length one of the Indians threw her across his back, and the march was resumed. Olive became so faint and weary that she felt she could not go on, but the fear of being separated from her sister gave her superhuman energy. At noon of the following day they halted until the cattle were brought up, killed, and cut in pieces. In the afternoon they again started, and journeyed until ten o'clock at night. During this time the sufferings of the girls were lessened by having pieces of skin tied upon their feet. At daybreak they continued their march.

Near noon, as they were passing through a dark cañon, a band of eleven Indians appeared, and approached them in great excitement. One of them drew his bow and let fly an arrow at Olive, which pierced her dress but did not harm her. As he fitted another to his bow the captors sprang forward and placed themselves before the girls, while one of them seized the would-be assassin. It appeared that this man had lost a brother in a recent attack upon some whites, and had sworn to avenge himself upon the first white that he met. The captors, however, had other uses for their captives, and finally succeeded in getting rid of the avengers, though not until there had almost been a general battle. They travelled until midnight. In the morning they hurried on till they came to a village of low, thatched huts. The captives, suffering and exhausted by two hundred miles of cruel marching, were placed on a pile of brush, around which all the inhabitants of the village, about three hundred in number, whirled in a dance of exultation and savage joy. Throughout it they took every means of humiliating the captives, by striking them, throwing dirt upon them, and spitting in their faces. Their insults had but little effect on the wretched girls, who had now reached the stage of indifference and desperation. The only apprehension that troubled them was the fear of torture. This was dispelled on the succeeding day. The jubilee and feast were over. A night's rest had somewhat

refreshed the captives and eased their pains. They were set
to work at the employments which must henceforth engage
them. Their fate was now clear. They were slaves.

It would be difficult to imagine a more oppressive slavery
than that in which they existed. The Tontos were a people
of the most degraded character, with customs which added
weight to the natural brutality of savagery. They had broken
off from the tribes to the southeast during the flowery days of
the Spanish power, and taken refuge in the wilderness, while
their brethren remained to fight the invaders. From the
Coyoteros, so they told the girls, they had received an Apache
name which means unruly, but this name had been corrupted
by the Mexicans into the word *tontos*, which means stupid or
foolish. They were a connecting link between their fierce
relatives on the east and the agricultural Mohaves on the
west; they had neither the wild, warlike habits of the one,
nor the good-natured indolence of the others. Their women
were obliged to do all the work, as in most of the tribes, and,
to make their lot more unenviable, the Tontos had a theory
that young females should not subsist on meat any more than
was absolutely necessary to prevent starvation. In consequence their women of all ages were dwarfed and dried up,
while their young girls frequently died from want of food.
To these enslaved and half-starved squaws the Oatman girls
were sub-slaves, and they found them most cruel mistresses.
They delighted in inventing new and unnecessary tasks, and
at the least provocation beat the helpless children unmercifully. The girls quickly learned that the children of the tribe
were their masters also, for the slightest complaint from one
of these youngsters was the signal for a severe beating. All
this, and their constant menial labor, had to be undergone on
the most stinted allowance of food. Even in feast times the
savages would contemptuously throw them refuse scraps of
food, saying: "You have been fed too well; we will teach
you to live on little." They would have died of starvation if
they had not appropriated for themselves, at every possible
occasion, the roots and other food that they were ordered to
gather for their owners.

Late in the fall of 1851 a party of Mohaves visited the

village on a trading expedition, and some talk was had about a purchase of the captives. When about a year had elapsed from the time of their capture, a second delegation of Mohaves, five men and the daughter of the chief, came to the Tonto village to negotiate for them. The question of sale was in dispute for some hours, but on the morning after the arrival of the Mohaves the Tontos concluded to accept the price offered, which was two horses, three blankets, some vegetables, and some beads.

Another long and weary march was before the girls, but what they suffered now was not a result of spite. The chief's daughter walked all the way, carrying a roll of blankets that she shared each night with the captives, while the two horses that remained to the party were carrying the gentlemen. For eleven days they trudged along, over rugged mountains and across dusty deserts, until they reached the Mohave valley, on the Colorado River. A beautiful valley it appears to the wayworn traveller across the desert, with the broad river gleaming beyond through its fringe of willows and cottonwood, and patches of grass relieving the brown, dead color that has become so tiresome. Here dwelt the new owners of the slaves. As masters they were far preferable to the Tontos. They seemed to lack much of that savage trait of torturing for the pleasure of seeing pain. They lived in rude but comfortable huts, made of logs set on end, thatched on three sides, and covered with mud roofs. These were usually surrounded by rows of cottonwood-trees and plots of grass, and near them were placed cylindrical osier granaries in which they stored their edibles. The Mohaves raised wheat, corn, melons, and vegetables. They did not till the ground, but planted everything in hills scraped up by their fingers, the annual overflow of the Colorado keeping the valley in a state of great fertility. The girls were obliged to work much as before, but they had more to eat and were beaten less.

One day the Mohaves heard the girls singing, and were curious about this accomplishment of their slaves. At their request the girls sang several songs. Afterwards they were frequently importuned to sing, and were usually rewarded for complying with strings of beads, pieces of red flannel, and other gifts that have a value to the savage. The flannel was valuable to the girls also, enough of it being acquired to make additions to their very limited wardrobes. The Indians often asked them questions about the whites; and though they usually concluded their inter- views by telling the captives that they were outrageous liars, like all the Americans, they lis- tened with apparent in- terest to the descriptions of the white man's hab- its. The idea of a heaven above the stars struck them as an especially foolish thing, because the heavenly hosts would necessarily all drop out. They also questioned the girls

IRATABA, MOHAVE CHIEF.

closely as to their contentment with their lot, and professed to be fearful that they would attempt to escape. Finally, they imparted the unwelcome information that they were about to tattoo the girls' faces, so that they would know them wherever they found them. The Mohaves tattoo their own women only when they marry, marking them with vertical blue lines on the chin, but Miss Oatman stated that their markings were differ- ent from those of the Mohave women, and that they were not treated as wives by their owners.

The chief labor of the girls, through the summer, was col- lecting mezquite (pronounced *mez-kee-tay'* by the natives) beans and storing them in the granaries. There are two kinds of mezquite. The common, or straight-pod, is very similar to the common honey-locust in growth, foliage, and the armor of sharp spines. It occurs as a shrub, in dense thickets, or as a tree from ten to forty feet high. It is invaluable to the inhabit- ants of Arizona for fuel, principally furnished by the roots, which remain intact long after the tree has disappeared, and are found everywhere. The pods or beans, when ripe, contain a sweet, mealy pulp, which, when dried and powdered, is used for sweetening pinole (ground parched corn), or as a food direct. The other is called the tornillo, or screw-pod mezquite. It is similar to the first, except that the beans are twisted in a close spiral, resembling a screw. During the spring, when the winter supplies had been exhausted and the new growth was not matured sufficiently for food, there was ordinarily destitution among the Mohaves. Their chief reliance was in gleaning the mezquites from which beans had been gathered in the preceding autumn. The summer of 1853 brought a failure of crops to them, and they looked forward to the approaching winter with well-grounded fears of a famine. The unhappy slaves were taxed to their utmost to gather provisions, and the failure to return in the evening with loaded baskets was sure to be paid by a beating. Mary was fast failing under this barbarous life, and the starvation which was peculiarly their lot. She wasted away to gauntness, and became more and more feeble. As starvation became more imminent, those of the Indians who were able to travel made a journey of sixty miles in search of food. Mary tried to accompany them, but gave out and went back. The party secured a tolerable supply of food, but it was soon exhausted. The Indians were growing so desperate that savage selfishness prevailed. Each one provided strictly for himself and ate all he could get. They would let their nearest kin starve, and then rend the air with the dismal howling that their customs make appropriate in time of death.

Mary became helpless and Olive was distracted. She was obliged to go away to procure food, yet she feared to leave her sister. The Indians would give Mary nothing to eat, and some of them advocated killing her in order that Olive might have more time to procure food for them. When Olive found anything to eat the Indians would take it from her, if they saw it. Whole days passed when neither of them had a morsel. Their pangs of hunger were almost beyond endurance, and their strength was ebbing. Olive could remain on her feet but a short time, while Mary was fast approaching death.

She fixed all her thoughts on a future life—a reunion with her father and mother, her sisters and brothers, in a beautiful land where pain and want would never come. Every day, so long as her strength would permit her, she sang the hymns that were used in the Sabbath-schools of thirty-five years ago. Wan and weak, with flesh wasted and skin drawn tightly over her bones, with unnatural fires gleaming in her eyes, her voice would carry, pure and clear, the words of "Jesus, lover of my soul," or, "The day is past and gone," until she seemed some supernatural being, striving to throw off the covering that held her, and rise above the earth. The Indians, even those who thought it an injury to themselves for her to live, would gather about her and stand enchained by the weird sight, although close by their relatives were dying unheeded. At times some of them would be overwhelmed with unknown emotions, and give way to outbursts of weeping and moaning as they looked on the dying girl. Death came at last, and she passed to the abode of spirits peacefully and quietly, as if sinking to sleep. Instead of burning her body, as is their custom, they gave Olive the privilege of burying her remains in the little garden-spot that had been set off for their use.

Oppressed by a terrible feeling of loneliness, Olive lived on through the famine. The next year was one of plenty, but it brought her a new torture. When the growth of the year had advanced sufficiently to furnish the Mohaves with food, and they had recovered strength and spirit, they decided to make an expedition against the Cocopahs. This was the first one that they had undertaken since the purchase of the captives, and Olive was informed that in case any of the warriors were killed she would be sacrificed, in accordance with their custom, which requires a warrior who falls in battle to be furnished with a slave in *Hippoweka*—the spirit-land. For five months the war-party was absent. For five months Olive was tortured by the constant contemplation of the thread on which her life depended. There seemed hardly a possibility that all the war-party would return, for the Cocopahs were reported to have been joined by new and powerful allies since the Mohaves last attacked them. At length, one day, as she was gathering roots, she saw a messenger coming to the village.

He brought news, but of what? She knew not what to do. For a moment she thought of flight, but abandoned that chance as hopeless. In desperation she went to the village to learn her fate. She sat in silence through the convening and opening of a council, that Indian decorum made necessary before the news was told. At length the messenger spoke. The Mohaves were returning in triumph with five prisoners. None of them had been killed. Tears of joy and relief rolled down the poor girl's cheeks, and she bowed her head in thankfulness for her deliverance.

Soon after this, Olive was forced to behold a shocking spectacle. The captive Cocopahs were all young girls but one, who was a woman about twenty-five years of age and unusually beautiful. She appeared almost frantic with grief. Olive succeeded in communicating with her, and learned that her distress was caused by her separation from her husband and infant child. Their village had been attacked in the night, and the Cocopahs had fled. As she ran along, her husband took the child from her arms and ran ahead. She followed, but was overtaken. After remaining in the Mohave village for a week, she made her escape in the night. She swam down the river for several miles and concealed herself in a willow thicket during the day. In this way she swam about one hundred and thirty miles down the Colorado, in less than a week, travelling only at night. She had passed almost through the country of the Yumas, when one day a Yuma warrior discovered her lying under a shelving rock near the river. He secured her, and, as obliged by the intertribal relations, brought her back to the Mohaves. The Mohaves crucified her. That is one thing that the Arizona Indians have learned from missionaries, at any rate, and they seem to think it an improvement on their own barbarities. She was raised to the cross-beam, about eight feet above the ground, and her hands fastened by driving coarse wooden pegs through them. Similar pegs were driven through her feet. Her head was tied to the upright by strings of bark stuck full of thorns. The other captives and Olive were then brought before her and told to behold the fate that awaited them if they attempted to escape. For two hours the unfortunate lived, the Mohaves meanwhile dancing about her, shooting her with arrows, and mangling her body with burning brands. After death they took her down and burned her body on a funeral pyre.

After this Olive gave up all thought of escape. She lived on in the usual way, though with one improvement; the Mohaves had been awakened to the necessity of greater care in their planting, by the famine of 1853, and there was no more suffering from want of food. In February, 1856, she was startled to hear that a Yuma Indian had arrived in the village with a message from the fort, demanding her release. This

PASQUAL, YUMA CHIEF.

assistance had come from an unexpected source. When Lorenzo Oatman reached Camp Yuma, his story attracted the sympathy of a number of officers and men, who desired to attempt the rescue of his sisters, but the garrison was soon to move and there was no time for any protracted search. Colonel Heintzelman, the commander, sent out a small force under Captain Davis and Lieutenant Mowry, but they failed to find the captives. In June the garrison removed to San Diego, except about a dozen men, who were left to guard the ferry. In a short time these men were driven away by the Yumas, who retained control of the ferry for several months.

A chief named Antonio Garra, a man of resources and ability, undertook to unite the Yumas and Coahuillas, of Southern California, in an alliance to sweep the Americans from the country. This failed through the treachery of Juan Antonio, a Coahuilla chieftain, in whom Garra trusted. Colonel Heintzelman was sent back to chastise them, a work that required over a year. By October, 1852, Garra was killed and the Yumas subdued. Lorenzo had gone to San Francisco with Dr. Hewitt. He remained there and in the mines for three years, trying to devise some plan to rescue his sisters; but though he received much sympathy, he could get no material assistance. In October, 1854, he went to Los Angeles, still intent on this object. He joined several parties of prospectors organized to search for gold beyond the Colorado, and one of them penetrated the country bordering on Bill Williams Fork in 1855, but without getting any trace of the captive girls. In December of the same year he searched in Southern California for them, but with no success. He then tried the newspapers, by which he succeeded in arousing public sympathy somewhat, and in learning that his sister was reported to be a captive among the Mohaves. Thereupon he prepared a petition to Governor Johnson, of California, for men and means to recover her, which was signed by many of the people of Los Angeles county. The governor replied that he had no authority to grant the request, and referred him to the Indian Department. He prepared a memorial to the Indian Department and forwarded it about the first of February, 1856.

During this time an unknown friend was at work. In 1853 there came to Fort Yuma, as carpenter, a Mr. Grinnell, who was known to the Indians as "Carpintero" on account of his occupation. He was a nephew of Henry Grinnell, whose princely philanthropy fitted out the *Advance* and *Rescue* for De Haven's search after Sir John Franklin's exploring party. A similar spirit of humanity actuated the humble carpenter, and led him to take a lively interest in the fate of the Oatman girls. He continually questioned emigrants and Indians for tidings of them. One night in January, 1856, a friendly Indian, named Francisco, came to his tent and asked him:

" Carpintero, what is this you say so much about two Ameri-
canos among the Indians?" Grinnell informed him that the
whites well knew of the existence of the girls and would certainly make war upon the Indians unless they were surrendered. Producing a copy of the Los Angeles *Star*, in which
Lorenzo had made his first published appeal for assistance,
Grinnell translated the article to Francisco, and, still appearing to read, told him that a large army was being prepared
which would annihilate the Mohaves and all tribes who assisted them in concealing the captives. Francisco was visibly
impressed. Grinnell kept him in his tent all that night, and
in the morning took him to Colonel Burke, who commanded
the fort. Francisco said: "You give me four blankets and
some beads, and I will bring her in just twenty days, when the
sun is there," indicating about four o'clock in the afternoon.
Burke thought it was some trickery on the part of the
Indian, but Grinnell said to give him the goods and charge
them to him. The goods were furnished and Francisco departed.

The arrival of Francisco caused no little tumult in the
Mohave village. A council was called and Olive was shut
up in a distant part of the valley. Francisco urged her release eloquently, but the Mohaves were not yet acquainted
with the power of American arms, besides feeling strong in
their remote location. Late at night the council broke up
with a refusal to surrender her, and an order to Francisco to
cross the river and return no more on penalty of torture.
He crossed the river but did not abandon his purpose. All
night he argued with the chiefs on that side and in the morning they asked him to return with them, saying they would
do all they could to procure her surrender. They went back,
and, after some consultation, another council was called, which
Olive was permitted to attend. The Mohaves had devised a
new project. They stained her skin and ordered her, on pain
of death, not to speak to Francisco in American, Mohave, or
any other language that he could understand. To him they
represented that she was an Indian of a distant tribe. She
summoned all her courage and told him who she was and
what they had ordered her to do. Francisco sprang from his

A MOHAVE DWELLING.

seat in fury.   He launched upon the Mohaves a most vehement and eloquent address.   He reproached them for their
attempted deception; told them the whites knew that the
girl was there; that they would destroy the Mohaves and the
Yumas if she were not given up; that the Yumas had
fought the Americans for many months and knew that they
were more powerful than all the Indian tribes; that he had
come to them out of mercy for his own tribe; and that they
had endangered their own lives and those of their friends the
Yumas by this treachery.   To Olive he gave the following
note, which she deciphered with much difficulty:

"Francisco, Yuma Indian, bearer of this, goes to the Mohave nation to obtain a white woman there, named Olivia. It is desirable she should come to this post, or send her reasons why she does not wish to come.

"MARTIN BURKE, Lieut.-Col. Commanding.

"HEADQUARTERS, FORT YUMA, CAL., 27th *January*, 1856."

The Mohaves wanted to know what was in this letter. Olive told them, and also informed them that the Americans would certainly send an army to destroy them if they did not let her go with Francisco. The Mohaves began to be cowed. They proposed that they should kill Olive and that Francisco should report her as dead, but this Francisco refused to do. The night dragged on in that fierce debate, where a feather's weight might give the captive liberty or doom her to death. After sunrise Francisco and Olive were told to retire, and when called back they were informed that the Mohaves had decided to surrender her. Unable to repress her emotion, Olive burst into tears. She was not allowed to take any mementoes with her. They took away even the beads and cloth that had been given to her and Mary for singing. She had only the privilege of a last visit to her sister's grave. There were few preparations to make. They got breakfast, secured a little food, and started. They were accompanied by Francisco's brother and two cousins, who had come with him, and by the chief's daughter, who went to the fort to obtain a horse that Francisco had promised to her father.

The twentieth day arrived and found Grinnell waiting patiently. He had been the subject of many jests by his comrades, who thought that Francisco had cleverly worked on his sympathies to the extent of the goods furnished him. At noon three Yumas appeared and announced that Francisco was coming. "Is the girl with him?" asked Grinnell, eagerly. "Francisco will come here when the sun is there," answered the Indians, indicating the point Francisco had designated, and no more satisfaction could be had from them. The sun crept down the west never so slowly. As the hour neared, Grinnell's strained eyes caught sight of three Indian men and two women approaching the ferry, on the opposite side of the river. He sprang forward with the glad shout:

" They have come; the captive girl is here!" Olive, who did
not wish to come to the fort in her scanty bark dress, was
quickly furnished with clothing by an officer's wife, and was
soon presented to the commander amid wild enthusiasm.
Men cheered, cannons boomed, and the assembled Yumas,
carried away by the general joy, gave vent to shrill whoops.
There remained a yet more affecting meeting. Two days after sending his memorial to the Indian Department, a friend
handed Lorenzo a copy of the Los Angeles *Star* containing a
brief statement of Olive's recovery. He mounted a horse
and hastened to the editor. The report was reliable. It was
based on a letter from Colonel Burke. A kind friend furnished him with transportation and accompanied him to Fort
Yuma. Ten days of riding, along the western slope and
across the Colorado desert, and the brother and sister were
clasped in a fond embrace. What a meeting! Five years before they separated amid the groans of their dying kindred,
in the moonlight, on the desert. Now they meet, the sole
survivors, after weary days and nights of hardship and despair, in safety, and surrounded by friends. Tears came un-
bidden to the eyes of strong men who stood about them, but
they were not ashamed to weep.

There remains but little more to tell. Lorenzo and Olive
returned to Los Angeles, and thence went to Southern Oregon, to live with a cousin who heard of their trials and invited them to make his home their own. They afterwards
attended school in the Santa Clara Valley, in California, and
in 1858 removed to New York. Francisco received praise
and reward from the whites, and this led the Yumas to make
him a chief. He was commonly known as El Sol Francisco,
possibly from his indicating the time of his return by the
sun. He was very arrogant in his new station, but remained
friendly to the whites while he lived. In 1857 the Yumas
and Mohaves determined on a grand expedition against the
Maricopas. They raised a large band, including a number
of Yampais and Diegenos, and attacked the Maricopa villages
about the first of September. They burned some houses, and
killed some women and children, but a swift vengeance overtook them. The Pimas and Maricopas hastily congregated,

OLD FORT YUMA.

and were reinforced by Papagos until their numbers were about equal to those of the invaders. At Maricopa Wells they fought a great battle, in which the river Indians were defeated with a loss of over two hundred warriors. Out of seventy-five Yuma warriors who went to battle only three returned alive. Francisco fell on this field, killed, it is said, by his own men, who thought he had brought disaster on them by befriending the whites. The Yumas and about half of the Mohaves still remain along the Colorado. They are not under charge of any agent, and are subdued to a state of abject servility. The remainder of the Mohaves and most of the Chemehueves are on the Colorado River reservation and are commonly known as the Colorado River Indians. The Tontos remained at large for many years, but at length, reduced by war and disease to less than seven hundred, they were placed on the White Mountain reservation in Arizona. They never acquired any weapons, except a few knives and lances, and were never formidable. The Pimas and Maricopas have had a reservation set off for them, including their cultivated lands on the Gila, and still remain there. The Papagos have a reservation of 6000 acres, including San Xavier del Bac. These three tribes have always remained friendly, and have been at times the only bulwarks of the whites against the hostile Apaches. They offered to raise a regiment for the Union during the civil war, but the government contented itself with furnishing them arms to fight the Apaches. They have often served as scouts and guides.

CHARLES D. POSTON.

After the remains of the Oatmans were covered up by Wilder and Kelly, they were dug out by coyotes, and lay scattered until the arrival of Dr. Webb's party of the Mexican Boundary Commission, a few months later. They were then reinterred. A second time they were dug up by the desert scavengers and scattered over the mesa. In 1854 they were again gathered by Mr. Poston, an early settler of Arizona, and buried in the flat below the scene of the massacre. A small enclosure marks the spot, and a board with a rudely carved inscription tells the traveller that there are buried the remains of the unfortunate family whose terrible calamity gave a name to Oatman Flat.

CHAPTER VII.

THE ROGUE RIVER, YAKIMA, AND KLICKITAT WARS.

OREGON was organized as a territory in 1848 by Congress, and its territorial government went into operation in the following spring, on the arrival of the governor, General Joe Lane, an Indianian who had won distinction in the Mexican war. Under the organic act, it embraced the country west of

GENERAL JOE LANE.

the Rocky Mountains north of parallel 42. The part of this north of parallel 46 to its intersection with the Columbia, and north of the Columbia thence westward to the ocean, was organized as Washington Territory in 1853. At the time of

the organization of Oregon, the part afterwards erected into
Washington Territory was still virtually in the hands of the
Hudson's Bay Company, except that a few families had settled in 1844 at Tumwater, now a suburb of Olympia, and one
or two more at the latter place. Its first governor, Isaac I.
Stevens (the Brigadier-general Stevens of the Union army
who fell at Bull Run), arrived, overland, in the fall of 1853,
with a surveying-party, examining the country which they
traversed with regard to its availability as a railroad route.
To these territories we must now return, for, while a restless
peace has been maintained in Washington and Northern Oregon for several years, trouble has arisen in the South.

Along the southern boundary, extending into both California and Oregon, were several warlike tribes, who, though
not very friendly among themselves, were in general sympathy
in their hostility towards the whites. On the Rogue River were
several bands of the Shasta family, sometimes known by the
names of their chiefs, but almost always called "the Rogue
River Indians." There were two principal clans of them, the
Upper and Lower Rogue Rivers; the former were led by
"Joe," whom they called Apso-kah-hah (the Horse Rider); the
latter were under "Sam" (Ko-ko-kah-wah—the Wealthy), a
wily and avaricious old man, who generally restrained them
from hostility to the whites, and managed to reap a heavy
harvest of presents and profits for himself. South of these,
on the Klamath River, were the Lutuami or Klamaths (Klamet,
Klamac, Clammat, Tlamath), the several tribes included under
the name having no close relationship. Those nearest the
ocean, called the Lower Klamaths (Eurocs, Youruks or Poh-
liks), were a dark people, inferior to their relatives above, a
distinction which is always marked between the tribes who
subsist on fish and roots and those who eat flesh. Above
them, on the river, were the Upper Klamaths (Cahrocs, Kah-
ruks or Pehtsik), a finely formed, energetic, and cleanly race.
The Modocs (Moädocks, Moahtockna), formerly included in
the Klamaths, but really a branch of the Shoshonee stock, lived
about the lakes in which the Klamath heads, and others near
them, extending to the bounds of the Bannocks and Pah-Utes.
In their own language they are called Okkowish, their com-

mon name (pronounced *Mo'-ah-dock'*) being a Shasta word
which means strangers or enemies, a coincident signification
that has doubtless caused them to be blamed for many wrongs
which they did not commit. South of the Klamaths were the
remainder of the Shastas (Tshastl, Chasta, Shasty, Sasté, Shas-
teeca), of whom a part were friendly, especially a band of the
Scott's River Indians (Ottetiewas), under their chief, Tolo, who
was called by the whites "Old Man" or "Charley." The
Shastas, Rogue Rivers, and Scott's Rivers have all one language, and had formerly one head chief, who was accidentally
killed a short time before the discovery of gold in California.
After his death a contest arose as to the chief command between John, the old chief's son, Sam and Joe of the Rogue
Rivers, and Scarface of Shasta, Tolo remaining neutral.
When the whites began to come in they separated, each
aspirant retaining supreme control of his own faction. These
bands were further subdivided under various sub-chiefs, and
with them had confederated the Umpquas, who lived north of
the Rogue Rivers.

These Indians had never been friendly to the Americans.
Away back in 1834 the Umpquas attacked a trading party of
fourteen men under Captain Smith, of Smith, Sublette, &
Jackson, and killed eleven of them. In 1835 a party of eight
was assailed in the Rogue River Valley; Daniel Miller, Edward
Barnes, Mr. Sanders, and an Irishman called Tom were killed;
the other four escaped, badly wounded. In 1838 they attacked
the first party sent out by the Wallamet Cattle Company to
bring in stock from California, but were beaten off after
wounding Mr. Gay, one of the survivors of the party of
1835. In 1845 the Klamaths attacked Fremont's third exploring expedition, in camp, at Klamath Lake, and killed
three men before Kit Carson's trained ear caught the sound,
and the party was awakened to win safety in a hand-to-hand
conflict. In the spring of 1851 the Rogue Rivers killed two
men on Grave Creek, and two or three on Rogue River, in
consequence of which Major Phil. Kearny, the same gallant
cavalier who fell at Chantilly, was sent against them with a
detachment of regulars. He defeated them in two actions;
the men fled to the mountains and about thirty women and

children were captured. He was taking these prisoners into
California when he was met by General Joe Lane, who

persuaded him to permit
them to return with him
to the Rogue River. Lane
arrived at Rogue River
shortly after the commis-
sioners who were treat-
ing with the various tribes
arrived at the same place.
The Indians had refused
to make any terms with
Major Kearny; but when
they saw their women and
children returning, under
charge of a "tyee" in
whom they had great

PHILIP KEARNY.

confidence, they came in, and a treaty was made. Just
about this time, unfortunately, the commission received instructions to discontinue its labors, and the treaty was never
ratified. Nevertheless, the Rogue Rivers committed no further serious depredations for about two years.

The other tribes were not so quiet. In June, 1852, the Pitt
River Indians killed four men who were locating a wagon road,
and in August the Modocs massacred an emigrant party of
thirty-three persons, of whom several were Californians who
had gone out to assist the emigration. Volunteer companies
were at once organized at Yreka and Jacksonville and despatched to the scene of the affair, near Tulé or Rhett Lake.
The California company, under Captain Ben Wright, reached
Bloody Point, on the lake, just in time to relieve an emigrant
train of sixteen wagons which had been surrounded by the
Indians for several hours. At the approach of the volunteers
the Indians took to their canoes and continued the fight from
the lake, which is shallow, full of islands, and bordered with
a heavy growth of tulé reeds. They soon discovered that
they were playing an unequal game, and after losing a dozen
or more warriors they retired out of range. The next day the
volunteers found and buried the bodies of eighteen murdered

emigrants and settlers. They remained in the locality for three months, together with the Oregon company, under Captain Ross, which had arrived after the battle and consolidated with the Yreka Company, with Captain Wright commanding. They employed their time in escorting emigrant trains through the more dangerous places, and concluded an otherwise meritorious campaign by a most disgraceful massacre. It was on the morning that they left for home that they had, as one of their number reported it, " a smart engagement, in which we killed about forty of them, impressing upon the minds of the balance, no doubt, the opinion that we had avenged the wrongs their tribe had committed towards the whites, at least during that season." In reality Wright sent out a captured squaw by whose representations forty-eight of the Modocs were induced to come to the camp to have a feast and make a treaty. The original plan was to poison the food given to the Indians, and so be rid of them, but it did not succeed. Some say that the squaw got an inkling of what was going on and notified the warriors, who thereupon refused to eat. Others say that they ate, but the poison did not operate ; that Wright used to swear afterwards over the way he had been imposed on by the druggist. At any rate, the feast part of the programme passed and they sat down to talk. While the talk was going on Wright opened fire with his revolver, killing two of the principal Indians. At this prearranged signal his men fired, their rifles having been charged afresh for the occasion, and thirty-six more of the Modocs fell. The remaining ten managed to escape before the volunteers could reload. Wright broke camp and returned to Yreka in triumph, his men carrying the scalps of the Indians on their rifles. He reported that he had demanded the return of stolen property of the Modocs, and, on their failure to surrender it, had punished them. A general welcome was extended by the citizens of Yreka, and the legislature of California paid the volunteers for their services, but Wright met his punishment four years afterwards, when the Rogue Rivers killed him, at his agency, with twenty-three others. The Modocs never forgot this outrage, and the bad faith shown bore fruit long afterwards, as we shall see hereafter.

From these conflicts no very peaceable disposition had been produced in either whites or Indians, but, aside from this, there was a continuing cause which was the chief occasion of both the wars that followed. In 1852 President Fillmore said, in his message to Congress: "The Senate not having thought proper to ratify the treaties which had been negotiated with the tribes of Indians in California and Oregon, our relations with them have been left in a very unsatisfactory condition. In other parts of our territory, particular districts of country have been set apart for the exclusive occupation of the Indians, and their right to the lands within those limits has been acknowledged and respected. But in California and Oregon there has been no recognition by the government of the exclusive right of the Indians to any part of the country. They are, therefore, mere tenants at sufferance, and liable to be driven from place to place at the pleasure of the whites." What the President thought "liable" to occur was at that time occurring. During the controversy with England, as to the ownership of the country, and afterwards, strong representations of future benefits had been held out to emigrants, by statesmen who favored an occupation of Oregon, and these had been made good by Congress, by allowing each actual settler before 1850 to pre-empt three hundred and twenty acres of land, with an equal amount for his wife, if married, while settlers from December 1, 1850, to December 1, 1853, took half that amount. As there was no restriction in regard to what lands were to be taken, the settlers naturally took the best they could find, and, as gold was discovered at various points, farms were opened about the diggings, and all of the better part of the country was overrun by the enterprising immigrants. In the meantime treaties were not ratified, and the Indians failed to receive the promised consideration for the lands of which they had been dispossessed. Of course, the same possessory title remained in them as had always been recognized in the eastern tribes, and disinterested persons, particularly the army officers, regarded them as being imposed upon. In 1852, Brevet Brigadier-general Hitchcock, commanding the Pacific division, wrote: "As matters now stand the United States troops are placed in a most delicate and awkward position.

The whites go in upon Indian lands, provoke the Indians, bring on collisions, and then call for protection, and complain if it is not furnished, while the practical effect of the presence of the troops can be little else than to countenance and give security to them in their aggressions; the Indians, meanwhile, looking upon the military as their friends, and imploring their protection." The courts, of necessity, took much the same view of the question as the military authorities. In 1851 several Klickitats were indicted for malicious trespass, for destroying some timber in the Wallamet Valley, which a settler, named Donald McLeod, had prepared for a house. They maintained that it was their own timber, grown on their land, and that they had warned McLeod not to attempt to settle there. The United States District Judge held that they had a possessory title to the land, not yet extinguished by the government, and that the action would not lie. Another attempt to have the Indians punished for trespass was made by one Bridgefarmer. He had built a fence across an Indian trail, and they had torn it down and followed their customary highway. It resulted as the other case had.

The situation was one from which warfare was certain to result. The settlers had come to get their three hundred and twenty acres of land and go to farming, but no matter where they settled they were on Indian land. They saw other settlers peaceably established on their farms, under the same circumstances, and they settled also. But they went to inexcusable lengths in their appropriations. Nearly all of the Indians had adopted agriculture to some extent, and particularly the cultivation of the potato, of which they were very fond. In many tribes each family had its little patch of a quarter of an acre or more, which was carefully tended and quite productive. In pre-empting farms many of these were enclosed by the settlers, and so notorious had this evil become, in 1853, that Lieutenant Jones, commanding Steilacoom barracks, gravely writes: "The practice which exists throughout the territory, of settlers taking from them their small potato patches, is clearly wrong and should be stopped." One is almost inclined to ask what he was there for, but it is well to remember that military interference, in the United States, has

13

ever been regarded as the climax of evils, and no officer could be expected to do more than call the matter to the attention of the government.

The Indians of Oregon had, from the first, treated the Americans remarkably well. The Whitman massacre was the first serious trouble that had occurred, and, in Northern Oregon, almost the only one. But as the Indians saw their lands being taken without compensation, their treaties unfulfilled, and the men who " spoke with authority " to them being constantly changed, and unable to carry out their agreements, they lost all confidence in their white friends. One Rogue River chief said: " We have waited and waited, because the agents told us to be patient; that it would be all right by and by. We are tired of this. We believe Uncle Sam intends to cheat us. Sometimes we are told there is one great chief and sometimes another. One superintendent tells us one thing, and the great chief removes him. Then another superintendent tells us another thing, and another great chief removes him. Who are we to believe? Who is your great chief, and who is to tell us the truth? We don't understand the way you act. With us, we are born chiefs; once a chief we are a chief for life. But you are only common men, and we never know how long you will hold your authority, or how soon the great chief may degrade you, or how soon he may be turned out himself. We want to know the true head, that we may state our condition to him. Let him come here himself and see us. So many lies have been told him that we think he never hears the truth, or he would not compel us to suffer as we do."

The Rogue Rivers chafed more than the others, because there were more miners in their country, and consequently more aggression. The road from California to Oregon lay across their lands; placers had been found on them; and miners and settlers had flocked in. Jacksonville was a flourishing town; villages had sprung up at several points; farms were opened all through the Rogue River Valley. The Indians saw but one chance for relief. On August 4, 1853, they began remedying the evil by killing Edward Edwards in his house, on Stewart's creek; and rapine and destruction were the order from that time forward. On the next day Thomas

MOUNT SHASTA FROM VALLEY OF SACRAMENTO.

Wills was killed within three hundred yards of Jacksonville, and, on the 6th, Richard Nolan was murdered about a mile from the same town. By this time the alarm had been sounded everywhere, and the people gathered together for protection, while the torch was applied to their buildings and haystacks, and their stock was being driven off to the mountains. Captain B. R. Alden, commanding at Fort Jones, in Northern California, was notified, and at once repaired to the scene. He brought ten regulars, all that were available at the fort, and some volunteers from Yreka, who, together with the volunteers at Jacksonville, made a force of about two hundred. On August 11 this force had prepared for a night attack on the Indians, who were strongly posted near Table Rock, but at dusk a messenger appeared, at full speed, announcing that a band of Indians was raiding the valley and that the families there were in imminent danger. As he spoke his words were verified by the red glare of burning buildings on the western sky, and the volunteers, without waiting for orders, hurried to the defence of their homes. The force could not be collected again for work till the 16th, and then the Indians had retired into the mountains, firing the pine forests behind them.

On the 20th, while preparations were being made for an extended chase, General Lane arrived and took command. At daybreak of the 22d the troops moved forward in quest of the savages. For two days and a half they searched through an almost impassable country, where nearly all traces of the trail had been destroyed in the forest fires. Near noon of the 24th, General Lane, who was in advance, heard a sound of voices, about four hundred yards away, in a dense forest. The troops were quietly dismounted, and, dividing into two parties, made their attack. The Indians quickly recovered from their first surprise and took positions behind logs and trees, from which they returned the fire vigorously. The battle was thus carried on for nearly four hours, and during it General Lane, Captain Alden, and three others were badly wounded and three killed, the Indians losing eight killed and twenty wounded, of whom seven died. While General Lane was at the rear, having his wound dressed, the Indians called to the

13*

troops that they wanted to make peace. Two men went to talk with them, and, on learning that General Lane was in command, they wanted him to come also. He went over, and, as there was no prospect for a victory over the Indians, he made arrangements by which they were to come to Table Rock and make peace. Both parties remained on the ground over-night, good faith being mutually observed, and in the morning the Indians moved off. They appeared at Table Rock as agreed, and a treaty was concluded there on September 10. The Indians were by no means conquered, but treated on equal terms, being influenced by their confidence in General Lane more than by any other consideration.

Discontent soon became an active force again, for all the old causes were in operation. Force seemed to be the only arbiter for which either party had any respect. There were murders committed by Indians, and murders committed by white men. On January 16, 1854, a party of citizens from Yreka undertook to chastise a party of Shastas for an alleged theft of cattle, but were driven back with a loss of four men. Over on the Oregon side, at daybreak of the 28th, a party of thirty miners, under a discharged sergeant of dragoons, named Abbott, attacked three lodges of friendly Indians at the mouth of the Coquille; killed sixteen, and wounded four. These Indians had only three good guns among them, and the number of warriors in the district was less than half of that of the whites. The assassination of some thirty men is attributed to the Shastas, Rogue Rivers, and Modocs between the treaty of September 10, 1853, and the outbreak of 1855. It may safely be assumed that at least as many Indians were murdered by whites, for there were many white men among the pioneers who, when a safe opportunity presented, shot an Indian as they would a wolf. In addition to these home affairs, the whites were greatly inflamed, all through the coast, by the barbarous massacre of an emigrant party of nine men, two women, and eight children on August 20. This crime was committed near Fort Boisée by the Snake Indians. Before it occurred there had been murders all along the emigrant trails, and, in the summer, a company of militia had been sent out under Captain Jesse Walker. He attacked the Modocs at their rancherias on Tulé Lake, forced them to take to the water, and destroyed their buildings and all their provisions. From August 18 to September 4 there was more or less skirmishing between them, and, on the latter date, the Indians, being wholly out of provisions, made peace, and promised to rob and kill no more. He then marched against the Pah-Utes and chastised them at Warner's Rock, but was unable to bring them to terms. But troubles in Oregon were beginning to be more important than those along the trails.

Until 1855 the Klickitats (Robbers) had been friendly to the whites. In 1851 they had tendered their services during the Rogue River troubles, but had not been used. In 1853, sixty of their warriors, armed and mounted, had gone to assist General Lane, but they did not arrive until the treaty of Table Rock had been completed. These Indians, though not great in numbers, were among the most powerful and influential of the tribes, well supplied with fire-arms, and very expert in their use. From their home on the eastern slope of the Cascade Mountains, north of the Columbia, they had sallied forth, at about the time the missionaries came into the country, and fallen on the weaker tribes below. They first attacked the Cowlitz, Chinooks, and other inferior tribes along the Columbia, and in five years had reduced them to tributaries. In 1841 they began raiding south of the Columbia, west of the Cascades, where the coast tribes, reduced by disease, were unable to resist them. They subdued the Clackamas, Yamhills (Che-am-ills, meaning bald hills, now hopelessly corrupted in the form given), Santiams, and other tribes of the Wallamet Valley, and forced them to pay tribute. The Umpquas next fell before their conquering arms, and the Klickitats controlled the country from the Columbia to the Rogue River Mountains, exercising possession and claiming title by right of conquest. In their palmy days they maintained a state more nearly approaching regal magnificence than did any savage tribe of America. Casino, one of their chiefs, was frequently attended on his travels by a hundred slaves, and, on visiting Fort Vancouver, it is said, his slaves carpeted the way from the landing to the fort, a quarter of a mile, with furs, and, on returning, the Hudson's Bay men carpeted the same path with blankets and other goods. In 1851 treaties were made with the coast tribes at Shampoag, in which the Klickitats were entirely ignored, notwithstanding their possessory title had been judicially recognized, as before mentioned. Nevertheless they retained their actual sovereignty. They maintained an extensive trade in furs and slaves with all the neighboring tribes, roamed the country at will, and exacted tribute on all fish and furs taken in their territory, as well as on all increase of stock. Their chief highway was through the valley of the Wallamet, and here, during the winter season, they usually kept their families. As the country settled up, their excursions became annoying to the whites, and, in 1853, Governor Palmer represented to the government that the property of the whites, as well as that of their subject tribes, suffered at their hands. In the spring of 1855, reduced by disease to a comparatively small band, they were compelled to remove to their original home, and from that time they were ready for war.

Several of the tribes east of the Cascade Mountains were dissatisfied with the treaties which had been made with them, for their lands, by Governor Stevens, in the spring of 1855. They did not understand the bargain as the whites did. Chief among these were the Yakimas (Black Bears), a strong tribe of Washington Territory, whose country lay just north of the Klickitats. They were closely united by intermarriage and interest with both the Klickitats and the "King Georges," or British, and carried on an extensive commerce through all the northern country from the coast to the Rocky Mountains. Their chiefs, Kamiaken, Owahi, Skloo, and others, had signed the treaty of Walla-Walla under strong pressure from Governor Stevens, and almost immediately repudiated it. The Indians claimed that the chiefs who signed it had been bought up, a practice occasionally resorted to by the representatives of the government; they were indignant and alarmed. To the representations of the Hudson's Bay people, that the Americans would take their lands, the Yakimas lent a credent ear. In fact, they had only to look across the mountains to see the lands of other tribes taken without recompense, while disease was sweeping the expelled owners from the face of the earth. Disaffection was rife everywhere, and there was scarcely a tribe from the British possessions to California but had its grievance. Mormon emissaries aided in diffusing enmity, nor was their part merely that of advisers, for in the succeeding war guns and ammunition bearing Mormon brands were captured from the Indians. The more intelligent and resolute chiefs urged a union of all the tribes for war. Among these none was more influential than Leschi, a Nasqualla chief, who, with half a dozen of his tribe, crossed the mountains and preached a crusade to the interior tribes. "Bold, adventurous, and eloquent, he possessed an unlimited sway over his people, and, by the earnestness of his purpose and the persuasiveness of his arguments, carried all with him who heard him speak. He travelled by day and night, caring neither for hunger nor fatigue; visited the camps of the Yakimas and Klickitats; addressed the councils in terms of eloquence such as they had seldom heard. He crossed the Columbia, penetrated to Southern Oregon, appealed to all the disaffected there. He dwelt upon their wrongs; painted to them, in the exuberance of his imagination, the terrible picture of the '*polakly illeha*,' the land of darkness, where no ray from the sun ever penetrated; where there was torture and death for all the races of Indians; where the sting of an insect killed like the stroke of a spear, and the streams were foul and muddy, so that no living thing could drink of the waters. This was the place where the white man wanted to carry them. He called upon them to resist like braves so terrible a fate. The white men were but a handful now. They could all be killed at once and then others would fear to come. But if there was no war, they would grow strong and many, and put all the Indians in their big ships, and send them off to that terrible land where torture and death awaited them." On the other hand, there were chiefs in all the tribes who opposed war; some tribes refused to take any part in the matter, and others acted as auxiliaries to the whites. The Nez Percés were particularly faithful. They escorted back to Walla-Walla Governor Stevens, who had gone to treat with the Blackfeet and other tribes, and for whose safety there was much apprehension.

They also organized for active work against the hostiles when they should be called upon.

A union in sympathy, at least, was effected between a majority of the tribes, but before any definitely arranged plans for simultaneous action were matured the impatient tribes of the North opened the contest. The Colville mines were discovered in the summer of 1855, and the usual rush for the new diggings ensued. Among others who started was a Mr. Mattice, who had been operating a coal-mine on the Dwamish. He had just crossed the mountains, by Snoqualimie Pass, with a considerable amount of money and provisions, when a party of Indians, supposed to be Yakimas, killed him and carried off his property. About the same time his partner, Fantjoy, was also murdered by the Indians, and thereafter miners were cut off at every opportunity. In September, Indian agent Bolen went from the Dalles into the country of the Yakimas, and had a talk with Kamiaken, Owahi, and other chiefs. On the next day, as he was returning, three Indians came up with him, and, while two talked to him, one fell behind and shot him in the back. He was scalped and his body partially burned. As soon as this outrage was heard of, a plan was formed to send 100 men into the Yakima country from Fort Steilacoom, while Major Rains (afterwards a Confederate general), commanding at Fort Vancouver, advanced by way of the Columbia, and to unite the two forces in the enemy's territory. The force from Steilacoom was confronted in the mountains by an overwhelming body of Indians, and retired to the western slope. Under instructions from Major Rains, Major Haller advanced from the Dalles, with 100 men on October 3. On the 6th he was surrounded in a position where he had neither wood nor water, and was forced to retreat, reaching the Dalles on the 10th. He lost three killed, nineteen wounded, thirty pack animals, and was obliged to cache a mountain howitzer, which, however, was afterwards recovered. Major Rains then came up and took the field in person, with 350 regulars. He pushed forward to the Catholic mission on the Yakima, had a few skirmishes with the Indians, and burned some of their stores, but failed to accomplish any satisfactory result.

In the South, war was precipitated by a foolish and fiendish attack on the friendly Rogue Rivers of Old Sam's band. Some of the whites decided that sub-chief Jake's ranche was a harbor for unfriendly Indians, who had been burning fences and buildings, and also for friendly ones who had been guilty of pilfering, so, early on the morning of October 8, a party of them under "Major" James Lupton attacked it. They left behind them, as proof positive of their prowess, the bodies of

THE DALLES.

eight men (four very aged) and fifteen women and children, besides several whose bodies were thrown into the river. They also fired into sub-chief Sambo's camp, killing one woman and wounding two boys. This latter party was on the way to the reservation, the men having gone ahead. A large number of the remaining friendly Indians fled in terror to Fort Lane, where the troops saved them from destruction in the war of extermination that followed. The rest joined

"John" (Te-cum-ton—Elk-killer), the hostile fourth chief
of the tribe, and at once began retaliating. On the 9th
they burned every house from Evans' Ferry to Jump-off-Jo
Creek, and robbed and destroyed every wagon along the road.
They killed eighteen people, of whom six were women and
children, at Jewett's Ferry, Evans' Ferry, Wagoner's Ranch,
and neighboring points. This descent is known as the "Wagoner massacre." On the next day they killed Misses Hudson
and Wilson, on the road between Crescent City and Indian
Creek, and thenceforward a most sanguinary war was waged
by both whites and Indians on unprotected parties of stragglers, while both parties oppressed the friendly Indians who
desired only to remain on the reservation in peace, the whites
murdering them at every opportunity, and the Indians destroying their houses and other property. Among other atrocities a party of volunteers, on December 23, 1855, surrounded
the camp of some Indians, whom they had visited the day
before, and knew to be friendly and unarmed, with the exception of a few bows and arrows; they killed nineteen men,
and drove the women and children out into the severe cold,
from the effects of which the little remnant that gathered at
Fort Lane were all suffering with frozen limbs. The openly
expressed policy of the volunteers, and of many of the citizens,
was the extermination of all neighboring Indians.

At the North the volunteers blundered as badly as in the
South. A company of them, under Nathan Olney, an Indian agent, had organized on the call of Major Rains, and
pushed up the Columbia early in the winter. They reached
Fort Walla-Walla on December 3, and on December 5 met the
band of the Walla-Walla chief Pio-pio-mox-mox (Yellow Serpent, Serpent Jaune). This chief had formerly been a good
friend of the Americans. He had assisted Colonel Fremont
in California; he had refused to join the hostile Cayuses after
the Whitman massacre; he was emphatically the chief of the
Columbia country whose influence was most worth having.
But he had recently plundered Fort Walla-Walla (still a Hudson's Bay Company post), and was understood to be in sympathy with the hostiles. He advanced under a white flag and
desired to treat, but a question arose over the terms, and the

whites told him he must go back and fight. This he refused to do, so he and four of his men were held as prisoners, still repeatedly refusing to leave the camp and fight, still promising to return the property plundered from Fort Walla-Walla, and still insisting on peace. On the 7th, the volunteers were attacked by about three hundred Indians and fought them on the march all day. At evening an attempt was made to bind Yellow Serpent and his companions, but they refused to submit to this indignity; they drew knives and attempted to resist, but were shot down, except one young Indian who made no resistance. Yellow Serpent's scalp and ears, and the scalps of the others, were sent into the settlements as trophies. This action settled the question with many hesitating Walla-Wallas, Umatillas, Cayuses, Pelouses, and Des Chutes, who forthwith joined the hostiles. On the 8th, the attacking force numbered nearly six hundred, but they were driven across the Columbia with little loss to either side. Aside from this these volunteers accomplished nothing beyond creating dissatisfaction among the friendly Cayuses and Nez Percés, who had acceded to their terms, and who accused them of taking their property wrongfully. After two months' service this company was disbanded, but a large force of volunteers was kept in the field in various parts of Oregon, most of them still determined on the policy of extermination.

In the latter part of January the Indians about Puget's Sound suddenly began war, having been incited to it by the chiefs Leschi, Kitsap, Stahi, Nelson, and others. So unlooked-for was this outbreak that a number of unsuspecting settlers were cut off while supposing themselves in entire safety, and much valuable property was destroyed before any organization could be made for mutual protection. Some of the settlers took refuge on shipboard, and others in the town of Seattle. The Indians, meantime, devastated all King County, and even attacked Seattle. It was a situation, seemingly, of great peril, with active hostilities thus in progress from the Sound to Northern California, but the sources of safety were among the Indians themselves. They were hopelessly divided. There was not a tribe in which there were not some chiefs and some warriors who favored the Americans, and preferred

peace, while the great majority of the Flatheads and Nez
Percés were of this mind. This enabled the army officers
afterwards to accomplish by diplomacy what could only have
been accomplished with the greatest difficulty by war. Besides, these Indians were not the Indians of the East. Perhaps three thousand warriors in Oregon could be counted as
hostile, but one thousand Shawnees, Delawares, Seminoles,
Sioux, or Apaches would have done ten times as much damage.

Major-general John E. Wool, who succeeded General Hitchcock in the command of the Department of the Pacific, had
little sympathy with the extermination policy, and less with
the plan of sending troops into the country of the hostiles
while the settlements were left unprotected. He disregarded
the voluminous plans which Governors Stevens and Curry
prepared for carrying on the war, refused to make a winter
campaign, declined to recognize the volunteers as United
States troops, insisted that their presence in the field was
wholly unnecessary, concentred the regulars at Fort Vancouver, and used as many of them as he considered necessary
in protecting the friendly Indians, who remained on the reservations, from the aggressions of the whites. Governor
Palmer took substantially the same view of the matter as
General Wool, and also urged the establishment of the Grande
Ronde and Siletz reservations near the coast; and, in consequence, petitions of the Oregon Legislature were forwarded
to Washington, asking the removal of both. They further
charged against Palmer that he was a "Know-nothing Whig,"
and had been guilty of not voting the Democratic ticket at
local elections; while they characterized E. R. Geary, whom
they recommended for his successor, and whom Palmer had
discharged from the office of secretary for abetting the opposition, as a "sound, consistent, and reliable national Democrat."
Governor Palmer was succeeded, for other reasons, by George
L. Curry, as Governor, but was retained as Superintendent of
Indian Affairs. A spicy wrangle ensued between Wool and
Governors Stevens and Curry, which was protracted for
months in the newspapers and in their official reports. It
must have been painful to the governors, in after-times, to
learn that Wool's reports had uniformly gone to the Secretary

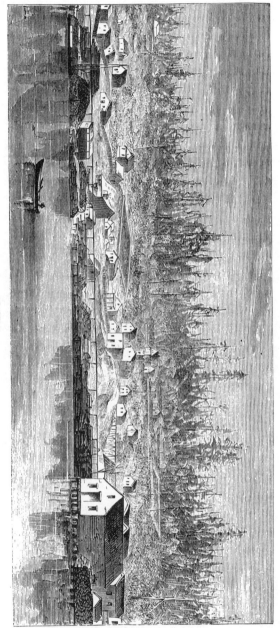

SEATTLE.

of War endorsed, "Respectfully submitted. I fully approve the views of Major-general Wool. WINFIELD SCOTT."

The regular troops and the volunteers acted independently of each other, the former endeavoring to bring the war to a close by treaty, making what the settlers considered undue conces- sions to the Indians, and the others trying to accomplish the extermination project, or, at least, to make "an indelible im- pression." Neither did anything of importance during the winter, but the Indians had more success. On February 22, 1856, at dawn, when most of the volunteers of the force en- camped on Rogue River, three miles above its mouth, were gone to a "Washington's-birthday ball" at the mouth of the river, the hostiles surprised the camp and killed Captain Ben Wright, special agent, Captain Poland, and twenty-two others, among whom was Mr. Wagoner, whose family had been murdered in the preceding October. Charles Foster alone escaped from the camp, and succeeded in reaching a place of safety, after hiding all day in the bushes. He esti- mated the attacking party at three hundred. They also sacked and burned all the ranches along the river, the whites who escaped fleeing to Port Orford and the mouth of the river, where they fortified themselves, and remained on the defensive for a while.

As the spring opened, and General Wool got ready to act, Colonel Wright, of the 9th Infantry, went up the Columbia and took charge of the campaign. He passed the Cascades, leaving only a command of nine men, under Sergeant Kelly, to protect the portage. The river from the Cascades to the Dalles was the key to the Columbia country, as it afforded the only connection between eastern and western Oregon. The river here breaks through the Cascade range. From Celilo to Dalles City, fifteen miles, it rushes through a narrow chan- nel of basaltic rock with an impetus that makes navigation impracticable; then comes a stretch of quiet water for forty miles; and then between five and six miles of rapids, known as the Upper, Middle, and Lower Cascades. The mode of passage is now, as it was from the earliest days, by boats, making portages at the Cascades and the Dalles. In 1855–6 the intermediate forty miles was traversed by two little

14

steamers, the *Mary* and the *Wasco*. The force left by
Colonel Wright was located in a block-house at the Middle
Cascades. On May 26 Wright left the Dalles, and on the
same day a party of Yakimas under Kamiakin, assisted by
some of the supposed friendly Indians, attacked the settlement at the Cascades. They first fired on the steamer *Mary*,
lying at her landing, and killed one man and wounded three.
The boat was run out into the stream, before they could accomplish their purpose of boarding and destroying it, leaving
the captain and mate on shore, and steamed up to the Dalles,
picking up a number of families on the way. The Indians
next turned their attention to the citizens, a part of whom
were killed and a part escaped to the block-house at the Middle Cascades. The block-house was attacked and fired on all
that day and the succeeding night, but without damage. A
messenger reached Wright, five miles above the Dalles, and
he countermarched on the 27th. The portage was cleared,
after a warm skirmish, and on the morning of the 28th the
besieged block-house was relieved. In this affair, known as
the "Cascade massacre," seventeen whites, including one
soldier and several women and children, were killed.

Colonel Wright found there was satisfactory evidence that
some of the supposed friendly Cascade Indians had aided in
the massacre, and ordered a military commission, by which
their chief, Chimoneth, and eight braves were found guilty
and hanged. He then resumed his march against the hostiles,
leaving detachments to guard the fisheries, and a stronger
force at the Cascades—the latter under an officer with whom
the American public is now well acquainted, Lieutenant P. H.
Sheridan. One of his first duties was to report on the murder of six Indians, the father, wife, niece, and little child of
Spencer, a friendly chief, and two friendly Vancouver Indians in company with them, by six white men. These Indians were bound, short cords with slip-nooses were placed
about their necks, and then, by pulling on both ends of the
cords, they were, to borrow an expression from Balzac, "deli-
cately strangled between the head and the shoulders." The
younger woman was also outraged.

By May 23 Governor Stevens appears to have had hopes

SPEARING SALMON AT THE CASCADES.

THE CASCADES.

that General Wool's plan would be as dismal a failure as the winter campaign had been. On that date he wrote to the Secretary of War: " It is not to be disguised that the tribes east of the mountains thus far consider themselves the victors. When Colonel Wright commenced his march into the Yakima country, early this month, they practically held the whole country for which they had been fighting. Not a white man now is to be found from the Dalles to the Walla-Walla; not a house stands; and Colonel Wright, at the last despatches, was in the Nahchess, in presence of twelve or fifteen hundred warriors, determined to fight. Colonel Wright met the hostiles on the 8th of May, and made an effectual [ineffectual] attempt to treat with them till the 11th. On the evening of the 11th he despatched an express to the Dalles for reinforcements. His force probably now numbers some four hundred and seventy-five effective men." Nevertheless the Indians would not fight, and Wright was unable to bring on a general engagement. But while they were able to avoid the troops, the Indians were distressed by the loss of their supplies and their fisheries. After numerous talks, in which the sub-chiefs were promised preference over the hostile head-chiefs, bands of the hostiles began coming in and agreeing to live at peace, it being understood that their lands were not to be taken away from them. In this way the summer was passed.

At the same time, Lieutenant-colonel Buchanan, assisted by Superintendent Palmer, was pursuing a similar course in the South, but the hostiles there were more pugnacious. John, their leader, said the whites would kill him if they got him in their power, and declared he would never surrender. On May 27 his band surrounded the camp of Captain Smith at Big Bend, on the Rogue River, and held him besieged for thirty-six hours, although Smith had ninety men and a how-itzer. Their situation was one which would have resulted in their total destruction if assistance had not arrived, but word had reached the troops below, and a detachment under Cap-tain Augur was sent to relieve the beleaguered company. He routed the Indians by a dashing charge, in which he lost two killed and three wounded. Smith's company had been with-out water for twelve hours, and had lost eight killed and eighteen wounded. This was the only engagement in the en-tire war that was worthy of being called a battle. On June 21 all of the friendly Indians who had been near Port Orford, and all the Lower Rogue Rivers, were gathered together and removed by steamer to their new reservation of Grande Ronde, between the Wallamet and the coast. The hostiles then con-cluded to treat also, and John's band surrendered on June 29. By July 19 all the remaining Indians, to the number of twelve hundred and twenty-five, were on the way to the Grande Ronde, where they remained until the spring of 1857, and were then removed to the Siletz reservations on the coast. In the North a few of the hostiles fled to the interior, but, by the efforts of Lieutenant-colonel Casey, the main body were paci-fied and put on the several small reservations set off for them along the Sound, a few being held as prisoners. Late in the fall arrangements were concluded with the interior Indians, by which they were permitted to retain their former territory, the army officers recommending that the treaties made by Governor Stevens be not ratified. No whites were to remain east of the Cascade Mountains but those who had ceded rights from the Indians, except the miners at Colville, and these were to be punished if they interfered with the Indians. Military stations were established among the tribes, however, and maintained, although they occasioned some dissatisfaction. Lieutenant Sheridan was put in command of the one in the Yakima country.

This war was little more than a succession of massacres and outrages on both sides, so far as collisions between the hostile parties were concerned. The loss of life was not great, but the destruction of property was enormous, on the southern coast, on the Columbia, and on the Sound. Not only was there serious loss from destruction, but also from the desertion of property. A gentleman who passed over the road from Cowlitz Landing to Olympia, in 1857, wrote : " Notwithstanding this region was exempt from any actual collision with the Indians, the effects are nearly the same as in other parts of the territory. All along the road houses are deserted and going to ruin ; fences are cast down and in a state of decay ; fields, once waving with luxuriant crops, are desolate ; and but little, if any, stock is to be seen on the broad prairies that formerly bore such inspiring evidences of life." It was a costly war, and, as usual with Indian wars, the loss and injury had fallen heaviest on the innocent, both red and white.

The treaties for the cession of land, which were largely the cause of the hostilities by the interior tribes, were very extensive, the land relinquished being about equal to all of New England, with the State of Indiana added. They were divided as follows : the Wallamet Valley tribes, 7,500,000 acres, for $198,000 ; the Walla-Wallas, Cayuses, and Umatillas, 4,012,- 800 acres, for $150,000 ; the Yakimas, Pelouses, Klickitats, and others, 10,828,000 acres, for $200,000 ; the Nez Percés, 15,- 480,000 acres, for $200,000 ; the Des Chutes, 8,110,000 acres, for $435,000 ; the Flatheads, Kootenais, and Upper Pend D'Oreilles, 14,720,000 acres, for $485,000. The sums paid, in aggregate, look rather large, but, viewed with reference either

to the price per acre or the number of grantors, they are trifling.   Viewed with reference to the result they are supposed
to accomplish, the subsistence of the Indians till they are initiated in civilized methods of support, they are ridiculous.
The treaty with the Rogue Rivers of September 10, 1853, by
which 2,180,000 acres was relinquished for $60,000, was about
on a par with them—three cents an acre, more or less—and it
was ratified.   The grantors, at the time of the treaty, numbered nearly two thousand ; four years later they had dwindled away to nine hundred and nine, and $40,000 of the pur-
chase-money was still to come, in sixteen annual payments
of $2500 each.   In other words, the Indians were getting
$2.75 each per year.   Of course they had their reservation
lands, and the usual treaty adjuncts of schools, blacksmith-
shop, etc., but, if the Indian profited much by his education, he
certainly would not find much consolation in reflecting on his
treaty.   An annual income of $2.75 can hardly be considered
a princely recompense for the surrender of a principality.
There is no greater foundation than this for the oft-repeated
claim that these treaties of Governor Stevens were made on a
grandly liberal basis.

CHAPTER VIII.

ASH HOLLOW AND THE CHEYENNE EXPEDITION.

In 1856, eight years after our last look at the eastern
edge of the mountain country, there had not been much
alteration in its appearance in the matter of settlements.
There still remained the two pueblos on the Arkansas, one
at the mouth of the Fontaine Que Bouille, the present city
of Pueblo, Colorado, and the other some thirty miles farther
up the stream, called Hardscrabble. The former was established in 1840, and the latter two or three years later. Their
character may be gathered from the following extract from
a letter of Indian agent Fitzpatrick, in 1847: "About seventy-five miles above this place [Fort Bent], and immediately
on the Arkansas River, there is a small settlement, the principal part of which is composed of old trappers and hunters;
the male part of it are mostly Americans, Missouri French,
Canadians, and Mexicans. They have a tolerable supply of
cattle, horses, mules, etc., and I am informed that this year
they have raised a good crop of wheat, corn, beans, pumpkins,
and other vegetables. They number about one hundred and
fifty souls, and of this number there are about sixty men,
nearly all having wives, and some have two. These wives
are of various Indian tribes, as follows, viz., Blackfoot,
Assineboines, Arickeras, Sioux, Aripohoes, Chyennes, Snake,
Sinpitch (from west of the Great Lake), Chinock (from the
mouth of the Columbia), Mexicans and Americans. The
American women are Mormons: a party of Mormons having
wintered there, and, on their departure for California, left
behind two families. These people are living in two separate
establishments near each other; one called 'Punble' [Pueb-
lo?] and the other 'Hardscrabble;' both villages are fortified
by a wall twelve feet high, composed of *adobe* (sun-dried

brick). Those villages are becoming the resort of all idlers and loafers. They are also becoming depots for the smugglers of liquors from New Mexico into this country; therefore they must be watched."

CHEYENNE VILLAGE.

There were also the trading-posts, as formerly, but the chief trace which the white man had left was by the wearing of thousands of wagon-wheels along the Platte and the Arkansas. There was also a well-marked road along the foothills from north to south. The country was still occupied by the same Indian tribes, but their boundaries were fixed to a certain extent. The Cheyennes and Arapahoes, by the treaty of Fort Laramie, in 1851, held the lands east of the mountains, between the North Platte and the Arkansas, as far as the junction of the South Platte on the former, and the old Santa Fé road crossing (near Dodge City) on the latter. To the south of the Arkansas were the Kiowas and Comanches, and north of the Platte were the Sioux. These Indians belong to the plains, but their conflicts with the settlers of the mountains and foot-hills are within our province. The Arapahoes have lived in this general locality from the period of our earliest knowledge of them. They call themselves Atsina ("Good Hearts"). They are also called the Fall River Indians and the Gros Ventres of the South. In origin they are allied to the Caddoes. Their number in 1822 was estimated at 10,000, which was probably about three times their real number, and in 1842 at 2500.

The Cheyennes, though closely confederated with the Arapahoes, are of entirely different stock. They belong to the great Algonquin family, and, when first known to the whites, lived on a branch of the Red River of the North. Here, about a century ago, they became embroiled with the Sioux through a collision between two of their hunting parties. The Sioux were far the stronger, and the bloody war that resulted seemed so certain to destroy the Cheyennes that they retired west of the Mississippi. Their powerful foe still pursued and oppressed them, so they determined to move again; this time to the west of the Bad Lands, where they hoped to rest in peace. The main body of the nation started in the spring, leaving a large party which was to remain for four months, to hunt and to keep back the Sioux. When these last went after the others the Sioux followed on their trail, and overtook them on the Big Cheyenne. The Cheyennes were besieged for many days; at length their warriors made a night sortie, while the squaws and children escaped across the river; many of the warriors were killed, but the remnant reached the main band. The Cheyennes located along the eastern border of the Black Hills, and grew in wealth and numbers. They acquired horses, and joined their neighbors in raiding the Mexican settlements. Their men ranked among the best warriors, and their squaws were the most chaste women of the plains. In 1822 they were

estimated at 3250, and in 1847 at 5300.   These numbers
would be more nearly correct if reversed.   Their number
did not exceed 3000 in 1847, and they were then complaining
of their decrease.   Previous to this date differences had
arisen among them, growing out of their southern journeys
for the purposes of trade and war, and they separated into
two bands, one remaining about the North Platte, in coalition with the Ogallalla Sioux, and the others ranging gener-

INDIAN VILLAGE ON THE MOVE.

ally on the Arkansas.   The Arapahoes also separated into
north and south bands, on account of a factional fight, and
both bands allied themselves to the Cheyennes.   Although
these tribes were dissimilar in many respects, their confederations proved close and lasting ones.   They fought each
other's battles and shared each other's triumphs; treated
together, went on reservations together, and still remain in
the same close communion.

Although living thus, each tribe retained its own language, and very few of either learned the language of the other. Their means of communication was the universal sign language of the Indians, which has been brought to a remarkable state of cultivation by the Indians of the plains. This distinctiveness of language is probably due to the character of the Arapahoe tongue, which is harsh and guttural, and very difficult to learn or understand. It has even been said that two Arapahoes have difficulty in understanding each other in the dark, when signs cannot be used, but this is doubtful, and, if true, is due to the constant use of the sign language and not to scantiness of vocabulary. Sign language is used among all savages, and, to a greater or less extent, by all civilized peoples. Among them all it is in many respects similar, and, what is more remarkable, duplicate signs for the same idea are often duplicated in the same way in different continents. This indicates that certain signs are the natural expressions for certain thoughts, and that such communication is in fact less artificial than vocal language. The experiment of bringing Indians and deaf-mutes together has often been tried during visits of Indians to the East, and they always communicate readily, the signs being, of course, ideographic. A very wonderful demonstration of the extent of natural meaning in signs and expression was a test exhibition by President Gallaudet, of the National Deaf Mute College, at Washington, in which he related intelligibly to a pupil the story of Brutus ordering the execution of his two sons for disobedience, without making a motion with hands or arms, or using any previously determined sign or other communication, but simply by facial expression and motion of the head. To illustrate the natural sign theory, let us take the expression of peace or friendship. To the savage the obvious natural thought would be to show that he had no weapons, which is easily done by exposing the empty hands. When one is mounted, or it is inconvenient to lay down the weapons, the same thought is conveyed by exposing the opened palm of the right hand; this is sometimes supplemented by moving the hand towards the party communicated with, signifying that although armed, you are disarmed as to him. This is the sign that Logan made to the white hunters on the Juniata, more than a century ago, at the same time further expressing the thought by spilling the powder from the pan of his rifle, and they understood him at once.

On the other hand the long-distance signal of friendship, when mounted, is an illustration of purely artificial signs. The person desiring to communicate the message of amity turns his horse and rides him back and forth two or three times, over a space of forty or fifty paces. If the approaching party be friendly, he clasps his hands above his head, or interlocks the fingers as far as the first joints, and rests his hands on his forehead, as though shading his eyes from the sun. The first answer is possibly derived from the white man's habit of shaking hands, but this is not certain; the Natchez Indians used it in 1682 in saluting La Salle's party, as they descended the Mississippi. The second answer is of uncertain origin, but is also ancient; an Illinois chief used it on the occasion of a visit by Father Marquette, who mistook it for a sign of reverence indicating that he was dazzled by his visitor. Another artificial sign is that for white man, which is made by drawing the horizontal, flattened hand, palm down, or the index finger alone, across the forehead from left to right, just above the eyebrows. Other signs are derived from the verbal expressions of ideas. Thus, the common Indian expression of deceit is to say one has a double or forked tongue; this is expressed in sign language by touching the left breast with the right hand, and carrying it thence to the mouth, from which a forward motion is made with the hand closed, excepting the first and second fingers, which are extended and slightly separated. So, with the Klamaths, the word for crazy or mad is from a root signifying a whirling motion, and the sign is a rotary motion of the hand close to the head.

The signs for the different tribes usually correspond with the tribal name, though they are sometimes indicated by reference to their mode of dressing the hair, or other tribal peculiarities. The Crows are designated by bringing the flattened hands to the shoulders, and, by a wrist movement, imitating a bird flapping its wings. The Arapahoes or "Good Hearts" are designated by touching the left breast with the fingers. They are also called "Smellers" by some bands, and the corresponding sign is seizing the nose with the thumb and index finger, or touching the first finger to the right side of the nose. The Cheyennes are usually called "Cut-arms" or "Cut-wrists," from the mutilations they practise in the sun-dance and other religious ceremonies, and are designated by drawing the first finger of the right hand, or the bottom of the flattened hand, across the left arm, as though gashing it. They are also called "Dog-eaters," which is signified thus: make the sign for dog, by extending the hand in front of and below the hip, and drawing it back, marking with the extended first and second fingers the upper contour of an imaginary dog, from head to tail; then make the sign for eating, by bringing the thumb together with the first and second fingers, above and a little in front of the mouth, and moving them quickly to the mouth several times. A motion of the hand or the first finger across the throat, as if cutting it, indicates the Sioux or "Cut-throats"—the *Coupes-Gorges* of the French trappers. The Brulé (Burnt) Sioux, or Si-can-gu ("Burnt Thighs"), are designated by rubbing the palm of the hand, fingers down, in a small circle on the upper part of the right thigh. This band received its name from being caught in a prairie fire about the year 1763. The Nez Percés and Caddoes are both designated by passing the extended index finger from right to left under the nose, referring to their ancient practice of piercing the nose. A forward motion of the index finger towards the left, in a sinuous course, indicates the Shoshonees or "Snakes."

There is a tradition among the plains Indians that the sign language originated with the Kiowas, who were originally the go-betweens in the commerce of northern and southern Indians and Mexicans, but this is not within the range of possibility. They could not have communicated it so universally over the continent, and it is certain that the language existed in many places before there was any extensive commerce on the plains. There is little doubt that they extended and improved it, as other tribes in other localities have done also, so that no tribe at present uses purely natural signs. It is certain that there are divergencies in meaning in many cases; that some tribes have carried the language to greater perfection than others, and that many signs are altogether conventional. The reader must also remember that what would appear natural to one accustomed to signs, might not appear so to one who had given the matter no thought. A slight, unintentional gesture may entirely alter the meaning that an amateur sign-talker is desirous of conveying. Thus, Baillie-Grohman undertook to say to an Arapahoe, "How has it come to pass that the bravest of the brave, the man of all men, the dearest friend I have among the Arapahoes, has grown such a flowing beard?" but only succeeded in informing the gentle savage, "that his face was like a young maiden's, and his heart that of an old squaw."

For communicating at long distances the Indians have devised many ingenious expedients. When a party is searching for anything, its discovery is usually communicated by riding rapidly in a circle; the same sign is also used as a signal of danger, or when it is desired for the party communicated with to be on the alert. Horsemen riding to and fro, passing one another, inform the beholder that an enemy is at hand. If riding back and forth abreast, the meaning is that game is discovered. Blankets are frequently used in long-distance signalling. The discovery of buffalo is announced by facing the camp and spreading the blanket, the upper corners being held in the out-stretched hands. Instruction to pass around a place is given by pointing the folded blanket in its direction, drawing it back towards the body, waving it rapidly in front of the body only, and then throwing it out to the side on which the party signalled is desired to go. When it is desired to signal the discovery of something sought, and the discoverer has no blanket, the information is communicated by throwing a handful of dust in the air. A novel mode of signalling at night, in use among the Sioux, is by fire-arrows, which are prepared something like sky-rockets, by attaching moistened powder to the arrow-heads. The meaning given to various flights of these arrows is always agreed upon for special occasions. Another very common mode of signalling is by columns of smoke, sometimes rising steadily, and sometimes in puffs, made by covering the fire briefly with a blanket. Perhaps the most ingenious method ever used was signalling by the reflections of the sun on hand-mirrors, which was highly perfected among the Sioux. General Dodge once saw a Sioux chief put his warriors through a long drill, giving his directions entirely by the reflections of a small glass. This system has never been communicated to the whites, though the Indians say they have no further use for it, having abandoned war. It was much used in their operations against Fort Phil Kearney.

The government of western tribes is rather complex. They have usually a head chief, whose power in ordinary matters is supreme, but still not sufficient to crush an organized opposition of large extent. Below him are sub-chiefs, who control various bands of the tribes and have absolute control over their immediate followers. Any change of the settled policy of the tribe, or matter affecting the common interest, is controlled by the council, or assembly of all the warriors who choose to attend. The police power is in the hands of certain chosen men whom they call " soldiers," from their analogy to the warriors of the whites. Says Parkman, in speaking of the Sioux soldiers, " The office is one of considerable honor, being confided only to men of courage and repute. They derive their authority from the old men and chief warriors of the village, who elect them in councils occasionally convened for the purpose, and thus can exercise a degree of authority which no one else in the village would dare to assume. While very few Ogillallah chiefs would venture without risk of their lives to strike or lay hands upon the meanest of their people, the ' soldiers,' in the discharge of their appropriate functions, have full license to make use of these and similar acts of coercion." With the Cheyennes this body is enlarged and performs many other duties, partaking of the nature of a fraternity rather than an official organization. They are called " dog-soldiers," which is equivalent to Cheyenne soldiers, the name of the tribe being an Anglicism of the French *chien*, or rather of the feminine form, *chienne*, which was given them on account of their

15

fondness for dogs as food.   The name is always pronounced, and formerly was frequently written, Shian.   Of this body General Dodge says, "Among these 'dog-soldiers' are many boys who have not yet passed the initiatory ordeal as warriors.   In short, this guild comprises the whole working force

SQUAWS CURING ROBES.

of the band.   It is the power which protects and supplies the women and children.   A war-party is under the command of the chief.   The home, or main camp, with its women and children, horses, lodges, and property of every kind is under the control and protection of the 'dog-soldiers.'   From them emanate all orders for marches.   By them the encampments are selected.   They supply the guards for the camp, designate the hunting-parties and the ground they are to work over, and when buffalo are sought, they select the keen-eyed hunters who are to go in advance and make all the arrange-

ments for the surround. One of the most important functions of the 'dog-soldiers' is the protection of the game. . . .
Crimes against the body politic, or violations of the orders of
the chief, are punished severely: sometimes by death, at other times by beating and destruction of property. In these
cases the chief acts; but he must have at least the tacit consent of the Council, and the active assistance of the 'dog-soldiers.' Nearly all crimes against individuals are compound-
ed by the payment of damages, the amount of which is
assessed generally by the chief, assisted in important cases
by two or more prominent men. A violation of the 'dog-
soldiers'' rules is at once met by a sound beating." The independence of this organization and its ability to defy the
power of the chiefs has caused the name of "dog-soldiers"
to be applied, in some instances, to bands of renegades; but
this is a perversion of the real meaning of the term, and it
is never used in that sense by the Cheyennes.

Between the Cheyennes and Arapahoes and the white
trappers of early days there was peace or war as happened
to suit the parties respectively. In 1841 the Indians had
become quite hostile, and a severe engagement occurred between Cheyennes and Sioux and sixty men under Mr. Frapp,
of St. Louis, on Snake River, in which the Indians lost eight
or ten warriors, and the whites four, besides their leader.
Fremont found them hostile at the times of his several expeditions, but avoided trouble by threatening the vengeance
of the "Great Father" in case of any injury to his party.
In 1845 Colonel Kearny marched along the foot-hills from
Fort Laramie to Fort Bent, and summoned the Indians to a
grand council. When convened, he informed them that any
future injury to the whites would be severely punished, and
showed his power by parading the dragoons, firing a howitzer, and sending up a rocket. The Indians were much impressed and promised good behavior, which promise they
kept for many months. During the summer of 1847 the
Kiowas, Apaches, Pawnees, and Comanches were at war with
the whites, and doing much damage; it was estimated that
they killed 47 men, destroyed 330 wagons, and run off 6500
head of stock. In the winter, efforts were made to bring

SIOUX HUNTING BUFFALO.

the Cheyennes and Arapahoes into a coalition against the whites, but Lieutenant-colonel Gilpin (afterwards governor of Colorado) marched two companies of cavalry into the midst of their villages, and camped there all winter. This movement, with their enmity to the Pawnees, determined them in the course of friendship, and they abandoned all intercourse with the hostile tribes. Before this time a party of Arapahoes, under circumstances of base treachery, had murdered two trappers named Boot and May. Their tribe was much frightened over the anticipation of vengeance by the whites, and hastened to send a valuable present of horses to Fort Laramie in atonement. Bordeaux, the trader there, declined to accept them. Still more terrified, they sent in offering to surrender the murderers, but Bordeaux declined this also. They then returned to their lodges in despair, expecting a terrible punishment, but weeks passed, and no dragoons came, so their courage rose again. They grew more insolent and bold, and this feeling spread to the neighboring tribes until all were ready for the hostilities which broke out in 1854, beginning with the Sioux.

The Sioux were the most extensive of the western nations. Their name in their own language is Dakota, the word Sioux being an abbreviation of Nadowessioux, which is a term of contempt given them by their Algonquin enemies, the Chippewas. They also call themselves O-ce-ti Sa-kow'-in, or the Seven Council Fires. Their tradition is that in the far past they were all of one council fire, but separated on account of intestinal strife. These council fires, as usually counted, are: (1) The Mde-wa-kan-ton-wan, or Village of the Holy Lake; (2) the Wah-pe-ku-te, or Leaf-Shooters; (3) the Wah-pe-ton-wan, or Village in the Leaves; (4) the Sis-se-ton-wan, or Village in the Marsh; (5) the I-hank-ton-wan-na, or End Village; (6) the I-hank-ton-wan, or End Village; (7) the Te-ton-wan, or Prairie Village. Some count only six fires, esteeming the 5th and 6th, which are commonly called Yanktonnais and Yanktons, to be the same. The first four are called by the other Sioux I-san-ti, or, as it is commonly written, Santee, meaning People of the Leaves, on account of their forest homes. The French called them Gens du Lac. We have to deal only with the last division, though in all the Sioux wars there were always more or less of the other sections among the hostiles. The ending of the names above given signifies a village, from *ton-wan-yan*—to form a village, to dwell. Ordinarily the last syllable is dropped, and the Indians referred to are called the Sissetons, the Tetons, etc. As to pronunciation, the letter *n* in these names, preceded by *a* or *o*, has the French nasal sound. The Tetons (the word means Boasters or Arrogant Ones) or prairie Sioux have also seven principal divisions: (1) The Si-can-gu, Brulé, or Burnt Thighs; (2) the I-taz-ip-co, Bowpith, Sans Arcs, or Nobows; (3) the Si-ha-sa-pa, or Blackfeet; (4) the Mi-ni-kan-ye (Min-ne-con-jous) or Those who Plant by the Water; (5) the Oo-hen-on-pa, Two Boilings or Two Kettles; (6) the O-gal-lal-las, Wanderers or Dwellers in the Mountains; (7) the Unk-pah-pahs (Oncpapas), or Those who Camp by Themselves. The student is cautioned not to be misled into the belief that the 6th tribe is of Irish origin, by the fact that their name is put "O'Gallalla" in one of their treaties with the government. The country of the Tetons was west of the

Missouri, north of the Platte, and east of the mountains; the Yanktons and Yanktonnais held the eastern side of the Missouri from Sioux City to about the line of the Northern Pacific railroad; the Santees were in Minnesota and Eastern Dakota, gradually retiring before the settlements.

In the late summer of 1854 a large number of Brulés, Ogallallas, and Minneconjous were camped below Fort Laramie, waiting for their annual presents. On August 18th an ox belonging to some Mormon emigrants was taken and killed by a Minneconjou, who was camped with the Brulés. The whites said it was stolen, and the Indians that it had given out and been abandoned. The Bear (Mah-to-I-o-wa),* chief of the Brulés, came to the fort, reported his version of the story to Lieutenant Fleming, commanding, and said that if a detachment were sent for the Indian he would be surrendered. Lieutenant Grattan, with eighteen men and two howitzers, was sent after him. The Indians were camped between Gratiot's and Bordeaux's trading-houses, distant respectively five and eight miles from Fort Laramie, between the Oregon road and the river. The Ogallallas were nearest the fort and the Brulés farthest from it, with the Minneconjous between. The Brulé camp was semicircular in form, with the convex side to the river, and was bordered by a slight, abrupt depression, heavily grown with bushes. The Bear came out, but either could not or would not surrender the accused, as he had promised. Grattan then moved forward towards the centre of the camp, where the teepee of the accused stood, with the intention of taking him by force, and as he did so the warriors of the camp and many from the other camps pressed angrily forward and massed around the teepee and in the bushes, to resist the attempt. At this show of resistance, Grattan ordered his men to fire, and their guns were scarcely discharged before their commander and the greater part of themselves fell dead from a return volley,

---

* "The Bear" is not a full translation of this name, that being the signification of Mah-to. Mr. Reed translated it "The Bear that Scatters," but I-o-wa means a pen, or pencil, or other instrument for writing. The name has been printed, perhaps as a result of illegible writing, "Mah-to-Lo-wan." Lo-wan is the Sioux verb "to sing."

while the remainder were surrounded by a thousand or more of infuriated warriors, and exterminated in an inconceivably short time. Only one man escaped, and he died of his wounds two or three days later. The Indians menaced the fort for a time, but withdrew without accomplishing any damage, and the fort was soon afterwards reinforced by troops

ON THE OREGON TRAIL.

from Fort Riley. The Bear was killed in this affair, and Little Thunder succeeded to the chieftainship. The band separated from the other tribes, though accompanied by many of their warriors, and struck the whites whenever opportunity presented. Their principal successes were the destruction of a mail party and the murder of Captain Gibson. The latter was leading a train of Missourians up the Platte in June, 1855, when, at Deer Creek, thirty miles below the North Platte bridge, two Indians rode up and asked where the captain was. He was pointed out, and while one shook hands with him, the other shot him dead, after which they fled. Several days later an emigrant party was attacked at the same place by eighteen Indians, who lanced one man and one woman, and drove off sixteen head of horses.

On August 4, 1855, Kansas matters having become more quiet, General Harney marched from Fort Leavenworth with thirteen hundred men for the country of the hostiles. As he rode out of the fort he remarked to Mr. Morin, " By God, I am for war—no peace," and he experienced no change in his sentiments. He had learned Indian fighting thoroughly in the Black Hawk, Seminole, and other wars, and believed in decisive measures. He had brought the Seminole hostilities to a close by hanging thirteen of the hostile chiefs. The Indians are not long in learning the character of an opponent, and they knew what to expect from Harney. Billy Bowlegs used to say, " Harnty catch me, me hang; me catch him, he die." The command reached Fort Kearney without incident, and having replenished their supplies continued their march on the 24th. On September 2d they reached Ash Hollow, a celebrated point in the early history of the plains. It is the lower valley of Ash Creek, a tributary of the Platte, in North-western Nebraska, and was afterwards the location of old Sidney Barracks; it must not be confounded with the town of Sidney, that lies to the south-west, on Lodge-pole Creek. Here information was received that the hostile Brulés were encamped in force on Bluewater Creek (Me-ne-to-wah-pah), a stream on the north side of the Platte and two miles above Ash Hollow. General Harney at once prepared for an attack. Colonel Cooke, the former commander of the Mormon battalion, was sent at three o'clock in the morning, with four companies of cavalry, to cut off their retreat. Under the guidance of Joe Tesson, an old trapper, the command approached the creek several times, but found a succession of villages for four miles up the stream. About sunrise they succeeded, without attracting attention, in reaching a position half a mile above the upper village, in the bed of a dry gulch which opened to the creek. At half-past four Harney moved forward with the infantry. As he approached the lower village, the Indians struck their lodges and began retreating up the creek, while Little Thunder came forward and began a parley. To this Harney was not averse, knowing that their retreat was cut off. He told the chief that his warriors had insulted our citizens and murdered our troops, and now, these warriors, whom he said he could not control, must be surrendered or they must fight. While they were talking, a commotion among the more distant Indians announced to the soldiers that the cavalry had been discovered. Little Thunder returned to his warriors, and, without waiting for any answer to his demand, Harney advanced, firing. At the first volley the dragoons rode out of the defile and charged down the valley. As they came in sight, the infantry gave one wild yell and dashed forward. The Indians saw their danger and fled towards the bluffs on the west side of the valley, pursued by the infantry, while the cavalry directed their course to cut off the fleeing Indians. The battle then became a chase, the Indians urging their fresh ponies to their utmost speed, and throwing away everything that could hamper their flight. The dragoons pursued them from five to eight miles, until scattered and far beyond the support of the infantry; they then turned back to camp. In this engagement the Indians lost eighty-six killed, of whom a number were women and children, five wounded, and seventy prisoners, women and children, besides fifty horses and mules captured, a large number killed, and all their provisions, robes, camp utensils, and equipage destroyed. In the camp was found a lot of the plundered mail, some of the clothing taken at the Grattan massacre, and two white women's scalps. The loss to the troops was four killed and seven wounded.

Such a dreadful blow had never before been struck at the plains Indians, and it produced a valuable result. Harney marched on to Fort Laramie, and thence across the country to Fort Pierre, but before he left Laramie he sent word to the Indians that the murderers must be surrendered. After he started, the Indians came in numbers to Fort Laramie, and asked permission to camp in the neighborhood. This was granted, and soon after the garrison was surprised to see five warriors in full war costume approach the fort, chanting their death-songs. They were a part of the murderers whose surrender had been demanded, and came, as they said, to throw their lives away for the good of the tribe. They were Red Leaf, Long Chin, two brothers of the dead chief Mahto-Iowa, and Spotted Tail. Of the remaining two murderers, one had fled and one was too sick to be moved. After these had surrendered, Red Plume and Spotted Elk, two leading men, came in and offered themselves as hostages for the peace, and all seven, with their squaws, who had accompanied them, were sent to Fort Leavenworth for further proceedings. The Sioux of the plains were evidently conquered, and Harney was entitled to the credit of quieting them, for this action on the Bluewater, which has since become commonly known as the fight at Ash Hollow, was the only engagement that occurred. At Fort Pierre, General Harney held a council with all the Sioux bands, in March, 1856, at which they all agreed to be peaceable in the future. They made reparation for all property stolen, and agreed to surrender the man who killed the cow and the man who killed Gibson. At this time General Harney also authorized the appointment of a native police force, the first instance of the kind among the Western tribes.

The people—especially those of the West—accorded General Harney the praise which the results of his campaign merited, but the War Department appeared inclined to question the means rather than to admire the end. There appears to have been bad blood between Lieutenant-general Scott and General Harney, for some reason not satisfactorily explained, and it was understood throughout the army without much delay that Scott objected seriously to the killing of women and children that had occurred at Ash Hollow. Colonel Cooke, in his official report, which was not published for a year after Harney's, and then on express Congressional call, says, "I will remark that in the pursuit, women, if recognized, were generally passed by my men, but that in some cases certainly these women discharged arrows at them." Colonel Sumner, in his final report of the Cheyenne expedition, two years later, goes more bluntly to the point, saying, "I have the pleasure to report, what I know will give the Lieutenant-general commanding the army the highest satis-

faction, that in these operations not a woman nor a child has
been hurt." The matter drifted along until the summer of
1857. Harney had then received orders to take command of
the expedition into Utah, and was making his preparations,
when he received a summons to appear before a court-martial
in Washington, and the command of the Utah expedition
was turned over to Col. Albert Sidney Johnston. For a
time things looked gloomy for Harney; but he had friends,
and he was a fighter in a political way as well as on the field.

BEFORE THE DAYS OF STAGE STATIONS.

Soon there was felt in the case the power of William H. Russell, of the firm of Majors, Russell & Co. The greatness of
these names is but a memory now in the West, and in the
East they are forgotten, though people who knew Washington City thirty years ago may remember Mr. Russell, the
great contractor, who daily dashed along Pennsylvania Ave-
nue behind four blooded grays. They were the great
freighters of the plains, who, for several years before the re-

bellion, controlled all transportation of a public nature from
the Missouri to the mountains. They commenced business
early in the '50's with twenty wagons and two hundred oxen,
from which they grew until, in 1859, they employed 5000
wagons, 20,000 oxen, 10,000 horses and mules, and 4000 men.
They inaugurated and owned the famous Pony Express, by
which, with its 1000 fleet horses and 100 trusty men, the
mail was carried from St. Joseph to Sacramento. What a
change came over them! The failure of Congress to pass
the appropriation bills, in the spring of 1860, paralyzed their
business, which then amounted to $8,000,000 a year. Rus-
sell was arrested as a defaulter, and died so poor that his
friends paid his funeral expenses. Mr. Waddell of the firm
died penniless; A. B. Miller was recently living in Denver,
Colorado, in reduced circumstances; and Majors, the only
one of them that came up again, is a millionaire in Salt Lake
City. But to resume, Russell was very influential with the
administration, so much so that he procured the appointment
of Gen. Joe Johnston as quartermaster-general of the army
after the death of General Jesup. He induced Buchanan to
put a summary end to the court-martial, by making Harney
a brigadier-general, a rank he already held by brevet, and
putting him in command in the West. Harney went out to
Utah, but after a brief stay went on to Oregon, where he
was soon quarrelling with Scott again over the occupation of
the island of Haro and the cashiering of Lieutenant De Hart.

Terrorizing as was the blow struck on the Bluewater to
the Sioux, it seemed to have no effect on the Cheyennes and
Arapahoes. It was too late in the season of 1855 to proceed against them, and the expedition which was planned, for
the spring of 1856, "to compel them to release the captives
held by them, restore the property taken, and deliver up the
criminals," was given up because the troops were needed in
Kansas again. Immunity from punishment only made the
Indians more bold. On August 24, 1856, a war-party of
eighty Cheyennes attacked a mail-party within a few miles
of Fort Kearney, and severely wounded the conductor. Capt.
G. H. Stuart was sent in pursuit of the marauders with forty-
one men, and overtook them at about four o'clock on the

following afternoon. Dividing his force, he charged their camp from two sides. The Indians fled, but were hotly pursued, and suffered a loss of ten killed, eight or ten wounded, twenty-four horses and mules and much other property captured. On this same day another party of Cheyennes attacked a train of four wagons on Cottonwood Creek, about thirty miles below Kearney. This train belonged to A. W. Babbitt, Secretary of Utah, who was conveying a large amount of public money and valuable property to Mormondom. The Indians here killed two men, wounded one, carried off Mrs. Wilson, and killed her child. On the 30th a party of Cheyennes and Arapahoes attacked a small party of emigrants eighty miles above Kearney, killed one woman, wounded one man, and carried off a child four years of age. On September 6th a party of Cheyennes and Arapahoes attacked a Mormon train on the Platte, and killed two men, one woman and a child, besides carrying off a woman. These particulars of outrages committed by the Cheyennes, long after the Sioux had made peace, are mentioned because an impression has been created by certain Indian-ring gentlemen, who will be mentioned more expressly hereafter, that the Cheyennes were ever friendly to the whites. Many well-meaning but poorly informed people have been drawn into this delusion. Mr. Loughridge, of Iowa, in descanting on the " Sand Creek massacre," even went so far as to say that the Cheyennes "had done more to make travel across the plains safe to the whites than any other class of people." Major-general Persifer F. Smith wrote from Fort Leavenworth, on September 10, 1856, " This tribe must be severely punished, . . . but no trifling or partial punishment will suffice, and as no one can be spared from this neighborhood I will postpone extensive operations until the spring." The beauty of a winter campaign was not yet appreciated.

In the summer of 1857, Col. E. V. Sumner was sent against them with six companies of cavalry and three of infantry. On July 29th, while marching down Solomon's Fork, the cavalry, which was about three miles in advance of the infantry, came suddenly upon some three hundred warriors, drawn up in line of battle across the valley. The troops wheeled into line and charged at once. "The Indians," says Colonel Sumner, "were all mounted and well-armed; many of them had rifles and revolvers, and they stood with remarkable boldness until we charged and were nearly upon them, when they broke in all directions and we pursued them seven miles. Their horses were fresh and very fleet, and it was impossible to overtake many of them. There were but nine men killed in the pursuit, but there must have been a great number wounded." The loss to the troops was two killed and nine wounded. On July 31st Sumner found their principal village, from which they had fled in great haste, leaving one hundred and seventy lodges standing, and in them a large amount of supplies of every kind, all of which were destroyed. Sumner then continued his search for the Indians, but they separated into small parties and avoided him, a move which they accomplished more easily because his troops had no provisions but fresh beef, the cattle being driven as they marched. Early in September he received orders to break up the command and detach all but two companies of dragoons to join the expedition into Utah. He obeyed with reluctance, for he said he thought the Cheyennes had "not been sufficiently punished for the barbarous outrages they have recently committed." The punishment was severer than it seemed, for the buffalo did not range in their country that summer, and the movements of the troops prevented them from making any preparation for the ensuing winter by hunting elsewhere.

For three or four years their behavior was quite exemplary, and this change of heart came at an opportune season, for in the next year was made the discovery of gold, which caused the settlement of the eastern slope of the mountains. In the summer of 1858 a party of about one hundred men, mostly Georgians and Cherokee Indians, led by Green Russell, started from the Missouri to look for gold on the eastern slope of the Rockies. They found indications, but no paying placers, and all but thirteen of them started back in disgust. On the next day Russell struck pay in Cherry Creek, and soon after in Dry Gulch, both on the plains near Denver. They took back enough gold to interest every one who learned of it, and in the spring of 1859 a considerable emigration began. Among those who turned from previously intended courses to look at the new diggings was John Gregory. He knew that placers on the plains were very certain to mean deeper deposits in the mountains, and made his search in the tangled ravines of the foot-hills, which resulted in the discovery of Gregory's Gulch. From that time the future of the mines was assured. The wildest stories were current concerning the wonderful riches of the region. Benton's jest about the "ankle-deep" and "knee-deep" gold in California was put in the shade by some genius who reported that the gold on Pike's Peak was in layers on the surface, and was collected by parties of men who slid down the mountain on a harrow, each tooth of the harrow cutting up a long shaving of gold. Within three years there were probably 80,000 immigrants to the "Pike's Peak" country, of whom, however, a large number returned to their homes, or went elsewhere.

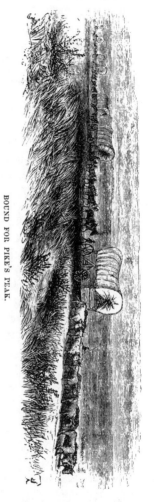

BOUND FOR PIKE'S PEAK.

Concerning these settlers there is one very extraordinary thing to be noticed — the Indians never complained of any bad treatment at their hands. The cause of the mutual good feeling was partly due to Ash Hollow and Sumner's expedition, but more than anything else it was due to the fact that the whites were locating on ground which lay between the territory of the mountain tribes and those of the plains, and was never per-

manently occupied by either.   The consequence was that the
settlers neither interfered with the Cheyennes and Arapahoes nor the Utes, but had their friendship sought by each
party for the purpose of acquiring arms and ammunition to
fight the other.   While the Indians fought each other the
prospectors made their way all through the foot-hills and
the mountains of the main range.   To this day the hunter
and prospector find their old workings and the decaying
boards of their flumes in the ravines on the western slope
of the Snow Mountains, which are the main divide in Colorado.   In time of war, when all provocations were summed
up, the Indians accused the whites, in a general way, of in-
truding on their lands and driving away the buffalo, but in
the " weak piping time of peace " they had nothing to say of
this.   On February 18, 1861, the Arapahoe and Cheyenne
chiefs made a treaty at Fort Wise, which contained this uncommon clause : " In consideration of the kind treatment of
the Arapahoes and Cheyennes by the citizens of Denver and
the adjacent towns, they respectfully request that the proprietors of said city and the adjacent towns be permitted by the
United States government to enter a sufficient quantity of
land to include said city and towns, at the minimum price of
$1.25 per acre."   The Senate struck out this clause, but in
the capacity of a solemn declaration by the Indians it stands
unimpaired by the amendment.   Of course it cannot be said
to be conclusive proof that the Indians were particularly anxious to do something for their white friends.   It was, more
probably, the result of a few presents by the town companies
to induce the Indians to recommend a favor that injured
them in no respect ; but in the absence of any accusation of
mistreatment by the whites, it is satisfactory evidence of the
real state of feeling.

This treaty is a celebrated one, and the reader will find
himself repaid in remembering some of its provisions, for it
was the foundation of the subsequent troubles with the
Cheyennes.   By it the southern tribes of Cheyennes and
Arapahoes ceded all their lands except a triangular tract,
bounded on the west, practically, by meridian 28° 30' west of
Washington, on the north-east by the Big Sandy, and on the

south-east by the Purgatoire or Las Animas.   It recited that these tribes were very desirous of adopting an agricultural life, and made provisions for such a change.   Finally it provided that right of way should be had across their lands for "all roads and highways laid out by authority of law."   In this phrase there was a world of significance.   Whether or not the chiefs understood that the right to build a railroad would be claimed under it is uncertain, but whether they did or not it is certain that their warriors wanted no railroad, no such cession of lands as had been made, and no agricultural life.   They said that they preferred to remain hunters, and would do so; that the buffalo would last a hundred years. Dissatisfaction was expressed at once, and depredations followed soon afterwards.   They threatened to kill their chiefs if they did not repudiate the treaty.   The war of the rebellion had its weight in increasing the hostile feeling, and at length the Kansas Pacific road was begun, directly through their country.   All these things worked towards war, and culminated in the open hostilities of 1864.

16

CHAPTER IX.

LOS NABAJOS.

Of all the interesting Indians of the Far West none are more interesting than the Navahos. The name is a Spanish one, in their orthography Nabajos or Navajos, and signifies ponds or small lakes. Their country, which abounds in these, most of them full in the rainy season and dry the remainder of the year, was originally called Navajoa, and the Indians, in the old New Mexican records, were called " Apaches de Navajoa," which has gradually given place to the present form. The Apaches proper call them Yu-tah-kah, and they call themselves Tenuai or " men," a title which nearly all the American tribes take to themselves in their respective languages. Their home, from our earliest knowledge of them, has been in the northwestern corner of New Mexico and the northeastern corner of Arizona. It may, in a general way, be described as lying between parallels 35 and 37 of north latitude and 107 and 111 of west longitude; or east of the Moqui villages, north of Zuñi, west of the divide between the Rio Grande and the Pacific slope, and south of the Rio San Juan. Across it, from southeast to northwest, is a ridge of high land which takes a mountainous shape at the northern end. It is there known as the Sierra Tunicha; farther south as the Chusca; still to the south and east as the Mesa de Lopos; and terminates at the southeast as the Sierra San Mateo. In the southern part is a low range called the Zuñi Mountains, and in the northwest a more rugged chain known as the Calabasa (Calavaser) Mountains.

The country is partially drained to the north by the San Juan, of which the Chelly and Chaco are the principal tributaries; on the southwest the drainage is to the Colorado Chiquito, by the Rio Puerco (Hog River) of the West and

Cottonwood Fork. Much of it is not drained at all, the surface water gathering in ponds during the wet season and passing off by evaporation. The higher land presents a succession of high peaks, sterile valleys, timbered table-lands, and fields of lava, with an occasional oasis. The lower lands have a yellowish composite soil, with outcroppings of sandstone, gypsum, and some coal. It is readily washed, converting the face of the land into a series of mesas (table-lands) separated by arroyos and cañons, with now and then a streamlet, to which the ground imparts a color varying from a rich cream to a dark buff. These are all called *rios*, though elsewhere they would be called brooks. In the rainy season, they at times develop suddenly into raging torrents, sweeping away dams and other obstructions, and then as quickly subside to their former feeble state. The vegetable growth is chiefly the wild sage or artemisia, with a fair allowance of cactus, and a sprinkling of pines, cedars, and piñons. On the mountains are some extensive forests of pines of large growth, with scrub oak, and rarely the valley of some mountain brook shows a fertility of soil and luxuriance of vegetable growth that makes it a paradise, as compared with the hot, dusty, dreary deserts about it.

The Navahos are well-formed, of good countenance, and light-colored, as compared with the average Indian. It has been claimed by some savants that they are a degenerated Pueblo people, an idea which has also been advanced in regard to the Nez Percés, the Natchez, and some other tribes that showed a marked degree of civilization, but, with due respect to the authors of the idea, there is little ground for the belief. The surest test of origin is language, and the language of the Navahos identifies them, as well as the Apaches and Lipans, with the Athabascan family of British America. Neither of these three southern tribes has any traditional account of occupying the old pueblos or *casas* that are found in their country, and the buildings themselves show a gradual decay, through centuries, without repair or occupancy. The dwellings of the Navahos, which they call *hogans*, are rude, conical huts of poles, covered with brush and grass, and plastered over with mud. They refuse to make any more substantial buildings on account of their nomadic habits and certain superstitions, which cause the destruction of their *hogans*, at times. With these facts in view, it is far more probable that there was an emigration of Athabascans from the North, and a partial adoption of the customs of the people they conquered, than that there was an emigration from the South, of a civilized race, which has fallen back into complete savagery, while, at the same time, the remainder of this Southern civilized race has retained all its civilization except the dwellings, that constituted its most desirable feature. The Navahos are of a more peaceful disposition than their cousins, the Apaches and Lipans—even more so than their timid relatives, the Tinné of the North. They devote their time to pastoral and agricultural pursuits almost exclusively. At the time of our conquest they possessed about 200,000 sheep, 10,000 horses, and many cattle. Their chief crop was corn, of which they sometimes raised 60,000 bushels in one year; it was estimated that they had 5000 acres under cultivation, in 1855. They irrigated very little, but secured crops by deep planting, the corn being placed about eighteen inches under the surface, and earing out soon after it came above the ground; in consequence of which their fields present an unfamiliar appearance to an American. In addition to corn, they raised wheat, peas, beans, melons, pumpkins, and potatoes, and had numerous peach and apricot orchards.

They dressed much more comfortably than other Indians. The men wore a double apron coat, like a shortened *poncho*, opened at the sides and fastened about the waist by a belt. It was of woollen cloth and frequently much ornamented. The legs were covered with buckskin breeches, close-fitting, adorned along the outer seams with brass or silver buttons. They extended to the knee, and were there met by woollen stockings. The feet were covered with moccasins, and often leggings, reaching to the knee, were worn. The attire was finished by a blanket thrown over the shoulders, as a mantle, and a turban or leather cap, surmounted by a plume that gave it the appearance of a helmet. They formerly carried a lance and a shield, which, with their costume, gave them the appearance, at a distance, of Grecian or Roman warriors. The

CAÑONS IN THE NAVAJO COUNTRY.

costume of the women was a sleeveless bodice, loose above, but fitting neatly at the waist, a skirt reaching below the knees, and moccasins, in summer; in winter they added leggings and a blanket. The bodice and skirt were usually of bright colors, the latter terminating in a black border or fringe. The costumes of both sexes have become more or less nondescript of later years, but many still retain their ancient fashions. They manufacture all their clothing, including their blankets. The blankets have been the wonder and admiration of civilized people for many years. They are very thick, and so closely woven that a first-class one is practically water-tight, requiring four or five hours to become soaked through. The weaving, which is all done by women, is very tedious, two months being consumed in making a common blanket and sometimes half a year for a fine one. They are worth from fifteen to a hundred dollars, varying with the quality of the wool and the amount of work put on them. They formerly manufactured cotton goods also, importing the cotton bolls from Santa Fé, according to Señor Donancio Vigil, but this has been discontinued for many years. They make some pottery, similar to that of the Pueblos, of whom they probably learned the art. They have numerous silversmiths, who work cunningly in that metal, and these have made remarkable advances in art of late years, since they added modern tools to their kits. They are singularly imitative, and will acquire a practical knowledge of any kind of work in a very short time.

Their superstitions are peculiar. They never touch a corpse if possible to avoid it. If a person dies in a *hogan*, they either burn it or pull out the poles and let it fall on the body; if on the open plain, they pile stones over the corpse and leave it. In consequence, they do not scalp or mutilate their victims, and, in fact, have little pleasure in killing, though they have a Spartan admiration for adroit thievery. They have a great aversion to the hog, and neither eat its flesh nor permit it to live in their country. This, with a few other peculiarities, has caused some to insist on their Israelitish origin. Perhaps some future sage may see in it evidence of relation to Bismarck. They are averse to bear meat also, on account of some religious scruple, and seldom kill the animal except it be in self-defence.

The most striking characteristic of the Navahos is their treatment of women. The life of an Indian squaw, ordinarily, is one of drudgery, with very few pleasures to relieve its monotony. She is so completely a slave that her husband has the right not only of selling but also of renting her. She does all the work, while her husband looks after the amusements for the family. In occasional instances women hold higher positions, but it is usually through some gift of prophecy or other "medicine" power; this is especially the case with the tribes of Oregon and Washington. There have also been a few tribes that admitted women to the council. William Penn mentions a council at which several women were present, and among them one, to whom remarkable deference was paid, known as "the ancient wise woman." He asked them if this were their custom. They replied that "it was, and that they never decided on any important matter without consulting their women, and that some women were wiser than some men." The Mohawks paid unusual attention to the opinions of the squaws, but with them their councils were held separately. In some tribes women have attained the supreme command, and in others, where they cannot become chieftainesses, they may have the right of naming the chief. Thus, Catharine Brant, widow of Joseph Brant, the Mohawk chief, named two successors in office to him. With the Navahos there is an equality of sex which is a close approximation to the "woman's rights" doctrine. The husband has no property in the wife, though he has invariably to pay her parents for her when he marries. The marriage ceremony consists simply in eating a meal together, and the tie is as lightly severed as made, when either wearies of it. The women hold their property independently, and in case of divorce an equitable division of goods is made, the children going with the mother. Incompatibility of temper is an excellent ground for separation. It is much on the principle of the French social system, where a woman is not free until she is married.

In consequence, women are well treated, and escape much

NAVAHO SQUAWS WEAVING A BLANKET.

of the drudgery that falls commonly to the lot of squaws. The men do the greater part of the out-door work, and the women look after the affairs of the house. If a Navaho wants his horse saddled, he does it himself, if he has no peon. Man and wife eat together. Stranger still, it is a common thing in their country to see a man carrying a pappoose—an extremely rare condescension in other tribes,. though sometimes seen among the Utes and Shoshonees. The women appear to have a special interest in the sheep. The flocks are looked after by the young girls, who employ their leisure moments in spinning a loose yarn that is used for the filling of blankets. They make very pretty and romantic shepherdesses. The sheep are never disposed of without the consent of the women; in fact, a Navaho never makes a bargain of any kind without consulting his wife or wives. They never strike their women. If a man quarrels with his wife, or she becomes careless of his wishes, or abandons him, he solaces his grief and assuages her anger by killing some gentleman of an adjoining tribe, or other outsider, which makes everything pleasant again. The doctrine of "free love" goes with "woman's rights" in their case. None of the women are chaste, and the nation has been badly infected with venereal disease, but they claim to be nearly rid of this, through the efficacy of their treatment, which consists of a decoction of herbs taken internally, an ointment made from a peculiar kind of clay, and sweat baths. In consequence of their better usage the women are much above the average squaw in looks. They are tall, straight, and well-formed. As a rule they are healthier than the men, which is probably due to their out-door exercise as shepherdesses in youth. Their treatment of women is the result of their religion. Their only god, Whai-la-hay, is a woman, and, according to their tradition, she taught them to weave blankets and mould pottery. Hence they are grateful to the sex. Besides, after death, the Navaho shade has to fight his way through a guard of evil spirits and get across a great water, neither of which he can do without the assistance of Whai-la-hay, and that they do not receive unless they have treated their women well. There appears to be some connection between this goddess and Ari-Zuña, the sun-maiden, the

beloved of Montezuma, who figures more or less extensively
in the different religions of Mexico. In calling her their only
god, I mean the only one of a beneficent disposition. They
have a masculine devil, called Chin-day, to whom they devote
much attention in endeavors of propitiation. They also repair
at stated seasons to a mountain in their country, called
Polonia, for the purpose of worshipping the spirits of their
ancestors, who are supposed to have a certain subordinate
power.

Another characteristic of the Navahos was their form of
government, or, rather, their lack of government. When they
came under our control they numbered about 12,000, of whom
2500 were warriors, but notwithstanding their numbers, and
the extent of country they occupied, they had scarcely any
central controlling power, and what power there was, was on a
democratic basis. The patriarchal form of government obtained among them, a man having as absolute control over his
children, while they lived with him, as of his slaves, but, once
a warrior, a man was his own master, and once married, a woman was largely her own mistress. Head chiefs were made
and unmade with little ceremony, and the pledges of a head
chief appeared to have little weight, either while he was in
office or afterwards. Every man had personal liberty of action,
by virtue of being a warrior. If he distinguished himself in
war, or acquired riches which enabled him to maintain a following, he became known as a chief. The head chief was
really a war chief, with no perceptible authority in time of
peace, and neither he nor any other governing power of the
tribe could compel the surrender or punishment of a man of
any influence among them. On account of this lack of executive power, there was no enforcement of law and little
law to enforce. Religious scruples were the chief restraining
power. Some men, from a naturally bad disposition, became
vagabonds, and lived wholly by theft, plundering their own
nation as well as others. Of these the remainder appeared to
be in perpetual dread, without any power of restraining them.
Major Backus once asked a Navaho chief how they punished
their people for theft. "Not at all," he replied. "If I attempt to whip a poor man who has stolen my property, he

will defend himself with his arrows and will rob me again. If I leave him unpunished, he will only take what he requires at the time."

This lack of government was the source of all their troubles with the Americans. We were obliged to consider them a tribe and to treat with them on that basis. When a treaty was broken it was necessary to treat them as a tribe in demanding satisfaction, but they were unable as a tribe to make the reparation we demanded. There were two other causes that prevented any lasting peace for many years. One was that they thought they outnumbered us. The reason they gave for this belief was that, in the beginning, a beaver dug a hole in the earth, from which there came five whites and seven Navahos, *ergo*, they are the more numerous. It required a score of years to satisfy them that figures could lie in regard to population. The other was hostile feeling between them and the Mexicans. The two nations had fought for centuries, and, as neither of them was afflicted with honesty, they were continually in conflict after they passed under our control. The blame of this is put on one or the other, as writers favor or oppose the Indians. The fact is, that each robbed and abused the other at every opportunity. When it came to reparation, it is reasonably certain that the estimates of damage done by the Navahos, especially as to the amounts of stock stolen, were generally exaggerated; and it is equally certain that, in the restitutions which the Indians were compelled to make, they culled the worthless animals from their herds to return. The Mexicans took the larger number of captives; the Navahos stole the more property. The territorial records from the time of our occupation to January 1, 1867, show the New Mexican losses from all Indian tribes to have been 123 persons killed, 32 wounded, 21 captured, 3559 horses stolen, 13,473 cattle, and 294,740 sheep, of a total value of $1,377,329.60; or an average of 6 killed, 1 captured, and $70,000 worth of stock stolen annually. The Apaches, Comanches, and Utes were, of course, responsible for a share of this, but the Navahos came in for at least one third of it. What does not appear on the records, and it is very essential for showing the burden of guilt, is how much the Mexicans stole from the Navahos. The fighting between them was not serious. The Navahos are not dangerous as warriors, although they have been so represented in the diseased literature of frontier life. The idea, so far as it had any basis, came from the Mexicans, and was due not so much to the bravery of the Indians as to the cowardice of their foes.

The relations of the United States with the Navahos begin with the occupation of New Mexico by General Kearny. The general, by his "annexation," assumed the protection of the New Mexicans from Indians, and gave them frequent promises, in public and private, to that effect. He did not remain there long enough to discover that a feud of centuries was not to be disposed of abruptly, but he did receive a taste of their predatory warfare. While visiting the settlements below Santa Fé, on the Rio Grande, with a detachment of troops, the Navahos swooped down on the valley, in sight of the command, and drove off a large number of horses and cattle, a part of which belonged to the command, before the troops could reach them. An expedition was sent against them under Colonel Doniphan, in October, but it did not return until after Kearny had left for California. It entered the country of the Navahos in two columns; one, under Major Gilpin, took the route up the Chama, by way of Abiqui, down the San Juan, and over the Sierra Tunicha; the other, under Doniphan, went up the Puerco of the East and spread over the country in three commands, gathering up the Indians as they moved. About three fourths of the Navaho nation were thus brought together at Ojo del Oso (Bear Spring—Ojo, literally "an eye," is commonly used by the Mexicans to signify a spring instead of the purer Spanish *fuénte* or *manantial*), and a treaty was made with them without any hostilities. The stealing went on as usual as soon as the soldiers were out of the country. Early in the following spring (1847) Major Walker marched against them with a force of volunteers, and penetrated as far as the Cañon de Chelly, but did not even succeed in making a treaty. In 1848, Colonel Newby, with a large force of volunteers, entered their country and made another treaty, which was promptly broken on his departure.

In 1849, Colonel J. M. Washington marched against them, with seven companies of soldiers and fifty-five Pueblo Indians. He was accompanied by Antonio Sandoval, chief of a band of about one hundred and fifty Navahos, who ever remained friendly to the Americans, and by Francisco Josta (Hos-ta, the Lightning), Governor of the Pueblo of Jemez. The cause of the expedition was that since their last treaty the Navahos had stolen 1070 sheep, 34 mules, 19 horses, and 78 cattle, carried off several Mexicans, and murdered Micento Garcia, a Pueblo Indian. The Navahos were first found on the Tunicha, a tributary of the San Juan, where Narbona, José Largo, and Archuletti, three of their chiefs, met Colonel Washington and Agent Calhoun in council. They agreed to meet at the Cañon de Chelly to form a permanent treaty, and were about to separate, when one of the stolen horses, owned by a Mexican volunteer then present, was noticed in the possession of the Indians, and a demand for it was made. The Navahos refused to surrender it, and Colonel Washington directed that one of theirs should be seized. At the attempt the Navahos fled and were fired on. Narbona, who was then head chief, was killed, and six others were mortally wounded. The command moved on and reached the Cañon

de Chelly on September 6. On the following morning, Mariano Martinez, representing himself as head chief, and Chapitone, second chief, with a number of their people, came into camp and sued for peace. It was granted, on condition that they gave up the stolen property and surrendered their Mexican captives and the murderers of Garcia. They gave up three Mexicans and part of the stolen prop-

CHAPITONE.

erty, agreeing to deliver the remainder at the Pueblo of Jemez within thirty days. The cañon was explored for a distance of nine and a half miles above its mouth, and it was learned that the previous idea of an impregnable fortress in it was erroneous. The command then returned by way of the Pueblo of Zuñi, which is situated seventy-five miles south of the cañon. Not only was the property not delivered at Jemez, but a party of Navahos hurried to the settlements before the troops returned, and ran off a large herd of mules from within sight of Santa Fé. Shortly afterwards, Chapitone was brutally murdered by some Mexicans, near Ciboletta.

Not discouraged by past experiences, Colonel Sumner and Governor Calhoun met a large party of warriors and chiefs at Jemez, in the winter of 1851–2, and proposed another treaty. The Indians ridiculed the proposition at first, but after an exciting council they agreed to ratify the treaty with Colonel Washington, which they said Martinez and Chapitone had no authority to make. The treaty was violated continually during the same winter, and, in the spring of 1852, Colonel Sumner marched against them, but being unable to bring on a general engagement, he employed his time in building Fort Defiance. This was the most effective stroke made against the Navahos for years, and had a perceptible effect in restraining them. It was located in the heart of their country, sixty miles north of Zuñi, fifteen miles south of the Cañon de Chelly, fourteen miles from the Laguna Negra (or Negrita), a deep and cool lakelet of dark water, much frequented by the Navahos, and three miles west of the present line of Arizona. It is in the highlands about the sources of the Rio Puerco of the West, at the base of a rocky range, which rises five hundred feet or more above the surrounding table-land, known as the Bonito Hills. Through these hills breaks the Cañoncito Bonito (Pretty Little Cañon), an abrupt gorge with perpendicular walls, and at its mouth is the fort. The cañon is half a mile long, averaging one hundred yards in breadth, with a level grassy floor. Near its head are two springs that feed a little stream which supplies the fort. This place and several fertile valleys of the vicinity had long been favorite haunts of the Navahos. The fort was simply a group of barracks, stables, and offices around a parade-ground, 300 by 200 yards in extent. There were no stockades, trenches, block-houses, or other fortifications. The buildings were principally of pine logs with dirt

FORT DEFIANCE.

roofs, though a few of them were of adobes. There was one stone building for the officers.

In May, 1853, Romano Martin was robbed and murdered by Navahos. The murderers were not surrendered when demanded by Governor Lane, and a campaign was being prepared for, when Colonel Sumner was relieved by General Garland and Governor Lane by Governor Meriwether. The new governor extended a general amnesty, after a talk with the chiefs, and matters proceeded much as usual. In 1854 a Navaho killed a soldier at Fort Defiance. Major Kendrick, the officer in command, demanded the offender with such sternness that the Indians concluded something must be done. The chiefs agreed to surrender the guilty party, and a day was appointed for his execution by hanging. Rather strangely, the Indians asked the privilege of doing the hanging, which was granted to them, and on the day appointed they brought forward and hung the alleged murderer in the presence of the troops. It was learned two or three years later that the man executed was a Mexican, who had been a slave among them for many years, and that the murderer, who was a man of influence among them, was still living. In 1855 Governor Meriwether met with the Navahos, for a talk, at Laguna Negra. Sarcillo Largo, their head chief, represented that his people would not obey him, and resigned his office at the council, whereupon the chiefs elected Manuelita to the position. The council proceeded quite boisterously, but a treaty was agreed on, the Indians promising to surrender offenders and keep within certain reservation limits, except that they had the privilege of gathering salt at the saline lake near Zuñi. Presents were then distributed, as is usual at treaties, a custom that may account for the great readiness of the Navahos to make them. This treaty was not ratified by the Senate, but that was immaterial, for the plundering went on just as if the treaty were in full force. It is but just to say, however, that these depredations were claimed to be—and to a very large extent certainly were—the acts of a small portion of the tribe. The real offense of the nation as a whole consisted chiefly in shielding the wrongdoers and exercising no control over them. The result was that while the mass of the nation was peaceable from inclination and the necessities of a largely agricultural life, the warlike and vicious members were exercising their violent ardor at will, and the force of American resentment was held in light esteem.

In the early part of July, 1858, a Navaho of prominence and influence had a difficulty with his wife. He desired her to accompany him on a visit, instead of which she went to a dance. Her husband repaired to the *baile* and reduced her costume to an ultra-fashionable style, by tearing every stitch of clothing from her. This failed to bring her to a sense of her conjugal duty, and it was about as far as Navaho customs permitted him to go in the way of direct coercion. The usage of the nation presented, as his next proper step, the killing of some outsider. He went to Fort Defiance on the following morning, July 12, with the avowed intention of selling two blankets that he carried with him. He was there for three or four hours, and had just sold one of the blankets to a camp-woman (an American compromise between a sutler, a laundress, and a vivandiere), when Jim, a negro boy belonging to Major Brooks, the post commander, passed to the rear of the camp-woman's quarters. He said nothing and did nothing to the Indian, nor had he ever before seen him. As he came out on the other side, with his back turned, the Indian, who meantime had jumped on his pony, let fly an arrow that passed under his shoulder-blade and penetrated his lung. The Indian fled at once. The boy, without making any outcry of any sort, undertook to pull the arrow from the wound, but broke it near the end, leaving the head in his body. The surgeon was unable to extract it, and four days later Jim was dead. On the day after the assault, Sarcillo Largo, former head chief, was sent for, and the assassin demanded. Excuses were made and action postponed from day to day, until, on July 22, Sarcillo and Huero (Juero or Huerero, literally, the Blacksmith—named Huero Miles by the soldiers on account of the analogy of his position to that of Lieutenant-colonel D. S. Miles, recently placed in command in that district) were summoned, and notified that they must produce the murderer within twenty days.

Preparations for a campaign were kept up, and Indian Agent Yost came up from Santa Fé to act in conjunction with the military. He was escorted by Captain McLane, with a dozen men, and, at Covero, was joined by Captain Blas Lucero with his company of Mexican spies, fifty in number. As this party approached Bear Spring (Ojo del Oso), on August 29, they found an encampment of Navahos at that point and attacked it. The spring lies to one side of the travelled road and is approached through a valley, about two hundred yards wide, on either side and at the extremity of which rise steep hills, covered with pine-trees. Down this the troops advanced and opened fire at long range, while the Indians deployed on both sides, under cover of the timber that skirted the valley. The firing was kept up until six Indians were killed and several wounded, when Captain McLane was struck in the side by a ball, and fell. It was supposed that he was mortally wounded, but he afterwards recovered, the ball having struck a rib and glanced off. A part of the command charged, and captured twenty-five ponies and a number of blankets, and the party then proceeded onward to Fort Defiance, where Colonel Miles arrived two days later and took command. On September 1, Juan Lucero, a Navaho chief, came to the fort to see if Major Brooks were not satisfied with the injury done to the Indians at Bear Springs, but was informed that he was not, and would not be until the murderer was surrendered, dead or alive. A block-house was built on the hill east of the fort, as an additional defence, the garrison being comparatively small. The Indians were now satisfied that something would really be done, and Sarcillo came in and promised to surrender the murderer. Sandoval, the friendly chief, made a desperate effort to keep on good terms with both parties. Every day he would rush breathless to the fort and announce his discoveries; now the murderer was at Ojo del Oso; now he was in a cave near Laguna Negrita; now he had fled to the Sierra Tunicha. On the morning of September 8, he announced, with great haste and bustle, that the murderer had been caught in the Sierra Chusca on the preceding day. Soon after, Sarcillo Largo arrived, and stated that the murderer had been desperately wounded and

17*

MESA OF CHUSCA MOUNTAINS.

had died during the night.   Could he have a wagon to bring
the body in ?   He could not; but a mule was furnished him,
and after much delay and display, a corpse was produced.
Every one in the garrison who had seen the offender was
called to identify him, and each one unhesitatingly testified
that this was the body, not of the murderer, but of a Mexican
captive who had often visited the post.   The surgeon gave
his opinion that the wounds on the corpse had been inflicted
that morning.   All of this was afterwards substantiated by the
Indians themselves, but, at the time, the chiefs protested that

the body was the one called for. Colonel Miles declined to hold any council with them, and active hostilities were prepared for.

On the next morning Colonel Miles went on a scout with three companies of mounted rifles, two of infantry, and Lucero's spies. They entered the Cañon de Chelly on the 11th, and marched through the lower half of it, occasionally killing or capturing an Indian, but meeting with no material resistance. When they camped for the night, in the cañon, the Indians gathered on the heights above and began firing at them. The attack did no harm, for the walls of the cañon were so high that the arrows lost their force and dropped horizontally on the ground, but it was thought better not to take any risks. Among the prisoners taken was the father of the leader of the attacking party, and to him notice was given that he would be hung if the firing were not stopped. He communicated his peril to his son, who withdrew his warriors, and left the soldiers in peace. On the next day they reached the mouth of the cañon, and were much relieved to be out of a place where the Indians could have done them much damage, if they had known how. At the mouth of the cañon, Nakrisk-thlaw-nee, a chief, approached under a flag of truce and proposed peace, but was informed that there could be no peace until the murderer was surrendered. The command then moved to the southwest twelve miles, over the Sierra de Laguna, a range of red sandstone hills, to the ponds where the principal herds of the vicinity were pastured. Here six thousand sheep were captured, and the troops camped, as they had been doing, in the corn-fields of the Indians. In the early morning of the 14th the Indians attacked the picket of the herd, but were driven off after wounding four men, one mortally. On the same day a bugler wandered away from the command and was killed. The troops returned to the fort on the 15th, having killed six Indians, captured seven, and wounded several, bringing with them six thousand sheep and a few horses.

On the evening of the 25th Captain John P. Hatch, with fifty-eight men, started for the ranch of Sarcillo Largo, which was situated nine miles from the Laguna Negra. They marched all night, and approached the Indians early in the morning, through an arroyo that crossed their wheat-fields, getting within two hundred yards of their *hogans* before they were discovered. About forty Navahos, all armed with guns and revolvers, hastily assumed the defensive. Captain Hatch brought his men within fifty yards of them, dismounted, and opened fire. The Indians stood gallantly until they emptied their rifles and revolvers, and then retreated, leaving six dead; the wounded, including Sarcillo Largo, escaped. There were captured fifty horses and a large number of robes, blankets, saddles, etc., of which all that could not be carried off were

NAVAJO IN WAR COSTUME.

piled on the wheat-stacks, near the houses, and the whole burned. Strangely enough, the Indians neither killed nor wounded any of the soldiers, which was due to their being unaccustomed to firearms. With their bows and arrows they would certainly have inflicted more injury. The Indians had just purchased their arms for war with the Americans, and had not yet learned to use them. Where did they get them? The cloven foot of Mormonism is again apparent; Utah was the only possible furnisher. The Mormon settlements joined the Navahos on the northwest, and the Saints extended their hands in fellowship to them as to other Indians. A year after this fight their criminal dealings with the Navahos were shown beyond question. On September 20, 1859, Captain J. G.

Walker reported from Fort Defiance that he had met a party of Pah-Utes, eighty miles west of the Cañon de Chelly, while exploring the San Juan River, who said that they had been sent out to invite the Navahos to a great council of Indians, at the Sierra Panoche, for the purpose of a union against the Americans. Sierra Panoche is a mountain southwest of the Calabasa range, and eighty miles east of the Colorado River. The Mormons had agreed to furnish all needed arms and ammunition for a general war against the United States. Captain Walker says: "That this report is substantially true I have every reason to believe, as the Pah-Utahs, to confirm their story, exhibited various presents from the Mormons, such as new shirts, beads, powder, etc. I was further confirmed in this opinion by meeting, the next day, a deputation of Navajos on their way to Sierra Panoche, to learn the truth of these statements, which had been conveyed to them by a Pah-Utah whom I saw in the Cañon de Chelly afterwards, who had been sent as a special envoy from the Mormons to the Navajos. He had in his possession a letter from a Mormon bishop or elder, stating that the bearer was an exemplary and regularly baptized member of the church of the Latter-Day Saints." This report was confirmed by the Indian agent at Fort Defiance, the Indians in that vicinity having been visited for the same purpose, during Walker's absence, by an Indian who said " the Mormons had baptized him into their church, and given him a paper certifying that he was a Latter-Day Saint and a good man."

On the 29th Colonel Miles went out on another scout, taking three hundred men, as before. On the first day they overtook a party of Indians with their herds, in the Chusca Valley, twenty miles northeast of the fort, and captured nine horses and one thousand sheep. On the night of the 30th, a detachment of one hundred and twenty-six men, under Captain Lindsay, was sent to attack the camp of Ka-ya-ta-na's band, which was at a laguna fifteen miles distant. The detachment reached the pond at about three o'clock in the morning, found the Indians gone, and followed on their trail. At daybreak they discovered them encamped in a deep cañon. The descent was very difficult. As the soldiers were making their way down, in single file, the foremost having just gained the bottom, three Indians rode up. With quick exclamations of astonishment and alarm, they wheeled their horses and fled to warn their people. There were but a dozen men down, but seeing that no great advantage could be gained without a sudden rush, Captain Lindsay boldly charged down the cañon with this handful. After a hard gallop of five miles they succeeded in overtaking the Indians and heading off their stock, amounting to seventy horses and four thousand sheep. Captain Lindsay took station, with his little band, on a wooded knoll in the cañon, and held the stock till the remainder of his command came up. The property in the camp which had been so hastily deserted, consisting of blankets, robes, and other supplies, was all destroyed. The Indians lost eight men killed; the troops four killed and one wounded.

Thus a series of expeditions was kept up, leaving the Indians no time for repose. On October 4, Major Brooks convoyed a number of trains towards Albuquerque and then circled through the Navaho country from Ojo del Gallo, in the western edge of the Rio Grande Valley. They had one engagement, in which, it was reported, twenty-five Indians were killed or badly wounded. On the morning of the 17th the post herd was attacked by three hundred mounted Navahos, who succeeded in killing two men and driving away sixty-four horses and mules. On the 18th Colonel Miles started out with two hundred and fifty soldiers and one hundred and sixty volunteer Zuñi Indians, who were to be recompensed by a small ration and what they could capture. The cupidity of the Zuñians prevented an engagement with the Indians, but one hundred horses were captured and the houses of Manuelita's band were destroyed. On the 23d Lieutenant Howland, with twenty soldiers and forty of Blas Lucero's Mexicans, marched south from the fort to Colites Mountain. At daybreak of the next morning he surprised the ranch of the chief Ter-ri-bio, capturing sixteen women and children, four men, including Terribio, ten horses, and twenty goats and sheep. An extensive expedition in two columns was then planned and was being carried out, when the Navahos

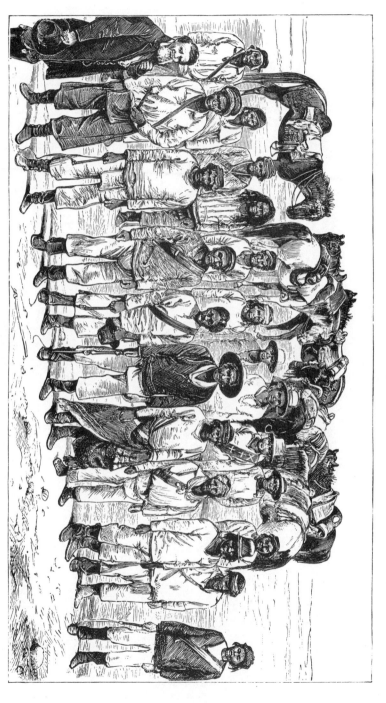

GROUP OF NAVAHOS.

sued for peace, and, on December 4, an armistice was granted to give them an opportunity to treat.

On December 25, 1858, a treaty was made, with conditions satisfactory to all parties. Eastern and southern limits were fixed which were not to be passed by the Navahos, except that Sandoval and his band retained their former location. They were to make indemnification for depredations on citizens or Pueblo Indians, since August, 1858, by returning the property taken or its equivalent in sheep, horses, or cattle. For the future the whole tribe was to be held responsible for the wrongs committed by any member, and reprisals were to be made out of any flocks, if satisfaction were not promptly given. All Mexican, Pueblo, and Navaho captives, who desired to return to their people, were to be surrendered. The assassin of the negro boy, Jim, being represented to have fled out of their country and beyond their power, his surrender was waived, but they agreed not to permit him to return under any circumstances. The right of the United States to send out military expeditions and establish posts in their country was formally recognized. Finally, the Navahos were earnestly urged to appoint either a head chief or some central power which could act for the tribe. This treaty lasted nearly five months, being broken hopelessly before the Senate had an opportunity to ratify it. It marks the close of the hostilities occasioned by the murder of the boy Jim, an important epoch in Navaho history.

Before leaving the subject, it may be well to correct an oft-repeated error connected with it. It has been said that the murder of Jim was in revenge for the killing of some cattle, some days prior, by the soldiers, but this is not true. The commander of the post had selected certain convenient grazing-grounds for the post-herds, and these the Indians had been ordered to keep away from, for the reason that there was no more grass than was needed for the post, and to avoid annoyance from the mixing of the herds. Manuelita refused to obey this order, and defiantly stated that he would pasture his cattle on these grounds. He was informed that if he did they would be shot. He drove them in and they were killed. This matter was smoothed over, and the Indians were visiting the post as usual, for some time before Jim was murdered. The murderer had nothing to do with the cattle, and, according to the Indians themselves, committed the crime solely on account of his trouble with his wife. He gained his point, for she accompanied him, as he had desired, when he returned to their camp with information of what he had done. He secured his domestic happiness and the tribe paid for it.

CHAPTER X.

MOUNTAIN MEADOWS.

DURING these years whose happenings we have been recording, there has been a community existing in the centre of our region that we have barely noticed. Their history, at any period, is a subject which a conscientious writer approaches unwillingly, for it involves a certain consideration of the merits of Mormonism and the Mormons, and that means wholesale denunciation, almost always of the Mormons, and very frequently of their enemies. Sweeping accusations must be made, and these, he knows, weaken alike the testimony of a witness, the plea of an orator, and the statement of an author. It is repugnant to man to believe that the majority of mankind are evil, and it is contrary to ordinary experience that any large class or sect of men should be radically bad. Besides this, all candid men will admit that the Mormons have at times been treated badly; that the killing of Joseph Smith, their prophet, was one of the most disgraceful murders ever known in this country; and that they were driven from their homes in Missouri and Illinois under circumstances of cruel severity. But candid men must also admit that past suffering is no excuse for continuing crime, and, leaving out of consideration all of their offences that preceded or followed it, it has not fallen, nor shall fall, to the lot of any man to record a more atrocious crime than that of the Mountain Meadows. For this crime all Mormondon has voluntarily shown itself responsible, offering no excuse but fanaticism and revenge; and, worse than nothing as these excuses are, the moral obliquity of the deed is, if possible, increased by the desire of plunder, which was also an actuating motive.

To themselves, the Mormons are, of course, justified in any act that is approved by their priesthood. They are the chosen people whose inheritance is the earth, and in spoiling the Gentiles they are simply taking their own. They are the appointed agents of a vengeful God, and can do nothing but their duty in obeying his mandates, as pronounced by his holy prophets. They are under a "higher law" and the direct control of an inspired guide. They carry the higher-law theory farther than even the extreme Jesuits, and in this dogma centre all the objectionable features of their religion. When any sect receives a dispensation which permits its members to transgress the laws of man, and the commonly recognized laws of God, "for righteousness' sake"—whenever it publicly confesses that it owns no obligation of truthfulness, or honesty, or humanity, to outsiders—it has put itself outside the pale of our civilization, and can no longer justly complain of the lawlessness of any person. More than that, none of its members can consistently ask to be believed in any statement, except its truth be otherwise established, and this is the only safe rule of procedure with the testimony of Mormons or persons who have ever been Mormons. It will be made manifest, in the course of this chapter, that Mormon declarations and oaths are worth less than the breath in which they are uttered, or the paper on which they are written. It does not follow that everything said against them is to be believed, nor that they cannot tell the truth when it is to their interest to do so; but it is evident that their statements must be received with the utmost caution. Put it in what language you may, no really harsher criticism of their veracity can be made than their own claims of obedience to a "higher law."

When the Mormons left Nauvoo it was not certain where they were going. They profess to have moved under divine guidance, which all may believe who choose. The common understanding was that they were going to California, and a statement to that effect was commonly made in newspapers at the time. It is known also that Governor Ford, of Illinois, gave Brigham Young a copy of Fremont's report of his second and third expeditions, and recommended him to go to some of the larger valleys of the Wahsatch. However that may have been, a party of explorers went out in 1847 and selected a place and a path for the mass of the people, who did not seem ready to trust divine guidance without an exploring expedition ahead. The Great Basin, in which they settled, was not wholly a desert, as they have claimed and as has been too commonly believed. Colonel Fremont had examined it carefully several years before the Mormons came, and he said of it: "Partly arid and sparsely inhabited, the general character of the Great Basin is that of a desert, but with great exceptions, there being many parts of it very fit for the residence of a civilized people; and, of these parts, the Mormons have lately established themselves in one of the largest and best. Mountain is the predominating structure of the interior of the basin, with plains between —the mountains wooded and watered, the plains arid and sterile. . . . These mountains had very uniformly this belt of alluvion, the wash and abrasion of their sides, rich in excellent grass, fertile and light, and loose enough to absorb small streams." Much of the land then considered sterile has since been made fruitful by irrigation, but it is erroneous to suppose that cultivation and improvement have been more rapid in Utah than in other equally sterile parts of the West. The contrary is the case.

The Indians who inhabited this country were diverse in character, although originally of the same stock and speaking dialects of the same language—the Shoshonee or Snake. They have three principal divisions, the Snakes proper, the Bannocks, and the Utes, but these relate only to race. In tribal government they were separated into more than a hundred small bands, each entirely independent. The country was divided among them in small districts, the boundaries being fixed by natural monuments. Only the principal divisions can be noticed here. The Eastern Snakes ranged from the South Pass to Bear River and Wind River; they numbered one hundred and twenty-five lodges, and subsisted largely on buffalo meat, for which reason they are called Kool-sa-ti-ka-ra, or Buffalo Eaters. They have been very reliable in their friendship to Americans, their chief, Wash-i-kee (Gambler's Gourd), otherwise known as Pina-qua-na (Smell of Sugar), having attained a wide notoriety on this account. He was a half-breed, tall, well-formed, superior to his people, and exercising strong control over them. The Took-a-ri-ka, or

18

WASHAKIE.

Mountain-Sheep Eaters, ranged high up on the mountains, usually, and had little to do with the whites. They were an extraordinary people, building their rude houses above timber line on the mountain heights, and seeming doomed to so cheerless a life that the Canadian trappers gave them the name "*les dignes de pitié*," or, the objects of pity. On the Salmon River was a mixed band, largely of their people, which numbered fifty lodges. Its principal chief was Qui-tan-i-wa (Foul Hand), and his sub-chiefs were " Old Snag," an Eastern Snake, and "Grand Coquin," a Bannock. Their friendship was always questionable. The Western Snakes were in two main bands, one under Am-a-ro-ko (Buffalo Meat under the Shoulder), ranging on Camas Prairie, and the other under Po-ca-ta-ra (White Plume), ranging in the Goose Creek Mountains and on the Humboldt. They numbered about one hundred and fifty lodges, and were on good terms with the Mormons, but not with other whites. They are commonly called Sho-sho-kos, or " White Knives," from the white flint knives they formerly used. A large band of the Bannocks ranging west of the Blue Mountains were known as the War-ra-ri-kas, or "Sunflower-Seed Eaters. They numbered one hundred and fifty lodges, were commanded by Pa-chi-co (Sweet Root), a mighty medicine man, and were hostile when favorable opportunities occurred. In the neighborhood of Fort Boisée were one hundred lodges of Bannocks, under Po-e-ma-chee-ah (Hairy Man), who were the most friendly of their race towards the Americans. Ranging about Salt Lake, especially on Bear River, was a band led by "Long Beard" and Pag-e-ah (The Man who Carries the Arrows), numbering about fifty lodges, and known variously as Ho-kan-di-ka, the Salt Lake Diggers, Southern Snakes, Mormon Snakes, or Cache Valley Indians. They were the worst of all these Indians, so far as Americans generally were concerned, but were hand-in-glove with the Mormons. Commonly associating with these were the Mo-pe-as, so called after their chief Mo-pe-ah (Bunch-of-Hair-in-the-Forehead), who boasted himself a friend of the Mormons. They numbered sixty lodges. The Utes were much the largest division, and held the country to the south of the other two, occupying practically all of Nevada, Utah, and the mountainous part of Colorado, with a considerable portion of Northern New Mexico. The eastern bands, the Tabequaches, Mohuaches, Grand Rivers, Capotes, Uintas, and others occupying the country east of the Wahsatch Mountains, were the best warriors among them; they were less influenced by the Mormons, and most friendly to Americans. The Pah-Utes, or Water-Utes, of the Sierra Nevada, and the western part of Nevada, commonly called the Monos and the Washoes, were also good warriors. Of intermediate grade were the Gosi-Utes (Goships, Goshoots) of Eastern Nevada, the Sanpitches (Sinpichi, or, as now corrupted in Utah, San Petes), Timpanagos, and others of Eastern Utah. The lowest as warriors were the Pah-Utes, or Pi-Utes of Southern Utah and the desert portions generally, several bands of miserable beings, who were getting into a more wretched state each generation, through starvation and their defenceless condition. They were decreasing in numbers, in stature, and in physical strength, and were constantly preyed upon by their neighbors. Their food consisted of snakes, lizards, roots, berries, grass-seed, worms, crickets, grasshoppers, and, in short, anything that could be chewed, swallowed, and partly digested.

The Mormons had but little trouble with Indians, for they approached them as brothers and equals, without any desire to force civilization upon them. The negroes, the descendants of accursed Ham, were originally barred from the Mor-

mon heaven, though latterly a revelation has been made which
lets them in, but the Indians were always brothers.   They are
"Lamanites," the "remnant" of the lost tribes of Israel, lin-
eal descendants of Abraham, sprays from the "fruitful bough
by a well, whose branches run over the wall," who are to be re-
claimed by Mormon righteousness, and in due time to become
"a fair and delightsome people."   The Mormons brought to
the Indians a religion and customs differing in but one essential respect from what they already had, and that was obedi-

UTE SQUAWS OF UTAH.

ence to the Mormon prophet.   This duty was largely bought
by presents (usually purchased with United States' funds) and
protection, and was further induced by missionary work and
intermarriage.   Their protection of the Indians who adhered
to them was sufficient to prevent any punishment for their
crimes.   The case of the murderers of Lieutenant Gunnison
will illustrate this.   Gunnison had wintered at Salt Lake in
company with the remainder of Captain Stansbury's party,

and all had been treated kindly by the Mormons. Gunnison repaid their kindness by serving as a volunteer in their Indian war during the winter, and by eulogizing them in his reports. But in 1853 he was on a mission which the Mormons did not wish accomplished, that of selecting a route for a Pacific railroad by way of Salt Lake, and he, with seven of his party, were killed by the Indians near Sevier Lake. In 1854 Colonel Steptoe reached Salt Lake with a body of soldiers, captured the murderers of Gunnison, and brought them to trial. A clear case was made against them; the judge charged the jury that they must either be found not guilty or guilty of murder; and the Mormon jury returned a verdict of manslaughter. The highest possible sentence, three years' imprisonment, was pronounced, but the murderers escaped " by oversight" of their jailers, and regained their tribes, where they remained undisturbed. The Mormons announced that they had treated Gunnison's party well, as he testified himself, and that they had done all they could to bring his murderers to justice, to which facts they still point with pride.

The war in which Lieutenant Gunnison assisted was the only real trouble that the Mormons ever had with the Indians. At that time there were but two settlements in the beautiful borders of Utah Lake, one on the American Fork, and one on Provo River. The Indians there, a band of Pah-Utes, did not appreciate good treatment, and from begging went to robbing. Finding they were not punished, they attributed their safety to the cowardice of the Mormons, and became so bold as to shoot people who tried to hinder them from taking what they wanted. They little dreamed of the claws of the velvet paw they had been playing with. The people on the Provo sent for assistance, and one hundred and fifty men went to them from Salt Lake. They found the Indians posted in the brush and cottonwoods along the Provo, and fought them there for two days. Then Sunday came, and the Saints rested, as is their custom, while the Indians fled. On Monday secular occupation was resumed. The Indians at the southern end of the lake were first proceeded against, and about thirty of their warriors killed. They then returned to their first opponents, who had fled up a cañon, and killed all but seven or eight of their men. Some fifty women and children were taken prisoners and distributed among the settlements, but afterwards allowed to join other bands if they so desired. After this there was no trouble that could be dignified by the name of war. Brigham Young was governor and *ex-officio* Superintendent of Indian Affairs. The agents, farmers, and interpreters were all Mormons. It was repeatedly charged that all the government annuities were represented to the Indians to be Mormon gifts, and numerous offi-

SNAKE INDIANS OF UTAH.

cial reports of this, based on the statements of the Indians and other evidence, show their truth. Pocatara told Superintendent Lander that "whenever he should feel certain that the White Father would treat him as well as Big-um (Brigham Young) did, then he would be the kindest friend to the Americans that they had ever known." The hostile Indians in Utah were often accompanied and led by painted whites, and emissaries were kept constantly at work among the more remote tribes. While the troops were fighting Indians, who were furnished with Mormon guns and ammunition, in the Yakima country, the people of Southern California were holding mass-meetings and denouncing the Mormon bishop, Tinney, who had been among the San Luis Rey and Carvilla Indians, telling them that the Mormons and Indians must act together against their common enemies, the Americans. While the Pelouses were receiving aid and bad counsel from Salt Lake, an Indian emissary to the Navahos, bearing letters which certified his conversion and membership of the Mormon Church, was taken in New Mexico, and confessed that he was sent by the Mormons to urge the Navahos to war. And so, in almost every war in the Rocky Mountains, the same complaint has been made, down to the last outbreak of the Utes in Colorado, when Ouray certified to its truth. To these charges no defence is made, except the denunciation of their authors as liars.

As might naturally be supposed, the Mormons did not feel kindly towards the people who had expelled them from their homes in the East and murdered their "prophet," and their friendship was not increased by the treatment which their missionaries occasionally received. But there was a more potent cause for their disloyalty than persecution, or mere allegiance to a Church which asserted and maintained temporal power. The Mormons are chiliasts, and for thirty years have been looking for the millennium to be ushered in very soon, their millenarian doctrines being perhaps the strongest feature of their religion as presented in missionary work. The millennium, by prophecy, is to follow at once on the disruption of the Union, which is to be caused by civil war, and "Zion" is to be set up on the ruins of this nation, with headquarters in Jackson County, Missouri. The principal basis of this belief is the following prophecy of Joseph Smith, said to have been delivered in 1832, and certainly published as early as 1854:

"WAR.

"Verily thus saith the Lord concerning the wars that will shortly come to pass, beginning at the rebellion of South Carolina, which will eventually terminate in the death and misery of many souls. The days will come that wars will be poured out upon all nations, beginning at that place; for, behold, the Southern States shall be divided against the Northern States; and the Southern States will call upon other nations, even the nation of Great

Britain, as it is called, and they shall also call upon other nations, in order to defend themselves against other nations: and thus war shall be poured out upon all nations. And it shall come to pass, after many days, slaves shall rise up against their masters, who shall be marshalled and disciplined for war. And it will come to pass, also, that the remnant which are left of the land [*i. e.*, the Indians] shall marshal themselves and shall become exceedingly angry, and shall vex the Gentiles with a sore vexation. And thus, with the sword and by bloodshed, the inhabitants of the earth shall mourn, and with famine and plagues and earthquakes, and the thunder of heaven, and the fierce and vivid lightning, also, shall the inhabitants of the earth be made to feel the wrath and indignation and chastening hand of an Almighty God, until the consumption decreed hath made an end of all nations; that the cry of the saints and of the blood of the saints shall cease to come up into the ears of the Lord of Sabaoth, from the earth, to be avenged of their enemies. Wherefore stand ye in holy places, and be not moved until the day of the Lord come; for, behold, it cometh quickly, saith the Lord! Amen."

It would be difficult to find, in the entire range of prophecy, a prediction more remarkably fulfilled in many respects, and more possible of explanation and delay as to the unfulfilled portions. The best proof of its earthly origin will be found in unfulfilled prophecies from the same source, by those who are curious enough to examine them. Its effect on the loyalty of the Mormons was necessarily disastrous. They could not feel an attachment for a country whose destruction must precede their entry into millennial bliss. When the civil war began, "We told you so" was heard wherever a Mormon was found; and when that war was concluded without embroiling "all nations," the ready interpreter showed that the time was not yet full. It has been expected to break out again at every national election, especially those of 1876 and 1884, each failure of fulfilment being only the result of misinterpretation. They cling to it still with more than "Millerite" patience, and its fulfilment is only a question of "a few more years." Then will come the time mentioned by Isaiah, when "Seven women shall take hold of one man, saying, We will eat our own bread, and wear our own apparel: only let us be called by thy name, to take away our reproach" —the reproach referred to being childlessness, by Mormon interpretation; the men Mormons, and the women Gentiles.

Decided changes took place in the Mormon community after the exodus from Nauvoo. There was a weeding out of a majority of the weaker brethren, to begin with, leaving the assemblage in Utah fairly united in credulity and fanaticism. Relieved of any prohibitory power, polygamy was openly announced as a doctrine in 1852 at Salt Lake City, and in the following year abroad. This caused a split in the Church, and an extensive desertion at all points outside of Utah. The dissenters maintained that the doctrine was an introduction of Brigham Young's, and in proof cited the express prohibitions of it in the "Book of Mormon," and also in the "Doctrines and Covenants," the latter adopted in open conference after Smith's death. The Brighamites showed that in fact it had been practised and taught by Smith and other leaders. Moreover, both sides proved their claims by the solemn statements of the principal men of the Church, made at different times, and thus it was demonstrated that the principal men, including Smith and President Taylor, were unblushing liars, no matter whether the doctrine were new or old. It is fairly assured, however, that the doctrine was privately promulgated from about 1844. Under this doctrine a woman may possibly attain salvation, but never an "exaltation," when not the wife of a saint, and, as a corollary to this proposition, it is both lawful and commendable to induce any woman, married or single, to leave her sinful relatives and seek the higher heaven in company with a Mormon. The doctrine was at first treated rather as a matter of privilege; but as months passed away, and its peculiar fitness to their theory of pre-existent spirits, anxiously waiting for earthly bodies, was seen, it became more and more a thing of duty. It reached its grossest form during the reform period of 1855–6.

The "Reformation" was the result of distress. The removal across the plains involved large losses; the work of the last two years had been rendered unprofitable by drought and grasshoppers; the Saints were reduced to a condition of general poverty. The leaders accounted for it as a punishment sent on them for sin and want of faith. Under the preaching of men who, in charity, may be called demented, the people were wrought up to an extravagant pitch of religious frenzy. Men were exhorted everywhere to repent, confess their sins, and be rebaptized, for the day of the Lord was at

PRESIDENT JOHN TAYLOR.

hand; and from all that land there rose a wail of, "Unclean! unclean!" It floated out over the desert, and over the mountains, and from the extreme southern settlements it was echoed back, "Unclean! unclean!" Men and women bared their hearts' darkest corners to the public congregations, and many, whom suspicion itself had marked pure, confessed the perpetration of horrible crimes. Polygamy took on its most revolting shape; children of twelve and thirteen years were married to gray-haired elders; whole families of girls were wedded to one man; uncles united with nieces; in at least one instance half-brother and sister were married; men met in the streets and exchanged daughters; divorce and remarriage became so common that some women had eight or ten husbands in almost the same number of months. All of the people were rebaptized, and started anew on their peculiar path, determined to gain heaven at any cost.

Out of this groaning for sin there arose the most villainous of all the doctrines of the Mormon Church—that of the "blood-atonement." It is, in brief, that there are certain sins which are unpardonable, except the blood of the sinner be shed; and the people were exhorted: "Let your blood be shed, and let the smoke ascend, that the incense thereof may come up before God as atonement for your sins." The chief of these unpardonable sins is the "shedding of innocent blood," which means the blood of Mormons, and possibly of

Gentiles who have not reached years of accountability, and whose parents have not been guilty of injuring Mormons or associating with people who have. Adultery, under certain circumstances, procurement of abortion, and the "violation of a sanctified oath" are also unpardonable, and for these offences many of these enthusiasts gladly submitted to death. But it did not stop there. They were not satisfied with throwing themselves under the wheels of Juggernaut, but must also have the privilege of sacrificing others to save them from their sins. "It is to save them," said Brigham Young, in a sermon reported in their Church organ, the *Deseret News*, on October 1, 1856, "not to destroy them. It is true that the blood of the Son of God was shed for our sins, but men can commit sins which it can never remit." Again, on February 8, 1857, he said: "I could refer you to plenty of instances where men have been righteously slain in order to atone for their sins. I have seen scores and hundreds of people for whom there would have been a chance (in the last resurrection there will be) if their lives had been taken, and their blood spilled on the ground as a smoking incense to the Almighty, but who are now angels to the devil, until our elder brother, Jesus Christ, raises them up, conquers death, hell, and the grave." These are but brief selections from the many blood-seeking sermons of those days, and the zealous churchmen took eager hold of this doctrine which the world had been growing out of for a score of centuries.

Just after the Church was fairly encompassed in this blaze of zeal, it was announced, on July 24, 1857, to the great gathering of Mormons at Cottonwood Park, where they had met to celebrate the anniversary of the arrival of their exploring party in the Basin, that there was an army under way for Utah, escorting the new territorial officers. It was true. Crime in the guise of religion had become so rampant in Utah, and its repression by the people there so hopeless, that an external executive agency had to be sought. The courts had been overawed by armed mobs and the judges had fled. A lawyer who protested against such proceedings had been murdered. Indian agent Hurt had reported something of their connection with the Indians, and, believing his life in danger, had slipped away through the mountain passes, guided by Indian friends. He resigned, declining reappointment. Such troubles had been growing since 1851, and almost every Gentile official that went there had died suddenly, or been driven away on account of "immorality." In his message of 1857, President Buchanan said : " Without entering upon a minute history of occurrences, it is sufficient to say that all the officers of the United States, judicial and executive, with the single exception of two Indian agents, have found it necessary for their own personal safety to withdraw from the territory, and there no longer remains any government in Utah but the despotism of Brigham Young." Whether the officials had been blameworthy or not is immaterial ; the fact remains that Utah was in a state of confusion and lawlessness, and it was necessary to send troops with the new officials, who should act as a *posse comitatus* on their call.

From the official instructions given at the time it is easily seen that, in the eyes of the administration, the state of affairs in Utah was very similar to what had recently existed in Kansas, with the difference that the trouble was over another question. But in reality the situation was very different. In Utah the people were united, but they wanted no government except that of their own leaders, no matter what the United States desired. The majority of them were ready for war. They had been apart from the Gentiles long enough to let the delusion of divine aid grow up again, and the belief was general, as it was in Missouri, that one should " chase a thousand, and two put ten thousand to flight." The leaders were not so pugnacious. The plan they adopted was to hold the army back until they were ready to move, and then desert the northern part of the territory, destroying everything behind them—to make a second Moscow of Salt Lake City. For this active preparations were made ; grain was hoarded up and cached in the mountains ; hiding-places were sought out ; and all the people prepared for a journey. The Mormons in California were recalled, and all returned to Utah. Fort Bridger and Fort Supply, under control of Mormon Indian agents, were vacated and burned down, in order that they might not furnish shelter to the troops when they came. The Nauvoo Legion was brought into active discipline, and a general martial spirit pervaded the entire community, such as is shadowed in this verse from one of their favorite songs:

> " Old squaw-killer Harney is on the way
> The Mormon people for to slay;
> Now, if he comes, the truth I'll tell,
> Our boys will drive him down to hell."

General Harney did not come until after the difficulty was adjusted. He was succeeded by Colonel Albert Sidney Johnston, who reached the army in the early winter. No resistance being anticipated, Captain Van Vliet, a discreet officer, was sent ahead to purchase supplies for the army and explain its purpose to the Mormons. He arrived at Salt Lake early in September and found them preparing for war. He was treated with consideration, but could purchase no supplies. They told him that they had been persecuted, robbed, and murdered in the East, and now would resist all persecution at the outset; " that the troops now on the march for Utah should not enter Salt Lake Valley." Van Vliet called their attention to the fact that resistance could only be temporary; that if the army were kept out over winter the government would send an overwhelming force which would crush them. Young replied: " We are aware that such will be the case, but when those troops arrive they will find Utah a desert; every house will be burned to the ground, every tree cut down, and every field laid waste. We have three years' provisions on hand, which we will cache, and then take to the mountains, and bid defiance to all the powers of the government." On Sunday Van Vliet attended their services, and when Elder Taylor, now President, after presenting the probabilities to them, " desired all present who would apply the torch to their own buildings, cut down their trees and lay waste their fields, to hold up their hands, every hand in an audience numbering over four thousand persons was raised at the same moment." He also stated that, " The Almighty had appointed a man to rule over and govern his Saints, and that man was Brigham Young, and that they would have no one else to rule over them."

On September 14 Van Vliet left Salt Lake City, and on the 15th Young issued a proclamation, in which he recited the wrongs and misfortunes of the Mormons, and "forbid— First, All armed forces of every description from coming into this territory under any pretence whatever. Second, That all the forces in said territory hold themselves in readiness to march at a moment's notice to repel any and all such invasion. Third, Martial law is hereby declared to exist in this territory

BRIGHAM YOUNG.

from and after the publication of this proclamation; and no person shall be allowed to pass or repass into, or through, or from this territory without a permit from the proper officer." A copy of this was sent to Colonel Alexander, commanding the advance of the army. On September 21 Van Vliet met the advance, on his return, and reported his failure. On September 29 Young again addressed the commanding officer, calling his attention to his disregard of the former proclamation, and adding: "I now further direct that you retire forth-with from the territory by the same route you entered. Should you deem this impracticable, and prefer to remain until spring in the vicinity of your present encampment, Black Fork, or Green River, you can do so in peace, and unmolested, on con-dition that you deposit your arms and ammunition with Lewis Robinson, Quartermaster-general of the Territory, and leave in the spring as soon as the condition of the roads will permit you to march." This was accompanied by a note from "Daniel H. Wells, Lieutenant-general commanding Nauvoo Legion," stating, "I am here to aid in carrying out the instruc-tions of Governor Young." The army was then in what is now the southwestern corner of Wyoming, straggling over a hundred miles or more of country, and not yet apprehensive of actual resistance; Colonel Johnston was at Fort Laramie; the supply trains were not guarded. On October 5 the Mor-mons, under Lot Smith, one of their great "war-captains," at-tacked and destroyed a train on Green River, another on the Big Sandy, and a number of wagons belonging to the sutler of the 10th infantry, also on the Sandy, making a total loss of seventy-five wagons, with their contents, and several hun-dred animals. About the same time it was learned that the mountain passes were barricaded and held by Mormon troops. It was considered impracticable to force them in the winter, so the army went into winter camp.

During the long summer days that the Mormons passed in preparation for war, an emigrant train, known on the road as Captain Fancher's train, was passing through Utah. It reached Salt Lake City in August, and took the "southern route" which led through Provo, Nephi, Fillmore, Beaver, and Cedar City, and at the last-named place joined the Spanish trail from Los Angeles to New Mexico, which ran thence southwest to the coast of California. These emigrants num-bered originally fifty-six men and sixty-two women and chil-dren, most of them being from Carroll, Johnson, Marion, and other northern counties of Arkansas. At Salt Lake City they were joined by several disaffected Mormons. They had thirty good wagons, about thirty mules and horses, and six hundred cattle. Dr. Brewer, of the army, who met them on the Platte, in June, said it was " probably the finest train that had ever crossed the plains. There seemed to be about forty heads of families, many women, some unmarried, and many children. They had three carriages, one very fine, in which ladies rode." Slowly this long line wound its way up the Jordan, around the sedgy border of Utah Lake, through Juab Valley, and down the long, dreary stretch of road from the Sevier to Little Salt Lake. At Beaver they were joined by a Missourian, who had been held in custody there for some alleged offense, and he urged them to hurry on beyond the power of the Mormons. They passed through settlements from day to day, but they were friendless as in the voiceless desert. They wished to buy grain and hay to recruit their failing stock, but the edict had gone forth for all supplies to be " hid up" in the moun- tains, and there was no grain to be bought by their money. One man did trade them a small cheese, but he was seen by the special policeman who was detailed to watch the train, and was " cut off " from the church for it. Sell supplies to these Gentiles? Oh, no! They were but a portion of the mob that would soon be battering at the gates of Zion. Rumor wearied her countless wings in incessant flight, carrying before them the reports of their evil deeds, which grew and spread until their original inventors might have blushed for them. It was said that they were taking property by force; that they broke down and burned fences; that they insulted men; that they ravished Mormon women; that they were a part of the mob that drove the Saints from Missouri; that they boasted of hav- ing the pistol with which the Prophet Joseph was killed; that they were connected with the recent murder of the apostle, Parley Pratt; that they threatened to return from California with enough men to destroy all the Mormon settlements; that they poisoned an ox with strychnine, causing the death of some Indians and one white man; that they poisoned the spring at Corn Creek with arsenic, causing the death of twenty Pah- Vant Indians; that they were, in short, a crowd of hardened, godless wretches, whose sins could never be washed away ex- cept in their own blood. The chief hierarch of Southern Utah announced that he believed there was not "a d——d drop of innocent blood among them." The charges made against them were to the people of Southern Utah as words of certain truth, for the fanaticism and bigotry of Northern Utah was only lukewarmness in the southern settlements. Men scowled and women glared their righteous hatred at the doomed party, and little children peered through half-opened doors, in curious fear, at the wicked people who had raised their hands against God's anointed. True, they saw none of this evil-doing as the emigrants passed them, but their belief in it was not shaken by that. They had Mormon testimony to its truth, and that was sufficient.

The emigrants kept on as fast as they could conveniently. They crossed the Great Basin; they climbed up the southern rim; and on this border of Mormondom they stopped for a few days to let their cattle revel in the rank, coarse mountain grass, before they went on into "the Ninety-Mile Desert." The location of the Mountain Meadows, their stopping-place, is in the southwestern corner of Utah, in the present county of Washington, about eight miles south of the village of Pinto. The place is a pass—sometimes called a valley—about five miles in length and one in width, but running to a rather narrow point at the southwest end. At about its centre, lengthways, is the "divide" between the Basin and the Pacific slope, the ascents being very gradual, and at each end is a large spring, the waters of the eastern one flowing into the Basin, and those of the western one to the Santa Clara, and thence to the Rio Virgen. At the eastern spring was the house and corral of Jacob Hamlin, Mormon sub-agent for the Pah-Utes, who, with some assistants, all Mormons, was pasturing cattle on the meadows. The train passed his place on the 3d of September, and camped at the western spring on the 4th. The spring, which is a large one, is in the southern end of the narrow part. The bank rises from it to a height of about eight feet, and from its top there reaches a level stretch of some two hundred yards. Beyond this there comes an irregular ridge or row of hills, fifty or sixty feet in height, back of which is a valley of considerable extent, which opens into the main Meadows three or four hundred yards below the spring. The emigrants were camped on the level ground just north of the spring. They were now on the edge of the Pa-

CACTUS IN DESERT.

cific slope, and must have felt the gladness of the wayworn
traveller who knows that another stage of his journey is finished.   Just across there, to the southwest, was golden California—they could almost see it—a few more miles of desert,
a few more days of dust and alkali water, and they would be
through.

In the chilly dawn of Monday, September 7, as they were
grouped about their camp-fires, preparing and eating their
breakfasts, they were stunned by a volley of guns from the
little gully through which the waters of the spring ran away.

Seven of their number were killed, sixteen were wounded, and the remainder thrown into confusion; but it was only for a moment. They were brave men, and they had lived too long on the frontier not to be ready for an Indian attack on short notice. The women and children were hastily placed in the shelter of the corralled wagons, and the rifles of the men were soon replying effectually to those of their foes. This was discouraging to their assailants, for they had counted on a massacre, not a fight. They were not warriors of much eminence. On the contrary, Captain Campbell afterwards classed them as "a miserable set of root-diggers," and said, "nothing is to be apprehended from them but by the smallest and most careless party." They were Pah-Utes from the neighborhood of Cedar City, under Moquetas, Big Bill, and other chiefs; and others from the Santa Clara settlements, extending thirty-five miles below, under Jackson and his brother; Upper Pi-Edes, under Ka-nar-rah, and Lower Pi-Edes under Tal-si-Gob-beth; but at this time they were all directed and controlled by John D. Lee, sub-agent, Nephi Johnson, interpreter, and two or three others, all disguised as Indians. It required all their efforts to keep the Indians at their work. Several were killed early in the engagement, and two of their war-chiefs had their knee-joints shattered by rifle-balls, from the effects of which both died. The Indians moved back to safer quarters, and, after driving away all the cattle that were out of range of the spring, vented their rage by shooting the remainder that they dared not attempt to drive away. An occasional shot was fired at the emigrants, as a reminder that they were still in the neighborhood. White reinforcements were sent for at once, after the first repulse, and began to arrive on the following day. They stopped out of sight of the emigrants to camp. Occasionally they would put on a little paint and go take a shot at the wagons; then they would return and amuse themselves by pitching quoits. The little party of the besieged meanwhile were improving their time. They drew their wagons close together, chained them wheel to wheel, and banked up earth to the beds, making a fortress which they could easily hold against all the Indians within a hundred miles of them.

On Wednesday night a young man named Aden, a son of

Dr. Aden of Kentucky, with one companion, stole out of the valley and started to Cedar City for aid. At Richards' Springs they met three Cedar City men, William C. Stewart, Joel White, and Benjamin Arthur. As their horses drank from the spring, Stewart shot and killed Aden, and White wounded his companion, but the latter escaped and made his way back to the camp. The emigrants now began to realize the desperation of their situation. Aden might surely have hoped for assistance if any one could, for his father was known to have saved the life of a Mormon bishop of the neighborhood ; yet he was assassinated by a Mormon. There could be little doubt that the white men, of whom occasional glimpses had been caught by them, were Mormons, and that they were aiding the Indians. They prepared a statement of their situation, giving their reasons for believing that the Mormons were their real besiegers, and directed it to Masons, Odd Fellows, the leading religious denominations, and to " good people generally." This they intrusted to three of their best scouts, who, on Thursday night, slipped down through the arroyo of the spring-branch, across the strip of valley, and off towards California. The paper implored assistance, if assistance could reach them, and, if not, that justice might be meted to their murderers.

While these men were endeavoring to slip through the meshes of the net that was drawn about them, a strange scene was to be witnessed just over the little divide of the Meadows. There were now fifty-four white men in the attacking party and about two hundred Indians, all of whom were satisfied that no direct assault on the camp could be successful. The resolute defence of the emigrants had made a change of procedure necessary, and they were now obliged to obtain " counsel " from those in authority, and the approval of the Lord. Up to this time every step had been taken in that way. George A. Smith, one of the Twelve Apostles, had gone through the settlements and arranged the preliminaries ; the day after the train passed through Cedar City a Church council was held, at which women were present, and, after due consideration, it was decided, by a unanimous vote, to be the will of the Lord that the Fancher outfit should be exterminated. The manner selected was an Indian massacre, but this had failed. A council of the Mormons in the Meadows was held on Thursday evening, and the orders from President Haight of Cedar City were read. They directed that the emigrants should be decoyed from their stronghold and exterminated. Haight was lieutenant-colonel of the militia, and had received his directions to this effect from Colonel Dame, commander of the militia of the district, which was known as "the Iron militia." The men in the Meadows were all members of it, and were commanded by Major John Higbee. There was some feeble remonstrance to the orders, so, after a little talk, they all knelt, with elbows touching, in "a prayer circle," and asked for divine guidance. On the still night air of that mountain pass, one voice after another rose in fervent prayer, asking God to say to them whether or not they should betray and murder one hundred and twenty of their fellow-men. The last voice ceased; a moment of silence ensued; then Major Higbee announced, in confident tone, "I have the evidence of God's approval of our mission. It is God's will that we carry out our instructions to the letter." In that declaration the "higher law" stands out in all its naked enormity. Mere polygamy is a virtue compared with such a devils' faith. The council remained in session until daybreak, and all the minutiæ of the following day's work were arranged for. A hasty breakfast was despatched, and the preparation for the Lord's work was begun at once.

The Indians were concealed in a thicket a mile and three quarters from the camp, on the road back to the Basin. The Mormons procured two wagons, with which they moved on towards the western spring. They stopped out of gun-shot, and John D. Lee and William Bateman advanced under a white flag. An emigrant came out to meet them. They talked over the situation. Lee said that the Indians were much excited, on account of injuries done them by former parties, and could scarcely be controlled, but he had got them to promise that no harm should be done to the emigrants if they surrendered to the Mormons. Part of them had left already. It would be necessary to make a form of surrendering; the guns could be placed in the wagons brought by the

Mormons, together with the sick, wounded, and small children; the men must march unarmed, each accompanied by a Mormon, to make the Indians believe they were captives. To this the emigrants consented. They were putting themselves wholly in the power of the Mormons, but it was all they could do. There was no escape without Mormon aid. Even if the

JOHN D. LEE.

Indians left them, their stock was all gone, and they were unable to move. Perhaps they thought the Mormons would be satisfied with getting their property and would save their lives, blaming what had happened to the Indians. Perhaps they did not suspect the Mormons any longer. No one knows. The book is sealed till the last day. The wagons are driven up; the corral is opened; the guns are loaded in, also the sick, the wounded, and the smaller children; the wagons drive on. The women and older children follow, on foot. The men, part of whom have just finished burying two of their number, who had died of their wounds, making ten deaths at the spring, come last.

It is just after noon, and the day is bright and clear. Tramp, tramp, tramp; they march down from the camping-place. The men have reached the militia, and give them three hearty cheers as they take their places, murderer and victim, side by side. Tramp, tramp, tramp. They are rounding the point of the ridge which has served as a screen for the Mormons and Indians for the past week. A raven flies over them, croaking. What called him there? Does he foresee that he shall peck at the eyes of brave men and gentle women who are looking at him? Tramp, tramp, tramp. The wagons with the wounded and the children are passing the hiding-place of the Indians. How quietly they lie among the gnarly oak bushes! but their eyes glisten, and their necks stretch out to see how soon their prey will reach them. The women are nearly a quarter of a mile behind the wagons, and the men as much farther behind the women. A half-dozen Mormon horsemen bring up the rear. Tramp, tramp, tramp. The wagons have just passed out of sight over the divide. The men are entering a little ravine. The women are opposite the Indians. They have regained confidence, and several are expressing their joy at escaping from their savage foes. See that man on the divide! It is Higbee. He makes a motion with his arms and shouts something which those nearest him understand to be: "Do your duty." In an instant the militiamen wheel, and each shoots the man nearest him; the Indians spring from their ambush and rush upon the women; from between the wagons the rifle of John D. Lee cracks, and a wounded woman in the forward wagon falls off the seat.

Swiftly the work of death goes on. Lee is assisted in shooting and braining the wounded by the teamsters Knight and McMurdy, and as the latter raises his rifle to his shoulder he cries: "O Lord, my God, receive their spirits, it is for thy kingdom that I do this." The men all fell at the first fire but two or three, and these the horsemen ride down, knock over with their clubbed guns, and finish with their knives. Their throats are cut, that the atoning blood may flow freely. The women and older children are not hurried out of the world quite so quickly as the others. Some are on their knees begging for life. Others run shrieking over the Meadows. They receive but two answers—the tomahawk crashing through the skull, and the knife plunging through the heart. These are all left to the Indians, for fear there may be " innocent blood " among them, which no Mormon may shed. There is alarm on this account already, for one of the emigrants had carried his infant child in his arms, and the bullet that pierced the father's heart went through the babe's brain. It is decided, however, that it was accidental and that no criminal wrong is done. Several of the Mormons run to the Indians, to see that they do their work properly. Among them is Lee. It is discovered that two of the girls are missing. Some one saw them run to a ravine fifty yards away. Lee and one of the Cedar City chiefs run to the place and find there the Indian boy, Albert, who lives with Hamlin. He says the girls came there, and shows where they hid in the brush. They drag them forth and brutally ravish them. This was the only act on that field that was not inspired. Was it wrong, under the Mormon code of morality? The question is too subtle for me to answer; certainly it was not punished. Lee next tells the chief the girls must be killed. The chief answers : " No, they are too pretty to kill; let us save them ;" but he meets a grim refusal. The unhappy child that Lee holds, with the terror of death upon her, flings her arms round his neck and promises to love him as long as he lives, if he will spare her life. The wolf has keener fangs but no more merciless heart. He throws her head back with his arm, and with one stroke of his keen bowie-knife severs her neck to the spine. The chief brains the other with his tomahawk.

This finished the slaughter at the Meadows, but there remained a little more to do. The trail of the three scouts, who went out on the night before, had been discovered, and Ira Hatch, with a party of Indians, was sent after them. The fugitives were found sleeping, in the Santa Clara Mountains, and, from the volley fired at them, two slept on in death. The third fled with a bullet-hole through his wrist. He met two Mormons, who were much afflicted over his sad plight, and persuaded him that he could not get across the desert. They induced him to turn back with them, promising to smuggle him through Utah. They soon met Hatch's party and the man was killed; but they did permit him to pray first. The paper calling for assistance, which he carried, was in Mormon custody for some time, and is said to have been destroyed by John D. Lee. The man killed by Hatch's party brings the number killed to one hundred and twenty-one—ten at the camp, young Aden at Richards' Springs, one hundred and seven on the Meadows, and the three messenger scouts. The main massacre was on Friday, September 11, 1857. There has been some confusion as to this, arising from a failure to consult calendars. Judge Cradlebaugh fixed the date as September 10; Dr. Forney as "Friday, September 9 or 10;" all the Mormon witnesses, and Lee, in his confessions, fixed the day of the week as Friday, and the second Friday in September was the 11th, in the year 1857. On the evening of the same day the surviving children, seventeen in number, ranging in age from three to eight years, were taken to Hamlin's, and afterwards divided out among Mormon families.

The property still remained to be disposed of. A part of it was given to the Indians, and for this, Lee as Indian agent, in his report of November 20, 1857, charged the government over fifteen hundred dollars. The bodies of the dead were searched by Higbee and Klingensmith, the Bishop of Cedar City, and the money found is supposed to have been kept by them. The remaining property was put in Klingensmith's custody temporarily, and afterwards, on instructions from Brigham Young, was turned over to Lee and sold by him for the benefit of the Church. The bodies were stripped entirely naked, and fingers and ears were mutilated in tearing from them the jewelry, to them no longer valuable. The bloody clothing and the bedding on which the wounded had lain were piled in the back room of the tithing-office at Cedar City for some weeks, and when Judge Cradlebaugh examined the room, eighteen months later, it still stank of them. These goods were commonly known as " property taken at the siege of Sevastopol." Carriages and wagons of the emigrants were in use long afterwards, and some of the jewelry is said to be worn yet in Utah. The value of all the property taken, as nearly as it can be ascertained, was over $70,000. People in Arkansas who saw the organization of the train estimated its value at $100,000.

It was for many years a hotly debated question whether Brigham Young was connected with this crime or not. To those who were familiar with the subordination of the Mormon Church, its system of espionage, its compulsory confessional, its obedience to " counsel," and its prompt punishment of everything contrary to the will of those in authority, his guilt was a matter of course. But many did not believe it. In 1875 he published a deposition in which he acknowledged himself accessory after the fact, saying that, within two or three months after the affair, Lee began giving him an account of it, and, says the deposition, "I told him to stop, as, from what I had already heard by rumor, I did not wish my feelings harrowed up by a recital of detail." Lee and Klingensmith say they reported it fully to him, and Hamlin says he did also. To Lee, by his account, Young professed to be much shocked by the killing of the women and children, but, after considering it over-night, he said : " I have made that matter a subject of prayer. I went right to God with it, and asked him to take the horrid vision from my sight, if it were a righteous thing that my people had done in killing those people at the Mountain Meadows. God answered me, and at once the vision was removed. I have evidence from God that he has overruled it all for good, and the action was a righteous one and well intended. The brethren acted from pure motives. The only trouble is that they acted a little prematurely ; they were a little ahead of time. I sustain you and all of the brethren for what they did. All that I fear is treachery on the part of some one who took a part with you, but we will look to that." There is testimony also that he was accessory before the fact, and his proclamation, that " No person shall be allowed to pass or repass, into or through or from this territory without a permit from the proper officer," surely indicates that he was in an aggressive mood at the time. But this is now immaterial. He has passed beyond human punishment, and his moral guilt is sufficiently established out of his own mouth. On occasions of self-gratulation he sometimes exposed his methods. On August 12, 1860, he said, in the Tabernacle: " All the army, with its teamsters, hangers-on, and followers, with the judges and nearly all the rest of the civil officers, amounting to some seventeen thousand men, have been searching diligently for three years to bring one act to light that would criminate me; but they have not been able to trace out one thread or one particle of evidence that would criminate me; do you know why? Because I walk humbly with my God, and do right so far as I know how. I do no evil to any one; and as long as I can have faith in the name of the Lord Jesus Christ to hinder the wolves from tearing the sheep and devouring them, without putting forth my hand, I shall do so. I can say honestly and truly, before God and the holy angels and all men, that not one act of murder or disorder has occurred in this city or territory that I had any knowledge of, any more than a babe a week old, until after the event had transpired; that is the reason they cannot trace any crime to me. If I have faith enough to cause the devils to eat up the devils, like the Kilkenny cats, I shall certainly exercise it. Joseph Smith said that they would eat each other up as did those cats. They will do so here and throughout the world. The nations will consume each other and the Lord will suffer them to bring it about. It does not require much talent or tact to get up opposition in these days; you see it rife in communities, in meetings, in neighborhoods, and in cities; that is the knife that will cut down this government. The axe is laid at the root of the tree, and every tree that bringeth not forth good fruit will be hewn down."

His guilt is most fully shown in the subsequent course of himself and the Mormon Church. It was unquestionably the intention of the Mormon Church to keep the participation of white men in the massacre a secret, and lay the blame on the Indians. On January 6, 1858, after he was acquainted with the general facts, according to his deposition, Brigham Young reported to Commissioner Denver: "On or about the middle of last September a company of emigrants, travelling the southern route to California, poisoned the meat of an ox that died, and gave it to the Indians to eat, causing the immediate death of four of their tribe, and poisoning several others. This company also poisoned the water where they were encamped. This occurred at Corn Creek, fifteen miles south of Fillmore City. This conduct so enraged the Indians that they immediately took measures for revenge. I quote from a letter written to me by John D. Lee, farmer to the Indians in Iron and Washington counties. 'About the 22d of September, Captain Fancher and company fell victims to the Indians' wrath near Mountain Meadows. Their cattle and horses were shot down in every direction; their wagons and property mostly committed to the flames.' Lamentable as this case truly is, it is only the natural consequence of that fatal policy which treats the Indians like the wolves, or other ferocious beasts." This plan was, perhaps, as ingenious as any that could have been adopted, but there is no possibility of keeping such a crime secret. A murder by a single hand, under carefully planned circumstances, seldom fails to come to light, but with a crime of this magnitude the exposure of the truth is only a question of time, and a short time at that.

On October 2, 1857, eleven men, partly Mormons, who were secretly escaping from Utah, passed through Mountain Meadows and saw the fruits of divine guidance. One of them afterwards described it, on the witness-stand, thus: "Saw two piles of bodies, one composed of women and children, the other of men; the bodies were entirely nude, and seemed to have been thrown promiscuously together; they appeared to have been massacred. Should judge there were sixty or seventy bodies of women and children; saw one man in that pile; the children were aged from one and two months up to twelve years; the small children were most destroyed by wolves and crows; the throats of some were cut, others stabbed with knives; some had balls through them. All the bodies were more or less torn to pieces, except one, the body of a woman, which lay apart, a little southwest of the pile. This showed no signs of decay, and had not been touched by

SCENE OF MASSACRE.

the wild animals. The countenance was placid and seemed to be in sleep. The work was not freshly done—supposed the bodies had been here fifteen or sixteen days." These men went on to California and told their story. A meeting of citizens at Los Angeles examined the testimony, decided that the Mormons had committed the crime, and called on the President for protection. The report flew on wings of the wind to every part of the country, which was already excited over the resistance offered to the army. How secret the brethren in Utah kept it! On December 31, fifteen brief weeks after it occurred, William C. Mitchell, of Dubuque, Arkansas, wrote to Senator Sebastian of that state: "Two of my sons were in the train that was massacred, on their way to California, three hundred miles beyond Salt Lake City, by the Indians and Mormons. There were one hundred and eighteen unmercifully butchered; the women and children were all killed with the exception of fifteen infants. One of my sons, Charles, was married and had one son, which I expect was saved, and at this time is at San Bernardino, I believe in the limits of California. I could designate my grandson if I could see him. . . . Four regiments, together with what regulars can be spared, is too small a force to whip the Mormons and Indians, for rest assured that all the wild tribes will fight for Brigham Young. I am anxious to be in the crowd—I feel that I must have satisfaction for the inhuman manner in which they have slain my children, together with two brothers-in-law and seventeen of their children."

The people of the neighborhoods whence the emigrants went were satisfied with the evidence they had. The press announced the organization of volunteer companies in a dozen counties of Missouri and Arkansas. The government, however, did not decide so quickly. Many wild reports concerning the situation in Utah had been current—reports of battles in which seven or eight hundred on a side had been killed—of the army being captured and the officers hung— and possibly this was only a canard too. It was decided to investigate first, and Dr. Forney, Superintendent of Utah, was instructed to look into the matter. The Western men did not let the case drop, however. On March 18, 1858, Mr. Gwin, of California, introduced a resolution of inquiry in the Senate, asking what steps had been taken to punish the murderers of the one hundred and eighteen emigrants.   He said he knew the Indians were guilty, and it had been charged, and was believed, that the Mormons were, but at any rate the guilty should be punished.   On June 22, 1858, Dr. Forney reported : "It affords me great pleasure to inform you, and the friends of the children in question through you, that I learned to-day where the children are.   In my inquiries about the children I met a gentleman who lives at or near where the massacre took place.   This gentleman, Mr. Hamlin, has one of the children, and informs me that all the children (fifteen) in question are in his immediate neighborhood in the care of whites. These unfortunate children were for some days among Indians; with considerable effort they were all recovered, bought and otherwise, from the Indians."   Forney was as impartial a man as the Mormons could have asked for—in fact, he was prejudiced in their favor.   He evidently believed Hamlin, of whom more anon, but, as he went south and gathered facts, here and there, the truth gradually forced itself upon him, and on May 1, 1859, when he had recovered sixteen of the children, he wrote: "Four of the oldest of the children know, WITHOUT DOUBT KNOW, enough of the material facts of the Mountain Meadow affair, to relieve the world of the white hell-hounds who have disgraced humanity by being mainly instrumental in the murdering of at least one hundred and fifteen men, women, and children, under circumstances and manner without a parallel in human history for atrocity."

Dr. Forney had cause to change his mind, outside of the evidence of the children.   He went first among the Pah-Vant Indians under chief Kanosh, at Corn Creek—the Indians who had been poisoned by the emigrants and taken vengeance on them.   He found that none of them had been poisoned by the waters of the spring; that the spring ran so strong that a barrel of arsenic would not have poisoned it; that an ox belonging to Dr. Ray, a Mormon living at Fillmore City, had died about the time the emigrants were camped at Corn Creek, from eating a poisonous weed—a not unusual occurrence—and some Indians who ate of the ox were poisoned, but they had made no complaints of the emigrants, and had no trouble of any kind with them; that none of the Pah-Vants were at the Mountain Meadow massacre; that the conduct of the emigrants all through Utah had been most exemplary; that none of the children had been with the Indians for an hour. And yet, as if desirous of adding a little more to the awful infamy of

KANOSH.

this affair, all the Mormons who had had custody of these children put in claims for the purchase-money expended in buying them from the Indians, as well as for their maintenance, the total claimed amounting to over $7000. Of this amount Forney paid $2961.77 for what he considered proper charges, and reported as to the rest that he "cannot condescend to become the medium of even transmitting such claims to the department."

In the spring of 1859 a company of dragoons and two companies of infantry, under Captain R. P. Campbell, passed through the Meadows and buried the remains. Theirs was the last view of the Lord's work. Dr. Charles Brewer, in charge of the burying-party, reported: "At the scene of the first attack, in the immediate vicinity of our present camp, marked by a small defensive trench made by the emigrants, a number of human skulls, and bones and hair, were found scattered about, bearing the appearance of never having been buried; also remnants of bedding and wearing apparel. On examining the trenches, which appear to have been within the

20

corral, and within which it was supposed some written account of the massacre might have been concealed, some few human bones, human hair, and what seemed to be the feathers of bedding, only were discerned. Proceeding 2500 yards in a direction N. 15° W., I reached a ravine fifty yards distant from the road, bordered by a few bushes of scrub oak, in which I found portions of the skeletons of many bodies—skulls, bones, and matted hair—most of which, on examination, I concluded to be those of men. 350 yards farther on, and in the same direction, another assembly of human remains were found, which, by all appearance, had been left to decay upon the surface—skulls and bones, most of which I believed to be those of women, some also of children, probably ranging from six to twelve years of age. Here, too, were found masses of women's hair, children's bonnets, such as are generally used upon the plains, and pieces of lace, muslin, calicoes, and other material, part of women's and children's apparel. I have buried thirteen skulls, and many more scattered fragments. Some of the remains above referred to were found upon the surface of the ground, with a little earth partially covering them, and, at the place where the men were massacred, some lightly buried, but the majority were scattered about upon the plain. Many of the skulls bore marks of violence, being pierced with bullet-holes, or shattered by heavy blows, or cleft with some sharp-edged instrument. The bones were bleached and worn by long exposure to the elements, and bore the impress of the teeth of wolves or other wild animals. The skulls found upon the ground near the spring, or position of the first attack, and adjoining our camp, were eight in number. These, with the other remains there found, were buried, under my supervision, at the base of the hill, upon the hillside of the valley. At the rate of 2500 yards distant from the spring, the relative position and general appearance of the remains seemed to indicate that the men were there taken by surprise and massacred. Some of the skulls showed that firearms had been discharged close to the head. I have buried eighteen skulls and parts of many more skeletons, found scattered over the space of a mile towards the lines, in which direction they were, no doubt, dragged by the wolves. No

names were found upon any article of apparel, or any peculi-
arity in the remains, with the exception of one bone, the upper jaw, in which the teeth were very closely crowded, and
which contained one front tooth more than is generally found.
Under my direction, the above-mentioned remains were all
properly buried, the respective localities being marked with
mounds of stone." Major (since General) Carleton afterwards
erected a monument in the Meadows, of a large pile of rocks
surmounted by a rude wooden cross, between twelve and fifteen feet in height, bearing the inscription: "Vengeance is
mine; I will repay, saith the Lord." On one of the stones he
caused to be engraved: "Here lie the bodies of one hundred
and twenty men, women, and children, from Arkansas, murdered on the 11th day of September, 1857." It is said that
the cross and the inscribed stone mysteriously disappeared
the first time Brigham Young came into the southern settlements.

On June 29, seventeen of the children having been recovered, fifteen of them were sent East, overland, in spring-wagons,
escorted by soldiers. Every possible provision was made for
their comfort, and four women were sent with them to attend
to their wants. Two boys about seven years of age, John C.
Miller, known to the Mormons as John Calvin Sorel, and
Milum Tackett, who was known to the Mormons as Ambrose
Miram Taggit, were retained as witnesses. Those returned
were Mary Miller, called by the Mormons Mary Sorel; William
Tackett, known to the Mormons as William Taggit; Prudence
Angeline Dunlap and Georgiana Dunlap, known to the Mormons as Angeline Huff and Annie Huff; Sophronia Jones,
called by the Mormons Sophronia Huff; T. M. Jones, called
by the Mormons Ephraim W. Huff; Kit Carson Fancher, called
Charley Fancher by the Mormons; his cousin Tryphena Fancher, called Annie Fancher by the Mormons, and supposed by
them to be Charley's sister; Betsy Baker, Sarah Jane Baker,
William Baker, Rebecca Dunlap, Louisa Dunlap, Sarah Dunlap, and Joseph Miller, called by the Mormons Samuel Dunlap. They were met at Fort Leavenworth by Mr. Mitchell,
whose great bereavement by this horrible affair has been mentioned. His little grandchild was not among the saved, as he

had hoped. With heart bowed down by the completeness of his loss, he bore the little ones tenderly on to Carrollton and gave them into the arms of their friends. It was a sad day in the little county-seat. Nearly every one had lost some relative in the massacre, and bitter tears were accompanied by bitter curses on the murderers. The two boys kept as witnesses were afterwards taken to Washington, and then returned to their homes. In addition to these children, two others were made orphans at the Mountain Meadows, although they were not there; they were Alfred Rush and his sister Martha—now Mrs. Campbell—who live at present in Texas. The misfortunes of these children did not end with their return. In attempting to justify themselves the Mormons have forged most shameful lies about them, and have so often repeated them that they have obtained credence with outsiders. It was told, and currently believed in Utah, that Idaho Bill, a noted desperado who served a long term in the Utah penitentiary for horse-stealing, was Charley Fancher, and yet it can be proven by a large number of witnesses, whose characters are above reproach, that this boy was raised by his uncle, H. B. Fancher, in Carroll County, Arkansas, and died at his house some years ago. It was told that the children were sent to the poor-house in St. Louis. There was just one of them that went to St. Louis, but not to the poor-house. Sarah Dunlap, blind from her birth, and with one arm shattered and crippled for life by a Mormon rifle-ball, went to the Institute for the Blind in that city. They were all raised by their relatives and friends, and most of them still live in the neighborhood of their former homes. William Baker, Betsy Baker, now Mrs. Terry, and Sarah Baker, now Mrs. Gladden, live at Harrison, Arkansas; Rebecca Dunlap, now Mrs. Evans, is at Hampton, Arkansas; Louisa Dunlap, now Mrs. Lynton, is at Scottsville, Arkansas; her sister Sarah lives with her. Samuel Dunlap is at Lead Hill, Arkansas. Tryphena Fancher is the wife of J. C. Wilson, of Rule, Arkansas. The Huff children live in Eastern Tennessee. William Tackett is at Protem, Missouri; Milum Tackett lived for some years in Texas, but is now in Arizona.

There is nothing in the character of any of them that any

one need apologize for, and if there were, the Mormons should be the last ones to upbraid them for it. Whatever any of them may lack of the comforts or the accomplishments of life is due to the Saints. They have the money, the cattle, the jewelry, and the other property that should have gone for the education and maintenance of these orphans. Is it not enough that they should have been made to eat the bread of charity, and to make their own ways over the rugged paths of struggling poverty, without being weighted down with slander? There is something, too, most strangely inconsistent in the fact that while the whole country has raved about the murder done at the Mountain Meadows, and clamored for the punishment of the criminals, nothing has been done for the relief of the unhappy survivors, whose property, as well as protectors, was swept away on that bloody day. It is true that Congress passed a law donating 320 acres of land to each of them, but any citizen can have that for little more than the taking, and besides, as one of them writes to me, "Public lands in this country (Arkansas) are almost worthless, and but few of them are able to emigrate." Congress ought to make the Mormon Church disgorge the $70,000, or more, that it took from these people, with usury, and if it be not able to do so, it ought to make good the loss from the public treasury. It is notorious that the Church received the greater part of the proceeds of that butchery. It has been proven by the testimony of Mormon witnesses. It was done at a time when the Mormon Church was in armed resistance to the government. It was done when the government was not enforcing its laws in that portion of its territory. The wronged people are unable to obtain redress by any authorized means. They are poor; and it would take fortunes to prosecute their claim. Why should the Mormon Church be allowed to retain the plunder, while its victims still live in poverty? If it is permitted so to do, the government should make them whole. If the "Gentiles" of Utah wish to make an issue on which they will have the sympathy of the whole American people, let them demand the righting of this wrong. It is a far more urgent cause than preventing the Mormons from hanging a flag at half-mast on the Fourth of July. Ay! it is far more worthy of attention than prohibiting a half-dozen female cranks from living with a male fanatic, that the Mormon Church should give back to the rightful heirs the property that it took with bloody hands, on September 11, 1857.

At the same time that Forney was pursuing his inquiries, Judge John Cradlebaugh, one of the associate justices of the Supreme Court of Utah, came south to hold court there, and to aid in investigating the massacre. He was accompanied by Brigham Young, who was "extending every assistance in ferreting out the perpetrators of the crime." John D. Lee says that while on this trip Young said to a congregation of the faithful, at Cedar City: "I am told that there are many of the brethren who are willing to swear against the brethren who were engaged in that affair. I hope there is no truth in this report. I hope there is no such person here under the sound of my voice. But if there is I will tell you my opinion of you, and the fact so far as your fate is concerned. Unless you repent at once of that unholy intention, and keep the secret of all that you know, you will die a dog's death, and be damned, and go to hell. I do not want to hear of any more treachery among my people." Inasmuch as Young admits in his deposition that he was familiar with the facts of the affair long before this; inasmuch as apostates from that section corroborate Lee's statement; inasmuch as no one was brought to justice at the time, we may fairly believe this statement to be true. There was evidence obtained, nevertheless, and apostates in the South promised that, if Judge Cradlebaugh would hold court with enough troops at hand to protect the witnesses and the court, they would insure the conviction of nearly all the guilty parties. Warrants were issued for thirty-eight of the assassins, but just then another complication occurred. A great outcry had been raised because troops had been stationed near the court in Provo, during some recent Danite trials, and General Johnston received instructions that the troops must be used only as a *posse comitatus*, on due call of the executive department. He notified Judge Cradlebaugh of this fact, and the judge, having had experience in holding a court of justice in a Mormon community, without protection, very sensibly dropped the Mountain

Meadows investigation for the time. Indeed, it was a matter of necessity, for no witness would have dared to testify without protection.

Investigation was smothered temporarily, but the affair was too horrible for any ban of Church or State to keep it down, especially among such a people as the Mormons; for from their intense superstitions it is but a step to others, and they are believers, with scarcely an exception, in spirits, goblins, ghosts, visions, trances, and other supernatural phenomena. It is admitted, by the most bitter anti-Mormons, that a thrill of horror was felt by many Mormons, especially in the northern settlements, as the truth concerning the Fancher train was gradually revealed in mysterious whispers; but that was little to the feelings of those in Southern Utah from whose consciences the impressions of the teachings of earlier and better days had not been wholly effaced. The war feeling quieted down, and they realized that the day of the Lord had not yet come. They saw their leader openly pretending friendship with the officers of justice, who were searching, not for priests of the atoning blood, but for murderers. They saw men of their neighborhoods riding away on midnight expeditions, and heard reports of other murders that appeared more like the deeds of pirates than of priests. They heard of the attack on Shepherd's train, in Hedspeth's cut-off, where a child of eighteen months was wantonly tossed on the rocks and its limbs broken, three of the attacking party being recognized as painted whites. They heard of Lieutenant Gay's party, intentionally led into an ambuscade by a Mormon guide. They heard of a white woman of one train, ravished by five men, and then shot, who lived long enough to tell the next party that her assailants were all painted whites. They heard of the attack on Miltimore's train, in Lander's cut-off, where five were killed, three carried or driven off so that they were never found, and one child of five years was left with its legs and ears cut off, scalped, and its eyes gouged out, and that these Indians, by the affidavits of those who escaped, all spoke good English—that some had light hair and several had beards. Was the atoning blood always to flow? Was there to be no end of sacrifices? It was not strange that the Mormons came to believe the Meadows were haunted. It was not strange that men told in low tones how the spirits of the dead met nightly at the old camp and re-enacted the bloody tragedy. It was not strange that the lives of those who neither dared to speak while living, nor to die without speaking, became hideous nightmares. It was not strange that a lad of Beaver drank deeply of rum, without staggering, and horrified his acquaintances with recitals of the visions that he saw. It was not strange that young Spencer, the school-teacher at St. George, wasted to a skeleton, and, after writing piteously to his bishop and to Brigham Young for some assurance that could drive away the terrors that haunted him, died in grewsome tortures of remorse. It was not strange that, from time to time, as opportunity offered, Mormons escaped from the territory, apostatized, and relieved their guilt-laden souls by confession. But it was strange that the Mountain Meadows, whose verdant heath had induced its name, became barren and sterile, and to this day remains the abode of desolation.

And what did the Mormons all this time? They bent every power to show that the massacre was the deed of Indians who had been incensed by outrageous conduct of the emigrants. They slandered the victims in the most vindictive manner. They said the relatives of the surviving children refused to receive them, saying that "they were the children of thieves, outlaws, and murderers, and they would not take them, they did not want anything to do with them, and would not have them around their houses," and that in consequence the children were sent to "the poor-house in St. Louis." There was not a Mormon of any prominence who did not know the truth about the massacre, and not one who did not take part in this deception. George Q. Cannon, late Representative in Congress, wrote articles to prove the Indians guilty. Brigham Young maintained it for years, and then swore that he knew the truth within three months after the crime occurred. William H. Hooper, for some time Representative in Congress, asserted it again and again in the most solemn manner; he denounced the enemies of his people as the basest of liars, and extolled the Mormons as "the most peaceful and persistently industrious people on the continent ;" and yet it was proven that he traded boots and shoes for forty of the cattle taken at the Meadows, soon after the murder was done. The Mormons, from the first, assumed an air of injured innocence. While the army was in winter quarters, Colonel Kane, an old friend of the Saints, went into Utah, by way of California, to negotiate with them. Under his care Governor Cummings started to

GEORGE Q. CANNON.

Salt Lake City, accompanied by two servants, on April 5. He received military salutes as he passed the Mormon troops ; the walls of Echo Cañon were made light with bonfires in his honor, and on April 15 he was duly installed in his office and received ceremonial calls from leading Mormons. The people, who were all moving from the northern settlements, were begged to come back. L. W. Powell and Ben McCulloch were sent as commissioners to treat with them, and it was agreed that the army should not be further resisted, it being understood that it would not camp close to any town or city. The army entered the Basin and went into camp in Cedar Valley, three miles west of Utah Lake, and thirty-six miles south of Salt Lake City. The government resumed operations. Haight and Lee came to Salt Lake City as Senator and Representative, and each received a young wife from the hands of Brigham. All the murderers retained respectable standing in the community and in the Church—Lee, Haight, and Dame all being bishops for years.

But conscience did not die, and people did not forget. Instead of growing faint with age, the color of the crime seemed to heighten. The civil war did not result in the destruction of the Gentile men, and seven women did not take hold of one man. Gentiles kept settling in Salt Lake City, and apostates no longer fled. The younger generation of Saints did not hold to the faith of their fathers with much steadfastness. Something more of conformity to the ideas of the world at large was necessary, and the more extreme doctrines of the Church were put in the background. Lee was "cut off" from fellowship; so were Bill Hickman and other Danites. Lee went on a "mission" outside the limits of Utah. He kept a ferry on the Colorado, down in the deserts of Arizona, where for convenience he was known as Major Doyle. In January, 1874, the Gentiles held a public meeting in Salt Lake City, and a committee of forty-five drafted a memorial to Congress, showing the utter perversion of justice in the territory. Congress passed a law which took the selection of jurors out of the control of the Mormon Church, and it was left with no refuge but the perjury of witnesses, and such Mormon jurors as came on in regular order. In the same year Lee came up to Panguitch, on the Sevier, to visit some of his younger wives (he had eighteen, besides one whom he married "for her soul's sake," and did not count). While there, Deputy-Marshal William Stokes received warrants for the arrest of Lee, Haight, and others. He located Lee, and went after him with a posse of four men. The object of their search was found concealed in a log chicken-coop, and taken away peaceably, after much talk and threatening. He was brought to trial in the following summer.

The trial was a farce. Three of the jurors were Gentiles, and nine were Mormons who took their seats by dint of sturdy swearing. Men who had lived in Utah for years and never heard of the massacre—men who resided in the southern settlements before and ever since the crime, and formed no opinion about it—men who long lived in the same town with Lee and never heard much about him—men who had seen the monument in the Meadows and never asked what it was for, were accepted as jurors. They were "counselled" beforehand that Lee was not guilty. The prosecution made a much stronger case than had been anticipated. They had witnesses who, it had been supposed, would not dare to return to Utah. The Mormons tried to get hold of them by arresting them on various charges, but the United States Marshal ordered his deputies to prevent their removal for any cause, and they did so. Philip Klingensmith, ex-Bishop of Cedar City, who had fled into Nevada and thence to California, went on the witness-stand and told the whole story. He was corroborated by other witnesses. The defence tried to prove the old stories of poisoning the spring and the ox, but under cross-examination the perjured witnesses broke down. The Church authorities became alarmed and decided to sacrifice Lee, but no opportunity for communicating with the jury was allowed them. The jury went out, and these nine Mormons, who knew nothing about the case, and had formed no opinions, proceeded to demonstrate from facts within their own knowledge that Lee could not have been guilty. The Gentiles held out for two days, and consented to a disagreement. Then came an era of excitement. The Mormons and their friends through the country claimed that they were vindicated, but the evidence that had been sent out over the wires every day, and printed in every corner of the country, was too strong to be cried down in that way. Public sentiment grew bitter. There were still many who believed that Brigham Young was innocent, but Lee had been proved guilty and should have been punished; he had been saved from punishment by Mormon jurors.

The second trial was a worse farce than the first. In fatal folly the Mormon authorities permitted themselves to be persuaded that they could sacrifice Lee and better their own standing. They forgot that in so doing they must give the lie to their professions of nineteen years. They forgot that they must give testimony which would implicate themselves. They forgot that though a prosecuting attorney may promise immunity, he cannot prevent cross-examination or restrain public opinion. They forgot everything except that the country demanded the punishment of John D. Lee, and they dared no longer refuse it. Of course, Lee was not informed of this. He passed the fourteen months that intervened between his two trials relying on the protestations of friendship

of the leading men.   The first thing was to fix the jury.   A
list of the *venire* was obtained, and submitted, by the defend-
ant's attorneys, to a Mormon committee of professed friends
of Lee, who were to mark with a dash (—) those who would
convict, with an asterisk (*) those who would rather not convict, and with two asterisks (* *) those who would not convict under any circumstances.   There was no trouble in getting that jury.   The defence thought they knew who they
wanted, and the prosecution seemed willing to humor them.
Every juror was a * * man.   The jury was impanelled and
the testimony began.   Then the defence realized that they
were entrapped.   The depositions of Brigham Young and
George A. Smith, which had been objected to by the prosecution in the former trial, were now offered by the prosecution.
Mormons who previously had known nothing of the massacre,
and had aided Lee in the former trial, now became possessed
of remarkable memories—as to Lee.   Samuel Knight, who
lived at Hamlin's, and drove one of the wagons at the massacre, but who formerly knew nothing about the matter, now
recollected that he saw Lee shoot a woman in his wagon.   He
saw a number of white men at the place, but no one that he
knew except Lee.   Nephi Johnson, another shining example
of previous ignorance, now remembered enough as to Lee and
Haight and two or three who were dead, but as to others his
memory was fatally defective.   Finally, under cross-examination, he said : "I don't want to bring in new names."   He was
further tortured sufficiently to cause him to drop the facts
that the few Mormons who objected, at the councils, did not
dare to say anything ; that persons had been injured for not
obeying counsel ; that the whole matter was talked over afterwards, and it was decided to keep it secret.   Jacob Hamlin
recollected that Lee told him all about the massacre, within a
few days after it occurred ; he recounted Lee's story to the
jury.   On cross-examination he remembered that he reported
the matter fully to Brigham Young and George A. Smith,
"pretty soon after it happened," and that Brigham Young
said : "As soon as we can get a court of justice, we will ferret
this thing out, but till then don't say anything about it."   In
accordance with this injunction he kept quiet until the sec-

ond trial. He said: "It is the first time I ever felt any good would come of it. I kept it to myself until it was called for in the proper place. . . . I had an idea that if I came here that it would be a pretty good place to tell it." This man's story to Dr. Forney has been given. To Judge Cradlebaugh and various military officers who investigated the affair he professed to know nothing that would implicate any white man. He did not feel called upon to speak at Lee's first trial. He gave to the jury the statement of the Indian boy Albert, who saw the massacre and the killing of the two girls, yet this boy told Dr. Forney that it was all done by Indians. The inference is irresistible that Hamlin induced him to lie about it, and this although anti-Mormons concede Hamlin to be an unusually honorable Mormon. This boy Albert, by the way, first revealed the fact that the children were brought directly to Hamlin's house on the evening of the massacre. The good people, who had bills for purchasing them from the Indians, had probably forgotten to instruct him on that point.

When Lee heard the testimony of these men he knew that the Church had abandoned him and he was lost. He broke down completely and was taken to his cell, where he paced the floor, cursing the Mormon leaders. The defence offered no testimony; their witnesses of the previous trial had forgotten everything. The jury was out three hours, and brought in a verdict of guilty of murder in the first degree. The prisoner was brought to the bar, and, after a few impressive words, Judge Boreman informed him that, under the statute, he had his choice of being hung, shot, or beheaded. Lee said: "I prefer to be shot." He was accordingly sentenced, and on March 23, 1877, the sentence was executed in the Mountain Meadows, at the scene of the massacre. At the last moment Lee confessed to his attendant minister, Mr. Stokes, that he killed five of the emigrants with his own hands. This was his fourth confession, each one differing from all the others, and yet each one lifting the veil from around the affair enough to give a glimpse of its actual horrors. He made a short speech, declaring his faith in Mormonism, as originally taught by Joseph Smith, and his assurance of a place in the Mormon heaven, but stated that

Brigham Young was leading the people astray. He closed, and sat down on his coffin. A prayer was offered, the word was given, five rifles were discharged, and he fell back without a struggle.

So justice was done—not rightly justice either, for this man was not convicted as men are required to be convicted under our laws. The jury that pronounced him guilty had morally no more right to do so than the Sultan of Turkey had legally. They were murderers as truly as Lee was. John D. Lee was not a victim to justice. He was murdered by his accomplices for their own safety—as much so as if they had shot him themselves. Personally they attained safety, though not as they expected. The greater criminals of the active participants hid for a time in the mountains, and are now probably in foreign countries. Brigham Young died peacefully in his home, five months after Lee's execution. The remainder were not molested. But in the public eye the Mormon Church stands as the guilty criminal, and it seems destined to expiate the crime. In that respect the Mountain Meadows massacre has had a mission. It is the one complete and unanswerable exposure of Mormon deceit, hypocrisy, and crime, under the " higher law " dogma. Every other crime charged against them they can defend, not having admitted their guilt, but in this one they have been forced, step by step, from an indignant denial to a defiant confession. They cannot evade it; their apologists can make no explanation of it; and in its lustration their denials of other crimes become faint and sickly. It is admitted that they are industrious and thrifty, but the American people realize that thrift has its crimes as dark as any of those of dissipation. Jonas Chuzzlewit was thrifty; so was Judas Iscariot. It is true that, according to their standard of virtue, they are fairly virtuous, but the people understand that, under the "higher law," their virtue is, to the civilized world, crime. They understand it so well that the American heart, which warms most quickly to any persecuted for religion's sake, is icy towards the Saints. Only a few weeks since, a murderous attack was made on one of their meetings in Tennessee, and a bitter local persecution followed. Had the

EXECUTION OF JOHN D. LEE.

people assailed been Buddhists, or Brahmins, or Voudooists the country would have been in an uproar of indignation. What comment did it receive? Generally, none; and occasionally a growl that it would be well to follow the example elsewhere. The Mormons are right in their superstition that a Nemesis stands, ever threatening them, on the mountains of Southern Utah. She does stand there, and in her outstretched hands, for the ash-branch and the scourge, she holds a blight and a curse over the doomed theocracy, while from her ghastly lips there comes the murmur of those words, which no prophet can still: " Vengeance is mine, I will repay, saith the Lord."

21

CHAPTER XI.

THE WAR WITH THE SPOKANES, CŒUR D'ALÊNES, AND PELOUSES.

WHILE the commissioners were negotiating with the Mormons, an extraordinary outbreak occurred in the eastern part of Washington Territory, which hitherto had been a scene of peace between the red man and the white. It had been the boast of the Spokanes and the Cœur d'Alênes that they had never shed the blood of a white man. In the winter and early spring of 1858, however, it was represented that there was much restlessness among the northern tribes, especially in the neighborhood of the Colville mines, and Brevet Lieutenant-colonel Steptoe, who commanded at new Fort Walla-Walla, determined to make an excursion in that direction. The new fort, which had been established as a military post after the last war, was on Walla-Walla Creek, thirty miles east of the old fort, the latter being now used as an agency by the quartermaster's department. In addition to looking after the northern inquietude, Colonel Steptoe also desired to investigate the recent murder of two American miners by a party of Pelouse (Paluce, Galousse) Indians, and, if possible, to bring the murderers to justice. These Indians lived just to the north of the Snake River, and were directly in his line of travel. Steptoe left Fort Walla-Walla on May 6th with one hundred and fifty-seven men, dragoons and infantry, the latter acting as gunners for two howitzers which were taken. They marched across the rolling prairies between the Walla-Walla and the Snake to the mouth of the Pelouse, where the crossing of the Colville road was located. From this point they proceeded northward and eastward to the divide between the Snake and the Spokane, and over the Grand Plateau of the Spokane, the Pelouses keeping out of their sight. While winding through the prairie hills that skirt Ingossomen Creek, on Sunday, May 16th, the command was suddenly confronted by about twelve hundred warriors, Pelouses, Spokanes, Cœur d'Alênes, Yakimas, and others, hideous in their war-paint, armed and defiant. This was a complete surprise, for no hostilities had been expected, except there should be some little altercation with the Pelouses. The little command moved on slowly, menaced by the hooting and yelling savages, who seemed desirous of provoking an attack. It approached a small ravine that led around the base of some hills, which were covered with Indians, when, seeing their intention to attack at that point, Colonel Steptoe turned his troops aside and encamped on one of the little watercourses common to this section, which are flowing in the spring and in pools during the drier season. The dragoons remained in the saddle until dark, an attack being expected at any moment from the howling mob, which continued to heap insults upon them. Towards evening several of the chiefs came to the camp to talk, and asked the reason of this invasion of their country. Colonel Steptoe assured them that he had no hostile feeling towards the Spokanes or any other of the friendly tribes; that they had always been our friends, and he desired them to so continue; that he was on his way to Colville to have a friendly talk and preserve peace there. The chiefs said they were satisfied with this, but they would not consent to let him have canoes at the Spokane, without which the crossing could not be made. The colonel therefore decided to fall back to the fort, and, having passed the night without molestation, began his return march in the morning.

On the evening of the 16th, Father Joset, one of the Jesuit missionaries, had arrived at the camp of the Indians from the Cœur d'Alêne Mission. In the morning he came up with the troops and talked over the situation with Colonel Steptoe, the Indians having assembled again and being massed on the flanks and rear of the column in a threatening manner. He proposed a talk with the chiefs, to which the colonel replied that his pack-animals were too wild for him to stop long. Father Joset said they could talk while marching, and the colonel responded that he would see them

in that way willingly. Joset then went for the chiefs, but
could find only Vincent, the head chief of the Cœur d'Alênes.
They came back together, and Vincent received an assurance
that the troops were desirous only of returning to the fort in
peace. He returned to the Indians, who, according to Father
Joset, agreed to go to their homes, and the priest with several chiefs did so, but a few minutes later the Indians opened

THE JESUIT MISSIONARY.

fire on the rear guard, just as they filed into the valley of a
small tributary of Ingossomen Creek. The firing was caused
by Mil-kap-si, a Cœur d'Alêne chief, who became infuriated,
probably because he was not consulted, and struck Victor
and Jean Giene, two other chiefs, who were in favor of going
home. One of his relatives said to him, "What are you
doing? You strike your own people! There are your enemies," pointing to the soldiers, whereupon the Indians com-

menced firing. The troops fell back for three miles more, under a constant fire. They were hampered by their pack-train. The country gave every advantage to the Indians. The stock of ammunition was low, and the raw recruits, of whom there were a number in the command, were firing wildly. It was decided to fall back to Ingossomen Creek, where a good position, with wood and water, could be had, and there make a stand. Two companies under Captain Taylor and Lieutenant Gaston were thrown out as flankers, between whom and the Indians a succession of charges and countercharges was kept up, with loss to both sides. About noon Gaston fell, and his company was driven back in confusion. Half an hour later Captain Taylor was brought in, shot through the neck and mortally wounded. The troops were now close to the crossing of the creek, and Colonel Steptoe at once took position on a small hill, to hold the Indians at bay until night.

The provisions were placed in the centre of the top of the hill, which was flat, and around them the horses and pack-animals were picketed in a circle. In a much larger circle, along the crest of the hill, in skirmish line, were the dismounted men and the howitzers, one at the front and one at the rear. The situation was growing more desperate every minute. The Spokanes were massed on the north, the Cœur d'Alênes on the east, and the Pelouses on the west, covering all the neighboring heights. They took advantage of every hillock, depression, and tuft of grass to work along closer to the hill. The soldiers lay flat on the ground, having no other protection, while the Indians crept closer and closer, and two or three times made ineffectual attempts to charge the hill. The officers crawled from one point to another on their hands and knees, giving orders and encouraging the men. Two of the companies were armed with musketoons, which were of no use for this sort of work, and the cartridges of the remainder were nearly all gone. The wounded were constantly increasing in number. The soldiers were becoming dispirited. At length darkness came, and brought them some relief; but they could not relax their vigilance, and they had before them the certainty that another day's

21*

fighting would result in the destruction of the entire force. A hurried consultation concluded with a decision to retreat with all expedition to the Snake River, and make sure of a crossing before the Indians could reach the same point. Everything that could impede flight was abandoned. The howitzers were buried; the supplies, except such as each man carried, were left on the ground; the disabled animals were left picketed; and between nine and ten o'clock, stealthily, but in good order, the force moved down the hill at the rear, across the creek, and away. Most of the night they rode at a gallop, nor did they stop till they reached the Snake, ninety miles below. There they were met by Timothy's band of friendly Nez Percés, who assisted them in crossing the river. They could not have crossed without their aid. In this affair they lost two officers, five men and three Nez Percés Indians killed, thirteen wounded, and one missing. The Indians admitted a loss of nine killed and forty wounded, but there must have been more; there were twelve dead ones counted at one point where the two flanking companies met in a cross-charge.

The attack on the troops caused much excitement in the West, for war by these tribes, hitherto so peaceable, seemed certain proof of a general outbreak. The expectation of a great war was the more reasonable because no cause could be given for the attack on Steptoe. To this day, with all investigation made and reasons suggested, it is impossible to say certainly why the Spokane and Cœur d'Alêne Indians joined in this assault. It was known that there was discontent and dissatisfaction among them, for some cause, but no one anticipated open hostilities, except, it may be, Father Joset. He stated that he had anticipated trouble, and had started several days before to warn Colonel Steptoe of it, but returned because Chief Vincent feared that the Pelouses would kill the young men who went with him, and charge the Americans with the deed, after which it would be impossible to restrain the Cœur d'Alênes. This priest was accused of furnishing powder to the Indians—a quite improbable story, but believed by many who had not forgotten the Whitman massacre, and explained all Indian disturbances by the influence of the Jesu-

PEND D'OREILLE MISSION.

its and the Hudson's Bay Company. He did give some color
to this report by attempting to put the blame of the outbreak
on the Protestant Nez Percés, who were the best friends the
whites ever had in the North-west. He circulated every tale
the guilty Indians invented concerning them, and related
some experiences of his own which, to say the least, are improbable. ' In a letter to Father Congiato, of June 27, 1858,
he says, " Towards the beginning of April it was learned that
an American had been assassinated by a Nez Percé. Immediately rumor commences to circulate that the troops were
preparing to cross the Nez Percé to obtain vengeance for
this crime." In a letter to Father Hoecken, of June 17th,
ten days earlier, he says Vincent told him the Pelouses and
Nez Percés killed the two miners, who were the only Americans killed by the Indians in that locality. As a matter of
fact, it was well known all through the Indian country that

the Pelouses killed them. Again he says, in his account of his attempted journey of warning to Steptoe, "In the mean time I saw several Nez Percés. Their conversation was generally against the Americans. One of them said in my presence, 'We will not be able to bring the Cœur d'Alênes to take part with us against the Americans; the priest is the cause; it is for this we wish to kill the priest.'" Does a would-be assassin usually notify a desired victim thus? Was an Indian ever known to do such a thing? Aside from its unreasonableness, the Nez Percés were not at war with the Americans, but were acting as auxiliaries to them. Again he says, concerning his visit to Colonel Steptoe with Vincent just before the firing began, "One of the Indians [Nez Percés] who accompanied the troops gave Vincent a blow over the shoulders with his whip, saying to him, 'Proud man, why do you not fire?' then accused one of the Cœur d'Alênes who had followed Vincent of having wished to fire upon a soldier." Such a thing would be very unnatural for a member of a small command, surrounded by an enemy that outnumbered them ten to one. Besides, nothing of the kind occurred. Every effort was made by the entire command to avoid a fight, and the soldiers did not return the fire of the Indians for several minutes. Finally, he taxes credulity by this: "The Cœur d'Alênes say, also, that it was cried to them from the midst of the troops, 'Courage! you have already killed two chiefs;' that one of the Nez Percés who had followed the troops came back to say to his people, 'It is not the Cœur d'Alênes, but, indeed, the soldiers who killed the two Nez Percés.'" The intended presumption is, of course, that one of the Nez Percés made the encouraging call from the hill, but the fact that one-third of the killed, on the side of the troops, were Nez Percés, is sufficient evidence of the feeling between them and the attacking party. The offence of Father Joset may be summed up in this, that in trying to get his wards out of a bad scrape, in which they were placed by their own fault, he strained facts a little in their favor and became a trifle mixed. The hostile Indians took the same line of defence. Milkapsi sent word to General Clarke concerning a proposed talk: "Tell your friends, the Lawyer's

band, to be quiet; if you come with a good mind, let none
of them be along. I want to have a good talk with the soldiers, but I can't when they are along; I don't want to hear
any more of their lies." The Lawyer was celebrated for
his constant friendship to the Americans, and was known
all over the North-west as an unusually reliable Indian. This
talk deceived no one, though it made people distrustful of
both Indians and Jesuits, but there is no ground for supposing that the Jesuits, or any of them, used any influence to
bring on hostilities. There is no doubting that Joset tried
to prevent the attack, or that he and the other priests were
of much service in finally adjusting the difficulty.

The Mormons were a disturbing element, and in all
probability gave active assistance to the Indians, as well as
incendiary instructions. On November 27, 1857, George
Gibbs, Esq., whose name is sufficient guaranty of the truth of
his statements, wrote: " A very curious statement was recently made me by some of the Indians near Steilacoom. They
said that the Klickitats had told them that Choosuklee (Jesus
Christ) had recently appeared on the other side of the mountains; that he was after a while coming here, when the
whites would be sent out of the country, and all would be
well for themselves. It needed only a little reflection to connect this second advent with the visit of Brigham Young to
the Flathead and Nez Percé country." Between the Oregon Indians and Utah were the Snakes, who were in so
close connection with the Mormons that the first knowledge
of Utah affairs at Fort Walla-Walla was usually through the
Indians. On December 1, 1857, Captain Kirkham wrote
from that point: " The Snakes tell our Indians that they
are well supplied with ammunition, and that they can get
from the Mormons any quantity they wish; and they further tell our Indians that the Mormons are anxious to supply them—to wit: the Nez Percés, the Cayuses, and Walla-
Wallas, with everything that they wish. I would not be
surprised if the Mormon influence should extend to all the
tribes in our neighborhood, and if they are determined to
fight we may have trouble among the Indians on the coast
again." These, with numerous similar complaints from oth-

er points, caused General Clarke, commanding the Department of the Pacific, on January 1, 1858, to recommend that all Indians be detached from Mormon influence and control. A singular confirmation of Captain Kirkham's report was made in the following summer, when a band of Bannocks

GENERAL ISAAC I. STEVENS.

committed some depredations on the Mormons of Northern Utah, and gave as a reason for this extraordinary proceeding that the Mormons had sold arms and ammunition to their enemies, the Nez Percés; that the Nez Percés had stolen their property; and that now they were getting reparation from the original source of the evil. It was learned positively that the hostile Indians had large supplies of ammunition, which they could have obtained only from the Mormons or the Hudson's Bay Company's post at Fort Colville. The company's agent exchanged ammunition with the Indians for some of the property abandoned by Colonel Steptoe, but on complaint at their head-quarters both the purchase of plunder and the sale of ammunition were stopped.

The chief basis of discontent was in the treaties agreed on by Governor Stevens with the various tribes, but which had not yet been ratified. The exact nature of the discontent was in controversy. One set of officials kept insisting that the Indians were angry because the treaties were not ratified and carried out, while another set, equally numerous, insisted with equal vehemence that the Indians were angry because they feared that the treaties would be ratified. On October 19, 1857, Colonel Steptoe reported from Fort Walla-Walla, "It is my duty to inform the general that Mr. J. Ross Browne, acting, I believe, as agent of the Indian Bureau, did, in a recent conversation with 'Lawyer,' the Nez Percé chief, assert that Governor Stevens's treaty of Walla-Walla would *certainly* be ratified and enforced. . . . I will simply add that in my opinion any attempt to enforce that treaty will be followed by immediate hostilities with most of the tribes in this part of the country." This information was received with some indignation by General Clarke. He had taken command of the department in June, and soon after had a consultation with Indian Superintendent Nesmith in regard to this very matter. Nesmith told him there were two causes for the hostile feelings then existing. One was that while the Indians understood that amnesty had been granted to the murderers of agent Bolen by Colonel Wright, there was still an endeavor on the part of some civil officers to apprehend them. The other was a fear that the treaties with Governor Stevens would be enforced, although they held them void, on the ground that the chiefs who made them had no authority to do so. On this information the general used his influence to have the treaties left inoperative, and permitted the Bolen murderers to remain at large. "It is under these circumstances," he wrote, in complaint to army head-quarters, "that Mr. J. Ross Browne makes (with what authority I know not) the declaration to the Indians that the treaties will certainly be ratified and enforced."

Mr. Browne was a special agent of the Interior Department, who was sent into Oregon and Washington to inspect the condition of the reservations, and who incidentally reported on the causes of the wars of 1856. He believed that the war resulted from the irrepressible conflict between savagery and civilization. He said, "The treaties were not the cause of the war. I have already shown that the war had been determined upon long before. If Governor Stevens is to blame because he did not so frame the treaties as to stop the war, or stop it by not making treaties at all, then that charge should be specifically brought against him. My own opinion is, that he had no more control over the course of events than the Secretary of War in Washington." Mr. Browne was a pleasing writer and a man of discernment, but like most men who have a fixed idea, to begin with, he was inclined to bend everything to it. Still there was much of truth in his views, as, indeed, there is in everything he has written on the Indian question, but he is at times carried away by enthusiasm. It is not to be supposed that he was alone in his views of the treaties. A large party in the Northwest had the same opinions, and so had several persons who reported specially on the subject. For example, Lieutenant Mullan, who accompanied Colonel Wright in the campaign of which an account follows, after personal investigation, wrote the Commissioner of Indian Affairs on September 5, 1858: "To this day the labors of Governor Stevens are disregarded and uncared for, and the treaties containing the solemn promises of the Indian on the one side, and binding obligation of the government on the other, lie among the dusty archives of Congress, while a war rages in every quarter of the North-west coast. The Indians feel that their rights have been trifled with by promises made by agents armed and vested with authority to act, which the government has not ratified. And will it, I ask, longer remain in this passive mood? Will it longer act inertly [!] while lives are sacrificed and millions squandered, and still longer hesitate to act? For one, I trust not. Let these be ratified."

The cause of this conflict of opinion is found in the fact that the Indians were not agreed as to the treaties. The more friendly Indians, chiefly Nez Percés, wanted the treaties ratified, partly because they thought the whites desired it, and partly because they were ready to adopt a quasi-civilized life. These Indians were more often seen by " visiting statesmen," and were more communicative; in consequence of which their ideas were more apt to be taken as an expression of Indian sentiment by casual visitors. The military, on the other hand, were largely in contact with the Indians who desired to retain their wild life, and were acquainted with their views. The objections of those who opposed the treaties were not to a continuance of friendship, or a surrender of part of their lands, but to the surrender of the entire country of certain tribes and a removal to other locations. Unquestionably those who opposed the treaties were much more numerous than the others. Their view was thus set forth by Garry, the Spokane chief, in a message carried to General Clarke by Father Congiato: " When you [Clarke] meet me, we walk friendly, we shake hands. Two years after you met me, you, American, I heard words from white people, whence I concluded you wanted to kill me for my land. I did not believe it. Every year I heard the same. Now you arrived, you my friend, you, Stevens, in Whitman Valley; you called the Indians to that place. I went there to listen to what should be said. You had a speech—you, my friend Stevens, to the Indians. You spoke for the land of the Indians. You told them all what you should pay them for their land. I was much pleased when I heard how much you offered; annual money, houses, schools, blacksmiths, farms, and so forth. And then you said, all the Cayuses, Walla-Wallas, and Spokanes should emigrate to Layer's [Lawyer, or Hal-al-ho-sote, the Nez Percé chief] country; and from Colville and below all Indians should go and stay to Camayaken's [Kam-i-a-ken, the Yakima chief] country; and by saying so you broke the hearts of all the Indians; and hearing that, I thought that you missed it. Should you have given the Indians time to think on it, and to tell you what portion of the land they wanted to give, it would have been right. Then the Indians got mad and began to kill the whites. I was very sorry all the time. Then you began to war against the Indians. When you began this war all the upper country was quiet. Then every year we heard something from the lower Indians. I told the people hereabout not to listen to such talk. The governor will come up; you will hear from his own mouth; then believe it. Now this spring I heard of the coming of Colonel Steptoe. I did my best to persuade my people not to shoot him. He goes to Colville, I said, to speak to the whites and to the Indians. We will go there and listen to what he shall say. They would not listen to me, but the boys shot at him; I was very sorry."

This difference of opinion among the Indians naturally resulted in perpetual misunderstanding. One Indian would tell a special agent that he wanted the treaties ratified, and would be assured that they should be ratified. Another would explain his objections to the treaties to some officer, and be assured that they should not be ratified. These Indians would then come together and find themselves in a conflict of fact, which showed that some one was deceiving them. Suspicion and discontent grew apace. The treaty Indians wanted the goods and money that had been promised them, but not paid; the opponents of the treaties watched with jealous eye every appearance of an encroachment on their lands. One thing that they desired, and they insisted on it at their council with Stevens, was that "the soldiers should not come north of the Nez Percés River." They did not object much to small parties, but they wanted no large ones, and no cannon. The stream they referred to is the Snake, or Lewis Fork of the Columbia. The Indians called it the Nez Percés, the Pelouse, and the Snake, in the parts which flowed through the countries of those tribes respectively. The whites applied the name "Snake" to it throughout its length, and gave the name Pelouse to its first large affluent, above its mouth, on the north side, otherwise known as Flag River.

With all these causes for discontent, there was still no satisfactory reason for the attack on Steptoe, and this the

VIEW OF THE COLUMBIA ABOVE THE DALLES.

Indians themselves admitted. Says Father Joset to Father Hoecken : "Vincent arrived. I asked him what provocation they had received. 'None; all the fault is on our side.' 'You are the murderers of your own people, not the Americans.' 'It is true. I would rather die as the Americans, as our people are dead. I had no intention to fight, but at seeing the corpse of my brother-in-law I lost my head. What will be the consequences? If we are pardoned we will faithfully restore all that has been taken; if not, we will remain home, and if we are attacked we will defend ourselves to the last, and when we are all killed the Americans will have our lands. Fools that we are, we have always doubted the truth of what the Father told us; now we have seen it. The Americans do not want to fight us.' " Again he says to Father Congiato, "The next day I asked those that I saw, 'What provoca-

tion have you received from the troops?' 'None,' said they.
'Then you are only murderers, the authors of the death of
your own people.' 'This is true; the fault can in no way
be attributed to the soldiers; Malkapsi is the cause of all
the evil.'" There were some, however, who claimed that the
soldiers were the aggressors, because they had come into their
country and brought cannon with them.

One thing, of course, is to be remembered—there were all
degrees of offending, from the active hostile to the almost
neutral, just as there are in every Indian war. The worst of
them all were Kamiaken, his brothers Skloom and Shawawai,
Owhi and his son Qualchian, the Yakima malcontents of 1856,
who had been roaming among the tribes, exciting discontent
and committing depredations where they could. Kamiaken
was the most influential of them all. He was a man of unusual stature and remarkable strength. No man in the tribe
could bend his bow. He was rated the best orator from the
Cascades to the Rockies, and appears to have been inspired
by a patriotic hope of throwing off the supremacy of the
whites. In later years, when his plans were miscarried and
his hopes of a great combination of the Indians against the
common foe dashed to the ground, he refused to return to
his own country, and, apparently broken-hearted, passed the
rest of his days east of the Columbia. The Pelouses were
next in culpability. They were a tribe of about five hundred, living along the north side of the Snake River. They
were in three bands: Que-lap-tip, with forty lodges, camped
usually at the mouth of the Pelouse; So-ie, with twelve lodges,
was located thirty miles below on the Snake; Til-co-ax (Tel-
ga-wax, Til-ca-icks), with thirty lodges, lived at the mouth of
the Snake. The remaining Indians in the country between
the Snake and the Columbia, some half-dozen bands, were
commonly called Spokanes by the whites, but the Indians
gave that name only to the band that lived about the forks of
the Spokane River. This was the location of that old land-
mark "the Spokane House," an old Hudson's Bay Company
fort, which appears on the old maps. The chief of this band
was the celebrated Garry, often called Spokane Garry, who
had been sent by Sir George Simpson to the Red River set-

CHARGE OF CAVALRY AT FOUR LAKES.

tlements for education at the age of twelve years. He lived there five years. At this time he was about forty-five years of age, was intelligent, spoke English well, and had more control over his Indians than any chief in the North-west. He and his band usually dressed in the fashion of civilization and were still Protestants in religion. Their conversion was the work of Reverends Walker and Eels, who established the Mission of Ishimakin (Chemakane, Cimiakin) while Whitman and Spalding were laboring among the Cayuses and Nez Percés. This Mission was on a little tributary of the Spokane a few miles west of Garry's village, and was abandoned after the Whitman massacre. There was considerable coolness between the Spokanes and their then allies the Cœur d'Alênes, whose country joined them on the east, on account of religious differences, but they lived at peace with each other. The latter numbered about one hundred lodges and were under Vincent, who has been mentioned.

The Indians must be punished—that was evident—and active preparations were begun for putting a large force into the field. The priests came down and waited on General Clarke, to explain the situation and offer their services in smoothing " the wrinkled front of war." Father Joset and Father Congiato, who was at the head of the Jesuit Missions, were sent back to the hostiles with instructions to tell them that the general did not ask permission to send troops through their country—that was his right; that he did not ask them to permit the road to be built through their country from the Missouri—that was the right of the government; but if they desired peace they must drive Kamiaken and all other hostiles of other tribes from their country, return all the property taken from Steptoe's troops, and surrender the men who first fired on the troops in disobedience to their chiefs. To these terms, especially the surrender of the prisoners, the Indians were not ready to submit. Their replies were written down and sent back by the priests. Polot-kin (Saulotken, a Spokane) said, " The practice of the Indians is different from what you think; when they want to make peace, when they want to cease hostilities, they bury the dead and live again on good terms. They don't speak of more blood. I speak sincerely, I, Saulotken, let us finish the war; my language shall not be twofold; no; I speak from the heart. If you disapprove my words you may despise them. I speak the truth; I, Indian; I don't want to fight you. You are at liberty to kill me, but I will not deliver my neighbors. If it should be my practice, I would do according to it, and deliver them. But that's a practice of your own." Milkapsi said, "I feel unwilling to give you up my three brother, for I think though we fought, I won't begin to make peace. I want you to begin if you want to make peace; come into my country." Garry said, "You ask some to be delivered up. Poor Indian can't come to that. But withdraw this one word, and sure you will make peace." In fact, the Indians were more defiant than these messages would indicate. Agent Owen, who was among the hostiles on the Spokane, and could not get away without endangering his life, wrote on July 16th, "I have just returned from one of the blackest councils, I think, that has ever been held on the Pacific slope. Five hundred fighting men were present, elated with their recent success; the dragoon horses were prancing around all day; the scalp and war dance going on all night long." He reported the Indians as saying, "Let Steptoe come; bring plenty of men; it will be dark, too dark to see; father and son will fall together. We will meet him on Snake River; burn the grass around and before him. We want more fine horses; the soldiers are the people we want to take them from. Steptoe may want peace; has he sent you here to ask for it? If so let us know on what terms. We will consider his proposition; perhaps we will make peace."

Preparations for the campaign were not delayed while the Fathers were on their mission. All available troops were brought up from California, and the 6th and 7th infantry were ordered across from Utah. Colonel George Wright, commanding at the Dalles, was put in command of the main column, which was to move from Fort Walla-Walla. At the same time a smaller column, having for its base Fort Simcoe, on the Yakima, was to scour the country north and west of the Columbia, and drive all the hostiles to the other side. It required some weeks to prepare for the march, as the stock of supplies at Fort Walla-Walla was very low and everything had to be transported overland. A steamboat had been running on the Columbia above the Dalles, but it had recently gone over the cascades, and there was left no available means of transportation by water. The friendly Indians along the river were talked to and presented with medals. Among others thus munificently rewarded was Spencer, the unfortunate chief whose family had been so mercilessly murdered during the last war, and who yet had remained firm in his friendship to the whites. On August 4th a treaty of alliance, offensive and defensive, was made with the Nez Percés under Lawyer, Timothy, Joseph, Eagle from the Light, Captain John, and others, and thirty of them volunteered to accompany the expedition. On the 7th the column moved. It consisted of five hundred and seventy regulars besides the friendly Indians and one hundred employés, with two six-pounders and two howitzers. They struck the Snake at the mouth of the Toukannon, three miles above the mouth of the Pelouse, and there built Fort Taylor and established a ferry. One company was left as a garrison, with most of the supplies, and the remainder, after spending three days in crossing, marched on northward. They found the grass burned for about twenty miles back from the river, but beyond that it was undisturbed. No resistance was offered to them, though they occasionally caught sight of parties of the hostiles, until September 1st.

The troops were then camped on the south side of the Four Lakes, ten or twelve miles south-west of Lahto or Ned-whuald Creek, a tributary of the Spokane. The largest lake is at the west, the second in size is two miles or more east of it; between them lie the two smaller ones, which are about equal in extent, one of them half a mile north of the other. At the north-western corner of the second lake is a high hill, on which the Indians were seen in force on the morning of the 1st. Colonel Wright at once prepared to advance against them. Two companies of dragoons, under Major Grier, were sent around the hill on the west side to cut off retreat; two companies of riflemen, one howitzer, and the Nez Percés were

22*

thrown to the right between the hill and the lake; and four companies of infantry, under Captain Keyes, charged the hill from the south-west. The Indians retired before him, and on gaining the summit it was seen that the woods on the north-eastern base were full of Indians, while on the open plain to the north-west were four or five hundred mounted warriors, riding furiously to and fro, and apparently eager for a fight. The riflemen dashed through the woods on the east, driving the Indians before them to the open plain. Captain Keyes's command advanced steadily down the hill until they passed the dragoons, who dismounted and followed in the rear, leading their horses, until well on the plain. They then mounted and charged the Indians, who fled in every direction and were soon out of reach. They had lost about twenty killed and a number wounded. The troops had met with no casualty of any kind.

On the 5th the troops moved northward again. They passed the lakes, and, two miles beyond, entered the open prairie, where the Indians soon appeared, moving to intercept the force before it reached the next timber. They fired the grass on both sides and in front, quickly surrounding the little army with smoke and flame, under cover of which some seven hundred warriors opened fire on them. An advance was ordered, and the dragoons rode through the flames, chasing the Indians back to the forests. The pack train with its guard moved forward as speedily as practicable, and at every available point the howitzers opened fire, driving the Indians from their cover. The command was kept as much concentrated as possible, and charges were made from the lines at every opportunity. In this way the troops marched north for five miles, and north-east seven, going into camp below the mouth of the Lahto, after a march of twenty miles without water, fourteen of it under fire. The fighting lasted seven hours, and resulted in a loss to the hostiles of two chiefs and many warriors, including two brothers of Garry. The only casualty to the troops was one man wounded.

The Indians were now much discouraged. On the morning of the 7th they called across the Spokane that Garry wanted to talk with the colonel. An interview was granted,

FALLS OF THE SPOKANE.

in which Colonel Wright told him, "I did not come into this country to ask you to make peace; I came to fight. Now, when you are tired of the war, and ask for peace, I will tell you what you must do. You must come to me with your arms, with your women and children, and everything you have, and lay them at my feet; you must put your faith in me, and trust to my mercy. If you do this I shall then dictate the terms upon which I will grant you peace. If you do not do this, war will be made on you this year and next, and until your nation shall be exterminated." Garry went away, and soon Polotkin, who had led in the battles of the 1st and 5th, and had been conspicuous in the fight with Steptoe, came over with nine warriors. This chief was held as a prisoner, and also one of his men, who was recognized as having been recently at Walla-Walla with Father Ravalli, and was strongly suspected of being one of the murderers of the two miners.

On the 8th the march up the Spokane was continued. After proceeding nine miles, a great dust was observed in front and to the right, and Major Grier was despatched towards it with three companies of dragoons and the Nez Percés, Colonel Wright following with a part of the infantry. The dragoons found the commotion to be caused by the Indians driving their herds into the mountains; they charged, and after a brief skirmish succeeded in capturing eight hundred horses. The command then went into camp on the river. The case of the Indian taken with Polotkin was examined into, and it being found that he was one of the murderers, he was hung at sunset. On the next day Colonel Wright, finding it impracticable to keep the captured horses with him, many of them being very wild, selected a few to replace broken-down animals in the command, and ordered the rest shot. The slaughter took up that day and the next, and during its progress the troops also killed a large number of cattle and destroyed several barns full of grain, and many caches of camas and other roots, berries, and other supplies. The horses belonged to and constituted almost the entire wealth of Tilcoax, the Pelouse chief, so that the blow fell in a good place. He had never been friendly, and for more than two years he and his young men had been stealing horses and cat-

tle from the settlements, as he boldly admitted to Colonel
Steptoe. On the 10th a messenger came from Father Joset
saying that the hostiles were "down and suing for peace,"
which caused a cessation of the work of destruction for the
time.

The army moved on up the Spokane, without any resistance, to the north-western extremity of Cœur d'Alêne Lake,
and thence around the north-eastern side of the lake, over
one of those most difficult of all highways, a mountain Indian
trail. It was encumbered with fallen trees and bowlders below, and obtrusive branches above, to such an extent that the
expedition was obliged to move in single file almost the entire distance to the Mission, which is thirty-one miles from
the outlet of the lake. This Mission was established in 1841,
on St. Joseph's River, but owing to overflows in that valley
it was removed, in 1846, to its permanent location, on the
right bank of the Cœur d'Alêne River, a sluggish stream
one hundred yards wide and twenty-five feet deep. The
Mission is on a small hill, a fragment of an east and west
spur of the Bitter Root Mountains, looking towards the north;
below it is a small prairie, a mile in width and three in
length, which at this time was under cultivation in crops of
wheat, oats, barley, and vegetables, and dotted here and there
with houses and barns. The principal building, the Church
of the Sacred Heart, was quite an imposing edifice for such a
location. The church proper was forty-six feet wide and
sixty feet long, with thirty feet more in length, supported by
heavy pillars. It was designed by Father Ravalli, formerly a
professor of chemistry and philosophy in the Jesuit College
at Rome, and was two years in construction. The only workmen were the priests and a few Indians, having for tools a
saw, an auger, an ax, and an old jack-plane. To the left of
the church was the house of the priests, and again to the left
were the storehouse, hospital, workshop and a building for
the use of the Indians. The lake about which the country
of the Cœur d'Alênes lies is some fifteen miles west of the
Mission. It is irregular in shape, thirty miles long, varying
in width from one to five miles. It is embosomed in beautiful mountains. The shores that are protected from the pre-

CŒUR D'ALÊNE MISSION. (FROM THE PAINTING BY STANLEY.)

vailing winds shelve rapidly; the exposed ones are shallow, with a pebbly beach extending a short distance out. It has two principal feeders, the St. Joseph's and the Cœur d'Alêne, both deep streams with scarcely any current. This is caused by the nature of the outlet of the lake, the Spokane River, which at a point ten miles west of the lake is confined in a narrow rock cañon, where it has an abrupt fall of eight or ten feet, known as the Upper Falls. Above this natural dam the water is really back-water, extending for a consider- able distance up the principal feeders. It also causes quite extensive marshes, and in the spring season produces general overflows, the water having no ready outlet. The streams and lake abound in trout and are great resorts for water- fowl, as also are the marshes. The hills, which were largely covered with forests of pine and fir, abounded in large game. Such was the home of the Cœur d'Alênes, a tribe of about five hundred, of whom one hundred and thirty could bear arms. Their country was not easily accessible, and they were very jealous of intrusion, not even permitting the French Canadians of the Hudson's Bay Company to enter it. Probably for this reason they received their name Cœur d'Alêne—Heart of an Awl, or, as it is more commonly ren- dered, Pointed Heart. They were brave and warlike, and had many horses and cattle.

On the 17th, some four hundred Indians having assem- bled at the Mission, a council was held and Colonel Wright imposed his own terms, which were that they should surren- der the men who began the attack on Steptoe; give up all property, public or private, in their hands, that had been taken from the whites; permit whites to pass through their country unmolested; and give a chief and four men, with their families, as hostages. These terms were accepted, and on the next day the march around the lake was resumed. The Cœur d'Alêne and St. Joseph's were both ferried, and from the latter, which enters the southern extremity of the lake, the troops marched south-west to the Lahto. There, on the 23d, the Spokanes were met in council. Garry and Polot- kin were both present. There were with them some Calispels or Pend d'Oreilles (this name was probably Pendues Oreilles, or Hung Ears, originally), and members of other small tribes. Milkapsi was there also. He had lost all his haughtiness, and begged to be admitted to peace with the rest. His prayer was granted, but Colonel Wright took occasion to remind him of his letter to General Clarke, and call his attention to the fact that the whites were not asking for peace. The Spokanes were all very penitent, and made fervent promises of future good behavior. They were treated with on the same terms as the Cœur d'Alênes.

While these movements were being made, Major Garnett had marched up the Yakima in search of the few hostiles who were on the west side of the Columbia. They were chiefly Yakimas, with a few Pelouses and other renegades. On the morning of August 15, 1858, Lieut. J. K. Allen, a popular and efficient young officer, with fifteen men, surprised the camp of Ka-ti-ho-tes, one of the hostile chiefs, and captured twenty-one men, fifty women and children, seventy-five horses, fifteen cattle, and all their other property. Lieutenant Allen was killed in the surprise; it is probable that in the darkness, it being at three o'clock in the morning, he was accidentally shot by one of his own men. Three of the warriors captured were found to have been in the party that murdered the two miners, and were shot. Another of the murderers had been killed while trying to escape during the surprise. It was ascertained of these Indians that twenty-five in all were engaged in the attack on the miners. On the 21st a detachment of sixty men went up one of the branches of the We-nat-che River, and, with the assistance of Ski-nar-wan, a friendly chief, succeeded in entrapping five more of the murderers, all of whom were shot. Another was found alone in the forest, and killed by the soldiers. A great terror fell upon all the wrong-doers. One of the murderers of Agent Bolen committed suicide. Six of the murderers of the two miners fled into the fastnesses of the Cascade Mountains; the remainder escaped across the river and joined Kamiaken.

On the evening of the 23d, Owhi, the hostile Yakima chief, came into Colonel Wright's camp on the Lahto. He said he had come from the lower Spokane, and had left his son Qualchian there. Qualchian was an Indian that Colonel Wright wanted. He had been actively engaged in murders and robberies since 1855, besides stirring up discontent among the friendly Indians. In the preceding June he had been severely wounded in an attack on some miners on the We-nat-che, but had recovered quickly and at once resumed his evil course. Owhi was put in irons, and word was sent to Qualchian to come in at once; that if he did not come his father would be hung. He arrived at nine o'clock the next morning, and at half-past nine was hung. From this camp three troops of dragoons were sent to Steptoe's battle-ground. They brought in the two abandoned howitzers, and also the remains of Captain Taylor and Lieutenant Gaston, which were conveyed to Fort Walla-Walla for burial.

On the 25th a number of Pelouses came into the camp. They represented that they had been with the hostiles, but that Kamiaken had fled over the mountains and they had seceded from him. The colonel seized fifteen of them, all of whom, on investigation, were found to have left their own country and waged war against the United States. In the troubles of 1856, which he had settled so leniently as to arouse the resentment of the Oregonians, Colonel Wright had promised these Indians severe punishment if found again with the hostiles. He accordingly hung six of the worst ones and kept the remainder in irons. On the 26th the command proceeded south-westerly to the Pelouse. Here, on the 30th, all of the Pelouses remaining in the country were met in council. Colonel Wright addressed them, reproaching them severely for their thefts and murders, and demanded the murderers of the miners among them. One man was produced, and hung at once. All the property taken from the whites was then restored. The prisoners seized as Pelouses were brought out, and three, who were found to be renegade Yakimas and Walla-Wallas, were hung. A chief and four warriors, with their families, were demanded as hostages, and surrendered. It was then announced to the Indians that no treaty would be made with them at that time, but if they did as commanded, a treaty would be made in the following spring; they were ordered to allow whites to pass through their country unmolested, and to apprehend and deliver into custody any of their nation guilty of theft or murder. This they agreed to do, and, after warning them that if he ever had to come into their country again he would annihilate them, Colonel Wright dismissed them. The objects of the expedition being now accomplished, half of the troops were left temporarily at Fort Taylor, and the remainder rendezvoused at Fort Walla-Walla, where they were reviewed on October 5th by Colonel Mansfield, Inspector-general of the Army.

Thus ended one of the most remarkable Indian campaigns ever known. In it two battles and a number of skirmishes occurred, all resulting in the defeat of the Indians with heavy losses; about one thousand horses and many cattle were captured, and either destroyed or confiscated; enormous quantities of supplies of the hostiles were destroyed; eleven murderers and robbers were executed; the Indians who commenced the hostilities were surrendered; three large tribes and several small ones were reduced to abject submission; hostages were given by each tribe for their good behavior; and all this without the loss of a man. The expedition of Major Garnett resulted in the punishment of ten of the murderers, and greatly aided in the successful issue of Colonel Wright's movement, but it met with some loss, chiefly in the untimely death of Lieutenant Allen. Still a further and more signal result of this war was yet to come. Lawyer wrote from Walla-Walla to Governor Stevens, then in Washington, as follows: "At this place, about three years since, we had our talk, and since that time I have been waiting to hear from our big father. We are very poor. It is other people's badness. It is not our fault, and I would like to hear what he has to say. If he thinks our agreement good our hearts will be thankful. Colonel Wright has been over after the bad people, and has killed some of the bad people and hung sixteen; and now I am in hopes we will have peace." The letter was submitted to the Department of the Interior. There was a general move in favor of the ratification of the treaties. Lieutenant Mullan, who was with Stevens in the railway exploration, reiterated his prayers to the department in that behalf. Superintendent Nesmith, who had strenuously opposed them, now wrote that "after a careful investigation of the subject" he was satisfied that the treaties ought to be ratified, the country thrown open fully for settlement, and the Indians removed to reservations. The Indians, completely cowed, were ready to do anything to please the whites. With every force favoring the movement there was no longer reason for delay, so, on March 8, 1859, the Senate ratified the treaties with the Dwamish and their allies, the S'Klallams, the Makahs (of Cape Flattery), the Walla-Wallas, Cayuses, and Umatillas, the Yakimas, Pelouses, Klickitats, and their allies, the Nez Percés, the Des Chutes, Wascoes, and their allies, the Qui-nai-elts, the Flatheads, Kootenais, and Pend d'Oreilles, and the Molels. Thus, Governor Stevens was vindicated at last, to his own satisfaction, and the North-west was put at peace for many years. Nevertheless it is true that peace could not have been made in 1856 if these treaties had been insisted on, and that war would have resulted from any attempt to enforce them during two years afterwards. The trouble was not that the general provisions of the treaties were not good, but that they provided for removing part of the tribes entirely from their native homes to the country of others. In fact this provision was not enforced for years after the treaties were ratified, and it produced trouble when it was enforced, as we shall see hereafter. There is little room for doubting that Garry was right in his theory, that in this particular Stevens "missed it."

23

CHAPTER XII.

DEATH TO THE APACHE!

No more serious phase of the Indian problem has presented itself to the American people than that offered by the Apache tribes. Aided by the desert nature of their country, they have resisted the advance of the whites longer than any other Indian nation. They have fought with bravery and inconceivable cunning. They have committed atrocities that devils alone would seem capable of, and have been subjected to atrocities that devils might blush to commit. They have made their name a terror and a thing of execration to a section of country five times larger than all New England. They have kept miners for years from treasure deposits that have been regarded as of fabulous richness. They have gained the reputation of being the most treacherous, cruel, and inhuman savages that have been known in the United States. People who have been willing to extend sympathy and assistance to other Indians, have stood aghast at the murderous work of the Apaches, and given their opinions that nothing but the extermination of the tribe could ever rid Arizona and New Mexico of a constant liability to outrage and devastation. In noteworthy connection with this reputation is the fact that the Apaches are among the least known of the Indian tribes. Not only has their hostile attitude prevented white men from associating with them, but even when brought in contact with the whites they maintain a jealous reserve as to their habits, particularly those of a religious character. By way of example, it is commonly believed that they do not bury their dead, and never touch a dead body except in case of necessity ; yet Colonel Cremony, who had excellent opportunity for knowing, insists that they bury their more prominent men, at least, with great ceremony, though he was unable to learn exactly what the formalities were.

The Apaches, as has been previously mentioned, speak the same language as the Navahos and Lipans; and all Southern Indians using this common tongue are often called Apaches. The Apaches proper call themselves "Shis Inday," or People of the Woods, a rather strange name for a tribe living in a country where three trees constitute a *bosque* or forest, but taken by them probably because the principal timber growth of the region is on the mountains which have long afforded them safe retreats. They were in nine tolerably distinct tribes through the earlier part of the present century, though by confederations and factional separations, in the course of their long warfare, some of this identity has been lost. At the beginning of our intercourse with them they were best divided as follows: Chiricahuas (Chiricagüis), Gileños, Mimbreños, Mescaleros, Jicarillas (Xicarillas, Hickorias), Pinaleños, Mogollons, Coyotéros, and Tontos. These names refer chiefly to their geographical positions. The Chiricahuas lived in South-eastern Arizona, about the Chiricahua Mountains. They are sometimes called Cochees, from their noted chief Cochise or Cheis, who was gathered to his fathers several years since, much to the relief of neighboring settlers. East of these, in the mountains about the headwaters of the Gila, was a small band of about two hundred warriors, known as the Gileños or Gila Apaches. The name Gileños is also sometimes used generically, including two or three additional tribes. North-east of these, in South-western New Mexico, lived the Mimbreños or Mimbres (Miembres —Willows) Apaches, otherwise known as the Copper Mine Apaches, from the fact that they infested the celebrated copper mines of Santa Rita del Cobré. To the east, beyond the Rio Grande, and west of the Pecos, dwelt the Mescaleros, who derived their appellation from their extensive use of the mescal (maguey, American aloe, or century-plant) for food, and in the manufacture of the intoxicating drink known by the same name. The Jicarillas lived in the mountains of Northern New Mexico, above Taos, and were closely associated with the Southern Utes. North-west of the Chiricahuas

was a tribe sometimes called the Pinaleños or Pinal (Penole)
Apaches, and sometimes the Arivapas (Aribaipais), from the
Rio Arivapa which flows on the south-west of the Pinal
range to the Gila. The Mogollons (Mogayones) lived directly north of these in the Mogollon Mountains and the deserts
about them. Westward along the Gila River, and through
the country north of it, roamed the Coyotéros, the most considerable of the tribes, who are said to have their name from
their habit of eating the coyote or prairie wolf. It is possible,
however, that the name is a corruption of Garrotéros (club
men) which was formerly applied to some of the western
tribes. The Tontos, who lived chiefly in the rough country
south and west of Bill Williams Mountain, say that they
broke off from the Coyotéros many years ago, and that their
Indian name, which means "unruly," has been corrupted into
the Spanish word *tonto*, which means "stupid."

No little confusion has arisen from the numerous names,
of different languages, given to these and kindred tribes.
The Indians east of the Pecos, called Llaneros or Apaches,
are properly Lipans. They have always been confederated
with the Comanches and Kiowas in our dealings with them,
and are now located in Indian Territory with those tribes.
The Faraones or Taracones, mentioned in old Spanish books,
were probably Navahos; the word *Yutajenne* is given as the
Apache synonym of the name, and *Yutajenne* or *Yutakah* is
the Apache name for the Navahos. The Yampais or Yavipais are now known as Apache Mohaves. The Cajuenches
were probably the same as the Cuchanos or Yumas. The
Hualapais (Hualpies, Wallapais) have been called Apache
Yumas since 1868, when that name was given them by General Gregg, who was then commanding in Arizona.

The Apaches were always known as wild Indians. It is
doubtful if the Spaniards ever obtained any control over
them, and certain that the Mexicans never retained any.
Between these two peoples there was almost continuous war.
The condition of the people of the Northern Mexican settlements was such that there was little chance of successful
opposition to the Apaches. They were poor, and hardly
more advanced in knowledge than their Indian enemies.

The central government exacted heavy taxes from them, but did nothing for their protection. The supreme power in their settlements was in the hands of the *ricos* or wealthy men, who often resisted the government and often contended among themselves. Some of the *ricos* were of quite pure Spanish blood, but the great mass of the people were the mongrel Mexicans, and these were nearly all in the state of peonage or bondage for debt. As a general rule it was found cheaper and more consonant with the warlike spirit of the Mexicans to buy peace of the Apaches than to fight them. Instead of uniting and making an effort for common defence, it was usually the case that when the State of Chihuahua was at war with the Indians, the State of Sonora would be at peace, and vice versa. The property and even the captives taken in the one State would be purchased in the other. General Carasco, military governor of Sonora after the Mexican war, on one occasion broke into this system. Sonora was at war with the Apaches, and Chihuahua was not only at peace but also was issuing rations to them quarterly at the village of Janos, near our border. Carasco advanced on this place by night marches, and succeeded in surprising them during the feasting that ensued upon the issue of rations. He killed a number and took ninety prisoners. Medina, the governor of Chihuahua, made complaint to the general government of this breach of inter-state customs, but the authorities sustained Carasco. This was a fortunate decision for the Northern Mexicans, for Carasco did more to protect their frontier than any ruler they had for years. He impressed the poor as soldiers, and forced the rich to supply the means for keeping them in the field. His methods were unpopular, however, and he was poisoned.

Many anecdotes are related by travellers of the poltroonery of the Mexicans in their contests with the Apaches. It is not strange that they appeared cowardly. They were poor, without organization, and with nothing in life to stimulate them to bravery. They were obliged to support themselves mainly by agriculture and stock-raising, and these pursuits put them continually on the defensive, while they scattered the people so as to make defence difficult. The Americans who went into the Apache country prior to our conquest were on a different footing from the Mexicans. They were chiefly trappers or traders, and though many of them had Mexican wives or mistresses, quite as many had their mar-

ital companions from among the Indians, while their business interests were quite diverse. The traders had more cause for sympathy with the Mexicans than the trappers, and yet the traders were so seldom attacked that the Mexicans accused them of having treated secretly with the Apaches. Their immunity was really due to constant preparation for attack; the Apaches never attack except by surprise. The trappers acted with one side or the other, or remained neutral, as their temporary interests demanded.

In 1837 the Mexicans of both Sonora and Chihuahua were at war with the Apaches, and both were becoming desperate over the successful incursions of the enemy. Chihuahua promulgated a law called the *Proyecto de Guerra*, or project for war, by which the State offered one hundred dollars for the scalp of an Apache warrior, fifty for the scalp of a squaw, and twenty-five for that

AN APACHE WARRIOR.

of a child. Sonora was also paying a bounty for scalps,
and both gave to the captor any booty he might take from
the Indians This liberality was produced mainly by the
many atrocities of Juan José, a Mimbres chief, who had
been educated among the Mexicans, and used his knowledge
of their customs to great advantage in his warfare.   One
favorite scheme of his was robbing the mails, for the purpose of obtaining information as to the plans of the Mexicans. At this time there were several parties of trappers
on the head-waters of the Gila, and the captain of one of
these, a man named Johnson, undertook to secure a number
of Apache scalps. It is said that in addition to the scalp
bounty he was induced to this by pay from the owners of the
Santa Rita copper mines. At any rate he made a feast and
invited to it a number of Mimbreño warriors, who accepted
his hospitable bidding. To one side of the ground where his
feast was spread he placed a howitzer, loaded to the muzzle
with slugs, nails, and bullets, and concealed under sacks of
flour and other goods. In good range he placed a sack of
flour, which he told the Indians to divide among themselves.
Unsuspicious of wrong, they gathered about it. Johnson
touched his lighted cigarrito to the vent of the howitzer, and
the charge was poured into the crowd, killing and wounding
many. The party of trappers at once followed up the attack
with their rifles and knives. A goodly number of scalps
were secured, that of Juan José among others, but the treachery was terribly repaid. Another party of fifteen trappers
was camped on a stream a few miles distant. The surviving
Mimbreños went to these unsuspecting men and murdered
every one of them. Their vengeance did not stop at this.
The copper mines of Santa Rita were furnished with supplies
from the city of Chihuahua by guarded wagon-trains (con-
ductas) that brought in provisions and hauled back ore. The
time for the arrival of the train came and passed, but no train
appeared. Days slipped away; provisions were almost exhausted; the supply of ammunition was nearly gone. Some
of the miners climbed to the top of Ben Moore, which rises
back of the mines, but from its lofty summit no sign of an
approaching *conducta* was visible. Starvation was imminent.

The only hope of escape for the miners and their families was in making their way across the desert expanse that lies between the mines and the settlements. They started, but the Apaches, who had destroyed the train, hung about them, and attacked them so persistently that only four or five succeeded in reaching their destination.

The scalp bounty was not always so effective in procuring the death of Apaches as in this case. A few years after our conquest, when the vigilance committees of California had filled Arizona with the most villainous collection of white men that ever breathed, there was enacted a comic tragedy in which the principal performer was John Gallantin. He was a desperate scoundrel, and had gathered about him a band of cut-throats whose infamous characters were excelled only by his own. The governor of Chihuahua undertook to make these men useful to the State by paying them thirty dollars for each Apache scalp they secured. They brought scalps in profusion, but the Apache raids were nowise diminished. On the contrary, large numbers of Mexicans and friendly Indians were assassinated and scalped in the midst of the settlements. The suspicions of the Chihuahuans were excited, and Gallantin was at length discovered taking the scalps of some Mexicans whom his people had murdered. This accounted for the extraordinary activity of "the Apaches," and Gallantin and his band left the country. They gathered up some twenty-five hundred sheep as they went along, and with these made their way to the Colorado at the mouth of the Gila. They were met with professions of great friendship by the Yumas, who were then (1851) commanded by Caballo en Pelo (Naked Horse), a chief of great prowess. Having placed themselves in favorable positions in the camp of the desperadoes, the Yumas suddenly fell upon them and murdered the entire party. The scalp-bounty system was not given up by the Mexicans, and, what is more remarkable, man-hunters were allowed to pursue their occupation on our side of the line for the scalp markets of Chihuahua and Sonora. In 1870 Lieutenant Drew was visited by such a party from Janos, Chihuahua, who coolly proposed to massacre the Indians who were then under his protection, preparatory to going on a reservation. He said,

BLACK KNIFE. (FROM THE PAINTING BY STANLEY.)

" These people do not care a straw for the depredations committed in this or any other country ; they work for the money a scalp brings, and one from a friendly Indian is worth as much as one of any other." Orders were soon after issued which lessened this business as an international commerce.

When the Americans invaded the country during the Mexican war, the Apaches welcomed them as allies, though their professions of friendship were not much believed. At San Lucia Springs, near the Santa Rita mines, General Kearny was met by Mangas Colorado (Red Sleeves—in defective Spanish), chief of the Mimbreños, who vowed eternal friendship to the Americans. It was noticed, however, that they kept shy of howitzers, and that one of them wore a shirt made of a Henry Clay campaign flag, which doubtless signified a dead American somewhere. The Apaches were overwhelmed with admiration of our soldiers and their weapons. Said one of their chiefs to General Kearny, as they prepared to leave, " You have taken New Mexico and will soon take California; go, then, and take Chihuahua, Durango, and Sonora. We will help you. You fight for land ; we care nothing for land; we fight for the laws of Montezuma and for food. The Mexicans are rascals ; we hate and will kill them all." This feeling, though somewhat advantageous to us during war, was a disadvantage as soon as peace was made. We were bound by the treaty of Guadalupe Hidalgo to protect our newly-acquired Mexican citizens, and also to prevent our Indians from depredating in Mexico. Americans who settled in New Mexico lived, of course, in the Mexican settlements, and had interests much in common with the Mexicans. The Apaches in the neighborhood of these settlements were not very troublesome for several years, but the western bands pursued their old vocation of plunder with unabated vigor. The settlers below the Gila, and the emigrants who passed over the southern road, retained their lives and property only by eternal vigilance.

After the massacre of the miners, the Mimbreños held possession of the Santa Rita mines for a dozen years undisturbed. The place became known as their great stronghold, and no white men were able to break through its surrounding wilds.

In 1850 there came an invasion. The American half of the
Mexican Boundary Commission, under charge of Mr. J. R.
Bartlett, decided to make the copper mines their head-quarters for a time, and a force of three hundred men took possession of the place. The Mimbreños, under the leadership
of their great war-chief Cuchillo Negro, or Black Knife, were
disposed to resist at first, but thought better of it, and received the Americans with professions of friendship. A short
time after the commission was established in these quarters,
there came along three Mexican traders, who had been among
the Pinal Apaches, and purchased of them a young Mexican
girl named Inez Gonzales. This girl, who was about fifteen
years old, had been a captive for nine months. Her parents
lived at the town of Santa Cruz, whence she had started in
company with her aunt and others, with an escort of soldiers,
to attend the feast of San Francisco at Magdalena. They
were ambushed by the Pinaleños; the men were killed, and
the women and children carried away. The Mexicans were
taking her to Santa Fé, probably to sell her or to keep her for
immoral purposes, as was the common practice with female
slaves. Mr. Bartlett had no hesitancy as to releasing her,
inasmuch as the United States had expressly agreed, in the
treaty of Guadalupe Hidalgo, to release all such captives and
to suppress the traffic in them. Inez was returned to her
parents by the commissioner when he arrived in Santa Cruz.
She subsequently became the mistress of Captain Gomez, who
commanded the troops in Northern Sonora. He married her
on the death of his wife, and after his death Inez married the
Alcalde of Santa Cruz, her social standing not having been at
all affected by her romantic adventures.

The release of this captive did not directly affect the Indians, but a few days later two Mexican boys, who were held
as slaves by the Mimbreños, took refuge in the tent of Colonel Cremony, with the commission, and appealed to him to
save them from their masters. These children, Saverro Aredia and José Trinfan, had heard the Indians speaking of the
release of Inez, and determined to seek the same protection.
Protection was given to them. There were some indications
that the Apaches, thwarted in recovering them, might murder

them, and on account of this Mr. Bartlett sent them away at
night, under guard, to the camp of General Condé, the
Mexican commissioner. Condé at once forwarded them into
Mexico. The Mimbreños were very indignant at this summary release of their property—a rather inconsistent interference, too, at a time when the Fugitive Slave Law had just
gone into operation—but after holding a council, and being
informed that they could not help themselves, they concluded
to accept about two hundred and fifty dollars' worth of goods
for the two boys.

As this institution of slavery in the West has been the
cause of much trouble with the Indians, a glance at its features and extent will be advantageous in considering the difficulties between the two races. The system obtained with all
the tribes of the Rocky Mountains, and also with the Kiowas and Comanches who sprang from mountain stocks. Instead of dooming their captives to death, or adopting them
into their tribes, as the Eastern Indians did, they held them
for barter and the performance of menial duties. The slave
was the property of his immediate captor, but in case he was
taken by a band he was the property of the tribe. Ownership was frequently changed by sale or gambling. The slave
was wholly subject to the caprices of his owner, even to his
life. "Women," says Captain Johnson, speaking of the Apaches, "when captured, are taken as wives by those who capture them, but they are treated by the Indian wives of the
capturers as slaves, and made to carry wood and water; if
they chance to be pretty, or receive too much attention from
their lords and masters, they are, in the absence of the latter, unmercifully beaten and otherwise maltreated. The most
unfortunate thing which can befall a captive woman is to be
claimed by two persons. In this case she is either shot or
delivered up for indiscriminate violence." This latter abrupt
method of deciding controversies was adhered to by the Apaches to prevent quarrels among themselves. Other property
was treated similarly. If a horse were claimed as booty by
two warriors, they must adjust their differences speedily or
the animal was shot.

The case of Inez Gonzales was not an exceptional one,

wherein Mexicans who had been captured by Indians were bought and held as slaves by Mexicans. It was the almost universal rule. In the preceding summer, Indian agent Calhoun released four Mexicans, three boys and a woman, all of whom had been bought by Mexicans from the Apaches. He reported: "The trading in captives has been so long tolerated in this Territory that it has ceased to be regarded as a wrong; and purchasers are not prepared willingly to release captives without an adequate ransom. In legislating upon this subject it should be distinctly set forth under what circumstances captives shall be released, and limiting the expenditures that may be incurred thereby. Unless the Mexicans are paid for such captives as they have purchased, and have now in possession, but very few of them will be released; nor will it answer well to allow captives to make their election as to a release, for their submission to their masters is most perfect, and they are well instructed as to proper replies to interrogatories. . . . I may, in conclusion, mention that there are a number of Indian captives held as slaves in this Territory, and Congressional action may be necessary in relation to them, and I respectfully submit the question for appropriate consideration." The Mexicans could never see any great evil in slavery. Their system of peonage, or bondage for debt, amounts to life servitude in most cases, for wages are so low that a peon ordinarily earns only enough for his subsistence. There was no public sentiment against the subjection of women to the pleasures of their owners, for virtue is almost unknown among them. It is the common mode, to this day, for one who desires a Mexican mistress, to select the girl and make arrangements with her parents by the payment of a small sum monthly.

The Americans who settled in the country held very similar ideas in regard to Mexicans and Indians, both of whom were considered as inferior races. The trapper or trader who desired a squaw purchased one, and the settler who wanted servants very commonly purchased them. They took to the system so naturally that legislation was made necessary to prohibit it. Many of the more reckless characters engaged in the business of catching and selling slaves, as is illustrated

in the following extract from the journal of Colonel Cooke:
"I had lately a conversation with old Weaver, which was not
official. He said, 'The Tontos live in that range over there;
I never see them with more than one or two lodges together;
they are a band of the Coyotéros, and are called fools for their
ignorance. When I went over once, from the Pimas to the
Cochanos and Mochabas [Mohaves], I met some lodges and
had a fuss with them.'—'What sort?'—'Oh, we killed two or
three and burned their lodges, and took all the women and
children and sold them.'—'What!'—'Yes, I have often
caught the women and children of Digger Indians and sold
them in New Mexico and Sonora. Mr.—— of Tucson told
me a squaw I sold him ran off, and was found dead, famished
for water I s'pose, going over from the Pimas to the Colorado.'—'What! have you no feeling for her death, trying to
return to her father and mother you tore her from?'—'I
killed her father and mother, as like as not; they stole all
our traps; as fast as we could stick a trap in the river, they'd
come and steal it, and shoot arrows into our horses; they
thought we would leave them for them to eat, but we built a
big fire and burned them up.'" The weaker tribes of course
suffered most in this business. The wretched Diggers of the
Salt Lake Basin were especially the victims of it, in an early
day, as was often testified to by travellers. Farnham says,
"These poor creatures are hunted in the spring, when weak
and helpless, by a certain class of men, and when taken are
fattened, and carried to Santa Fé and sold as slaves. A 'likely girl,' in her teens, often brings three or four hundred dollars. The men are valued less."

The Diggers fell under the control of the Mormons,
and to their honor be it said that they made an effort to
ameliorate the condition of these captives. The evil to
be remedied is thus set forth in the preamble of an act
passed in January, 1852:

"*Whereas*, from time immemorial, the practice of purchasing Indian
women and children of the Utah tribe of Indians by Mexican traders has
been indulged in and carried on by those respective people until the Indians consider it an allowable traffic, and frequently offer their prisoners
or children for sale; and

"*Whereas* it is a common practice among these Indians to gamble away their own children and women; and it is a well-established fact that women and children thus obtained, or obtained by war, or theft, or in any other manner, are by them frequently carried from place to place, packed upon horses or mules, lariated out to subsist upon grass, roots, or starve, and are frequently bound with thongs made of rawhide, until their hands and feet become swollen, mutilated, inflamed with pain, and wounded; and when with suffering, cold, hunger, and abuse they fall sick, so as to become troublesome, are frequently slain by their masters to get rid of them; and

"*Whereas* they do frequently kill their women and children taken prisoners, either in revenge, or for amusement, or through the influence of tradition, unless they are tempted to exchange them for trade, which they usually do if they have an opportunity; and

"*Whereas* one family frequently steals the children and women of another family, and such robberies and murders are continually committed in times of their greatest peace and amity, thus dragging free Indian women and children into Mexican servitude and slavery, or death, to the almost entire extirpation of the whole Indian race; and

"*Whereas* these inhuman practices are being daily enacted before our eyes in the midst of the white settlements, and within the organized counties of the Territory; and when the inhabitants do not purchase or trade for those so offered for sale, they are generally doomed to the most miserable existence, suffering the tortures of every species of cruelty, until death kindly relieves them and closes the revolting severity:

"Wherefore, when all these facts are taken into consideration, it becomes the duty of all humane and Christian people to extend unto this degraded and down-trodden race such relief as can be awarded to them," etc.

The act following this argumentative recital provides that any white person having a captive in his possession, shall go with it before the select-men, or the probate judge, and bind the captive to some proper person, in the discretion of the select-men, for a term of not over twenty years. The person to whom he is bound is required to send him to school three months in the year, from the age of seven to sixteen, and to clothe him in a suitable manner. The select-men are also empowered to obtain such captives from the Indians for the purpose of binding them out.

In the North slavery prevailed everywhere, and was abetted and encouraged by the Hudson's Bay Company. Said Mr. Slocum, of slavery in Oregon, "The price of a slave varies from five to fifteen blankets. Women are valued higher than men. If a slave dies within six months of the purchase, the seller returns one-half the purchase-money.

... Many instances have occurred where a man has sold his own child. . . . The slaves are generally employed to cut wood, hunt and fish for the families of the men employed by the Hudson's Bay Company, and are ready for any extra work. Each man of the trapping parties has from two to three slaves, who assist to hunt and take care of the horses and camp. They thereby save the Company the expense of employing at least double the number of men that would otherwise be required on these excursions. . . . As long as the Hudson's Bay Company permit their servants to hold slaves, the institution of slavery will be perpetuated." Slavery was, in fact, more extensive in Oregon than anywhere else in the West, and more similar to the African and Oriental systems. Stanley says of Casino, the celebrated Klickitat chief, "In the plenitude of his power he travelled in great state, and was often accompanied by a hundred slaves, obedient to his slightest caprice." The same authority says, "It is a very common practice of the Shaste, Umpqua, and Rogue River Indians, to sell their children in slavery to the tribes inhabiting the banks of the Columbia River. During my tour through the Willamette Valley in 1848, I met a party of Tlickitats (Klickitats) returning from one of these trading excursions, having about twenty little boys, whom they had purchased from the Umpqua tribe." The Oregon Indians also preyed upon the degraded tribes of California in this trade, and the Modocs, Klamaths, and Pitt River Indians obtained the reputation of fierce and cruel slave-drivers in procuring captives for sale to their Northern neighbors.

All through the Rocky Mountains, except in what we have called the north-eastern triangle, this system of human slavery extended, and it had obtained such a root that it was very hard to extirpate. In Colorado it was brought to a summary end, so far as white slave-holders were concerned, in 1865, through the efforts of the government. Indian Agent Head, accompanied by Deputy Marshall E. R. Harris, visited all owners of Indian slaves and informed them that they must be released. Says Mr. Head, " I have notified all the people here that in future no more captives are to be purchased or sold, as I shall immediately arrest both parties caught in the

24

transaction. This step, I think, will at once put an end to
the most barbarous and inhuman practice which has been in
existence with the Mexicans for generations. There are captives who know not their own parents, nor can they speak
their mother tongue, and who recognize no one but those
who rescued [!] them from their merciless captors." In New
Mexico and Arizona the slaves have not yet been fully emancipated. There were twenty Mexican slaves released from
among the Navahos in 1883. In 1866 the number of Indians
held as slaves and peons by the whites was estimated officially
at two thousand. There are undoubtedly many Indian slaves
held among the Mexicans in those Territories now, but the
system of peonage, and the fact that they are kept in fear of
expressing discontent, makes it difficult to release them. In
Northern Mexico there are numbers of Indians, of our tribes,
still held in slavery, and the officials of Arizona reservations
are continually besieged with appeals to restore to our Indians their captive kindred.

The condition of these slaves was as shocking as proclaimed in the Mormon document quoted above. The female captives were nearly always subjected to indignities,
both among the Indians and the whites, and among the latter
they were frequently made public prostitutes for the gain of
their owners. Among the Indians there was also the constant liability of sacrifice for religious purposes. At the death
of any person of prominence it was customary to kill one or
more captives, who should serve as slaves to the deceased in
the spirit world, as has been recounted herein, in the narrative of the captivity of Olive Oatman. Walker (Wacca), the
noted Ute chief, who died in 1855, and was buried on a high
mountain about twelve miles south-east of Fillmore, Utah,
was accorded full honors of this kind. Four Pi-ede slaves,
three children and one woman, were buried in the grave with
him. Three of them were killed and thrown into the grave;
the other was thrown in alive. Among the Chinooks the
burial custom was to bind a slave hand and foot and tie him
to the corpse, after which they were deposited together in the
place of sepulture; after three days the victim was strangled by another slave. The particulars of the treatment that

might be anticipated by captives were known to both races, and, as may be imagined, the whole system tended to make their hatred intense. When people are killed, and out of the way, warfare may to some extent be forgotten, but when relatives and friends are held in slavery, there is a constant pressure to rescue them or be revenged. This was a feeling common to both sides, and in regard to women it was perhaps more strong with the Apaches than with the Mexicans. The Apache women were noted for their chastity. In this respect they were far superior to the Mexicans, and equal, if not superior, to any Indians on the continent. The fate to which their captive wives and daughters was doomed often caused poignant sorrow among them. Of course there was not the same effort made by the whites to restore Indian slaves to their tribes that there was to recover Mexican or American slaves. The "axiom" of Aristotle, that "Barbarians are designed by Nature to be slaves," is one that has always been adopted by superior races when thrown in contact with inferior ones.

The forcible purchase of the Mexican boys by the Boundary Commission, was not forgotten by the Mimbreños, who considered it an invasion of their rights. The relations of the parties were soon further complicated through the killing of an Apache by Jesus Lopez, a Mexican teamster. The Apaches insisted that the Americans should hang this man, who undoubtedly deserved hanging. Mr. Bartlett objected to performing such summary justice, but promised to have the offender tried at Santa Fé. The Indians contended, with much show of reason, that he ought to be hung there, where the crime was committed. After a lengthy discussion, in which it was urged that the Apaches had recently killed an American on the road between Janos and the mines, for which they had made no reparation, the matter was arranged by paying the mother of the murdered man thirty dollars, and twenty dollars per month thereafter, being the amount of the murderer's wages. Three weeks later the Indians began stealing the horses and mules belonging to the Commission. They vehemently denied that they were guilty, at first, but soon a pursuing force overtook one of the bands of thieves,

and found it commanded by Delgadito (the Slender), a Mimbreños chief, who had slept in the Commissioner's camp only
two nights before.   In the course of a month nearly two hundred horses and mules were taken, and at the end of that
period the advancement of the work caused Mr. Bartlett to
move on with his almost dismounted command.   The Mimbreños considered his departure as a victory for them, and
always thought that they drove the Americans away.

During the stay of the Commissioner's party, a number
of miners had settled at the Pino Alto gold mines, north-west
of the Santa Rita mines, and these remained there when the
copper mines were abandoned.   They grew in numbers, and
the Mimbreños were unable to dislodge them.   After several
years Mangas Colorado tried to accomplish this end by deceit.
He would approach a miner and tell him in a confidential
way of wonderful gold mines to which he would escort him,
out of personal friendship, only they two must go alone.   No
one risked a trip with the kind-hearted chief, but after several
weeks some of the miners happened to compare notes, and
the probable treachery was revealed.   The next time Mangas
appeared at the mines, he was tied up and soundly whipped.
It would have been far more politic to have killed him.   He
never forgave this injury—the greatest that could be inflicted
on an Indian—and he certainly avenged it on a royal scale.
For years he was the greatest and most vindictive leader of
the Apaches.   He united himself by marriage with Cochise
(Cheis), the principal chief of the Chiricahuas, and also made
a marital alliance with the Navahos that gave him great influence in that tribe.   Murders and robberies innumerable
were committed under his leadership.   He succeeded for a
long time in keeping together larger bodies of warriors than
had ever been known among the Apaches, and in devastating
all the regions through which they roamed.

During all this time the Jicarillas were disturbing the
peace on the northern side of the Rio Grande settlements.
In October, 1849, they committed the massacre of the White
party which attracted wide-spread attention at the time.   Mr.
White, with his wife and child, was coming to Santa Fé, where
he had formerly been a merchant, in company with a wagon

SILVER MINES OF SANTA RITA.

train belonging to Mr. Aubrey. They had passed the country considered dangerous, and the Whites started ahead, accompanied by a German named Lawberger, an unknown American, a Mexican, and a negro. While camped between Rock Creek and Whetstone branch, a party of Jicarillas approached them and demanded presents. White refused, and drove them out of camp. Presently they returned, and were again refused and ordered out. Instead of going they opened fire, killing the negro and Mexican. The others tried to fly, but were killed, excepting Mrs. White and the child, who were taken prisoners. The dead bodies were laid along the road, but were not scalped or stripped, and the Indians concealed themselves. A party of Mexicans soon came along, and began plundering the wagons. The Indians fired on them, but succeeded only in wounding one boy, who was left for dead. He lay quiet until the Indians went away, and then came to Santa Fé and reported the occurrence. A company of dragoons, with Kit Carson as guide, followed the Indians for three or four days before they found them. They made an attack and killed several, but the Indians murdered Mrs. White and the child before they fled. A severe snow-storm came on, from which both sides suffered severely, and rendered farther pursuit impossible. In 1851 these Indians murdered a party of eleven persons who were carrying the mail. After some further hostilities they entered into a treaty with Agent Calhoun, and went on reservations near Fort Webster and Abiquiu, but the treaty was not ratified. Mr. Meriwether, who succeeded Mr. Calhoun in August, 1853, found the Jicarillas on his hands, with no money to provide for them. He told them he could do nothing for them, and turned them out. As they had made no provision for winter, they proceeded to support themselves by theft. In a few months their depredations became so insufferable that the troops were sent after them. Lieutenant Bell had a successful skirmish with them on March 5th, but on March 30th Lieutenant Davidson's command of sixty men was attacked by two hundred Jicarillas and Utes, and only nineteen men escaped, most of them wounded. A large force of regulars and volunteers was then put in the field, and, on July 30th General Garland reported that the Jicarillas had been subdued and had sued for peace. There was one band, however, that escaped and took refuge among the Utes; these renegades with their allies destroyed the settlement on the Arkansas, and were punished as recorded in the sketch of the Utes hereafter.

The Mescaleros, to the south-east of the Rio Grande settlements, were the Apaches for whose civilization there seemed the best prospect. They were more devoted to agriculture than the others, and consequently had more to lose by war. They exercised the ancient prerogative of thieving to a limited extent for some years, but in the winter of 1854–55 their depredations became so extensive that they could not be tolerated. Captain Ewell, of the 1st Dragoons, was sent against them with one hundred and eighty men. The Mescaleros met them on the Peñasco, on the night of January 17th, and fought them all the next day as they advanced. The troops lost three killed, and the Indians were seen to bear away fifteen dead bodies. The Mescaleros retreated in the direction of the Guadalupe Mountains. On February 23d a party of fifteen warriors attacked a grazing camp of four soldiers, surprising them and pulling their tent down upon them, but the soldiers extricated themselves and drove the Indians off with heavy loss. The Mescaleros then concluded that their mission was not fighting the Americans. They came to Agent Steck at Fort Thorne, and begged for peace. Peace was granted, and a reservation was given them in their own country, between the Pecos River and the Sacramento Mountains. The Mescaleros thereafter behaved quite well until the Texan invasion, early in the civil war, but the Mexicans gained in blood-thirstiness what the Indians had lost. In February, 1858, a militia party from Messila, known as the "Messila Guard," attacked a peaceful Mescalero camp close by the village of Doña Ana, and pursued the Indians into the houses of the Doña Anans, where they fled for refuge. Eight or nine Indians were killed and one child taken captive. The citizens of Doña Ana denounced this affair as a riotous and wanton outrage, though they seemed to object more to the disturbance of themselves than to the wrong done the Indians. In April these same *valientes* attacked the Mescalero camp on the reserva-

tion near Fort Thorne, killed seven and took several prisoners.   The garrison was promptly called to arms, and after a
brief chase captured thirty-five of the attacking party, including Juan Ortega, their leader.   The military authorities were
now thoroughly indignant.   The officers at the fort knew
that these Indians had been peaceable and well-behaved, so
that Mexican affidavits of outrages committed by them were
not effective; and the prisoners were held, notwithstanding
the writs of habeas corpus that were issued for their release.
General Garland also determined to withdraw his troops from
Fort Thorne and let the valiant Messilans have their fill of
Indian fighting.   This called forth a petition from the people, in which assertions of their own valor and prayers for
protection are ludicrously blended.   General Garland left two
companies to protect settlers innocent of outrage, but informed others that they "have no claims to the protection of
the military, and will receive none."

The eastern Apaches remained at peace until the beginning of the war of the rebellion.   They were not making any
material progress towards civilization, except in the matter
of becoming drunkards.   The intercourse laws could not be
enforced in New Mexico because there were no "Indian
lands."   The Mexicans had treated the Indian title as extinct,
and we had taken the Mexican title, in consequence of which
our legislators assumed that the Indians, who actually held
the country, and had held it from the "time when the memory of man runneth not to the contrary," had no title whatever.   To make this absurdity more serious in its results, none
of the treaties made with the Apaches were ratified, and therefore the reservations designated for them did not come within the protection of the intercourse laws.   The result was
that the most of the property that the Jicarillas and Mescaleros got hold of went for *aguardiente*.   The Western tribes
continued their piratical warfare.   Several expeditions were
sent against them, but none resulted in any permanent advantage or any material punishment to the Indians.

At the opening of the war a Pandora's box of evils was
opened over every square mile of New Mexico and Arizona.
Among the officers of the army were many Southerners, and

these did not hesitate to return to the South. Some tried to take their soldiers with them, but these attempts were generally unsuccessful. Immediately after came an order withdrawing the troops from the frontier posts. This meant a desertion of nearly all the country, for life in it had only been made possible by the presence of the soldiers. The overland mail company abandoned its line through the two territories (one at that time), thus putting an end to all communication. The Western Apaches seemed to have awakened to new life. They pursued their work of murder and robbery with such daring that no safety was possible. Men were killed and ranches plundered in the midst of well-settled districts. The Indians seemed to be everywhere.

This activity was occasioned in the first place by a military blunder. In the spring of 1861 some Apaches stole a cow and a child from the Mexican mistress of an American, and, on complaint of the latter at Fort Buchanan, seventy-five men were sent to demand the property of the Chiricahuas, who were accused of the theft. The party went to Apache Pass and camped, with a white flag flying over the tent of the commander. Under its protection Cochise and five other chiefs came in to talk. They professed absolute ignorance of the theft, and stuck to it, on account of which obduracy orders were given to seize them. Cochise seized a knife, slit the canvas, and escaped, carrying with him three bullets. One chief was knocked down and spitted on a bayonet while attempting to follow. The other four were bound. The Indians at once began hostilities by killing some prisoners. The captive chiefs were hung in retaliation, and the Apaches attacked the troops. The latter were badly whipped, and obliged to return to the fort. The abandonment of the posts by the troops soon after on the order of recall was believed by the Indians to have resulted from their hostilities, and they were satisfied that they need only fight if they desired to rid themselves of the Americans. The Arizona settlements, which were at that time all within the Gadsden Purchase, and chiefly in the Santa Cruz Valley, were made desolate. At first ranches were destroyed one after another, and travellers waylaid and murdered. Having accomplished this work thor-

oughly, the Apaches began operations against the strongholds
of their enemies. The silver mines east of Tubac were held
for a few weeks; but it was necessary to arm the peons to accomplish this, and arming them forced the Americans in
charge to stand guard constantly, to preserve their lives from
their employés. The mines were abandoned as soon as their
business affairs could be arranged. Tubac was deserted soon
afterwards. Tucson dwindled away to a village of two hundred souls.

What was lacking in the desperate nature of the situation
was added by the invasion of the Texans. They occupied
all of the southern part of New Mexico, and all of what is
now Arizona that was occupied by the whites. On the southeast they occupied Fort Stanton, the only post in the Mescalero country. All the Apache tribes except the Jicarillas
were within the region held by them, and the Jicarillas were
the only Apaches that remained at peace. It is worth remembering that but for the friendly attitude of the Jicarillas
and the Utes, New Mexico must almost certainly have fallen
into the hands of the Texans. The Mescaleros, who had been
behaving well previously, became involved in a quarrel with
the Confederate soldiers, and a fight resulted in which several
were killed on both sides. The Mescaleros then began an
Ishmaelitish war, sparing no one. The settlements which had
grown up on the Rio Bonito were quickly devastated, and the
war was carried to the villages of the Rio Grande country.
On the south-west Mangas Colorado prevented the settlers
from suffering the pangs of ennui. Most of the Mimbres
went to war immediately after he was flogged by the miners,
and the Chiricahuas and Gileños made common cause with
them. On the morning of September 27, 1861, a force of
over two hundred warriors attacked the mining village of Pino
Alto, but fortunately for the people Captain Martin had arrived the night before with a detachment of the Arizona
Guards, a volunteer organization, and after several hours' hard
fighting the Indians were driven off with considerable loss.
Soon after one hundred and fifty warriors attacked a large
wagon train, one day out from Pino Alto, and besieged it for
fourteen hours. The train escaped destruction by the timely

arrival of the Arizona Guards, who escorted it to the Mimbres River.

Any long continuance of this state of affairs must have been ruinous to New Mexico; but aid was at hand. The Colorado Volunteers marched down from the North, turned back the Texans, and joined Canby in driving them from the Rio Grande. At the same time General Carleton, with a column of three thousand Californians, was advancing by way of Fort Yuma, driving all hostiles before him, and opening communication through to the coast. The combined forces of Mangas Colorado and Cochise made a desperate resistance to his advance at Apache Pass, in the Chiricahua Mountains, but the Californians were supplied with howitzers and shells, and the Apaches found that their positions, which they had made almost impregnable to direct attack, afforded them no protection from these new missiles of their white foes. They fled with a loss of sixty-six killed; the Californians had two killed and three

A RECORD OF MANGAS COLORADO.

wounded. Just after this engagement Mangas Colorado was seriously wounded while trying to cut off a messenger that was carrying back news of the fight at the pass. He was taken to the village of Janos, in Northern New Mexico, by his warriors, and put under charge of a physician there, with notice that if he did not recover, every one in the place would be killed. He recovered. A short time after his recovery, early in 1863, he was captured by Captain Shirland of the California Volunteers, and killed while attempting to escape. It is said that the sentinel stirred him up with a heated bayonet and then shot him. It was time for him to die. He was about seventy years old, and had secured all the revenge to which one man is entitled. His skull is said to ornament the phrenological museum of Prof. O. S. Fowler.

General Carleton arrived at the Rio Grande settlements in September, 1862, and relieved Canby, who went to take a glorious part in the great struggle in the South. Carleton, being rid of white enemies, devoted his attention to the subjugation of the Indians. He first sent Col. Kit Carson, with five companies of New Mexican volunteers, to occupy Fort Stanton, from which he was to operate against the Mescaleros and any Navahos that were in that region. Captain McCleave, with two companies of California Volunteers, was sent into the Mescalero country by way of Dog Cañon (Cañon del Perro), from the south-west. Captain Roberts, with two companies of Californians, was sent into the same region from the south, by way of the Hueco (Wacco) tanks. The orders to each command were: "The men are to be slain whenever and wherever they can be found. The women and children may be taken prisoners, but, of course, they are not to be killed." Carson took possession of Fort Stanton with no material hinderance. McCleave encountered the Apaches at Dog Cañon, which was one of their greatest strongholds. There were about five hundred of them—over a hundred warriors— and they were completely routed by the Californians. They fled to Fort Stanton and surrendered to Carson, who took them under his protection, rather against the sanguinary instructions of Carleton, and sent five of their chiefs to Santa Fé to treat for peace. General Carleton required them to go on a reservation at the Bosque Redondo, on the Pecos River. The spokesman of the Mescaleros was Gian-nah-tah (Always Ready), known to the Mexicans as Cadéte, or the Volunteer. He was a son of Palanquito, their former head chief, who died soon after they were first treated with, in 1855. Gian-nah-tah said, "You are stronger than we. We have fought you so long as we had rifles and powder; but your weapons are better than ours. Give us like weapons and turn us loose, we will fight you again; but we are worn out; we have no more heart; we have no provisions, no means to live; your troops are everywhere; our springs and water-holes are either occupied or overlooked by your young men. You have driven us from our last and best stronghold, and we have no more heart. Do with us as may seem good to you, but do not forget we are men and braves."

The Mescaleros were sent to the Bosque Redondo with the promise that if they should remain there peaceably until the war was finished, so that they would not be confused with the hostiles, they should be given a reservation in their own country. At the Bosque they came under charge of Colonel Cremony, formerly with the Boundary Commission, to whose intelligent labor the world is indebted for much of its knowledge of Apache customs. It may be mentioned, by-the-way, that he collected a valuable vocabulary of the Apache language and forwarded it to the Smithsonian Institution over twenty years ago, but it has not yet been published. The Indians came to the Bosque rapidly; by spring four hundred Mescaleros were on the reservation, and the remainder were reported as having fled into Mexico or joined the Gila tribes. The disposal of the Mescaleros gave some opportunity for proceedings against the Mimbreños. An expedition was sent into their country in January, 1863, which resulted in the defeat and capture of Mangas Colorado, with a loss of twenty of his warriors. Fort West was established in the Pino Alto country, and scouting parties were kept in the field. By the latter part of April, forty of the band had been killed, includ-

PAPAGO CHIEF.

ing a brother and one of the sons of Mangas. The attention of the greater part of the troops was turned to the Navahos during the year 1863 and the early part of the next year. By March, 1864, there were 3600 Navahos and 450 Apaches at the Bosque. By the twentieth of that month 2600 more Navahos were reported captured and on their way. Events were occurring in Arizona, however, that soon carried the seat of active operations to that territory. In 1862 Pauline Weaver, the pioneer prospector of Arizona, discovered the placers on the Colorado near La Paz, and in 1863 he found the district that bears his name, south-west of Prescott, and the remarkable mines of Antelope Peak. In the spring of 1863 a party of prospectors under Captain Walker, an old California mining celebrity, left the Rio Grande settlements and went into the same region. The new mines attracted many people, to whom General Carleton gave all the protection and assistance in his power.

In the summer of 1864, his hands were comparatively free in New Mexico, and the troops were centred on the western Apaches. The extermination policy then received as full and fair a trial as could possibly be given to it. The forces were adequate, for every one joined in the movement. On April 20th General Carleton detailed his plans to Don Ignacio Pesquira, Governor of Sonora, saying, "If your excellency will put a few hundred men into the field on the first day of next June, and keep them in hot pursuit of the Apaches of Sonora, say for sixty or ninety days, we will either exterminate the Indians or so diminish their numbers that they will cease their murdering and robbing propensities and live at peace." To Don Luis Perrazas, Governor of Chihuahua, a similar request was forwarded. The miners in the new districts of Arizona agreed to keep a force in the field if the government would furnish provisions, and this General Carleton did. The Pimas and Maricopas were furnished with American leaders, and given over two hundred muskets, with ammunition. The governors of Arizona and New Mexico were requested to aid, and did so. To Governor Goodwin, of Arizona, Carleton wrote: "Pray see the Papagos, Pimas, and Maricopas, and have that part of the programme well and effectually executed.

You will be able to secure the efforts of the miners without trouble. Let us work earnestly and hard, and before next Christmas your Apaches are whipped. Unless we do this, you will have a twenty years' war." For his own part Carleton located a force of five hundred men on the Gila, north of the Chiricahua Mountains, to operate from that point. Could a plan be more perfect? Here was a combination of the military, citizens, and friendly Indians of two nations against the Apaches. They all went into it heartily, with a sincere hatred of the enemy, and with many old scores to pay off. The oft-repeated orders were to kill every male Indian capable of bearing arms, and capture the women and children. It is not possible to give here even a synopsis of the fights that occurred. The brief mention of the encounters with Indians in the general orders for the year covers six such pages as these, in fine print. The results of the year's work, so far as they could be obtained, were officially summed up thus: Indians killed, 363—wounded, 140; soldiers killed, 7—wounded, 25; citizens killed, 18—wounded, 13; recovered from Indians 12,284 sheep, 2742 horses, 35 mules, 31 cattle, and 18 burros; taken by Indians, 4250 sheep, 26 horses, 154 mules, and 32 cattle. The greater part of the damage done was to the Navahos, who, to the number of over two thousand, were sent to the Bosque Rodondo, taking with them most of the sheep that were reported as captured. For the Apaches alone the returns sum up, 216 Indians and 16 whites killed; 146 horses captured by Indians, and 54 recovered; 17 cattle taken by Indians, and 21 taken from them; 3000 sheep taken by Indians, and 175 recovered. The loss to the whites was not fully reported, and the Indians were much damaged in addition to this by the destruction of their crops. Nearly all the Apaches planted to some extent in the sheltered valleys of their wildernesses.

This war was conducted on strictly extermination principles. It is true that removal to the Bosque was named as an alternative, but only thirty western Apaches ever reached the Bosque, from all sources. The troops were constantly stimulated to activity. Failure was the only offence that could be committed, and success was approved, no matter how obtained.

APACHE CRUCIFIED BY PAPAGOS.

By way of example, the general orders for 1864 contain the following: "January 24th.—A party of thirty Americans and fourteen Pima and Maricopa Indians under Col. King S. Woolsey, aid to the governor of Arizona, attacked a band of Gila Apaches, sixty or seventy miles north-east of the Pima villages, and killed nineteen of them and wounded others. Mr. Cyrus Lennon, of Woolsey's party, was killed by a wounded Indian." That does not read badly, but it is not the whole truth. This party started out to hunt for stock supposed to have been stolen by the Indians. They were signalled by a party of Coyotéros and Pinals, who dared them to come and fight. Woolsey sent an interpreter to them to tell them that he did not wish to fight, but to make peace. On his invitation thirty-five of them came into the camp with their arms. The chief, Par-a-muck-a, insolently ordered Woolsey to clear a place for him to sit upon, as he was a great chief. Woolsey calmly folded up a blanket and handed it to him. He then told the Apaches that he would make a treaty with them and give them certificates of good conduct such that no white man would ever molest them. His men were gathered about in preparation for the treaty. Woolsey drew his revolver and gave Par-a-muck-a the Arizona certificate of a "good Indian" at the first shot. His men signed on the bodies of the others. Only one Indian—a lame man who could not run away—affixed his signature. He did it with his lance, on the person of Mr. Lennon. This is historically known as "the Pinal treaty," and the place is appropriately called "Bloody Tanks."

This occurrence is not mentioned in any spirit of "mawkish sentimentality," but merely to show that the extermination policy had a fair trial. These Indians would undoubtedly have murdered their new white friends if they had obtained the opportunity. They are entitled to no compassion on the ground of treachery used against them. The Apache makes war by treachery. His object is to harm his enemy but to escape uninjured, and he thinks that a man who walks up to open danger is a fool. He will go into dangerous places himself, but he goes by stealth. He never attacks except by surprise. He is brave, but he has no ambi-

tion to die a soldier's death.   Apache glory consists strictly
in killing the enemy.   A wounded or helpless Apache will
fight like a demon to protect his friends, but a sound Apache
would never take such risks to bear away a
wounded compatriot as a Sioux or Cheyenne
warrior would.   Of necessity, this warfare had its effects on the Apaches, in
the way of making peace seem more
endurable, but they were
neither exterminated nor conquered.   In April, 1865, Inspector-general Davis held a
parley with Victoria, Acos-
ta, and other chiefs, among
whom were Pasquin, Cassari,
and Salvador, the sons of
Mangas Colorado.   The Indians were very destitute, and
wanted peace, but they did
not wish to leave their coun-

APACHES WATCHING A TRAIN.

try. The iron rule, of removal to the Bosque, staggered them. They agreed to send four chiefs to inspect the reservation and report to the tribe, but none of them came back, as they promised, and the war went on as before.

At the close of the war of the rebellion the United States was divided into five Military Divisions, and these were sub-divided in nineteen Departments. New Mexico was put in the Department of the Missouri, commanded by Major-general Pope, which was a part of the Military Division of the Mississippi, commanded by General Sherman. Arizona was in the Department of California, commanded by Major-general McDowell, which was a part of the Military Division of the Pacific, commanded by Maj.-gen. H. W. Halleck. The extermination theory was believed in by General Halleck, so far at least as the Apaches were concerned. He said, "It is useless to negotiate with these Apache Indians. They will observe no treaties, agreements, or truces. With them there is no alternative but active and vigorous war, till they are completely destroyed, or forced to surrender as prisoners of war." The hostile Apaches were nearly all in Arizona, which was commanded by Brigadier-general Mason, and the war there was prosecuted much as before, or, if possible, more bitterly. Both sides were becoming more and more exasperated, and vented their spleen in ways that only served to make matters worse. The Indians were adopting the practice of mutilating the dead, which was formerly contrary to their customs. The whites frequently killed inoffensive Indians on general principles. In 1868 a man named Mitchell causelessly killed Waba Yuma, head chief of the Hualapais, and that tribe, which had been peaceable, went to war. They had been looked upon with the contempt that frontiersmen commonly feel for peaceable Indians, but they proved vicious enemies. General McDowell reported that, "the officers from Prescott say they would prefer fighting five Apaches to one Hualapais."

In the mean time trouble had come at the Bosque. The question of a permanent reservation at that point became a political one, and everything connected with it passed into the realms of misrepresentation, so that the truth is hard to

25*

reach. It is clear, however, that the reservation crops failed, or were destroyed by insects, year after year. It is also clear that the Navahos and Apaches did not get along well together. The Navahos were the stronger in numbers, and appeared to have the ear of the commanding officer. After the Mescaleros had been at the Bosque for two years, the land which they had been cultivating was taken from them and given to the Navahos, while they were assigned to another location. This was done to prevent quarrelling, but to the Mescaleros it appeared an act of favoritism. There could be no harmony between them and the Navahos. They had long been at war, and their customs were totally different. The Mescaleros claimed the fulfilment of General Carleton's promise that they should have a reservation in their own country; indeed, Agent Labodie testifies that they had looked forward to this all the time, and had used their influence in bringing in their own hostiles solely for that purpose. They were not removed. The Bosque reservation for all Apaches and Navahos had become General Carleton's pet scheme. On November 3, 1865, the entire tribe of Mescaleros left the Bosque and went to their own country. They went to war because they knew that leaving the reservation would be considered an act of war, and that they must fight or go back. One of their leading men, Ojo Blanco (White Eye*), had left several weeks prior to this time with a small party. After several years of desultory warfare, during which the anti-Bosque party had gained their point, and the tribes were returned to their former homes, the Mescaleros were settled on a reservation in their own country.

The military operations of the '60's were not devoid of results. New Mexico had a season of comparative quiet, in the better settled parts, and Arizona was yielding to the progress of civilization. The valley of Santa Cruz was again filled with ranchemen. Tubac was reoccupied, and Tucson

---

* The Apache words for "white eye" are *Pin-dah Lick-o-yee,* and this is the name they use to designate Americans, in their own language. We are "white eyes," not "pale faces," to them. They also use the word Americano in common with other tribes who are more or less versed in Spanish.

TUBAC.

regained its lost population. The mining regions on the Colorado and about Prescott were held by the whites. Yet, in fact, there was merely a change in the seat of war. The Apaches held mountain fastnesses, as yet unknown, from which they sallied forth to raid into the very heart of the settlements. No one dared to travel the roads unarmed, and small parties were not safe when they had arms. Horses were run off in broad day from within half a mile of Prescott. Men who were not vigilant were liable to be killed anywhere. No Apache tribe was subdued. The later years of this period found them at war from the Pecos to the Colorado. The bitterness and want of confidence which had been instilled into the Indians by this system of warfare are results which are not subject to measurement, but it must, in fairness, be admitted that they did follow in some degree. On the whole the policy of extermination in Arizona, coupled with concentration in New Mexico, proved a dismal failure, after a full and fair trial. The army officers began to realize this, and Indians who were willing to make peace were permitted to gather about Fort Goodwin, Camp Grant, and in the White Mountains. This marked the beginning of a new era in Arizona, which will be considered in a subsequent chapter.

APACHE BOOT, HEAD-DRESS, ETC.

CHAPTER XIII.

SAND CREEK.

On the night of November 28, 1864, about seven hundred and fifty men, cavalry and artillery, were marching eastward across the plains below Fort Lyon. There was a bitter, determined look on their hard-set features that betokened ill for some one. For five days they had been marching, from Bijou Basin, about one hundred and fifty miles to the northwest, as the crow flies, but some fifty miles farther by their route. When they started the snow was two to three feet deep on the ground, but, as they progressed, it had become lighter, and now the ground was clear. The night was bitter cold; Jim Beckwith, the old trapper who had been guiding them, had become so stiffened that he was unable longer to distinguish the course, and they were obliged to rely on a half-breed Indian. About one third of the men had the appearance of soldiers who had seen service; the remainder had a diversity of arms and equipments as well as of uniforms, and marched with the air of raw recruits. About half a mile in advance were three men, the half-breed guide and two officers, one of the latter of such gigantic proportions that the others seemed pygmies beside him. Near daybreak the half-breed turned to the white men and said: "Wolf he howl. Injun dog he hear wolf, he howl too. Injun he hear dog and listen; hear something, and run off." The big man tapped the butt of his revolver in an ominous way, and replied: "Jack, I haven't had an Indian to eat for a long time. If you fool with me, and don't lead us to that camp, I'll have you for breakfast." They found the camp. There were one hundred and twenty Cheyenne and eight Arapahoe lodges in it, stretched along the bank of a shallow stream, which crept sluggishly down a broad bed of sand. On each side of the camp, ranging out perhaps a mile, was a herd of ponies, the two numbering about eleven hundred. It was between daybreak and sunrise; the Indians were just beginning to move. A squaw heard the noise of the approaching horses, and reported that a herd of buffalo was coming. Others ran out, who quickly discovered that the rumbling was the tread of horses, and that a large body of troops was approaching. In a moment all was confusion. Men, women, and children ran here and there, getting their arms in readiness or preparing for flight. The principal Cheyenne chief hastily ran up an American flag over his teepee, with a white flag above it. A white trader, who was in one of the teepees, came out and hastened towards the soldiers. At the same time two detachments of cavalry were galloping towards the herds, and some of the Indians were running in the same directions.

Firing began between these parties. The white trader seemed confused, and stopped. A cavalryman said: "Let me bring him in, major," and, starting from the ranks, galloped towards him, but a bullet from the camp tumbled him from his horse, and the trader turned and ran back. The herd of ponies on the farther side of the camp became alarmed and ran towards the camp, the soldiers cutting off only about half of them. The main body of troops pressed forward, firing as they came, led by their giant commander, who rode through the ranks, calling out: "Remember our wives and children, murdered on the Platte and the Arkansas." The Indians were beginning to fall rapidly under the deadly fire. Part of them caught the straggling ponies which had reached the camp, and fled. The remainder, warriors and squaws, with some children, retired slowly up the creek, fighting as they went. They continued thus for about three quarters of a mile, to a point where the banks rose from three to ten feet, on either side of a level expanse of sand, some three hundred yards wide. Along the banks the Indians made their stand, protected by them on one side, and on the other by heaps of loose sand which they had scraped up. Most of the troops were now in confusion, each doing about as he liked. About one half of them were firing on the line of Indians in the creek bed, and squads were riding about, killing stragglers, scalping the dead, and pursuing the flying. No prisoners were being taken, and no one was allowed to escape if escape could be prevented. A child of about three years, perfectly naked, was toddling along over the trail where the Indians had fled. A soldier saw it, fired at about seventy-five yards distance, and missed it. Another dismounted and said: "Let me try the little —— ——; I can hit him." He missed too, but a third dismounted, with a similar remark, and at his shot the child fell. At the creek bed the fight was at long range and stubborn. A private was firing at an Indian who climbed up on the bank from time to time, and made derisive gestures at the soldier's fruitless efforts. "Let me take that gun of yours for a minute, colonel," said the soldier. The colonel handed him his rifle, an elegant silver-mounted one, presented him by the citizens of Denver; the Indian showed himself again; the rifle cracked and he dropped dead. The squaws were fighting along with the men. One had just wounded a soldier with an arrow, and a comrade put his rifle in rest, remarking, "If that squaw shows her head above the bank again, I'll blow the whole top of it off." An officer, standing by him, said: "I wouldn't make a heathen of myself by shooting a woman." The words had hardly dropped from his lips when the same squaw sent an arrow through the officer's arm, and his philanthropic remark changed to a howl of "Shoot the —— ——," and the soldier did it. The Indians could not be dislodged by the small arms, but towards noon two howitzers were brought into action and they broke the line. The Indians fell back from one position to another, the combat becoming gradually a running fight, which was kept up for five miles or more, and abandoned by the pursuers a short time before dusk. The soldiers then gathered at the Indian camp, where they remained until the second day following. Most of the corpses were scalped, and a number were mutilated as bodies are usually mutilated by Indians, with all that implies. Near evening, on the day after the battle, Jack Smith, the half-breed who had guided the soldiers to the camp, and a son of the white trader who was in the camp, was shot by one of the men. He had tried to run away during the fight, but had been brought back. The

TEXAN RANGERS.

colonel commanding was warned that he would probably be killed if the men were not ordered to let him live. He replied : " I have given my orders, and have no further instructions to give." There were, at the time, seven other prisoners in the camp, two squaws and five children, who were taken to Fort Lyon and left there. They were the only prisoners taken. When the camp was broken, the buffalo-robes were confiscated for the sick, the soldiers took what they wanted for trophies, and the remainder was burned. The Indians lost three hundred, all killed, of whom about one half were warriors and the remainder women and children. The whites lost seven killed and forty-seven wounded, of whom seven afterwards died.

This was " the massacre of the friendly Cheyenne Indians at Sand Creek, by the Colorado troops, under Colonel John M. Chivington," or " the battle on the Big Sandy, with the hostile Cheyennes and Arapahoes," as you may be pleased to consider it. That is to say, it is a statement of what occurred there, as nearly as the truth can be arrived at, without favor or reservation. It is but just to add that the great majority of the troops who participated in it say it was not so bad as here represented, and that the witnesses of the action and events connected with it, who subsequently denounced it, make it no worse, notwithstanding the fact that many, who knew nothing of the facts in the case, have added much to the statement above given. The number killed was the point most in controversy in the investigations of the matter, ranging from about seventy, in Major Wynkoop's estimate, to six hundred, in Colonel Chivington's original report. The Indians conceded a loss of one hundred and forty, of whom sixty were warriors, and the testimony of all who counted bodies, after the battle, indicates the number stated above. Concerning this affair there has been much of exaggeration, much of invective, much of misunderstanding, and much of wholly unfounded statement. Indeed, so much has been said in regard to it that the controversy is far more extensive than the original trouble, and the historical shape that it has assumed is the creation of the controversy, not the fight. Now that twenty years have passed away—that the Indian is only a memory where he then roamed—that a new generation has taken the place of the old—let us try calmly to unravel the thread of truth from the fantastic fabric which has so long concealed it; and to do this we must first know something of the actors on that field.

Who was Colonel Chivington? In 1840 he was a rough, uncouth, profane child of nature, just stepped across the threshold of manhood. He lived in Warren County, Ohio, about two miles south of the line of Clinton. At a log-rolling in the neighborhood a good old Methodist brother reproved him, one day, for profanity, and the sturdy youth answered defiantly: "I will swear when I please and where I please." But he brooded over the rebuke, and a few days later he went to his reprover's house, determined to swear there, before his family. He did not do as he intended. Some unknown power beat down his resolution, and the curse died trembling on his tongue. He went away, but the mysterious influence followed him; his eyes were turned inward on his guilty soul; he could not rest. He struggled against it, but in vain, and soon he sought at the altar the pardon for his sins. Scoffers may smile at the change of heart by divine grace, but sure it was there was a change in him. He became an industrious, orderly man; he joined the Methodist Church and lived consistently with its discipline; he apprenticed himself to a carpenter and thoroughly learned the trade. Towards 1850 he determined to move West and enter the ministry, and this he did, working meantime at his trade. At the end of the second year of his clerical service he was transferred to the Missouri Conference and continued his labors there. It was a troubled field for him, for he was peculiarly a Northern man. Mobs collected at various times to hinder his preaching, but his apparent abundance of "muscular Christianity" kept him from serious trouble, and his intended disturbers often remained to hear him preach.

His kindly nature helped him to preserve peaceful relations, also. One day he met an old planter, hauling logs, with his team mired down. Chivington dismounted, tied his horse, waded into the mud, and helped him out. The planter desired to know to whom he was indebted, and, on being told, exclaimed: "Come right home with me. A preacher that

will get off in the mud to help a stranger won't steal niggers."
They were good friends thereafter. A few years later Chivington was in Kansas, taking an active part with Lane and
his friends in the border war. After the Kansas troubles were
settled, we find him serving acceptably, for two years, as a
missionary to the Wyandot Indians, and afterwards, as interpreter and guide, travelling through the West with the
Methodist bishops who were establishing missions among the
Indian tribes. Soon after the beginning of the war he went
to a quarterly meeting at Denver, being then a Presiding
Elder in Western Kansas and Colorado, and, while there,
preached to the soldiers at their barracks. They liked his
style and urged him to stay with them. Governor Gilpin
offered him a chaplaincy, but he said that if he went with the
soldiers he wanted to fight, so he was made a major instead.
There is one point in his character that must not be lost
sight of, if his history is to be understood. He was, like
other Kansas free-soilers, an uncompromising Union man,
and had no use for a rebel, white or red. His dislike to anything savoring of treason got him into trouble time and
again, but he never held back on that account. On one occasion, after the war, he seriously disturbed his domestic peace
by peremptorily shutting off some reminiscences from his
brother-in-law, an ex-confederate.

And what of the Colorado troops? They included men
from all ranks and classes in life; many of them are prominent and respected citizens of Colorado now. About two
thirds of those at Sand Creek were one-hundred-days' men, of
the 3d regiment; the remainder were veterans, mostly of the
1st regiment. These last had established a military reputation beyond all cavil, and, without referring to other services,
a brief sketch of their work in New Mexico will satisfy the
reader that no equal body of men ever did greater or more gallant service for the Union. In the early part of 1862 General
Sibley invaded New Mexico with an army of twenty-five hundred, including a large number of Texan Rangers, having evidently in view the conquest of the entire mountain country.
Our government had been paying little or no attention to the
Far West; its hands were full in the East. Even the official

communications in some departments had not been replied to
in a year past. The Confederacy was more watchful. Full information of the situation in the West had been given to its
leaders by officials, civil and military, who had been located at
various Western points, and had hastened to the South as soon
as the war opened. The United States troops in the country
were few in number. The Indians were ready for war whenever an opportunity presented itself. The Mexicans were
supposed to be friendly to the South, and the lower classes
were known to be ready for rapine and pillage, at any time
and against anybody. The Mormons were in ecstasy over the
apparent fulfilment of their late Prophet's war prophecy, and
were willing to help on the " Kilkenny-cat fight." Besides,
they were still sore over the troubles of 1857, and had no love
for the national government. The Secession element in California was quite strong, especially in the southern part, which
was to have been a slave state under the Calhoun plan. These
facts at once determined the policy of the South, and the invasion was begun. If it had been successful—what an awful
possibility !—the South would have had a coast-line impossible of blockade, the entire line of Mexico for external communication, the mines to fill her depleted treasury, and an
extensive country which could have been reconquered only at
immense cost of life and money. The Texans entered New
Mexico from the south. They took Fort Fillmore without
resistance, and marched up the Rio Grande unchecked, until
they reached Fort Craig, where General Canby awaited them.
They decided not to attack the fort, and were flanking it, to
go forward, when Canby came out and attacked them at
Valverde. They rather worsted him, and he retired to the
fort, while they pursued their march up the river. They occupied Santa Fé, and found that the Mexicans were not nearly so glad to see them as they had anticipated ; still, little discouraged, they pushed on towards Fort Union, some sixty-five
miles northeast, on the edge of the plains, the arsenal and supply depot for that section.

Governor Gilpin, all this time, had been moving in the
mining camps of Colorado, and, on February 22, the 1st Colorado regiment, under Colonel Slough, left Denver through

OLD FORT UNION.

snow a foot deep. They reached Fort Union on March 11, after a journey of great hardship, and were there armed and equipped. They pressed forward, and, on the 23d, reached the mouth of Apaché Cañon, the location of "Pigeon's Ranch," or, more properly, the ranch of M. Alexandre Vallé; the Texans had by this time reached the opposite end of the cañon. In this cañon, where Armijo had failed to meet Kearny, the Greek miner met the Greek cowboy. It was a contest the like of which never occurred elsewhere. The Southerners had adopted as their favorite name, "Baylor's Babes;" the Coloradoans gloried in their chosen title of "Pet Lambs"—grim satires these, as well on the plainsmen who charged McRae's Battery with revolvers and bowie-knives, as on the mountaineers who never learned what it was to be whipped. On the 26th the advance of the Texans met two hundred and ten cavalry and one hundred and eighty infantry under Major Chivington, and, in the words of a local writer, it "was more like the shock of lightning than of battalions." Said M. Vallé, who witnessed the fight, "Zat Chivington, he poot down 'is 'ead, and foight loike mahd bull." Both detachments reeled back from this hard bump, and on the 28th, the main forces having arrived, they went at it again. The Texans surprised the Coloradoans' camp, but the Lambs stood their ground, and, after a desperate fight, the Babes were forced to retire, and they retired to a little surprise-party at home. While they had been making their attack, Chivington had led a force of one hundred men up the precipitous side of the cañon, along a rugged and dangerous path, and down on the Texan rear-guard of some six hundred men. It was a desperate charge to make, but it resulted in a brilliant success, and the Texan train of sixty-four wagons and two hundred mules, with all their supplies and ammunition, were destroyed. The Texan invasion was ruined. Sibley began his retreat, and Slough fell back on Fort Union for his supplies, but only for a breathing space. On April 13 the Coloradoans had joined General Canby and begun a pursuit of the retiring Texans, which was kept up for one hundred and fifty miles; a pursuit so disastrous to the pursued that one half of their original force was left behind, dead, wounded, and prisoners, together with all their stores, public and private. So much for the Colorado troops.

The Cheyennes we know something of already. The village attacked was that of Black Kettle (Moke-ta-ve-to), the principal chief of the southern Cheyennes, and the few lodges of Arapahoes were under Left Hand (Na-watk), second in rank of the southern chiefs. There had been trouble in these tribes ever since the treaty of Fort Wise, in 1861. The warriors denounced the chiefs for making the treaty, and were particularly opposed to the construction of the Kansas Pacific Railroad through their lands, as they knew it would drive away the buffalo. The chiefs were threatened with death if they undertook to carry out its provisions, and so the intense desire of the Cheyennes and Arapahoes for an agricultural life, which is recited as the cause of the treaty, had to go ungratified. The first serious troubles, after Sumner's campaign, occurred after this treaty was made, and all the succeeding troubles grew out of it. The Cheyennes began committing minor offences in 1861, and, as they were unpunished, they gradually grew bolder, until, in 1863, Agent Lorey reported that the Cheyennes were dissatisfied, and that the Sioux were urging them to open war. In other words, the war feeling had grown so strong that it was necessary to treat with them anew. Governor Evans went out, by agreement, to treat with them, on the head-waters of the Republican, but they failed to come as agreed. The governor sent his guide, a squaw-man named Elbridge Gerry (a grandson of the signer of the Declaration of Independence, of the same name), in search of them. He returned after an absence of two weeks, and reported that they had held a council and decided not to treat. One chief, Bull Bear (O-to-ah-nac-co), the leader of the "Dog-soldiers," had offered to come in, but his warriors would not allow him to do so. The Cheyennes afterwards confirmed this statement fully; they said they were going to remain at peace, but would make no treaty that they had to sign; that they were going to have their lands; and even if a railroad was built through their country, they would not allow any one to settle along it. The chiefs who had signed the treaty of Fort Wise said they were obliged to repudiate it or their warriors would kill them. Minor depredations were committed during the remainder of 1863 and the early part of

1864, and, during the winter, word was received, from spies among them, that a coalition was being formed among all the plains tribes, to drive the whites out of the country. This information proved true, for in the spring and summer of 1864, the Sioux, Comanches, Kiowas, Cheyennes, and Arapahoes were engaged in active hostilities. The reader will note here, that no one has ever pretended that any of the eighteen hundred Southern Cheyennes, except the six hundred at Sand Creek, were not open enemies at the time.

The effect of this warfare on the whites was distressing. Nearly every stage was attacked, emigrants were cut off, and the settlements were raided continually. The overland trains, on which the entire settlements depended for supplies, were deterred from moving by fear of attack. On June 14 Governor Evans applied for authority to call the militia into the United States service, or to call out one-hundred-days' men, which was not granted. Matters became worse. All the set-

STANDING OFF THE CHEYENNES.

tlements from the Purgatoire to the Cache la Poudre, and for two hundred miles on the Platte, were in consternation. The settlers left their crops and built block-houses for mutual protection. Those near Denver fled to that place. The governor was besieged with petitions for arms and authority to organize for protection. On August 8 all the stage lines were attacked. On August 11 Governor Evans issued a proclamation, calling the people to organize for self-protection, and under this several companies were formed which were considered sufficient for the defence of the settlements. But they could not protect the settlements from famine. On August 18 Governor Evans despatched Secretary Stanton: "Extensive Indian depredations, with murder of families, occurred yesterday thirty miles south of Denver. Our lines of communication are cut, and our crops, our sole dependence, are all in exposed localities, and cannot be gathered by our scattered population. Large bodies of Indians are undoubtedly near to Denver, and we are in danger of destruction both from the attack of Indians and starvation. I earnestly request that Colonel Ford's regiment of 2d Colorado Volunteers be immediately sent to our relief. It is impossible to exaggerate our danger. We are doing all we can for our defence." There was no favorable answer received to this, and, on September 7, a second despatch followed: "Pray give positive orders for our 2d Colorado Cavalry to come out. Have notice published that they will come in detachments to escort trains up the Platte on certain days. Unless escorts are sent thus we will inevitably have a famine in addition to this gigantic Indian war. Flour is forty-five dollars a barrel, and the supply growing scarce, with none on the way. Through spies we got knowledge of the plan of about one thousand warriors in camp to strike our frontier settlements, in small bands, simultaneously in the night, for an extent of three hundred miles. It was frustrated at the time, but we have to fear another such attempt soon. Pray give the order for our troops to come, as requested, at once, or it will be too late for trains to come this season." The troops were not sent, but, in the mean time, authority had been given by the War Department to raise a regiment of one-hundred-days' men, and the 3d Colorado was organized and impatiently waiting for arms and equipments, which they did not get until a short time before their march to Sand Creek.

But were the Cheyennes responsible for all this? Quite as much so as any of the tribes. They began stealing stock early in the spring, and, on April 13, a herdsman for Irving, Jackmann, & Co. reported that the Cheyennes and Arapahoes had run off sixty head of oxen and a dozen mules and horses from their camp, thirty miles south of Denver. Lieutenant Clark Dunn was sent after them with a small party of soldiers. He overtook them as they were crossing the Platte, during a heavy snow-storm. A parley was commenced, but was interrupted by part of the Indians running off the stock, and the soldiers attempting to disarm the others. A fight ensued, in which the soldiers, who were greatly outnumbered, were defeated, with a loss of four men, the Indians still holding the cattle. After this fight, there was not a word nor an act from any member of the Southern Cheyennes indicative of peace, until the 1st of September, when the Indian agent at Fort Lyon received the following:

"CHEYENNE VILLAGE, *Aug.* 29, 1864.

"MAJOR COLLEY,—We received a letter from Bent, wishing us to make peace. We held a council in regard to it. All come to the conclusion to make peace with you, providing you make peace with the Kiowas, Comanches, Arapahoes, Apaches, and Sioux. We are going to send a messenger to the Kiowas and to the other nations about our going to make peace with you. We heard that you have some [Indian prisoners] in Denver. We have seven prisoners of yours which we are willing to give up, providing you give up yours. There are three war-parties out yet, and two of Arapahoes. They have been out for some time, and are expected in soon. When we held this council there were few Arapahoes and Sioux present. We want true news from you in return. That is a letter.

"BLACK KETTLE, *and other chiefs.*"

This letter was written for the chiefs by Edmond Guerrier and George Bent, Cheyenne half-breeds. Black Kettle was head chief of all the Southern Cheyennes, and conceded by all to be the most friendly of the chiefs towards the whites, with, possibly, the exception of Bull Bear. Yet, by this letter, he and the other chiefs admit fully that they were hostiles; that three Cheyenne war-parties were then out; that they were in coalition with the other tribes, and would consult them before treating; that they would treat only if all the other tribes treated. Indeed, why should the Cheyennes deny that they were hostile? They had been raiding in every direction; had run off stock repeatedly; had attacked stages and emigrant trains; had killed settlers; had carried off women and children; had fought the troops under Major Downing; had defeated those under Lieutenant Dunn and Lieutenant Ayres; and had been evading other bodies of troops all summer. They attacked the settlements on the Little Blue, and, after killing the men, they carried off Mrs. Ewbanks, Miss Roper, and three children. It was almost certainly they who killed Mr. and Mrs. Hungate and their two babies at Running Creek. They carried off Mrs. Martin and a little boy from a ranch on Plum Creek. General Curtis prepared two or three times to march against them, but was diverted from his purpose by rebel raiders from Arkansas. He sent General Blunt after them, and they ambushed his advance-guard at Pawnee Fork and almost annihilated it. On November 12, after Black Kettle had gone to Sand Creek, a party of Cheyennes and Arapahoes approached a government train on Walnut Creek, east of Fort Larned, and, after protesting friendship and shaking hands, suddenly fell upon the teamsters and killed fourteen of them, the only person who escaped alive being a boy who was scalped and left for dead. He recovered, but became imbecile, and died from the effects of the injury.

The Cheyennes never denied that they were hostiles; that they were was a discovery of the Indian ring, perpetuated by Indian worshippers. When they sent in the letter quoted above Major Wynkoop went out to them, and brought in Black Kettle, his brother White Antelope, and Bull Bear, of the Cheyennes, and Neva and other Arapahoes, representing Left Hand, for a talk with Governor Evans. They said then: "It was like going through a strong fire or blast for Major Wynkoop's men to come to our camp; it was the same for us to come to see you." From this talk I quote the following: " Gov. EVANS. 'Who committed the murder of the Hungate family on Running Creek?' NEVA. 'The Arapahoes; a party of the northern band who were passing

WHICH TRIBE DID IT?

north. It was Medicine Man or Roman Nose and three others. I am satisfied, from the time he left a certain camp for the North, that it was this party of four persons.' AGENT WHITELY. 'That cannot be true.' Gov. E. 'Where is Roman Nose?' NEVA. 'You ought to know better than me; you have been nearer to him.' Gov. E. 'Who killed the man and the boy at the head of Cherry Creek?' NEVA (after consultation). 'Kiowas and Comanches.' Gov. E. 'Who stole soldiers' horses and mules from Jimmy's camp twenty-seven days ago?' NEVA. 'Fourteen Cheyennes and Arapahoes together.' Gov. E. 'What were their names?' NEVA. 'Powder Face and Whirlwind, who are now in our camp, were the leaders.' COL. SHOUP. 'I counted twenty Indians on that occasion.' Gov. E. 'Who stole Charley Autobee's horses?' NEVA. 'Raven's son.' Gov. E. 'Who took the stock from Fremont's orchard and had the first fight with the soldiers this spring north of there?' WHITE ANTELOPE. 'Before answering this question I would like for you to know that this was the beginning of the war, and I should like to know what it was for. A soldier fired first.' Gov. E. 'The Indians had stolen about forty horses; the soldiers went to recover them, and the Indians fired a volley into their ranks.' WHITE ANTELOPE. 'That is all a mistake; they were coming down the Bijou and found one horse and one mule. They returned one horse, before they got to Gerry's, to a man, then went to Gerry's expecting to turn the other one over to some one. They then heard that the soldiers and Indians were fighting somewhere down the Platte; then they took fright and all fled.' Gov. E. 'Who were the Indians who had the fight?' WHITE ANTELOPE. 'They were headed by the Fool Badger's son, a young man, one of the greatest of the Cheyenne warriors, who was wounded, and though still alive he will never recover.' NEVA. 'I want to say something; it makes me feel bad to be talking about these things and opening old sores. . . . The Comanches, Kiowas, and Sioux have done much more injury than we have. We will tell what we know, but cannot speak for others.' Gov. E. 'I suppose you acknowledge the depredations on the Little Blue, as you have the prisoners then taken in your possession.' WHITE

ANTELOPE. 'We [the Cheyennes] took two prisoners west of Fort Kearney, and destroyed the trains.' . . . NEVA. 'I know the value of the presents which we receive from Washington ; we cannot live without them. That is why I try so hard to keep peace with the whites.' Gov. E. 'I cannot say anything about those things now.' NEVA. 'I can speak for all the Arapahoes under Left Hand. Raven has sent no one here to speak for him ; Raven has fought the whites.' " Little Raven (Oh-has-tee) was head chief of the Southern Arapahoes, and was notoriously hostile. Even Major Wynkoop conceded that he had, during the summer, killed three men and carried off a woman.

But even if most of the Cheyennes had been hostile, were not the Indians at Sand Creek friendly? It is usually difficult to disprove an Indian's protestations of friendship in a satisfactory way, but if ever it was done it was here. Black Kettle had admitted his hostility, as shown above. So had his brother, White Antelope. War Bonnet, a chief who was killed there, was identified as one of the most active hostiles in the attack on General Blunt at Pawnee Fork. The testimony shows, without contradiction, that there were at least two hundred warriors in the camp, and it would be very difficult to point out a Cheyenne warrior who had been friendly. It had been the plea of the chiefs, all along, that they desired to carry out the treaty of Fort Wise, but were deterred by fear of their warriors. But more satisfactory than the established reputation of these Indians was the testimony of scalps, women's and children's dresses, and stolen goods, which were found in profusion in the teepees. Perhaps medical testimony will be most convincing as to the condition of the scalps. Dr. Caleb S. Birtsell, Assistant Surgeon, testified : " While in one of the lodges dressing wounded soldiers a soldier came to the opening of the lodge and called my attention to some white scalps he held in his hand ; my impression, after examination, was that two or three of them were quite fresh ; I saw, in the hands of soldiers, silk dresses and other garments belonging to women." Major Anthony, commanding at Fort Lyon, considered that there were three Indians in the camp who were friendly, Black Kettle, Left

Hand, and One Eye, and these he desired to be spared. Black Kettle escaped unhurt; Left Hand received a wound from the effect of which he afterwards died; and One Eye was killed. He was in the camp as a spy; placed there, on a salary of $125 per month and a ration, by Major Wynkoop, to watch these "friendly" Cheyennes, and continued in the same position by Major Anthony.

And this brings us to another equally serious question. Although these Cheyennes at Sand Creek had been hostile, were they not at Sand Creek under a promise of protection by the military? To this the testimony answers clearly, "No." That is a rather startling statement to one who is familiar only with the current version of Sand Creek, but it is true, nevertheless. Both the congressional and departmental investigations were peculiar. The former was conducted by a committee of men whose minds were made up before they began; the style of their questions, the inaccuracy of their findings, and the fact that they condemned every one for prevarication who differed from what they expected in testimony, prove this. The latter was conducted by Major Wynkoop, who had been displaced by Major Anthony at Fort Lyon but a short time previous to the fight, who was one of the leading prosecuting witnesses, and who was, immediately after the investigation, appointed to the Agency, a position which is very rarely forced on men against their wishes. There was also a military commission appointed, which took testimony at Denver and Fort Lyon; it was presided over by Colonel Tappan, of the 1st Colorado Cavalry, who was recognized as a personal enemy of Chivington. This was the only one of the tribunals before which Chivington appeared and was given opportunity to cross-examine or produce witnesses. The reports of the other investigations were made without any knowledge of its proceedings; in fact, its proceedings were not published for two years after the reports were made. In the testimony at both of the earlier investigations, scheming and jealousy crop out at many points. The prosecuting witnesses who were out of office charged the prosecuting witnesses who were in office with stealing from the Indians, and selling them their own goods. The fullest latitude was given

to hearsay, and expressions of opinion were courted.   But
the most striking thing in all that testimony was the adroit
manner in which several witnesses confused the relations of
Black Kettle's Cheyennes, to Fort Lyon, with those of Little
Raven's Arapahoes.   Their real relations were explained to
the Committee on the Conduct of the War, clearly enough to
have been understood by men who were not blinded by prejudice, but the committee only carried on to perfection the
work which the witnesses had begun.   The testimony of all

LITTLE RAVEN.

the witnesses, taken together, shows that the Indians who
came to the fort and were subsisted by Major Wynkoop were
six hundred and fifty-two of the Southern Arapahoes, under
their head chief, Little Raven.   That this chief had been hostile is not questioned; Major Wynkoop himself blames him
and his warriors for all the depredations committed by the
Arapahoes.   On November 2 Major Anthony arrived and
assumed command; he found these Arapahoes camped two
miles from Fort Lyon, with all their arms, and coming daily
to the fort for provisions; he told them they must surrender

their arms, and they gave up a lot of old and worn-out weapons, which, they said, were all they had. After ten days he concluded that he was exceeding his authority in this, returned their arms to them, and told them to go away. They went; Major Wynkoop says that Little Raven's band went to Camp Wynkoop, and Left Hand's joined the Cheyennes. The Arapahoes who went with Left Hand numbered about forty.

The most satisfactory evidence in regard to this is not in the testimony of any one, but in the official report of Major Anthony, made at the time, when there was no "Sand Creek" to attack or defend. On November 6, in a letter to headquarters, after recounting his disarming the Arapahoes, he says: "Nine Cheyenne Indians to-day sent in, wishing to see me. They state that six hundred of that tribe are now thirty-five miles north of here, coming towards the post, and two thousand about seventy-five miles away, waiting for better weather to enable them to come in. I shall not permit them to come in, even as prisoners, for the reason that if I do I shall have to subsist them upon a prisoner's rations. I shall, however, demand their arms, all stolen stock, and the perpetrators of all depredations. I am of the opinion that they will not accept this proposition, but that they will return to the Smoky Hill. They pretend that they want peace, and I think they do now, as they cannot fight during the winter, except where a small band of them can find an unprotected train or frontier settlement. I do not think it is policy to make peace with them now, until all perpetrators of depredations are surrendered up, to be dealt with as we may propose." This, then, was the true state of affairs; on November 6 there was not a Cheyenne at Fort Lyon; there were six hundred and fifty-two Arapahoes under the hostile chief Little Raven, who was then playing friend; there were six hundred Cheyennes under Black Kettle, thirty-five miles north, proposing to come in. And what was done in regard to the Cheyennes? They came on down after some further parleying; they were not allowed to come into the fort at all, or camp in the vicinity of the post. They were told that they might go over on Sand Creek, forty miles away, and camp,

27

and if the commandant received any authority to treat with them he would let them know. They were not in the camp two miles from Fort Lyon at any time; they were never disarmed; and they were never held as prisoners.

Neither did these Indians have any promise of immunity from Governor Evans or Colonel Chivington, as is intimated by the committee. They met but once, at the council in Denver, on September 28. It has been stated over and over that the Cheyennes came to Sand Creek, in response to Governor Evans's circular, calling on the friendly Indians to take refuge at the forts—friendly Cheyennes and Arapahoes at Fort Lyon. This statement is absolutely and unqualifiedly untrue. The circular was dated June 27. Three months later the chiefs appeared in Denver to talk peace, in consequence of the circular, but were plainly told it was too late for any treaty. Governor Evans said to them: "Whatever peace they make must be with the soldiers, and not with me;" and the entire talk was on that basis. I quote again: "WHITE ANTELOPE. 'How can we be protected from the soldiers on the plains?' Gov. E. 'You must make that arrangement with the military chief.' WHITE ANTELOPE. 'I fear that these new soldiers who have gone out may kill some of my people while I am here.' Gov. E. 'There is great danger of it.'" Again, Governor Evans said: "I hand you over to the military, one of the chiefs of which is here to-day, and can speak for himself to them if he chooses." The chief referred to was Colonel Chivington, Commander of the District—it should be noted, however, that Fort Lyon was not in Chivington's district. He said: "I am not a big war chief, but all the soldiers in this country are at my command. My rule of fighting white men or Indians is to fight them until they lay down their arms and submit to military authority. They are nearer Major Wynkoop than any one else, and they can go to him when they get ready to do that." If any one can torture those utterances into promises of immunity he is welcome to do so.

Some five weeks later the messengers of the Cheyennes arrived at Fort Lyon and were turned away, as above stated. They did not arrive there until after Major Wynkoop was superseded by Major Anthony. They did not make any arrangement with Major Wynkoop; it was impossible for them to do so, as he was not in command. More than that, Major Wynkoop never, at any time, had any authority to make any treaty with them, and the Indians knew it. White Antelope said, in the council: "When Major Wynkoop came, we proposed to make peace. He said he had no power to make a peace, except to bring them here and return them safe." The Cheyennes went over to Sand Creek and camped, not anticipating any trouble, because there were no soldiers near them, except the garrison, and it was too small to risk an attack. Indeed, they were ready for an attack from it, and sent word that, "If that little —— —— red-eyed chief wants a fight, we will give him all he wants." The chief referred to was Major Anthony, who was af-

flicted with sore eyes at the time. The Indians were not allowed to visit the fort, and none of their friends or supposed allies, except on first being blindfolded. This was under general orders which were adopted a few weeks previously, after a Sunday - morning performance by friendly Indians at Fort Larned. On that occasion the Indians had drawn supplies for the week, and some squaws were executing a dance

FRIDAY—A GOOD ARAPAHOE.

for the edification of a part of the officers and men, when the braves stampeded the cattle belonging to the post, with all the horses and mules, and succeeded in getting away with them. At the first whoop of the stampede the dancers jumped on their ponies and scampered away, demonstrating that the affair had been planned in cold blood. Major Anthony testified that he had no friendly relations with these Cheyennes; that he should have attacked them before Chivington came if his force had not been too small; that he told Chivington it was only a question of policy whether they should be attacked or not, as it would probably cause an attack by the large band, which was not far distant. So far as the propriety of attacking these Indians was concerned, there is not the least question but that Chivington was justified in his attack, under all the rules of civilized warfare. They were hostiles, and there was no truce with them. There is another matter—it seems almost absurd to mention it, but it were well to prevent any further misunderstanding—and that is the display of flags by Black Kettle, which some persons have seemed to lay much stress upon. The uniform testimony of the soldiers was that they saw nothing of the kind, but that is immaterial. No one of common understanding would profess that the display of a flag of any kind was cause for stopping troops in the midst of a charge, and especially in the midst of a surprise of an enemy's camp.

Having now shown the propriety of the attack, we arrive at the question of the propriety of the manner in which it was made, a question much more difficult of solution. One point is certain—every one in authority felt that the Indians ought to be punished. Major Wynkoop testifies that Governor Evans at first objected to seeing the chiefs at all, but finally consented to hold the council which has been mentioned. His feelings on the subject were exposed to the Indians at the council in these words: "The time when you can make war best is in the summer time; when I can make war best is in the winter. You, so far, have had the advantage; my time is just coming." He told them, as before stated, that they would have to talk to the military authorities, and his action was approved by the Indian Bureau. The military had no desire for peace at the time. It is quite true that the field orders of General Curtis directed hostilities only against hostile Indians, and expressly stated that "women and children must be spared," but "hostile Indians" meant Indians who had been hostile, and neither he nor any other commander in the West was in favor of treating till the Indians had been punished. On the day of Governor Evans's council with the chiefs, General Curtis telegraphed the District Commander: "I fear agent of the Interior Department will be ready to make presents too soon. It is better to chastise before giving anything but a little tobacco to talk over. No peace must be made without my directions." The last telegram Chivington received from him, before marching, was: "Pursue everywhere and punish the Cheyennes and Arapahoes; pay no attention to district lines. No presents must be made and no peace concluded without my consent." The reader will observe that General Curtis is not by these directions made responsible for killing the women and children, or deciding that the Sand Creek camp was hostile, but his desire to punish the Indians was clear and decided. And it was so all through the West. A few weeks later, when Colonel Ford wanted to make peace with the Kiowas and Comanches, General Dodge, his Department Commander, telegraphed him: "The military have no authority to treat with Indians. Our duty is to make them keep the peace by punishing them for their hostility. Keep posted as to their location, so that as soon as ready we can strike them." So, in New Mexico, General Carleton had instructed Colonel Kit Carson: "If the Indians send in a flag and desire to treat for peace, say to the bearer that when the people of New Mexico were attacked by the Texans, the Mescaleros broke their treaty of peace, and murdered innocent people, and ran off their stock; that now our hands are untied, and you have been sent to punish them for their treachery and their crimes; that you have no power to make peace; that you are there to kill them wherever you can find them; that if they beg for peace, their chiefs and twenty of their principal men must come to Santa Fé to have a talk here; but tell them fairly and frankly that you will keep after their people and slay them until you receive orders to desist from these head-quarters." On September 19 Curtis writes to Carleton: "General Blunt is at or near Fort Larned looking out for Indians, and may co-operate with you in crushing out some of

the vile hordes that now harass our lines of communication."
On October 22 Carleton writes to Blunt, hoping he will effect
a union with Carson, "so that a blow may be struck which
those two treacherous tribes will remember."   On January 30,
1865, Curtis writes to Governor Evans: "I protest my desire
to pursue and punish the enemy everywhere, in his lodges especially; but I do not believe in killing women and children
who can be taken."

It is equally certain that the desire of punishing these Indians was increased, with loyal people, by the belief that their
hostility was produced by Southern emissaries. How far their
hostility was so produced will never be definitely known, but
there was reason for the belief, without doubt. Soon after
the beginning of the war the insurgents had occupied Indian
territory and enrolled many Indians in Confederate regiments.
The loyal Indians tried to resist, but, after two or three engagements, about seven thousand of them were driven into
Kansas.   From the men among them three regiments were
organized, and the women and children were subsisted out of
the annuities of the hostiles. In the latter part of 1862, John
Ross, head chief of the Cherokees, announced officially that
the Cherokee nation had treated with the Confederate States,
and, as is well known, there were several regiments of Indians
in the regular Confederate service, besides numbers in irregular relations, among whom were Cherokees, Creeks, Choctaws,
Chickasaws, Osages, Seminoles, Senecas, Shawnees, Quapaws,
Comanches, Wachitas, Kiowas, and Pottawattamies, and none
of them regained friendly relations with the United States
until the treaty of September 21, 1865. On the south of Colorado the Comanches and Kiowas were at war, with Southern
sympathies. The Mescaleros had taken the war-path on the
advance of the Texans. To the north it was the same. The
Sioux troubles all originated in Minnesota, and concerning
them our Consul-general in Canada, Mr. Giddings, wrote at
the time: "There is little doubt that the recent outbreak in
the Northwest has resulted from the efforts of secession agents
operating through Canadian Indians and fur-traders." The
war feeling was so strong among the Sioux that the friendly
Yanktons, in 1862, refused to receive their annuities unless a

force of soldiers was brought, to protect them from the other Sioux, who insisted on their becoming hostile. As the Minnesota Sioux were driven west the feeling spread everywhere, and in the winter of 1863–64 ripened into the coalition "to clean out all this country," while the government had its hands full with the South. With the Indians on all sides of them moved to war by Southern emissaries, the natural supposition is that the Cheyennes and Arapahoes were at war from the same reason, and especially as the Sioux, Comanches, Kiowas, and Apaches were their friends and allies, while the Pawnees, Kaws, and Osages, their hereditary enemies, were in the service of the United States. It was certain that the South had hopes of opening hostility in this region, for, in 1863, nineteen rebel officers were killed by friendly Osages, and on their persons were found papers authorizing them to organize the sympathetic in Colorado and Dakota. White Wolf, a friendly Arapahoe, informed Agent Whitely, in the latter part of August, that the Cheyennes had "declared their intention to take all the forts on the Arkansas when joined by the Texan soldiers," and this indicated that some one had told them a move in that direction was contemplated. Finally, George Bent, half-breed Cheyenne, son of Colonel Bent, had served under Price in Missouri, had been captured, and, after being paroled, had joined the Cheyennes. He had taken part in their depredations, and helped write their letter to Colley, and was reported and believed to be a rebel emissary to them. Chivington spoke of them as "red rebels" in official correspondence, long before the Sand Creek fight, and to men of

GEORGE BENT.

his feelings there was just this one crime of treason that could add anything to the atrocity of Indian warfare.

There are two reasons given for killing women and children, and for mutilation, which are worthy of consideration. First, as a matter of policy, it is believed by frontiersmen that Indians should be fought just as they fight. They look contemptuously on the policy of treating them according to the rules of civilized warfare. They believe that the only way to make Indians sign a treaty which they will keep, is, when at war with them, to kill them at every opportunity, destroy their property, and make their homes desolate; in short, to make them suffer. The plains Indians have given more cause for this belief than other tribes. They have repeatedly shown a disposition to go to war in the spring, when their ponies were getting fat, and subsistence was easily had, but as winter came on, and hardship began, they were ready to treat. They have had cause, too, to laugh at the silly whites, who bought their friendship with presents, while the blood of slaughtered innocents was hardly dried. They took advantage of the white man by killing his helpless people, while, for the safety of their own, they relied on the white man's ideas of warfare. Their women took advantage of him by fighting, as they did at Sand Creek, Ash Hollow, and many other places, along with the men, and, when the battle went against them, proclaiming their sex and claiming immunity. There is not a bit of doubt that killing women and children has a very dampening effect on the ardor of the Indian. In this very case of Sand Creek they said "they had always heard that the whites did not kill women and children, but now they had lost all confidence in them." Their "loss of confidence" grows a trifle amusing, when it is remembered that they had been killing women and children all summer themselves. Scalping and mutilation also strike terror to the Indian heart. Their religious belief is that the spirit in the next world has the same injuries that are inflicted on the body here. For this reason they almost invariably mutilate corpses, besides taking the scalp, which is almost an essential for entrance to the happy hunting-grounds. The greatest acts of daring ever shown by plains Indians have been in carrying off the bodies of their dead to prevent these misfortunes. That the Sand Creek affair inspired them with terror is beyond question. The Cheyennes and Arapahoes got over into Kansas and Indian Territory as quickly as possible, and stayed there. A party of Sioux raided down into Colorado once afterwards, but when they heard that the Colorado troops were after them they scampered off as though the evil spirit were at their heels.

Secondly, is the matter of vengeance. There is a certain amount of justice in the theory of meting to a man in his own measure, and the people of Colorado had old scores to pay in the accounts of murder, robbery, and rape. The treatment of women, by any Indians, is usually bad, but by the plains Indians especially so. When a woman is captured by a war-party she is the common property of all of them, each night, till they reach their village, when she becomes the special property of her individual captor, who may sell or gamble her away when he likes. If she resists she is "staked out," that is to say, four pegs are driven into the ground and a hand or foot tied to each, to prevent struggling. She is also beaten, mutilated, or even killed, for resistance. If a woman gives out under this treatment, she is either tied so as to prevent escape, or maimed so as to insure death in case of rescue, and left to die slowly. That there may be no question of the guilt of these Sand Creek Cheyennes, I quote the statement of Mrs. Ewbanks, who was captured at the same time as the prisoners surrendered by them, as taken down by Lieutenant Triggs, of the 7th Iowa Cavalry, and Judge-advocate Zabriskie, of the 1st Nevada Cavalry. "Mrs. Lucinda Ewbanks states that she was born in Pennsylvania; is twenty-four years of age; she resided on the Little Blue, at or near the Narrows. She says that on the 8th day of August, 1864, the house was attacked, robbed, burned, and herself and two children, with her nephew and Miss Roper, were captured by Cheyenne Indians. Her eldest child, at the time, was three years old; her youngest was one year old; her nephew was six years old. When taken from her home was, by the Indians, taken south across the Republican, and west to a creek, the name of which she does not remember. Here, for a short

ON THE LITTLE BLUE.

time, was their village or camping-place. They were travelling all winter. When first taken by the Cheyennes she was
taken to the lodge of an old chief, whose name she does not
remember. He forced me, by the most terrible threats and
menaces, to yield my person to him. He treated me as his
wife. He then traded me to Two Face, a Sioux, who did
not treat me as a wife, but forced me to do all menial labor
done by squaws, and he beat me terribly. Two Face traded
me to Black Foot (a Sioux) who treated me as his wife, and
because I resisted him his squaws abused and ill-used me.
Black Foot also beat me unmercifully, and the Indians generally treated me as though I was a dog, on account of my
showing so much detestation towards Black Foot. Two Face
traded for me again. I then received a little better treatment. I was better treated among the Sioux than the Cheyennes; that is, the Sioux gave me more to eat. When with

the Cheyennes I was often hungry. Her purchase from the
Cheyennes was made early last fall (1864), and she remained
with them (the Sioux) until May, 1865. During the winter
the Cheyennes came to buy me and the child, for the purpose of burning us, but Two Face would not let them have
me. During the winter we were on the North Platte the
Indians were killing the whites all the time and running off
their stock. They would bring in the scalps of the whites
and show them to me and laugh about it. They ordered me
frequently to wean my baby, but I always refused; for I felt
convinced if he was weaned they would take him from me,
and I should never see him again."

Mrs. Ewbanks's daughter died in Denver, from injuries
received among the Indians, before her mother was released.
Her nephew also died from his injuries, at the same place.
Miss Roper, who was surrendered with the children, had experienced the same treatment that no white woman was ever
known to escape at the hands of the plains Indians. Mrs.
Martin, another prisoner surrendered by them, was taken by
the Cheyennes on Plum Creek, " west of Kearney," as testified by herself and admitted by White Antelope in the council. Mrs. Snyder, another captive, had grown weary of the
friendship of these Cheyennes, and hung herself before Major Wynkoop arrived. These things were known to the people of Colorado, and two thirds of the troops who went there
were citizen-soldiers, raised for the express purpose of fighting Indians. Be it known, also, that these offenses were
committed without any provocation from settlers, beyond occupying the lands which the chiefs of the Cheyennes had relinquished in treaty. There is absolutely not on record, from
any source, a single charge, let alone an instance, of aggression or injury to any Cheyenne or Arapahoe, by any settler
of Colorado, prior to Sand Creek. The sole troubles had
been with the soldiers in chastising the Indians for past offences. The people of Colorado did want revenge, and these
men, who had been cooped up all summer in towns and block-
houses, whose crops were ruined, whose stock had been run
off, whose houses had been burned, who had been eating
bread made of forty-five-dollar flour, who had buried the

mutilated bodies of their neighbors, in helpless wrath, who
had heard the stories of the women captives—these men
marched to Sand Creek, with the fire of vengeance in their
hearts, and quenched it in blood.

Let us now look for a moment at the report of the Joint
Committee on the Conduct of the War. It states, first, that
these Indians wished "to deliver up some white captives they
had purchased of other Indians." The Indians did not pretend to have purchased them. They admitted in the council
that they had captured them, and the captives themselves testified to the same, as shown above. It states that after the
council these Indians went to Fort Lyon, where they " were
treated somewhat as prisoners of war, receiving rations and
being obliged to remain within certain bounds." As has
been shown, the Cheyennes were never treated as prisoners
of war, received no rations, and did not remain within any
bounds. The Indians who did so were Little Raven's Arapahoes, who were hostile, by the declarations of the Arapahoe
chiefs in the council, and the testimony of Major Wynkoop.
These Indians went away before the Cheyennes came, but
eight lodges of them, under Left Hand, who was friendly,
went to the Cheyennes and camped with them at Sand Creek.
This wrongful and unjust confusion is kept up all through
the report. It states that "all the testimony goes to show
that the Indians under the immediate control of Black Kettle and White Antelope, of the Cheyennes, and Left Hand, of
the Arapahoes, were and had been friendly to the whites, and
had not been guilty of any acts of hostility or depredation."
Not only does the testimony show the opposite to be true,
but also there is no testimony whatever to that effect. There
was testimony to the friendly character of these chiefs, but
not to that of their Indians, and, in fact, no Indians could be
separated out as theirs, for at the time of their letter, and the
council, and afterwards, the Cheyennes were all together, and
all under their "immediate control." Even when the party
at Sand Creek came in ahead, it was reported by them that
the remainder of the tribe was a short distance back, waiting
for good weather.

It states that "a northern band of the Cheyennes, known

as the Dog Soldiers, had been guilty of acts of hostility; but all the testimony goes to prove that they had no connection with Black Kettle's band," and that "Black Kettle and his band denied all connection with or responsibility for the Dog Soldiers." As shown in a former chapter, the Dog Soldiers were not a separate band, but were a department in the tribal government. Black Kettle and his band did not deny connection with them or responsibility for them; many of the band at Sand Creek were Dog Soldiers. Bull Bear, the leader of the Dog Soldiers, was at the council in Denver as one of Black Kettle's sub-chiefs. The only time that any of the Indians had an opportunity to make a statement which could go to the committee, was at the council in Denver, and there the Dog Soldiers were mentioned but once, and in this passage: " BLACK KETTLE. 'We will return with Major Wynkoop to Fort Lyon; we will then proceed to our village and take back word to my young men, every word you say. I cannot answer for all of them, but think there will be but little difficulty in getting them to assent to help the soldiers.' MAJOR WYNKOOP. 'Did not the Dog Soldiers agree, when I had my council with you, to do whatever you said, after you had been here?' BLACK KETTLE. 'Yes.'" The committee is far more kind to Black Kettle than he is to himself. It had determined that he should not be connected with them. Senator Doolittle pressed this question on John S. Smith, one of the most bitter of the prosecuting witnesses: " Is the northern band the same that are commonly called the Dog Soldiers?" Smith, who had been among them twenty-seven years, answered: " No, sir; the Dog Soldiers are mixed up promiscuously; this is a band that has preferred the North Platte and north of the North Platte, and lives over in what is called the bad land, *mauvais terre*." The same fact was shown by Major Wynkoop in his cross-examination, by Chivington, before the Military Commission, as follows: " Q. Will you explain what the Dog Soldiers are and how they are controlled? A. I understand that the Dog Soldiers are a portion of the warriors of the Cheyenne tribe, and presume that they are controlled by the head men."

It states that " these Indians, at the suggestion of Governor

Evans and Colonel Chivington, repaired to Fort Lyon and placed themselves under the protection of Major Wynkoop." Enough of the council proceedings has been quoted to show the falsity of this. They told the Indians that they could not treat with them, but that they must go to the military, and when they got ready to lay down their arms and surrender as prisoners of war they might go to Major Wynkoop. But, in fact, the Cheyennes did not even send in their messengers until after Major Wynkoop was suspended. They

INDIANS ATTACKING STAGE.

were never under his protection at all. It states that Jack Smith, the half-breed son of John S. Smith, was in Black Kettle's camp, at the time of the attack, as a spy, employed by the government. As shown above, he guided the troops to the camp to make the attack. This man was the only prisoner killed after the fight, and it was in evidence before the committee that he had led an attack on a stage a short time previously. That he was present he did not deny, but said he approached the stage for some information, and, on being fired on, fired back in self-defence. But it is not necessary to particularize further. The report abuses every one who, in telling the truth, happened to differ from the preconceived judgment of the committee; it distorts and colors every matter of fact involved so as to injure Chivington and his men; it omits or glosses over all the injuries to the people of Colorado; and, having arrived at a proper pitch of indignation and misrepresentation, it assails Colonel Chivington in a gush of sanguinary rhetoric, that reads more like the reputed address of Spartacus to the gladiators than the impartial judgment of rational men.

But, outrageous as was the report of the committee, it was dignified, just, and proper by the side of the ornamental misrepresentation that outsiders have added. It has been said that Sand Creek "brought on the general war of 1865, which cost the government $35,000,000 and much loss of life," and this statement has become a part of the "history" of the affair. Sand Creek brought on that war just about as much as the battle of Gettysburg brought on the late civil war. It was an event in the war, and no amount of misrepresentation can make it anything else. Leaving the Cheyennes out of consideration altogether, the general war had been in progress since the early spring of 1864. But, as a matter of fact, it did not even aggravate the war. It has already been shown that the Cheyennes had been at war all summer, and no other tribe went to war on account of it. On January 12, 1865, on receipt of orders to investigate Chivington's action, General Curtis despatched to Washington: "Although the colonel may have transgressed my field orders concerning Indian warfare, and otherwise acted very much against my views of propriety in his assault at Sand Creek, still it is not true, as Indian agents and Indian traders are representing, that such extra severity is increasing Indian war. On the contrary, it tends to reduce their numbers and bring them to terms. . . . I will be glad to save the few honest and kindly disposed, and protest against the slaughter of women and children; although, since General Harney's attack of the Sioux many years ago at Ash Hollow, the popular cry of settlers and soldiers on the frontier favors an indiscriminate slaughter which is very difficult to restrain. I abhor this style, but so it goes, from Minnesota to Texas. . . . There is no doubt a portion of this tribe assembled were occupied in making assaults on our stages and trains, and the tribes well know that we have to hold the whole community responsible for acts they could restrain, if they would properly exert their efforts in that way." Again, on January 30, he wrote to Governor Evans: "Let me say, too, that I see nothing new in all this Indian movement since the Chivington affair, except that Indians are more frightened and keep farther away. By pushing them hard this next month, before grass recruits their ponies, they will be better satisfied with making war and robbery a business." On the same day he wrote Major-general Halleck: "There is no new feature in these Indian troubles except that Indians seem more frightened." General Curtis commanded the department; he had all the information as to the state of the hostilities that could be had; he evidently was not inclined to defend Chivington; and therefore his testimony on this point ought to be conclusive.

Said Hon. Mr. Loughridge to the House of Representatives: "Some of the few captured children, after they had been carried many miles by the troops, were taken from the wagons and their brains dashed out. I gather this from the records and official reports, and blush to say that its truth cannot be questioned." Mr. Loughridge might well blush for other reasons. There is not one word in all the testimony, records, and official reports, to substantiate this statement. The nearest and only approach to it, in the report of the Joint Committee, is this statement by Lieutenant Cannon, who accompanied the expedition: "I heard of one instance of a child, a few months old, being thrown into the feed-box of a wagon, and, after being carried some distance, left on the ground to perish." In the testimony taken by the Military Commission, Lieutenant Cramer and Private Louderback give similar hearsay evidence, in almost the same words. Only one witness was examined, at any time, who professed to have personal knowledge of this abandonment, and that was Sergeant Lucian Palmer, who was introduced by the prosecution, before the Military Commission. He said: "They [the two squaws] took care of it [the pappoose in question] the first

INDIAN SCOUTS CELEBRATING.

day after we left Sand Creek; they had it in bed with them the night we stopped this side of Sand Creek; they left it themselves, as no one else had anything to do with it, to my knowledge." Thus the prosecution disposed of the feed-box story, and left Mr. Loughridge without even that faint support for his slander. It was distinctly testified, by every witness who was questioned on the subject, that no one was killed after the fight except Jack Smith. It was also established, without contradiction, that the two squaws (wives of white men) and five children, who were said, by every witness except those mentioned, to have been the only prisoners taken, were conveyed to Fort Lyon and left there. These are but samples that show the extraordinary extent to which this delusion has been carried. The wealth of epithets and invectives that has been gathered to damn the reputation of this man Chivington, by people who have, at best, but superficially examined his case, constitutes a veritable treasury of vituperation. If everything that was said against him by the witnesses were true, and much of it, on its face, was not, he is still the colossal martyr to misrepresentation of this century.

The sequel to Sand Creek throws some valuable light on the character of the case. On October 14, 1865, a treaty was made with the Cheyenne chiefs on the Little Arkansas, on which occasion John S. Smith and Major Wynkoop were figuring prominently. The treaty, in its original draft, went out of the way to attack Chivington and the troops, and this feature the Senate omitted by amendment. The treaty was made on behalf of the entire tribe, but the majority of the Dog Soldiers were not present and never formally accepted its provisions. The most striking feature of it is that, while they were assigned a reservation with the privilege of roaming over their original territory, these friendly Indians were prohibited from camping within ten miles of a main travelled road, night or day, and were pledged not to go to any town or post without permission of the authorities there. Special remuneration was given to every one who had lost relatives or property at Sand Creek, and annuities of goods and money to the tribe in general, to the amount of $56,000 annually until they moved to the reservation, and $112,000 annually afterwards. Thefts, murders, and other offences were perpetrated by Indians in the following summer, and, so far as could be learned, they were committed by a party of Dog Soldiers, numbering some two hundred lodges, who had joined with about one hundred lodges of Sioux, under the chief Pawnee Killer. In the spring of 1867 General Hancock started with an expedition into the plains with the intent of making a peaceful demonstration of power, which would induce all doubtful and hostile Indians to go on reservations. Agents of the Indian bureau were invited to accompany the expedition, to assist in talks with the Indians, and did so.

They found the band of Dog Soldiers and Sioux on Pawnee Fork, about thirty miles above Fort Larned. After negotiating, and making several appointments for councils, which they did not keep, the Indians slipped away one dark night with all their property that they could carry. Spring was not their season for treating. The next heard of them was that they had burned several stage stations on the Smoky Hill route and killed, after torturing, three station keepers at Lookout Station, near Fort Hays. On receipt of information of this, General Hancock destroyed what was left of their village, and troops were kept in search of the Indians all summer, under command of General Custer. There were a number of engagements between them, and considerable loss of life, with no material advantage to either side. At the same time a severe pen-and-ink contest was being waged between war people and peace people in the East, and the peace people got the upper hand. The result of it all was that at the end of the season Custer was under arrest on a charge of leaving Fort Wallace without orders, while the Indians, who had had no opportunity to lay in supplies for the winter, made another treaty, in which the whole tribe, Dog Soldiers included, joined. This time they took a reservation wholly within Indian Territory, a triangular tract bounded by the Kansas line and the Cimarron and Arkansas rivers. They were to receive a suit of clothes for each Indian, and $20,000 annually, besides teachers, physicians, farmers, millers, carpenters, blacksmiths, and other guides to civilization. It was not agreed that they were to be given any arms or ammunition, and this the reader will remember. They agreed not to molest any coach or wagon, carry off any white woman or child, nor kill or scalp any white man; to surrender any wrong-doer for punishment, and not to interfere in any way with the building of the Kansas Pacific Railroad.

In the spring of 1868 it was learned that arms and ammunition were being issued to Indians, and a military order was made prohibiting it. The agents raised a cry that the Indians could not hunt the buffalo without arms and ammunition (they prefer the bow and arrow for this, and seldom used anything else); the peace people joined in the chorus that the Indians were being starved, and the order was revoked. On August 1 the Arapahoes received 100 pistols, 80 Lancaster rifles, 12 kegs of power, a keg and a half of lead, and 15,000 caps. On August 10 Colonel Wynkoop, our old acquaintance, who had been promoted, and appointed Indian Agent after the investigations, wrote: "I yesterday made the whole issue of annuity goods, arms, and ammunition to the Cheyenne chiefs and people of their nation; they were delighted at receiving the goods, particularly the arms and ammunition, and never before have I known them to be better satisfied, and express themselves as being so well contented previous to the issue. . . . They have now left for their hunting-grounds, and I am perfectly satisfied that there will be no trouble with them this season." What hunting-grounds had they left for? On September 10, just thirty days later, Colonel Wynkoop, in explaining that the Indians had gone to war because "their arms and ammunition" had not been issued promptly, writes: "But a short time before the issue was made a war-party had started north from the Cheyenne village, on the war-path against the Pawnees; and they, not knowing of the issue, and smarting under their supposed wrongs, committed the outrages on the Saline River which have led to the present unfortunate aspect of affairs." It was rather unfortunate. The inference from his letter is that it was all right for them to use their weapons, furnished for the purpose of hunting, in making war on the Pawnees,

who had been, for several years, our most valuable allies and
friends on the plains; but that they should attack the whites
was unfortunate.   Two hundred Cheyenne, four Arapahoe,
and twenty Sioux warriors raided down the Saline and the
Solomon, killing, ravishing, burning, and torturing.   They
carried off two young women, who were afterwards recovered
from Black Kettle's band, if he can be said to have had any
particular band, by threatening to hang some of their principal chiefs, who were captives.   Much of the plundered property was found in Black Kettle's camp.

Wynkoop then proposed to locate the friendly Indians
near Fort Larned, in order to separate the good ones from the
bad ones, Larned being about as near to the seat of war as
they could be placed; but General Sherman would have
nothing of that kind.   He said the Indians who were peaceable should stay on their reservation, where they belonged.
Never was a better opportunity for friendly Indians to
separate themselves from the bad ones and let themselves
be known: and they did it.   After some hard fighting in the
summer and fall, notably the eight days' fight between General Forsyth's party and four hundred and fifty Cheyennes,
aided by Sioux and Arapahoes, on the Arickaree fork of the
Republican, the bad Indians went into winter quarters, and a
winter expedition was sent against them under Custer, who
was reinstated for the occasion.   The reservation was vacant.
The good Cheyennes were not visible.   The entire southern
tribe was camped away south on the Wachita, on lands where
they had not even the right to hunt, with the hostile Kiowas,
Arapahoes, Comanches, and Apaches, forming an almost continuous camp for twelve miles.   Custer followed the trail of
a returning war-party into Black Kettle's camp, and, in the
early dawn of November 27, surprised the Indians, while
they were sleeping off the effects of the previous night's cele-
bration over fresh scalps and plunder.   Here, as at Sand
Creek and Ash Hollow, women fought with the men, and
a number of them were killed, but their fighting did no
good.   103 Indians were killed, and 53 squaws and children were captured, together with 875 ponies, 1123 robes,
535 pounds of powder, 4000 arrows, and arms and goods

THE CHARGE ON BLACK KETTLE'S CAMP.

of all descriptions, constituting all their possessions. What could be advantageously kept was retained, and the remainder, including 700 ponies, was destroyed. The entire Indian force attacked Custer, but he succeeded in getting his troops and captives safely away. And what did the irrepressible Wynkoop after this affair? He affirmed that the Cheyennes were martyrs ever, and that on this occasion they were peaceably on their way to Fort Cobb to receive their annuities when attacked! He also resigned his position as Indian Agent, feeling, probably, that it would be forced on him again. But Hancock and Custer were bigger game than poor Chivington. Their brother officers and officials examined their cases more carefully than they did that of the volunteer colonel, and Custer himself ventilated the matter in a series of articles in the *Galaxy* that made some people open their eyes.

After the war, Chivington returned to his old home in Ohio and settled on a small farm. A few years later his house was burned, and he afterwards moved to Blanchester, Clinton County, where he purchased the *Press*, and edited it for two or three years. In 1883 he was nominated on the Republican ticket for Representative to the legislature, and in the campaign "Sand Creek" was used for all it was worth. It began in the contest for the nomination and was continued until Chivington withdrew from the race. It was believed, and still is, by good judges of politics, that he would have been elected by a majority of five hundred or more, but there was a large Quaker population in Clinton, and, as is well known, the Society of Friends considers itself the special guardian of the Indian. He had an up-hill fight on his hands, and the opposition was very bitter. I can but think another thing influenced his determination. While this fight was being pressed upon him, he received an urgent letter from Colorado, asking him to attend and address a meeting of old settlers, on the twenty-fifth anniversary of the settlement of the state. There he would find old friends, who knew the true history of Sand Creek, and felt as he did. He went. There were hearty welcomes given to distinguished pioneers by the people assembled in Jewell Park on that day, but none so demonstrative as Colonel Chivington's. The chairman introduced him with these words: "We all remember the Indian wars of 1864 and '65, and with what joy we received the news that some of them at least had met the reward due to their treachery and cruelty. The man who can tell you all about those wars, who can tell you all you want to know of the Indians, and who can give you the true story of Sand Creek, is here. I have the honor, ladies and gentlemen, to introduce Colonel Chivington, one of Colorado's 'Pet Lambs.'"

He began his speech amid enthusiastic cheers, but as he proceeded the attention grew breathless. He told his story in a simple, straightforward way, and nods of assent and approval, from all parts of the pavilion, silently indicated that he need not prove the truth of his statements to the people gathered there. He did not reply to the thousand charges made against him, nor did he assume an argumentative style until he closed in these words: "But were not these Indians peaceable? Oh, yes, peaceable! Well, a few hundred of them have been peaceable for almost nineteen years, and none of them have been so troublesome as they were before Sand Creek. What are the facts? How about that treaty that Governor John Evans did not make with them in the summer of 1863? He, with Major Lorey and Major Whiteley, two of his Indian Agents, and the usual corps of attachés, under escort, went out to the Kiowa to treat. When he got there, they had gone a day's march farther out on the plains and would not meet him there, and so on, day after day, they moved out as he approached, until, wearied out, and suspicious of treachery, he returned without succeeding in his mission of peace. He told them by message that he had presents for them, but it was not peace and presents they wanted, but war and plunder. What of the peaceableness of their attack on General Blunt's advance-guard, north of Fort Larned, almost annihilating the advance before succor could reach them? What of the dove-like peace of their attack on the government train on Walnut Creek, east of Fort Larned, under the guise of friendship, till the drivers and attachés of the train were in their power, and at a signal struck down at once every man, only a boy of thirteen years barely escaping, and he, with the loss of his scalp, taken to his ears, finally died. What of the trains captured from Walnut Creek to Sand Creek on the Arkansas route, and from the Little Blue to the Kiowa on the Platte route, of supplies and wagons burned and carried off, and of the men killed? What of the Hungate family? Alas! what of the stock of articles of merchandise, fine silk dresses, infants' and youths' apparel, the embroidered night-gowns and chemises? Ay, what of the scalps of white men, women, and children, several of which they had not had time to dry and tan since taken? These, all these, and more, were taken from the belts of dead warriors on the battle-field of Sand Creek, and from their teepees which fell into our hands on the 29th day of November, 1864. What of the Indian blanket that was captured, fringed with white-women's scalps? What says the dust of the two hundred and eight men, women, and children, ranchers, emigrants, herders, and soldiers, who lost their lives at the hands of these Indians? Peaceable? Now we are peaceably disposed, but decline giving such testimonials of our peaceful proclivities, and I say here as I said in my own town, in the Quaker county of Clinton, State of Ohio, one night last week, I stand by Sand Creek."

Said the *Rocky Mountain News*, of the following day, "Colonel Chivington's speech was received with an applause from every pioneer which indicated that they, to a man, heartily approved the course of the colonel twenty years ago, in the famous affair in which many of them took part, and the man who applied the scalpel to the ulcer which bid fair to destroy the life of the new colony, in those critical times, was beyond a doubt the hero of the hour." This is the simple truth. Colorado stands by Sand Creek, and Colonel Chivington soon afterwards brought his family to the Queen City of the Plains, where his remaining days may be passed in peace.

What an eventful history! And how, through it all, his sturdy manhood has been manifest in every action. Through all the denunciation of that Indian fight, he has never wavered or trembled. Others have dodged and apologized and crawled, but Chivington never. He has not laid the blame upon superior officers, as he might do. He has not complained of

misinformation from inferior officers, as he might do. He
has not said that the soldiers committed excesses there which
were in no manner directed by him, as he might do. He has
simply stood up under a rain of abuse, heavier than the shower
of missiles that fell on Cœur de Leon before the castle of
Front de Bœuf, and answered back: "I stand by Sand
Creek." And was it wrong? To the abstract question,
whether or not it is right to kill women and children, there
can be but one answer. But as a matter of retaliation, and a
matter of policy, whether these people were justified in killing women and children at Sand Creek is a question to which
the answer does not come so glibly. Just after the massacre
at Fort Fetterman, General Sherman despatched to General
Grant : "We must act with vindictive earnestness against the
Sioux, even to their extermination, men, women, and children.
Nothing less will· reach the root of the case." Was it right
for the English to shoot back the Sepoy ambassador from
their cannon? Was it right for the North to refuse to exchange prisoners while our boys were dying by inches in
Libby and Andersonville? I do not undertake to answer
these questions, but I do say that Sand Creek is far from being "the climax of American outrages on the Indian," as it
has been called. Lay not that flattering unction to your souls,
people of the East, while the names of the Pequods and the
Conestoga Indians exist in your books; nor you of the Mississippi Valley, while the blood of Logan's family and the
Moravian Indians of the Muskingum stain your records; nor
you of the South, while a Cherokee or a Seminole remains to
tell the wrongs of his fathers; nor yet you of the Pacific
slope, while the murdered family of Spencer or the victims of
Bloody Point and Nome Cult have a place in the memory of
men—your ancestors and predecessors were guilty of worse
things than the Sand Creek massacre.

CHAPTER XIV.

CAÑON DE CHELLY AND BOSQUE REDONDO.

WE left the Navahos in their chronic state of war, that is to say, the state of robbing their neighbors and being robbed by them while the troops were absent, and of making peace when the troops marched against them. From the mass of conflicting testimony taken in 1865, in regard to the Indian history of New Mexico, and from other sources, it appears that one side made aggressions about as often as the other, the common opinion being that the Navahos captured the greater number of sheep, and the Mexicans the greater number of slaves. The Navahos were preferred to other Indians for slaves on account of their tractable nature, intelligence, light skins, and the voluptuousness of the females. Dr. Louis Kennon, whose opportunities for observation had been good, testified, " I think the number of Navajo captives held as slaves to be underestimated. I think there are from five to six thousand. I know of no family which can raise one hundred and fifty dollars but what purchases a Navajo slave, and many families own four or five—the trade in them being as regular as the trade in pigs or sheep. Previous to the war their price was from seventy-five to a hundred dollars, but now they are worth about four hundred dollars. But the other day some Mexican Indians from Chihuahua were for sale in Santa Fé. I have been conversant with the institution of slavery in Georgia, but the system is worse here, there being no obligation resting on the owner to care for the slave when he becomes old or worthless." Of course the Mexicans grumbled continually about the awful incursions of the savages, but there was little disposition on the part of the military to use any great violence against the Navaho nation. They understood the situation, having had the best of opportunities for hearing the Navaho side of the question; many of the officers had Navaho mistresses.

Occasionally there would be a rupture between the Indians and the soldiers, the most noted of these being the fight at Fort Fauntleroy, in September, 1861. This trouble arose over a horse-race, on which there had been very heavy betting. The soldiers backed a horse ridden by Lieutenant Ortiz, one of the post officers, and the Indians the other. The Indians' horse ran off the track after running about one hundred yards, the result, it was said, of a broken bridle, and they claimed a draw. The commanding officer, on the refusal of the winners to draw the race, gave orders that the Navahos should not be allowed to enter the post. The winners filed into the post, whooping and hallooing, with fifes screeching and drums beating, and as they did so a shot was fired, and an Indian killed. Who fired the shot is not certainly known, but it was said to be a sentinel, past whom the Indian was trying to make his way. The soldiers armed themselves, and attacked the Indians in a confused way, without any orders. Says Captain Hodt, of the 1st New Mexican Cavalry : " The Navahos, squaws, and children ran in all directions, and were shot and bayoneted. I tried my best to form the company I was first sergeant of, and succeeded in forming about twenty men—it being very hard work. I then marched out to the east side of the post; there I saw a soldier murdering two little children and a woman. I hallooed to the soldier to stop. He looked up, but did not obey my order. I ran up as quick as I could, but could not get there soon enough to prevent him from killing the two innocent children and wounding severely the squaw. I ordered his belts to be taken off and him taken prisoner to the post. On my arrival in the post I met Lieutenant Ortiz with a pistol at full cock, saying, ' Give back this soldier his arms, or else I'll shoot you, G—d d—n you,' which circumstances I reported to my company commander, he reporting the same to the colonel commanding, and the answer he received from the colonel was ' That Lieutenant Ortiz did perfectly right, and that he gave credit to the soldier who murdered the children and wounded the squaw.' Meantime the colonel had given orders to the offi-

GIANT'S ARM-CHAIR.

cer of the day to have the artillery (mountain howitzers) brought out and to open upon the Indians. The sergeant in charge of the mountain howitzers pretended not to understand the order given, for he considered it as an unlawful order; but being cursed by the officer of the day, and threatened, he had to execute the order or else get himself in trouble. The Indians scattered all over the valley below the post, attacked the post herd, wounded the Mexican herder, but did not succeed in getting any stock; also attacked the expressman, some ten miles from the post, took his horse and mail-bag, and wounded him in the arm. After the massacre there were no more Indians to be seen about the post, with the exception of a few squaws, favorites of the officers. The commanding officer endeavored to make peace again with the Navahos by sending some of the favorite squaws to talk with the chiefs; but the only satisfaction the squaws received was a good flogging. An expressman was sent shortly after the affairs above mentioned happened, but private letters were not allowed to be sent, and letters that reached the post-office at Fauntleroy were found opened, but not forwarded. To the best of my knowledge the number of Navahos killed was twelve or fifteen; the number wounded could not be ascertained."

In the winter of 1860–61, Colonel E. R. S. Canby (soon afterwards General Canby) proceeded against the Navahos and inflicted severe punishment upon them until February, 1861, when an armistice of three months was agreed upon, and later this was extended to one year. In September Governor Connelly, Colonel Canby, and Superintendent Collins had a long talk with thirty of their leading men, in which the usual assurances of their peaceful intentions were given, but the peace was not lasting. They were not, in fact, in a condition that encouraged peace. Owing to constant hostilities, they had planted but little for three years, and much of what they had planted had been destroyed by the troops, as also many of their herds; they were obliged to steal or starve, and adopted the former alternative. In 1862 their agent reported that they had "driven off over one hundred thousand sheep, and not less than a thousand head of cattle, besides horses and mules to a large amount." In these depredations he said they had "murdered many persons, and carried off many women and children as captives." In consequence of this plundering, Governor Connelly made a call for militia in September, and some independent expeditions were also organized, but the latter were stopped by the authorities for the reason that these irresponsible companies invariably attacked friendly Indians and hostile ones indiscriminately. General Carleton assumed command of the district at this time, and took charge of all military operations. His forces were chiefly occupied with the Mescalero Apaches during the winter, but in the spring of 1863 he was ready for the Navahos.

General Carleton's plan was to remove all who would consent to the Bosque Redondo, on the Pecos River, in Eastern New Mexico, and to place the others with them as fast as they were captured. This plan had the merit of sparing the innocent the horrors of war, at least. That General Carleton was actuated by motives of humanity in adopting it can scarcely be questioned. He said : "They have no government to make treaties; they are a patriarchal people. One set of families may make promises, but the other set will not heed them. They understand the direct application of force as a law; if its application be removed, that moment they become lawless. This has been tried over and over again, and at great expense. The purpose now is, never to relax the application of force with a people that can no more be trusted than the wolves that run through the mountains. To collect them together, little by little, on to a reservation, away from the haunts and hills and hiding-places of their country ; there be kind to them ; there teach their children how to read and write ; teach them the arts of peace ; teach them the truths of Christianity." If there were any fault in this plan it was only in their removal from their native country, but for the purpose of separating the peaceful from the hostile during the war this could not very well be avoided. The Navahos were given ample warning of General Carleton's intentions. He notified part of the chiefs himself, and sent messengers among them to inform them that they might have until the 20th day of July, 1863, to come in, but that "after that day every Navaho that is seen will be considered as hostile, and treated accordingly."

Quite a number of Navahos accepted the proffered terms, and against the others the troops were kept operating from Forts Stanton, Craig, Canby, Defiance, and the post at Los Pinos; and the troops at all other posts were ordered to be constantly on the lookout for prowling bands of Navahos, which were liable to appear in any part of the country. They went everywhere in their expeditions. One band of a hundred and thirty warriors even penetrated the Mescalero country, southeast of the Rio Grande settlements, and, passing north, drove off cattle and sheep from the Bosque Redondo; they were followed by a few troops and some Mescaleros, and the property was retaken, with other plundered goods. The orders to the soldiers, everywhere, were to kill every male Navaho capable of bearing arms, whenever and wherever he might be found; women and children were to be captured and held as prisoners. These orders were often repeated, and the officers were urged to the utmost activity by praise to the successful, and reproaches to the unsuccessful. The following, issued to Colonel Rigg, commanding at Fort Craig, on August 4, 1863, is a sample of the instructions: "I have been informed that there is a spring called *Ojo de Cibolo*, about fifteen miles west of Limitar, where the Navahos drive their stolen cattle and 'jerk' the flesh at their leisure. Cannot you make arrangements for a party of resolute men from your command to be stationed there for, say, thirty days, and kill every Navaho and Apache they can find? A cautious, wary commander, hiding his men and moving about at night, might kill off a good many Indians near that point." Such orders seem harsh, and yet they afforded the only means of bringing the Navahos to terms. The great difficulty was to get any opportunity to fight them. They were separated in small bands, under their patriarchal system, and, being constantly on the move through a country with which they were thoroughly acquainted, they were usually able to avoid the soldiers, for whom they kept a vigilant watch. After a few weeks of slight success, the soldiers were further stimulated to activity by a bounty of twenty dollars for each good horse turned over to the quartermaster's

CAÑON DE CHELLY.

department, and one dollar for each sheep. The principal
offensive force was that operating from Fort Canby, under
Colonel Kit Carson, but, notwithstanding the ability and activity of that noted Indian fighter, the results obtained during
the summer and fall of 1863 were not important, and Carleton
consoled the colonel with the hope: "As winter approaches
you will have better luck." Still, as winter approached, success did not increase very materially, and the Navahos were still
able to keep out of the way of the troops. It was therefore
decided to strike them in the Cañon de Chelly, which was re-

puted to be their greatest stronghold, and Colonel Carson was ordered to prepare for this movement, which was to be made in January.

The Cañon de Chelly is one of the most remarkable works of nature in the United States. The Rio Chelly may be found, not very accurately traced, on any fair-sized map of Arizona, in the northeastern corner of that territory. Its headwaters are in the Sierra Tunicha, of Northwestern New Mexico, and it flows thence almost due west, for some thirty miles, then swings abruptly to the north, and empties into the Rio San Juan near the northern line of Arizona. The line of its western flow indicates the position of the cañon, which extends throughout that distance, the northward bend of the river being just beyond its mouth. The main cañon is counted as beginning at the union of three small streams, each of which has a cañon of its own. They are the Cienega Negra (Black Meadow), or Estrella (Star), on the southeast, the Palo Negro (Black Timber), or Chelly Creek, on the east, and the Cienega Juanica, or Juanita, on the northwest. The most easterly entrance used by the Indians is near the head of Chelly Creek; by it, the bottom of that stream is reached above the junction of the others. It is not accessible for animals. The Cienega Negra enters about three miles below the head of the Chelly proper, and the Juanica half a mile lower. At places above the entrance of the last-named stream the chasm is so narrow that one might almost leap across it, but the beholder involuntarily recoils from the dizzy view of over one thousand feet of unbroken descent to the yellow floor beneath. About half a mile below the Juanica there is another descent, where the wall of the cañon, there only seven hundred feet high, is broken and sufficiently sloping to permit a zigzag descent to pack-animals. Below this point the walls increase in height to fifteen hundred feet, and the width of the cañon from two hundred to three hundred and fifty yards. The next approach is by a side cañon that enters on the south side, about eleven miles below the Juanica; it is commonly known as Bat Cañon, but the Indians and Mexicans call it Cañon Alsada, or Cañon of the High Rock, from a natural obelisk, one thousand feet high, with a base of one hundred and fifty feet, that rises ma-

29*

jestically at the mouth of the cañon, a hundred feet distant from the wall. This needle leans so much that it seems about to topple over. The Alsada entrance is the one commonly used in approaching from Fort Defiance, and the trail is cut deep in the sandstone by thousands of feet of men and animals that in past generations have followed it. The descent here is along ledges on the cañon wall, so narrow that animals are always driven ahead, for fear they may slip and carry the owner over. Occasionally, below this point, there are lateral openings in the cañon walls, but none of them extend more than a few hundred yards back, and there is no other entrance until about three miles above the mouth, where the Cañon del Trigo (Wheat Cañon) enters from the north. Below the Trigo the walls sink rapidly, and the cañon opens out into a rolling country, barren and unprepossessing.

The formation is all sandstone, which is the "country rock" for miles in every direction. From above, at almost any point, the traveller comes suddenly on this mighty chasm, without any warning of its presence in the rock plain over which he is passing. The sudden view of the awful depths is startling beyond description. From below, the stupendous height of the walls, which often project above the head of the beholder, cannot be fully comprehended. The floor of the cañon is comparatively smooth and very sandy, the general appearance being that of a river of sand flowing between the rock walls and circling around occasional islands of green. There is no detritus along the foot of either wall, as is common in other cañons. The rocks are apparently disintegrating and gradually filling the chasm, but the only agents in this work are the wind and the loose sand, and their progress is so slow as to be almost imperceptible. The particles of sand, whirled along in the air, are constantly eating away the walls and detached blocks of stone, and in the course of centuries have made a very wonder-land of weird shapes and fantastic sculpturing. The amount of water in the cañon depends wholly on the season. In years of drought there is none above the surface, but the sand is moist, and the Indians obtain what water they need by digging. In moderate seasons there is an occasional show of running water, which sinks again in the sand.   In wet seasons there is a considerable stream, and about a mile below the Cañon Alsada there is seen a magnificent fall of water from the top of the cañon, sheer a thousand feet, swaying in the wind and breaking by the resistance of the air, until it is completely lost in a fine mist at the bottom.   The Navahos say the stream has decreased of later years, and the remains of ancient acequias indicate the truth of their tradition.   There is a slight growth of underbrush throughout the cañon, with grass at intervals, and now and then the corn-fields and peach-orchards of the Indians.

This place was inhabited long before Columbus set his sails to seek the Indies.   Along its walls are perched the strange cliff-dwellings of that ancient and unknown race which once peopled the present deserts of Arizona.   Some of them are on ledges only forty or fifty feet above the cañon floor, with parts on the floor, and others are six or seven hundred feet higher.   How the higher ones were constructed is an unsolved problem, for there appears now no way of access to man but by ropes from above, or by broken flights of ladder-like steps cut in the rock at various places, and these houses are built of stone and heavy wooden beams.   The timber in them is in excellent preservation, and the whitewash on the interior walls looks as though it had been put on within a year, yet the Navahos say that these buildings were there, just as they are now, when their forefathers came into the country. The architecture is that of the Pueblos, with similar masonry, the usual fragments of pottery, and the universal estufa.   The Navahos have never used them, and, so far as is known, have never been able to reach some of them, to which, indeed, there appears no feasible approach, except possibly by balloon.   The enterprising archæologist would probably find them just as the cliff-dweller left them when he departed on his last migration.

This cañon was not explored throughout until 1859, although the troops had often been in its vicinity, and the Navahos thought it afforded them an inaccessible retreat in time of war.   Still it was not a place of retreat to which they all gathered, as was generally supposed, nor were there any fortifications in it, as rumor had declared.   It is not probable that

there were ever more than a thousand Indians living in it, for
no large numbers were ever found there, and there was not
the grass in it to support the large herds that they owned.
Nine tenths, at least, of the Navaho nation made their homes
at such other points in their extensive territory as afforded
pasturage for their flocks; the Cañon de Chelly was merely
the residence of a small portion of the tribe; but none of the
whites knew just what was there, and the great chasm was regarded in all circles as the mysterious stronghold of the Navahos. The first recorded entrance into it by troops was made
in September, 1849, by Lieutenant Simpson, of Colonel Washington's expedition, escorted by Major Kendrick, with sixty
men. They entered at the mouth, went a short distance up
the Cañon del Trigo, and then ascended the main cañon for
nine and a half miles, in search of the fortifications of the
Navahos. To confirm the stories of the guides about an impregnable fortress on a plateau so high that fifteen ladders
were required to reach it, they found nothing but the cliff
houses, and, on returning, announced that the mystery of the
Cañon de Chelly was solved. In 1858, Colonel D. S. Miles
entered it at the Cañon Alsada and marched to the mouth
without any casualties, but he was so impressed with the advantages it afforded for attack from the summits of the walls
that he reported: " No command should ever again enter it."
In July, 1859, Captain Walker, commanding an expedition
against the Navahos, entered the cañon half a mile below the
entrance of the Juanica, and marched to the mouth. Two
weeks later he returned to the head of the cañon and explored
it to the point of his former descent. In view of these explorations it seems remarkable that General Carleton should
have written, after Carson's expedition: " This is the first
time any troops, whether when the country belonged to Mexico
or since we acquired it, have been able to pass through the
Cañon de Chelly, which, for its great depth, its length, its
perpendicular walls, and its labyrinthine character, has been
regarded by eminent geologists as the most remarkable of any
'fissure' (for such it is held to be) upon the face of the globe.
It has been the great fortress of the tribe since time out of
mind." In reality, however, this misinformation was uni-

CLIFF HOUSE IN CAÑON DE CHELLY.

versal. No officer who entered the cañon (judging from their reports) had any definite knowledge of what his predecessors had done. Carson surely should have been acquainted with the history of so famous a place, but, with an inaccuracy that is strikingly illustrative of the unreliability of traditional history, he reported that his troops had " accomplished an undertaking never before accomplished in war-time—that of passing through the Cañon de Chelly from east to west."*

Colonel Carson started from Fort Canby on January 6, 1864, with a force of three hundred and ninety officers and men, for the mouth of the cañon. Just before starting he sent Captain Pfeiffer, with one company, to operate from the eastern end. The depth of the snow on the divide between Fort Canby and the Pueblo Colorado was so great that his command was three days in reaching the latter place, a march that was usually made in one day. He had started his supply-train on the 3d, expecting that the oxen would be recuperated by the time of his arrival, but the train had taken five days in making the twenty-five miles, and had lost twenty-seven oxen. Reorganizing, and leaving part of the train, he pushed on to the cañon, which he struck on the 12th, about six miles above the mouth. On the night of the 11th he sent out Sergeant Andres Herrara, with fifty men, as scouts. In the morning this party found a fresh trail, and, following it rapidly, they overtook the Indians just as they were entering the cañon, and attacked them ; they killed eleven and captured two women and two children, with one hundred and thirty sheep and goats. On the 13th Carson divided his force into two commands : one, under Captain Berney, was sent up the north side of the cañon, and the other, under Captain Carey, accompanied by Carson, moved up the south side, with the view of ascertaining the topography of the country and the position of the Navahos, if they had undertaken to make a stand. The latter party found and captured five wounded Indians at the scene of Herrara's fight. On the 14th they returned to the mouth of the cañon and found Pfeiffer there, he having come

* Carson's report has never been published. I quote from the manuscript copy on file in the office of the War Department, at Washington, to which the department has courteously afforded me access.

through the cañon successfully, without any casualty to his command; they had killed three Indians, and brought in nineteen women and children prisoners.

While returning to camp, Carson was approached by three Indians, under a flag of truce, who asked if they might come in with their families and surrender. He told them that they might if they came by ten o'clock the next morning, but not later. About sixty came in by the appointed time and acceded to the terms of surrender and removal to the Bosque. Says Carson: "They declared that, owing to the operations of my command, they are in a complete state of starvation, and that many of their women and children have already died from this cause. They also state that they would have come in long ago, but that they believed it was a war of extermination, and that they were equally surprised and delighted to learn the contrary from an old captive whom I had sent back to them for this purpose. I issued them some meat, and as they asked permission to return to their haunts and collect the remainder of their people, I directed them to meet me at this post [Fort Canby] in ten days. They have all arrived here according to promise, many of them, with others, joining and travelling in with Captain Carey's command. This command of seventy-five men I conferred upon Captain Carey at his own request, he being desirous of passing through this stupendous cañon. I sent the party to return through the cañon from west to east, that all the peach-orchards, of which there are many, might be destroyed, as well as the dwellings of the Indians." About three thousand peach-trees were destroyed in the cañon; and one hundred and ten Navahos came in with Carey's command. On January 23 Carson reported the results of the expedition as follows: "Killed, 23; captured, 34; voluntarily surrendered, 200; captured 200 head of sheep."

This expedition has passed into the realms of romance, like many other events in New Mexican history, and the facts have been lost sight of in the rosy coloring of imagination. Illustrative of this I quote the following from a popular biography of Kit Carson, that is introduced by what purport to be certificates to its accuracy by such well-known New Mexicans as Colonel Ceran St. Vrain and Judge Charles Beaubien:

COLONEL KIT CARSON.

"The Navajo Indians were very troublesome. For a whole decade they had defied the government, and now, enlisted as savage cohorts of the rebels, they were especially dangerous. They numbered several thousand warriors, and roamed over an immense tract of country. General Carleton selected Carson to command two thousand picked men, consisting of Californians, Mexicans, and mountaineers, to operate against these Indians. The campaign was a most brilliant one. After a succession of skirmishes, Carson succeeded in getting the enemy into a bed or ravine, and had his own forces so disposed as to command every approach, and in doing this compelled the surrender of ten thousand Indians, being the largest single capture of Indians ever known. The entire tribe, men, women, and children, was disposed of by this magnificent operation. This greatly increased the fame of the

mountain leader, and the official reports to the War Department very justly sounded his praises in flattering terms, but
none too extravagantly." This leads to the thought that if
there be anything more unreliable than traditional history it
is written history.

There is a generally prevailing impression, in regard to the
results of Carson's expedition, similar to the above statement,
and possibly derived from it. The great success of the expedition was not in immediate effect, but in the ulterior results
of the campaign, which Carson, with his keen foresight, anticipated. He said, in his report of January 23, 1864: "But
it is to the ulterior effects of the expedition that I look for
the greatest results. We have shown the Indians that in no
place, however formidable or inaccessible in their opinion,
are they safe from the pursuit of the troops of this command,
and have convinced a large portion of them that the struggle
on their part is a hopeless one. We have also demonstrated
that the intentions of the government towards them are eminently humane, and dictated by an earnest desire to promote
their welfare; that the principle is not to destroy but to save
them, if they are disposed to be saved. When all this is understood by the Navajoes, generally, as it soon will be, and
when they become convinced that destruction will follow on
resistance, they will gladly avail themselves of the opportunities afforded them of peace and plenty under the fostering
care of the government, as do all those now with whom I
have had any means of communicating. They are arriving
almost hourly, and will, I believe, continue to arrive until the
last Indian in this section of the country is *en route* to the
Bosque Redondo." This prediction proved substantially a true
one. The Navahos came in so fast that General Carleton's resources were taxed to the utmost to support them. By February 20, 750 had surrendered at Los Pinos and been forwarded
to the Bosque. On February 24, 1650 were reported surrendered at Fort Canby. On February 24, 1300 more were reported from Los Pinos. By March 11, 1500 more had come
in at Fort Canby, and Carleton notified Carson that he could
not take care of more than one additional thousand. By July
8, there were 6321 at the Bosque, and 1000 more at Fort

Canby. The war was evidently ended; Fort Canby was ordered abandoned in August, and the troops sent into Arizona. Carson was sent to the plains to fight Kiowas and Comanches, with 200 Ute warriors, who had volunteered to go if allowed what they could capture.

The evil qualities of the removal and concentration began to show as soon as success had been attained. The number of Navahos had been underestimated by Carleton. Carson maintained that there were at least 12,000 of them, and, if any credit can be given to subsequent statistics, he was right, but Carleton insisted that there could not possibly be over 8000; there must not be; it would spoil the Bosque system if there were. The greatest number ever at the Bosque Redondo was between nine and ten thousand; the remainder of the nation lurked in their old haunts, or fell back to the desert regions of Arizona and Utah, to avoid the troops. Of course, under the system of voluntary surrender, the worst Indians, the ones whose surveillance was most desirable, did not come in; but the removal of the others left them plenty of room in their own country, and this, with the fear of the troops, kept them quiet. The troops attacked them whenever they met them, for several years afterwards. The expense of caring for the exiled Navahos was very great. The New Mexicans offered to relieve the government of a portion of this burden by a system of "binding out," but the offer was declined; and also all the Navahos who had been kept at the army posts, "for whatever purpose," were required to be sent to the Bosque. There was difficulty between the Navahos and the Mescaleros at their new home. They had been enemies of old, and there was nothing to bring about a reconciliation. Their customs differed. The Mescalero women were chaste, but had no part in the control of the tribe; the Navaho women were very dissolute, and exercised a strong influence in the tribal government. The Mescaleros were the bolder warriors, but they were far inferior in numbers. The tribal jealousies were aggravated by petty aggressions and hectoring. The Apaches accused the Navahos of trampling down their crops, and otherwise annoying them. The reservation authorities made the matter worse by

removing the Mescaleros from the land they had been cultivating, and giving it to the Navahos. The Mescaleros then
claimed the fulfilment of the promise to them of a reservation in their own country, and when this was refused they
went without permission, and began hostilities.

Agriculture at the Bosque did not result successfully; the
crops usually promised well enough, but something always
spoiled them. One time it was drought, another cut-worms,
another bad irrigation, or overflows, or hail-storms. The Indians were, of necessity, a great expense to the government.
The cost of feeding them for seven months, March to September inclusive, in 1865, was $452,356.98. The cost for a
year previous to this time averaged higher than this, but the
exact figures cannot be given, on account of the large amount
of stores transferred from other departments and not reported
as to value. All this time it was well known that they could
support themselves in their own country. The principal
cause of their helplessness in their new homes was that they
were a pastoral, not an agricultural, people. In their own
country their chief food is goats' milk and the roots of certain
herbs of wild growth. Their flocks had been largely destroyed
during the war. Tradition puts the number of sheep killed by
soldiers at fifty thousand, but the Navahos say that the Utes
and Mexicans stole the greater part of them. The Bosque
did not afford grazing facilities for the sheep and goats they
still had, and these gradually decreased in number. It has
been proven since then that they can and will take care of
themselves, very easily, if they can get ample pasturage; and,
unless stock-raising is to be considered a less civilized pursuit
than agriculture, there is no reason why any forcible attempt
should be made to change the natural bent of their industrial
instincts.

The fitness of the Bosque Redondo for a reservation is
something that has been the subject of great controversy and
of misrepresentation on one or both sides. The following
description of it, given by Captain Thomas Claiborne in 1859,
when there was talk of establishing a military post there, may
fairly be considered as impartial: "The Bosque Redondo is
an elbow of the river [Pecos]; the molts of cottonwoods are

mostly on the left bank of the Pecos, extending for perhaps six or seven miles, in clusters. The river is very crooked, and stretched from side to side of the valley, which, midway of the Bosque, is two miles or over wide. The appearance of the Bosque in that desert country is very agreeable. The lower half of the valley is tillable, the upper is filled with drift sand. A secondary mesa, twelve hundred yards wide and a mile and a quarter long, lies on the right bank of the river, about midway the Bosque, about thirty feet above the river-bottom, and is curtained by sand-hills about twenty-five feet higher than itself. A kind of red-top grass grows in the lower bottoms, mixed with bunch grass; the hills are covered with brown sedge grass; the mesa above spoken of is well covered with mesquite grass. The water of the river is bad and the surrounding country is most desolate. The place is altogether unfit for a post." That the water of the Pecos at this point is alkaline, and charged with certain salts, is unquestionable; this comes from the Aqua Negra, which debouches into the Pecos at Giddings's Ranch, above the Bosque. The water of the Aqua Negra, however, has always been used, more or less, at Giddings's Ranch, both by men and animals, without bad results, though it is somewhat diuretic. Dr. Warner, physician at Fort Sumner, testified that the water of the Pecos at the Bosque is wholesome. Cadéte (Gian-nah-tah), the Mescalero chief, testified: "It is not good, too much alkali, and is the cause of the sickness in the tribe and losing our animals." The Navahos sometimes said the water was all right, and sometimes that they thought it was bad, but they always unanimously expressed a preference for their old country.

The head of the opposition to the Bosque was Dr. Matthew Steck, a well-known settler in New Mexico, at that time Superintendent of Indian Affairs. He favored giving the Mescaleros a reservation in their own country, as had been promised them, and opposed the removal of the Navahos to the Bosque. He advocated his views in New Mexico, and, when he found he could do nothing there, he went to Washington to secure the same ends. Carleton complained bitterly of this attempted interference with his plans, and insisted on the enforcement of the ultra-humane policy; that is, on com-

30

pelling the Indians to do what the white man in authority—
in this case himself—may think to be best for them.   He said:
"Dr. Steck wants to hold councils with the Navajoes!   It is
mockery to hold councils with a people who are in our hands
and have only to await our decisions.   It will be bad policy
to hold any councils.   We should give them what they need,
what is just, and take care of them as children until they
can take care of themselves.   The Navajoes should never leave
the Bosque, and never shall if I can prevent it.   I told them
that that should be their home.   They have gone there with
that understanding.   There is land enough there for themselves and the Apaches.   The Navajoes themselves are Apaches,
and talk the same language, and in a few years will be homogeneous with them."   He was proven to be mistaken as to
the two tribes becoming homogeneous; whether he was wrong
in other regards is a question about which people will differ;
in brief, it is simply the question whether the concentration
policy is the right one—whether it is better to place Indians
where they do not wish to be, oblige them to do things which
they do not wish to do, and force them to abandon the pursuits by which they had formerly supported themselves.
General Carleton also accused Mr. Steck of acting from interested motives, but he did not specify in what regard.

In the winter of 1864–65, the Navahos at the Bosque were
reduced to terrible straits through the destruction of their
crops by cut-worms.   There was want all through that portion of the country from various causes.   Neither the War nor
the Indian Department was able to relieve them adequately.
There was no relief from natural sources, for the acorns, ce-
dar-berries, wild potatoes, palmillas and other roots, mescal
and mesquite, on which they could rely in their old home in
times of famine, were not found at the Bosque.   Cattle and
sheep were issued to them for food, "head and pluck," and
the blood of the slaughtered animals was ordered to be saved
to make "haggis and blood-puddings" for the orphan children.   To add to their distress these people, who make the
most serviceable blankets in the world and usually have plenty
of them, were destitute, by the ravages of their enemies, of
both blankets and clothing.   They had no houses, and, as sub-

stitutes, holes were ordered to be dug, in which they might be sheltered from the wind.   In spite of all his efforts and ingenuity, General Carleton knew that they must suffer, and, on October 31, 1864, he directed the commandant at Fort Sumner to explain his good intentions to the Indians.   " Tell them," he said, " to be too proud to murmur at what cannot be helped.   We could not foresee the total destruction of their corn crop, nor could we foresee that the frost and hail would come and destroy the crop in the country ; but not to be discouraged ; to work hard, every man and woman, to put in

NEAR THE HEAD-WATERS OF THE NAVAHO.

large fields next year, when, if God smiles upon our efforts, they will, at one bound, be forever placed beyond want, and independent.   Tell them not to believe ever that we are not their best friends ; that their enemies have told them that we would destroy them ; that we had sent big guns there to attack them ; but that those guns are only to be used against their enemies, if they continue to behave as they have done."

With all his good intentions, General Carleton was inexcusable, under analogy of the laws that are daily administered in every state and territory of the Union.   There is no excuse known for failure under such circumstances. When a man is restrained of his liberty, or deprived of any right, for the purpose of benefiting him, there is no extenuation except he be in fact benefited, or, at least, not injured. Good intentions never excuse a wrong; and though, as a war measure, placing the Navahos at the Bosque may be justified, keeping them there against their will, in time of peace, is clearly an infringement of natural right. Our government must actually benefit the Indians by the reservation system in order to justify itself. Still, General Carleton stuck to his theory, and said that if the Navahos were moved from the Bosque at all they ought to be sent to Kansas or the Indian Territory. In 1865 the worms destroyed the crops again, and on July 18, after giving directions for husbanding all food, Carleton instructed the officer in command: "You should tell the Indians what a dreadful year it is, and how they must save everything to eat which lies in their power, or starvation will come upon them." The Indians had been slipping away from the place in small parties since midwinter of 1864–65, and in July a large party, under Ganado Blanco (White Cattle), broke away forcibly, but they were pursued and driven back. In August Carleton concluded to let the few Coyotero Apaches on the reservation return to their own country, as they desired. In the summer of this year a commission, consisting of Senator Doolittle, Vice-President Foster, and Representative Ross, visited New Mexico, and made a full investigation of the Indian affairs there, but nothing resulted from it.

In 1865 Felipe Delgado succeeded Mr. Steck as Superintendent; he was in harmony with General Carleton, and reported that, "It is fair to presume that next year their [the Navahos'] facilities will be greater," etc. He had the good sense to recommend the purchase of sheep for them. In 1866 the crops failed again—this time, as Superintendent A. B. Norton and their agent reported, from bad seed, improper management, and overflows of the Pecos. There were reported to be 7000 Indians on the reservation, and the cost of keeping them was estimated at $1,500,000 annually. In 1867 the crops failed, from bad management and hail-storms, as reported; the Comanches attacked and robbed the Navahos several times; and many of their horses died from eating poisonous weeds.   There were 7300 Indians reported as on the reservation, and their property had become reduced to 550 horses, 20 mules, 940 sheep, and 1025 goats.   In 1868 Superintendent Davis reported: "The Navahos were located several years ago upon a reservation at the Bosque Redondo, by the military, and after expending vast sums of money, and after making every effort for more than four years to make it a success, it has proved a total failure. It was certainly a very unfortunate selection for a reserve; no wood, unproductive soil, and very unhealthy water, and the Indians were so much dissatisfied they planted no grain last spring, and I verily believe they were making preparations to leave as the Apaches did."

Fortunately for all concerned, General Sherman and Colonel Tappan, Peace Commissioners, reached New Mexico in May, 1868.   They satisfied themselves that the Navahos would never become self-supporting or contented at the Bosque Redondo, and, on June 1, entered into an agreement with the tribe by which they were to be removed to their former country.   The reservation then given them was included between parallel 37° of north latitude and a parallel drawn through Fort Defiance, for north and south lines, and parallel of longitude 109° 30' and a parallel drawn through Ojo del Oso, as east and west lines.   The Indians were to receive five dollars annually, in clothing, for each member of the tribe, and ten dollars for each one engaged in farming or mechanical pursuits.   Each head of a family was entitled to select one hundred and sixty acres of land, if he desired to hold in severalty, and in such case he was to receive one hundred dollars in seeds and implements the first year, and twenty-five dollars each for the second and third years. Buildings of the value of $11,500 were to be erected, and the Navahos pledged themselves to compel all their children between the ages of six and sixteen to attend school.   A separate school-house and teacher was to be provided for every thirty pupils; $150,000 was to be appropriated at once to the Indians, part of which was to be expended in the purchase of 15,000 sheep and goats and 500 cattle, and the remainder to be used for the expenses of their removal and in such other ways as should appear most beneficial.

Under this liberal treaty the tribe was removed in 1868, and since then there has been a continuous improvement in their condition. They had very bad luck with their crops for several years, but their herds increased steadily. By 1873 they were reported to have 10,000 horses and 200,000 sheep and goats. In 1872 an Indian police force was organized at the agency, on recommendation of Captain Bennett, and placed under command of Manuelito, their war-chief, providing, for the first time in their history, for a control of offenders by tribal authority. It was discontinued in 1873 for a short time, but was soon put in force again, with beneficial results. A few years later the Indians abandoned it on account of the small pay given to the policemen. About fifteen men are now employed, and they appear to be all that are needed. In 1876 the Navahos were reported as self-supporting, notwithstanding they had lost 40,000 sheep by freezing during the past winter. In 1878 their agent said : " Within the ten years during which the present treaty with the Navahos has been in force they have grown from a band of paupers to a nation of prosperous, industrious, shrewd, and (for barbarians) intelligent people." They were reported at that time as numbering 11,800, and owning 20,000 horses, 1500 cattle, and 500,000 sheep ; they were tilling 9192 acres of land, and obtained ninety-five per cent. of their subsistence from civilized pursuits.

In fact, they were increasing so rapidly that there was an urgent call for more room, and, as there was desert land to spare in all directions, it was given to them. By executive order of October 29, 1878, there was added to their reservation the land between the northern line of Arizona, parallel 110° of west longitude, parallel 36° of north latitude, and the western line of the reservation. Still there was a call for more land, and on January 6, 1880, they were given a strip fifteen miles wide along the eastern side of the reservation, and one six miles wide along the southern line. In the latter year three windmill pumps and fifty-two stock pumps were put in at different points on the reservation, which have stopped

MOQUI PUEBLO.

much of their wandering in search of water, and added greatly to the value of their grazing-lands. Their march of improvement has not stopped, and in 1884 the nation, estimated at 17,000, cultivated 15,000 acres of land and raised 220,000 bushels of corn and 21,000 bushels of wheat; they had 35,000 horses and 1,000,000 sheep. In 1884 the reservation was extended west to 111° 30', and the northern boundary was made the Colorado and San Juan rivers. By this addition the reservation encloses the Moqui Pueblo reservation on two sides, and the agencies for the two have been consolidated. This order, increasing the reservation by 1,769,600 acres in Arizona and Utah, was supplemented by one taking away 46,000 acres in New Mexico; the reservation as now established includes 8,159,360 acres, mostly desert land.

With their advancement in wealth the Navahos have made but little progress in civilization, and their condition is one that might well call for more extended mission work than has been done among them. The government is maintaining an industrial school at present, and the Presbyterian Church, to which they were assigned, has established a mission school two or three times, but it has been discontinued through the failure of Congress to furnish a suitable building. The Navahos, however, have repeatedly asked to have schools established, and the Presbyterian Board of Foreign Missions has recently decided to establish a school, whether the government complied with its promises or not. There were twenty-five reported, in 1884, as being able to read, but the report is not very reliable; only five were reported as able to speak English in 1883. Their manners, customs, and religion are practically unchanged, except that they have adopted civilized clothing to a large extent. They still plant with sharpened sticks, but this has been conceded by farmers to be the best way of planting in their country; seed must be planted deep in order to obtain moisture to insure growth, and ploughing only makes the ground dry. They never wash their sheep, and still chop the wool from them with case-knives, pieces of tin, or anything else that will cut, obtaining about one pound from each animal.* Their horses are seldom

---

* A large number of sheep-shears were sent to them in 1885, and will probably be used.

used except in travelling; three fourths of them are never broken, and are of no use whatever, except in the purchase of wives. Attempts have been made to introduce improved looms among them, but the women adhere tenaciously to their old modes. About fifty of the men were induced to build houses, in 1884, but the vast majority still adhere to their temporary *hogans,* and desert them when a death occurs. Their morals are as loose as ever, except that the consumption of liquor has decreased materially. These are the chief signs of advancement, and yet it has been said repeatedly that the Navahos afforded the best material for civilization among our Indian tribes. After forty years of our guardianship they are still barbarians—self-supporting while kept separate from the whites, but as helpless and as easily swindled as children, except in the most ordinary business dealings, and scarcely better fitted for the duties of citizenship than when we first knew them. They were always among thieves, and thus far Christianity and civilization have passed by on the other side. Possibly that is why they are now so prosperous.

CHAPTER XV.

FORT PHIL KEARNEY.

UNTIL the close of the War of the Rebellion, the great northeastern triangle of the mountain country, lying between the continental divide and the plains, had been subject to little encroachment from the white man, but civilization had been pressing up about it on all sides. On the east, the Sioux had been pushed back gradually until the great outbreak of 1862, in Minnesota, and then, by one stroke, forced into the confines of Dakota. At the south, the mining settlements of Colorado had grown populous and strong enough to entirely dispossess the Indian. On the southwest, the Saints had planted themselves immovably, and converted what hunting-grounds there were in that section into farms. On the west, the gold-hunters had crowded up to the continental divide and were moving down its eastern slope. They had advanced from the Pacific coast, passing from one point to another in wild stampedes, as new discoveries of the precious metal were made, but always growing in numbers and always pressing towards the east. The discovery of the Colville mines was followed in 1857–58–59 by the Frazer River excitement, which carried a large population into the Northwest. Then came the rush for the Salmon River mines in 1861–62, sending the adventurers into Southeastern Washington, to such an extent that in 1863 Idaho was organized as a territory, including the new settlements. The overflow from the Salmon River country, across the divide, began in 1861, and the prospectors soon found ground that was worthy their time and attention. In the following year the wonderful placers of this section became known, and there ensued a rush for the new Golconda that surpassed anything ever known in the Northwest. The richness of the mines justified the great immigration; it is estimated that the placers of Alder Gulch alone produced $50,000,000 of gold in the four years following their discovery. Helena, Virginia City, Bozeman, and other camps sprang up, with populations that produced nothing but gold, and which must be supplied with everything else from the outside.

There were two ways of reaching the Montana settlements from the East: one was by following the established

PROSPECTORS IN THE MOUNTAINS.

emigrant road through the South Pass, to Fort Hall, and thence north; the other was by boat, on the Missouri and Yellowstone rivers, to the head of navigation, and thence through the country of the Crows to the mines. Both these routes were very circuitous, being over five hundred miles longer than the direct road which was physically practicable, from Fort Laramie to Bozeman, along the eastern base of the

Big Horn Mountains. Several parties had gone into Montana by this route, which was at first called "Bozeman's Route," and afterwards, when definitely located, "the Montana Road." Besides the extra distance, the South Pass route, which was virtually the only road used by emigrants with teams, required crossing and recrossing the continental divide, a very considerable hardship to the way-worn emigrant. For these reasons it became desirable to open a direct road, and preparations for it were commenced in 1865, by negotiating with the Indians for the right of way.

The country through which the proposed road was projected belonged, when first known to the whites, to the Crows, or, as they call themselves, Absaroka or Upsaroka. It is sometimes called by the same name, which is then translated "the land, or home, of the Crows." The tribe is a branch of the Dakota family, numbering about three thousand five hundred, and is in three divisions; the Ki-kat-sa, or Crows proper, commonly known as the Mountain Crows; the Alla-ka-weah, and the Ah-nah-a-ways, who live farther to the east, and are termed the River Crows. These Indians are tall, well-formed, expert horsemen and good hunters. The fur traders had troubles with them at times, and gave them the reputation of rascals and thieves, but of later years they have been faithful and honorable friends of the whites. They had all the fighting they could attend to from their cousins, the Sioux, who waged relentless war upon them. On this account they cultivated the friendship of the whites, from whom they could procure arms and ammunition, and even had several reputable white chiefs, among whom were the celebrated Bridger and Beckwith. By the time that the early emigration to the mountains began, a large portion of the southern and eastern parts of the northeastern triangle had been deserted by the Crows as a habitation, though still held in common with the Sioux as a battle-ground and hunting-ground. By 1865 the Sioux, with their allies the Northern Cheyennes and Arapahoes, had gained control of these sections, and the Crows were virtually expelled from the country east and south of the Big Horn Mountains.

That part of the country, thus gained by the Sioux, which

lies between the Black Hills, the Big Horn Mountains, and the Yellowstone River, was known as the Powder River country, from its principal stream, whose valleys, together with those of the Tongue River and the Rosebud, constituted the best hunting-ground remaining to the Sioux. For over thirty miles north from Fort Reno this country is much like the great plains, with little vegetable growth except sage-brush; north of that it is more fertile, covered with grass, and abounding in all the vegetable growth of the latitude. The monotony of evergreen forests is broken by groves of cottonwoods, willows, ashes, and red-birches. All kinds of berries, with grapes, cherries, and plums, grow wild, in pro-fusion. The streams are clear and wholesome, instead of muddy and alkaline, as in the lower country. This beautiful region extends along the eastern and northeastern bases of the Big Horn Mountains, in a strip of varying width. Off to the northeast, at an average distance of perhaps twenty miles, begin the "bad lands," and the country takes on a dreary and desolate aspect. In this entire region large game was still abundant. The most extensive herds of buffalo yet re-maining pastured there. Elk, deer, and antelope were to be met with everywhere. The terraced buttes were the favorite home of the big - horn. Bears rioted among the fruits and berries. Of small game, such as rabbits, grouse, and water-fowl, there was an abundance that can scarcely be imagined. Naturally enough, the Indians did not desire to lose this sports-man's paradise, but the government did not appear to know it.

It was the era of peace—in Washington. The Indians, in the annual reports, were doing nothing but defending themselves from the encroachments of lawless whites. They were ready and willing to do anything, if they could only se-cure schools and churches. Mr. Bogy, the Commissioner of Indian Affairs, sat back and smiled sarcastically at reports of hostilities. The peace people were busy, working themselves into a white heat over the wrongs of the Cheyennes. The entire country looked contemptuously on the strength of the red men. What! we, who had just put down the greatest rebellion the world ever knew, to be terrified by a few half-starved Indians? Oh, no! The army was cut down to its lowest possible figure, and much of it was employed in the late insurrectionary states. Its arms were chiefly old-fashioned muzzle-loaders, notwithstanding the wonderful improvements that had been made in weapons during the war. The Indians were better armed. On one occasion a cattle guard excused themselves for not firing on Indians who were attacking their herds, because the Indians had revolvers, while they had nothing but muzzle-loading muskets, and would be at the mercy of the Indians if they discharged them. "Judicious men" were sent out to treat with the Sioux for the right of way through to Montana. They met at Fort Sully, and, from October 10 to October 28, made treaties with the Minneconjous, Lower Brulés, Two Kettles, Blackfoot Sioux, Sans Arcs, Oncpapas, and Ogallallas, by which these Indians agreed to "withdraw from the routes overland already established or hereafter to be established through their country," and not to interfere "with the persons or property of citizens of the United States travelling thereon." The chief striking features about these treaties were the small number of signatures appended to them, and the absence of names of prominence among these. The Ogallalla treaty had but three signers—Long Bull, Charging Bear, and Man that Stands on a Hill—neither of whom, as was notorious, had any control over the tribe. In the mean time General Connor had marched into the Powder River country to chastise the Indians who declined to treat, but he had little success, and was forced to be content with establishing Fort Reno on the head-waters of Powder River.

The matter drifted on through the winter, the opposition growing somewhat less during that annual period of starvation, when the presents from the Great Father looked so much more enticing. The leader of the anti-cession party was Red Cloud (Mock-peah-lu-tah), who was at that time known only as the chief of the Bad Faces, one of the three bands into which the Ogallallas were divided. He was a warrior, not of hereditary rank, who was raised to the leadership on his merits, and was already exerting a wide influence. His influence was largely due to his medicine powers, which were not of the ordinary stripe. In common with many other Indians, he professed the power of seeing spirits, but, in excess of them, he claimed direct communication with the Great Spirit, who guided him in all matters of importance. Shrewd in all things, he was especially keen in his foresight. He realized that the building of the road meant the destruction of the game in their best hunting-ground, and the reduction of his people to the beggarly condition of the Indians who hung about the government posts. He bitterly opposed the treaties from the first. An able second was found in Ta-shun-kah-Ko-ke-pah (Man Afraid of his Horses), the warlike chief of the Honc-pah-te-lah band of Ogallallas. The name does not mean that he fears his horses, as it is often understood, but that he is fearful of losing them. It was given him because, on occasion of an attack by the Shoshonees, he abandoned his family in order to save his herd of ponies.

The most influential of the chiefs that favored the treaties was Spotted Tail (Sin-ta-Gal-les-sca), who, like Red Cloud, was not of hereditary rank, but a warrior who had risen by his courage and ability. He and his coadjutor Standing Elk (As-hah-kah-nah-zhe) will be remembered as among the Brulés who surrendered themselves, for the safety of their tribe, after the battle of Ash Hollow. When a young man of twenty, Spotted Tail quarrelled with one of the boldest and fiercest chiefs of his tribe, about a young girl, whom both admired. Meeting one day alone, outside the camp, the chief demanded of him that he should abandon his pretensions to the lady, on pain of instant death. The young brave did not stop to bandy words. Burning with rage and hatred, he snatched his knife from its sheath and defied his rival's prowess. The chief's keen blade had flashed in the air as quickly as his own; with a bound he was upon the presumptuous youth, and they were in the struggle for life or death. A few hours later an Indian, who passed that way, found them locked in each other's arms and covered with gaping wounds; the chief was dead, and Spotted Tail was senseless. He soon recovered from his wounds, and at once rose to prominence. It is pleasing to know, also, that he married the girl for whom he fought so well, and through life treated her with such kindness and affection as are rarely known among these In-

SPOTTED TAIL.

dians. On the death of the head chief the tribe put aside the hereditary claimants, and elected Spotted Tail, by an almost unanimous vote, to the highest command. He had proved an able chief and remained friendly to the whites, but at the present juncture the sentiment against the road was so strong that his authority was reduced to a nominal control, even of his own tribe.

In the spring the commission located itself at Fort Laramie, being still engaged in efforts to get signers to its treaties, and especially to conciliate the Ogallallas. The idea prevalent among officials, both in the East and the West, was that there must be peace, and accordingly it was said with assurance that there would be. According to the statement of Special Agent Chandler, " Commissioner Taylor repeatedly asserted that he was sent there by the government for the purpose of making a treaty, and it should be accomplished, if made with but two Indians," as could be " proved by numerous officers and citizens at and near this post, who heard him." Every effort was made to induce the Indians who opposed the road to consent to it, but in vain. Colonel Taylor promised " that the travel on said road should be confined strictly to the line thereof, and that emigrants and travellers generally should not be allowed to molest or disturb the game in the country through which they passed ;" but this offer, so evidently impossible of performance, did not deceive the Indians, and they still refused to treat. So certain, however, were all parties that the right of way would be granted, that the military occupation of the country began while the negotiations were pending. Colonel H. B. Carrington was ordered up from Fort Kearney, with about two thousand men, of whom eight companies were assigned to the new route. They numbered about seven hundred men, five hundred of them raw recruits. This command passed through Laramie in June, while the negotiations were going on, and marched directly for the Powder River country.

As soon as the destination of these troops was announced to the Indians, Red Cloud, Man Afraid, and their followers withdrew from the council and refused to return. The only ones of the Prairie Sioux who remained and agreed to abide by the treaties were the Lower Brulés, with a few stragglers from other tribes. At that time they numbered about two thousand five hundred, but a year later Spotted Tail, Standing Elk, and Swift Bear, the treaty chiefs, had with them only one hundred lodges, mostly of old women and squaws, the young men having gone to swell the ranks of Red Cloud. Included among the Indians that treated was the mixed band under Big Mouth and Blue Nose, which had lived about Fort Laramie so long that they were known as the "Laramie Loafers." They numbered about six hundred, but less than a hundred of them were men, and more than a hundred were half-breed children. So rapid was the defection of warriors to the hostile camps, that, within two weeks after the passage of the troops, Spotted Tail and Standing Elk told the whites that their young men had left them and gone to the Powder River country, and that parties who went far from home had best "go prepared, and look out for their hair."

The commissioners were right in insisting that a treaty should be made and the road opened. There was no existing treaty with the Sioux by which the United States relinquished the right of opening roads through their country, as has sometimes been stated. The United States does not often make treaties of that kind with Indians, and it is doubtful whether it ought at all. The reason for the law of eminent domain extends to the right of way over Indian lands, whether reserved or not, as it does to that over the property of the citizen, and the Indian should submit to it as the white man does. After land is reserved for the use of Indians, however, the law of eminent domain comes in conflict with another dogma of public policy, which is that the Indians should be kept separate from the whites until they become civilized. The damage done by the intrusion is held superior to the benefit resulting from the road, but in such cases right of way is almost invariably obtained by treaty. When a new railroad is to be built, it is pushed through the country with very little regard for the feelings of property owners. It may spoil the old spring, ruin the orchard, and wipe the beloved homestead out of existence, and this although in fact the road may be a mere speculation, and not a necessity at all. To this the white

man must submit; why then should a much-needed road be
left unmade for fear of spoiling the hunting-preserves of the
red man? Certainly the Montana road ought to have been
opened; the wrong done was in failing to report the actual
feelings of the Indians to the government. If we may judge
by the letters of Commissioner Bogy, he was in absolute ignorance of the condition of affairs. It was understood in Washington that the treaties were properly made and that everything was going on smoothly. The troops received assurances
to that effect.

The detachment for the Powder River country was moving on. The soldiers were splendidly furnished with everything except arms, ammunition, and horses. Nearly all of
them were armed with old, muzzle-loading, Springfield muskets; though the regimental band had Spencer breech-loading
carbines, and a few of the officers had Henry rifles. Of ammunition only a small amount was taken from Fort Kearney,

ON THE BOZEMAN TRAIL.
31*

in the expectation that a supply could be obtained at Fort Laramie, but unfortunately there was none there of proper make
and calibre.   There was no cavalry in the command, and only
two hundred horses available for cavalry purposes.   On these
two hundred infantrymen, armed with muskets, were mounted.
Verily this expedition was on a strictly peace basis.   The Indians were proceeding on a different theory.   On the morning
after the command reached Fort Reno, one hundred and sixty-
seven miles northwest of Fort Laramie, the peaceful Sioux
ran off all the sutler's horses and mules.   They were pursued,
but none of the stock was recovered; the only thing the pursuers captured was a pony, so heavily laden with the presents
recently distributed at Fort Laramie that he could not keep
up in the chase.   On July 14 the troops, who had then
reached Piney Creek, received notice from the Indians that
they must leave the country; that Fort Reno would not be
disturbed, but that no new forts could be built.   On the next
morning the new fort was located at the mouth of Little
Piney Creek.   It was named Fort Phil Kearney, in honor of
the distinguished cavalry officer, though the orthography does
not indicate it.*   Preparations for defence were at once begun by mowing the parade-ground and putting up signs to
" Keep off the grass."

On the morning of the 17th, at daybreak, part of the post
herd were stampeded, and the party that went in pursuit was
surrounded by a large force of Indians, who killed two and
wounded three of the soldiers.   Later in the day, the same
party of Indians came upon the travelling trading establishment of Louis Gazzous, commonly known as " French Pete,"
an old trader with a Sioux wife, and killed all the men, six in
number.   From that day until the 29th, five emigrant trains
were attacked, fifteen men killed, and much stock run off, part
of it from Fort Reno.   On the 29th Carrington appears to
have awakened to the fact that the hostile Indians were doing
some damage.   He telegraphed the Adjutant-general of the
army, on that day, for Indian auxiliaries and additional force.
On the 31st he requested reinforcements of General P. St.

---

* The family name is Kearny, but both the Nebraska post, which was
named after Stephen W., and this one, are universally spelled Kearney.

George Cooke, commanding in that district. On August 3, Fort C. F. Smith was located on the Big Horn, ninety-two miles northwest of Phil Kearney, by two companies sent from the latter point. During August the hostilities were chiefly horse and cattle stealing. Only three men were killed on the line, one of them being Grover, the artist-correspondent. In the latter part of August General Hazen visited and inspected the post. He stated that two companies of regular cavalry had been ordered up from Fort Laramie, and a regiment of infantry was on the way from St. Louis. In September more than a dozen men were killed on the line, about five hundred horses, mules, and cattle were run off, and five mowing-machines, with much other property, were destroyed.

During all this time active work was continued on the fort, which was being constructed on an extensive and elaborate plan. Large parties of men were kept busy cutting timber and hauling it in; others were working on the stockades and buildings; saw-mills were running at full speed; hay was being cut and stored for the coming winter. The timber was cut about seven miles from the fort, and the men detailed to cut and bring it in were called "the wood train." It was used in such enormous quantities, and so much of their time was consumed in Indian attacks and alarms, that from seventy-five to one hundred men were employed almost constantly in this branch of the work. By the last of October the fort was enclosed. It stood on a little plateau, elevated fifty or sixty feet above the surrounding bottom lands, in the point at the mouth of the Little Piney. Its length was sixteen hundred feet, northwest and southeast, parallel to the Big Piney. The northwestern part of it, or fort proper, was eight hundred feet in length by six hundred in width, and surrounded by a stockade of heavy pine logs, which were eleven feet long and planted three feet in the ground. The logs were hewn to a touching surface of four inches, loop-holed, and pointed. At the eastern and western angles were block-houses. Enclosed in this stockade were quarters for the troops, cavalry stables, store-houses, and a few other buildings. The southeastern half of the fort was of the same length, and of nearly equal width, where the two parts joined, but narrowing to about four hundred feet at the southeastern end. It was enclosed in a rough cottonwood stockade, and was used for a corral, teamsters' quarters, stables, shops, and similar purposes. The amount of work in all this was very great, there being forty-two distinct buildings in the fort proper, while the stables and other buildings of the corral extended entirely around it, except at the gates, abutting on the stockade.

The country about the fort is hilly. Some six miles west of it the Big Piney comes down in a northeast course, till it passes Piney Island; then it turns to the southeast and flows in a direct line for over six miles, to the mouth of Little Piney, where it swerves and flows away almost due east. North of the fort, on the opposite side of the Big Piney, is Lodge Trail Ridge, trending northwest and southeast, and forming the divide between Piney and Peno creeks. The latter is a tributary of Goose Creek, which, in turn, flows into Tongue River. East of the fort is Little Piney Creek, then a few low hills, then Starling Creek, and beyond it Lake De Smet. Southeast of the fort is an island of seven or eight acres in Little Piney, and beyond the creek rises a high knoll called Pilot Hill, which was used for a lookout station. South of the fort are two or three hills, and then the Big Horn Mountains, rising in successive ridges till they culminate in Cloud Peak, miles to the south. To the west is Fort Ridge, seven hundred feet above the valley, separating the head-waters of the Big and Little Piney. It is so called from the supposed remains of an Indian fort on its summit. Just to the northwest of the fort begin the Sullivant Hills, which extend away in that direction to the Big Piney. Beyond them the creek is divided by the large island called Piney, which was the principal place for cutting timber. Beyond the creek in this direction are Peno Head and Rocky Face Ridge, two branches of a spur of the Big Horn. Between these and Lodge Trail Ridge are the head-waters of Peno Creek. The Montana road crosses the country described from southeast to northwest, running south of Lake De Smet, north of Pilot Hill and the fort, crossing the Big Piney just above the fort, swinging around the northeastern slopes of Lodge Trail Ridge, and down Peno Creek.

The amount of work done by the force at Phil Kearney

was astounding, but the Indian fighting was limited, and of a
defensive nature. In one sense it was right enough that such
should have been the case, for Carrington was sent out to
build forts, and the work he did was in the line of his duty;
but he might, at least, have kept scouts enough out to have
known when thousands of warriors were in his immediate
vicinity. The men were obliged always to go armed to their
work, and accompanied by an escort guard. The wood trains

TORTURE BY PRAIRIE INDIANS.

were attacked repeatedly, in the woods and on the road, and
several men were killed in these assaults. Private Johnson
was cut off from his party and no trace of him found afterwards, which was almost conclusive evidence that he had been
taken alive and reserved for torture. The Sioux have an unpleasant method of torture. They fasten a man, naked, to
the ground, lying on his back, with arms and legs stretched
out and fastened to pegs; then they build a fire on his stomach,

and keep it up till he dies, occasionally touching a burning brand to other portions of his body, gouging out an eye, or otherwise adding to the agony of the victim. Private Smith was scalped and left for dead in the pinery, but recovered sufficiently to drag himself to the block-house, built for the protection of the axe-men, there to die. Two other private soldiers were cut off near the same place, and scalped before the eyes of their comrades. The men grew impatient, and longed for the time when they might quit carpenter-work, and seek revenge. The Indians grew bolder. Sometimes they contented themselves with attacking the wood train; sometimes they rode tantalizingly near the fort and challenged the soldiers to fight; two or three times they charged the picket that was kept on Pilot Hill to watch their movements. On these occasions a shell or a canister would be dropped among them, and the guard, which was on duty with horses saddled and bridled, would rush to the relief of the threatened watchmen. The simple expedient of placing a block-house or a small stockade on the hill, which would have made the picket perfectly secure, did not occur to any one. Carrington said he desired to assume the offensive, but wanted reinforcements, and these, though long-promised, were slow in coming. The only ones that reached the fort at all were sixty men of Company C, 2d cavalry, armed with Springfield muskets and old-fashioned Star carbines, who arrived in November.

Among those at the fort who were impatient for a fight was Brevet Lieutenant-colonel William J. Fetterman, a soldier by birth, instinct, and profession, who joined the command at the fort in November. He had his first opportunity on December 6. The wood train was attacked two miles from the fort, and forced to corral for defence. Fetterman was sent, with thirty-five cavalry and a few of the mounted infantry, to relieve the wood party, and drive the Indians across Lodge Trail Ridge, in which direction they usually withdrew, while Carrington, with twenty-five mounted infantry, crossed the Big Piney, to intercept the Indians on Peno Creek. Fetterman's party put the Indians to flight and chased them for about five miles, when they faced about and attacked the troops. Nearly all the cavalry fled, leaving Fetterman, assisted by

Captain Brown and Lieutenant Wands, with a dozen men, to face over a hundred warriors. They stood at bay until Carrington's force came in sight, when the Indians retired. In the mean while Lieutenant Bingham, joined by Lieutenant Grummond, with two or three men from Carrington's command, pursued a single dismounted Indian into an ambuscade, two miles from the remainder of the troops, where Bingham and Sergeant Bowers were killed. In this affair Red Cloud commanded in person. He had lookouts on all the neighboring hills, signalling the progress of affairs, and it is probable that he had planned a more extensive ambuscade, but that his plans miscarried.

The Indians made their arrangements better the next time. It was Friday, December 21, 1866. The morning was bright and pleasant, though there was snow on the hills. There was still little of the humdrum of army-post life about Fort Phil Kearney. The office building and one of the company quarters were not yet finished, and there were touches to be added at many points, before this chief architectural feature of the Powder River country was in condition to admit of Indian fighting. A force of some ninety men started to the pine woods for more material, little dreaming that the pine woods, the ravines, and the brush coverts all around were full of bloodthirsty warriors. About eleven o'clock an alarm was given, and the lookout signalled: "Many Indians on wood road; train corralled and fighting." A detachment was at once organized for their relief. At the same time Indian pickets were seen on the neighboring hills, and a score or more appeared at the crossing of the Big Piney, but these were quickly dispersed by a few shells. Colonel Fetterman asked permission to take command of the relief party, which was granted. Lieutenant Grummond volunteered, and was put in charge of the cavalry. Captain Fred H. Brown joined of his own motion. He had been at the post all summer, as regimental quartermaster, and was then engaged in closing up his business before going to Fort Laramie, whither he had been ordered. He was an enthusiastic Indian-fighter, and was particularly ambitious to get Red Cloud's scalp. Wheatley and Fisher, two frontiersmen who were at the post, went with Brown, making the entire party eighty-four men. The soldiers were of different companies; fifty of them had Spencer carbines and revolvers; the remainder carried Springfield muskets, except the two civilians and one of the officers, who had Henry rifles.

The corralled train, at which the fighting was going on, was south of the Sullivant Hills. Instead of proceeding directly to it, the command took a course back of these hills, across Big Piney Creek, on the southwestern slope of Lodge Trail Ridge, to cut off the Indians who were attacking the train. As they moved along, Indians appeared on their front and on their flanks, retiring before them, out of range, across Lodge Trail Ridge, whose crest Fetterman reached fifteen or twenty minutes before noon, and occupied, with his men deployed in skirmish line. At the same time the lookout signalled that the Indians had left the train, which had broken corral and moved on towards Piney Island. The train returned to the fort after dark without having been subjected to any further annoyance. Fetterman's halt on the crest of Lodge Trail Ridge was of very brief duration. His men disappeared over the summit and firing began soon after, which grew more and more rapid until, at noon, there was an almost continuous rattle of musketry. This was heard plainly at the fort, and conveyed the intelligence that a hard fight was in progress in Peno Creek Valley. The people at the fort grew anxious. Surgeon Hines, with one man, was sent to the wood train, with instructions, if it were safe, to join Fetterman. He found the wood train undisturbed, and started across the country to Peno Creek, but found many Indians on Lodge Trail Ridge, preventing him from further progress. He went back for reinforcements, and Captain Ten Eyck, with seventy-six men, all that were considered available, was sent out. The anxiety of all who were on the fort side of the ridge was intense. The relief party galloped on, but they seemed to crawl. Instead of taking the road they went straight to the ridge and ascended it. The firing was becoming less and less in volume. Who was giving way? What was silencing the guns? They knew at the fort which side had a small supply of ammunition. Just before Ten

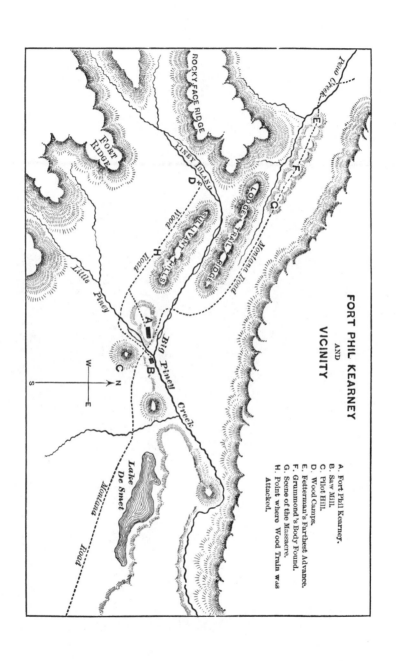

FORT PHIL KEARNEY
AND
VICINITY

A. Fort Phil Kearney.
B. Saw Mill.
C. Pilot Hill.
D. Wood Camps.
E. Fetterman's Farthest Advance.
F. Grummond's Body Found.
G. Scene of the Massacre.
H. Point where Wood Train was
    Attacked.

ROCKY FACE RIDGE
FORT RIDGE
PINEY ISLAND
LODGE TRAIL RIDGE
SULLIVANT HILLS
Little Piney
Wood Road
Montana Road
Big Piney Creek
Lake De Smet
Montana Road
Piano Creek

Eyck reached the summit of the ridge, at a quarter before one o'clock, two or three straggling shots were fired in the valley beyond; after that came silence. The struggle was evidently ended.

The relief party looked from the summit over the valley of Peno Creek. No soldiers were to be seen. The whole valley was filled with frenzied savages, who shook their weapons at the new arrivals, and challenged them to come down. A sergeant was despatched to the fort to report the situation and ask for a howitzer, which was not sent. For some cause, probably their losses, the Indians then began to withdraw from the valley of their own accord, and the relief party descended to the battle-field. The fight had taken place on a little ridge, three quarters of a mile in length, five to six miles from the fort, on the east side of Peno Creek, running parallel to it and to Lodge Trail Ridge, but beyond the latter. The road runs along its summit, rising to it opposite the northwestern extremity of Lodge Trail Ridge. Just beyond this point, on the road, a large number of Indians had been closely grouped when Ten Eyck's party first came in view, and here was the first intelligence of the ill-fated command which rode so gallantly from the fort but two hours before. Clustered on a space less than forty feet square were the bodies of Captain Brown, Colonel Fetterman, and sixty-five of the men. A more horrible sight could not be imagined. They were stripped naked, scalped, and so terribly gashed and mangled as to be almost unrecognizable. Years afterwards the Sioux showed a rough, knotty war-club of burr-oak, driven full of nails and spikes, which had been used to beat their brains out. It was still covered with brains and hair, glued to it in clotted blood. But with all the mutilation there were no signs of a struggle here. No empty cartridge shells were found around the bodies, though there were a few full cartridges. A few yards away the bodies of several of their horses were found, all heading towards the fort. All the appearances indicated that they had been suddenly overwhelmed by a rush of greatly superior numbers. Bullet-holes through the left temples of Colonel Fetterman and Captain Brown, from weapons held so close that the powder

had burned into their faces, showed that these officers had
" saved a shot for themselves," as they had often said they
would do, rather than fall into the hands of the Indians.

A messenger was sent to the fort for wagons, and his report, though meagre and indefinite, caused the hearts of the
garrison to sink. After dark Ten Eyck's party returned,
bringing forty-nine of the bodies, and the announcement that
all were killed. No advance had been made, however, beyond the point where the bodies lay grouped, so that, while
reasonably certain of the death of the others, there was no absolute assurance. The painfulness of the uncertainty was increased by the fact that among the bodies still unaccounted
for was that of Lieutenant Grummond, the only married man
of the detachment, whose wife was at the fort and in delicate
health. The night of mourning and suspense passed away,
and morning came. A party went out to learn the fate of
the remaining members of Fetterman's command. They advanced cautiously to the point gained on the day before, and
then on down the ridge. On the road, a quarter of a mile or
more beyond the first pile of bodies, was found the corpse of
Lieutenant Grummond. Still beyond, where the road made
its abrupt descent to Peno Creek, were found the remains of
half a dozen of the oldest and most experienced soldiers, with
many empty cartridge shells scattered about them ; and a little to one side, behind a pile of rocks, were the bodies of
Wheatley and Fisher, with more than fifty empty shells by
their sides, telling that they had not died tamely. Within a
few hundred feet in front of this position were found ten
dead ponies and sixty-five great gouts of blood, which had
flowed from the death - wounds of as many Indians. No
ponies and no blood-spots were found elsewhere. The bodies
here were scalped and mutilated as the others, the mutilations
being so shocking that they have never been made public,
further than the general announcement that the bodies were
gashed with knives, chopped with hatchets, and shot full of
arrows ; the rest is covered up in the statement that, " No
such mutilation is on record." The bodies were brought in,
and lay in ghastly array until the next Wednesday. The
weather turned so intensely cold, on the night after the mas-

THE LAST STAND.

sacre, that the men who were digging the great grave for this heap of slain had to be relieved every half-hour, and the work went but slowly. On Wednesday they were laid away in their common resting-place, fifty feet long and seven feet deep, in the little cemetery at the foot of Pilot Hill.

Just what happened after Fetterman's command passed the top of Lodge Trail Ridge no one can say, for no man lived to tell it. The movement was in disobedience of orders, as directions were given, at least twice, not to pass the ridge. No one is left to tell why those orders were disobeyed, or how the snare was closed about the gallant band, or who attempted to fly, or who fought doggedly to the death. As read in the position of corpses, the record of cartridge shells, and the register of blood-stains, and confirmed by the Indians, it would seem that Fetterman moved down to the road with little resistance; that he advanced up the ridge beyond Peno Creek, leaving a part of his force at the crest to guard his rear, and followed down the road with the remainder; that at the farther end of the ridge the battle raged for almost an hour; that meantime a large force of the Indians, who numbered about two thousand, gathered in his rear at the other end of the ridge; that the ammunition of the majority of the soldiers became exhausted; that a retreat was determined on; that Wheatley, Fisher, and five or six of the older soldiers decided to remain where they were, either from the knowledge that retreat under such circumstances was certain death, or from a voluntary determination to stay behind and "stand off" the Indians until the others escaped; that the remainder, as they rode back, found themselves suddenly confronted by a force that made escape impossible; that Brown and Fetterman shot each other, and the rest were cut down by the savages. Only six of the entire command appeared to have been killed by bullets, a fact which indicates that their ammunition had been expended, and that the Indians could not be kept from coming to close quarters.

The Indians say that this massacre was accomplished by a special expedition, organized among the Minneconjous, under the direction of their head chief, High Back Bone. It was their intention to kill all of the garrison and destroy the fort, their hope being to decoy nearly all of the soldiers out, and, having massacred them, to attack the great stockade on all sides, as a small force would be unable to defend it.   In addition to the Minneconjous, nearly all the warriors of the Upper Brulés, Ogallallas, Sans Arcs, Oncpapas, Two Kettles, Blackfoot Sioux, Northern Cheyennes, and Arapahoes, and stragglers from several other tribes, were on the war-path at the time, but only a part of them engaged in this affair.   The party, as stated by the Indians, was composed of 350 lodges of Minneconjous, 100 lodges of Cheyennes, 100 of Arapahoes, 3 of Crows, and a part of the Ogallallas and Brulés, numbering in all about 2000 warriors.   It will be observed that the percentage of warriors to a lodge, in a war-party, is much greater than under ordinary circumstances.   When out for war the old men and women are left at home with the younger children.   Only active squaws, and children old enough to be of service, accompany a war-party at any time, and very frequently only warriors go.   The Indians say that Red Cloud was not in the attack, but had gone towards Fort Buford with his own band, the Oncpapas, and the others. They concede a loss of four Minneconjous, three Brulés, three Ogallallas, one Cheyenne, and one Arapaho, killed, and about sixty wounded, of whom several died and many were permanently maimed.   They lost twelve horses killed, and fifty-six so severely wounded that they died within twenty-four hours.   This estimate is unquestionably below the reality.   There is scarcely a doubt that each of the sixty-five blood spots on the field meant a dead Indian.   Wounded Indians leave a battle-field with wonderful celerity, and one who cannot move, until he has bled freely, may safely be counted as dead or mortally wounded.

The tragedy was over, but who was to be blamed for it. There was a murmur from all the land, partly of rage against the Indians, and partly of disapproval of the military mismanagement that had made such a slaughter possible.   A thorough investigation was ordered by General Grant.   The off-hand impression was that the officer commanding at the post was in fault.   He was at once superseded by Brevet Brigadier-general Wessels, then commanding at Fort Reno, who had orders to investigate. There was much said about Carrington at the time that was unjust and absurd—so much that it enabled him to pose as a martyr later on. The most remarkable statement was made by Indian Commissioner Bogy, who hastened to explain the affair without waiting to learn the facts. He demonstrated that the Indian force must have been small; that the only hostiles in that part of the country were a part of the Ogallallas, under Red Cloud, with a few individuals from other tribes; that the idea of the wood train being attacked by three hundred warriors, on December 6, was preposterous; that the statement that they challenged the troops to fight was a wild absurdity; that the only things that made the report credible at all were the corpses of the soldiers, which seemed to be in conflict with his theory. He accounted for them thus: "These Indians, being in absolute want of guns and ammunition to make their winter hunt,

RED CLOUD.

were on a friendly visit to the fort, desiring to communicate with the commanding officer, to get the order refusing them guns and ammunition rescinded, so that they might be enabled to procure their winter supply of buffalo. . . . I regret the unfortunate death of so many brave soldiers, yet there can be no doubt that it is owing to the foolish and rash management of the officer in command at that post."

The matter of guns and ammunition was referred to because, in the preceding autumn, General Sherman had ordered Indian traders to discontinue the sale of weapons and ammunition to the Indians.   This procedure raised the wrath of the Indian ring, for the greatest profit in the Indian trade is from this source.   Commissioner Bogy explained how cruel and unnecessary the order was, as follows: " No Indian will buy two guns.   One he absolutely needs; and as he has no means of taking care of powder, he necessarily will take, when offered to him, but a very limited quantity.   It is true that formerly they hunted with bows and arrows, killing buffalo, antelope, and deer with the same; but to hunt successfully with bows and arrows requires horses, and as the valleys of that [the Powder River] country are now more or less filled with white men prospecting for gold and silver, their means of subsisting their horses have passed away, and they now have but few horses.   I mention these facts so as to place before the country, as briefly as possible, the condition as well as the wants of the Indians."   This statement, made so positively by Mr. Bogy, needs some correction.   At that time, and for years before and afterwards, every plains Indian would buy as many guns and revolvers as possible, and would take all the ammunition he could get.   Bows and arrows were still their favorite weapons for hunting buffalo, and were always carried, no matter how well armed they were otherwise. There were no white men prospecting in either the valleys or hills of the Powder River country, and the Indians had as many horses as ever, besides what they had stolen from the whites.   Otherwise Mr. Bogy's statement appears proper enough.   His theories about the Fetterman massacre are equally correct.   His proposed remedy for any evil that might exist was to send out " a commission of judicious men."

The press, as usual, gave circulation to numerous wild stories concerning the affair, and made impossible pictures of the massacre.   One even went so far as to report that the massacred men fell at the gates of the fort, begging for assistance, while the people on the inside dared not open the gates for fear the Indians would rush in.   The commission which investigated the matter exonerated Carrington altogether, and the responsibility drifted over to his superior officer, General Cooke, commanding in the Department of the

Platte; at least, the latter was relieved by General Augur soon afterwards. Carrington was a good enough civil engineer, but he was a dress-parade style of officer, who would have been more in place as a teacher in a military school. He built a very nice fort, but every attack made on him and his men, during the building, was a surprise. There is nothing to indicate that he ever knew whether there were a thousand or only a hundred Indians within a mile of the fort. He seems to have disapproved of Indians. Perhaps he would have ostracized them socially, if he could have had his way. It is no excuse for this want of watchfulness to say that he had asked for reinforcements and not received them. He might have spared men enough from some of the ornamental work about the fort to have attended to that. Besides, he had been authorized, on August 11, to enlist fifty Indian scouts, on cavalry pay and allowances. The fact is, that reinforcements were not asked for the purpose of defending the fort and the work about it, but for an expedition of offence that had been instructed by General Cooke. There is nothing to show that Carrington apprehended any danger near the post. On December 19 he telegraphed Fort Laramie: " No special news since last report. Indians appeared to-day and fired on wood train, but were repulsed. They are accomplishing nothing, while I am perfecting all details of the post and preparing for active movements." That was all he said—no call for reinforcements; no worry about arms; all complacency and promise. Two days later he telegraphed: "Do send me reinforcements forthwith. Expedition now with my force impossible. . . . I hear nothing of my arms that left Leavenworth September 15. The additional cavalry ordered to join me has not reported. . . . I need prompt reinforcements and repeating arms. I am sure to have, as before reported, an active winter, and must have men and arms. Every officer of this battalion should join it. . . . Give me officers and men; only the new Spencer's arms should be sent; the Indians are desperate; I spare none (!) and they spare none." No more complacency; no more promise; only a recollection that he had asked for arms, ammunition, and reinforcements long before. It is but fair to say that no one fully realized and understood the feelings and intentions of the Indians; the news of the massacre came like a thunderbolt in the night, waking the whole nation from a sleep. But Carrington should have known more about the Indians in his immediate vicinity, and probably would, if he had paid more attention to them than firing shells into the woods to scare them away. There was fault everywhere. The Indian agents were wrong in misrepresenting the feeling of the Indians; so were the treaty commissioners. Carrington and Cooke were wrong in permitting the troops to go into a hostile country equipped as they were. Cooke, and officers higher up, were wrong in not seeing that arms, ammunition, and reinforcements were furnished when regularly called for.

After General Wessels took command at Phil Kearney, he undertook a winter campaign against the hostiles, but the weather was so intensely cold that it had to be abandoned. Neither side was able to make any movements of importance for several months. It was known that the Indians had attacked Fort Buford, at the mouth of the Yellowstone, five days after the massacre at Phil Kearney, and for two months it was commonly believed that the garrison had all been killed. Then messengers came through with the glad news that the one company of soldiers stationed there had beaten Red Cloud's army off, and held them back, until the cold drove them to their winter camps. In the spring a peace commission was sent out. It met Man Afraid of his Horses and others on June 12. They all said they had reformed, and were going to join Spotted Tail's Brulés; they wanted ammunition for hunting. They got no powder, and they fell from grace, if they had ever attained it. Hostilities were kept up all summer, with such vigor that the frontier was in continual alarm. The troops on the line of the Montana road had actually to fight for their wood and water, but they had one day of bloody revenge. On August 2 Major Powell, of Fort Phil Kearney, was guarding a wood train, on the road to the pinery, around the south side of the Sullivant Hills. He had divided his force, keeping thirty men in reserve in a little fortress, made of fourteen iron wagon-beds placed in a circle; the remainder were to retreat to this if attacked. Sud-

SIOUX VILLAGE IN WINTER.

denly 800 Indian warriors swept down from the hills. The forces of the soldiers were separated; all fled to the fort except the reserve, in the corral of wagon-beds. At this the Indians rode, but the errors of 1866 had been remedied. The soldiers had breech-loading arms and plenty of ammunition. The Indians broke under their rapid and deadly fire, and drew off. Back in the hills were 1200 more of Red Cloud's warriors, who joined with the first attacking party and charged again, led by the great chief in person. The corral was a blaze of fire from the moment they came within five hundred yards, and the fire was far more effective than the Indians were used to, because they were massed together and hard to miss. Closer and closer they came, but there was no sign of giving way at the corral, and no cessation of that awful fire. The nerve of the Indians gave way, and they fled again. For three hours they kept at it, their courage always failing at the critical moment. Then they withdrew, and soon the little garrison was relieved by a party from the fort. They had lost but three killed and two wounded. The loss of the Indians was very heavy. A chief told Colonel Dodge that they had 1137 killed and wounded— but this is incredible. The Indians called it the "medicine fight," suspecting that their white friends had worked in some supernatural assistance.

In the fall the commission made up its report, and decided that the government had no right to put a road through the Powder River country. It cited Supreme Court decisions that have no bearing on the case, and made of importance ancient treaties that never existed. Nevertheless, their ideas prevailed. The country, and particularly the army, was anxious to have the Pacific Railroad completed, and the Indians would agree not to interfere with it, in consideration for our surrendering the Powder River country. With the railroad built, Montana would be more accessible from the south than from any other direction, and the Bozeman road would be of comparatively little use. Accordingly a treaty was made, at Fort Laramie, on April 29, 1868, relinquishing all claims to the country east of the Big Horn Mountains, in which all the chiefs joined, though the wary Red Cloud did not affix his name until November 6, when he had satisfactory assurance that the white man would keep his promises. In the summer of 1868 the troops abandoned the Montana road, whose opening had cost so much money and life, and the Sioux burned down the forts which had been planned with such mathematical nicety, and constructed in such architectural perfection. We gave up an unquestionable right, though perhaps not then worth asserting. A few years later we broke our faith and reasserted it. Then the work had to be done again.

CHAPTER XVI.

PUNISHING THE PIEGANS.

OF all the tribes within the Rocky Mountain region, the people of the Sakitapix or Blackfoot nation are most like the Eastern tribes, and this similarity is natural, for they are most probably an offshoot of the Algonquin family, and formerly lived much farther east. There are traces of their migration from above the sources of the Mississippi to the Upper Saskatchewan country, in which they lived when the era of credible history began with them. The two great branches of the Saskatchewan (Kisiskachewan—a Cree word, meaning swift current) rise in the Rocky Mountains, one about fifty miles and the other one hundred and eighty miles north of our line; they unite near longitude 105° West, and the main stream flows thence two hundred miles east to Lake Winnipeg. The home of the Blackfoot nation was between and about the two forks of the stream, when, before the whites had any acquaintance with them, the nation was separated by a great feud that arose on the death of their head chief, in battle with the Assinaboines. The older warriors followed the black banner of the hereditary claimant to the chieftaincy, but the younger ones generally ranged themselves under the red or bloody flag of a warrior who claimed succession by reason of prowess and ability. The supporters of the black-flag interest were defeated, and moved south to the Missouri. The migration was in the fall, after the prairies had burned over, and the black color received by their moccasins and leggings caused them to be called Satsika (Siksika), or Blackfeet, by the Crows. The victorious portion received the name of Kena (Kanaans) or Bloods. The Blackfeet were again divided through the ambition of a chief named Piegan (the Pheasant) who claimed the position of chief. He was defeated, and separated from the tribe, with his adherents, who were thereafter called Piegans (Peigans, Pagans, Pecaneaux). Later, the Gros Ventres of the North confederated with the Blackfeet. They were a band of Arapahoes who seceded from their tribe early in the current century, and after some ten years of wandering, during which they suffered severely at the hands of the Crows and Kootenays, they were relieved and taken into friendship by the Blackfeet.* In 1853 the numbers of these tribes were variously estimated as follows: Blackfeet, 250 to 500 lodges; Bloods, 350 to 400 lodges; Gros Ventres, 360 lodges; or a total of from 6500 to 12,000 souls. The lower estimates are probably more nearly correct. Their number at present is not definitely known, owing to the fact that they are partly in British America, but the most recent estimates are from 6000 to 7000. Those now in the United States are reported at 2300, and are consolidated under the name of Piegans; for comparison with the earlier population, 1100 Gros Ventres, who are now separated from the Piegans, must be added to this number.

These Indians were of high reputation as warriors, and esteemed themselves superior to the surrounding tribes, with whom they waged continual war. The men are tall Apollos, with large eyes and straight black hair. They pluck the beard from the face, and often remove the hair from the head, excepting the scalp-lock. Usually they were well clothed in garments made of dressed skins. The women are short and inclined to corpulency. The organization of the nation is quite complicated. Each tribe is divided into bands, and each band has a chief and a *mina maska*, or priest of the sun. Each tribe has a general council, called the Exkinoya, which meets once a year, when the tribe is assembled for the sun-dance and other religious ceremonies and festivities. The men are divided into seven ranks or degrees, according to their prowess, their skill, and their wisdom. Only members of the seventh or highest class are allowed in the Exkinoya, in which the legislative and judicial power of the tribe are centred.

---

* The Blackfoot Sioux have no connection with this nation. The similarity of name is purely accidental.

The sixth class includes the band chiefs, and entrance to it requires both valor and statesmanship. It is charged with the execution of the tribal laws. In enforcing orders, use is made of the entire police or "soldier" force of the tribe, including all unmarried warriors. The fifth class has charge of hunting and the moving of camps. The four lower classes mark merely the advancement of the warrior, as evinced by his deeds and ability. Four years is the ordinary time of probation required in each class, but this rule is sometimes broken over. Their chiefs are to some extent elective, but they have much regard for hereditary rank, especially if coupled with ability. In religion they are sun-worshippers, their deity being personified under the name of Napea. To this god they formerly offered annually a sacrifice of a young virgin, but this practice was long since abandoned, and of later years they have satisfied themselves with the mutilations of the sun-dance. Their religious nature is well developed, and their men have that peculiar dignity that is characteristic of the Indian in his wild state.

The Blackfeet have long had the reputation of being among the most treacherous and bloodthirsty of our savages, but it came chiefly from the statements of the tribes with whom they fought. This reputation has been widely extended through the "yellow-backed novel," that generally condemned, and more generally read, school-book of American youth, in which the Blackfeet are always at war and always very dangerous. As a matter of fact there was never any general or formal war between these people and the Americans. Their relations have been of a very friendly nature, Appleton's Encyclopædia to the contrary notwithstanding. In the early days of the fur trade they often fought with American trappers, but at that time they had no treaty with us, and considered the trapper an invader of their country, who was no better than a thief, for he came to take the furs which they were accustomed to gather and sell to the Hudson's Bay Company. In the struggle for supremacy between the rival fur companies, the Americans formed associations with the Nez Percés, Crows, and other enemies of the Blackfeet, and the latter, with other tribes, naturally fell under the influence

BLACKFEET AND TRAPPERS.

of the British company, though there is little to show that they preferred the English personally to the Americans. The fight recounted by Irving, between them and Sublette's and other trappers, including Wyeth's party, which was brought on by the treachery of a Flathead and a half-breed, allies of the Americans, is a good example of the manner in which they were almost forced into a hostile attitude. Their early hostility to the trappers was also increased by the killing of one of their warriors by Mr. Lewis, of Lewis and Clarke's expedition. From similar causes, and from the fact that in stealing horses the Blackfeet made little distinction in owners, the unfriendly feeling became such that the American Fur Company was obliged to maintain a force of sixty or seventy men at its post on the Marias River.

The Blackfeet were cruel, in the manner of Indians, but not more so than their neighbors. An illustrative instance of this fact is recorded by Mr. Cox, who happened among the Flatheads at a time when they were torturing some Blackfoot prisoners. He says: "Having been informed that they were about putting one of their prisoners to death, I went to their camp to witness the spectacle. The man was tied to a tree; after which they heated an old barrel of a gun until it became red-hot, with which they burned him on the legs, thighs, neck, cheeks, and belly. They then commenced cutting the flesh from about the nails, which they pulled out, and next separated the fingers from the hand, joint by joint. During the performance of these cruelties the wretched captive never winced, and instead of suing for mercy, he added fresh stimulants to their barbarous ingenuity by the most irritating reproaches, part of which our interpreter translated as follows: 'My heart is strong. You do not hurt me. You can't hurt me. You are fools. You do not know how to torture. Try it again. I don't feel any pain yet. We torture your relations a great deal better, because we make them cry out loud, like little children. You are not brave; you have small hearts, and you are always afraid to fight.' Then, addressing himself to one in particular, he said, 'It was by my arrow you lost your eye;' upon which the Flathead darted at him, and with a knife in a moment scooped out one of his eyes; at the same time cutting the bridge of his nose nearly in two. This did not stop him; with the remaining eye he looked sternly at another, and said, 'I killed your brother, and I scalped your old fool of a father.' The warrior to whom this was addressed instantly sprang at him and separated the scalp from his head. He was then about plunging a knife in his heart, until he was told by the chief to desist. The raw skull, bloody socket, and mutilated nose now presented an horrific appearance, but by no means changed his tone of defiance. 'It was I,' said he to the chief, 'that made your wife a prisoner last fall; we put out her eyes; we tore out her tongue; we treated her like a dog. Forty of our young warriors—' The chieftain became incensed the moment his wife's name was mentioned; he seized his gun, and, before the last sentence was ended, a ball from it passed through the brave fellow's heart, and terminated his frightful sufferings. Shocking, however, as this dreadful exhibition was, it was far exceeded by the atrocious cruelties practised on the female prisoners; in which, I am sorry to say, the Flathead women assisted with more savage fury than the men."

On the other hand, while the Blackfeet were savages, they occasionally performed acts of unexpected generosity. Shortly

before the arrival of Governor Stevens's party in the Blackfoot country, in 1853, a feud had arisen between the Blackfeet
and Gros Ventres, on account of the murder of a Gros Ventre
warrior by a member of the former tribe. The Gros Ventres
retaliated, and open war resulted, during which several Gros
Ventres were captured by the enemy. They expected death
by torture, but the Blackfeet fed them, treated them kindly,
gave them horses, and sent them to their homes. This humane
action paved the way for the reconciliation of these tribes, and
a treaty between them and the tribes west of the main range,
which Governor Stevens was desirous of effecting, and the
Indians all agreed to meet him in council two years later. At
this time, also, it was made apparent by the testimony of white
men who had been among them, that the reports of their evil
disposition had arisen from their hostile attitude towards the
tribes with whom the Americans had been on terms of friendship. Mr. Doty summed up their feeling in 1853, thus:
"Their present disposition towards the whites is unquestionably friendly. Undoubtedly a party of white men may travel
through this country in perfect safety. The only danger
would be that the Indians might take them for Indian enemies
and rush upon them in the night. Their horses might be
stolen, unless under the protection of a chief or an influential
white man, one who is friendly and well known to them. The
only white inhabitants of this country are the traders and employés at the American Fur Company's post, Fort Benton, and
at Mr. Harvey's, or the opposition fort. These are on friendly
terms with the Indians, as is evidenced by the fact that they
are constantly sending traders with large quantities of goods
to remote points in the Blackfoot country, who are not only
permitted to go and come without molestation, but are treated
with much kindness and hospitality at the camps. The horses
at this post [Benton] are always turned out to pasture without
a guard, and are seldom or never stolen. So far as has been
ascertained, their present relations with the Hudson's Bay
Company are simply those of a limited trade, which is entirely confined to a portion of the Blackfeet and Blood bands.
These Indians procure in the northern part of their territory
a considerable number of small peltries, and in the summer—

at which season they go farthest north—trade them at one of the Hudson's Bay Company's posts on the Saskatchewan River —'Chesterfield House,' I think.   This trade is carried on for two reasons: First, because the Indians are paid there a higher price for their small peltries than is given by American traders.   Secondly, they procure at that post an abundance of whiskey; and it is undoubtedly this latter consideration that induces them to go."

TRADER'S CAMP.

At this time the Bloods and Blackfeet occupied the country about the head-waters of the Marias and Milk rivers, as far north as latitude 50°; the Piegans were in the country between Milk River and the Missouri, on the Marias and Teton rivers; the Gros Ventres occupied the country between Milk River and the Missouri, from the mouth of the former to the country of the Piegans.   All this region was well supplied with game, and the natural growth of grass afforded ample pasturage for the horses, of which these tribes owned many—· about ten to each lodge. In character the land is much the same as the ordinary foot-hill country on the eastern slope of the Rockies, requiring irrigation for successful cultivation. The names given to its natural formations are usually Canadian French, instead of English or Spanish, as at the South. A divide or watershed is called a coteau ; a table-land, or mesa, is always a plateau ; a hill is a butte ; a gulch, ravine, or arroyo is a coulie. The name teton (a breast) is also sometimes given to hills, and the probability is that the Teton tribes had their name from the French fur-traders.

In October, 1855, Governor Stevens met with the tribes on the Upper Missouri, near the mouth of Judith River. The Indians attended, as they had promised two years before. There were represented the Bloods, Blackfeet, Piegans, Gros Ventres, Flatheads, Pend d'Oreilles, Kootenays, and Nez Percés. Common amity was declared by the United States and these tribes, and the Indians also agreed not to make war against any other tribe except in self-defence. A great common hunting-ground was agreed upon, east of the main range, between the Mussel-shell and the Yellowstone, to which all the tribes were to have access, but in which none were to reside. White men were given the right of travelling unmolested everywhere, and the government was conceded the privilege of making roads of any description, through any part of the country. All the land north of the Mussel-shell and Missouri rivers, between the main range and a line drawn north from the mouth of Milk River, was declared to be " the territory of the Blackfoot nation, over which said nation shall exercise exclusive control." In consideration for the rights relinquished, the government was to pay the Blackfoot nation $20,000 annually for ten years ; the further sum of $15,000 annually, for ten years, was to be expended " in establishing and instructing them in agricultural pursuits, and in educating their children, and in any other respect promoting their civilization and Christianization."

Under this treaty the Indians preserved a strict peace with the whites, though there was a disposition to carry on war with the Crows and Assinaboines. The Bloods were at first determined to pay no attention to their promises, as to these Indians; but on finding that the Piegans and Gros Ventres were standing firmly by the treaty, they abandoned their designs, and thereafter the only troubles between the tribes were occasioned by young men who would not listen to the advice of their chiefs and older warriors. These gradually decreased in frequency, and faith with the government was so admirably preserved that, in 1860, the Blackfeet were pronounced "the most peaceable nation on the Missouri River." Their annuities were brought up on boats each year, and distributed to them. Farming was tried by the agency people, but without success. The climate was too dry to permit successful farming without irrigation, and there was no money to be applied to making ditches. The money promised for schools might well have been used for that purpose, for they had no schools and no missions. It would be interesting to know what became of that $150,000. The Indians subsisted as before, wholly by the chase. One chief tried to cultivate eight or ten acres, but his crops failed, and he quit in disgust. This appears from the official records to have been the only step made towards that education for which $15,000 annually was agreed to be expended. Just at the close of the ten years, in October, 1865, the agent for the Blackfeet reported: "The moral condition of the Indians in this country is truly lamentable. Not one spark of civilization appears to have dawned upon their ignorant minds, and their capacity for improvement, if they ever had any, seems to have risen and set in total darkness." And yet he closes the same paragraph with the following sentence, which is one of the most touching expressions extant of the fervent, unconquerable faith of the average Indian agent: "Let us hope that success will yet crown our efforts to ameliorate the condition of these unfortunate and degraded savages, and place them and their children on the road to a better, brighter, and more glorious future." There has been a sorry crown for all the efforts made thus far.

During our civil war even the state of peaceful savagery into which the Blackfeet had lapsed was disturbed. The troubles with the Sioux prevented the Blackfoot annuities from reaching their destination. The tribes fell out among

33*

themselves and fought one another.   The Sun River farm, as
the agricultural experiment in their country was called, fell
into decay, but the agency farmer made a comfortable living
by keeping hotel and trading with the Indians.   The gold
discoveries of 1862–63 attracted a large white population to
the southern borders of the Blackfoot country, and the new-
comers furnished the Indians with all the whiskey they would
pay for.   There was still no war with the whites, who ran
through the country at will, without molestation. In the spring
of 1864 the Blackfeet showed their good-will by offering to
aid General Sully in fighting the Sioux.   In May of this year
the white population had so increased that Montana was cut
off from Idaho and organized as a separate territory.   In December, 1864, trouble arose with the Bloods.   A band of fourteen of them stole the horses of twenty white trappers, who
were hunting near the Little Rocky Mountains.   Nine of the
trappers followed them, overtook them at daylight, killed two
of them, and recovered the horses.   From that time on, bad
feeling increased among the Bloods.   In April, 1865, they
stole forty horses from Fort Benton.   On May 10 they stole
all the horses and mules from Sun River farm, and that school
for agricultural instruction was abandoned.   On May 22 a
party of drunken white men at Fort Benton attacked a party
of Bloods, who came there, and killed three of them.   Three
days later a large party of Bloods attacked ten white men,
who were cutting logs on the Marias, and killed every one of
them.   These hostilities were all confined to a small portion
of the Bloods, whose homes were properly in British America.
The Blackfeet proper, the Gros Ventres, and the Piegans all
remained at peace, a matter of no little importance at that
time, on account of the large amount of freighting that was
being done from the mouth of Milk River to Fort Benton,
there being two hundred and fifty wagons steadily engaged
in this business.

   In the fall of 1865 Agent Upson made a new treaty with
the Sakitapix, which was never ratified, the Indians, it was
claimed, having gone to war before the treaty reached Washington.   There was not, in fact, any war, except one between
the Piegans and Gros Ventres, resulting from reciprocal horse-

"NO HORSES TO SPARE."

stealing.   There were no troops in the country to protect any
one or enforce any order.   The country contained many lawless white men.   The better class of whites formed vigilance
committees to protect themselves against both white and Indian marauders.   The Gros Ventres had preserved a closer in-
timacy with the whites than the Piegans had, and in January
two white men who happened to be in company with Gros
Ventres were killed by Piegans.   With horse-stealing, intertribal war, occasional raiding by the Bloods, and no troops,
things went from bad to worse until the feeling of the white
population was that the Blackfoot nation, excepting the Gros
Ventres, was at war, but, in truth, the Blackfeet proper had
gone into British America prior to the treaty, and had nothing to do either with the treaty or the subsequent troubles.
A militia organization of five or six hundred men was made,
for the protection of the settlements, but they never took the
field against any of these Indians.   In April, 1866, a party,
supposed to be North Piegans, burned the buildings at the
Sun River farm.   In June, 1866, Little Dog, head chief of the
Piegans, who had labored faithfully to preserve peace, returned to the Indian agent twelve horses that had been stolen
from the whites.   As he was returning to his camp he was
ambushed by some of his own warriors, and he and his son
were killed.   There were several other acts of violence during the year, but hostilities were brought to a close by the orders stopping the sale and issue of ammunition, on account of
the Sioux war over the Montana road, coupled with the non-
issuance of supplies that had been expected under the new
treaty.   The Indians, with their usual improvidence, had made
no adequate preparations for the winter of 1866–67, and they
suffered much from want in that season, in consequence of
which they were in a more peaceable condition in the following year.   Both military and Indian authorities who investigated the situation in 1867 pronounced the apprehensions of
war without foundation, which was true enough then.   People were travelling the road from Helena to Fort Benton, and
thence to Cow Island, without being troubled in the least.
There was a party of ten emigrants killed in this year, but
within the British line, and by Bloods.   The fact is that no

considerable portion of the Blackfoot nation had been hostile
to the whites since 1853, nor were at any subsequent period.
In 1867 the Gros Ventres were separated from the Blackfoot
nation and placed with the River Crows, where they have
since remained.

The years 1867 and 1868 passed with a peaceful condition of affairs in the Blackfoot nation. The whiskey-trade
flourished at Fort Benton as it had never flourished before.
Some of the Bloods and Blackfeet stole horses and sold them
to the Hudson's Bay Company, but the southern bands returned many stolen horses to the whites, so that a reasonable
balance was preserved. Three annual appropriations, of $7000
each, were made under the treaty of 1865, and in the fall of
1868 another treaty was made, which was not ratified, but for
several years appropriations of $50,000 were made for the
education and civilization of the nation. So far as subsistence
was concerned, they were supposed to be taking care of themselves, but in reality what they did receive, which was not
very much, was in supplies. The lawless part of the white
population continued to act in a way that would bring on war
if the Indians had any spirit. While the Piegans were at
Fort Benton, in 1868, after signing the treaty, two white men
assaulted and shot at Mountain Chief, the principal chief of
the tribe, which produced a very angry feeling among them.
Special Commissioner Cullen tried to have these men arrested,
but, rather than take any part in such an unusual proceeding,
the sheriff and justice of the peace at that point resigned
their offices. The Indians soon after stole eighty horses from
the whites at Diamond City, and other points, on account of
which eighteen Piegans were seized by Cullen and held until
the horses were returned. An attempt to enforce the intercourse laws was repressed in a most effective way. The principal witness who had been subpœnaed to testify in the matter of a seizure of two bales of buffalo robes, that had been
purchased with whiskey, was followed by men from Fort Benton and hung until he was nearly dead, in consideration of
which he agreed to leave the country in silence.

The year 1869 was ushered in with a bad state of feeling,
which had been produced by the evil deeds of bad men on

both sides, and this feeling grew worse during the summer. That part of the Indians were stealing horses was not even questioned by the tribes. The chiefs said it was done by men whom they could not control, and that they could not return the horses, because they were run off into British America and sold. Edmonton House and Mountain House, both on the Saskatchewan, were the two posts of the Hudson's Bay Company at which this traffic was carried on principally. It was shown by the affidavits of half a dozen white men, who had lived in the vicinity of these posts, that the trade was a regular and notorious one. It was shown that the factors of the company well knew that the horses were stolen, and that Hickland, the chief trader at the Mountain House, encouraged the thievery, and told the Indians what kind of horses he wanted them to get for him. All of the best of these horses were kept by the officers and employés of the company. Wells, Fargo, & Co. involuntarily supplied our neighbors over the line with seventy-three animals during 1868 and 1869. An officer of the company drove a fine pair of grays, bearing the " W., F., & Co." brand, and another pair was used in one of the company's grist-mills. From other parties there were reported stolen, during the summer and fall of 1869, two hundred and twenty-seven horses and mules, nearly all of which went into British America. It was also shown that the company sold the Indians arms and ammunition, in any quantity desired. The only way in which our government could reach this evil was by punishing the Indians, but there was another evil which might have been mitigated, at least, if proper attention had been given to it.

The misconduct of white men still continued, and gave the Indians a ready excuse for their misdeeds. In fact, nearly all of the horse-stealing occurred after barbarities which had been committed by these lawless people. All of the government authorities saw this wrong, and tried to have it righted, but the force which was authorized was directed against the Indians, and the settlements were left to purge themselves by natural progress. General Sully, Superintendent of Indian affairs, wrote, on August 3, 1869: " There is a white element in this country which, from its rowdy and lawless character, can-

not be excelled in any section, and the traffic in whiskey with
Indians in this territory is carried on to an alarming extent.
This frequently causes altercations between whites and Indians,
resulting often in bloodshed; and as they occur in sections
where the civil authorities acknowledge themselves to be pow-
erless to act, nothing but military force can at present put a
stop to it. . . . From reliable reports, that increase daily, it is a
wonder to me that open war with the Indians has not broken
out already. . . . Nothing can be done to insure peace and
order till there is a military force here strong enough to clear
out the roughs and whiskey-sellers in the country." General
Hardie, who was sent out by General Sheridan to investigate,
testified to the same thing, in these words : "There are unprincipled and unscrupulous men of all classes who speak and
act without reference to the truth and right, in pursuit of their
private ends or the gratification of their passions. . . . There
are plenty of lawless and unprincipled men upon the border
who supply Indians with whiskey surreptitiously, if not openly, in defiance of the law." General De Trobriand, commanding in Montana, said : "There is in the territory a certain number of people whose pecuniary interest is intimately connected
with the Indian trade, licit or illicit. Therefore they are
averse to any Indian policy which can hurt their purse."

With these surroundings in view, the rise of the Piegan
troubles of 1869 are simple of explanation. The Piegans of
Mountain Chief's band, still smarting under the attack on him,
were openly hostile; and they were aided and abetted by the
bands of Bear Chief, Red Horn, and some others. On July
16, 1869, some of these Indians, while stealing horses, killed
two white men near Fort Benton. In retaliation the whites
there hung two suspected Piegans, and, a few days later, murdered an old man and his nephew, who were generally known
to be innocent and inoffensive people. Depredations at once
grew numerous. Horses were stolen everywhere. A freight
train was attacked on Eagle Creek; one man and twenty oxen
were killed before the Indians were driven off, with a loss of
four of their warriors. On August 17 great excitement was
caused by the murder of Malcolm Clarke, and the wounding of
his son, at their ranch, twenty miles above Helena. It was re-

EDMONTON HOUSE.

ported that the place had been attacked by hostiles, and wild rumors of war prevailed for a time, but the opinion soon gained ground that the murder was due to a family quarrel. Clarke had married a Piegan woman, and was killed by a nephew of hers, named Peter, a notorious ruffian, of a very quarrelsome disposition. He was shunned by his own people on account of having killed his father-in-law, Bear's Head, a brother of the Chief, Heavy Runner. There were some twenty Piegans present at the time, among them Pal, a son of Mountain Chief, who, in the melée, shot one of Clarke's sons. Another son of Clarke escaped unharmed, as did also Miss Clarke, an estimable young woman, who leaped through a window and fled during the quarrel. Young Clarke, who was left for dead by the Indians, afterwards recovered. The excitement in the settlements cooled down for a time, but in September it was raised again by the murder of James Quail, near Silver City. It was reported at the time that he was scalped and mutilated, and no doubt was entertained that the Piegans were guilty of the crime. Later reports established the untruthfulness of the report of scalping and mutilation. His horse was found near him, and, as it was known that he had a valuable watch and four or five hundred dollars with him, the presumption arose that he had been murdered by some white man. Still, many believed that Indians had committed the crime, and it was reported as talked among the Piegans that a warrior named Little Eagle was the murderer. There were two stage-robberies in the early fall, but it was definitely learned that they were the work of white bandits. The horse-stealing lessened perceptibly after the Clarke tragedy. It was learned later on that the hostile bands had left the vicinity of the settlements about September 1, part of them going to the Yellowstone, and part to the North. The friendly Piegans remained on the Marias.

The military authorities had been called on for assistance, by the Indian Bureau, in August, and again in October. They investigated carefully at the outset, and gave General Sully full opportunities to have the murderers surrendered, and stolen property given up, before taking any steps. It was determined to do nothing until the hostiles returned to the

Marias, which they were expected to do in January or February, but for some cause they came back about the middle of December. Within ten days after their return a party of ten hunters was attacked near the head of Sun River Valley, thirty mules were stolen from a government contractor at Dearborn, and the cabin of a wood-chopper, near Camp Cooke, was robbed, the last resulting in a fight. It was decided to strike them at once, as this could be done without interfering with the peaceable Indians. The Blackfeet were all in British America. The Bloods were in two parties, one across the British line, and one above the Red Coulie, on the Marias. The Piegans were on the same stream, but lower down, and in separate bands, the hostiles being located at the Big Bend. The camps of Heavy Runner, Big Lake (Big Leg), Little Wolf, and The Boy were ordered to be left unmolested, as these chiefs had proven themselves friendly. Only the camps of Mountain Chief, Bear Chief, and Red Horn were to be struck. The expedition was put in charge of Colonel E. M. Baker, of the 2d Cavalry, at Fort Ellis. He left that post on January 6, with four companies of cavalry, and proceeded to Fort Shaw, at which point he was reinforced by two companies of mounted infantry, and departed thence to the north on the 19th.

The weather was intensely cold, and, as the success of the expedition depended largely on its secrecy, the marching was done at night after reaching the Teton River, on the 19th. On the night of the 20th the command proceeded to the mouth of Muddy Creek, a tributary of the Teton. On the night of the 21st they marched across the country towards the Big Bend of the Marias, but were unable to reach it. They lay all that day in a ravine, on the Dry Fork of the Marias, and at night marched on again. About eight o'clock on the morning of the 23d they reached the camp of Bear Chief and Red Horn, consisting of thirty-seven lodges, in the valley of the Marias. The attack was a complete surprise. Smallpox had broken out among the Indians, causing them to omit even the slight precautions that they would have naturally observed in a secure winter camp. The herd of ponies, over 300 in number, was cut off and secured. 173 In-

FORT BENTON.

dians, including Red Horn, were killed. Only 9 escaped from
the place. All the rest, men, women, and children, were either
killed or captured. Leaving Lieutenant Doane with a detachment to destroy the camp, Colonel Baker hastened down the
river in search of Mountain Chief's camp, which was said to
be four miles away, but he found nothing until he had gone
sixteen miles, and then only seven deserted lodges. These
were destroyed, and the command then marched to the post
of the Northwest Fur Company, near the Red Coulie, where
the Blood chiefs were summoned, and required to give up
the stolen horses in their possession, after which the troops returned to their quarters. The captives that had been taken
were released at once, on learning that the smallpox was
among them, and found their way to other camps. Thus far
the details of the "Piegan War" are as stated above, by the
concession of all parties concerned, but beyond this there is
some controversy, and the matter has been left in that unde-

34

cided state which forces a recourse to the calculation of probability.

The principal point in dispute was the age and sex of the
persons killed. The report from the Indians was first received, it having been collected from them by Lieutenant
Pease, their agent, and was as follows: "Of the 173 killed on
the 23d, 33 were men ; of these, 15 only were such as are called
by them young, or fighting, men ; these were between the ages
of twelve and thirty-seven ; the remaining 18 were between
the ages of thirty-seven and seventy; 8 of the latter were
between the ages of sixty and seventy ; 90 were women—
35 between the ages of twelve and thirty - seven, and 55
between the ages of thirty-seven and seventy; the remaining 50 were children, none older than twelve years, and many
of them in their mothers' arms. Out of 219 belonging to Red
Horn's camp, only 46 survived; among them are 9 young
men who escaped during the attack, and 5 who were away
hunting. The lives of 18 women and 19 children (none of
them more than three years of age, and the majority of them
much younger), some of whom were wounded, were spared
by the soldiers. Red Horn himself was killed. At the time
of the attack this camp was suffering severely with small-
pox, having had it among them for two months, the average
rate of deaths among them having been six daily." The
original report of Colonel Baker was limited, in this regard,
to the statement: "The result of the expedition is 173 Indians killed, over 100 prisoners, women and children." He
never furnished a detailed report of the sex and age of the
killed, such as General Sherman said was "proper and usual,"
any further than the following, by telegraph: "I am satisfied
that the following numbers approximate as nearly to the exact truth as any estimate can possibly be made. That the
number killed was 173. Of these there were 120 able men,
53 women and children; that of captives (afterwards released), there were of women and children 140." At least, no
further report was submitted to the House of Representatives,
which called on the War Department for all papers and correspondence connected with the affair. On February 3,
General De Trobriand wrote, presumably from the infor-

mation he had been able to acquire by that time : " The execution was made against 36 lodges, and there 173 were killed ;
about 100 squaws and pappooses were captured, and, after the
action, turned loose unhurt."

It is apparent that both the first and second statements
are exaggerated, and probable that the information on which
the third was based was somewhat colored. As to the first,
if the Indians had been dying at the rate of six a day, for
two months, the camp would have been completely depopulated before the troops reached it. As to the second, the estimate of 120 able men, out of a total of 313, is a proportion
that was never known to exist in any winter camp in the
country. As established by all preceding and succeeding estimates and censuses of the Blackfoot nation, the ordinary
proportion of warriors was two to each lodge, a lodge being
estimated at seven people. The variations from this proportion in any recorded enumeration are very slight. We would
therefore naturally expect, in a village of 37 lodges, 259 people, of whom 74 would be warriors. Smallpox might have
decreased this total to 219, as stated by the Indians, but there
is scarcely a possibility that there should have been only 29
fighting men belonging to the band, as stated by them, i. e.,
15 killed, 9 escaped, and 5 absent. The fair inference from
all considerations, it being remembered that Colonel Baker's
statement purports to be an estimate only, and that the examination of a camp in which there was smallpox would probably be brief, is that about 60 of the killed were warriors,
and 113 women and children. The number of nominal captives was not probably more than 85.

The attack on the Piegans created a sensation in the East,
or, more properly, a sensation was created by a letter of Vincent Colyer's, concerning it, which found its way into print.
What Lieutenant Pease had reported merely as the statement
of the Indians, this letter stated as fact, in these direct terms :
"The facts were received to-day from Lieutenant W. B.
Pease, United States Army, the agent of the Blackfeet, and
is endorsed by General Sully, United States Army." This
was a palpable misrepresentation. Lieutenant Pease expressly stated the sources of his information, and General

Sully's endorsement said: "The report that Lieutenant Pease sends is entirely what the Indians say of the affair, and of course it is natural to suppose it is prejudiced in their own favor. It is the Indians' side of the question, and, as I am here as their only representative, I consider it my duty to give them a hearing." On Mr. Colyer's letter the action of the troops was severely criticised in Congress, as it would probably have been also on the facts, for the criticism was addressed to the manner of making war which involved the killing of women and children. Said Mr. Voorhees: "When the Indians were a power in this land we made war on them according to civilized warfare. We struck them in manly battle. Now, when they are poor, broken, and miserable remnants, corrupted and demoralized, it is proposed to change our mode of warfare, and smite not merely the warrior, but the woman and the babe in her arms. I have thought much on this subject, and the more I think of it the more it fills me with horror. If, however, we are to change the policy of the government, let it go forth to the country now; . . . if the administration is to call home its peaceful agents who are endeavoring to civilize the Indians, and to send instead the sword and the fagot into their midst, when they are in their lodges, in the dead of winter; to strike them when dying of disease, sparing neither mother nor babe, till the scream of the last expiring infant shall be heard in its helpless agony on the gale, then avow it, avow it here, avow it boldly, and say that Indian warfare in these days means extermination,— extermination without regard to age, sex, condition, or health, or anything else that usually protects non-combatants in war."

Mr. Mungen said: "In looking at the accounts of the inhuman sacrifices of those 'savages' who were women and children, I cannot see in it any mercy, or justice, or humanity, or Christianity, or any godlike attributes. As for the savages who murder and destroy our women and children, I would fight them to the last, but I would not torture even them; and I certainly would not jump upon a little Indian child, having the smallpox, and kill it." The debate, which was in Committee of the Whole, resulted in nothing but a

call for the correspondence from the War and Interior departments, it having been shrewdly treated as a Democratic attack on General Sheridan, by the friends of the administration, although a Republican began the criticism and others
aided in it. There was an attempt made also to interpose
General Hancock, then commanding the Department of Dakota, as the responsible superior officer. In truth, General
Sheridan was the responsible superior, he having sent Inspector-General Hardie to Montana to investigate, and, on receiving his report, having issued instructions to him, on January
15, in these words: "If the lives and property of citizens
of Montana can best be protected by striking the Indians, I
want them struck. Tell Baker to strike them hard."

LIEUTENANT-GENERAL P. H. SHERIDAN.

Neither General Sheridan nor any other officer advocated or defended any unnecessary killing of women and children, although they justified the attack. Colonel Baker reported: "I believe that every effort was made by officers and men to save non-combatants, and that such women and children as were killed were killed accidentally." General De Trobriand reported: "Quarter was given to all known in time as women and children." General Sheridan, after referring to women and children who save themselves during the bombardment of cities by hiding in cellars, said: "Should any of the women and children of the Piegans have lost their lives, I sincerely regret that they had not similar places of refuge, though I doubt if they would have availed themselves of them, for they fight with more fury than the men." General Sherman said: "There is no question at all of responsibility, save and except only as to whether Colonel Baker wantonly and cruelly killed women and children unresisting, and this I never believed." With all this unanimity of sentiment, and though Baker may not have directed it, it seems impossible that so many women and children should be necessarily killed, whether the number was 53, as estimated by the military, or 140, as claimed by the Indians, or a medium between these extremes, as is most probable. 173 Indians are too many to be necessarily killed out of thirty-seven lodges, especially when the only casualty to the attacking party was one man killed. Whether the results justified it is another question, but there is hardly room for doubt that but for the determined stand of all the officers in defence of the action, the attack on the Piegan village would have rested in the same category with Sand Creek.

To the conservative mind the justice of the criticisms made will depend largely on the question whether there was or was not existing a state of war. If there were, the military view that a single effective blow is the most humane way of ending a war, is certainly worthy of consideration. If not, the movement should have been confined to the arrest of criminals. As to this there was a difference of opinion. On August 18, when the first reports of the killing of Clarke reached him, General Sully telegraphed: "I

fear we will have to consider the Blackfeet in a state of war."
With subsequent reports his opinions changed, and on January 13 he thought that all difficulties might be ended by the seizure of Mountain Chief and half a dozen of his warriors. On October 6, General De Trobriand said: "The first fact, which I think must be admitted by all, is that there is actually *no Indian war* in the territory," and he then favored the arrest of a few men, as an adequate measure. With the depredations in December his opinions changed, and in January he favored chastising the hostile bands. General Hardie, at the latter period, thought a single severe blow "would be more sparing of blood, and better on all accounts," but he reported the facts and the opinions of both sides impartially, with the question: "Under all the circumstances, how far should the opinion of General Sully, as to scope of operations, govern the military?" To this General Sheridan replied by the telegraphic instructions above quoted, and the attack was made in pursuance of his order. In connection with the question as to the propriety of indiscriminate attack, it is to be remembered that Mountain Chief and the worst of the offenders, as conceded by all, escaped altogether. It is also noteworthy, as a probable result of the criticism, that there has not occurred since that time any such indiscriminate attack. However just may be the feeling of some that this method is the more effective, and therefore the more humane, the general sentiment of the country is against it. As Mr. Voorhees said: "It cannot be justified here or before the country; it cannot be justified before the civilization of the age, or in the sight of God or man."

Since the infliction of this severe punishment there has been no trouble reported from the Piegans, though they have had ample cause for it. While this result is to some extent attributable to that punishment, it is more largely explained by other things. Indians are usually obedient to their own laws; the lawlessness that white men object to arises from the fact that their laws differ from ours, and from the fact that our laws have not covered offences committed among them. The Indian tribes have been left to regulate their own behavior so long as they did not interfere with the whites. If a tribe had good laws the results were always beneficial, but with those whose laws were of a barbarous type there have occurred many crimes, from our stand, for which there was no redress. The Blackfeet, as has been mentioned, had a remarkably complete tribal organization, and when this was supplemented by a code of good laws, which they were induced to adopt in 1875, a most admirable state of quietude resulted. Their code prohibits intemperance, polygamy, sale of women, theft, and assault. Murder is punished by death. Their police force has executed these laws effectively. Not only this, but they have arrested a number of Indian and white criminals, who had committed crimes in the settlements and undertaken to escape across the reservation.

The Sakitapix have not advanced much in civilization, but what advance they have made has been due to their own efforts. They were assigned to the Methodist Church for missionary work, but none has been done among them. An alleged government school has been reported as being in operation at their agency for some fifteen years, at an expense of $1200 a year, paid out of their appropriations, and satisfactory results have been reported from year to year; but in 1884 comes the statement that sixteen of the Blackfoot nation—think of it, sixteen!—can actually read, and that fourteen of these have learned all of that during the past year. We have then, presumably, two children taught to read as the result of the work of the fourteen years previous, and an outlay of some $17,000. It is a great achievement to get $8500 worth of reading into one child's head. He ought to become an elocutionist of high degree—an ornament to any reservation. The chances are about one hundred to one that the Indians have been robbed by their agents, but it is also evident that the aid given them by the government has been inadequate. It is a fact that ought to be considered a reproach to the nation that peaceable tribes, as a rule, have received little assistance, no matter what their needs may be or their services have been. As to this nation, the statistical tables have furnished information which on its face is unreliable, but still is enough to show something of their sufferings from want. The deaths have repeatedly been in excess of the births, and in 1884 the terrible disproportion was reached of 247 deaths, chiefly from starvation and its concomitant ills, against 46 births. It has not needed statistical tables to prove their wretched lot; again and again the newspapers have published the item: "The Piegans are reported to be starving, notwithstanding the assistance furnished them by the government," and similar brevities. It is notorious that we have been starving these people, and it is true that Congress, which waxed so furious over the slaughter of a few dozens of women and children, is largely responsible for the death of a much greater number, by the more lingering and more cruel mode.

There has been no excuse for this neglect. The matter has been called to the attention of Congress several times, in the most urgent language, and Congress, in response, has cut down their appropriation. From 1871 to 1878 the appropriation was $50,000 annually; in the latter year it was cut to $40,000; in 1881 it was cut again to $35,000. All the expenses of the reservation, including the pay of from six to eight employés and teachers, were paid out of this sum. At the same time their other sources of support have been decreasing even more rapidly. The buffalo, which was formerly their main reliance, is entirely gone, and other game has so decreased that it can no longer be counted on for material support. The situation has been growing worse constantly until, in 1884, R. A. Allen, who took charge of the agency on April 1 of that year, reported as follows: "When I entered upon the duties of agent I found the Indians in a deplorable condition. Their supplies had been limited, and many of them were gradually dying of starvation. I visited a large number of their tents and cabins the second day after they had received their weekly rations, looked through them carefully, and found no provisions, except in two instances. All bore marks of suffering from lack of food, but the little children seemed to have suffered most; they were so emaciated that it did not seem possible for them to live long, and many of them have since passed away. To feed these Indians, about 2300 in number, from April 1 to June 30, I had 19,080 pounds bacon, 44,700 pounds beef, and 62,565 pounds flour, being only 1½ ounces bacon, 3½ ounces beef, and less than 5 ounces

flour per day for each individual. I had no beans, rice, hom-
iny, salt, nor any other articles of food, except sugar, tea, and
coffee (of which I had only enough for the sick and infirm) to
give them, the supply of such articles having been exhausted
before this time, nor have I yet [August 14] received any. In
the fore part of May I was reduced to such a strait that I was
compelled to issue over 2000 pounds of bacon which had been
condemned by a board of survey the past winter, but which
I found not to be in as bad condition as had been supposed.
In the latter part of June and fore part of July, so great was
their destitution that the Indians stripped the bark from the
saplings that grow along the creeks and ate the inner portion
to appease their gnawing hunger." Do you grasp the dreadful import of these words? Here, in free America, in the
year of grace 1884, when a surplus of so many millions had
accumulated in the national treasury that financiers were
frightened, this occurred, and nothing was done to relieve
their sufferings. If the people had understood this, and had
known how to reach the Piegans, they would doubtless have
responded as cheerfully and as liberally to their cry of distress
as they have to the calls of the famine-stricken elsewhere, but
they did not. We have been trusting our authorized representatives to look after such things, and they have not done it.
We ought to have known it, or rather it ought never to
have occurred. There is something radically and horribly
wrong in the management of Indian affairs to make such
a thing possible. The Board of Indian Commissioners
ought to assume the responsibility of calling on the people
for aid in such a case, and it would be well if standing committees were appointed in each state and territory where Indians live, to see that such destitution is promptly reported to
the Board.

An adequate relief of these Indians is not merely a matter
of humanity and charity. We owe it to them to put a stop
to this worse than inquisitorial cruelty. We confirmed to
them by treaty, in 1855, all the land north of the Mussel-shell
and Missouri rivers, from the mouth of Milk River to the
main range of the Rockies, and to them, in common with
other tribes, hunting-grounds between the Yellowstone and

SUMMER CAMP ON MARIAS RIVER.

the Mussel-shell, from the Rockies to Twenty-five Yard Creek. Under the unratified treaties of 1866 and 1868, and the executive orders of July 5, 1873, and August 19, 1874, we took from them all the land between the Mussel-shell and the Marias, as well as their hunting-grounds below—the best hunting-grounds they had—for which we gave them nothing but the annuities mentioned. By Act of Congress of April 15, 1874, the reservation was made to include only the land north of the Missouri and the Marias, from the western line of Dakota to the main range of the Rockies, and the eastern part of this was reserved for the Gros Ventres and River Crows, who are located there. It is true that the reservation was increased by executive order of April 13, 1875, but nearly all the increase was restored to the public domain by executive order of July 13, 1880. We took their land because we had power to do so; they were the wards of the nation, and the nation could do as it pleased. If an ordinary guardian should thus appropriate his ward's property the courts would not be slow in forcing him to disgorge, but there is no court, except the people, to supervise the doings of the Indians' guardian. Did the Blackfeet object to this? Certainly they did, but their protest availed them nothing. Not only did these orders take away their lands, but they left the reservation buildings outside the reservation, and new ones had to be built out of the miserable pittance—four cents a day to each individual—provided for their education, civilization, and support. Would not justice have been better here than the humanity that was exercised?

But, it may be asked, why do not these Indians do something for themselves? They have done all they could. In 1879, their agent reported: "Some of the most influential chiefs set an example to the rest by going into the field and working themselves, instead of simply standing by and seeing their squaws work." In 1882, he reported: "In all the work the agency requires the Indians are an efficient help, such as cutting and hauling firewood, also saw-logs from the mountains, and hauling in hay from the nearest hay-field, which is some ten miles from the agency. Our hay crop will be about one hundred tons. The Indians use their own ponies in hauling, and soon become fair teamsters." The trouble is that there is nothing for them to do by which they can support themselves. They are in an isolated position, where there is no call for un- skilled labor from neighboring settlements. Farming has been tried on their reservation for over twenty years, and it has usually failed from drought or grasshoppers. In the few years that crops have looked hopeful, the Indians have been driven by starvation to eat them long before they matured, or the Indians from the British side of the line so preyed upon them that they were forced to abandon cultivation and come in to the agency, in order to protect their few remaining horses. Congress has been informed a number of times that farming in this country was hopeless without irrigation, and that no funds had been provided for making irrigation ditches or pro- curing implements, but Congress has just as often failed to do anything. How long is this to continue? There seems to be no help for it from the government. A deaf ear has been turned to the prayer of the living and the groan of the dying alike. The government too seldom moves until accumulated wrongs have brought on bloodshed. In this case we have been, and now are, writing one of the most damning pages in our Indian history. We are making either spectres to haunt our firesides, or demons to revenge their shameful wrongs. The time may come when they will light the frontier with the red torch of war. If it should, will any white man be able to say that their warfare " cannot be justified before the civilization of the age, or in the sight of God or man "?*

---

* Since the above was written, in August, 1885, it was reported that some of the Piegans (by which name the entire Blackfoot nation is now known) had been stealing horses, and had fought with white pursuers. Possibly the report was false. It is only surprising, however, that they have not stolen everything they could lay hold of.

CHAPTER XVII.

THE TRAGEDY OF THE LAVA BEDS.

No other tribe of American Indians ever leaped into notoriety so suddenly and unexpectedly as the Modocs, and no tribe has excited more interest since their appearance before the public. They were almost unknown in the East until 1873. There had never been more than four or five hundred of them since the whites knew them, and as they occupied a country which was not very desirable, and were known to be warriors who could not be bullied or intimidated, they were not much disturbed by adventurers. They were peculiar people; good-natured, as a rule, but high-tempered; industrious, and yet as haughty as the laziest Indians on the continent. They had more of that commendable pride which makes men desire to be independent and self-supporting than any of their neighbors. They were inclined to be exclusive in their social relations, but even among themselves there was little merry-making. They took a more serious view of life and its duties. Stubbornness and strong will were tribal characteristics. In feature they are rugged and strong, the cheekbones large and prominent, the hair thick and coarse, the face heavy and not much wrinkled in old age. Their vitality is remarkable. The tribe lost about one hundred and fifty members by small-pox in 1847, and they were often at war with other tribes and with the whites, yet they number now about the same as when we first knew them, while other tribes, formerly stronger than they, have passed almost out of existence. There was no trouble with them, of any consequence, from 1856 to 1872. They lived in comparative peace, and the civilized world went on in its hurry and bustle, all unconscious of their existence. They hunted and trapped in their mountain wilds. They paddled their dug-out canoes over

their lakes and streams, dragging their seines or seeking for
water-fowl. In these same canoes they gathered the *wocus*,
an aquatic plant peculiar to their lakes, with a pericarp like a
poppy capsule, full of farinaceous seeds. This they threshed
out and made into flour, or parched entire. They dug *kace*
and *camas* and other roots. They dwelt in their curious conical houses, half underground and half covered with dirt, unmolested and unmolesting.

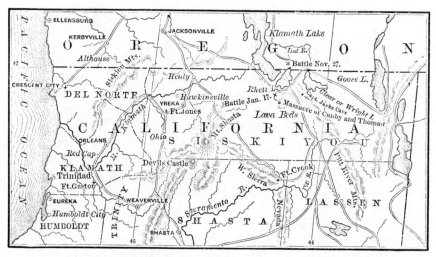

MAP OF THE MODOC COUNTRY.

On October 14, 1864, a treaty was made with the Klamaths, the Modocs, and the Ya-hoos-kin band of Snakes, by
which they surrendered all their lands and accepted a reservation in Lake County, Oregon, in the military district known
as the District of the Lakes. The Wohl-pa-pe Snakes and the
O-che-o Pi-utes were afterwards placed on the same reservation. In the ordinary delay of Indian business, the Senate
did not ratify the treaty until July 2, 1866. Two amendments
were made to it which were simply grammatical corrections,
not affecting the substance in any respect. It was then turned over to the active and vigilant Indian Bureau, in whose
care it reposed for three years and a half. On December 10,
1869, it was submitted to the Indians for consent to the

amendments. By that time trouble had arisen and a part of the Indians had become suspicious. Captain Jack, or Krent-poos (Kient-poos), thought that the treaty had been materially altered. The testimony of the other chiefs satisfied him, however, and it was accepted by all of them. On February 17, 1870, it was proclaimed—only five years and four months after it had been made. Thus do we attend to business of importance. The Indians, in the mean time, had all moved to the reservation, and settled down to work in good earnest, building cabins and enclosing plats for cultivation. Annuity goods were issued to them in the fall of 1867 and thereafter, though it appears that Captain Jack's band did not receive their portion. In a short time trouble arose. The Klamaths and Modocs were ancient enemies. The former were in two divisions, one under Captain George, and one under La-Lake, called respectively the Muck-a-lucks and the La-Lakes. The recognized head chief of the Modocs was Schonchin; but only a small portion of them acknowledged his authority, and his rank was contested by Captain Jack, on grounds of lineage and tribal choice. The reservation was on land which had formerly belonged to the Klamaths. The Klamaths began to devise and practise petty annoyances on the Modocs. They called them "strangers" and "beggars," who had come to the land of the Klamaths for support. They "hectored and bullied them, obstructed their fishing operations, insulted and beat their women whenever they could do it safely, and, in short, did everything that savages are so ingenious in doing to make another tribe miserable."

The Modocs complained to the agent, but the annoyance was not stopped. Schonchin endured the insults with the fortitude of a Stoic, but Jack's royal blood was not so tame. He left the reservation, taking a considerable number of the tribe with him. The agent then undertook to remedy the evil by moving the Modocs. He put up new reservation buildings in Sprague River Valley, in the eastern end of the reservation, and to this point, known as Yainax Agency, Schonchin's Indians removed. Jack and his Indians were also induced to return to the same place. They went to work on their new location, but they did not escape their tormentors.

35

By some blunder a band of Klamaths was located at the same place. After enduring the old annoyances for some time, they again complained to the agent that their treatment was unbearable. The agent, Captain Knapp, could see no better remedy than to move them again, and accordingly selected another location. The Modocs looked at it and declined to accept it, saying it was nothing but a trap to put them in the power of the Klamaths. They had lost their little crops, and failed to gather enough food for their support, on account of these annoyances and their removals, and were reduced almost to starvation. As no other relief was proposed, Jack announced his intention of leaving the reservation, and a majority of the tribe went with him. They went to their old homes on Lost River and about Tulé Lake, into which Lost River empties. The lake is also known as Rhett Lake and Modoc Lake. Once afterwards they were induced to return to Yainax Agency by Agent Meacham, but soon after a member of the tribe became sick and died. He was attended by a Klamath doctor, whom Jack either killed or caused to be killed, as is common with the Indians of the North-west. The Klamaths insisted that he should be arrested and tried for this offence, in consequence of which he again left the reservation, and was followed by two-thirds of the tribe. After some negotiation it was agreed that they might remain off the reservation so long as no complaints were made of them.

Besides Jack's Indians there was another band of Modocs off the reservation, living in Northern California, and known as the Hot Creek Indians, who had little to do with any of the others. They numbered about forty-five. There was also a little band of nine or ten warriors, with their women and children, led by the Curly-headed Doctor. They had broken off from Jack's band, but still fraternized with its members to some extent. They were the worst of the Modocs, and paid very little attention to the authority of any one. The conduct of the Modocs off the reservation has been a matter of some controversy, but it is pretty well established that whatever lawlessness can be attributed to them was committed by Curly-headed Doctor's little band. The charges of bad conduct against any of the Modocs off the reservation finally

MODOC SQUAWS.

settled down to these : that they scared women and children by boisterous conduct when they came to the houses of the settlers; that they killed cattle; and that they used and carried off hay belonging to certain settlers. Major Elmer Otis investigated these charges in the spring of 1872. It was testified by some settlers that Jack and his band claimed their old home on the theory that they were not bound by the treaty, and demanded compensation from those who settled on these lands; that they were insolent and threatening; that they were guilty of thefts and of stealing cattle. On the other hand, one settler testified that he had never paid anything for settling on their lands, and did not believe that any one was asked to pay; that the Indians were no more insolent to whites than whites are to whites; that from inspection of the trails made by marauders, he believed that the Klamaths were the parties who were guilty of killing the cattle. Another settler testified that he had lived near the tribe for ten years, and did not consider that there was any danger to settlers from them; that the parties whose hay was taken had agreed to pay the Indians for cutting hay on lands claimed by them and had failed to do so. It may be mentioned, in this connection, that the general charge was made, all through the Modoc troubles, that the Indians were influenced by "low whites," who advised them to resist removal to the reservation. This position is hardly tenable. On his trial, when there was every inducement to state anything that would excuse him, Captain Jack solemnly denied that he had ever been advised to resist by any white man. He denied always that he or his tribe had been guilty of wrong-doing, and said that if any thefts had been committed, the Klamaths or Curly-headed Doctor's men were the guilty parties. Certain it is that all these Modocs lived off the reservation, without causing any serious trouble until the winter of 1872. They roamed over a large extent of country at will. On the 4th of July they usually turned up at Yreka, in California, where their friends and advisers, Judge Roseborough and Judge Steele, resided; and on the national birthday in 1871, when that town was destroyed by fire, the Modocs did good service at the engine and elsewhere, in aiding to fight the flames.

550 MASSACRES OF THE MOUNTAINS.

No complaints were made of their conduct anywhere, except those mentioned, which were by some of the settlers near their usual homes.

During all this time an effort was being made by the local military and Indian authorities to have a small reservation set off for these people, where they might live without the continual annoyance of the Klamaths. It was their desire to have their lands in severalty and become citizens, though it was questionable whether all of them were sufficiently advanced in the white man's ways for that. They had, as all Indians had, a true friend in Gen. E. R. S. Canby, commanding the Department of the Columbia. He had served continuously in the army since 1839; had won notice in the Seminole and Mexican wars; had stood firmly for the Union in New Mexico, at the outbreak of the civil war, when his senior officers went over to the South; had led the forces that drove the Texan invaders from the mountains; had commanded at the capture of Mobile; and had compelled the surrender of the rebel forces in the Southwest. During his long service he had many dealings with Indians, and had treated them with uniform fairness and honesty. One tribe had named him "the Indian's Friend." He said, on February 7, 1872, "I am not surprised at the unwillingness of the Modocs to return to any point on the reservation where they would be exposed to the hostilities and annoyances they have heretofore experienced (and without any adequate protection) from the Klamaths; but they have expressed a desire to be established upon Lost River, where they would be free from this trouble, and the superintendent informed me last summer that he would endeavor to secure such a location for them." The land they wanted was about three miles long by one mile wide, bordering on Lost River. There were less than two thousand acres of it, and it was not occupied by settlers. In addition to the reasons mentioned, they wanted their reservation on Lost River because that stream and Tulé Lake abounded in fish, a staple food of theirs. "There are black, silver-sided, and speckled trout, of which first two species specimens are taken weighing twenty-five pounds; buffalo fish, from five to twelve pounds; and very large, fine suck-

MAJOR-GENERAL E. R. S. CANBY.

ers—such only in name and appearance, for they are not
bonier than common fishes. In spawning time the fish
school up from the lake in extraordinary numbers, so that
the Indians have only to put a slight obstruction in the river,
when they can literally shovel them out."

Superintendent Meacham desired and urged that a separate reservation be established for them, but in the spring of
1872 he was relieved by F. B. Odeneal, who appointed two
agents to hold a council with the Modocs and report. He
accepted all complaints against them as true, and enlarged
them, without seeing the tribe himself; he reported that the
leaders of the Modocs off the reservation were "desperadoes,"
and foes to civilization. "As well," says this eloquent and

judicious man, "might we expect our own youth to grow up
in the practice of Christian virtues under the tutorship of
the 'road-agents' of Montana, or the guerillas of Mexico, as
to think of instilling any good into the minds of the Modocs
while under the exclusive control, as they have been, of their
present leaders." He advised that the leaders be arrested
and the others compelled to go on the Klamath reservation.
This advice was taken by the Indian Bureau, although General Canby had reported, but a few weeks before, that the
previous Commission had "authorized the Modocs to remain
where they were until the superintendent could see them.
This has been understood as a settlement of the question until some permanent arrangement could be made for them;
and unless they have violated some subsequent agreement, I
do not think that the immediate application of force as asked
for would be either expedient or just. They should at least
be notified that a new location has been selected for them, and
provision made for their wants."

Troops had already been placed in the vicinity of the Modocs, on account of the complaints before mentioned, and to
them was assigned the task of bringing the Indians to the
reservation. The instructions from General Canby to the
officer commanding the District of the Lakes, were: "If the
military force is to be used, it will only be in aid of the Indian Department and after peaceable means have been exhausted, but you should be prepared for the possibility that
the attempt to remove them may result in hostilities, and be
able to act promptly in that event for the protection of the
frontier." It was thought necessary, however, by the commanding officer, to surprise their camp, which was on Lost
River—at that point a deep stream three hundred feet wide.
Jack's Indians were located on one side and the Doctor's on
the other. In the night of November 28th, Captain Jackson
with forty men and ten citizens quietly made their way to
the camp. On the 30th the captain reported concerning the
outcome of this strategic movement. "I have the honor to
report that I jumped the camp of Captain Jack's Modoc Indians yesterday morning soon after daylight, completely surprising them. I demanded their surrender and disarming,

and asked for a parley with Captain Jack. Captain Jack, Scar-faced Charley, Black Jim, and some others, would neither lay down their arms nor surrender, and some of them commenced making hostile demonstrations against us, and finally opened fire. I immediately poured volley after volley among the hostile Indians, took their camp, killed eight or nine warriors, and drove the rest into the hills. During the engagement I had one man killed and seven wounded, three of the last severely and perhaps dangerously. The band that I attacked was on the south side of the river; another small band on the north side was attacked by a party of ten or twelve citizens, and their surrender demanded; but when the firing commenced in Captain Jack's camp, these Indians opened on the citizens and drove them to the refuge of Crawley's ranch. One citizen was killed during the fight, and two others coming up the road, unconscious of any trouble, were shot; one (Mr. Nuss) mortally wounded, and the other (Joe Pennig) badly. My force was too weak to pursue and capture the Indians that made off, owing to the necessity of taking immediate care of my wounded, and protecting the few citizens who had collected at Crawley's ranch. . . . From the best information I can get, Captain Jack, Scar-faced Charley, and Black Jim are killed or mortally wounded." Neither one of them was killed, but the Curly-headed Doctor's band was made furious. The leadership of this band was shared, to a certain extent, by Hooker Jim (Hooka, Jooka, Hocker, Hawkey), who was probably the worst man of the lot. There was no control over them by any one. They acknowledged Jack to be chief of the tribe, as they had always done, but they did what they chose, without regard to his orders. They at once began attacking the scattered settlers, and within forty-eight hours had killed twelve men. No women or children were killed by either Indians or soldiers, except one Indian child, reported as accidentally shot. With the killing of these settlers Captain Jack and his band proper had no connection. Judge-Advocate Curtis said, at the trial, "I do not accuse Captain Jack of any participation in those murders. I acquit him of them entirely. I know almost to a demonstration that he was ignorant of their occurrence until after they had taken place. I have investigated that matter somewhat since I have been here, and I do not believe he was concerned in them or knew of them in advance."

It was at once realized that the surprise was a mistake. Lieutenant-colonel Wheaton, commanding the district, placed the blame on Superintendent Odeneal and his agents. There is no room for doubt that the fighting qualities of the Modocs were underestimated by the military as well as by the agents of the Indian Bureau. Captain Jack's band moved at once to the Lava Beds, on the south side of Tulé Lake, where they were soon joined by Hooker Jim's party, who had added six more to their list of victims. This now celebrated stronghold of theirs covers about fifty square miles of country in Northern California, partly in Siskiyou County and partly in Modoc County. It is what is known in scientific parlance, as also locally in the West, as a pedregal (pay-dray-gahl'), a name adopted from the Spanish, meaning a stony place. It is impossible to give any adequate idea of the place by words. The rock is volcanic, and appears to have been broken in fragments again and again by explosions, as the lava was cooling; after each explosion the fragments dropped back into the gradually solidifying lava, to be again thrown up and again fall, until the whole became cool, and the explosive element lost its force. If you will go to the end of a slag dump at a blast-furnace, where the refuse has been tumbled from the slag pots, chilled outside and molten within, bursting, shooting in the air, hissing, crackling, rolling, and flowing, there to cool and solidify—if looking at such a ragged surface you can imagine with what ease an ant could make its way over it, you will have an idea of the progress of a man across the Lava Beds—only you must remember that an ant has three times as many legs as a man, and that its feet have the power of suction, by which it is enabled to walk as easily on a window-pane or a ceiling as on a floor. There are rocks, from the sharp-edged pebble that cuts through a cowhide boot, to the bowlder as large as a church. They are in heaps, of all sizes and shapes. This is the surface; but it is cut in every direction by innumerable chasms and crevices, some of them a hundred feet deep, with occasionally a wholly subterranean

passage, through which a man can pass from one point to another. Such is this mighty pedregal, and in the northern end
of it, near Tulé Lake, the Modocs had established their camp,
in what were called the Modoc Caves.

Against the Modocs, in this Gibraltar, troops were soon
preparing to move. In the middle of January they were on

A VIEW OF THE CAVES.

the ground, anxious for the attack. There were four hundred of them, two hundred and twenty-five regulars, all well-
armed and equipped, with a battery of howitzers. They were
confident and determined. Said their commander: "If the
Modocs will only try to make good their boast to whip a

thousand soldiers, all will be satisfied." Over in the chaotic heap of lava were fifty Modoc warriors, and about one hundred and seventy-five women and children. They were armed with muzzle-loading rifles and revolvers. On the morning of the 17th, the advance into the pedregal was begun by three hundred of the troops, including twenty Indian scouts, the remainder being employed in guarding the stores and as a reserve. The advance was well planned, but the nature of the country had not been realized. It is impossible to realize it without going over the ground. The movements contemplated could not be made. The junction of detachments was prevented by deep chasms. The troops could move only at a snail's pace. Constantly before them were the Modocs, picking their shots and firing carefully. They were not exposed to a return fire, for they were behind lava bowlders, shooting through crevices. The troops had no targets but puffs of smoke. After hours of painful creeping they would gain the place of the smoke, but nothing would be found. A hundred yards away would be another puff, spitting out its leaden missiles. All day the troops heroically advanced under these difficulties, protected to some extent by the dense fog that rested over the lake and the Lava Beds until two o'clock, now lifting a little and now settling again—an almost constant phenomenon of the place. At evening the soldiers were withdrawn. They brought out their wounded, twenty-eight in number, but ten dead were left behind, after strenuous attempts to bring them away. Officers and men now understood that they had a serious task before them, and Colonel Wheaton reported: "In the opinion of any experienced officer of regulars or volunteers, one thousand men would be required to dislodge them from their almost impregnable position, and it must be done deliberately, with a free use of mortar batteries." He asked for three hundred more men and four howitzers.

On receipt of reports of this attack, the authorities at Washington decided to "give the peace men a chance." Pity it had not been done three months earlier. The Modocs were now confident and well supplied with ammunition. They obtained powder and lead from cartridges found on the field.

VIEW OF CAMP AND LAKE.

They captured also some breech-loading guns. They swore afterwards that they obtained caps from the Klamaths. They had been made suspicious by the surprise of their camp in November. They had been kept in a continual state of distrust by the people in their neighborhood. In December the band of Hot Creek Indians, who had no connection whatever with the troubles, had started for the Klamath reservation, under care of authorized agents. At Link River, Oregon, they were met by an Indian agent, who informed them that the citizens were collected beyond, to mob them. On hearing this the Indians became frightened and scattered into the mountains. It was with the utmost difficulty that a portion were gathered and placed on the reservation. The remainder fled to the Lava Beds and joined Jack's Indians. The Modocs testified that whites told them they would be executed, and that one, Nate Beswick, informed them that the commissioners wanted to get them out to kill them. They swore (those who were tried and others) that the Klamaths encouraged them to fight, and furnished them with ammunition. General Gillem says he learned, on what he considered good authority, that Sam Blair, a man of the neighborhood, sent word to them, " That he had an order in his pocket from the governor of Oregon to hang the nine Indians engaged in killing the citizens as soon as they came in." Notoriously, almost all the Pacific slope was clamoring for their extermination, and Governor Grover, of Oregon, on February 10th, in a pathetic open letter to the commissioners, protested against any settlement of the matter on terms which did not include the surrender for trial of the men who massacred white settlers "on the 29th and 30th of November last," although they "had not been attacked by the soldiery or otherwise molested." The reader will remember that Captain Jackson's surprise was at daybreak on the 29th.

On January 30th instructions were given for the suspension of hostilities, and a commission was ordered. It was made up of A. B. Meacham, Jesse Applegate, his nephew Oliver Applegate, agent at Yainax, and Samuel Chase. They were all men whom the Modocs distrusted and disliked except Meacham. Nothing could be done under the circumstances. The Modocs were afraid to meet where they would be in the power of the whites, and the commissioners declined to meet where they would be in the power of the Modocs. So they dawdled along until the 1st of March, by which time General Canby had arrived, and the authorities at Washington had been made to understand that the Commission would be useless until its personnel was altered. It was decided to change it, and Judge Roseborough, of Yreka, Rev. E. Thomas, of Petaluma, and

THE REV. DR. THOMAS.

L. S. Dyer, of the Klamath Agency, were substituted for the Applegates and Chase. The Commission, as it now stood, was unexceptionable from the peace people's stand-point—also from the stand-point of unbiased people; the Indian-haters did not like it—"too much milk-and-water and all that." Five weeks were consumed in completing these changes, and during this time a change was going on among the Modocs also. This statement will be disapproved both by those who have decided that all the Modocs were always good, and by those who have ordained that all the Modocs were always bad; nevertheless it is true. There were in the Modoc camp eight men known as "the murderers," which meant that they were the men who killed the settlers, after the surprise by Captain Jackson. These men knew that they were considered guilty of murder by the white people, and that all the people who lived about them were in favor of trying, convicting, and hanging them. They knew also that if they made peace, and had a reservation set off for them on Lost River, it was very questionable whether the United States could protect them. The offences had been committed within the State of Oregon; Lost River was within the State of Oregon; and the people and authorities of Oregon, while always very ready to claim monetary recompense from the General Government for injuries by its "wards," were ever jealous of any interference with its jurisdiction over those wards. These things were explained to the Indians by the Commission, or members of it, from time to time. The explanation was necessary in order to try to induce them to move elsewhere. It was proposed to them that they should be temporarily located on Angell's Island, in the Pacific, and subsequently placed on a reservation in Arizona or Indian Territory. They agreed to this at first, but there still remained the trouble that they must surrender to the soldiers, to begin with. They were afraid to do this. They knew that the soldiers, both regulars and volunteers, "had bad hearts towards them," on account of the deaths of their comrades. Consequently "the murderers" objected to surrender and urged war, and they were gradually bringing the other Indians over to their views.

It was a situation where two parties were desirous of peace, on a basis of amnesty for the past and harmony for the future, but neither dared trust the other. The Indian-hater may say that the idea that they were afraid to trust our commissioners and officers is preposterous, but it is not. Just around the lake, in constant view when the fog lifted, was Bloody Point, where Ben Wright invited them to make a treaty, and murdered thirty-eight of them, in 1852. Just there, on the

36

edge of the Lava Beds, were sons and nephews, neighbors and friends of men who took part in that "lesson to the Modocs." In command of a part of those volunteers was General John Ross, who led the Jacksonville volunteers that operated with Ben Wright. It is idle to talk of the Modocs having no reason to fear bad faith, especially in consideration of the fact that a part of them were afterwards murdered while they were prisoners. On March 6th Captain Jack sent a message to the commissioners then present by his sister Mary. He said, "I am very sad. I want peace quick, or else let the soldiers come and make haste and fight. . . . I am nearly well; but I am afraid of the soldiers on the road. There are so many soldiers around. There are soldiers on Lost River, on Clear Lake, and Bernard's soldiers. Wouldn't they be afraid if they were in the same situation? . . . I wish to live like the whites. Let everything be wiped out, washed out, and let there be no more blood. I have got a bad heart about those murderers. I have got but a few men and I don't see how I can give them up. Will they give up their people who murdered my people while they were asleep? I never asked for the people who murdered my people. I only talked that way. I can see how I could give up my horse to be hanged; but I can't see how I could give up my men to be hanged. I could give up my horse to be hanged, and wouldn't cry about it; but if I gave up my men I would have to cry about it. I want them all to have good hearts now. I have thrown away everything. There must be no more bad talk. I will not. I have spoken forever. I want soldiers all to go home. I have given up now and want no more fuss. I have said yes, and thrown away my country. I want soldiers to go away so I will not be afraid."

Of course the soldiers could not be sent away. It would have been inconsistent with the position the government had taken—inconsistent with the usages of every civilized nation —to withdraw its forces pending a treaty, while the submitting force remained as it was. Besides, there was the fear that the Indians intended treachery. It was impossible that the Commission should overcome these obstacles, but it hoped on. If the Modocs had felt that they were whipped—if they had realized the hopelessness of their struggle—they might have submitted to the chance of life or death that they saw in a surrender; but they did not. They had more and better arms and more ammunition than before. Their confidence in the strength of their position was unbounded. The Klamaths were promising to assist them. It was reported that the Indians of Washington, Oregon, and Idaho were on the verge of declaring war. It was evident, however, that the Modocs were not united; that there was a war party and a peace party. Jack and part of his followers wanted peace; the murderers wanted war, and Schonchin John, Scar-faced Charley, and others leaned towards them. The commissioners were satisfied that Jack was under duress; that he was in fear of the others. Others thought that he was trying to gain time; but he had no object to gain by that. Certain it was that he acted like a man in great trouble: he was sad and gloomy; much of the time he was weeping. Finally the Modocs offered a new solution; they would take the Lava Beds for a reservation. This could not be accepted. To the whites it meant establishing a den for wild beasts, from which they could issue for rapine and plunder; to the Indians it meant a home in a castle where no sheriff's posse could arrest them for killing the people in November. The commissioners were satisfied that no permanent settlement of the trouble could be made if the Indians remained in that part of the country, and so matters drifted along until the second week of April.

Captain Jack sat on a rock in the Lava Beds. His heart was bowed down. He had talked with the commissioners and was no nearer a solution of his troubles. He had been informed that the soldiers could not be sent away. He had been told that his people could not remain in the Lava Beds. He could find no answer to the arguments of the murderers, for from his stand they were not much to be blamed. They had not killed the settlers till the soldiers had surprised his camp. They had not killed women and children. They had fought the soldiers like brave men. If he surrendered they would probably be hanged, and that was a dreadful death; it killed both the body and the soul. The rope closed up a man's throat so that his spirit could not come out, and take

up its journey to the happy hunting-grounds. It must die
in his body. He could not feel satisfied that the soldiers
would not shoot all the Modocs when they came out, as they
had done twenty-one years before. The murderers came
around him. They saw that the time for argument was past,
and the time for appeal to passion had come. They taunted
him. Hooker Jim said, "You are like an old squaw; you
have never done any fighting yet; we have done the fighting
and you are our chief. You are not fit to be a chief." Then
came George, another of the murderers, and said, "What do
you want with a gun? You don't shoot anything with it.
You don't go any place to do anything. You are sitting
around on the rocks." After a while Scar-faced Charley
came up. He was a Rogue River Indian, of the Tipsie Tyee's
(Bearded Chief) band, who had joined the Modocs many years
before, after the separation of his tribe. He had been with
Captain Jack's band, and was the oldest of his warriors. He
said, "I am going with Hooker Jim. I can fight with them.
You are nothing but an old squaw." Jack winced a little
when they called him a squaw. They brought a dress and a
squaw's bonnet and put them on him. They mocked and
jeered their squaw chief. He had sat there through the
morning, bearing it all. Now the fog had parted and risen,
and the sun was shining on them. He rose and threw the humiliating garments from him. With blazing eyes he turned
on his tormentors and hissed: "I will show you that I am
no squaw. You say you want war. We will have war, and
Krent-poos will not be the one who asks for peace." He had
fought his temptation and it had proved too strong for him.
The perplexity pushing on one side and the eight devils tug-
ging on the other had started him in the evil path. The
dormant savage in him waked with renewed strength. His
good angel fled from him, as Vivian from old Merlin, who lay
in the dark spell "of woven paces and of waving hands,"
shrieking back, "Oh, fool!" From that hour on his heart
was bad.

Arrangements were being made with the commissioners
for another meeting. Judge Steele, of Yreka, an old resi-
dent, in whom the Indians had the utmost confidence, who

had been the arbiter of their petty troubles for many years, acted as one messenger to them. Riddle, the interpreter, and Toby, his squaw wife, acted also on behalf of the Commission. At Steele's last visit to the cave the Indians became angry, and his life was saved only by Captain Jack and Scar-faced Charley standing guard over him during the night. He told the commissioners that the Modocs meant treachery and refused to go to their camp again. As Toby left the cave, on the occasion of her last visit, a Modoc named William—they called him "Whim"—followed her and warned her to keep away, and to keep the commissioners away; that the Indians were going to kill them. The commissioners were in a quandary. There had been acts that appeared evidences of treachery before, but they had come to nothing. They had consulted the Commissioner of Indian Affairs then, and he had replied, on March 5th, "I do not think the Modocs mean treachery. The mission should not be a failure." An agreed meeting had not been attended by the Commission on April 8th, because the lookout had discovered twenty armed Modocs in ambush near the place of conference. On the 10th, Bogus Charley came from the Modocs, proposing that General Canby and the commissioners, unarmed, should meet an equal party of Modocs, unarmed, at the council tent, about three-quarters of a mile from General Gillem's camp, and on the day after they would all come in and surrender. The Commission discussed this plan. They all felt that the meeting would probably be dangerous. Mr. Thomas said they ought to go; that it was a duty which they could not conscientiously evade. General Canby thought that the importance of the object justified some risk. He believed that the Indians would not kill them, though he considered them capable of it, because it was not to their interest. Meacham and Dyer insisted that the meeting ought not be held; that it was going to certain death.

Riddle told them that the Indians meant to kill them, possibly not that day, but probably then; that if they went they must free him from all responsibility. Meacham then proposed that they should go armed, and add John Fairchild, a frontiersman of the neighborhood, to the party, but Dr. Thom-

as protested that this would be a breach of faith.   Meacham
then proposed that in case there appeared indubitable evidences of treachery, they should agree to anything that the
Indians might ask, until they could make their escape.   Dr.
Thomas replied, " I will be a party to no deception under any
circumstances ; this matter is in the hands of God."   General
Canby said, " I have dealt with Indians for thirty years, and

GENERAL ALVIN GILLEM.

I have never deceived an Indian.   I will not consent to it—
to any promise that cannot be fulfilled."   Riddle insisted
that the commissioners accompany him to General Gillem's
tent, and there, again, he repeated his warnings, and called
Gillem to witness that he washed his hands of the whole matter.   He added that if they were determined to go, he would
go with them rather than be called a coward.   Gillem thought

the Indians would not dare to commit the anticipated treachery. Canby and Thomas said they would go. Meacham and Dyer said they would go also rather than subject themselves to a charge of cowardice, or have the Commission fail for want of action on their part. Before starting, Meacham and Dyer gave John Fairchild what valuables they had about them, and indicated their last wishes, as men preparing for death. Each of them also put in his pocket a small derringer pistol. Some have said that Canby and Thomas were foolhardy to do as they did. To those who are incapable of understanding lofty motives it must ever appear so. They went to their fate drawn by a destiny as irresistible as that which led Krentpoos to his, but of an opposite nature. They knew that the trouble had been caused by the wrong-doing of white men, and their consciences would not permit them to throw their personal safety in the balance on the question of going. They felt bound to leave no stone unturned in their attempt to right this wrong peacefully.

The place of meeting was at what was called the peace tent, or council tent. It was in a little open space at the foot of a high bluff, in the edge of the pedregal. The approach was sufficiently level and clear to permit of riding a horse into it, and a tent had been placed there for the use of the Commission. Thither the little party of peace-makers started at eleven o'clock. General Canby and Dr. Thomas, with Boston Charley, who came to the camp that morning, walked ahead; Meacham, Dyer, and Toby rode; Riddle and Bogus Charley, who had been in the camp over night, came last, on foot. At the tent they found six Modocs: Captain Jack, Schonchin John, Ellen's Man, Black Jim, Hooker Jim, and Shack-nasty Jim. It was at once noticed that they were armed with revolvers, but as they had been armed at previous councils, no remark was made concerning this. Twenty or thirty feet from the tent a small fire of sage brush had been made, and around it was a row of stones, in a half-circle. On these the party seated themselves, excepting Dr. Thomas, who reclined on the ground. They talked together about the proposition for this meeting and the surrender on the morrow. Captain Jack made a speech, the substance of which was that he did not want anything from the President, but wanted the soldiers taken away. As he concluded, Hooker Jim stepped back and fastened Meacham's horse, which had been left loose. He took Meacham's overcoat from the pommel of the saddle and put it on, remarking, "I am Meacham." This was understood as a bid for an objection on which a quarrel might be based, but Meacham merely said, "Take my hat, too." Jim replied, in Modoc, "I will, presently." General Canby, apparently understanding the meaning of this by-play, arose and began to speak. He told them how he had dealt with other Indians, and had been named by them "the Indian's Friend;" how he had met those Indians afterwards and been thanked by them for his just treatment of them; how he hoped that in some future time the Modocs would thank him for getting them happy homes. He said he could not send away the soldiers—that the President had sent them there—but that whatever the commissioners promised should be done, and the citizens should not interfere. Dr. Thomas rose to his knees, rested his hand on Meacham's shoulder, and, with uncovered head, said, "I believe the Great Spirit put it in the heart of the President to send us here to make peace. I have known General Canby fourteen years, Mr. Meacham eighteen years, and Mr. Dyer four years. I know all their hearts are good, and I know my own heart. We want no more war. I believe that God sees us, what we do; that he wishes us all to be at peace; that no more blood should be shed."

Jack said that he did not want to leave that country; that he did not know any other country. If he could not have a reservation on Lost River, he would take one on Willow Creek and Cottonwood Creek. Meacham tapped him on the shoulder, and said, "Jack, let us talk like men, and not like children. You are a man that has common-sense; isn't there any other place that will do you except Willow Creek and Cottonwood?" Schonchin interrupted, and told him to hush; that he could talk a straight talk; to let him talk. As he began, Jack stepped back to the horses. Schonchin said, "Give us Hot Creek for a home, and take away your soldiers." The commissioners tried to explain that they would have to see first whether they could get lands there, but Schonchin cried, very excitedly, " Take away the soldiers and give us Hot Creek, or stop talking." Just then two Indians, Barncho and Slolox, jumped up from some rocks fifty yards away, and came running forward, each carrying three guns. At the same time Steamboat Frank and another Indian appeared from another direction. The commissioners turned, and one said, " What does this mean, Captain Jack ?" As he did so Jack stepped forward, cocking his revolver; said, "*At-we*" (all ready); and levelled his revolver at General Canby, within three feet of his face. The cap snapped at the first attempt, but quick as thought it was cocked again. At the second the ball struck General Canby under the eye, and he fell back.

At the word each of the Indians sprang at his appointed victim. Dr. Thomas was shot in the left breast by Boston Charley. He rose and ran, followed by Boston Charley and Bogus Charley. At about seventy yards he fell, killed by a rifle shot from Bogus. Schonchin John fired at Meacham, at a distance of three or four feet, and missed him. Meacham ran back, drawing his pistol. Schonchin and Black Jim followed him, firing, and Meacham fired back once. He had gone about fifty yards when a ball struck him in the head and he became unconscious. General Canby also sprang to his feet and fled after the first wound: the ball had ranged down and come out at the back of the neck. He ran about as far as Dr. Thomas, when Ellen's Man shot him with a rifle, and Captain Jack killed him by a stab in the neck. Dyer ran, pursued by Hooker Jim, who fired as he ran. At about two hundred yards, Dyer faced on his pursuer and pointed his derringer at him, whereupon Jim ran back and Dyer escaped. Riddle was followed by Shack-nasty Jim and Barncho, who were joined by Ellen's Man after Canby fell. They were all firing at him, but he escaped with the touch of a rifle-ball on his ear. Toby was struck across the back with a rifle by Slolox, who was trying to get possession of her horse, but was saved from further violence by Captain Jack, who ordered that she should not be injured. By this time the wild excitement of the assassination was over. The Indians quickly stripped all the clothing from the bodies and started to move away. Boston Charley ran back and began to scalp Meacham, but Toby cried out, "Soldiers! soldiers!" and they all fled. The soldiers were not yet in sight. She used this stratagem in order to prevent the mutilation.

The soldiers were coming, however, at a double-quick; the camp had received the alarm before the assassination began. Around on the east side of the lake, where Major Mason's command was posted, two Indians had appeared, under a flag of truce, at a little after one o'clock. Lieutenant Sherwood and Lieutenant Doyle went out two or three hundred yards to meet them. The Indians said they wanted to talk to the "Little Tyee" (Major Mason), but were informed that no one there could talk to them. Scar-faced Charley and another Indian, who were concealed in the rocks, then opened fire, inflicting wounds in Lieutenant Sherwood's arm and thigh, from which he died three days later. This treachery was signalled to General Gillem's camp. A message was being prepared to send to Canby when the firing was heard, and the signal officer reported that the commissioners were being murdered. The soldiers sprang to their arms at the sound of the shots, and advanced towards the council tent on a run. In a few minutes Dyer appeared, almost exhausted, reporting that all the others were killed. A little farther on Riddle reached the lines. The soldiers hurried on to the scene of the tragedy. About seventy yards from the tent were found the bodies of Canby and Dr. Thomas, stripped of everything. The former had two bullet wounds through his head and a cut in the neck; the latter had several wounds in his body. A little farther on was Meacham, also stripped. He had one bullet wound under his right eye, one in the side of the head, one through his right arm, a grazing shot on the temple, a finger shot from his left hand, one ear cut, and a long knife-wound on his head, where Boston had begun to scalp him. It was not expected that he would live, but, after four bullets had been extracted from his head, he grew better and rapidly recovered. The soldiers advanced a short distance beyond the council tent, and then withdrew, bearing the remains of the victims in sadness to the camp.

There has never been an occurrence in any of our Indian wars that excited such wide-spread indignation as this act of treachery. The high esteem in which both General Canby and Dr. Thomas were held, their disinterested efforts in behalf of these Indians, and the atrocity of the assassination stirred public feeling to its depths. The Modocs were the objects of universal execration, and their outlandish names quickly became household words. For a time there was but one sentiment, and that was that the tribe should be exterminated. The soldiers had the same feeling, but extermination was not so easily accomplished. The entire force moved forward on the 14th, in the face of a stubborn resistance by the Indians, to positions from which the mortar batteries could reach the caves. The stronghold was shelled during the 15th and 16th. On the morning of the 17th the troops advanced again and took possession of the cave, all of the Indians having moved away, except a small rear-guard, which was driven out by a dashing charge. The famous retreat was found to be a long crevice, extending for more than a mile in a north and south direction, connected at various points with deep sink-holes. All along it were fragments of bursted shells, and here and there the body of an Indian. The body of one man was literally torn to pieces. It was learned afterwards that the man had picked up a shell and was trying to bite off the fuse when it exploded. Another man was killed by the same explosion. Altogether there were eleven bodies found, three of them men, as the product of the three days' work. There were no wounded reported. No quarter was given. The loss to the troops, from the morning of the 14th, was six men killed and fourteen wounded. In addition to this the Indians had cut off Eugene Hovey, a young citizen, killed him, and captured four horses. The Indians took a new position about four miles south of their old place, but kept closely hidden for several days.

Prior to this time the troops had been reinforced by a party of sixty Warm Springs Indians, under Donald McKay, their interpreter. They proved invaluable assistants, the only objection to them being that they absolutely refused to do anything on Sundays. Supposed discoveries of the new hiding-place of the Modocs were made on several occasions, but they were not found until the morning of the 23d. Early on the 26th, a party under command of Captain Thomas of

DONALD McKAY, LEADER OF THE SCOUTS.

the 4th Artillery was sent on a reconnoissance to a sand-hill in the centre of the Lava Beds, to ascertain the practicability of taking the pack-train with the mortar battery to that point. The command consisted of six officers, sixty-four men, and thirteen of the Indian scouts, under McKay. They marched in column of twos, with a company deployed across the front, and flankers on either side. It was soon apparent that many of the men were inspired with a dread of the foe, which had been dealing death among them from its hidden fastnesses. The skirmishers kept lagging until the column was upon them, and the flankers continually edged in from the sides, notwithstanding the orders of the officers. The base of the sand-hill was reached by noon, without sight of the enemy, and the party stopped for luncheon. They were in comparatively low ground. On all sides of them but the front, which was occupied by the sand-hill, were rough lava ridges, from four to six hundred yards distant. Two men were sent to reconnoitre the ridge to the east of the sand-hill. When about half-way to it, two shots were fired at them from the rocks to which they were going, and immediately fire was opened from the lava ridges all about them. A large portion of the men became panic-stricken. They rushed to and fro, crying, "We are completely surrounded," and paid no attention to commands. A number sought hiding-places, and sneaked away as soon as the engagement of the Indians with the others gave them opportunity. The rest, with the officers, at first pushed up the sand-hill.

Lieutenant Wright was ordered to advance with one company and occupy the ridge to the west. Lieutenant Cranston, with five men, volunteered to take the ridge to the north. All of this party were killed, the position of their bodies indicating that they had died while bravely trying to accomplish the task they had undertaken. The main body, now reduced to less than thirty men, soon started to follow Lieutenant Wright, but Wright's command had gone to pieces, and no trace of them could be found. The others reached a little hollow about fifty yards from the ridge, supposing it to be occupied by Lieutenant Wright's men, but on calling for them received a volley of rifle-shots for an answer. By death and desertion they had been cut down to only twenty, and these saw that they were lost. Captain Thomas said, "We are surrounded. Let us die like brave men." They sheltered themselves as best they could behind rocks and sage bushes, but they were helpless. There were twenty-one Indians here. They separated and, by paths known only to them, gained positions on two sides—fourteen on one side and seven on the other—from which they maintained a deadly cross-fire, they being in perfect safety. About the time the firing began, the Warm Springs Indians, who had been scouting, came up and tried to join the troops. They were mistaken for Modocs and fired upon. They used every device to show who they were, but in vain. They captured an escaping bugler and made him sound the whole list of bugle calls, but the soldiers did not understand. Being under two fires the scouts could do nothing but keep concealed. All of them escaped unhurt. In the mean time Major Green, with all available forces, was hastening in the direction of the firing. They reached the place in time to save but few of the party. Captain Thomas (son of Gen. Lorenzo Thomas), Lieutenant Howe (son-in-law of General Brady), Lieutenant Wright (son of Gen. George Wright), and Lieutenant Cranston were dead. Lieutenant Harris was mortally wounded. Dr. Semig, who had performed his duties everywhere, regardless of flying bullets, received a wound in the leg which necessitated amputation below the knee. Eighteen enlisted men were killed and seventeen wounded, several mortally. The troops held the ground through the night, but the Modocs crept through the lines to scalp and rifle the dead. In the morning the Indians retired and the troops withdrew to the lake. All the wounded and the greater part of the dead were brought in. Over twenty of the soldiers of Captain Thomas's command straggled into camp, reporting that they had been "cut off." Gen. Jeff. C. Davis, who arrived a few days later to take General Canby's place, denounced them as "cowardly beef-eaters."

When Davis took command of the troops, he found them so dispirited over this series of failures and losses, which left always the same desperate task before them, that he considered it injudicious to move actively at once. There was much raillery at the time at the army's want of success; but the outside world had no idea of the situation, or of the high order of courage in the common soldiers that it called for. There have been many thousands of men who dared to march up to the cannon's mouth, but what if such marching be required to be done by inches, when there is no opportunity for harming the cannoneer, and with the certain knowledge that when the cannon was reached it would be whisked away to another safe position, there again to belch out its iron death? The Modocs added not a little to the apprehensive feeling by keeping perfectly quiet. They gave no intimation as to what part of that wilderness of stone they occupied. They might be hidden in its nearest edge; they might be resting peacefully in the centre. No one knew. On May 6th two friendly squaws were sent into the pedregal. They returned after two days, almost exhausted, and reported that the Modocs had moved towards the southeast. On the evening of the 8th some Warm Springs Indians were sent out. They confirmed the report of the squaws, and also reported that fifteen or twenty Modocs had attacked and captured a supply-train of four wagons, attended by an escort equal in number to the attacking party, on the east side of Tulé Lake. The casualties to the escort were three men wounded. Two squadrons of cavalry, with the Indian scouts, were at once sent in that direction. They discovered some signs of Indians near a small, dry lake, and pitched their camp there for the night. At daybreak the next morning (the 10th) the Indians attacked them. The troops were surprised, but the men seized their

GENERAL JEFFERSON C. DAVIS.

guns and returned the fire so gallantly that the Indians began to retreat. They were followed for three miles, fighting all the way, till they reached the Lava Beds. The troops followed them in at a distance, and at the same time detachments were thrown in on the other sides, the plan being now adopted of making permanent camps in the pedregal. By this means the Indians were kept continually on the watch, which, owing to their small number, was a great hardship to them.

There was a more serious trouble than this in the Modoc camp. Over at the dry lake there had occurred a quarrel between Hooker Jim and Jack, in which the murderers sided with Jim. The bad feeling then created grew with the hardships of the fighting, and these warriors began to think that Jack was tyrannical. The quarrel became so bitter that the band separated about the 15th. Thirteen warriors, with sixty-two women and children, composed the murderers' party; thirty warriors, with fifty-two women and children, followed Jack. Both parties left the Lava Beds, thereby throwing away their greatest protection as completely as did Roderick Dhu when he cast down his targe and bared his breast to Fitz-James's blade. The trail of the murderers' party was soon discovered. Hasbrouck's cavalry followed it, and overtook them after a hard march of fifty miles. For seven miles or more a sharp running fight was kept up, and then the Indians scattered for safety. The cavalry horses were so exhausted that further pursuit was abandoned for that night. Some Indians captured in this chase said the band desired to surrender. Messengers were sent to them in the morning. They asked for terms, but none were given, except safe conduct to General Davis's quarters. On May 22d they all came in and laid down their arms. Hooker Jim volunteered to go to Jack's camp and secure his surrender; he wanted eight men to go with him for protection, but only three were allowed. He was assured, through a mistake of the interpreter, it is said, that they would have immunity from punishment. Under this arrangement Hooker Jim, Bogus Charley, Shack-nasty Jim, and Steamboat Frank were furnished with horses and Springfield rifles, and started on their search for Jack's band, which, it was believed, had either gone south towards Pitt River, or east towards Goose Lake. The latter supposition proved correct. The four scouts found them, on the 28th, on Willow Creek, one of the head-waters of Lost River, east of Wright's Lake. The scouts had a stormy interview with Jack, in which he denounced them as cowards and squaws, who had induced him to go into this war and deserted him in the hour of peril. He said that he would never surrender; that he would die with his gun in his hand.

The scouts returned to the troops, who were moving in the same direction. At two o'clock the next day the command surprised Jack's band in the cañon of Willow Creek, near the crossing of the old emigrant road. Boston Charley came out and held up his hands in token of surrender. He was permitted to come into the lines. Seven women were captured also, including Jack's sister Mary, commonly known as "Queen Mary," or "Princess Mary." The rest escaped by running down the cañon, which is about forty feet deep and impossible of access to horses. On the next morning the troops followed their trail over hill and valley, through cañons and across beds of sharp lava rocks, to a bluff bordering on Langell's Valley. As they approached the bluff four shots were fired from it, and immediately after two warriors came bounding down the rocks, crying, "We surrender; don't shoot!" Five warriors came in. With these Dr. Cabanisse, who was well acquainted with the Modocs, went into the rocks to make arrangements for the surrender of the rest. He remained with them overnight. In the morning twelve warriors, including Schonchin and Scar-faced Charley, surrendered. Jack, with three warriors, fled in the night. There were nine others who scattered in different directions.

On June 1st, an hour or so before noon, a Warm Springs scout, with Colonel Perry's squadron of the First Cavalry, struck a fresh trail three miles above the mouth of Willow Creek. The squadron followed it, and in a short time found and surrounded the Modocs, who occupied a small pedregal. A warrior bearing a white flag appeared from among the rocks. He said that Jack desired to surrender. The scouts went in to meet him. He came out cautiously, glared about him for a few moments, and then, with the hopeless, desperate air of a man

> "Who had thrown, and had missed
> His last stake,"

he came forward and extended his hands to the scouts. His only remark was, "My legs have given out." He was taken

37

to the camp at Applegate's ranch, near Clear Lake. The news of the capture had been carried before them, and was received with enthusiasm and rejoicing. Jack was the centre of attraction. Dressed in old, dilapidated clothes, and wrapped in a faded army blanket, it was still the universal sentiment that he looked every inch a chief. He stood apart, silent as a statue. The Indians said he was insane.

There surrendered with Jack two warriors, fifteen squaws, and seven children; the remainder of the band were captured during the two days following, excepting Long Jim and his father, who were caught on the 11th. The Modoc war was ended. In it the whites had lost in killed eight officers, thirty-nine enlisted men, sixteen citizens, and two Warm Springs scouts; in wounded sixty-seven. This was the loss to the army proper. To it should be added eighteen killed and about as many wounded, for the settlers who were attacked in November. The loss of the Modocs from the massacre of the commissioners to the close of the war was five warriors. Three were killed during the advance on the cave—two by the explosion of a shell, and one by a rifle-ball; one was killed at the dry lake, and one during the attack on Thomas, of the 26th. Their other killed were all women and children. The cost of the war was over half a million of dollars. The quartermaster-general reported the cost to his department at $355,000. We paid Oregon and California $76,000 for the services of their militia. Then there were the claims for destroyed property and other contingent expenses. The reservation that the Modocs asked for was of less than 2000 acres. If they had been settled in severalty the cost, including the value of the land, would have been about $10,000. An agency might perhaps have come as high as $20,000. Beyond dispute, the Modoc war would have been prevented at a cost of not to exceed one-twentieth of the outlay that occurred. It is, in fact, usually cheaper to be fair and honest with Indians, just as in other affairs in this world.

Governor Grover was on hand, demanding that the Modocs should be turned over to the civil authorities for trial. General Davis was not in favor of "the law's delay," and decided to hang eight or ten of them without any formality of

CAPTAIN JACK AND HIS COMPANIONS.

judge or jury. While the scaffolds were being prepared, a
telegram came from Washington, directing their trial by a
Military Commission. The Commission sat from July 5th to
July 9th, at Fort Klamath, Oregon. The prisoners arraigned
were Captain Jack, Schonchin John (Schonchis), Black Jim,

Boston Charley, Barncho, *alias* One-eyed Jim, and Slolox, *alias* Lolocksalt, *alias* Cok. Ellen's Man was dead. The charges were murder and assault to kill, in violation of the rules of war. The prosecution made a clear case by the testimony of Riddle, Toby, Meacham, Dyer, Shack-nasty Jim, Hooker Jim, Bogus Charley, Steamboat Frank, William, Lieutenant Anderson, and Surgeon McEldery; the defence introduced Scarfaced Charley, Dave, and One-eyed Mose, who testified that the Klamaths furnished them gun-caps and were guilty of other acts of treachery. This may have been introduced in mitigation of their offence, or from an ignorant belief that they could shift the guilt to others. There is another possibility, which is very strong. Jack may have intended his defence solely for futurity. He may have been actuated by the same desire of a justification by posterity that moved Robert Emmet to the words, "Let not my epitaph be written till other times and other men can do me justice." He did not deny his guilt; he admitted that he had done wrong. He did not hope for a realization of his motives by his judges. He told them as much. The members of the Commission were strangers to him; they did not know his past surroundings or the events that had driven him on. He saw around him the men he had attempted to assassinate, the whites he had fought, and his enemies the Klamaths, who had urged him on. In the midst of them he saw the men who had brought him to ruin and betrayed him, sitting as his accusers. What room had he to hope for mercy there? He addressed the Commission. He tried to tell how he had been adopting the customs of the whites; how he had treated them generously; how he had dealt so fairly with all men that no one called him mean except the Klamaths. He said, " I have always lived like a white man, and wanted to live so. I have always tried to live peaceably and never asked any man for anything. I have always lived on what I could kill and shoot with my gun and catch in my trap. Riddle knows that I have always lived like a man, and have never gone begging; that what I have got I have always got with my own hands, honestly. I should have taken his advice. He has always given me good advice, and told me to live like a white man; and I have al-

ways tried to do it, and did do it, until this war started. I
hardly know how to talk here. I don't know how white people talk in such a place as this; but I will do the best I can."
The Judge-Advocate said, in a kindly way, "Talk exactly as
if you were at home, in a council." Jack went on to tell how
he and his people had become fearful of treachery on account
of Captain Jackson's surprise, on account of the treatment of
the Hot Creek Indians, on account of the threatening word
sent to him by white men, on account of the misrepresentations of the squaw messengers. He told how his warriors refused to obey him; how they attacked the settlers without his
knowledge; how they taunted him; and, as he came to the point
where he gave way under the awful pressure that was brought
upon him, he broke down. His throat choked up; he could
speak no further. At his request the Commission adjourned
to the next day, with permission to him to continue then. On
the next day he resumed his address, but the flood of tender
feelings that had overwhelmed him on the preceding day
had given way to the stoical desperation which characterizes
his race when the shadow of death is over them. In a few
curt sentences he pointed out the guilt of the four informers,
and sat down.

The Judge-Advocate submitted the instructions and detailed report of Captain Jackson, showing that he had acted
in accordance with his instructions when he surprised the
camp on Lost River. He acquitted Jack of any complicity
in the attack on the settlers immediately following this occurrence, and submitted the case without argument. There
could be but one result. The prisoners were found guilty on
both charges and sentenced to be hanged. A strong influence was exerted with President Grant for a commutation of
the sentence. The National Association to Promote Universal Peace, the American Indian Aid Association, and many
individuals, petitioned in their behalf. One good Quaker
brother offered, if the President would commute their sentence to imprisonment on some ocean island, to go there and
devote his life to their enlightenment and salvation. For the
information of the President, the Judge-Advocate, H. P. Curtis, reported that Barncho and Slolox were common soldiers,

who appeared to have acted under the orders of their chief; that they were ignorant and devoid of perception—in short, little above the level of the brute; that they did not seem to understand the nature of their trial or appreciate their danger; and that Slolox, from choice, sat on the floor during the trial, much of the time asleep. Under this statement the sentences of Barncho and Slolox were commuted to imprisonment for life on the Island of Alcatraz, in the harbor of San Francisco. The others were executed at Fort Klamath on October 3, 1873, in accordance with the sentence. They were all hanged from one long scaffold. They mounted it firmly, and with no tremor stood through the preliminary proceedings, though Jack showed the signs of internal torment in his face. He had asked for delay that morning, but on being assured that it could not be granted—that he must die—he said, "I am ready to go to the Great Father." The orders for execution and the reprieve for Barncho and Slolox, which had arrived the night before, were read from the scaffold. The chaplain prayed fervently and the signal was given. As the drop fell, an involuntary cry of horror went up from the throats of over five hundred Klamaths, who had assembled to witness the execution. From the stockade, where the Modoc captives stood, in full view of the scene, rose shrieks and wails of anguish. It was over. The white man's justice was satisfied.

The decision of the President was just. It seems wrong that these men should be hanged for the very offence for which Ben Wright and his men were fêted and rewarded, but the wrong done was in failing to punish the white assassins. If criminals were to be pardoned because equally guilty men have escaped, there would be an end to all punishment. They knew they were committing a crime. Few criminals have a keener sense of their offending than did Captain Jack. He would not have debated so long before taking the fatal step if he had not known its evil nature. It was right that he should be hanged—and yet we killed him much as you would kill the mad dog that bites the hand extended to caress him, and we had helped to make him mad. Was it strange that the son of Dr. Thomas said, "The wickedness of white men caused my father's death?" The remainder of the tribe, excepting those who were murdered while prisoners, were sent east. Most of them were located at the Quapaw Agency, where, under chief Bogus Charley, they have become models of industry and good-behavior. Several of the worst men were sent to Fort Marion, at St. Augustine, Florida, and put under charge of Captain Pratt, of training-school fame. Under his labors they were converted to Christianity, and if testimony can be believed they underwent an actual change of heart. In 1879 Steamboat Frank, the unhanged murderer of 1873, was installed as pastor in the Modoc church on the Quapaw reservation. It is well that by penance and good works they should expiate their wrong-doing, but great must be the grace that has come upon them if the face of Krent-poos does not haunt them. Unfortunate man! Drawn by forces whose power we can scarcely imagine, he fell—fell hopelessly. Who shall reproach his memory? It was a divine wisdom that taught us all to pray, "Lead us not into temptation," for if the right temptation come, in open strength, or hidden under deceptive covering, who shall withstand it?

CHAPTER XVIII.

THE LITTLE BIG HORN.

THE Sioux war of 1876 was more like the wars between civilized nations, in its inception, than any conflict that ever occurred between the whites and the Indians. There were the same violations of compacts on both sides, the same diplomatic skirmishing, and the same deliberate preparation for wholesale killing, that the civilized world has decided to be proper when two nations have reached so belligerent a feeling that peace is no longer satisfactory to either. On paper, our relations with the Sioux remained as they were established in 1868, when we abandoned the Montana road. There was then set off to the western tribes, as a reservation, all of Dakota Territory west of the Missouri River and south of parallel 46—practically, the southwest quarter of the territory. This reservation, by the treaty, "is set apart for the absolute and undisturbed use and occupation of the Indians herein named, and for such other friendly tribes or individual Indians as from time to time they may be willing, with the consent of the United States, to admit amongst them; and the United States now solemnly agrees that no persons except those herein designated and authorized so to do, and except such officers, agents, and employés of the government as may be authorized to enter upon Indian reservations in discharge of duties enjoined by law, shall ever be permitted to pass over, settle upon, or reside in the territory described in this article, or in such territory as may be added to this reservation for the use of said Indians; and henceforth they will and do hereby relinquish all claims or right in and to any portion of the United States or Territories, except such as is embraced in the limits aforesaid, and except as hereinafter provided." The subsequent provision referred to is Article 16, as follows:

"The United States hereby agrees and stipulates that the country north of the North Platte River and east of the summits of the Big Horn Mountains shall be held and considered to be unceded Indian territory, and also stipulates and agrees that no white person or persons shall be permitted to settle upon or occupy any portion of the same; or without the consent of the Indians, first had and obtained, to pass through the same." The land covered by this article is "the Powder River country," and the article closes with the agreement that the Montana road, and all the posts along it, shall be abandoned.

During these eight years material changes had been taking place in other respects which altered the relations of the two races. The completion of the Pacific Railway, and the wonderful advance of minor lines into the plains, had carried an enormous population into the West. Kansas, Iowa, Nebraska, Colorado, Wyoming, Montana, and Eastern Dakota were filling up rapidly, and assuming the appearance of long-settled countries. The whites were strong in their numbers and their facilities for transportation. They had grown used to the Indian as the loafer and drunkard, and had no great fear of him in any character. Among the whites were many miners who looked with longing eyes on the Black Hills (a literal translation of the Sioux name, Pah-sap-pa), which lay wholly within the reservation. This tract of mountain country was almost unknown. It was partially surrounded by the Bad Lands, which formed a barrier that the emigrant shunned. The Indians went into the Hills but little. They considered it a "medicine" country, inhabited by their supernaturals, and not to be rashly invaded, though they occasionally hunted in its borders, or cut lodge-poles in its pine woods. Lieutenant Warren (afterwards a Confederate general) attempted to go into it in 1857, but when in the neighborhood of Inyan Kara, a peak on the western side, he was met by a delegation of Sioux chiefs and warned back. They said it was sacred ground. It was commonly believed that there was gold in the Black Hills, even before gold was discovered in California. In 1847, Parkman recounted how his trapper friend, Reynal, had stood on one of those mountains and said: "Many a time, when I

THE BAD LANDS.

was with the Indians, I have been hunting for gold all through
the Black Hills.   There's plenty of it here ; you may be certain of that.   I have dreamed about it fifty times, and I never
dreamed yet but what it came out true.   Look over yonder
at those black rocks piled up against that other big rock.
Don't it look as if there might be something there?   It won't
do for a white man to be rummaging too much about these
mountains; the Indians say they are full of bad spirits; and
I believe myself that it's no good luck to be hunting about
here after gold.   Well, for all that, I would like to have one
of those fellows up here, from down below, to go about with
his witch-hazel rod, and I'll guarantee that it would not be
long before he would light on a gold mine."

No one knew whether there was gold in the Hills or not,
but there grew up that strong faith in its existence which
miners always have in regard to a country difficult of access.
Man ever hopes for much from the unknown.   Imagination

furnishes the only statistics by which it may be judged, and imagination is liberal. The first recorded discovery of gold in the Black Hills was made by Toussaint Kensler, a half-breed who had worked in the placers of Alder Gulch, Montana. He had been under arrest for murder, but escaped, and for a long time was not seen in the haunts of men. He then reappeared at the agencies on the Missouri, with several goose-quills full of gold dust, and a fossil skull which he said he had found in the Bad Lands, when returning from these diggings that he had discovered. He was rearrested, convicted, and hung for the murder, but he left a map which shows a full acquaintance with the country he claimed to have examined. He said he found the gold on what is now called Amphibi-ous Creek, a tributary of the South Fork of the Cheyenne, about ten miles above its mouth. The Indians sometimes brought in pieces of rock, bearing gold, and trappers occasionally reported discoveries of the metal. It is quite probable that Wetmore, the man who started the story of the " Lost Cabin," that great *ignis fatuus* of the miners, obtained the gold, which he brought home, from the Black Hills.

The interest in the country grew so strong that influence was brought to bear on the government, and an exploring expedition was ordered. It consisted of over twelve hundred men, with four Gatling guns and a large supply-train, accompanied by sixty Indian scouts, all under command of General George A. Custer. The movement was called a military re-connoissance, and said to be a military necessity ; but the expedition certainly devoted more time to investigating the mineral and agricultural resources of the region than to anything else. It was accompanied by a number of miners and prospectors, who carefully examined the country along the lines of march and exploration. Custer mentions one instance in which they excavated to a depth of eight feet in their exploitations. They demonstrated the existence of gold beyond all reasonable questioning, but owing to some controversy that arose afterwards, the government sent another party to the Hills, in the following year, for the express purpose of investigating the gold indications. If this fact does not lift the thin disguise of military necessity from the first expedition, one could hardly imagine what would. The Custer expedition did not return until September, and the reports from it were so golden-hued that the excitement grew feverish. Parties were organized to go into the Hills, treaty or no treaty, and some of them did go. The Indians complained, and threatened to attack them if they were not removed. The military authorities denied for a time that any one had gone in, but on December 24 it was conceded that one party of twenty-one had evaded their watchful eyes. A company of cavalry was sent after them, but returned, after almost perishing from cold, without finding them. They remained in the Hills all winter and greeted many others in the spring.

There was no little dissatisfaction among the Indians over this invasion, and war was seriously contemplated. The far-sighted Red Cloud sent men to ascertain the probable number of buffalo, and their report showed that no reliance could be put on this food supply for any great time. The slaughter of buffalo in the past six or eight years had been prodigious. Careful investigators have estimated it at a million a year. It may have been less than that, but it was enormous. The buffalo had disappeared from the eastern side of the mountains altogether. The plains of Kansas, Colorado, Nebraska, and Dakota, which had once been alive with them, no longer shook beneath their migrations. The valleys of the Arkansas, Platte, Cheyenne, and their tributaries were deserted. The buffalo range was limited to the Powder River country. Red Cloud took in the situation. He decided for peace. In January, 1875, he and Spotted Tail expressed a desire to visit Washington and make arrangements for selling the Black Hills. To this request the government acceded. In the spring, miners began to flock into the Hills. The Interior Department called on the military to put them out. The troops made several trips for this purpose, brought out the gold-hunters, and turned them over to the civil authorities for trial. The civil authorities turned them loose, and they went back. Each time they went back their numbers were greatly increased. During the summer Professor Jenney made his exploration of the Hills, to settle the question of the existence of gold. He had no difficulty in learning that there was gold, from the miners who were there extracting it. The Hills contained probably a thousand miners in the fall of 1875. Custer City had been laid out, and people were coming in, with but little show of resistance.

It has often been claimed that the Black Hills question had nothing to do with the Sioux war of 1876, but the claim is partisan and untrue. In June, 1875, a commission was appointed by the President to secure from the Indians the right of mining in the Black Hills. They met with all the Teton tribes, the Northern Cheyennes and Arapahoes, and representatives of the Yanktons and Yanktonnais, September 17, 1875, at the plain north of Crow Butte, eight miles east of Red Cloud agency, on White River. They found the Indians in two parties, as to the sale. The larger party favored sale, but demanded sums ranging from thirty to fifty millions in payment. The smaller party, nearly all young men, opposed selling, on any terms. Their dissension became so bitter that a fight would probably have ensued but for the efforts of Young Man Afraid of his Horses, the leader of the " soldiers," or police force. The form in which the Indians who were willing to sell put their demand was, " Subsistence for seven generations ahead, or so long as we live." Their argument, as repeated by all the chiefs who spoke, was substantially as made by the Cheyenne chief, Little Wolf. He said : " You are here to buy the gold regions in those Black Hills. There has been a great deal stolen from those Hills already. . . . If the Great Father gets this country from us, it is a rich country and we want something to pay us for it. We want to be made rich too. There is gold and silver and a great many kinds of mineral in that country. The Great Father gets that for the whites. They will live on it and become rich. We want him to make us rich also." They refused absolutely to sell the Powder River country, and it was dropped from consideration on the first day. They dwelt much on the value of Pah-sap-pa. It was their " house of gold." It was " worth more than all the wild beasts and all the tame beasts in the possession of the white people." Said Crow Feather : " Even if our Great Father should give a hundred different kinds of live-stock to each Indian house every year, it seems that would not pay for the Black Hills. I was not born and raised on this soil for fun. No, indeed. . . . I hope the Great Father will look and see how many millions of dollars have been stolen out of the Black Hills, and when he finds it out, I want the Great Father to pay us that." They offered to allow one road, and only one, which they designated as "the thieves' road." This, on inquiry, was found to be Custer's trail, over which several parties of miners had gone into the Hills. Little Bear claimed that white men had been in the Hills for four years, and Lone Horn said seven. The commission offered to lease the country at $400,000 per year, so long as the whites should use it, or to give them $6,000,000 in fifteen annual instalments for their title, which propositions the assembled Sioux received with derisive laughter. The commission was obliged to return unsuccessful. It reported: "We do not believe their temper or spirit can or will be changed until they are made to feel the power as well as the magnanimity of the government." It recommended that the government set its own price, and force the Sioux to accept it. In justice to the commission, it should be remembered that the same chiefs, who demanded $50,000,00 in the morning, would be begging for a shirt in the evening, and that it was believed that white men had urged them to ask this large sum. However, irrespective of all other questions, it is evident that the Sioux valued the Hills highly, part of them because they desired the country itself, and part of them on account of what they hoped to obtain for it. There appears no reason for supposing that either party would be contented to see it taken by the miners without payment to them, or for a much smaller payment than they considered it worth.

At this time the Sioux nation could hardly be said to have the same divisions that were formerly recognized. The Teton Sioux had become divided into four main bodies after the treaty of 1868, and had mixed largely with the Yanktonnais and Sissetons. Their agencies had all been on the Missouri until 1874, and then, on stated grounds of the contaminating effects of the settlements, Red Cloud and Spotted Tail agencies were removed to the southeast of the Black Hills. With the usual care that marks the transaction of Indian business, both agencies were located in Nebraska, off the reservation. At Red Cloud agency there were supposed to be 9100 Ogallallas and 3700 Cheyennes and Arapahoes. There was no such number of genuine Ogallallas. The tribe had been reinforced by other Sioux, attracted by Red Cloud's fame. At Spotted Tail (Whetstone) agency there were reported 8400 Brulés and 1200 Minneconjous. At Cheyenne River agency, on the Missouri, there were 7600 Two Kettles, Sans Arcs, Minneconjous, and Blackfeet Sioux. At Standing Rock agency, on the Missouri, were 7300, of whom 4200 were Yanktonnais, and the remainder Oncpapas and Blackfeet Sioux. At Fort Peck agency (Milk River), Montana, were 6000 Indians, sometimes called Tetons, but not, in fact, for 2000 of them were Assinaboines, and the remainder Yanktonnais and Sissetons, except about 400 who were Tetons proper. These were all the Tetons except the roaming tribes, which were estimated at 3000, as follows: Black Tigers, 150; Long Sioux, 200; Shooters, 900; Tatkannais, 700; Oncpapas, 450; White Eagles, 200; Yellow Livers, 350. These Indians lived in the Powder River country, and roamed extensively, all of which they had the right to do, under the treaty of 1868. The most celebrated chiefs of these bands were Crazy Horse and Sitting Bull. Crazy Horse was an Ogallalla, although the Indians with him, in the spring of 1876, were chiefly Northern Cheyennes and Minneconjous, numbering not more than five or six hundred. Sitting Bull's band was still smaller, consisting of only thirty or forty lodges in times of peace, but in war times increasing rapidly.

Sitting Bull (Ta-tan-kah-yo-tan-kah) was a born fighter. He is said to be a half-breed Oncpapa, though he signed the treaty of 1868 as an Ogallalla. At this time he was somewhat broken by disease, but he was still of fine physique. His hair was brown, his complexion light, his face badly scarred by small-pox. There was probably no other Sioux who could make so proud a showing of individual prowess as he. About the year 1870 a Yanktonnais Indian brought to Fort Buford an old roster of the 31st Infantry, which had, on the blank sides of the leaves, a series of portraitures of the doings of a mighty

warrior. They were quite skilfully executed, in brown and
black inks, with coloring added for the horses and clothing.
The totem in the corner of each pictograph, a buffalo bull on its
haunches, connected with the hero by a line, revealed the fact
that it was a history of Sitting Bull, who, with a following of
sixty or seventy warriors, had been depredating in the neighborhood for several years. The Yanktonnais finally admitted
that he had stolen it from Sitting Bull, and sold it for a dollar
and a half's worth of supplies. The first twenty-three pictures

SITTING BULL'S FIRST ADVENTURE.

showed his slaughter of enemies of all descriptions, men,
women, and children, Indians, teamsters, mail-men, frontiersmen, railroad hands, soldiers. He was as impartial as death
itself. The next twelve show his exploits as a collector of
horses, a pursuit in which he displayed good taste and an in-
satiable craving for horse-flesh. He may fairly be considered
one of the ablest horse-thieves the country ever produced.
The last two pictures show him as leader of the Strong
Hearts, a Sioux fraternity for war purposes—Knights of the
Terres Mauvaises, as it were—storming two Crow villages.

SITTING BULL STORMS A CROW ENCAMPMENT AND TAKES THIRTY SCALPS.

In one of these fights thirty scalps were taken. These picture records are usually accurate. Ordinarily they are made
on buffalo robes, and kept by the hero for display among his
own people, who are acquainted with the facts of which he
boasts. In this case the pictorial history was confirmed by
knowledge that the whites already had of this doughty warrior.

While, therefore, Sitting Bull was not a chief of any particular prominence during times of peace, he had a record as
a fighter, and a reputation as a skilful commander, that made
him a loadstone to the discontented Sioux of the agencies.
Even the agency Sioux who were not discontented were not
averse to the society of their roaming brethren. Every summer they would slip away in small parties for a few months'
sport with the bad Indians. Sometimes they would massacre
a few Crows, or Blackfeet, or Arickarees. Sometimes they
would practice shooting at the miners of Montana. Sometimes they would gather some cattle and horses from the settlers in Wyoming. These statements are not flights of fancy.
The official records for seven months, from July 1, 1875, to
the spring of 1876, show seventeen attacks on the whites in

Yellowstone Valley alone, nine men killed, ten wounded, and a large amount of property stolen. These depredations caused general complaints from whites and friendly Indians. The Crows, especially, who were trying to adopt civilization, suffered severely from these attacks. We were under obligations to protect them, and all other tribes that had accepted reservations in good faith, but we neglected to do so for many years. It was an established custom of the early days for the whites to stand neutral when two or more Indian tribes were at war among themselves. Each tribe would object to any interference except as an ally to it, and interference could therefore result only in making one or all the tribes hostile. It was clearly politic for the whites to stand back and permit them to enjoy themselves; so the mountain tribes and plains tribes kept up a perpetual warfare, as they had done from traditional times.

As the country became more settled these wars became more annoying. If a band were disappointed in its search for Indian enemies, it was liable to take some lonely settler as a substitute. Many such affairs occurred, one of the most

SITTING BULL SCALPS A TEAMSTER.

SITTING BULL STEALS A DROVE OF HORSES.

celebrated being the Rawlin's Springs massacre of June 28,
1873. On that occasion a party of Arapahoes went on the
war-path against the Crows, but hearing that *les Corbeaux*
were on the alert, they turned to try the Utes. Near Rawlin's Springs they crossed the Pacific Railroad, and chanced
to meet a lone teamster driving four mules. They attacked
him, but he fired on them and escaped. A party at once
started after the Indians, who, on being overtaken, claimed to
be friendly Utes. They would have gone unharmed, on that
theory, had they not happened to have some stolen horses
which were recognized by the whites. These were demanded, and during the controversy that ensued the Arapahoes undertook to run, firing back with their pistols as
they went. The whites opened fire, killed four of them,
and returned in triumph with eight captured horses. As
we placed the more tractable tribes on reservations and endeavored to lead them into civilized ways, our duty of
protection became stronger. The reservation Indian who
honestly desired to work had to go to the field with his
rifle in one hand and his hoe in the other. They complained
bitterly. The Crows said: "We might just as well go out
and kill white men as to try to be good Indians, for we get

neither protection nor reward for being good." The depredations of the roaming Sioux were infractions of the treaty,
justifying hostilities on our part. The only bad-looking feature of our sudden resolve to make them behave was that it
came so quickly on the heels of the failure of the commission
to purchase the Black Hills and the Powder River country.
This feature is the more striking because the reservation
Sioux refused to consider the sale of the latter, on the ground
that the roaming bands would not consent to it. It was also
pretty well established that the roaming bands were not guilty
of all the depredations, and that Indians from the reservations were doing their share of these misdeeds, yet Sitting
Bull's band got credit for nearly every wrong committed, a
false reputation to which, however, they had little objection.

It was determined that the roaming tribes, or, as they were
often called, " the hostiles," should be forced to go on the reservations. This determination was the immediate result of a
report on their behavior by Inspector Watkins, on November
9, 1875. On December 6 of the same year, after consideration of this report by the Interior Department, orders were
sent to all the Sioux agencies to notify " Sitting Bull's band
and all other wild and lawless bands" that " unless they shall
remove within the bounds of their reservation (and remain
there) before the 31st of January next, they shall be deemed
hostile, and treated accordingly by the military force." This
notice was given, and the roaming bands refused to comply
with it. They were then turned over to the military, and for
this they were ready. Sitting Bull coolly sent word to General Terry to come on. " You need not bring any guides,"
he said; "you can find me easily. I will not run away." It
was the original intention to strike the Indians before the
spring opened, while their ponies were in bad condition and
the weather prevented them from travelling, but movements
from General Terry's department were made impracticable
by the cold. General Crook prepared an expedition from
Fort Fetterman, from which point, it was supposed, the
troops could operate at any time.

The expedition was composed of ten troops of cavalry and
two of infantry (700 men), with a large train, it being neces-

sary to carry all forage for the horses and pack animals. The command marched down Tongue River almost to the Yellowstone. A trail was discovered, and Colonel Reynolds, with nine troops of cavalry, pushed forward over it, on the night of March 16. In the morning they discovered the camp of Crazy Horse, near the mouth of Little Powder River. The situation of the village, beneath the precipitous bluffs of the river, made it impossible to charge at once. The horses had to be conducted to the valley through almost impassable gorges, a work which required two hours, and even then Captain Moore's battalion of dismounted men, which had been assigned a position on the eastern side, had not been led to the designated point by the commander. Only two officers and five men advanced to where they had been ordered. At nine o'clock Captain Egan charged the camp, with one company, while Captain Noyes, with another, drove off the herd. Both movements were successfully executed, though Egan was put on the defensive before the supporting column came up. On its arrival the Indians fled to the rocks, and the soldiers began destroying the camp. One hundred and ten lodges, with numerous buffalo robes and property of all kinds, were burned. The troops lost four killed and six wounded; the Indian loss was trifling. Immediately after destroying the village, the troops retired rapidly to Lodge Pole Creek, twenty miles away, where they expected to meet Crook, but he had not arrived. The soldiers had now been thirty-six hours in the saddle, or fighting, and were much exhausted. Supperless and blanketless, they rested as well as they could during the intensely cold night. No guard was stationed with the captured herd, in consequence of which nearly all of them escaped and were retaken by the Indians. The cold grew so intense as to make further operations impossible. The thermometer repeatedly fell to thirty degrees below zero, and on several occasions went below registry. The command returned to Fort Fetterman, and the troops were distributed to their posts.

This movement and its results have been subjected to spicy criticism, beginning with some sharp talk by the Indian Department. In his report General Crook said that the village was a "perfect magazine of ammunition, war material, and general supplies. . . . Every evidence was found to prove these Indians in copartnership with those at the Red Cloud and Spotted Tail agencies, and that the proceeds of their raids upon the settlements had been taken to those agencies and supplies brought out in return." This raised the wrath of the Indian Bureau. Agent Howard, of Spotted Tail agency, reported at once: "No proceeds of raids upon settlements have been brought here; no supplies taken north in return. No arms have been sold by the agency trader to Indians for more than two years, and but little ammunition; and, for two months, none of either. . . . I respectfully suggest that General Crook be requested to produce some of the abundant evidence which he found." Agent Hastings, of Red Cloud agency, was more savage. He said: "I learn from one of the half-breed scouts, who was with Crook's expedition against the hostile camp, that it was a complete failure, with the exception of the killing of an old squaw and two children, and the destruction of about forty lodges, with a loss to the troops of four killed and six wounded. Seven hundred Indian ponies were captured, but were recaptured on the following day, with the exception of about seventy head. A dozen or more officers have been placed in arrest for cowardice, and the command have returned to the railroad. . . . Five pounds of powder, twenty of lead, and six boxes of percussion caps comprised all the ammunition that was found in the abandoned camp." The truth probably lies between these extremes. While some of the statements of the latter extract are exact, its tone is so venomous as to destroy confidence in others. On the other hand, General Crook's statement savors more of opinion than of demonstration. It is difficult to conceive of any evidence that could possibly be in the Indian camp which would prove that the proceeds of raids on the settlements had been taken to the agencies and traded for goods. If such were the fact, the evidence would be at the agencies, not at the camp.

The plan adopted for the campaign was an advance in three columns, as soon as the weather permitted. General Crook was to march north from Fort Fetterman, with fifteen troops of cavalry and four companies of infantry, 1300

OLD FORT RENO—CROOK'S SUPPLY CAMP.

men; Colonel Gibbon was to come east from Fort Ellis, Montana, with four troops of cavalry and six companies of infantry, 400 men; General Custer was to move west from Fort A. Lincoln, with the 7th Cavalry, six companies of infantry, and three Gatling guns, 1000 men, besides the train men. This plan was followed, except that General Terry commanded the last force, Custer having been deposed by order of General Grant. The trouble between them was occasioned by Custer's testimony before the celebrated Heister Clymer committee, in the Belknap investigation. Clymer learned that Custer had reported his suspicions of certain transactions to the War Department, and that orders had been given that the transactions referred to be not interfered with. He at once summoned Custer, by telegraph. This was in the middle of March, and Custer was preparing to start his column early in April. He protested, and asked to be examined by deposition, but without effect. Mr. Clymer was gunning for big game, and did not propose to feel around in the dark by means of interrogatories. Custer had to go on to Washington. The main point elicited from him was that certain government contractors had turned over to him a large amount of grain, in sacks which bore the Indian Department's mark. He suspected that the sacks had been stolen from the Indian Department through a conspiracy between the Indian ring and the contractors, and reported the matter through his superior, General Terry, in accordance with military etiquette, at the same time refusing to receive the grain. He received peremptory orders to take the grain, which orders, he naturally believed, came down from the Secretary of War. This belief, however, was erroneous, as Custer learned of General Terry, on his return. Terry had given the orders himself, under certain instructions intended for the protection of the government. Custer at once telegraphed this fact to Clymer, and asked that the telegram be made part of his testimony, but the evil had already been done.

Grant was furious. He considered the attack on Belknap as an attack on himself and his administration, as well as an unjustifiable assault on his personal friend. The same quality of persistence that made Grant successful as a general, got him into trouble as an executive. He stuck to his friends in rough weather just as when the sky was smiling. He always fought it out on the line he had begun with—an excellent policy if the line be correct, but very bad otherwise. The verdict of history will probably be that Grant was an honest man who fell an easy prey to tricksters. The partisan effort to defend his administration, and the partisan effort to involve Grant personally in its corruption, will both fail under the test of time. Whether, in fact, Belknap was guilty in the Fort Sill tradership affair, or whether the folly of his wife occasioned his ruin, is not very material. It is beyond doubt that he was saved from impeachment solely by the legal theory of the defence, that a man out of office cannot be impeached, for of the twenty-five Senators who voted " not guilty," twenty-three explained their votes as being wholly on the ground of lack of jurisdiction. Whether guilty or not, there is clearly no reason why any one who knew any material facts should not be called as a witness, or why any witness should be reproached for telling what he believed.

Custer was in disgrace at court. In court opinion the probability of his antipathy to the administration was heightened by the fact that he was a Democrat in politics. He had joined that party soon after the war, on account of a feeling that the Southern States were treated unjustly. He now felt that he was misunderstood, but Grant refused to see him or hear any explanation. Three times Custer called at the White House and failed to obtain an audience. During the last call, as he waited in the anteroom, General Ingalls notified the President that Custer desired to speak to him, but Grant said he did not wish to see him. Custer then sent in a note stating that he desired the interview solely to correct certain unjust impressions which he believed were held concerning him. Grant still declined to see him. Custer started for his post. At Chicago he was overtaken by a despatch, through General Sheridan, ordering that he should stop and await further orders, while the expedition went on without him. A telegraphic correspondence ensued, which disclosed the fact that the instigator of the order was Grant, and that

Custer's offence as a witness was the cause of his hostility. The first concession obtained was that Custer might go on to his post, and remain there on duty. This did not satisfy the warrior. He appealed personally to Grant by telegram, saying: "I appeal to you as a soldier to spare me the humiliation of seeing my regiment march to meet the enemy and I not to share its dangers." This message General Terry kindly endorsed: "I do not know the reasons upon which the orders already given rest; but if those reasons do not forbid it, Lieutenant-colonel Custer's services would be very valuable with his command." This brought Grant around one step more, and Custer was permitted to go with his regiment, under Terry.

Unfortunately for Custer, the press got hold of the matter, and it became the subject of partisan dispute. The worst thing that can befall a man is to become a political martyr for the benefit of an opposition. His temporary friends cannot assist him, and usually care nothing for him, except as a viaduct for attack, while to the other and powerful side he becomes an object of execration. The Democratic papers attacked Grant for his treatment of Custer, and the Republican papers, as in duty bound, abused Custer, in defence of Grant. Between his policy friends and his unreasonable enemies poor Custer was well-nigh ruined.

The expeditions finally started. Crook met the enemy first. He moved to the hostile country, and, on June 8, established a large supply camp on Goose Creek. This he left under a strong guard, and marched on the 16th in search of the enemy, with nearly one thousand men. He had mounted his infantry on the train mules, and supplied each man with four days' rations. The Indians were believed to be on the Rosebud, about sixty miles away. Crook advanced for forty miles and went into camp. His Crow scouts refused to make a night march, having secured some buffalo during the day, and being determined to feast before they fought. The next morning an advance of seven miles was made, after which the troops camped at the mouth of a deep and rocky cañon with steep, timbered sides. The scouts were out ahead. Suddenly the reports of guns were heard, and soon the scouts came racing over the hills, chased by a large force of Sioux. The soldiers were quickly formed in line of battle, and the right centre was advanced to the summit of the bluffs, the position of the camp being untenable except these were held. In this general position the fight was carried on from eight in the morning until two in the afternoon. At the latter hour the left wing was ordered to retire, or connect with the main body. This movement was effected with considerable loss, the Sioux at once occupying the deserted position, and pouring a heavy fire into the retiring troops. Their advance was checked by a charge of the infantry and Indian allies from the left centre. Orders were then given for an advance, the purpose being to strike the Indian village, which was supposed to be about six miles ahead, but this was abandoned on account of the shortness of the supply of ammunition, and the discovery that the advance would have to be made through a cañon where the troops would be at the mercy of the enemy. After a brief pursuit of the Indians, who were now withdrawing, General Crook went into camp on the field. The loss to the troops was nine killed and twenty-one wounded. Eleven dead Indians were found on the field. The surprise of the village being now impossible, the wounded needing care, and the enemy being in much greater force than had been expected, Crook determined to fall back on his supply camp, which he did without further molestation.

Communication had not yet been established with the other two columns, and this withdrawal took Crook out of the range of practicable communication. Terry and Gibbon had communicated on June 1. On the 7th Terry established his supply camp at the mouth of Powder River. From this point Major Reno made a scout up Powder River to the mouth of the Little Powder, about one hundred and fifty miles, thence across to the Rosebud, and down it to its mouth. He could find nothing of Crook and nothing of the Indians, but on the Rosebud he found a heavy Indian trail, about nine days' old, which he followed for a short distance. In the mean time the main command had proceeded up the south bank of the Yellowstone to a point opposite Gibbon's camp,

ROSEBUD RIVER.

the steamer *Far West* moving up the river at the same time. A conference was held, and it was determined to make a grand surround, it being now reasonably certain that the Indians were between the Rosebud and the Big Horn, probably on the Little Big Horn. Gibbon was to cross the Yellowstone near the mouth of the Big Horn, march to the mouth of the Little Big Horn, by June 26, and then up the last-named stream. Meanwhile Custer was to march up the Rosebud with the 7th Cavalry, to the trail discovered by Reno. Beyond that point Custer had virtually *carte blanche*, by his written orders, but it was understood that if the trail were found to lead to the Little Big Horn he would pass it and continue southward long enough to allow Gibbon, who had all the infantry, to reach the mouth of the Little Big Horn. This he could not do before the 26th. This understanding is substantially set forth in Custer's orders, as the views of General Terry, with the desire that Custer should "conform to them" unless he should "see sufficient reason for departing from them." It was evidently the object of the movement to get the Indians between the two forces, but it is equally evident that either command was supposed to be large enough to safely engage all the hostiles. The object of division of forces was to prevent the escape of the Indians, to surround the hostiles, and bring the campaign to a close at one blow. No one, as yet, had any suspicion of the number of Indians they were to meet.

Custer moved up the Rosebud on the afternoon of the 22d twelve miles, and encamped. On the next day he advanced thirty-three miles, striking the lodge-pole trail that Reno had found. On the 24th he followed this trail for twenty-eight miles, still up the Rosebud, and went into camp. The scouts were kept ahead. At half-past nine a council was called, and Custer announced his intention of crossing the divide to the Little Big Horn that night, in order to avoid detection by the hostiles. At eleven o'clock the regiment moved on, up one of the small feeders of the Rosebud, towards the Little Big Horn. The divide between these two streams is only about twenty miles across at this point, but by the course followed, up the tributary of the Rosebud, and down a tributary of the Little Big Horn, it was thirty-three miles from Custer's camp, on the evening of the 24th, to the Indian village. At two o'clock in the morning, after making ten miles, the column again halted until five o'clock in the morning, the scouts reporting that the divide could not be crossed until daylight. Coffee was made, and the troops moved on. At eight o'clock the first Indians were seen. It was then evident that no surprise could be made, but it was determined to attack the village, at any rate. The regiment was divided into four commands. Custer took five companies; Major Reno had three; Captain Benteen had three; and Captain McDougal, with one, was placed in charge of the pack train. Benteen was ordered to ride with his detachment to some bluffs on the left front, and to report if he could see anything of the village from there. He reached these bluffs, but could see nothing, and went on to some others beyond, making an offing of some ten miles. The rest of the command kept on down the creek until half-past twelve. Custer then sent word to Reno that the village was only two miles ahead and the Indians were running away. Reno says his orders were "to move forward at as rapid a gait as prudent, and to charge afterwards, and that the whole outfit would support me." He rode at a fast trot for two miles, crossed the river at a ford, halted ten minutes to gather his battalion, and moved on down the valley with his men in line of battle. The small number of Indians who appeared fled before him for two miles and a half, making scarcely any resistance.

"I soon saw," says Reno, "that I was being drawn into some trap, as they certainly would fight harder, and especially as we were nearing their village, which was still standing; besides, I could not see Custer, or any other support, and at the same time the very earth seemed to grow Indians, and they were running towards me in swarms, and from all directions. I saw I must defend myself, and give up the attack mounted. This I did, taking possession of a point of woods, and which furnished, near its edge, a shelter for the horses; dismounted, and fought them on foot, making headway through the wood. I soon found myself in the near vicinity of the village, saw that I was fighting odds of at least five to one, and that my only hope was to get out of the wood, where I would soon have been surrounded, and gain some high ground. I accomplished this by mounting and charging the Indians between me and the bluffs, on the opposite side of the river. . . . I succeeded in reaching the top of the bluff, with a loss of three officers and twenty-nine enlisted men killed, and seven men wounded." Benteen had struck the trail of the main body, just in advance of the train, and come on at a trot. He met a messenger with orders to McDougal to bring on the train as rapidly as possible. A mile farther on he met another messenger with the order: "Benteen, come on; big village; be quick; bring packs. P. S. Bring packs." Says Benteen: "A mile or a mile and a half farther on, I came in sight of the valley and Little Big Horn. About twelve or fifteen dismounted men were fighting on the plain with Indians, charging and recharging them. This body (the Indians) numbered about nine hundred at this time. Colonel Reno's mounted party were retiring across the river to the bluffs. I did not recognize till later what party this was, but was clear that they had been beaten. I then marched my command in line to their succor. On reaching the bluff I reported to Colonel Reno, and first learned that the command had been separated, and that Custer was not in that part of the field, and no one of Reno's command was able to inform me of the whereabouts of General Custer."

The two united commands, numbering three hundred and eighty men, now moved down the river, keeping on the bluffs. Firing had been heard in that direction, and the inference was that Custer was engaged. On reaching the summit of the highest bluff nothing could be seen of him, and no more firing was heard. Reno stopped until the pack train came up, meanwhile sending Captain Weir, with one company, to open communication, but he quickly sent back word that he could make no progress; that the Indians were surrounding him. A heavy fire from his force showed that his enemies were not imaginary. It now seemed certain that Custer had been driven back and had retired down the river. Weir was called back, and the whole force moved to Reno's first position after retreating across the river, which was the

39

most available point for defence yet found. Here they were
rejoined by scout Herndon and thirteen men, who had become separated from the command in the timber. The place
was a small depression, surrounded by the crests of the hills
that formed it. The animals were scarcely placed in the depression, and the men stationed on the crests, when the Indians attacked them in strong force They maintained an incessant fire from six till nine o'clock in the evening, during
which the troops lost eighteen killed and forty-six wounded.

All through that night the soldiers worked at their in-
trenchments, making rifle-pits and barricading with dead animals. Below them, in the valley, the Sioux were holding a
scalp-dance over those already fallen, and the wild sound
came plainly on the night air to the little band, who knew
that their scalps would be in demand on the morrow. Day
broke at half-past two, and the attack was renewed at once,
by a part of the enemy. The remainder came in crowds,
riding up the valley from the scene of their orgies of the
night, until all the élite of Sioux chivalry had taken their
places about the tiny fortress. For seven hours they maintained a continuous fire of rifles, themselves out of reach of
the carbines of the cavalrymen. At half-past nine they
made a desperate charge, advancing close enough to use their
bows and arrows, but were driven back by a counter-charge
from the lines, led by Captain Benteen. They then charged
on the other side, but were repulsed by a like counter-charge
under Major Reno. It was now ten o'clock, and the men,
especially the wounded, were suffering for water. Volunteers
were called for, and a party was soon scrambling down to the
river, under cover of the fire of their comrades. They secured enough to moisten the lips of all, but they left half a
dozen brave men on their road. The Indians then began
moving to the valley, presumably either to get something to
eat or more ammunition, and the soldiers hastened to get a
good supply of water before they should return. They did
not come back. At two o'clock they fired the grass in the
valley, and under cover of the heavy smoke began preparations for their final departure. About sunset they emerged
from the clouds of smoke and filed away in the direction of

the Big Horn Mountains. Reno moved his position that
night, so as to secure a full supply of water, but the Indians
had gone to stay. The only arrival during the night was
Lieutenant De Rudio, who had become separated from the
command in the timber, where he had been hiding ever
since. In the morning Terry and Gibbon came up. They
had seen nothing of Custer.

Until this time no one had felt any serious apprehension
for Custer's command. Reno and Benteen supposed he had
fallen back, down the river, and united with Terry. Terry
and Gibbon had received word by the Crow scouts that Custer had been defeated, but did not believe it. Captain Benteen was sent out with a company of cavalry to make a
search. He struck the broad trail that Custer had left, and in
that trail was read the record of their progress to death, as
plainly as though it were written in words. From the point
where Reno crossed the river, Custer had marched rapidly
down the north bank, keeping back of the crests of the bluffs,
for a little more than three miles. Then his trail swung
around to the river, but did not cross it. It turned back on
itself and still bore down the river. The fighting began at
this turning-point, as was shown by the bodies of men and
horses first appearing there. Custer had probably intended
to strike the lower end of the village, but, not knowing its extent, had attempted to cross the river near the middle of the
village. He had been ambushed and driven back. He had
been pressed so closely that there was no opportunity for a
stand. Three quarters of a mile back from the river Captain
Calhoun's company had been thrown across the line of retreat
as a rear-guard. They died at their posts. Stretched across
the trail in irregular line, with Calhoun and Lieutenant Crittenden in place at the rear, were the bodies of all the company—dead, where they had been stationed, in the attempt to
save the remainder of the command. Under cover of this
check, the rest of the force had fallen back a mile farther and
gained a better position; but the remorseless Sioux were on
their heels. The force was now disposed in something like
military order. The centre, on a small ridge, was held by
Yates's company. On the left was Keogh's company, with its

right flank resting on the ridge. On the right was Smith's company. Captain Tom Custer's company was probably in the right centre.

The brunt of the attack came first on Keogh's company, which went down, as Calhoun's had, in line. There was no chance to aid them. The Indians were pressing on every side. It has been learned from Sitting Bull that at this point the Indians captured most of the horses, by circling the hill to the right (of the Indians) and driving them away from the rear. The superior forces of the Indians, and the shrewdness and daring of their fighting, can be judged from this movement. They knew where the horses were and that they wanted only these to make their prey secure. The plains Indians have not the nerve to ride to certain death, but they charge as gallantly as any cavalrymen that ever rode, when they are confident of success. They had trampled down Keogh's men like ripened grain, as they dashed to the rear to secure the horses. The attack now came on the left centre—from the front, rear, and left flank. The fire poured in on the little ridge must have been terrific. Custer fell there, with nearly all his officers. Around his body were those of Captain Yates, Colonel Cook, and Lieutenant Riley. Close by were Boston Custer, the general's brother, Autie Reed, his nephew, and Kellogg, the *Herald* correspondent, all civilians who had accompanied the expedition. Around these were the bodies of Yates's company. Just beyond was the corpse of Tom Custer, the general's brother, with part of his men; and a little farther on lay Captain Smith. The positions of the bodies showed that the remnants of Custer's and Smith's companies, their officers all dead, and themselves surrounded on three sides by the foe, had fallen back through a ravine to the river, leaving twenty-three dead along the line of retreat. Near the river they stopped. They had all the surviving uncaptured horses with them. It is probable either that the sight of the village, extending yet below them, showed them there was no chance for escape, or that they were here met by some new force. Here, at least, they died.

The only man of the entire command that escaped was "Curly," a Crow scout. When Custer was surrounded on the

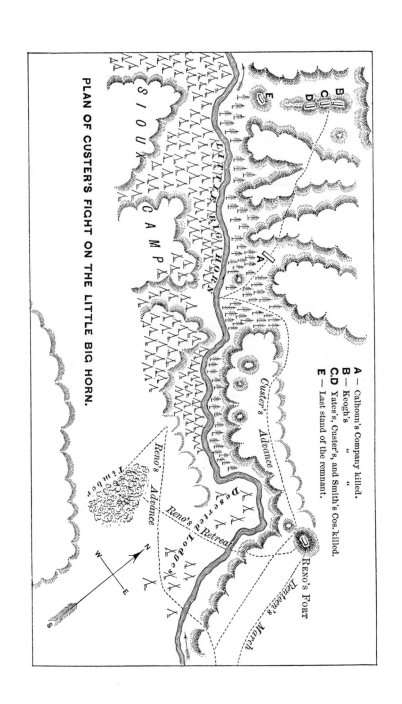

PLAN OF CUSTER'S FIGHT ON THE LITTLE BIG HORN.

A — Calhoun's Company killed.
B — Keogh's   "
C,D Yates's, Custer's, and Smith's Cos. killed.
E — Last stand of the remnant.

hill, he slipped down a ravine, let down his hair in Sioux fashion, changed his paint, secured a Sioux blanket, and succeeded in getting among the enemy during a charge. He mounted the horse of a fallen warrior and made his escape during the confusion of the battle. He says he did not leave Custer until the fight on the hill was almost ended. He saw Custer sink to a sitting posture, from a shot in his side, and then fall back, struck by a second bullet. It has been reported as having been claimed by some of the hostiles who fled into British America, that Custer was the last to fall; and that he died, sabre in hand, shot by Rain in the Face. The story is hardly credible. Custer was not the last to fall, beyond question. The evidence that has been obtained all goes to show that he was not even the last officer who fell on the ridge, but that Lieutenant-colonel Cook survived the others. Curly says that as he rode away, when nearly a mile distant, he looked back and saw a dozen or more soldiers, in a ravine, fighting the Sioux, who hemmed them in on all sides. This was after Custer's death, as the position of the bodies and the trail itself proved. The opinion most prevalent among Dakota people, to whom the talk of the Indians drifts, sooner or later, is that no one knows certainly who killed Custer—that he died by some bullet that could never be identified among the hundreds that were flying.

Of course it is possible that Rain in the Face shot him; but the real basis of this story was the imprisonment of this Indian, and his probable desire for revenge. In 1873 Custer had been sent with an expedition to protect a surveying-party of the Northern Pacific Railroad Company, from the Missouri to Montana. They crossed the country which had been guaranteed the Sioux, by the treaty of 1868, and which was consequently occupied by "hostiles." On this expedition the troops were attacked by the Sioux, and, at the time of the attack, two non-combatants were killed while separated from the command. They were Dr. Honzinger, the veterinary surgeon, and Mr. Baliran, the sutler of the 7th Cavalry. They were elderly men, of scientific tastes, and were searching for fossils, in which the bad lands abound. Their slayer was unknown; but, eighteen months later, while Custer was in winter quarters at Fort Abraham Lincoln, he was discovered at Standing Rock agency. The Sioux were there drawing rations, and, as usual, held dances in which they recounted their prowess. In one of these Rain in the Face, a young brave, described how he had killed these two men, and displayed articles that had belonged to them. Unfortunately for him, Reynolds, the scout —Lonesome Charley Reynolds, he was called; a brave man with a pathetic history, who fell in Reno's first skirmish on the Little Big Horn — was looking on, and understood the story. He notified Custer, who sent a company to arrest the man. They brought him out, after many threats and much begging by the Indians, and took him to Fort Lincoln. His arrest caused much anxiety to the Sioux, who expected him to be hung. He was a great brave, and so were his five brothers; one of them, Iron Horn, being a chief of prominence. He had especially distinguished himself in the sun dance—the Sioux test of endurance—by remaining suspended for four hours and refusing to be cut down, although the judges decided that he had passed the test.* He confessed his guilt to Custer, and was retained in the guard-house. In the spring of 1875 some white hay-thieves, confined in the same place, made their escape by cutting through the side of the building, and Rain in the Face slipped out after them. When next heard from he was with Sitting Bull, and sent in word to his tribe that he was awaiting an opportunity for vengeance.

It is to be regretted that Major Reno and General Terry should have felt it necessary to reflect on the course of Custer in attacking the Indians before the other troops were within supporting distance, and equally so that Custer's friends should have returned the attack by accusations of disobedience and cowardice against Reno and Benteen. There was no occasion for either. The affair is pardonable on one account, and one

---

* The tortures of the sun dance are about the same as those of the Mandans, described and illustrated by Catlin. The suspension test is made by hanging the candidate on cords passed under various muscles or sinews, until the flesh gives way under the strain and he falls to the ground. Sometimes weights are attached to the limbs to hasten the desired result. Rain in the Face was hung by cords passed under the muscles at the base of the shoulder-blades.

only; and all of its minor happenings fall under the same excuse. No one with Custer's command, or with Terry or Gibbon
or Crook, had any thought that there was so large a force of
hostiles; and none of them had any reason to suspect its real
strength. The roaming Indians were reported by the Indian Department to number 3000, which meant a fighting force of 600—
possibly 800. The information from other sources did not indicate any excess over this figure. On March 22, General Crook,
reporting the attack on Crazy Horse's village, said: "Crazy
Horse had with him the Northern Cheyennes and Minneconjous, probably in all one half the Indians off the reservation."
This camp consisted of 110 lodges, or less than 600 people.
From this statement it would appear that the military expected a hostile force of not to exceed 1200, or a fighting force of
about 250. Agent Howard, of Spotted Tail agency, replying
to Crook's report, said, on April 1: "Very few, if any, of these
Indians have been north this season, and I have heard of none
who were in copartnership with those of the North." Agent
Hastings, of Red Cloud agency, in a similar communication, on
April 3, said: "The agency Indians appear to take but little
interest in what has transpired north; but the disastrous result may have a tendency to awaken the old feeling of superiority. I have experienced no difficulty whatever in taking
the census, but have been somewhat delayed on account of the
weather." There was in these reports no cause to anticipate
that the hostiles would be materially reinforced from these
agencies. General Sherman, whose position put him in possession of all the information that could be had, referring to
Custer's departure on June 22, said: "Up to this moment
there was nothing official or private to justify an officer to expect that any detachment could encounter more than 500, or,
at the maximum, 800 hostile warriors." There was nothing,
after that moment, from which Custer or any of his officers
had any reason to change that estimate, until they were fairly
within the clutches of the enemy.

This was a wide miscalculation. The Indians from all the
Sioux agencies began slipping away to the hostiles as soon as
spring gave signs of approach, and when Custer struck them,
there were together, as nearly as can be judged, about one

half of all the Sioux in Dakota. As soon as the fight on the Little Big Horn had shown what the real state of affairs was, the military authorities insisted on taking control of the agencies, and, on July 22, the Secretary of the Interior acceded to the demand. The soldiers at once took possession of the agencies, and made a careful census of the Indians remaining on the reservations. At Red Cloud, instead of 12,873 Indians, there were 4760. At Spotted Tail, instead of 9610, there were found to be 2315. At Cheyenne River, instead of 7586, there were found 2280. At Standing Rock, instead of 7322, there were found 2305. In other words, there were 25,800 less Indians at these four agencies than belonged there, according to the reports of the Indian Bureau. These, with the 3000 roaming Indians, who were always off the reservations, make 28,800, to which there could safely be added a considerable number as representatives from other agencies, notably from Fort Peck. It is certain that a large portion of the Indians, off the reservations when the censuses were taken by the military, had left after reports of the Little Big Horn fight reached them and stimulated them to a desire for war, but, deducting one half for this, we may still count at least 3000 warriors for that engagement. Reno says, of the horde that surrounded his intrenchment on the 26th: "I think we were fighting all the Sioux nation, and also all the desperadoes, renegades, half-breeds, and squaw-men between the Missouri and Arkansas, east of the Rocky Mountains, and they must have numbered at least 2500 warriors." This is more probably an underestimate than an overestimate. The hostiles had assembled at this point, Crazy Horse, Sitting Bull, and all the rest. The Indians say so, and the scouting that had been done previously had shown that all the hostiles were in that neighborhood. The two main bodies joined about the 23d, as was shown by a heavy trail into the valley, about five days old, discovered by Captain Ball, on the 28th. The village extended three miles down the river, and in addition to the lodges there were a large number of brush shelters, such as are commonly called wick-i-ups in the West. Officers who estimated from the size of the village thought there were at least 3000 warriors.

MASSACRE MONUMENT.

The belief has been held by some military men that the Indians were not expecting an attack when the soldiers struck them, but this theory is not supported by the facts. The inference from all the evidence is irresistible that Custer advanced into a remarkably complete and well-planned ambuscade. The Indians had ample notice of his approach. He did not advance on them rapidly. At five o'clock in the morning, when he re-began his march, he was twenty-three miles from the village. At half-past twelve, when Reno was ordered to charge, they were still four miles from it. In seven hours and a half they had advanced nineteen miles. They first saw Indians at eight o'clock, and at their rate of marching they were then about fifteen miles from the village, with the Indians still nearer. If we suppose these first Indians seen to have been the first Indians who saw the troops, it is evident that they could have notified the village with ease by ten o'clock. No one at all acquainted with Indian methods will believe that the troops were out of sight of Indian scouts at any time after eight o'clock. There are two facts going to show that they desired the troops to suppose that the village had not been alarmed. They did not make any signal-fires for communication, as they usually do. These would have informed the soldiers that their presence was known to all the Indians in the vicinity. Secondly, Trumpeter Martin (the last white man who saw Custer alive), who brought back the message to Benteen, says he left the general at the summit of the bluff overlooking the village, and that, as he turned, " General Custer raised his hat and gave a yell, saying they were asleep in their teepees and surprised, and to charge." It is known that only a part of the village was visible from any point on the bluff that the soldiers reached before the fight, but the part Custer saw was quiet. It must have been kept quiet intentionally, for the warriors were at that time waiting for Custer below, and under such circumstances there would naturally have been an appearance of activity in the village, whatever its size might have been. Custer drew the correct conclusion on his theory of the number of Indians there. If there had been only from five to eight hundred warriors, and they had been notified of the coming of the troops, the squaws would have been taking down the lodges and packing at that time. The only inference that could be drawn was that they were surprised, and Custer acted on it, as they probably desired that he should.

The Indians were in at least two bodies before the fight began, one at the upper end of the village, and one at the ford where Custer attempted to cross. When Reno retired across the valley from the timber he was pursued by all the Indians there, who followed him until he reached the top of the bluff. His heaviest loss occurred while ascending the bluff. From the summit he heard firing, down the river, where Custer had gone. Custer was on the retreat from the time he was attacked, as is shown by the trail. Consequently, an overwhelming force of Indians was fighting each party at the same time. The number of Indians fighting Reno was estimated by Benteen at 900, and by Reno to be at least that number. So far as is known, the remainder, numbering probably 2000, were fighting Custer. The record of time given by Reno also shows that they were fighting simultaneously. Custer ordered Reno forward at half-past twelve. His own command followed Reno's to a point near the ford, and then moved rapidly three miles down the river, in all five miles. He must have been engaged by two o'clock, and probably was fighting from half-past one. It was half-past two when Reno reached the top of the bluff and was joined by Benteen. It is not probable that Custer's fight lasted long after that time. There has been published an account of this massacre, purporting to come from a trapper named Ridgely, who was a prisoner in the Sioux camp and escaped during the jubilee on the night of the 25th, in which it is stated that the fight with Custer lasted only fifty-five minutes. This story contains numerous errors, and is therefore unworthy of belief except as corroborated. In this particular it is corroborated by Reno and Benteen, who say the firing had ceased when they advanced on the bluffs, and Captain Weir was sent beyond to learn Custer's whereabouts. This movement was made shortly after Reno and Benteen united, and before the pack train had come up. Another fact which shows conclusively that Custer's fight was short, was the small number of Indians killed. The estimates of their killed, in the entire affair, by the officers engaged, were from forty to one hundred. The Indians conceded a loss of thirty-five. Most of these were killed by Reno's command in the fight on the 26th.

With these points in mind, it is easy to see the plan of the Indians. They knew that a force of about six hundred men was approaching. They saw Benteen's detachment leave the others and ride to the left. They arranged their forces, part at the end of the village nearest the soldiers, and part at the first accessible ford below the approach to the upper end of the village. If the soldiers reunited they might possibly charge through at either place, but if they did they would be surrounded on all sides. If they came in two detachments there would be enough warriors at both points to overwhelm them. At the upper end a few Indians remained among some scattered teepees, above the main village. As the soldiers advanced these were to retreat, and draw their pursuers into

the midst of the main body at this point.   They failed in this,
because Reno became suspicious of their action, and, seeing
nothing of Custer, who, he understood, was to follow him,
halted before reaching their ambuscade.   They then advanced
on him, passing constantly to his rear, to surround him, whereupon he cut through them to the bluffs.   At the other end

MAJOR-GENERAL GEORGE A. CUSTER.

Sitting Bull had his main force at the ford, with a strong band
advanced six hundred yards on the right bank, and concealed
in the timber.   Sitting Bull so states, and his statement is
verified by the fact that Custer, instead of falling back by the
road over which he advanced, retired farther down the stream.
This he would not probably have done from choice, for it took

him away from Reno and Benteen, and placed him in very bad ground, much cut up by ravines. He was struck in the rear by this band, turned down the river, and hurried on by a force vastly outnumbering him, until completely swept away.

It has been quite commonly believed that Custer recklessly charged his command into a force that outnumbered him from five to ten times over, and that his recklessness was more or less due to his trouble with General Grant. That this last made him more anxious for action is probably true. One can readily see how the soldier, who has unwittingly been drawn into the muddy pool of politics, would wish for an open field and the enemy before him. The people understood that, and they looked on the attack as some of "Custer's dash," but they did not blame him, for it was that same "dash" that carried him into their hearts long before. There was another consideration, too, that might well have palsied the tongue of criticism—the terrible loss to the Custer family. The general, his two brothers, his brother-in-law, Captain Calhoun, and his nephew, were certainly sacrifices enough to have expiated any common mistake. But this estimate, though it may be intended to be a kindly one, is unjust to Custer's memory. In fact, there has been injustice done to all the officers engaged in the battle, and it has arisen chiefly from the efforts of themselves or their friends to evade the supposed fault in the affair. There was not fairly any fault in it. It is evident that Custer attacked a force which he believed, and had every reason to believe, was about equal to his own. In that belief he concluded logically that the Indians were surprised when he saw their quiet camp. With that belief his division of his force into detachments, to strike on two sides, was a most excellent plan. He had not overmarched his command. His advance was only sixty-one miles, from five o'clock on the morning of the 24th, to the time of the fight, or about thirty-two hours. It is plain enough that Terry's plan was to get the Indians between Custer and Gibbon, but this was not from any supposition that either command was not large enough to handle the Indians singly. It was for the purpose of preventing their escape. Terry had no more knowledge of the number of the Indians than Custer had, and neither Terry nor Custer can justly be blamed for relying on what information they had.

On the other hand, Reno and Benteen are equally justifiable. Reno saw that he was being drawn into a trap, and fell back in time to save the greater part of his command. It was most fortunate that he did so as quickly as he did. Army officers, in blaming one another for failures, almost invariably weaken their common defence, and this case is no exception. Custer's biographer, Captain Whittaker, in assailing Reno for falling back, labors to prove that the number of all the Indians at the village, including squaws and children, was about 4500. If this were correct, the maximum number of warriors that could fairly be counted would be 1500. The number assailing Reno, by the estimates of both Reno and Benteen, was about 900. The result of Whittaker's argument, therefore, would be that Custer was driven back by a party smaller than that assailing Reno, and Custer had two companies more than Reno. Benteen's course is also attacked by Captain Whittaker, but in this his premises are incorrect. His argument is based on the time consumed in Benteen's movements, and his time and distances are fixed by the time when Benteen watered his horses, which he assumes to have occurred when crossing the river. The horses were watered at a morass, some distance back on the main trail. The unjustness of the estimate of our officers has been increased by an underestimate of the Indian leaders. That they were men of ability to handle their forces is certain. That was a matter of notoriety all through the campaign of 1876. No more complete evidence of their skill could be given than the fact that neither of the three armies searching for them secured any knowledge of their numbers or position in advance. Crook had no idea of their strength until they fought him and turned him back on the 20th of June. Custer did not suspect it until they swarmed about him on the 25th. Terry and Gibbon did not believe it possible for Custer to have been defeated, when the Crow scouts brought them word of it. It is a task requiring much tact and skill for a commander to conceal 15,000 people from the scouts of armies which are on all sides of him.

The struggle with the Sioux was protracted. The hostiles

of the Little Big Horn separated into two bands, Sitting Bull's Indians remaining in the west, and Crazy Horse's moving towards the east. The war spirit was awakened throughout the Sioux nation, and warriors were constantly leaving the reservations. Colonel Merritt intercepted and drove back a party of 900 Cheyennes, that had started from Red Cloud, but many others gained the hostile camps. In a short time small parties were raiding in all directions. Reinforcements and supplies for the troops were hurried forward, but autumn had arrived before they were ready for active operations. On September 29, Captain Mills, of Crook's command, with 150 men, surprised the camp of American Horse (Wa-se-chun-Ta-shun-kah, *i. e.*, Washington Tashunkah) at Slim Buttes, Dakota. American Horse was mortally wounded, four of his men killed, and a dozen captured. The Indians lost their lodges, supplies, arms, ammunition, and 175 ponies. A number of articles belonging to the 7th Cavalry were found in this camp. In October, after a desperate and fruitless attack on a large supply train, escorted by Colonel Otis, Sitting Bull

SITTING BULL. (FROM A PORTRAIT BY D. F. BARRY, BISMARCK, DAKOTA.)
40

met Colonel Miles with propositions for peace. Miles, who
had been put in command of the active troops in Dakota, told
him that he could have peace if he would go on a reservation,
or camp near the troops, where he would be in subjection to
the government. Sitting Bull said he would come in and
trade for ammunition, but wanted no rations or annuities, and
desired to live free, as an Indian. The council dissolved with
the assurance to the Indians that non-acceptance of the government's terms would be considered an act of hostility. Both
parties took positions for action, and a battle ensued, in which
the Indians were routed, and chased for over forty miles. On
the 27th more than 400 lodges surrendered. Sitting Bull,
with his band proper, escaped to the North, and was afterwards joined by several others. One band of 119 lodges, under
Iron Dog (Shon-ka-Ma-za) gained the Yanktonnais reservation
and dissolved. Just previous to this time the Indians on the
reservations were disarmed and dismounted. The same policy
was pursued towards all the hostiles that came in subsequently.
Red Cloud, who had remained at his agency, was deposed for
his hostile bearing, and Spotted Tail was put in charge of all
the Indians at both agencies.

Late in the fall a new expedition was fitted out by General
Crook. The cavalry with this force (ten troops), under Colonel
Mackenzie, surprised the camp of Dull Knife, a Cheyenne
chief, at daybreak, on November 25. The Indians escaped
with heavy loss, but their village of 173 lodges was destroyed,
and 500 ponies were captured. Owing to cold weather, operations were thereafter suspended in this department, but were
maintained in the Department of Dakota. On December 7
Lieutenant Baldwin, with 100 men, attacked Sitting Bull's
camp of 190 lodges, and drove him across the Missouri into
the bad lands. On the 18th Baldwin surprised their camp
and captured all its contents, together with 60 horses. The
Indians escaped across the Yellowstone in a state of destitution. Hearing of the reverses of Sitting Bull, Crazy Horse
sent him word to join his camp, as he had plenty of men and
supplies; but General Miles learned of this from spies, and
kept a force between the two bands which prevented their
union. On Dec. 29, Miles started with 436 men and two can-

nons against Crazy Horse, who had his winter camp on the Tongue River. The Indians abandoned their village on his approach, and were driven up the river from January 1 to January 7. On the evening of the 7th, the advance captured a young warrior and seven Cheyenne women and children, who were relatives of one of the Cheyenne head men. The Indians made a desperate attempt to recover them that evening, and on the following morning 600 warriors engaged Miles. This fight occurred on a spur of the Wolf Mountains. The ground was covered with snow and ice, and a blinding snowstorm came on during the action. The Indians were driven back over three rugged bluffs, which horses could not cross, and which men could surmount only with great difficulty. They then fled, having lost heavily, and went through the Wolf Mountains in the direction of the Big Horn range.

Communication was opened with them through the captives. On February 1 Miles sent word to them that they must surrender unconditionally or he would attack them again. In March, after consultation, they concluded to submit, and left nine men as hostages for their surrender, either to Miles or at the agencies. 300, under Two Moons, Hump, and other chiefs, surrendered to Miles on April 22. Over 2000, under Crazy Horse, surrendered at Red Cloud and Spotted Tail agencies in May. Sitting Bull fled into British America with his little band, and was there joined by Iron Dog, Gall, and other chiefs. Crazy Horse remained on the reservation near Camp Robinson, until September. It was then learned that he was trying to bring about another war. He was arrested, but tried to escape, while on his way to the guard-house, by running amuck through the crowd, striking with his knife at all who opposed him. He received a fatal wound, and died on September 7. The only band remaining at large was Lame Deer's. They were Minneconjous, with some renegades, who broke off from Crazy Horse's band when he determined to surrender, numbering in all 51 lodges. Colonel Miles surprised and routed them, on the morning of May 7, on the Rosebud, near the mouth of Muddy Creek. They lost 14 killed, including Lame Deer, all their supplies, and 450 ponies. The remaining Indians scattered, and Miles was soon after called away to stop

the Nez Percés, who were retreating through Montana.   On
September 26, 1876, the "hostile" feeling having become
somewhat subdued, the Sioux concluded the agreement by
which they surrendered the Black Hills and the Powder
River country to the government, and accepted in lieu thereof a substantial ration for each member of the tribe until they
should become self-supporting.

Sitting Bull's party was visited in British America by a
commission, with the object of inducing them to return and
surrender.   They returned a defiant refusal to the emissaries
of the government which "had made fifty-two treaties with
the Sioux and kept none of them," declaring their intention to
become subjects of her majesty.   The new situation did not
long suit them.   The British government gave them protection merely, with no assistance, and this on the understanding
that they would not be allowed to depredate across the line.
One by one they concluded to come back to the flesh-pots of
the republic.   They kept coming in small parties and surrendering to the troops until, on July 20, 1881, Sitting Bull, with
his little band, reduced to 45 men, 67 women, and 73 children,
surrendered at Fort Buford.   Two days later all the captive
hostiles, numbering 2829, were turned over to the agent at
Standing Rock.   There has been no trouble of any importance with the Sioux since 1877, and they are reported to be
making remarkable progress in civilization.

CHAPTER XIX.

JOSEPH'S NEZ PERCÉS.

THE meanest, most contemptible, least justifiable thing that the United States was ever guilty of was its treatment of the Lower Nez Percés. It will not be necessary to tell the reader of the preceding pages that the conduct of the Nez Percés had been of uniform friendship and kindness towards the Americans. Their call for missionaries, their support of the settlers against the overbearing Hudson's Bay Company, their offer of protection to the Lapwai Mission when Whitman had fallen a victim to the Cayuses, their protection and escort of Governor Stevens's party in 1855, their stand for peace when the other tribes were for war in 1855 and 1856, their rescue of Steptoe's party in 1858, their assistance to our troops against hostile Indians, have all been recorded. They also rejected proposals for hostilities from the Mormons, both before and during the civil war. It may also be remembered that their friendship was of older date than the matters treated of in the foregoing chapters; that they gave Lewis and Clarke a reception which brought joy to the hearts of those weary explorers; that they furnished them food and refused pay for it; that they cared for the horses and other property while the expedition made its way down the river, and returned them safely in the spring. It is true that there was some difference of opinion among these Indians in regard to adopting the white man's religions and customs, but not one whit as to remaining his friends. Our history ran its cycle of a hundred years with the record of but one American's blood being shed by a Nez Percé—a case of manslaughter, about the year 1862. Seventy years of friendly intercourse—seventy years in which the Indians patiently en-

dured what they justly considered hardships, for their friendship to the white man—seventy years of self-sacrifice, of for-
bearance, of sacred faith on their part—before the folly or
weakness or dishonesty, whichever it may have been, of our
governmental agents roused them to madness, and the worms
we so knavishly trod upon turned to sting us.

The Nez Percés, while one in feeling, were composed of

YOUNG JOSEPH.

several independent, confederated tribes. The most common
method of dividing them, used by the whites, was into the
Upper and Lower Nez Percés, a distinction referring to their
lands, as the names imply. The chief of the Wal-lam-mute-
kint (Wal-lam-wat-kin) band, which was usually called the
Lower Nez Percés, was Joseph, the chief who came to meet
the Oregon volunteers after the Whitman massacre, and said

to them, "When I left my home I took the Book in my hand and brought it with me; it is my light. I heard the Americans were coming to kill me. Still I held my Book before me and came on." There was never any head chief who claimed full control over all the bands, and none in whom we recognized such power, except those who had been appointed through our agency. The first one was appointed by Elijah White, their first agent, a man who meant well enough, but who was probably mistaken in his idea that he had discovered the Northwest passage around all Indian troubles. He appointed Ellis head chief in 1842; but Ellis had no control over the tribe, and after his death, in 1847, there was no head chief until 1855. The authority of Lawyer as head chief was formally recognized in the treaty made by Governor Stevens in 1855, but it was never understood by the Indians that this gave him any authority to dispose of their lands. As a matter-of-fact he was arbitrarily appointed by Governor Stevens for the purposes of the treaty, and was never acknowledged by half of the Indians. Among the Indians, the Lower Nez Percés were conceded to own the country south and east of the Blue Mountains, and west of the Snake River, as far south as the Powder River, a tributary of the Snake. It is true that the other bands had the privilege of hunting and fishing there, just as the Lower Nez Percés had the privilege of roaming over or camping in the upper country, but the right of control—their highest idea of a fee-simple—of both sections was never disputed to be in the bands respectively. The Lower Nez Percés moved to the upper country when Whitman and Spalding came, in order to receive "the Book" from their hands, but there was no change in the ownership of the lands; and afterwards, when jealousies arose between Joseph and Big Thunder, a chief of the Upper Nez Percés, Joseph was unceremoniously ordered to return to the land where he belonged, and he did so.

Joseph and his people seemed to love that country of theirs. It was not the most attractive region in the world to the white man, but it suited them. On one side of it the Snake surges and foams over its rocky bed. On the other the Blue Mountains rise majestically, and along their eastern

base the Grande Ronde River sweeps through its great arc to
the Snake.   Between them is a rugged country impossible of
cultivation.   Through it, towards the east, runs the Imnaha
(Immaha), down a narrow, rugged vale; through it towards
the northwest flows the Wallowa (Wall-low-how, Way-lee-
way—the Winding Waters), with a valley larger and better
than that of the other stream.   The valley of the Wallowa
was the very best of the land claimed by the Lower Nez
Percés, and it was not much to be desired.   Captain Whipple
reported of it, on August 28, 1875, "The valley is only fit
for stock-raising, as a business, and not desirable for that in
consequence of the long winters; but the Indian horses would
live through where the white man's cattle would perish."   It
was even so worthless that Americans did not desire it.   Says
Captain Whipple, "The average American is not, as a rule,
slow to take advantage of eligible openings to secure land
'claims' which may probably become valuable, but none of
them seem anxious to locate them in Wallowa Valley. . . .
The population is less than it was a year ago.   Since the valley was restored to settlement, three families have disposed
of their improvements for a trifle, and moved away; nor do
I believe any others have come in.   Not a man has taken a
claim in the valley since that time.   One of the most enterprising, reliable, and best citizens in the settlement, has told
me, within the past week, that he thought the people of the
valley were disappointed to learn it was not to be taken for
an Indian reservation; that he regretted it for one; that
he should sell out at first opportunity, and settle in a more
promising locality.   This shows how the white people who
reside here regard this valley.   On the other hand, the Indians love it."

A strange man was old Joseph, a sturdy, strong-built man,
with a will of iron and a foresight that never failed him but
once—when he welcomed the Americans to his country.   He
had some strange notions too, one of which was that "no
man owned any part of the earth, and a man could not sell
what he did not own."   He was an aboriginal Henry George
in his idea that ownership in land should be limited to occupancy, and, if we may judge by the converts that gentleman

is making, he was not without reason. Joseph continued friendly to the whites, but he grew suspicious of their trading abilities, and bade his people be careful how they made bargains; the land he would look after himself. Surely the white man would not get it away from him. He was very careful, indeed. He would not join in the treaty with Governor Stevens until his own land was reserved out of the cession. To be candid, he and his tribe claimed that he did not sign the treaty at all, though his name is affixed, but they evidently mean that he never signed a treaty ceding his land, which is true. After the ratification of the treaty, in 1859, the other Indians received presents from the government and annuity goods; they had tools and bright clothing and guns, but Joseph and his people took none. He said to them, "These presents are the price of the land which is sold. If we take the pay, the white man will say he has bought our land also." So, for all those years after the treaty the Lower Nez Percés refused to receive any of the annuity goods, contented to know that the land of the Winding Waters was their own. Foolish Indians! to think that they could escape our clutches in that way.

In 1863 the whites had so encroached on the lands of the Nez Percés, and whiskey was doing so much damage, that another treaty was considered necessary. Calvin H. Hale, Charles Hutchins, and S. D. Howe negotiated it. The Upper Nez Percés accepted their present reservation of Lapwai, in Western Idaho. The Lower Nez Percés refused to join in the treaty. They had seen nothing to make them believe that their own course was not the best. The other tribes had been getting very few of the fine things that Governor Stevens had promised them, and what they did get was in gewgaws that they did not want; for the Nez Percés always asked for substantial and useful goods. It must be confessed that the Lower Nez Percés twitted them a little, too, which was annoying, though natural. Agent Hutchins said of this in 1863, "The old men of the tribe look with sorrow on the fact that they cannot rebut these flings by pointing to real evidences of the good faith of the white man's chief." But Joseph's band did not save their land by refusing to join.

The Upper Nez Percés sold all their land except the reservation, and that took away all the land of the Lower Nez Percés. Do you not understand it? It is the simplest thing in the world. Governor Grover discovered the way—the same Governor Grover that tried so hard to prevent the Republican party from stealing the government in 1876, by stealing the vote 'of Oregon himself—who was sent to the Senate for his distinguished services. This is the process. In 1855 Joseph joined with other chiefs in the treaty by which they sold a certain amount of land; hence the land that they did not sell belonged to all of the tribe in common. By joining in that treaty, Joseph acknowledged the tribal organization; hence the tribe had authority to bind him afterwards. A majority of all the chiefs, counting all the bands together, joined in the treaty of 1863, and sold all their land except the Lapwai reservation; hence they sold Joseph's land. You may be inclined to call that thieving; it is also idiocy.

There is no pretence that the Upper Nez Percés intended to sell the land of the Lower Nez Percés, or claimed any power to do so, or that the commissioners understood that they were purchasing it. It does not appear that any one anticipated such a result at the time, for this construction was not adopted for years afterwards. Old Joseph went to his grave in 1871, in blissful ignorance of the fact that his land was not his land. Captain Whipple says, "Uniformly and with vehemence, to his last hour, he asserted to his children and friends that he had never surrendered claim to this (Wallowa) valley, but that he left it to them as their inheritance, with the injunction never to barter it away." His son says, "I saw he was dying. I took his hand in mine. He said, 'My son, my body is returning to my mother earth, and my spirit is going very soon to see the Great Spirit Chief. When I am gone, think of your country. You are the chief of these people. They look to you to guide them. Always remember that your father never sold his country. You must stop your ears whenever you are asked to sign a treaty selling your home. A few years more, and white men will be all around you. They have their eyes on this land. My son, never forget my dying words. This country holds your father's body.

Never sell the bones of your father and your mother.' I pressed my father's hand, and told him I would protect his grave with my life. My father smiled and passed away to the spirit land. I buried him in that beautiful valley of

OLLACUT.*

Winding Waters. I love that land more than all the rest of the world. A man who would not love his father's grave is worse than a wild animal."

This son was worthy his father's legacy. His name was In-mut-too-yah-lat-lat — the Thunder-Travelling-Over-the

---

* This cut was originally published as a portrait of Joseph, Ollacut having been mistaken for his brother by the artist.

Mountains.   To the Americans he was known as Young
Joseph, and to the world, since 1877, he is Chief Joseph the
Nez Percé.   He was six feet in height, well-formed, of serious
and noble countenance.   He was grave and thoughtful, as becomes a ruler.   He was shrewd and cautious, as becomes one
who transacts business for a nation.   He was exact and resolute, as becomes one who must preserve peace between two
factions prone to misunderstanding and jealousy.   Nearest
and dearest to him, after the death of his father, was his
brother Ol-la-cut, a little younger than himself, tall, handsome,
and gay.   Both of these youths were students in Mrs. Spalding's school in the happy olden time.   Probably the good
seed which was sown then ripened into good deeds afterwards ; possibly it accounts for their honorable conduct when
war came.   If so, it were well worthy of record in some Ely
volume.   The white men grew more numerous in the West.
They came into the Nez Percé country to search for gold,
and many of them remained there.   They did not treat the
Indians well, but the young chieftain ruled his people so wisely that no warfare occurred.   Says Joseph, " They stole a great
many horses from us, and we could not get them back because
we were Indians.   The white men told lies for each other.
They drove off a great many of our cattle.   Some white men
branded our young cattle so they could claim them.   We had
no friend who would plead our cause before the law councils."   Still there were no hostilities.   In 1871 an Indian was
killed by a white man.   The Indians took no revenge, but insisted that the whites should leave their country.   Troops
were sent into the country for the protection of both parties.
In March, 1875, a white man named Larry Ott killed a Nez
Percé in a quarrel, and the grand-jury returned no bill
against him.   In August, 1875, one Benedict shot at some
drunken Indians who came to his house at night demanding
admittance, and killed one and wounded another.   This man
was accused of selling liquor to the Indians.   In the spring,
also, one Harry Mason whipped two Indians ; the council of
arbitration chosen in this matter—three white men—decided
against the Indians.   In June, 1876, a settler named Finley
killed a brother of Joseph.   None of these offences were pun-

ished, and for none did the Indians take revenge, still urging only that the whites should leave their lands.

The question of title had drifted along until 1873, when the Interior Department took steps to set the Wallowa off as reserved land for the Lower Nez Percés. The improvements of the eighty-seven squatters who were to be bought out were appraised at $67,860. For eighteen months the matter rested in that way, all parties satisfied, but in the spring of 1875 Congress refused to confirm the purchase and reservation. Why it did so is beyond imagination, except it may have been from the influence of Governor Grover, who had put his fine-spun theory before the Government in the summer of 1873. As we have seen, the disappointment was almost as great to the settlers as to the Indians. Some of my readers may not understand the theory of settling for the purpose of being bought out. If a man discover where a reservation is to be located, he cannot do better financially than to locate upon it. Appraisers for government purchases are usually liberal. The Indians were cast down in spirit. When Joseph learned of the decision, Captain Whipple says "he looked disappointed, and after a short silence he said he hoped I could tell something of a possible doubt of their being obliged to relinquish this valley to the settlers. I told him the case was decided against the Indians by higher authority than that of any army officer. This declaration did not make the countenances of the Indians more cheerful. They all realize that after they go to Lapwai reservation, or one similar, they will be obliged to give up their horses, which constitute their main wealth, and that as a community they will cease to exist."

The outlook for the Lower Nez Percés was gloomy, but there was yet one ray of hope. There were still a few people in Oregon who remembered the good services of the Nez Percés in the past, and did not wish to see them robbed. Rev. A. L. Lindsley, celebrated for his mission work in the Northwest and in Alaska, with others, asked that a commission be appointed to investigate the matter and make some equitable settlement with the Indians. Gen. O. O. Howard, commanding the District of the Columbia, endorsed the proposition, and suggested that he be made a member of the Commission. A commission was appointed, and General Howard was made a member. They came to Lapwai to talk with Joseph and the other "non-treaties" that had never been able to understand Governor Grover's logic. There was White Bird's band, which occupied the country adjacent to the Salmon River. There was a band that roamed over the rugged country between the Salmon and the Snake, under the old chief and "medicine-man" Too-hul-hul-sute. There was a small band on Ashotin Creek, north of Joseph's country, and above this were several small bands under the authority of the young chief Hush-hush-cute (Hus-es-cruyt, Hus-ses-kutte—the Bald Head). There was also the band of Looking Glass, on whose land the Lapwai reservation had been located, and who retained their home in common with the "treaties" who had been put with them. These bands were sufficiently confederated in interest, and sufficiently sensible of Joseph's ability, to make him the common leader of the "non-treaty" party. The Commission talked with them in November, 1876, in the mission church at Lapwai, but Joseph nonplussed the commissioners. They say, "An alertness and dexterity in intellectual fencing was exhibited by him that was quite remarkable." It was remarkable. They were unable to answer his arguments. He said "that the Creative Power, when he made the earth, made no marks, no lines of division or separation on it, and that it should be allowed to remain as then made. The earth was his mother. He was made of the earth and grew up on its bosom. The earth, as his mother

GENERAL O. O. HOWARD.

and nurse, was sacred to his affections, too sacred to be valued by or sold for silver and gold. He could not consent to sever his affections from the land that bore him. He was content to live upon such fruits as the Creative Power placed within and upon it, and unwilling to barter these and his free habits away for the new modes of life proposed by us. Moreover, the earth carried chieftainship (which the interpreter explained to mean law, authority, or control), and therefore to part with the earth would be to part with himself or with his self-control. He asked nothing of the President. He was able to take care of himself. He did not desire Wallowa Valley as a reservation, for that would subject him and his band to the will of and dependence on another, and to laws not of their own making. He was disposed to live peaceably. He and his band had suffered wrong rather than do wrong. One of their number was wickedly slain by a white man during the last summer, but he would not avenge his death. But unavenged by him, the voice of that brother's blood, sanctifying the ground, would call the dust of their fathers back to life, to people the land in protest of this great wrong."

The commissioners knew that Joseph's statements were true. His brother had been killed, as stated, in a quarrel about some stock, by a man named Finley, and the Indians had refused even to appear as witnesses against the murderer in court. Joseph said, "When I learned that they had killed one of my people I was heart-sick. When I saw all the settlers take the murderer's part, though they spoke of bringing him to trial, I told them that the law did not favor murder. I could see they were all in favor of the murderer, so I told them to leave the country. As to the murderer I have made up my mind. I have come to the conclusion to let him escape and enjoy health and not take his life for the one he took. I am speaking as though I spoke to the man himself. I do not want anything in payment for the deed he committed. I pronounce the sentence that he shall live." The causes for removal given by the Commission were not brought into prominence in the council. They were not of a nature that would admit of consistent urging. The first was of a religious character. A part of the Nez Percés had become

Catholics; a part adhered to "Mr. Spalding's religion;" and a part had become believers in a form of spiritualism which had recently been introduced in Eastern Oregon by Smo-hal-lie, a chief who dwelt with a little band of followers across the Columbia from Wallula, the village on the site of old Fort Walla-Walla. He was a small and deformed sorcerer, but the abnormally large head that surmounted his humped shoulders had evolved the mystic faith of the "Drummer-dreamers," which threatened to stop the progress of good, old-fashioned, orthodox conversion. They were a queer lot. Their young men saw visions and their old men dreamed dreams. They taught that land ought not be divided up, or forced by cultivation to yield more than its natural fruits; that schools and churches were innovations of the devil; and that a savior would be raised up in the East who would bring their dead to life, expel the white man from the country, and restore the Indians to their own. This last was probably a relic of the story of the second coming of Christ, which Brigham Young had left in their country twenty years before. These theories seem odd, but the Indians defended them in a way that was hard to answer. Said General Shanks to Joseph, "Do you want schools and school-houses on the Wallowa reservation?" "No," said Joseph, "we do not want schools or school-houses on the Wallowa reservation." "Why do you not want schools?" "They will teach us to have churches." "Why do you not want churches?" "They will teach us to quarrel about God, as the Catholics and Protestants do on the Nez Percé reservation, and at other places. We do not want to learn that. We may quarrel with men, sometimes, about things on this earth, but we never quarrel about God. We do not want to learn that." These tenets apparently stood in the way of an adoption of our customs, but there is certainly nothing about them that is either criminal or improper, notwithstanding they so impressed Father Wilbur in that way that he recommended that the Indians be "brought within the Christianizing influences of the reservation," even if force were necessary to accomplish the removal. Apropos of this, are not the Indians entitled to a share in the temporal comforts of spiritualism, considering the immense amount of service their disembodied spirits have to perform as "controls" in the white man's séances? Our spiritualistic brethren have not had any tribe assigned to them for missionary labor—in fact they do not appear to be ardent missionaries—and, in consequence, the red man has been obliged to get along without any rappings, or materializations, or dark cabinets.

Another objection was that they went every year to the "buffalo illahie"—the Powder River country—to procure their winter's supply of meat. They did not disturb any one in going or coming, but it made the "treaty" Indians jealous and restless to be thus reminded that they had sold their birthright for a mess of pottage. Their unhappiness was increased by the fact that they did not always get the pottage. A fellow named Langford had taken and held possession for months of the old mission claim of six hundred and forty acres, on which the agency buildings were situated, and shut down the mills, forcing the treaty Indians to sell their grain at a sacrifice and buy flour. One Finney claimed and occupied six hundred and forty acres of the reservation; one Colwell claimed and occupied seventy-five acres; one Randall claimed fifty acres, and had a permit to place a stage station on the land. The deeds which had been promised the Indians for their twenty-acre lots had never been issued to them. There was due them $4665 for services and for horses furnished the Oregon volunteers in 1856, which it had been definitely agreed should be paid in the treaty of 1863. It was only thirteen years since that treaty had been executed, and the governmental agents had not had time to attend to these minor details. It is quite possible that these things made the "treaties" jealous of the "non-treaties" also. In connection with the objection to the "non-treaties" going to hunt buffalo, it is interesting to remember that the Sioux and their allies were doing the same thing, and that we had kindly guaranteed them the right to do so, because they were strong, and fought back, and made our occupation of the buffalo illahie so uncomfortable that we were glad to abandon the Montana road and leave them as they were.

Now why did these Nez Percés object to going on the

41

Lapwai reservation ? The first reason was that they preferred their own country, and, in connection with this feeling, they knew that the money, goods, and the rest that were so glibly promised them in the councils, in payment for their country, would not be forthcoming. They had the experience of their "treaty" brethren constantly before them in proof of that. The second reason was that they desired personal liberty to go from one place to another. They knew that going on a reservation meant staying there, except on permission of the authorities, and also a practical dissolution of their tribal organization. After the wrong was consummated, when Joseph had been permitted to go to Washington and talk to our wise men, he said, "I have asked some of the great white chiefs where they get their authority to say to the Indian that he shall stay in one place, while he sees white men going where they please. They cannot tell me." The third reason was that their chief wealth was in herds of horses, from the increase of which they had a plentiful support, with but little labor, and these they would have to give up if they went on the reservation. Why? Because, on the reservation, twenty acres of land, and no more, were allotted to each head of a family, out of which he was to make his living. Stock-raising on twenty acres is necessarily a limited business. The care of these herds, the visits of the Indians to the settlements to trade, and their annual buffalo hunts, are what constituted the "nomadic habits" that the Commission objected to.

The "judicious men" came to a conclusion at last. They revamped that false and fallacious theory of Governor Grover's, that Old Joseph's joining in the treaty of 1855 "implied a surrender of any specific rights to any particular portion of the whole reserve." They adopted his monstrous proposition that from the treaty of 1863 a contract should be implied which neither of the contracting parties contemplated and neither had a right to make. The thing is too absurd for serious argument. Joseph disposed of it, though he did not put his case so strongly as he might, in this manner: "Suppose a white man should come to me and say, 'Joseph, I like your horses, and I want to buy them.' I say to him, 'No, my horses suit me; I will not sell them.' Then he goes to my

LAPWAI.

neighbor, and says to him, ' Joseph has some good horses. I want to buy them but he refuses to sell.' My neighbor answers, ' Pay me the money and I will sell you Joseph's horses.' The white man returns to me and says, ' Joseph, I have bought your horses and you must let me have them.' If we sold our lands to the Government, this is the way they were bought." In short, the Commission recommended that if the Lower Nez Percés did not peaceably take up their residence on the Lapwai reservation within a limited time, that they should "be placed by force upon the reservation, and, in satisfaction of any possible rights of occupancy which they may have, the same aid and allotments of land granted to the treaty Nez Percés should be extended to them on the reservation." The same commission recommends that the Umatilla reservation —the peaceful home of the Cayuses, Umatillas, and Walla-Wallas for twenty years past—be vacated, because it "would be eagerly purchased," was "of the best quality of land," and was "occupied by a mere handful of Indians who are incapable of developing its rich treasures." By all means, put all Indians on lands that have no rich treasures to develop. Then nothing will be lost. To be sure, there are a few millions of acres, with undeveloped treasures, that can be had for the pre-emption, but they are not quite so convenient.

But, it will be said, surely the commissioners did not understand the real state of affairs. Go softly. General Howard had been looking over the matter ever since he was put in command of the Department of the Columbia. Papers containing full statements of the historic services of the Nez Percés, of the rights of the " non-treaties," and of the influences actuating them, had passed through his hands and received his endorsement and approval. In his report of September 1, 1875, he had said, " I think it a great mistake to take from Joseph and his band of Nez Percé Indians that [the Wallowa] valley. The white people really do not want it. They wished to be bought out. I think gradually this valley will be abandoned by the white people, and possibly Congress can be induced to let these really peaceable Indians have this poor valley for their own." Lieut.-Col. H. Clay Wood was another member of the Commission who was fully posted. On August 1, 1876, he reported at length on "The Status of Young Joseph and his Band of Nez Percé Indians," and gave his opinion that the government had so far failed to comply with its agreements in the treaty of 1855, that none of the Nez Percés were bound by it. Let us also record, to his honor, that he made a minority report, as commissioner, recommending that although Joseph's band would have to be moved eventually, yet that "until Joseph commits some overt act of hostility, force should not be used to put him upon any reservation." The other commissioners were D. H. Jerome, William Stickney, and A. C. Barstow. What previous knowledge they had of the matter I cannot say; but there was leaven enough for the whole lump in the two military members.

The Commission made its report, and the Department of the Interior, acting on its recommendations, ordered the non-treaties to be placed on the Lapwai reservation. By virtue of his office, General Howard was the agent to enforce this order. He met the non-treaties in May, and found, as he must have anticipated, that they were unwilling to go to the reservation. He held three councils with them—the last on May 7th. Too-hul-hul-sute, the *too-at* ("Drummer-dreamer" priest) and chief, was their spokesman. He talked boldly, and as word came back to word he said, "The Indians may do what they like, but I am not going on the reservation." Howard threatened him with arrest. "Do you want to scare me with reference to my body?" asked the old man. He was arrested and led out of the council. The Indians murmured. Should they kill Howard and the rest? They were well-armed and self-confident. Joseph bade them not. The position of the government was now plain to the Indians. They must go to the reservation or fight. They decided to go. Would you have done so, reader? Would you have swallowed the injustice, and meekly agreed to go, without striking one blow at least for liberty and right? I remind you that the Nez Percés had never fought the white man, and Joseph was not the man to begin. He says, "I said in my heart that rather than have war I would give up my country. I would give up my father's grave. I would give up everything rather than have the blood of white men upon the hands of my people." The Indians were given thirty days from May 14th, in which to gather their cattle and move; Hush-hush-cute's band had thirty-five. They say it was not time enough, but that was of no consequence. We must have firmness in dealing with Indians, even if we have nothing else.

The Indians went to make their preparations. They looked on their old home, and their love for it doubled under the realization that they must leave it. Too-hul-hul-sute's spirit burned because of his imprisonment for the offence of telling his determination in the council. There was a warrior whose father had been killed by a white man, five years before, who brooded over the unavenged wrong. There were the two warriors who had been whipped by Harry Mason. There were the kinsmen of the murdered men. They assembled at Rocky Cañon. Several hundred of their horses and cattle were missing. They held councils. A desire to resist removal sprang up and spread rapidly. They determined, over Joseph's counsel, to fight the soldiers when they came. It was the desire of a part that the settlers should not be molested, in the hope that they would remain neutral, but the others overruled them; they said it was the settlers that had brought all the trouble. They bought arms and ammunition where they could. They practised military movements, in which they were already quite proficient. General Shanks says, that "Joseph's party was thoroughly disciplined; that they rode at full gallop along the mountain side in a steady formation by fours; formed twos, at a given signal, with perfect precision, to cross a narrow bridge; then galloped into line, reined in to a sudden halt, and dismounted with as much system as regulars." June 13th arrived; the thirty days were up; the soldiers had not arrived. Over on Salmon River three Indians killed an old hermit ranchman named Devine. The taste of blood whetted their appetites. On the morning of the 14th they killed three more, and in the afternoon another. They mounted the horses of their victims, and hurried to Camas Prairie, where the main body of Indians was encamped. They rode through the camp displaying the spoils of their bloodshed, and calling on others to join them.

Joseph and Ollacut were not in the camp; they had placed their teepees away from the others on account of Joseph's wife, who was sick. White Bird, the next in rank and influence, gave way. He rode through the camp, crying, "All must join now. There is blood. You will be punished if you delay." Seventeen warriors joined the three, and they hastened back to the Salmon River. Eight more fell victims to them, including Harry Mason, who had whipped the two Indians. On the night of the 14th another party attacked the people of the Cottonwood house—a ranch on the road between Mount Idaho and Fort Lapwai—who were trying to escape to Mount Idaho. Two men and a boy were killed and the others badly wounded, two men subsequently dying of their injuries. It is said that two women were outraged. Joseph denies it, by implication. It may have been done without his knowledge. He was not there. He protested against hostilities until they had gone so far that war was inevitable; then he took command, and the Indians moved to White Bird Cañon, where they prepared to fight soldiers.

They had not long to wait. Colonel Perry was hurrying down from Fort Lapwai with ninety men. He reached Grangeville, four miles from Mount Idaho, on the evening of the 16th, was joined by ten citizens, and marched on through the night to White Bird Cañon, sixteen miles away. He reached the head of the cañon at daybreak, and began his descent of the broad trail, to surprise the Indians and prevent their escape across the Salmon. Down in the cañon Joseph watched his approach through a field-glass. Some of the Indians became nervous, and suggested that it would be better to move across the Salmon, where the soldiers could not reach them. Joseph said, "We will fight them here." A party of mounted warriors were put in ambush behind a hill on the south side of the cañon. The rest, under Joseph, were crouched on the ground, squarely across the trail, hidden behind rocks and in hollows. On came the soldiers until well within range, when every bush and rock poured out its fire. At the same time the party of mounted warriors appeared on the left. The foremost ranks deployed to engage the force in front, and the rear wheeled to meet the flank movement. Men were falling; the Indians were moving up on the hills, making towards the rear; some one cried to fall back to the next ridge. The next ridge was gained, with the enemy on their heels. There was no time to stop. The attempts of the officers to rally the men were only momentarily successful. The Indians were pressing along the sides of the cañon to gain the head and cut off retreat. Part of the command reached the ascent and hurried out. The remainder, under Lieutenant Theller, were cut off. They saw the bar across the way, and wheeled into a ravine to the left. The Indians were upon them in a moment, thinning them out with their murderous fire, through which only a few stragglers made their way unscathed to the summit. Across the rugged country the Indians pursued the flying troops for twelve miles; but the soldiers were out of that dreadful cañon now and had regained their wits. The officers obtained control, and the retreat of the sixty-five who escaped from the cañon was conducted in order. Four miles from Mount Idaho Joseph withdrew his men. He had fought and won his first battle.

The military reputation of the Nez Percés was altered. It would require more men to whip them. Reinforcements were started from all neighboring points. Skirmishing and minor engagements continued. A detachment was sent to arrest Looking Glass, who had not yet joined the hostiles, and bring him in. His camp was destroyed and seven hundred and twenty-five ponies captured, but the Indians all escaped and went to Joseph. Lieutenant Rains, with ten men and a scout named Foster, was sent on a reconnoissance. The party was surrounded and every man killed. A company of volunteers, under Captain Randall, was attacked on the Mount Idaho road; two were killed and two wounded. The remainder would have been killed if relief had not arrived. On July 11th General Howard and his assembled troops were in sight of the enemy, who had crossed the country to the Lapwai reservation, and taken position on the Clearwater to give him battle. Howard had four hundred fighting men besides his teamsters and train men. He had a howitzer and two Gatling guns. Joseph had about three hundred warriors, with the squaws for assistants. The soldiers advanced in line of battle, leaving the supply trains unguarded. Joseph saw this and sent thirty warriors to attack them. The glass of an officer caught this movement just in the nick of time. A messenger was sent back to hurry them into the lines, and a company of cavalry galloped to their protection. The Indians gained the smaller train first, killed two packers, and disabled their animals, but the fire of the cavalry drove them off. The large train gained the lines uninjured. All that afternoon the battle raged, with its charges and counter-charges, its feinting and fighting. All night both parties strengthened their breastworks and kept up a desultory fire. In the morning the battle was renewed and kept up, with no perceptible advantage to either side until the middle of the afternoon. Then a fresh company of cavalry appeared to reinforce Howard. The artillery moved back to meet them, and, having made a junction, they struck the enemy's line on the left and charged down it. The Indians fought stubbornly for a few minutes, gave way, and fled. The victorious troops pressed after them so hotly that the artillery covered their camp, beyond the Clearwater, before their lodges could be struck. The Indians, however, made their escape with their herds, and sufficient supplies for their purposes, and, before the troops could cross, a large body of warriors was seen on the right front, apparently returning for an attack. While preparations were being made to meet this force, the remainder of the Indians continued their flight; and when the preparations of the soldiers were complete, the returning warriors, having accomplished their purpose by this feint, were found to have disappeared. In the morning the troops continued the pursuit of the retreating Indians, who were still in sight from the heights, only to fall into an ambuscade by the Nez Percés rear-guard and be thrown into confusion. Night found the Indians safely encamped, in an almost impregnable position, at the entrance to the Lolo trail. Joseph had fought his second battle, against heavy odds, and though beaten had brought off his forces most creditably.

What was to be done? There was another trail which formed a junction with the Lolo, fifteen miles back of Joseph's position ; send a detachment, by a masked movement, to that point, to cut off his retreat and strike him from the rear. General Joseph was not so easily trapped. The detachment was hardly under way, on its pretended march to Lapwai, before Joseph's camp was broken, and the Indians were falling back beyond the dangerous point. It was at first intended to follow him closely, but that plan was abandoned. A small force, which was started up the trail, ran into the rear-guard rather disastrously, and then that ubiquitous rear-guard dropped back on the settlements and carried off a lot of horses. The settlers were sure that as soon as the soldiers were started on the trail the Nez Percés would be back, by some other route, devastating the settlements. What a wonderful trail that was for a highway ! It begins on Lolo Creek, a tributary of the Clearwater, crosses the Bitter Root Mountains, and comes to the lowland again by the Lou-Lou fork of the Bitter Root River on the east. Any mountain trail, especially any Indian trail, is bad enough, with its sharp rocks, its fallen timber, its slippery pitches, and its roaring torrents; but this one seems to have been made for its sterling impassable qualities. Says General Sherman, "This is universally admitted, by all who have travelled it—from Lewis and Clarke to Captain Winters—as one of the worst *trails* for man and beast on this continent." The Nez Percés came safely across it. In the valley of the Lou-Lou they were confronted by a hastily prepared fort, held by Captain Rawn with a few regulars and some volunteers. Looking Glass talked to them. "We will not fight the settlers if they do not fight us. We are going by you to the buffalo country. Will you let us go in peace?" Rawn refused to let them pass, but the volunteers rebelled. The Nez Percés had always been "good Indians" on the Bitter Root. The settlers had no grounds for complaint in their conduct, as they had passed annually to and from the buffalo country. They decided that, in the expressive frontier phrase, "they had not lost any Indians," and consequently were not hunting for any. The Nez Percés might go by, and God speed them out of the country. The Indians not only passed in peace, but they stopped at the villages of Stevensville and Corvallis and

traded with these pacific whites. They also left a spy at
Corvallis, who stopped until Howard had come up and passed
on, and then sped away on his cayuse to General Joseph with
full particulars.

Meantime a potent ally of the white man had been at
work. The telegraph had ticked its message of alarm all
through the country to the east, and the troops at the various
posts were on the alert. General Gibbon, with one hundred and
ninety cavalrymen, had hastened from Helena across to Fort
Missoula, on the Bitter Root, but arrived too late to intercept
the Indians. They had gone on to the south, up the Bitter
Root valley, past Ross's hole, and into the valley of the Big
Hole River. Gibbon followed on their trail. He came close
up to them on August 8th, while they were all unsuspecting.
He waited through the night, and in the stillness of "the hour
before the dawn" he swept through their camp in a furious
charge, completely surprising them. Surely now the Nez
Percés were whipped. Not a bit of it. They rallied and re-
took their camp. They drove the soldiers back to a wooded point where, behind rude barricades and in hastily dug
trenches, they defended themselves through the following
day. At eleven o'clock that night, having captured Gibbon's
howitzer, they withdrew, leaving Gibbon wounded, and his
command so crippled that it could not pursue. Joseph had
fought and won his third battle. Howard joined Gibbon
here, and in the presence of officers and men, his Bannock
scouts scalped and mutilated the bodies of the Nez Percé
dead. There were many dead, men, women, and children, but
worst of all Looking Glass, their ablest diplomat, lay stark
upon that field. The Nez Percés neither took scalps nor
mutilated during this war. They were neither civilized nor
the allies of civilization. They were only defrauded Indians.
A few days later they captured an Indian scout attached to
Howard's command, and said to him, "Your men kill our
women and children; your men are worse than the Indians."
"No, no," said the scout, "my chief is kind. I saw him and
his officers bury the women and children with their own hands.
They don't want to hurt the women and children." Then
his captors released him unharmed.

PLAIN OF THE GEYSERS.

Sunday, August 19th, Joseph had crossed the continental divide again into Idaho, and camped on the great Camas prairie which lies west of the National Park, on the Yellowstone. He had captured two hundred and fifty good horses, replenished his supplies and put his forces in excellent condition. Howard's forces were one day's march behind him. They camped on the prairie also. A detachment had been sent ahead, under Lieutenant Bacon, to hold Tacher's Pass, the most accessible roadway across the divide into the park. The sentinels and pickets were properly posted and the weary soldiers slept peacefully. In the faint starlight swarthy forms crept through the long grass. Hobbles were cut and bells were removed from bell-mares. Off to the east a troop of horsemen came in sight, riding back over the trail of the Nez Percés. They rode in column of fours, regularly and without haste. "It must be Bacon's men coming back," said the pickets. They came within hailing distance and were challenged. Their answer betrayed them. The picket opened fire. Then arose a wild yell that startled the soldiers from their sleep, and a confused discharge of small-arms, after which all the horses and mules that were not fastened were seen scampering away with a crowd of Indians after them, yelling like demons. Fortunately enough horses and mules were left to mount three companies of cavalry. They hurried out into the night after the Indians, came up with part of them, and recovered half a hundred of the lost animals. Before morning the Indians were back after these, and stampeded a part of them. Then they went on with their retreat, leaving the soldiers with one dead and six wounded men to care for; also to wait till more horses and supplies could be obtained from Virginia City. We must credit General Joseph with a successful surprise.

On went the Nez Percés through Tacher's Pass, where Bacon had missed them, and into the park; on through the pleasant open country of the western portion to the region of the hot springs, the geysers, and the sulphur lands. Here they met Cowan's party, consisting of Mr. Cowan, his wife, sister-in-law, brother-in-law, and two others. Three of the men were left for dead; one and the two ladies were carried away. Horrible fate!—carried into Indian captivity. General Howard says they were "afterwards rescued." Joseph says, "On the way we captured one white man and two white women. We released them at the end of three days. They were treated kindly. The women were not insulted.

THE STINKING WATER.

Can the white soldiers tell me of one time when Indian women were taken prisoners and held three days, and then released without being insulted? Were the Nez Percé women who fell into the hands of General Howard's soldiers treated with as much respect? I deny that a Nez

Percé was ever guilty of such a crime." On went the Indians, down by Yellowstone Lake, over the Yellowstone River, burning Baronett's Bridge behind them, and then, after a feint in the direction of the Stinking Water, they slipped through a narrow cañon to Clark's Fork, and down it to the Yellowstone again. By this movement Joseph avoided Colonel Sturgis, who had been warned, and come over from the Powder River country with six companies of cavalry (three hundred and fifty men) and some friendly Crows. Deceived by Joseph's movement, and by the messages he had received, Sturgis hastened to block up the trail down the Stinking Water. He discovered his mistake quickly, however, and took up the chase at once. On September 13th he overtook the Nez Percés on the alkaline, sage-brush plains across the Yellowstone. The rear-guard of the Indians engaged

GENERAL S. D. STURGIS.

the troops, while the remainder turned into the narrow valley of Cañon Creek; but a detachment under Captain Benteen circled around the fight and pressed the retreating herds so closely that over four hundred ponies had to be abandoned. The Indians then reunited at the mouth of the cañon, posting themselves wherever there was a chance for shelter. There was but one way of reaching them, and that was direct pursuit. All day the Indians dropped back, fighting for every foot of ground, and at dark the exhausted soldiers withdrew to camp at the mouth of the cañon. In the morning Sturgis was reinforced by a large party of Crow Indians, who pressed the Nez Percés so vigorously that five hundred more of the ponies were abandoned. March as they would,

42

the soldiers could not lessen the distance between themselves and the Nez Percés, who retired up the Mussel Shell River, and then, circling back of the Judith Mountains, struck the Missouri at Cow Island on the 23d. Joseph had fought his fourth battle, had held in check a greatly superior force, and brought off his people in comparative safety.

Cow Island is the limit of low-water navigation on the Upper Missouri, one hundred and twenty-three miles below Fort Benton, which is the high-water limit. The boats that run up to it are little steamers that have, in addition to ordinary steamboat machinery, long wooden arms, which are thrust out and worked by steam windlasses, to push the boat off from sand-bars and snags. Their navigation is much like that of those big water-beetles, which swim where there is water enough, and crawl where there is not. The landing is close by the mouth of Cow Creek. There was no settlement at the place; only a landing, with a little intrenchment near by, held by twelve soldiers and four citizens. The Nez Percés attacked it, but drew off at night, after wounding two of the garrison and burning all the freight at the landing. Major Ilges came down from Fort Benton with a small force, and followed them for a day or two, but wisely abandoned the pursuit after a skirmish with them. The Indians moved on leisurely to the north. They were now coming into a beautiful country, a "very Eden" it has been called, lying about the Bear Paw and Little Rocky Mountains. It is a country of romance also, the reputed locality of the celebrated "Lost Cabin of Montana," that miners have been crazy over for the last decade. They established their camp in a crescent curve of Snake Creek, a tributary of Milk River, thirty-five miles south of the British line. They had rid themselves of every force that had attacked them, but the telegraph and the messengers of the whites had done their work again. From Fort Keogh, away over on the Yellowstone, Col. Nelson A. Miles was coming with nine companies of mounted men, a company and a half of infantry, a company of white and Indian scouts, a breech-loading Hotchkiss gun, and a 12-pounder Napoleon. They reached Carroll, on the Missouri, below Cow Island, and learned of the events at the latter place. On the evening of the 25th three hundred and seventy-five men began their march from Carroll to cut off the retreating Nez Percés. Joseph did not know of this new and powerful enemy. He was resting quietly only one day's march from his bravely-earned safety. If he had only known—but he had no telegraph wires.

On the morning of the 30th the camp of the Indians was attacked by the soldiers. The Nez Percés knew of their coming only long enough to gain the ravines which led into the creek valley along the bluffs. Their herd, to the number of eight hundred, was cut off by one battalion of cavalry, while two more, with the scouts, charged the camp. These barely reached the village before they recoiled under the fearful fire of the Indians, with one-fifth of their force killed and wounded. For four days and nights the forces remained facing each other. The whites controlled the situation. They were unwilling to attempt the capture of the camp by storm, for that would involve a heavy loss of life, but they had the Indians surrounded and were damaging them with shells. The Indians could not escape through the lines without abandoning their wounded and helpless. Says Joseph, "We could have escaped from Bear Paw Mountain if we had left our wounded, old women, and children behind. We were unwilling to do this. We had never heard of a wounded Indian recovering while in the hands of white men." How deftly does this spiritualistic heathen strike us, and how keenly do his blows cut! There was only one power on earth from which they could hope for aid. Over the British line was Sitting Bull, who had been fighting Miles all summer. Perhaps this chief, who had said, "There is not one white man who loves an Indian, and not a true Indian but hates a white man," actuated by enmity to the whites, would come to the rescue. So they sent messengers, improved their defences, and held their ground, occasionally parleying with Colonel Miles; but Sitting Bull did not come, and on the morning of October 5th they surrendered—those who were left. Ollacut had fallen here at Snake Creek, and so had the old Dreamer-drummer, Too-hul-hul-sute, with twenty-seven others. White Bird had fled in the night with a band which, it was afterwards learned, numbered one hundred and five. They reached British America. Joseph, be it understood, surrendered on honorable terms. Colonel Miles says, "I acted on what I supposed was the original design of the government to place these Indians on their own reservation, and so informed them, and also sent assurances to the war parties that were out, and those who had escaped, that they would be taken to Tongue River, and retained for a time, and sent across the mountains as soon as the weather permitted in the spring." The Indians understood also that they were to retain what stock they still had. General Howard had come up and was present at the surrender. The negotiations were conducted through his Nez Percé scouts. He issued directions to Colonel Miles to send the Indians to his department in the spring, unless he received "instructions from higher authority." " Thus," says General Sherman, " has terminated one of the most extraordinary Indian wars of which there is any record. The Indians throughout displayed a courage and skill that elicited universal praise; they abstained from scalping, let captive women go free, did not commit indiscriminate murder of peaceful families, which is usual, and fought with almost scientific skill, using advance and rear guards, skirmish lines and field fortifications."

Of course the Nez Percés were sent back to the Lapwai reservation, as Colonel Miles had agreed. Well, no. They were sent to Fort Lincoln; then to Fort Leavenworth, where they remained for a few weeks; and then to the Quapaw Agency in Indian Territory. Says Commissioner Hayt, in his report of November 1, 1877, " Upon the capture of Joseph and his Indians, the first question that arises is, ' What shall be done with them?' Humanity prompts us to send them back and place them on the Nez Percé reservation, as Joseph and his followers have shown themselves to be brave men and skilful soldiers, who, with one exception, have observed the rules of civilized warfare, and have not mutilated their dead enemies. There is, however, an insuperable difficulty in the way, owing to the fact that at the beginning of the outbreak of the Nez Percé war, twenty-one whites in the immediate vicinity of Joseph's home were murdered in cold blood

JOSEPH'S LAST BATTLE.

by the Indians, and six white women were outraged. Because of these crimes, there would be no peace nor safety for Joseph and his Indians on their old reservation, or in its vicinity, as the friends and relatives of the victims would wage an unrelenting war upon the offenders. But for these foul crimes these Indians would be sent back to the reservation in Idaho. Now, however, they will have to be sent to the Indian Territory; and this will be no hardship to them, as the difference in the temperature between that latitude and their old home is inconsiderable." How complacently does this gentleman sit in his easy-chair in Washington, and thrum the heartstrings of this outraged people. "Humanity," indeed! What did honesty and common decency prompt? Was it nothing that these warriors laid down their arms on Colonel Miles's promise, in General Howard's presence, that they should be returned to Idaho? Cannot a commander in the field plight the faith of this nation and have his word respected? "Foul crimes!" What men were "murdered in cold blood?" and what "six white women were outraged?" There seems to be a feeling here that an Indian should never shoot any one but a soldier. Had the soldiers done them any injury? Had any one injured them directly except these settlers who located on their lands and "wished to be bought out?" Had Harry Mason and Finley and the rest done them no wrong? But suppose there were here twenty-seven cold-blooded crimes, how many times over did the whites exceed that number in this trouble? What of the four Indians murdered before they lifted a hand? What of the stock-stealing? What of the scalping and mutilation, on three different occasions, by Bannock and white scouts? What of the treatment of captured women? What of our cold-blooded steal of their country? What of our cold-blooded violation of Colonel Miles's agreement? What of the one thousand or more of horses that they had when they surrendered, which were to be returned to them, and of which Joseph says only, "Somebody has got our horses?" What of the cold-blooded refusal of the authorities to return the Indians to Idaho, when Joseph told them he would never have surrendered if Colonel Miles had not promised this—when he begged them to keep that promise? We have too much "humanity;" it might be profitable to experiment with honesty and good faith for a time.

But passing the coloring of the commissioner's statement, what truth was there in his two reasons for locating the Nez Percés in Indian Territory; namely, that there would be no hardship from the change of climate, and the existence of a thirst for revenge in Idaho? To avoid question as to the truth of Joseph's sad story, we will take up only official statements. In his report of November 1, 1878, Commissioner Hayt says, "The number of prisoners reported by the War Department, December 4th last, was as follows: 79 men, 178 women, and 174 children, making a total of 431. A few scattered members of the band were subsequently taken by the military and also sent to Fort Leavenworth. . . . The number reported to have been turned over to the inspector and agent was 410, three of whom—children—died on the route. Inspector McNeil reported that the camping-place selected by the commandant for these Indians, and where he found them, was in the Missouri River bottom, about two miles above the fort, 'between a lagoon and the river, the worst possible place that could have been selected; and the sanitary condition of the Indians proved it.' The physician in charge said that 'one-half could be said to be sick, and all were affected by the poisonous malaria of the camp.' After the arrival of Joseph and his band in the Indian Territory, the bad effect of their location at Fort Leavenworth manifested itself in the prostration by sickness at one time of 260 out of the 410, and within a few months they have lost by death more than one-quarter of the entire number. A little care in the selection of a wholesome location near Fort Leavenworth would have saved very much sickness and many lives." In addition to the facts mentioned, the agent, H. W. Jones, reported that they had been without medicine, and concluded thus: "I am now glad to be able to say that their sickness is abating, and I believe the worst is over. They now number 86 men, 168 women, and 137 children." Was this all due to the malaria from the Missouri bottom-lands? Let us see.

In June, 1879, the Nez Percés were removed to a new

reservation, just west of the Ponca agency (strange that these two shamefully mistreated tribes should be thrown together), on the Salt Fork of the Arkansas River. The philosophic Agent Whiteman reported of them on August 31, 1879: " The location, I think, is a healthy one, and the Indians are as healthy as could be expected. There is this fact about the Nez Percés, which, perhaps, is hardly ever considered, viz., that most of the young, able-bodied men and women were engaged in their late war with the government, and many of them were killed and wounded, and a large proportion of the Nez Percés brought to the Indian Territory were old people and children, which accounts in a great measure for the many deaths which have occurred among them. I have also observed both among the Nez Percés and Poncas, who came from northern climates, that lung diseases are very prevalent. I think that seven Indians out of every ten have their lungs diseased so badly that they could not live in any climate; and while I do not desire to depreciate the fearful ravages made by malaria on Northern Indians in the Indian Territory, yet I give it as my opinion, which I believe will be borne out by statistics, that more Indians die from pulmonary diseases in the Northwest than die from the effects of malaria in the Indian Territory .... The Nez Percés number at this time three hundred and seventy." It is to be regretted that Mr. Whiteman did not explain why, under his theory, the Indians of the Northwest were not extinct many years ago. On August 31, 1880, Agent Whiting reported: " The old Ponca saw-mill was removed to the Nez Percé reservation in July last, and we are now sawing out lumber for the purpose of erecting houses for the Indians, and I hope to have them all comfortably housed before cold weather." The statistical tables for the same year show nine births and twenty-one deaths for the year, but give the total remaining on the reservation at only three hundred and forty-four.

On September 6, 1881, Agent Jordan reported: " The Nez Percés located at Oakland comprise three hundred and twenty-eight souls, and I am sorry to be compelled to report that there has been a large amount of sickness and many deaths among them during the last year. This arises from

the fact that they have not become acclimated, and are to a
great extent compelled to live in teepees, the cloth of which
has become so rotten from long wear and the effects of the
weather as to be no longer capable of keeping out the rain,
by which they were soaked during the last spring. The
tribe, unless something is done for them, will soon become
extinct. . . . They are greatly in need of a church in which
to hold services, and for want of one are compelled to meet
under an arbor covered with branches and leaves. They
keep the Sabbath - day holy, abstaining from all kinds of
work, and the service at the arbor is attended by every member of the tribe, whether a communicant or not. . . . Poor as
they are, they have contributed forty-five dollars with which
to buy the lumber, etc., necessary to build a house for their
pastor. . . . Love of country and home, as in all brave people,
is very largely developed in this tribe, and they long for the
mountains, the valleys, the streams, and the clear springs of
water of their old home. They are cleanly to a fault, and
most of them have adopted the dress, and as far as possible
the habits, of the white man. They keep their stock in good
order, and are a hard-working, painstaking people. I hope
by the time winter comes on to have them all in comfortable
houses." This is enough to show the justice of Mr. Hayt's
statement that a removal to Indian Territory would be " no
hardship" to them. It is probably enough for all present
purposes. Picture to yourself these wretched people, sick,
destitute, with no decent shelter, longing for the clear waters
and balmy breezes of their stolen home. God help the victims of our " humanity." In all seriousness, it would have
been far more humane to have put them in some penitentiary, where they could at least have had medical attention,
and shelter from the rain and snow.

Comment on Mr. Hayt's climate proposition is needless.
How about the revengeful whites? It does not appear that
the government took any active steps to find what the sentiment of their former white neighbors was. Mr. Hayt's theory was evidently put on paper before investigation, for it is
dated less than a month after the surrender. There was subsequently much difference of opinion, in a speculative way,

as to what the feeling was. In 1883 Rev. A. L. Lindsley set about ascertaining it definitely. He prepared a series of questions, which he submitted to prominent residents of the Wallowa and Salmon River country, and from their answers drew the following conclusions: "There appears to be no active ill-will cherished towards these Indians, nor any opposition to the return of the exiles. There was a general agreement, in Judge Leland's opinion, who thought the aggrieved whites will take revenge. This will excite the Indians to retaliation; and that again will probably occasion another outbreak, or at least create public disturbances. There is only one way of prevention: to surrender to the authorities of Nez Percé County the survivors of the thirty-two Indians who were indicted for outrage and murder committed before the war began. It is known that a number of these are still living; some of them are with White Bird, who is in Canada, and some with Joseph. The Attorney-general of the United States answered a former demand for them by advising a suspension of all action in the case, with which the Idaho court complied. It is a suspension only; the return of these indicted men free will not escape the notice of the court. Even if it should, there are men who would excite a popular demand for justice. There is great reason to fear, however, that there are men in Kamiah Prairie and Mount Idaho who would not wait for the court to take action if these indicted Indians return free. A frequent remark used to be heard that certain Indians would be 'shot on sight.' Agent Monteith and others have no doubt that some men would carry out their threats. One of them is well known— 'he don't think he'd hunt 'em up to kill 'em; he thinks it mean to shoot even an Indian in the dark; but it wouldn't be safe for any of them to come where he is.' I must restrain my pen and assume much. The sum is this: that the peace can be preserved in the return of these Indians by the surrender of the indicted ones to the Idaho authorities—or sending them off to join White Bird in Canada. What the full effect of the alternative would be it would be difficult to estimate."

I submit that there is here no desire for revenge which

would justify the nation in breaking its faith with these Indians. I submit that an American who is sufficiently civilized to admit that it is "mean to shoot even an Indian in the dark," is humane enough not to have harassed the wretched remnant of these victims when he had been informed of their sufferings in exile. But supposing it were otherwise, what force was there in this plea? Is the nation to be prevented from being just because a score of men threaten to be lawless? Where was our army? There was no trouble in finding soldiers when it was anticipated that the Indians would rebel under the outrage put upon them. There had been no trouble in finding soldiers to station in the South when it was claimed that negroes were deprived of the right of suffrage. There had been no trouble in finding soldiers when strikers interfered with the property of capitalists. Is it unlawful to protect Indians, or was the government afraid of these desperate people of the West? If the latter, would it not have been well to have appointed a committee of " judicious men " to beg them not to become murderers? There remains another matter for consideration back of this. Supposing that the blood-thirsty people of Idaho could have been satisfied only by leaving the Nez Percés in Indian Territory, and that it were necessary to satisfy them, why were these Indians left in such destitution? (The alternative of surrendering the indicted Indians is not considered, because the government could not honorably have adopted it.) Why were not their ponies returned to them? What became of the lumber that was sawed for them in 1880? How did it happen that they must deepen their poverty by purchasing lumber for their pastor's house in 1881, while they sat under the drippings of their rotten teepees? Why were they not paid for their share of the Nez Percés lands, if the government must persist in holding them bound by the treaty of 1863? They had certainly received none of the purchase-money before they were sent to Indian Territory.

It was not possible that Mr. Hayt's flimsy reasons for keeping them in exile should long be regarded by any one but himself, although the lack of information concerning their case was not supplied in the Indian Bureau for years. In

1882 Commissioner Price said of Joseph's band: "Not in the least excusing or attempting to palliate the crimes alleged to have been committed by them, it is but fair to say that their warfare was conducted with a noticeable absence of savage barbarity on their part, and that they persistently claim that when they surrendered to General Miles it was with the express stipulation that they should be sent back to Idaho. Whether this alleged stipulation be true or not [General Miles had said officially that it was], it is a fact that their unfortunate location near Fort Leavenworth, when in charge of the military, and the influences of the climate where they are

GENERAL N. A. MILES.

now located in the Indian Territory, have caused much sickness among them; their ranks have been sadly depleted, and it is claimed that if they are much longer compelled to remain in their present situation, the entire band will become virtually extinct. It is now about five years since the surrender, and a sufficient time has probably elapsed to justify the belief that no

concerted effort will be taken to avenge wrongs alleged to have been perpetrated by these people so many years ago. The band now numbers only about three hundred and twenty-two souls, and the reservation in Idaho is ample to accommodate them comfortably, in addition to those who are already there, who are substantially self-supporting and who have enough to spare a portion for their less fortunate brethren, and, as I understand, are willing to give them such aid. The deep-rooted love for the 'old home' which is so conspicuous among them, and their longing desire to leave the warm, debilitating climate of the Indian Territory for the more healthy and invigorating air of the Idaho mountains, can never be eradicated, and any longer delay, with a hope of a final contentment on their part with their present situation, is, in my judgment, futile and unnecessary. In view of all the facts, I am constrained to believe that the remnant of this tribe should be returned to Idaho, if possible, early next spring, and I respectfully suggest that this matter be submitted to Congress at its next session, with a recommendation that an appropriation be made sufficient to meet the necessary expenses of a removal thither."

No immediate action was taken on this recommendation, but in the succeeding year the work of undoing this great wrong was begun. When the agency school broke up for vacation in May, 1883, the teacher, James Reuben, started for Idaho with twenty-nine of the exiles, mostly widows and orphans. James Reuben, by-the-way, was a Nez Percé, who had been educated and converted through the labors of Miss McBeth, a lady who went among the Nez Percés many years ago, and has devoted her life and her fortune to their advancement. Success has attended her devotion, and her preachers and teachers have done excellent work among other bands. It was, indeed, chiefly to the efforts of native missionaries, whom she had prepared for the work and sent out, that the rapid growth of Christianity among Joseph's band in the Indian Territory was due. The remainder of the band was still left there to suffer and mourn. On August 15, 1884, Agent Scott reported: "They are extremely anxious to return to their own country. They regard themselves as exiles. The climate does not seem to agree with them; many of them have died; and there is a tinge of melancholy in their bearing and conversation that is truly pathetic. I think they should be sent back, as it seems clear they will never take root and prosper in this locality." Whether this report moved the government, or whether the pleadings of their friends in Oregon at last induced the authorities to abandon the cruel injustice of the past eight years, I do not know; but last spring the remnant of the band, now numbering only two hundred and sixty-eight, were sent back to their mountain homes. Joseph and a few others were placed at Colville

Agency, in Washington Territory, and the remainder were put with their brethren on Lapwai reservation. The return of the exiles was a great occasion at Lapwai. The Indians collected from every part of the reservation to greet them. Addresses of welcome were made by Silas Whitman and James Lawyer, native preachers, and then, says a witness of the scene, "an earnest response was made by 'Tom Hill,' on behalf of the returned wanderers. His heart was too full for him to command his words, but as it was, he made a most impressive speech, delivered with matchless oratory. He touched on their long confinement in a dreary land, a land of many sorrows; spoke feelingly of their constant longings for their mountain home, which they had given up all hopes of ever seeing again; humbly acknowledged the goodness and mercy of God in permitting some of them to stand once more on the banks of the Lapwai in the presence of so many old-time friends; referred gratefully to the interposition of the Church and the law in their behalf, and closed with the announcement that their only desire now is to be henceforth law-abiding people and believers in the God of heaven. At the close of the speech hand-shaking began, which lasted for over an hour. Headed by your correspondent (Rev. G. L. Deffenbaugh), the long procession of our people filed past, and took the hand of every man, woman, and child. Friend met with friend, fathers and mothers with their long-lost sons and daughters. It was very touching to watch the play of features as the mind went through the process of identifying the face of a relative or friend, and then, after the decision was made, to hear the glad expressions, 'Is this you?' mentioning the name; 'Is it you, father?' or 'Is that you, brother?' Only one who had a heart of stone could have stood by and not entered with spirit into the joys of the occasion. But to one standing near the end of the line a different scene presented itself. Some having taken the hands of all present, and missing the faces of those they had hoped to see, gave vent to their sorrow in uncontrollable weeping. Certainly, the most cruel-hearted Indian-hater could not have stood by unaffected." And Joseph could not share in even this small recompense for past suffering. It was feared that local prejudice would make it dangerous for him to come. Joseph—ah no! he had been guilty of fighting like a man for justice and for the right. He was a criminal—in Idaho.

Who is to be blamed for all this wickedness and wrong? Incidentally, various persons who have been mentioned, but the greatest responsibility is apparently with the Commission of 1876, sent out to arrange for an equitable settlement with these Indians, who, with the exception of Lieutenant-colonel Wood, reported that the Indians ought to be sent to the reservation, by force, if necessary. Their names are Gen. O. O. Howard, D. H. Jerome, William Stickney, and A. C. Barstow. It has been mentioned that in 1875 General Howard took the position that the Lower Nez Percés ought to have the Wallowa country. Why he changed his mind in 1876 does not appear. Joseph says that when Howard came back he said, "I will not let white men laugh at me the next time I come." Whether Joseph means that he used these words, or merely thus indicates his own guess at the general's motives, the chances are that he struck the correct theory. In the spring of 1879, when there appeared in the *North American Review* Joseph's statement of his case—the most magnificent piece of Indian eloquence that was ever known, with the exception of the much disputed speech of Logan—General Howard rushed into print with a reply. Therein he promised a book on the subject, which appeared in 1881. If the existence of the publications be not sufficient evidence of his sensitiveness to public opinion, the inquiring reader will find ample confession of it in the pages of both productions. I do not find that his part in the work of the Commission is brought prominently forward in either. If there is any mention of the fact that he was a member of the Commission, in his book I have failed to discover it. I do find his objection to the public holding responsible an "army officer who is subject to the requisition of the Indian Department," and his statement that "the Indian management did not belong to my department." I do find him giving a summary of Governor Grover's letter, the ideas of which the Commission adopted, and then adding these words, "So much for our ideas of justice. First, we acknowledge and confirm by treaty to Indians a sort

of title to vast regions.   Afterwards we continue, in a strictly
legal manner, to do away with both the substance and the
shadow of title.   Wiser heads than Joseph's have been puzzled by this manner of balancing the scales."   Who would
read these words and imagine that their author had sat as a
judge in this case, and recommended the injustice over which
he sighs.

I do not presume to criticise General Howard's conduct
of the campaign.   It is quite probable that he did the best
he could—possibly as well as any one would have done.   He
had for an enemy the hardest fighting Indians on the continent,
led by the ablest uneducated chief that the world ever saw.   I
do criticise him for his part in the Commission, where he could
probably have induced a recommendation of fair and honorable treatment of these Indians, instead of the mistreatment
that was recommended.   I do criticise him for writing in
1879, those cruel words: "Let them settle down, and keep
quiet, in the Indian Territory, as the Modocs have done, and
they will thrive as they do."   I do criticise him for evading
the real issue in his attempted defence.   I do criticise him
for trying to make a defence.   I would that he had been noble enough to say, "I was mistaken."   I would that he had
said to the government and the people, "When I recommended the removal of these Indians, I thought they would go
without fighting.   I thought that they would have real advantages on the reservation which would compensate them
for their loss of freedom.   I did not imagine that they would
be roused to madness by the wrong we were doing.   I did
not think that the plighted faith of Colonel Miles and myself
would be broken.   I did not dream that the Indians would
be taken to swampy bottom-lands and shelterless plains to die
of unknown diseases.   I was wrong, and I wish to have my
wrong righted, as far as possible, by having them sent back
to their mountain homes."   If he had said this, the wrong
would probably have been righted long ago.

The great majority of the American people desire that the
Indians should be treated fairly and honorably—not because
they are Indians, but because they are men, and we desire
that all men should be so treated.   It can but be humiliating

43

that our second century should begin with such a wrong against that race, which, it must be confessed, has suffered at our hands, despite the wishes of the people. Yet there is nothing to relieve its monstrosity. It was not committed by rude and lawless men of the border, but by men selected from the nation for their supposed fitness for the work. It was not done when public sentiment might have been supposed to sustain harsh and unjust measures, but in the day of " advanced ideas " and under the lauded "humanitarian Indian policy " of our government. How tarnished are the tinsel vauntings of the admirers of that policy, in the light of this case! Taking it all in all, from the first time an Indian was kidnaped on the New England coast, and sold into slavery, down to the present day, Conestoga, Sand Creek, Bloody Point, and all, the treatment of the Nez Percés is the worst crime that the white man has perpetrated upon the red man. Heedless of this beam in our own eye, we have groaned over the wrongs of the Bulgarian Christians, waxed indignant at the harrying of the Russian Jews, and raged about England's treatment of the Irish. Look to your hands! They are red with innocent blood and dark with the stains of plunder. We may seek to justify ourselves by shallow casuistry, but if the time shall ever come when a just God shall judge between us and the Lower Nez Percés, what answer can we make?

CHAPTER XX.

WHITE RIVER AGENCY.

"The Utes must go!" How that cry resounded through Colorado in 1879 and 1880. "The Utes must go!" Everybody said so. If any one had been rash enough to dispute the proposition he would have been denounced as an enemy to public peace and prosperity. The newspapers kept the words standing for head-lines. People talked it, met together and resolved it, and finally accomplished it. It was a sentiment that arose several years before and gained strength steadily. Its original basis was that their reservation was rich in minerals and included the best agricultural and grazing lands in the state; that the Utes did not and would not develop these resources; and that the whites desired to develop them. At first this feeling was not so strong, because the whites were not numerous; and there were hundreds of acres of arable land that had not been taken up, and thousands of acres of mineral land that had not been prospected. But Colorado and all the adjoining territory were destined to a mighty revolution. It originated in the obscure mining-camp of Slabtown, or Oro City, in California Gulch, on the head-waters of the Arkansas River. The place first attracted attention in the time of the Pike's Peak excitement, when hardy gold-hunters were searching all through the ranges nearest the plains for deposits of the yellow metal. California, Stray Horse, and Iowa gulches were discovered; the towns of Oro, Malta, and Granite were established; and a population estimated at 10,000 occupied the region. In the course of four years they took out about $13,000,000 of gold; but after that the placers decreased in value, and were gradually abandoned until, in 1874, they were practically deserted. Work was prosecuted on them at intervals, however, and ranches

which had been established along the Arkansas and its tributaries were still occupied.

During the placer mining in California Gulch, the miners
had been much annoyed by a peculiar heavy substance, resembling clay, that clogged their rockers and interfered with their
work. In 1878 it was ascertained that this stuff was carbo-
nate of lead, and that it carried enough silver to make it valuable. It was already known that there were large deposits of
it above the town. Then ensued the most remarkable mining excitement ever known in America. Times were hard in
the East. The country was still suffering from the financial
disorders of 1873 and 1875. Railroads afforded speedy and
cheap transportation almost to the mines. Why not try the
West? In August, 1877, the camp of Slabtown was composed of a score of shanties. In June, 1878, it had a population of 400. In October, 1878, the city of Leadville had
6000 inhabitants; in April, 1879, it had 12,000, with additions coming at the rate of from 300 to 500 per day. But
this represented only a fraction of the people coming West.
The rival railroad lines across the plains had placed before
the public everywhere their most alluring prospectuses of
the country bordering on their lines, and beyond their ter-
mini, inducing thousands, who had been originally awakened to the desirability of Western fields of labor by the
Leadville discoveries, to go to other points. It was as well
that they did, for Leadville was already overloaded, and the
neighboring country for miles was staked out in mining
claims, that were worth less, actually, than the cost of surveying them, though their market value was for a time quite
respectable. The same thing occurred in many other places.
There were hundreds of acres that looked like overgrown
prairie-dog towns, so covered were they with the dumps of
sanguine prospectors, who had about as much knowledge of
mining as they had of the precession of the equinoxes. "Got
any indications?" some new arrival would ask. "Nothin'
very good, but you've got to dig for it if you find it. That's
the way George Fryer struck it." Then the inquiring tender-
foot would seek the most convenient unclaimed spot, adjust
the red flannel rag around his neck, worn to prevent pneumo-

THE SNOW RANGE.

nia, and begin digging. He had the same answer stored away for any one who asked him the reason of his faith.

The immigration increased until the summer of 1880, before it began its gradual return to a natural basis. Every train over the Union Pacific, Kansas Pacific, and Atchison, Topeka, & Santa Fé roads was uncomfortably overloaded. It appears, from the best data that are obtainable, that by railroad and wagon there came into Colorado on some days as many as five thousand people, and very seldom less than one thousand. Many of these returned, after a short stay, but the major part remained, or pressed on into the wilder country beyond. The influx of humanity was like a rising river. It filled the eastern valleys, crept up the mountain ranges, and poured into the valleys beyond. Onward, ever onward, it moved, gaining strength continually, until it was beating against the barrier of the reservation lines. Then the sentiment that "the Utes must go" gained strength rapidly. It was told in mysterious whispers that the reservation was a very treasure-house; the Elk Mountains were full of silver; there were placers on all the rivers. It was known that there were large deposits of coal and iron, and gold generally goes with iron. The impossibility of verifying the stories made them ten times greater, and increased credence in an equal ratio. What was the use of having the Utes there? There was plenty of land elsewhere, not rich in mineral, that would do just as well for them. Blank blank the Utes, any way. They were a miserable, lousy lot of savages, and a detriment to the country. Still, the sentiment did not obtain universally until the outbreak of 1879; then the whole state was put in a furor. The Utes were strong in numbers, well-armed, well-supplied with horses, and were warriors of no mean repute. They could cross either the Saguache or the Snow range, and strike the eastern settlements by a dozen different routes. The northern and southern settlements were at their mercy. Information was meagre and contradictory. There were hundreds of wild rumors. The only way to be safe was to be prepared for anything. Accordingly, men abandoned their work and organized for defence, at dozens of points, where there was, in fact, no danger at all. After the trouble was all over, it was learned that two or three hundred Indians, who had no intention of fighting except on their own lands, had thrown into confusion a hundred thousand people; but the scare had settled the matter. There were few who knew who the Utes were, or cared what they were. It made no difference what were their rights or what had been their wrongs. They were an injury to the interests of the entire state. If the United States did not remove them the people of Colorado would. The Utes must go!

There is no doubt that the Utes had been treated badly; there is no doubt that at least nine tenths of the charges made against them were unfounded. On the other hand, it is clear that their mistreatment had little, if anything, to do with the outbreak. The country of the Utes was not affected by any of the transcontinental thoroughfares. It lay south of the South Pass routes, and north of the road through the Spanish settlements. To the settlements on their borders they had been of so little trouble that no treaty with them was considered necessary until 1863. In the early days of the West some bands of them engaged in marauding, jointly with their allies, the Navahos and Apaches. On Christmas Day, 1854, a hundred Utes and Jicarillas, under Tierra Blanco, destroyed the settlement on the Arkansas, above the mouth of the Huerfano, killing fifteen men, capturing two women and some children, and running off all the stock of the settlement. Colonel Fauntleroy marched against these Indians from Fort Massachusetts, which had been established as a threat, for the preservation of peace, in the San Luis valley. His force consisted of two companies of regulars, two companies of volunteers, and Kit Carson's scouts. They surprised the Utes on the night of April 28, 1855, on the Arkansas, near Chalk Creek, about twenty miles above Poncha Pass.* The Indians had been holding a

---

* This pass leads from San Luis Park to the South Arkansas valley. The name was originally *Puncha* or *Punché*, the Ute word for a small plant, that they use for kil-li-kin-nick, which grows abundantly in the pass. When the post-office was established at Poncha Springs, in 1879, some backwoods philologists thought the word was the Mexican *poncho*, a blanket cloak; and the Post-office Department, with an admirable spirit of compromise, named it Poncha, which does not mean anything.

scalp-dance all night, and were struck at daybreak. Forty were killed, many wounded, six children were made prisoners, and all their property was captured. This blow had a very salutary effect on them. There were afterwards some petty depredations by the southern tribes, occasional disturbances with the Colorado miners, and some rather serious troubles on the Utah side, arising from Mormon influence, but never anything in the way of a general war. It has been claimed that as many as forty men were killed by them from 1860 to 1879; but many of these were people who were found dead, or had disappeared, and their taking off was blamed to the Utes in the absence of any other known cause. It should be remembered, also, that the plains Indians often entered this country, on war expeditions, and were at times mistaken for Utes. The Arapahoes engaged in the Rawlin's Springs massacre claimed to be Utes, and were supposed to be until after that affair was over. On the whole, the Utes may be called friendly, and were so regarded; but they were not admirers of civilization, and, with the exception of a few of the New Mexican bands, never showed much disposition to adopt "the white man's road." They preferred to live by the chase.

In 1863 the Tabequache Utes made a treaty accepting, as a reservation, a part of the lands they had always held in Western Colorado. There was some dissatisfaction, because payments were not made to them as they should have been; but it was smoothed over, and peaceful relations were maintained. In a few years it was thought best to put all the eastern Utes together. A treaty to effect this purpose was made with the principal bands on March 2, 1868, by Kit Carson, N. G. Taylor, and Governor Hunt; and the western part of Colorado, included between longitude 107°, a line fifteen miles north of latitude 40°, and the southern and western boundaries of the territory, was set apart to be theirs forever. There were seven principal bands. The Yampas (Bear Rivers) and Grand Rivers were located in the northern part of the reservation, with their agency on White River. The Tabequaches and Uncompahgrés were in the central part, with their agency at Los Pinos. The Wee-mi-nu-ches, Mu-a-ches, and Ca-po-tes, who were Southern Colorado and New Mexican Indians, were located in the southern part of the reservation. They had their agency at Los Pinos, with the Tabequaches and Uncompahgrés, until the San Juan cession, in 1873, and then a separate agency was established for them in their own country. A number of these southern Indians, principally Muaches (Maquaches), had land under cultivation on the Rio La Plata and other tributaries of the Rio San Juan, of which they retained possession for several years, but were then forcibly dispossessed by settlers who claimed that the Indians had no rights off the reservation. The annuities promised in this treaty were not paid until after unreasonable delay. The lines established were claimed by the Indians to be fraudulent. They said the lines were explained to them as being on the tops of the mountains, *i. e.*, the continental divide, but the line as surveyed cut off the beautiful valleys of the Gunnison, Tomichi, and other streams. It took away also Middle Park and North Park, which they said they did not sell. Worst of all, the whites continually invaded the reservation. It had been the great desire of the Utes to have a country that was absolutely their own, and accordingly the following strong promise was put in the treaty: "The United States now solemnly agrees that no persons, except those herein authorized so to do, and except such officers, agents, and employés of the government as may be authorized to enter upon Indian reservations in discharge of duties enjoined by law, shall ever be permitted to pass over, settle upon, or reside in the territory described in this article." The Indians considered this treaty as giving them the fee-simple of these lands. The first proceeding of part of the bands was to move off the reservation, which they said they intended to keep for a hunting-ground. They abandoned this plan, after remonstrance by their agents, and located on their reservation, with the privilege of hunting outside of it.

Looking back through the years, it seems questionable whether the men who negotiated this treaty, or the senators who ratified it, had any expectation that these agreements would be kept, so repeatedly had similar ones been broken. The Utes had scarcely received their first payments before the mines of the San Juan country were discovered, and great crowds of people went to them, notwithstanding they were wholly within the Ute reservation. The Indians complained, and soldiers were ordered to remove the intruders. Before the enforcement of the orders began, the President was " informed that their chief, Ouray (Uré, Uray—The Arrow), had expressed a willingness to negotiate for the sale of a portion of the reservation," and the orders were countermanded. Who vouchsafed this information does not appear from the published records. A commission was at once sent to the Utes (in 1872), and they utterly refused to sell. The miners remained undisturbed, and in the following year Felix Brunot was sent to talk to the Indians. He persuaded

OURAY.

them that he came from pure friendship for them, and induced them to make a cession of the San Juan and San Miguel countries, a block of land sixty-five miles wide by ninety-five miles deep. This left them a strip fifteen miles wide along the southern line of the state, and one twenty miles wide along the western line up to ten miles north of parallel 38, above which the reservation stood as formerly. This cession was made on the express understanding that it was not to include any farming lands, but only the mines on the mountains. Most of the farming lands on the reservation were in the southern part. The Tabequaches and Uncompahgrés had only a limited amount of arable land—a strip on the San Miguel, the Uncompahgré Park, and a small tract on the Uncompahgré River. No one, white or Indian, thought at that time that the lands on the Gunnison and the Grand, in the western part of the reservation, which are now farmed so profitably, were worth anything for agriculture.

The Utes said they thought the north line of the proposed cession would cut off part of the Uncompahgré Park. To meet this objection it was agreed that, if it did, an offset would be made to exclude it from the cession. This understanding was inserted in the treaty in these words: "*Provided*, that if any part of the Uncompahgré Park shall be found to extend south of the north line of said described country, the same is not intended to be included therein, and is hereby reserved and retained as a portion of the Ute reservation." This agreement was ratified by Act of Congress, April 29, 1874, "treaties" with Indians being at that time prohibited by law. The former agreement as to the exclusion of white persons from the reservation was reaffirmed, but the Indians agreed to allow one road, across the southern part of the reservation, to the ceded lands. The Utes made this cession with much hesitancy, and chiefly in the hope that it would avoid any further trouble from miners, but they still feared that the miners would want more. Said Ouray to Brunot: " The lines in regard to the mines do not amount to anything; it is changing them all the time—taking a little now and a little again—that makes trouble. You said you do not know anything in regard to these lines [those established under the treaty of 1868], and it may be the same in regard to lines you make. There are many men talk about it to us; they say they are going to have the lines as they want, whether the Utes like it or not. It is common talk; everybody tells it to the Utes. The miners care very little about the government. It is a long way off in the States, and they say the man who comes to make the treaty will go off to the States, and it will all be as they want it." True old Arrow! He went straight to the mark.

This treaty was not complied with by us in three important particulars, not to mention minor ones. In the first place, the Utes were to receive $25,000 annually forever, in compensation for the cession, but Congress provided for this by placing bonds to their credit, the interest on which was to meet these payments, and the first instalment did not fall due for one year. Consequently the first, or cash payment, was not provided for. After several years of protestation and bickering this was made good, but by this time there had been twice that amount withheld from the annual payments under "the discretion of the President." The amount thereafter continuously due the Utes, under this agreement, fluctuated from $65,000 to $90,000. At the time of the outbreak it was $65,000. In the second place, the south line of the cession was run so as to cut off a large amount of farming and grazing lands. Sapavanari, a young Uncompahgré chief, went with the surveying-party, to protect them from interference, "until he saw with his own eyes" that the line was cutting off some 15,000 acres of farm lands, including some of the Ute farms. Then he left them, fearing that he would be compromised with his tribe, and his tribe compromised with the government, if he did not protest against the line. The Indians said that as the agreement was explained to them they were to have ten miles more on the south side, and twenty miles more on the west side, than was given them. In the third place, the north line of the cession was run through the centre of Uncompahgré Park, and no offset was made to cover the part cut off. This fact was pointed out to the surveyor, J. W. Miller, and he promised to correct it, but, instead of doing so, went on to Washington, had his survey approved, got his money, and dropped out of the controversy. The Indians were greatly disappointed, and begged to have justice done them in this matter. After much correspondence the authorities concluded to humor them by complying with the treaty, and on August 17, 1876, President Grant issued an order withdrawing from the public domain four miles square of the cession, including the part of the Park that had been cut off, and adding it to the Ute reservation.

By this time a number of settlers had located in this part of the Park, which was the only convenient farming land in the neighborhood of Ouray, the principal mining-town of the San Juan country. They declined to remove except at the point of the bayonet. Some of their attorneys advised them that the President had no right to add to a reservation after it had been established by Congress, and one, C. H. McIntyre, prepared and forwarded to the Interior Department a brief maintaining this proposition. It seems to have escaped Mr. McIntyre's notice that this had nothing to do with the question. The reservation as established by Congress included all of the Uncompahgré Park. The trouble was that an executive officer had wilfully failed to comply with the provisions

HENRY M. TELLER.

made by Congress, and this the Executive Department not only had the right, but was in duty bound to rectify. Under Mr. McIntyre's profound logic, a United States deputy surveyor had abrogated an Act of Congress. Troops were ordered to remove the intruders in the spring of 1877, but H. M. Teller, of counsel for the settlers, since Secretary of the Interior, of Backbone Land-grant fame, wrote a touching letter to Secretary Schurz, detailing the hardships that this would cause to these people, who " went on the land in good faith," and Mr. Schurz weakly allowed them six months of grace, in which to harvest their crops and move. None of them agreed to move—their attorney, even, did not promise it—in order to obtain this kind concession of the rights of a third party, and none of them did move. In the spring of 1878 another order was made for their dispossession, but by this time the Park was full of defiant settlers. They refused to move, and said that if the soldiers put them off before the commission, which had been sent to treat for the four miles square, had been heard from, they would kill Indians and precipitate an Indian war. This threat so terrified the Ute agent, J. B. Abbott, that he withdrew the troops.

The commission arrived in August, 1878, headed by General Hatch. Their mission was to purchase the four miles square and also the southern strip, below the San Juan cession. At first the Indians refused to talk to them. They had not yet received the first payment for the San Juan cession. They said they would not talk of selling land to people who would not pay for what they had already bought. Finally, on promise that this should be made right, they went into council. There was no difficulty about the southern strip. The southern Utes had already proposed to take another reservation, " provided the government would pay them the previous indebtedness," and this the commission did, to the amount of $15,534, letting the remainder stand. In this transaction the southern Utes gave up over 1,800,000 acres of land and took a reservation of something over 700,000 acres, with the understanding that they should have compensation for the excess of 1,100,000 acres. This was left out of the treaty by the commissioners, but shows in the minutes of the council, as the Indians claimed. (During the past summer, by the way, they have been reported as reduced to starvation and becoming desperate.) The four miles square was more troublesome. The Utes wanted all of the Park because it was their best, almost their only, winter range for their stock—they had about six thousand horses, besides cattle and sheep. In addition to this, it contained a hot spring which was valuable to them for medicinal purposes. It was urged by the commission that the President wanted to give the miners some land, on which to raise vegetables. Said Ouray: "I can't see that the President wants it: the settlers want it." It was urged that the settlers and their backers were making strong claims to the government. Said Ouray: "If the government wants to take it and break the treaty, all right." It was urged that the land was not of importance, but that it was very desirable to end all difficulty. Said Ouray: "I don't think that would end it. They would want more." The value of $10,000, the price offered, was dwelt upon. Said Sapavanari: "We don't want to sell it; don't want money." The commissioners said they were talking for the good of the Indians, not the white men. Said Ouray: "If you were talking for the Indians, you would put the settlers out." The commission abandoned the task, in despair, but a delegation of Utes was brought on to Washington in the following winter, and the purchase was accomplished. The Utes wanted one thing distinctly understood, and they had it put on record; it was that they consented to this sale, not because they desired it, but because the government did. They wanted the $10,000 paid in cash, but were informed that they would have to wait until it was appropriated by Congress. They got it several years later.

While all these things are true, and while they are very dirty spots on our enlightened Indian policy, it is not true, as some have inferred, that they caused the Ute outbreak. They were all settled several months before it occurred. The Indians simply agreed to submit to these wrongs, and as disturbing forces they were removed. Moreover, the Indians who made the outbreak were not materially affected by these wrongs. Soon after the establishment of the reservation the Indians divided themselves into three groups, with independent governments, corresponding to the three agencies. The smaller tribes, principally Pah-Utes, who were afterwards placed on the reservation, joined one or the other of these groups. Ouray was treated as head chief of all the Utes, by the whites, but he did not, in fact, have general authority. The Southern Utes did not recognize him at all. Their head chief was Ignacio, a Muache, who was aided by several sub-chiefs, including Ka-ni-a-che (The One Who was Taken Down), An-ka-tosh (the Red), and others. Ignacio would have nothing to do with Ouray. This was chiefly owing to the fact that, by the Brunot agreement, Ouray was to receive $1000 annually for his services, an arrangement at the time unknown to the other Indians. The Los Pinos and White River Utes did not even claim any interest in the southern and western strips of land. When the commission of 1878 desired to purchase these lands, they said they would agree to whatever Ignacio said; that they had no claim to the lower country. The Tabequaches, Uncompahgrés, and others of the Los Pinos agency recognized Ouray's authority fully. Among their minor chiefs were Sha-va-no (Chavanaugh, Shawana —Blue Flower), Guero (Wa-ro—Light hair), and Captain Billy, of the Tabequaches, and Un-com-mute (Un-kum-good, Uncom, Uncah, Unqua), and Sapavana-ri,* of the Uncompah-

CAPTAIN BILLY.

grés. The White River Utes recognized Ouray's authority to

---

* There is some confusion about this name. In official reports it is often mistaken for the Spanish Saponiere (Xaboniere—a soap-maker), Saponavero (which may be translated "genuine soap"), or Saponaria (soapwort). The agent at Ouray writes me, on August 13, 1885: "I have made inquiry and learn that 'Sappovanaro' means anything white, and I am free to confess there are many of the Utes who seem to know more about it than 'Old Sap' himself. One says 'something white, all same pony or paper,' and another explained by pointing to a white toad-stool. The interpreter says it means a water-cloud or water-spout. Sappovanaro says the name was given him by Kit Carson, and was taken from the Mexican Indians." In his correspondence Mr. Carson spelled the name Sa-pa-wa-ne-ri.

44

a very limited extent; in ordinary affairs not at all. They were in two factions; one led by Douglas, and the other by Jack. Among the lesser chiefs were Colorado (Red), commonly called Colorow, Piah (The Black-tailed Deer), Sa-rap (The Rainbow), Sah-patch (White Hot), and Johnson. These Indians had no real interest in the San Juan cession, the south-line dispute, or the four miles square. The first concerned both of the other groups; the second affected only the Southern Utes; and the last was the affair of the Los Pinos Indians. The White Rivers took very little interest in these matters. They received no part of the money for the San Juan cession, and claimed no interest in it. The lands ceded did not belong to them. They said the other bands were fools for selling their land, and that it was good enough for them if they were cheated. The Uintah Utes were not on this reservation. Their chief was called Tabby (Taw-vi), and they were located on a reservation in Utah.

The trouble with the White River Indians arose from disagreements with their agent, N. C. Meeker. He was best known as the leader of the colony that settled the town of Greeley, Colorado, under the patronage of Horace Greeley, and was, for a long time, a correspondent of the *New York Tribune*, over the initials N. C. M. His reputation for honesty was excellent, but he prided himself on his practical qualities, and greatly overestimated his ability to civilize savages. He said, in a letter to Senator Teller, on December 23, 1878: "When I get round to it in a year or so, if I stay as long, I shall propose to cut every Indian down to bare starvation point if he will not work. The 'getting around to it' means to have plenty of tilled ground, plenty of work to do, and to have labor organized so that whoever will shall be able to earn his bread." A friend characterized him thus: "A man of the Puritan stamp, an enthusiast in whatever work he undertook, he had given his whole soul to the work of civilizing the Utes. It is a waste of words to say that he was honorable and upright in all his dealings with them, for his life has been public and his character beyond reproach." Admitting this to be true, the fact still remains that he did not understand the Indian character, and could not manage them.

He took charge of the agency in May, 1878, and began operations by moving the agency to Powell's Valley, on White River, fifteen miles below the old agency. The Indians opposed this because they used this valley for a winter camp, it affording the best pasturage for their horses. Meeker studied the situation, and adopted the plan of playing one of the factions against the other. He first took up the Douglas faction, which was recognized as "the government," although Jack's party was the larger. The feeling had become such that whatever one faction favored the other would oppose. The next difficulty, after moving the agency, to which the Indians yielded a reluctant assent, on being assured that the commissioner would be "a heap mad" if they did not, was to get their consent to the appropriation of $3000 of their money, for an irrigating ditch. This was never obtained directly, but was taken for granted, because a part of the Indians were employed in the work, on the theory that by taking part in the work they consented to the appropriation, "as much so as, when a man marries a woman, they consent." The Indians who assisted in the work, for which they received in all $303, were twenty-five men of the Douglas faction. Jack's party not only refused to work, but also objected to the others working, on the grounds that it was the white men's business to do all the work, and that the Indians at Los Pinos did not work. After being threatened with report to the commissioner, he withdrew this objection, and all his party, with a number of the others, went on a hunting excursion off the reservation, as had been their custom every summer.

To understand what Meeker was contending against, it must be borne in mind that the Utes had not yet emerged from "the hunter state." They subsisted on game to the extent of fully fifty per cent., and derived most of their money from the products of the chase, particularly buckskin. Deer were yet very numerous in the mountains of Colorado, and the greater part of them made their way beyond the divide in the summer. Their habit is to spend the winter months in the foot-hills, bordering on the plains, but in the spring to run back into the mountains, ranging as far as the beginning of the desert lands in Western Colorado. Elks were quite abundant, and a small herd of buffalo remained in Middle Park. The Indians roved where they chose, but their best hunting-grounds lay between the reservation and the divide, in Middle Park, in North Park, and in the country west of it. This country, they claimed, belonged to them under the treaty of 1868, being west of the Continental Divide. North Park is east of it, but is drained to the north by the North Platte. They also hunted buffalo on the plains east of Denver, where these animals were quite numerous until 1875. Their last visit to the plains was in 1878. They prided themselves on being "peaceable," but their visits were regarded by settlers with much the same dread that Eastern people have of a camp of gypsies or a colony of tramps. Undoubtedly they committed some trespasses and frightened some timid people in 1879, but the reports that were made concerning them were so wildly exaggerated as to deserve the name of falsehoods. The principal charge that was urged against them was that they were setting out fires by which the forests were destroyed and the improvements of settlers put in jeopardy. It was explained by some that this was a custom of theirs, the object of which was to drive the game so that it could be more easily killed. The charge and explanation were untrue and absurd. The Utes never had such a custom. The existence of millions of acres of virgin forests ought to have been sufficient proof of it. No people preserve game more carefully than Indians, and none know better than they that continuous fires would drive it away. Their hunting was like the white man's; the chief object was to induce a deer to stand still long enough to be shot. There were great and destructive forest fires that summer, but the Indians were responsible for very few of them. Major Thornburgh, commanding at Fort Fred Steele, Wyoming, investigated this charge thoroughly, by writing to reliable settlers, and by sending out men to look for evidence of it, but the reports, without exception, were that the Indians had killed no cattle, offered no violence to settlers, and set no fires. One man went over their trail and satisfied himself that no fires originated from their camps. They did set fire to the grass at several places in Middle Park, "to make good grass next year," but they claimed that Middle Park belonged to them, and repeatedly ordered settlers and others to leave it. They ordered the miners out in 1869, the first year after the treaty.

The truth is that nearly all the fires were occasioned by the carelessness of white men, and particularly from the carelessness of men in the "tie camps," *i. e.*, men who were cutting ties for the Denver, Rio Grande, and South Park railways, which were then being pushed through the mountains. It was notorious that most of these fires occurred in localities where there were no Indians. Many a prospector,

SOUTHERN UTES.

who never saw a Ute, saw hundreds of acres of pine consumed. I resided in a district that was nearly all burned
over in 1879, and there was not an Indian in it, though it
was within fifty miles of the reservation. Old settlers said
there had not been a mountain fire in the region for seventeen years before. They also said the year was unusually
dry, and that fires travelled and caught easily. It is true,
however, that, owing to the reports, the whites generally believed that the Indians were firing the forests at other places,
to drive out the miners. It is true also that the Indians
killed large quantities of game, as was complained, but so did
every one. A man who failed to shoot at a deer because it
was against the law would have been laughed at. Venison re-
tailed, in season, at four and five cents the pound, while beef
was fifteen to twenty. There was not a mountain stream in
which dynamite was not exploded to kill trout, if there were
any trout in it. So with the forests. The United States law
against cutting timber on public lands was no more regarded
than if it had not been on the statute-books. The forests of
stumps are there to-day to prove the statement. The people
of Middle Park sent a memorial to General Pope, in 1877,
representing that the Indians were slaughtering the game,
" when a white man is not allowed to kill a pound more than
he can use to sustain life;" but if the people of Middle Park
were any more virtuous or law-abiding, in this respect or any
other, than the rest of the people in Colorado, no one ever
discovered it. It was not many months later that half the
county officials of Grand County (Middle Park) conspired to
murder the county commissioners, and did murder them. It
is notorious that two of the signers of that memorial have
committed suicide on account of their participation in that
crime, and that Grand County to-day is a slumbering volcano
of hate, remorse, distrust, and revenge, as a result of that awful tragedy enacted on the shore of Grand Lake. Let it be
distinctly understood that there were reputable, law-abiding
people in Middle Park, and elsewhere in Colorado—plenty of
them—but to all such representations of uniformly proper
whites and uniformly villainous Indians, coming from any frontier settlement, I say : " In the name of the Prophet—Bosh !"

While the Utes behaved comparatively well in their summer excursions, it cannot be questioned that these trips were a serious impediment to their civilization. Of course they would not settle down to farming while they could live by hunting. That would have been unnatural. But, worse than that, there were no restrictions to trade with them, off the reservation. There were four stores on Bear River, and many at other points, where they could obtain guns, ammunition, whiskey, or anything else that they were able to pay for. They were also thrown in contact with the worst class of whites, and there were some very bad white people for them to come in contact with. Aside from the ordinary riff-raff, there were a number of cattle-men about the reservation with more property than character. Two of these, who were the subjects of repeated complaints by the agent, were the Morgan brothers. They had large herds of cattle near the reservation, and were accused of permitting them to mix with the herd belonging to the White River agency, for the purpose of claiming the unbranded increase (mavericks) of the agency herd. They were also charged with taking branded cattle and burning their brand, a double box (□□), over the "I D" of the Indian Department. They were not the only ones. When the outbreak came, and the agency herd was scattered and uncared for, about twelve hundred of them disappeared. It was supposed at the time that the Indians had taken them. It was afterwards learned that they were stolen by white men, rebranded, and sold to the government for beef. I had the honor to be acquainted with Wes Travis, one of the men engaged in this robbery—since succumbed to the combined powers of bad whiskey and death—and have heard him tell, with great gusto, how he and a companion, after finishing the cattle job, killed an Indian that they met when coming out of the reservation. They cut him open, removed his intestines, filled him with stones, sewed him up, and dumped him into a deep hole in Grand River. Morgan's partner, W. B. Hugus, and John Gordon, *alias* Samuel Lemon, were brought to trial for this affair, in Denver, but they had the good fortune to be acquitted. The Morgans escaped from the country.

The complaints made against the Utes, in the summer of 1879, flew on wings of the wind, growing as they went. The only palpable foundation for them was the alleged destruction  of some property by two Utes called Bennett and Chinaman. It had been agreed by the Utes that they would deliver up accused persons for trial, and they had complied with this agreement usually, but on this occasion Douglas refused to surrender these men to the officer who came for them, and informed him that he could not make the arrest on the reservation. The treaty also contained this clause: "*Provided*, That if any chief of either of the confederated bands

JACK.

make war against the people of the United States, or in any manner violate this treaty in any essential part, said chief shall forfeit his position as chief, and all rights to any of the benefits of this treaty: *But, provided further*, Any Indian of these confederated bands who shall remain at peace, and abide by the terms of this treaty in all its essentials, shall be entitled to its benefits and provisions, notwithstanding his particular chief and band may have forfeited their rights thereto." Meeker, although he had no personal knowledge of what was occurring off the reservation, joined in these complaints. On March 17 he reported that part of the Utes were going north "probably to supply ammunition to the hostiles," *i. e.*, certain Sioux who were said to be on the war-path, and asked that the military send the Indians back to the reservation. Jack was several times confronted with reports of wrong-doing, and the statement that his party wanted to go to war. Being conscience clear, he, with three others, went to Denver to see Governor Pitkin. He complained of this treatment and asked for Meeker's removal; but being there confronted by Meeker's letters, complaining of some things of which he had no knowledge, and of others that he could meet only by denial, he became disheartened and went back to the agency. In this interview he backed up his claim of Meeker's evil deeds by the statement that Meeker wanted their children to go to school and learn to work, neither of which the Utes wanted. Meeker had also promised him a wagon, and failed to give it to him, which satisfied him that Meeker could not be trusted. At the agency he got no satisfaction, and became impressed with the idea that Meeker was responsible for everything that was said about the Utes in the newspapers, a theory which the other Indians soon adopted. A more oppressive burden could not be placed on any man's shoulders than such a responsibility. The Colorado press was sensational, to say the least, and the contents of the papers were frequently communicated to the Indians by their white acquaintances.

In the mean time a new trouble had arisen. Powell's Valley had been subdivided by Meeker with a view to its permanent settlement by the Indians. One street crossed it lengthwise, and another at right angles to the first. The agency was located at the crossing, but the cross-street was as yet on paper only. Several small plots had been marked off for Indians who desired to work. The first one provided for was Johnson, a chief with "three cows and two wives," who showed a commendable disposition to civilize. A log-house was built for him, near the agency buildings, and for several months he was the "brag Indian" of the place. Horses were broken for him, and fed from the agency supplies to keep them in condition for work; but, finally, Meeker discovered that Johnson was using these horses to race with the other Indians, whose ponies were picking a precarious living where they could find it. Johnson stock fell rapidly thereafter. Instead of cultivating the land set off for him, Johnson used it to pasture his ponies, of which he had about a hundred and fifty. Early in

September Meeker undertook to plough up a large amount of land near the agency, including that set off to Johnson and two or three others. These Indians objected, and could neither be talked out of their objections nor induced to take other locations. They got their guns, and ordered the ploughing stopped. The ploughing went on. In a few minutes a gun was fired in a clump of bushes near by, and a bullet whizzed unpleasantly near the ploughman's ears. Meeker then stopped the work and appealed to Douglas; but Douglas said the men who claimed land wanted it, and that Meeker should plough in some other place. Having exhausted his influence in that quarter, Meeker thought he would try the other faction. He sent for Jack, who came at once with his retainers. A council was held, and the conclusion reached that Jack and his men cared nothing about it, but that Meeker might plough a strip one hundred feet wide and half a mile long. He told them that this would do no good; that he wanted at least fifty acres, besides meadow land. He understood that they consented to this, but on the following morning the work was stopped again. Jack was sent for once more and another council was held. They finally decided that Meeker might have the land if he would give Johnson a stove, move his corral, dig a well, and help build a house, to which the agent consented. He said, however, "that it was the wish of all the Indians that ploughing might be stopped, and that no more ploughing at all shall be done; but that the conclusion which they reached was based upon the danger they ran in opposing the government of the United States."

This influence wore off and the bad feeling of the Indians grew. Two days later (September 10) Johnson assaulted Meeker in his own house, drove him out, and beat him badly. Meeker would probably have been killed but for the interference of the employés. He sent at once for military aid, and telegraphed the commissioner: "Ploughing stops. Life of self, family, and employés not safe; want protection immediately. Have asked Governor Pitkin to confer with General Pope." On the same day he wrote to W. N. Byers, of Denver, in regard to Johnson's attack, and added: "I think they will submit to nothing but force. How many are rebellious I do not know; but if only a few are, and the rest laugh at their outrages, as they do, and think nothing of it, all are complicated. I didn't come here to be kicked and hustled out of my own house by savages, and if government cannot protect me, let somebody else try it. You know the Indians and understand the situation. Please see Governor Pitkin," etc. From that time to the outbreak, work at the agency was at a stand still. The feeling of the Indians, with very few exceptions, was that they would do no work; that the ploughing must stop; that Meeker was their enemy; that the soldiers were coming to have the land ploughed, to arrest Johnson, Chinaman, Bennett, and others, and, probably, to make everybody work; that the soldiers ought not to come. Meeker's feeling may be inferred from his telegram to the commissioner, of September 17: "There is no particular change, either for worse or better. No ploughing is done, nor will until it can be done in safety. It remains to be seen whether the business and industries of this agency are to be conducted under the direction of the Indians or of yourself."

In response to Meeker's application for protection, Major T. T. Thornburgh marched from Fort Fred Steele with a hundred men—three companies of cavalry and one of infantry. This post is in Wyoming, at the Union Pacific Railroad's crossing of the Platte. The road, which was the only ordinary approach to the agency, runs to the southwest, crossing the Sierra Madre at Bridger's Pass; thence south, bearing east, to the crossing of Bear River, at the mouth of Elk Head Creek. From this point its general course is southwest, striking the reservation at Milk Creek. On the 26th, Thornburgh was met at Bear River by a party of five Utes, including Jack and Colorow. They wanted to know why he was coming. He explained that the agent had sent for him; that the Indians had been acting badly. They denied everything, and asked that the soldiers should not come on the reservation. They proposed that he should leave the soldiers and go to the agency, with four or five companions, to investigate the truth of the charges. Major Thornburgh informed them that his orders were to go on, but that he would find a good place to camp, closer to the agency, and leave his men there while he

went on.   After some conversation, by which he thought they
were brought into a pacific state of mind, they went away.
They returned to the agency and asked Meeker to stop the

COLOROW.

soldiers, but he said it
was none of his busi-
ness. Finally he yield-
ed to their importuni-
ties, and, on the 27th,
sent a letter to Thorn-
burgh advising him
that it would be the
better course to come
on alone.   To this
Thornburgh replied on
the 28th that he would
discontinue his march
on the 29th, and come
on with five men. On
the 29th, in the morn-
ing, the command
reached Milk Creek
and entered the reser-
vation. The road, after
Milk Creek is passed
half a mile, enters a

cañon, the sides and top of which are covered with oak brush.
It is called Red Cañon.   An Indian trail runs along the adjoining ridge, or " hog-back," and joins the road near the creek.
The Indians were in ambush along the tops of the cañon. Just
as the troops were beginning to enter it, shortly before noon,
the advance guard, under Lieutenant Cherry, discovered some
Indians moving over a hill, half a mile in advance, and separated to reconnoitre. After flanking the cañon about two hundred yards, the ambuscade was discovered and at once reported.
Cherry was ordered to make a reconnoissance on the right,
and, if possible, communicate with the Indians, on the supposition that hostilities might be averted by a parley.   At the
same time Jack started from the Ute position to talk with
the soldiers; but when Cherry's command galloped off to the

right a body of Indians went out to oppose the movement, and both parties deployed. An Indian fired, and the fighting began on both sides.

Captain Payne's company was at once thrown out on the left and Captain Lawson's on the right, in skirmish line. The wagon train, which was crossing a small plateau, between one and two hundred yards from the stream, was ordered to park. The Indians pressed the troops hotly. They were in strong force. Major Thornburgh saw that they were massing to cut off his retreat, and ordered his men to fall back on the wagon train. The movement was executed in excellent order, but in the midst of it the commander was shot and instantly killed. Captain Payne took command, being next in seniority. He set the entire force at work fortifying. Wounded horses were killed for temporary shelter for sharpshooters. Boxes, bundles of bedding, sacks of corn and flour, and everything available were piled up for cover, while pick and shovel were plied to make the protection more substantial. The men worked desperately—the groans of the dying, the agonized cries of the wounded, and the incessant cracking of the Indians' rifles serving only as incentives to greater activity. To add to the peril of the situation, the Indians fired the grass and sage brush, and the wind was hurrying the roaring flames upon the little band. They worked on with feverish haste. The fire reached them, and stretched out its forked tongues to lick them up. There was no water within reach. They dropped their tools, and smothered the flames with blankets, blouses, and sacks. Some of the wagons took fire; but, under cover of the stifling smoke, these were extinguished also. The greatest danger was now past. By burning the brush the Indians had deprived themselves of cover for close approach, and were compelled to do their firing from the surrounding bluffs, at a distance of from four to six hundred yards. They commanded the situation, but could inflict no material damage. So long as the soldiers remained in their trenches they were safe from the bullets that were poured in on them.

The news of the attack was carried to the agency, twenty-five miles below, by an Indian messenger who arrived at about one o'clock. The Indians did not breathe a word about it to the whites. They had held another council with Meeker, on the arrival of the messenger from Thornburgh, in regard to the advance of the soldiers, just as though nothing had occurred. Meeker prepared a note to Thornburgh, as follows: "I expect to leave in the morning with Douglas and Serrick to meet you; things are peaceable, and Douglas flies the United States flag. If you have trouble in getting through the cañon to-day, let me know in what force. We have been on guard three nights, and shall be to-night, not because we know there is danger, but because there may be. I like your last programme; it is based on true military principles." This message was dated September 29, 1 P. M. He little dreamed that Thornburgh was then lying cold and stark at the mouth of the cañon. The "last programme" referred to was Major Thornburgh's letter of the 28th, in which he informed Meeker that he would bring his troops "within striking distance" of the agency on the 29th. He said: "I have carefully considered whether or not it would be advisable to have my command at a point as distant as that desired by the Indians who were in my camp last night, and have reached the conclusion that, under my orders, which require me to march this command to your agency, I am not at liberty to leave it at a point where it would not be available in case of trouble." Meeker received this message at noon on the 29th. Previous to that hour, it seems certain that he was deceived in regard to Thornburgh's intentions. On the day of the attack, the 29th, he telegraphed Washington: "Major Thornburgh, 4th Infantry, leaves his command fifty miles distant, and comes to-day with five men. Indians propose to fight if troops advance. A talk will be had to-morrow. Captain Dodge, 9th Cavalry, is at Steamboat Springs, with orders to break up Indian stores and keep Indians on reservation. Sales of ammunition and guns brisk for ten days past. Store nearest sent back 16,000 rounds and 13 guns. When Captain Dodge commences to enforce law, no living here without troops. Have sent for him to confer."

Meeker knew that Red Cañon, to which he refers in the one o'clock message, was less than twenty-five miles from the agency, and within the reservation. If he knew that Thornburgh was within a day's march of it, he was trying to deceive the Indians. If he had not received Thornburgh's message of the 28th, before writing his telegram to Washington, of the 29th—which is most likely—he probably misunderstood Thornburgh's intentions, but communicated his understanding to the Indians. The Indians were misinformed by him in either event, and undoubtedly thought they were misinformed intentionally, for they were fully posted concerning Thornburgh's movements, by their scouts, and believed that Meeker was hostile to them. With this belief they decided to meet treachery with treachery. It is not within the range of credibility that the attack and massacre were planned before the 26th. If they had been, Ouray would have known it sooner. There was no evidence of it at the agency. According to Meeker's statement, guards were first posted on the night of

the 26th. It was the opinion of Mrs. Meeker, Josie Meeker, and the employés that the plot was arranged on the 28th, when the soldiers had passed the fifty-mile limit. There was a war-dance that night, in Douglas's camp, which continued till daybreak the next morning. The action of the Indians on Monday was marked by deep cunning; their behavior at the council deceived Meeker completely. He despatched his note to Thornburgh by Wilmer Eskridge, a man employed at the agency as a sawyer. He was accompanied by two Indians—

ANTELOPE.

Antelope (Wah-sitz) and Ebenezer. After going two miles the Indians murdered Eskridge, and hastened back to the agency. In the mean time the other Indians had managed to get into the store-room and secure all the agency guns, without attracting attention.

The people at the agency were wholly unsuspecting. Mrs. Meeker and Josie were washing dishes in their house. Mrs. Price was washing clothes outside. Shaduck Price, post-farmer, and Frank Dresser, laborer, were in a wagon, throwing dirt on the roof of the new building. Arthur Thompson, laborer, was on the roof, spreading the dirt. Meeker and William H. Post, storekeeper and carpenter, were in the larger storehouse. The other employés were scattered about the place, engaged in their various duties. As Ebenezer and Antelope returned, about twenty Indians, armed with guns, started up from the river. They met Douglas, who was walking towards his teepee, and all came on to the buildings together. They began firing as soon as they reached the new building—Ebenezer, Antelope, and others having by that time secured positions for attacking the other men. At the first volley Price was killed and Thompson fell from the building. Frank Dresser was wounded in the leg, but managed to run to Meeker's house through a rain of bullets. Mrs. Price picked up her little boy and ran to her room. Dresser followed her. She gave him Price's gun, which lay on the bed. As he came out, the windows of the dining-room were broken in. He fired through the window and mortally wounded Johnson's brother. The Indians then left them and began plundering the stores. The inmates of the house went into Josie's room and hid under the bed, but as soon as their wits cleared they saw that this position afforded no safety. They then ran into the milk-house, a small adobe building close at hand. Here they remained all the afternoon undisturbed, Frank Dresser, the three women, and the children. They had the entrance barricaded, however, so that they could not see what was being done outside. For half an hour the firing was kept up quite steadily; then there were intervals of quiet, broken by volleys. It is probable that some of this firing was from the explosion of cartridges in the burning buildings, and the rest was drawn by some of the employés who had secured weapons and were fighting for their lives.

Mrs. Price tells their story thus: "We were in the milk-

house until nearly sundown. They set Meeker's house on
fire first. The house sat east and west, with wings built on
the south and north sides. The south wing was Josie's bedroom, and on the north was my bedroom. In the east part
of the house was a room used as a dining-room and kitchen,
and on the north of that the milk-house. They set Josie's
room on fire first, and we stayed until we began strangling
in the milk-house, and had to go out. We ran into Meeker's
house. I do not think it is ten feet to the corner of my bedroom. We opened both doors and thought of secreting ourselves under the bed of Mr. Meeker. I said : 'No, that will
not do.' We looked out to the north. The blinds were open.
They were busy taking out goods ; they were taking the blankets, shirts, and everything else they could. I said : 'Let's
try and escape to the north, in the sage brush ; it will not do
to stay here ; they will be here in a minute.' Frank said,
'Let's go while they are so busy,' and we went. I ran outside of the fence ; Josie, Mrs. Meeker, and Frank opened the
gate and went into the field, and I crossed over through the
wire-fence. They then saw us ; we had not got more than
ten or fifteen steps from the corner of the fence north before
they saw us and fired. They came running, on foot and ponies, and fired at all of us, and hit Mrs. Meeker. The bullets
whizzed by my head and hit beside me. They shot at Frank
Dresser, and, as he would take a step, the dust would fly.
The last I saw of him he was about a quarter of a mile from
the agency, in the field, still running. The Indians took us,
and said we had to go with them. As I was going, I said I
had read so much about their treatment of captives, that I
was afraid they would want to burn me. They said : 'No
kill white squaw ; heap like them.' I said, ' You are going
to burn me,' and they said, ' No burn white squaw.' Then
they took me on through the brush to the river."

  Mrs. Price's captor was Ahu-u-tu-pu-wit, a small, ill-favored
Uncompahgré. Josie Meeker says of her capture: " One
called to me and said, ' Come to me ; no shoot you.' I said,
' Going to shoot?' He said, ' No.' I said, ' Better not.' He
said, ' Come to me.' And then they took me down to the
camp." This was Persune, a Yampa warrior. Douglas tried

to take his captive from him, but Persune pushed him away. They had an angry dispute, after which Douglas went away and took Mrs. Meeker, whom no one else had claimed. The Indians moved that night about twelve miles to the south, and camped on Pi-ce-ance Creek, on the Great Hogback of the Roan or Book plateau. They had all been drinking. They were laden with plunder and flushed with success. That night the three women were "taken for squaws" by their respect- ive captors, and were so held during their captivity. Mrs. Price was also outraged by Johnson.

The news of these affairs came to the settlements slowly. There were weary days of suspense, in which no trustworthy tidings could be had, and no assurance as to the extent of the war. Ouray was on a hunting expedition with his band. A messenger brought him word of the outbreak, and he returned at once to Los Pinos to report to the agent. A letter to the White River chiefs was prepared and signed by Ouray, direct- ing them to stop fighting. This was carried by Joseph Brady, miller at Los Pinos, accompanied by Sapavanari. On receipt of Ouray's message the Utes agreed to obey his directions. Brady also communicated with the soldiers, who were now under command of Colonel Merritt. The remnant of the original command had held their fortification alone, without further loss, until the morning of the 2d, when Dodge's company of colored soldiers arrived. These had marched from Grand River on September 27, on orders to report at White River agency. On the 1st of October they found a paper, on a sage bush by the road, with the words: "Hurry up. The troops have been defeated at the agency.—E. E. C." A few miles farther they reached the village of Hayden, which was deserted, but while here a party of citizens came up, and the facts of the situation were learned. The command moved on down Bear River and went into camp as usual, to deceive the Indian spies, if any should be watching. At half- past eight they packed up again. The train was sent to the supply camp on Fortification Creek, and the remainder of the force, forty in number, took an Indian trail for Milk Creek. They reached the intrenchment at daybreak, without moles- tation, and did gallant service there. Merritt arrived with

PLAN OF WHITE RIVER AGENCY.

(As Described by Chief Douglas.)

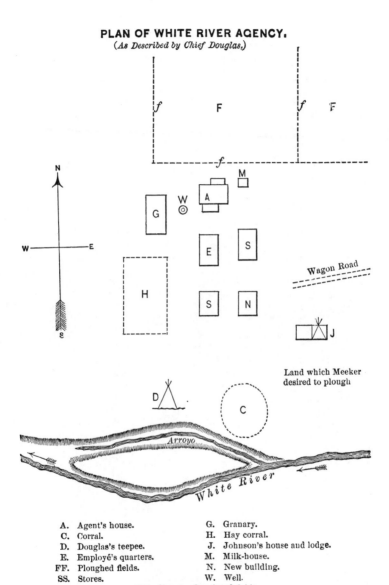

A. Agent's house.
C. Corral.
D. Douglas's teepee.
E. Employé's quarters.
FF. Ploughed fields.
SS. Stores.

G. Granary.
H. Hay corral.
J. Johnson's house and lodge.
M. Milk-house.
N. New building.
W. Well.

fff. Fences of enclosed fields.

reinforcements on the morning of the 5th. He found the besieged men in good trim. No more killed had been added to the thirteen who fell on the first day, though several had been struck. The wounded numbered forty-three, nearly all of the wounds being slight. The Indians were preparing to fight Merritt when Brady arrived with Ouray's order. No fighting was done afterwards, except that Lieutenant Weir and Captain of Scouts Humme were killed, and the scouting party of Lieutenant Hall, from which they had detached themselves, was attacked. The Indians claimed that this resulted from Humme's shooting at some Indians that he met, and this is the only evidence extant on the subject. On the 9th word was received at Los Pinos that the White Rivers would fight no more, and that the Southern Utes would not join in any hostilities.

On the 11th Merritt advanced to White River agency. All along the road were ghastly evidences of savage fury. In a gulch, six miles from the agency, lay the body of Carl Goldstein, a contractor who was taking supplies to Meeker. A hundred yards away was Julius Moore, one of his teamsters, with two bullet-holes in his breast, and his body hacked and mutilated. A little farther down the cañon the soldiers came to the old coal-mine, in which was found the body of Henry Dresser, engineer at the agency. He lay on his back, with his head pillowed on his folded coat. By his side was a Winchester rifle containing eight cartridges. In one of his pockets was Meeker's message to Thornburgh, with which Eskridge had started. It is evident that Dresser had escaped from the agency wounded. He found Eskridge's body, and, remembering that he bore a message, had taken the letter from his pocket to carry it forward. He had become weak, and crawled into the cave to rest, but his life was spent. The Indians had not found him. Two miles from White River Eskridge was found, naked, with a bullet-hole through his head. The agency was a scene of overwhelming desolation. All the buildings but one were burned down. No sign of life was near, and the absence of life was emphasized by the haphazard scattering of articles of all kinds over the ground, indicating a season of riotous pillaging before the burning. Lying here and there were the bodies of the victims. Father Meeker lay naked, on his back, one hundred yards from the ashes of his house. A bullet had pierced his brain, and the left side of his head was mashed in with a club. A barrel stave was driven into his mouth. Around his neck was a chain, by which he had probably been dragged from the store-house. These indignities to him meant that their hatred was directed chiefly towards him. Frank Dresser's corpse lay over in the field, with a bullet through the heart. George

Eaton, one of the laborers, lay naked, shot through the left breast. From some strange fancy, the Indians had placed a bundle of paper bags in his arms, after stripping him. The wolves had been eating him. These bodies, with those of Thompson, Price, and the others, were all picked up and buried.

The first object to which the government directed its attention, after the outbreak was checked by Ouray, was the recovery of the captive women.

DOUGLAS.

This was undertaken by General Charles Adams, special agent of the Indian Department, who, with an escort of fifteen Utes, started from Los Pinos for the hostile camp, on October 21, to secure their release. A stormy council was held on his arrival. Part of the Indians wanted to give up the captives and make peace. The rest wished to kill Adams and go on with the war. It was understood that the Uintahs, Shoshonees, and others promised assistance, but this was largely a result of Mormon misrepresentations. There were a few members of other tribes who would have aided the hostiles, but the majority favored preserving the peace. The Mormons unquestionably tried to help on the war. There were two of their emissaries in the hostile camp while Adams was there. The friendly Utes always said that the Mormons promised aid, and the hostiles would neither admit nor deny it. There was found, behind the breastworks of the Indians who besieged the force on Milk Creek, the body of an unknown white man, in the attitude of firing, just as he had been killed. He did not belong in that locality. The chances are about ten to one that he had a Mormon brand on his soul. Opposing these influences were Ouray's authority, the apprehension of being worsted by the soldiers, and the influence of a little knot of friendly Indians. Prominent among these were two squaws, Susan and Jane. Susan was a wife of Johnson and a sister of Ouray. She felt under obligations to the whites. Years before, when Governor Evans presided over the affairs of Colorado Territory, she had been captured by the Arapahoes. They were making preparations to burn her, when she was rescued by soldiers and taken to Fort Collins. Anxious to get to her people, she slipped away from the fort and narrowly escaped recapture by the Arapahoes, who were looking for her. She was saved by a ranchman, who hid her under some cabbages in his wagon when he saw the Arapahoes coming. She was taken to Central City, furnished with a horse, and returned in safety to her people. She not only treated the captives kindly, but also went boldly into the council, an almost unheard-of thing among the Utes, and insisted on their release. Jane was the wife of Pah-vitz. She had been cured of a serious illness by Mrs. Meeker, and had been treated kindly by her and her daughter. She manifested her gratitude by numerous acts of friendship.

There was another influence that affected the Indians. It was their rage over some pictures that they claimed to have found on the body of some dead person, but this was directed more particularly towards Meeker. The story is somewhat incoherent, and possibly was not correctly understood. It was to the effect that they had found, on this body, pictures of

Meeker, Mrs. Meeker, Josie, and Mrs. Price, each showing a wound in some mortal part, and each covered with blood. Meeker's showed a wound in the head, Josie's in the breast, and the others similarly. These, the Indians said, had been sent to make bad feeling against them. Whenever the subject was introduced they became furious. Some thought there was nothing in it, but Miss Meeker and Brady were both of the opinion that there was, because the story was repeated so often, by different Indians, and always the same. Captain Payne offered two possible explanations. One was that in his trunk, which was captured by the Indians, there was a picture of an Indian that had been given him a short time before by one of the scouts. When Thornburgh's body was recovered this picture was lying on his breast, held by a small stone. The Indian was not known to Payne, but was said by the Utes to be one of the Uncompahgrés. This occurrence, however, has so little identity with the story that it may be left out of consideration as an explanation. The second was that a teamster found on a bush a sheet of paper bearing rough drafts of the bodies of three or four men, with holes through them, that might have been meant for representations of bullet-wounds. Under the figures were wavy lines like writing. This was brought to Payne on the night of the attack at Milk Creek. The only objections to this are that the pictures were recognized by the Indians as those of the persons mentioned, and that this picture did not fall into the hands of the Indians. On the other hand, it may have been in the possession of the Indians before it was found, and the identity of the figures may have been indicated by some of the signs used in their system of pictography. It is possible that the body referred to may have been that of Eskridge, and he may have had in his pockets photographs, which had been defaced, as photographs sometimes are, by pencil or ink marks.

But to resume: the tribe at length decided that the captives should be given up, and there remained no objection except from Persune, who had become madly infatuated with Miss Meeker. He implored her to remain with him; promised that she should never do any work; that all his possessions should be hers, and similar rash vows. He wept like a

MAJOR T. T. THORNBURGH.

child, but his prayers and tears were of no avail. The other Indians regarded all this as a good joke on Persune, and afterwards, when the news of her death, while a Treasury clerk in Washington, came to them on Uintah Valley reservation, they nudged one another slyly, winked significantly, and said that Persune ought to put on his mourning paint for his wife. General Adams, with the captives, reached Merritt's camp on the night of the 23d, and conveyed them thence to Los Pinos. The captives then claimed that they had not been subjected to indignity, and General Adams stated afterwards that this was his reason for urging the withdrawal of the troops. They did not make a full statement of their treatment to any of the officials until their depositions were taken at Greeley, on November 4, and then very reluctantly, and under promise that the newspapers should not have information of it. The public did not learn the facts for several weeks.

The story of the remainder of the Ute trouble is mainly the record of the tedious sessions of two commissions. The government demanded the surrender of the parties guilty of the massacre and the attack on Thornburgh, but could get no legal evidence of their identity. The white survivors could not testify to the killing of any white man by any Indian. The Indians denied everything, except what favored them. They had learned the white man's maxim: "No man can be compelled to criminate himself," and had evidently added to it the words, "or any of his friends." Not a man could be found who knew any one that had been implicated. The chiefs who undoubtedly led in the attacks swore that they were not present, or, if present, were trying to preserve the peace. Finally, General Hatch demanded the surrender of the parties against whom there was the greatest show of evidence; *viz.:* Douglas, Johnson, Antelope, Ebenezer, Persune, Ahu-u-tu-pu-wit, Johnny (Douglas's son-in-law), Sah-witz (Sawa-wick, Sow-er-wick, Serwick, Serrick), Crepah, Tim Johnson, Thomas (an Uintah), and Pah-vitz. The proceedings were also delayed by the death of Ouray, on August 24, 1880, and of Ka-ni-a-che, who was struck by lightning two days after the death of Ouray. In one sense the death of Ouray furthered the final adjustment of the difficulty. He did not wish to move, though he finally consented to it, and he did not wish to leave his tribe. He had repeatedly said: "Ouray will never leave the great mountains." He and his tribe had the clear right to remain and retain the reservation, under the treaty. They had not only not been hostile, but also had prevented a general war. If Ouray had desired war—if he had even refused to interfere with the White Rivers—the frontier settlements would have been damaged incalculably. Inspector Pollock well wrote from the San Juan: "Saltpetre would not save this country but for the counsel of Ouray." No commissioner with a sentiment of decency or honesty could advise forcing him or his people to give up the reservation, and yet the rabble forgot his services, and could no longer see a distinction between good and bad Indians. Their skins are all of the same color, are they not? They are when the white man wants their property, at any rate.

The work of the commission was further complicated, and perhaps hastened, by the invasion of the reservation by armed bands of prospectors, and gangs of railroad graders. In the fall of 1880 war was almost precipitated by the murder of Young Johnson, a son of Shavano, by a drunken teamster, and the lynching of the teamster by the Indians. An adjustment was at length arranged, on the basis that none of the Indians should be punished, but that they should all move to new reservations. Strict justice would have required that the guilty Indians should be punished and the peaceable ones allowed to retain the reservation, but this would not have been satisfactory to either party. The Indians did not wish to be punished, and the whites wished to get the reservation. Under the circumstances, the solution arrived at was perhaps the best that could have been made. The Southern Utes were given land in severalty on the Animas, Florida, and other streams in Southern Colorado. The White Rivers were sent to the Uintah agency. The Los Pinos Indians were put on a new reservation on Green River, east of and adjoining the Uintah agency. It was stated by the Indians, accepted by the commission, and adopted by the government, that the guilty parties had fled beyond the jurisdiction of the United States. Of course this was a fiction. Those parties are all on the reservations in Utah; at least, they were eighteen months ago. But there was no special object to be gained by their surrender. There was not evidence to convict them, and the tribe was willing to purchase immunity by the surrender of the reservation. It is rare that any tribunal has an opportunity to settle a question so satisfactorily to all parties concerned, and, being so settled, it is to be hoped that our differences with the Utes are henceforth, forever, *res judicata.*

CHAPTER XXI.

CRUELTY, PITY, AND JUSTICE.

On July 20, 1867, was passed "an act to establish peace with certain hostile Indian tribes," providing for the creation of a board of peace commissioners. As members of this board, there were named in the act N. G. Taylor, J. B. Henderson, J. B. Sanborn, and S. F. Tappan, to whom the President was empowered to add four army officers. He named Generals Sherman, Harney, Terry, and Augur. The discussion connected with the emancipation and citizenship of the negroes had educated the people to a just appreciation of the natural rights of all men, and an awakening public conscience pointed to the Indian as a victim of past injustice. The "peace policy of General Grant," as it was commonly called, received the approval of a great majority of Americans. The labors of the peace commissioners were considered so valuable, and the advantages to be gained by authorizing a committee of citizens to aid in the conduct of Indian affairs were so evident, that by an act of April 10, 1869, a permanent Board of Indian Commissioners was organized. It was composed of ten civilians, who received no compensation for their services, but had their expenses paid, and were to assist in procuring and maintaining peace with the Indians, for which purposes an appropriation of two million dollars was made. Unfortunately for the Indian, the feeling in his favor wandered off into the channel of abstract compliment. From a demon he was raised to the position of a temporal deity by the extremists who were now given an opportunity to aid him. The gentlemen who wrote the reports of the commissioners revelled in riotous imaginations and discarded facts, as a part of the old and offensive *régime* which was henceforth to be abandoned. Take, for instance, this picture of the Indian's character from one of the reports: "His only compromise is to have his rights, real or fancied, fully conceded. To force he yields nothing. In battle he never surrenders, and is the more excusable, therefore, that he never accepts capitulation at the hands of others. In war he does not ask or accept mercy. He is then the more consistent that he does not grant mercy." This statement is astounding, in the face of the fact that for over three centuries the Indian had been yielding to force, surrendering, accepting mercy, and compromising his rights, if he ever had any. It is hardly possible that the commissioners ever read carefully the balderdash that has been printed over their names. Certainly the four military members of the peace commission did not realize to what they were assenting; it has been quoted to them at times when it must have been very embarrassing, from a logical stand-point, as, for example, in the case of Wendell Phillips's open letter to General Sherman during the Modoc war. These officers knew, as any sane man does, that the Indian is not an angel. He is merely an uncivilized man who has some good qualities and some bad ones, like other mortals. What he needs is honesty and justice, more than admiration or maudlin sympathy, and what success the peace policy has had has been in the line of the extension to the red man of that justice and reasonable aid to which Americans generally believe he is entitled.

The earlier years of commission work were devoted to the plains Indians and to those in the more settled parts of the country. During this time the extermination policy was pursued in Arizona. In June, 1869, Major-general Thomas relieved General Halleck, in command of the Military Division of the Pacific, and General Ord succeeded to the command of the Department of California. General Ord was an enthusiastic exterminator, so far as the Apaches were concerned. He writes, in September, 1869: "I encouraged the troops to capture and root out the Apache by every means, and to hunt them as they would wild animals. This they have done with unrelenting vigor. Since my last report over two hundred have been killed, generally by parties who have trailed them for days and weeks into the mountain recesses,

over snows, among gorges and precipices, lying in wait for
them by day, and following them by night. Many villages
have been burned, large quantities of arms and supplies of
ammunition, clothing, and provisions have been destroyed, a
large number of horses and mules have been captured, and
two men, twenty-eight women, and thirty-four children taken

HAUNTS OF THE APACHES.

prisoners; and though we have lost quite a number of soldiers, I think the Apaches have discovered that they are getting the worst of it." A more profitable result was obtained
in Western Arizona, where the less nomadic bands of the
Apaches were located. These Indians were more closely
surrounded by white neighbors and nearer to the locations
of the troops; besides which they were of a more peaceable
character than the other tribes. There were several bands
that were quite agricultural in their pursuits, notably that of

Miguel, who kept back in the mountain valleys and took little or no part in any of the wars. Miguel's village, with a white flag flying over each lodge, was found in the heart of the White Mountains by Captain Barry, whose forces were on an exterminating expedition, but these Indians showed so much sincerity in their professions of peace that even the Mexican scouts said they could not fire on them. For these Apaches the White Mountain reservation was first established, and to it others gathered as they learned that they could surrender and remain at peace in their own country.

Although extermination was not being satisfactorily accomplished in Arizona, the legitimate object of war was being obtained. The Apaches were gradually being brought to a realization that peace was a better mode of life than war. They were learning that their enemies could invade their homes, destroy their property, and keep them in constant apprehension of death. Some of them were ready to live peaceably at places where they could be protected, but for this result, which ought to have been the primary object of the war, there had been no adequate preparation. Indians who desired to surrender could go to the White Mountains, but Indians living elsewhere, who desired to make peace and settle in their old homes, had no one who could talk to them with authority. In February, 1871, a party of Indian women came to Camp Grant, near the junction of the San Pedro and Arivapa rivers, in search of a captive boy. They were treated kindly, and through them communication was had with Es-kim-en-zin, the chief of their band. They were Arivapa or Pinal Apaches, about one hundred and fifty in number. The chief said that they wished to make peace. Lieut. Royal E. Whitman, commanding the post, told them to go to the White Mountains. They were not willing to do this; some of their number had been there and found the locality unhealthy; the Indians there were people with whom they had never mixed. More than this, their home was on the Arivapa. They said, " Our fathers and their fathers before them have lived in these mountains, and have raised corn in this valley." Lieutenant Whitman told them that he had no authority to make a treaty or to promise them a per-

manent home at that place, but that they might surrender to
him, and he would feed and protect them as prisoners until
the authorities could be heard from. To this they agreed.
They came in about March 1st, and were immediately followed by other small tribes, bringing the number, by March

5th, to about three hun-
dred. Whitman ex-
pressed a full account
of the matter to Divis-
ion head-quarters, and
six weeks later received
an answer. The answer
was that his communi-
cation had not been en-
dorsed in accordance
with official etiquette,
and it was returned
therewith. There was
no comment on the con-
tents. The fate of three
hundred people was of
less importance than the
manner of addressing a
report.

Lieutenant Whit-
man had located the
Arivapas half a mile
from the post, and
counted them every oth-
er day. Their number
gradually increased till
it reached five hundred
and ten. They were
very destitute and al-

EFFECT OF EXTERMINATION POLICY ON ARIZONA
SETTLER.

most naked, but it was found that they were willing to work
to obtain clothing, so they were set to gathering hay. They
cut it with their knives and brought it in on their backs, but
by this slow method they furnished the post with one hundred
and fifty tons in less than two months, besides gathering large

quantities of mescal for their own use. As the weather grew warmer they were allowed to move four or five miles farther up the Arivapa, to some land that they wished to cultivate, and here they were counted and rationed every third day. About April 1st Captain Stanwood arrived and took command of the post, with instructions to hold and feed any Indians he might find there as prisoners of war. He examined the status of the Arivapas and left them as they were. On April 24th he started to the south, on a scout, leaving Lieutenant Whitman in charge of the post, with fifty infantry. The Indians were well-behaved, and the system of counting made it impossible for them to go any great distance from their camp. The ranchmen in the neighborhood were on friendly terms with them, and had made some contracts for their services in the coming harvest.

On April 28th a large party of Americans, Mexicans, and Papago Indians left Tucson, with the avowed determination of killing these Arivapas. Captain Penn, commanding at Fort Lowell, sent word of this movement to Lieutenant Whitman by a messenger, who arrived on the morning of April 30th. Whitman at once sent two men to the Indians to tell them to come in, but in an hour the messengers returned and informed him that it was too late. The camp was strewn with the mutilated bodies of women and children, and their lodges were burning. The post-surgeon, Doctor Briesly, with twelve men, was at once despatched to the place with a wagon, to bring in any wounded that might be found. Doctor Briesly said, "On my arrival I found that I should have but little use for wagon or medicine; the work had been too thoroughly done. The camp had been fired, and the dead bodies of some twenty-one women and children were lying scattered over the ground; those who had been wounded in the first instance had their brains beaten out with stones. Two of the best-looking of the squaws were lying in such a position, and from the appearance of the genital organs and of their wounds, there can be no doubt that they were first ravished and then shot dead. Nearly all of the dead were mutilated. One infant of some ten months was shot twice, and one leg hacked nearly off. While going over the ground,

46

we came upon a squaw who was unhurt, but were unable to get her to come in and talk, she not feeling very sure of our good intentions."

The next morning Lieutenant Whitman went out with a party to bury the dead. He says, " I thought the act of caring for their dead would be an evidence to them of our sympathy at least, and the conjecture proved correct, for while at the work many of them came to the spot and indulged in their expressions of grief, too wild and terrible to be described. That evening they began to come in from all directions, singly and in small parties, so changed in forty-eight hours as to be hardly recognizable, during which time they had neither eaten nor slept. Many of the men, whose families had all been killed, when I spoke to them and expressed sympathy for them, were obliged to turn away, unable to speak, and too proud to show their grief. The women whose children had been killed or stolen were convulsed with grief, and looked to me appealingly, as though I was their last hope on earth. Children who, two days before, had been full of fun and frolic kept at a distance, expressing wondering horror. I did what I could; I fed them, and talked to them, and listened patiently to their accounts. I sent horses into the mountains to bring in two badly-wounded women, one shot through the left lung, and one with an arm shattered. These were attended to, and are doing well, and will recover. Their camp was surrounded and attacked at daybreak. So sudden and unexpected was it, that no one was awake to give the alarm, and I found quite a number of women shot while asleep beside their bundles of hay which they had collected to bring in on that morning. The wounded who were unable to get away had their brains beaten out with clubs or stones, while some were shot full of arrows after having been mortally wounded by gunshot. The bodies were all stripped. Of the whole number buried, one was an old man and one was a well-grown boy—all the rest women and children. Of the whole number killed and missing—about one hundred and twenty-five—only eight were men. It has been said that the men were not there—they were all there. On the 28th we counted one hundred and twenty-eight men, a small number

being absent for mescal, all of whom have since been in. . . .
About their captives they say, 'Get them back for us; our
little boys will grow up slaves, and our girls, as soon as they
are large enough, will be diseased prostitutes, to get money for
whoever owns them. Our women work hard and are good
women, and they and our children have no diseases. Our
dead you cannot bring to life, but those that are living we
gave to you, and we look to you, who can write and talk and
have soldiers, to get them back.' I will assure you it is no
easy task to convince them of my zeal when they see so little
being done. I have pledged my word to them that I never
would rest easily, day or night, until they should have justice,
and just now I would as soon leave the army as to be ordered
away from them, or to be obliged to order them away from
here. But you will know the difficulties in the way. You
know that parties who would engage in murder like this,
could and would (and have already) make statements and
multiply affidavits without end in their justification. I know
you will use your influence on the right side. I believe with
them, this may be made either a means of making good citizens of them and their children, or drive them out to a hopeless war of extermination. They ask to be allowed to live
here in their old homes, where nature supplies nearly all their
wants; they ask for a fair and impartial trial of their faith,
and they ask that all their captive children living may be returned to them. Is their demand unreasonable?"

Unhappily for the good repute of Arizona, the press, and
apparently the people, justified or apologized for this monstrous crime. The frontier press does not always represent
the feeling of a majority of the community in these matters.
It is sensational on all subjects, and it is down on Indians on
all occasions, on the supposition that this course is popular.
It is popular in time of war. Misrepresentation may then be
carried as far as in politics, or farther, for then there is but
one side to be heard. But there is no community so de-
praved as to favor assassination in time of peace, and this was
downright assassination. Whatever provocation there existed was in the offence of other people. The massacre cannot
even be justified on the theory that it was an application of

lynch law, for lynching is resorted to for the purpose of just
punishment, irregularly of course, but still for the exclusive
purpose of punishment. The accompaniments of this deed
showed that no such motives actuated these murderers. The
camp was plundered, women were ravished, and the children
carried away were sold for the profit of their captors. Lust
and plunder are not motives consistent with the savage justice that sometimes makes lynching almost excusable. It
seems unjust to charge this wrong against the American people, for most of the perpetrators were Mexicans and Indians,
and there were Americans near by who would have given
protection to the victims if it had been in their power. It
ought to rank as a crime committed by criminals.

The offence of the people of Arizona was in defending it,
and the method of defence was worse than the abstract wrong
of defending a wicked and shameful action. The papers of
Arizona attacked Whitman, charging him with being a deb-
auchee and a consorter with Indian women. Even if these
charges had been true, they did not make the massacre any
less wrong; and they did not weaken Whitman's statements,
for these were confirmed in every particular by other men.
But the charges were not true, if we may believe the solemn
statements of the officers, men, contractors, and employés of
the post. Men of all classes, who voluntarily stated that they
had come to Camp Grant prejudiced against the Apaches,
swore that these Indians were peaceable and well-behaved,
and that the charges against Lieutenant Whitman were false.
One hundred of the participants in this affair, Americans,
Mexicans, and Papagos, were indicted and brought to trial
that year, in the December term of the United States District Court. The jury remained out for twenty minutes and
returned a verdict of "not guilty." It is such verdicts as
this that are bringing the jury system into disrepute. Nevertheless, the prosecution had some effect. It is a great step
towards civilization even to have men indicted for murder.
It tends to repress the light-hearted assassin. There is only
one consideration that affords any shadow of excuse for Camp
Grant: the Apaches made war similarly. With them it was
the highest science of war to lull an enemy's suspicions and

then murder him. Under similar circumstances hostile Apaches would probably have committed the Camp Grant massacre and gloried in it. This consideration is more than offset by the inexpediency of the act. This horrible warfare had to be ended in some way, and the military had the task to perform. There were but two ways of doing it; one was to exterminate the Indians; the other was to require both sides to observe the laws of civilization until confidence was restored. Years of warfare had shown the first to be impracticable. It was suicidal to place any obstacle in the way of attaining the second. As a matter of expediency, carrying away the children was worse than the murders, for this was a continuing wrong. Of the twenty-nine children taken, two escaped and five were recovered from Arizonians. The remainder were sold into slavery in Sonora.

An unfortunate misunderstanding occurred, soon after the massacre, that resulted in another attack on these Arivapas, and apparently gave them reason to believe that there were no white men who could be trusted. The grief-stricken remnant of the tribe gathered again in the valley, under promise of protection, and assurance that the soldiers had no part in the bloody work. Among them was Eskimenzin, the chief who first came to the post. In the massacre he lost two wives five children, and about fifty of his tribe. He came back during the burial and assisted in this mournful task, although nearly crazed with grief over his loss. As the Indians slowly returned, they camped in small parties, fearing to get together lest another attack should be made. On one of these parties, consisting of Eskimenzin and the remnant of his family, a party of soldiers suddenly came while returning from the White Mountains, about a month after the massacre, and by mistake, in the confusion of the moment, fired upon them. No one was killed, but Eskimenzin lost all confidence in the protectorate. He fled to the mountains with his remaining people, and killed a white man as he went.

The Camp Grant massacre naturally raised a whirlwind of indignation in the East among those who advocated peace, and even conservative people who had not been inclined to Indian-worship recoiled at this atrocity. In July, President

Grant gave Mr. Vincent Colyer plenary powers to go into Arizona and adjust the Indian troubles there as appeared proper to him. His advent as a representative of the government was heralded by the Arizona press with the same fiery defiance that used to characterize the Mormon papers when the government proposed to take a hand in Utah affairs. Still the government was not observed to tremble, and Mr. Colyer's policy was enforced. The Arizona papers simply weakened their cause by their absurd threatenings. Mr. Colyer was notoriously ultra in his peace theories, and evidently did not understand the situation in Arizona and New Mexico, but he was quite as correct as his assailants. There were in reality a large number of Indians there who were sufficiently humbled by war to be ready for reservation life, under control of the Indian Department. There were also many who had not been humbled, who had never been conquered, and who considered themselves the superiors of white men in all respects except numbers and equipments. It was as erroneous to suppose that the latter class would live peaceably on reservations, as it was barbarous to continue war against the well-disposed. No warlike Indian ever submitted to reservation restrictions until he had been whipped. He cannot be a savage ruler and an humble pupil at the same time. He cannot feel that fighting is the only work that a man ought to do, and yet take kindly to ploughing. His spirit must be broken in some way, or his nature changed, before he will submit to it. The right or wrong of breaking his spirit is another question; the fact remains that he must be born again into civilization, if he ever attains civilization.

It is but just to say that Mr. Colyer did not have full opportunity to talk with either the Indians or the people. The Indians were afraid to come in, being apprehensive of treachery, and Colyer did not care to interview the white population on account of the violent tone of the press. His changes of the location of the Indians were rather extensive, and none of them produced good results. The more peaceful portion of the Mimbreños had been living at and about Cañada Alamosa (Cottonwood Valley), and for these he selected a reservation in the Tularosa valley, to which the hostile Mimbreños with their allied Chiricahuas were also expected to come. None of the Indians wanted to go there, and many refused to go. Cochise, the Chiricahua chief, who had surrendered in September, 1871, with a band of about two hundred, went back to his old haunts in the spring of 1872, when the removal occurred. More than six hundred others followed their example. Less than half of the sixteen hundred Apaches gathered at Cañada Alamosa consented to go to Tularosa valley, and these were wretched and discontented. The water there was bad, the climate was cold, and the Indians were frightened by superstitions. They had warning legends of the destruction of the ancient races who once inhabited the ruins there, and they viewed the sickness which prevailed among them with great alarm. By fall their discontent was so great that the reservation was recommended to be abandoned, and the Indians placed on a reservation at Ojo Caliente, near their old home, which was done in 1874. Mr. Colyer established a reservation for the Pinaleños and Gileños at the mouth of the San Pedro River. It contained about one hundred square miles, extending west from the San Pedro and south from the Gila. These Apaches remained there for about a year, and then, on account of sickness, the proximity of settlers, and the inadequate supply of water, were established on a reservation on the Gila, south of and adjoining the original White Mountain reservation, and known as the San Carlos division. The Indians who had assembled in the White Mountains were gathered about Camp Apache (known at various times as Camp Ord, Camp Mogollon, and Camp Thomas), in the northern part of the present reservation, and these were left as they were. The Chiricahua reservation, in Southeastern Arizona, extending from the Mexican line to the Peloncillo Mountains, and including the Chiricahua range, was established in the following year by General Howard, as special agent. A very satisfactory reservation was set off for the Yampais, or Apache Mohaves, about Camp Verde, by Mr. Colyer; no other changes were made by him, except in the treatment of the hostiles.

As to these, his plans came in conflict with those which had been adopted by General Crook, who had taken command of the Department of Arizona on June 4, 1871. General Crook was the beau-ideal Indian-fighter of the frontiersmen at that time, and continued to be until his recent fair treatment of the Apaches has made him objectionable to the more rabid exterminationists—not that his treatment was not formerly fair; there has been no change in his expressed opinions concerning the Indians, though his opinion of their white neighbors in Arizona appears to have lowered somewhat. He was not an exterminator. His policy was to subdue the Indians and then treat them honestly. He said in September, 1871, "I think that the Apache is painted in darker colors than he deserves, and that his villainies arise more from a misconception of facts than from his being worse than other Indians. Living in a country the natural products of which will not support him, he has either to cultivate the soil or steal, and as our vacillating policy satisfies him we are afraid of him, he chooses the latter, also as requiring less labor and being more congenial to his natural instincts. I am satisfied that a sharp, active campaign against him would not only make him one of the best Indians in the country, but it would also save millions of dollars to the Treasury, and the lives of many innocent whites and Indians." General Crook had begun preparations for an active campaign against all hostiles when Colyer arrived, but Colyer's powers were made superior to his, and Colyer desired to try coaxing. Later on, Crook was given power to proceed

GENERAL GEORGE CROOK.

against all who failed to respond to Colyer's appeals, but finding that the prosecution of his plans would interfere with the negotiations of the peace agents, he undertook no active hostilities, and contented himself with pursuing and punishing, as far as possible, parties who made raids on the settlements. Mr. Colyer's plans for the procurement of peace were given a fair trial for over a year, and they failed. The hostiles did not come in, and they did not remain quiet. From September 1, 1871, to September 4, 1872, they made fifty-four separate attacks on the whites in Arizona, with recorded results as follows: soldiers killed, 3; citizens killed, 41; citizens wounded, 16; government horses and cattle stolen, 68; same stolen from citizens, 489. The actual depredations were slightly in excess of this statement. It may be remarked, parenthetically, that this damage and fourteen months' delay in obtaining peace, were caused by the Camp Grant massacre; but for that affair Mr. Colyer would not have been sent to Arizona, and General Crook would have conquered the hostiles in 1871. In view of the results mentioned, General Crook announced in September, 1872, his intention of proceeding to " punish the incorrigibly hostile."

For the first time in the history of that part of the country, the fair and sensible manner of dealing with the Apaches was adopted. Its results have proven this, and have shown General Crook to be the right man in the right place. It must be remembered that he had left to him a legacy of the hatred of three centuries between the peoples whom he had to pacify; that a large portion of the white population were as barbarous in their modes of warfare as the Apaches themselves; that Arizona was still a refuge for the criminal and lawless men of other states and territories; that war and pillage had been bred into the Apaches, until they were the most savage and intractable Indians in the country; that large bands of their nation still infested Northern Mexico, and had almost impregnable strongholds there; that Mexico pursued war in the old way, and still paid bounty for Apache scalps, no matter where procured; that slavery still existed in Mexico, and it was next to impossible to recover Indians once carried across the line. During the winter a vigorous campaign was prosecuted against the Tontos, Coyotéros, Yampais, and Hualapais, and by the summer of 1873 they were subdued.   Del-Shay's band of Tontos were captured in the Sierra Ancha by Captain Randall, on April 22d, with that notorious chief himself, who had played fast and loose with Mr. Colyer, and earned a reputation for unblushing treachery by his dealings with others.   Jemaspie's band of Hualapais surrendered to Captain McGregor, in the Santa Maria Mountains, on June 12th.   Lieutenant Babcock handsomely whipped the Tontos under Natatotel and Naqui-naquis, on June 16th, and forced their surrender.   Soon afterwards Captain Burns captured two hundred Yampais, the last organized band in Northern Arizona, and peace was practically established.

The Hualapais, or Apache Yumas, numbering about eight hundred, were gathered at Beale's Springs, whence the Indian Department moved them, much against their wills, to the Colorado River reservation.   When the removal was first proposed to them, they fled to the mountains and said they would resist to the death, but, through fear of the soldiers, they came back and were removed.   The Indians at this reservation were unfriendly to them, and the climate was unendurable to these people of the mountains.   In four months nearly all of them were afflicted with an epidemic eruptive disease; many of their children were nearly blind from a disease of the eyes, brought on by the heat and dust; and half of their horses had starved to death.   The troops stationed there suffered almost as much as the Indians.   After a year's residence there the Hualapais left the place in a body and went back to their old homes, but without committing any depredations.   They lived there on friendly terms with the whites for a time, and were then removed to San Carlos, through the intercession of General Crook.   The Yampais, or Apache Mohaves, and part of the Tontos, numbering nearly two thousand, were located on a reservation about Camp Verde.   The Pinaleños, with a few stragglers from other tribes, in all about twelve hundred, were sent to San Carlos, where they still remain.   There were about sixteen hundred Apaches, known as the White Mountain Apaches, grouped about Camp Apache.   It was estimated that about one thousand renegades, one-third of whom were warriors, still remained at large in various parts of the Territory, but there were not probably more than one-third to one-half of that number. Against these an unceasing war was waged.

The Indians placed on the reservations were kept under rigid surveillance. Each warrior was furnished with a metal check marked with his number and the name of his tribe. The officers in charge kept record of them and their families by these numbers, and as a full description of each man was recorded, and rations were issued on these checks, it was impossible for them to leave the reservation undetected. The remarkable success of General Crook in conquering these tribes so quickly was obtained by fighting Apaches with Apaches. The friendly White Mountain Indians and Hualapais were used against the others. They acted in the best of faith, rendering services that were invaluable. They knew the country as well as the hostiles, and could interpret all their signals, besides being adepts in the ruses of Apache warfare. After being brought on the reservation they were still used as police, with such gratifying results that the Indian police system has since been extended to all reservations. The Apaches were informed that their welfare would rest mainly with themselves; that white people punished their own offenders, and they must do the same. This was especially beneficial in the case of the Apaches, because they are thoroughly democratic in their tribal government. They have no hereditary chiefs; each warrior has a large amount of independence, and the rivalry between various aspirants for power usually affords any wrong-doer a certain amount of backing. The only way in which the guilty could be certainly singled out was by making the Indians the agents of the law. There were, of course, many who awaited only an opportunity to resume their old life, and the machinations of these could be detected and repressed by the Indians alone. In the spring of 1873, certain of these conspired to kill all the whites at San Carlos and make their escape. On May 27th the attempt was made prematurely, resulting in a failure. Chan-Deisi, a malcontent chief, tried to spear Agent Larrabee, but was prevented by Yomas, another Indian. He then shot and killed Lieutenant Almy. The bands of Cochinay and Chuntz, to which he belonged, at once fled to the mountains, and for over a year they were hunted by the troops and the reservation Apaches. Many of the Indians became worn out, and begged to return to the reservation, but they were met with the reply that they could come only when they brought Cochinay, Chuntz, and Chan-Deisi, dead or alive. One by one they joined the troops in hunting down their fugitive kindred. Cochinay was killed on May 26, 1874; Chan-Deisi was killed on June 12th; and Chuntz on July 25th. Del-Shay, the Tonto chief, tried to play treachery at the Verde reservation, to which he had been permitted to remove, by murdering all of the whites there. He had them surrounded, and would have killed them but for the prompt resistance of the police and other Indians. He was brought to bay and killed by his own people on July 27th. The punishment of these chiefs is conclusive evidence that a new era had dawned upon the Apaches.

The Apaches under General Crook's supervision were also giving other evidences of reformation. They were farming extensively and building houses for themselves. At Verde they made an excellent irrigating canal at no expense to the government. The White Mountain Indians, in 1874, raised 300,000 pounds of corn and 5000 pounds of beans, besides delivering 750 tons of hay to the post and making five miles of irrigating ditches. Everywhere they were quiet, except the few renegades, who were hunted diligently. For the first time in its history Arizona was at peace. The Indians were all on reservations that suited them, except the Hualapais, and they had seen the hopelessness of war. The whites also were satisfied, except that class who prey upon their fellow-men, and search out the helpless because they are the more easy and profitable victims. Governor Safford said, in his message of January 6, 1875, " At no period in the history of Arizona have our Indian affairs been in so satisfactory condition. Comparative peace now reigns throughout the Territory, with almost a certainty that no general Indian war will ever occur again. General Crook, in the subjugation of the Apaches, has sustained his former well-earned military reputation, and deserves the lasting gratitude of our people." Let it be remembered that this result was effected neither by the extermination policy nor by the so-called peace policy. It was the work of a man who said, "Vengeance is just as much to be deprecated as a silly sentimentalism." His policy was simple justice to red and white alike. Bear this in mind, as we proceed, and consider how fully its abandonment answers the question, Why did not this state of affairs continue?

The little cloud, like a man's hand, was already in the sky. In his report of August 31, 1874, General Crook said, "There are now on the Verde reservation about fifteen hundred Indians; they have been among the worst in Arizona; but if the government keeps its promise to them that it shall be their home for all time, there will be no difficulty in keeping them at peace, and engaged in peaceful pursuits. I sincerely hope that the interests that are now at work to deprive these Indians of this reservation will be defeated; but if they succeed, the responsibility of turning these fifteen hundred Apaches loose upon the settlers of Arizona should rest where it belongs." Although this was said of the Verde reservation only, it may be applied to the other Arizona reservations. The Indians were all at peace on reservations that suited them, and the responsibility of driving them to desperation by taking them from their native homes and placing them among enemies, in unhealthy and unpleasant localities, must rest where it belongs. We must turn our eyes to the Indian Bureau—our humanitarian, sympathetic, religious, peace and civilization Indian Bureau. It has been charged time and again that the Indian Department has been controlled by a corrupt ring, which manages to keep its hold on men of every profession and every party who are appointed to represent the government in this branch of its interests. It has been charged that they have had such a control over Congress that they can turn it whither they will, and break down any man who tries to stand up for honesty and justice. Considering the professions that various Indian Commissioners have made, it is but too evident that the control of that department has been in the hands either of men who "stole the livery of Heaven to serve the devil in," or of arrant fools who have been played upon like shepherds' pipes by the land-grabbers, who have secured the spoils. For present purposes it is immaterial which is the correct alternative.

In 1874 the reservations of Arizona passed from the control of the War Department to that of the Indian Bureau, and the latter inaugurated what it was pleased to call "the policy of concentration." In other words, it began taking away from various tribes the lands on which they were peacefully settled, and which had been promised them for their future homes. The interests that were at work to get the Verde reservation did get it, notwithstanding General Crook's hopes, and he was forced into the humiliating position of seeing the Indians taken away from the lands that had been promised them through him. He told the agent sent to remove them that he would give him all the assistance in his power except force; he would not use his soldiers to compel a removal. The Indians did not wish to go, but they went peaceably. They were informed that the President ordered their removal, and they had learned that what the President said must be obeyed. They gave up their houses, their irrigating ditches, and their fields, and went, because they dared not refuse. General Crook did not remain to see the undoing of his work. He was relieved, on March 22, 1875, by Colonel Kautz, and sent to the Department of the Platte, where the Sioux were beginning to be troublesome. Colonel Kautz held the same opinions as to the propriety of keeping faith with Indians that General Crook did, and managed to preserve peace for some months longer. To the statement of the Commissioner of Indian Affairs: "I believe now no one in the territory questions the wisdom of the removal of the Verde Indians," Colonel Kautz bluntly replied: "So far as my observation goes, I have seen no one who endorses it, except those connected with the Indian Department."

The next outrage committed by the Indian Bureau was the removal of the White Mountain Indians—that is, those who had been about Camp Apache, in the northern part of the White Mountain reservation—to the neighborhood of San Carlos agency. The advantages claimed to be gained by this were better and more extensive farming lands, a mild climate, excellent roads, a saving of the expense of an extra agency, and " last, but not least, to the people of the territory, it would avert the trade with these Indians from New Mexico to Arizona, where it properly belongs." The disadvantages were that these were mountain Indians, who were unused to the hot, stifling climate of the Gila Valley; that the region of the new location had proven so unhealthy to the soldiers at Camp Goodwin that the post had to be removed; that the Indians would be placed in close proximity to the white settlement of Pueblo Viejo; and that the Pinal Apaches, already at San Carlos, were their enemies by feuds of many years' standing. There were other considerations that would seem serious to some persons, though these humanitarians, who were desirous of having trade go in its proper channels, did not trouble their minds about them. A large majority, if not all, the Indians were bitterly opposed to the removal, and they had been good friends to us. These were the Indians on whom Mexican scouts had not felt willing to fire; who had helped General Crook to subdue the hostile Apaches; who were living on the little farms that had long supported them; who had raised greater crops than all the other Apaches together. Every inducement to move was used with them, except actual force, and that was refused by the military authorities. They were threatened with force, however, and their agency buildings were burned down by the representatives of the peace policy. Under these kindly arguments nearly half of the Indians consented to go. Their state of mind may be imagined from the fact that, on the way, they had a fight among themselves, in which five were killed and ten wounded—" Not a great loss where so much lead was expended," said the philosophic special agent, L. E. Dudley, who effected the removal. In the fall of the same year (1875) large numbers of these Indians left San Carlos and went to the Chiricahua reservation, stating that they were unable to live at the former place on account of the hostility of the Pinals. That winter they had a falling-out with the Chiricahuas; a Southern Chiricahua chief was killed; and our White Mountain Coyoteros had to flee from that reservation to escape the indiscriminating vengeance of his tribe.

The bands of Pitone, Eskyinlaw (*alias* Diablo), and Pedro, a majority of all the White Mountain Indians, refused to remove to San Carlos. They said that General Howard, as agent of the Indian Department, had promised them that they might remain there so long as they were peaceable; that they had not only been peaceable, but also had fought other Indians, in aid of the Americans. They did not want to leave their farms or their native mountains, and they begged Colonel Kautz to interpose for them at Washington. He did so, and his plea was met with the answer of "hostility of the War Department to the peace policy." Search you now the history of the whole world and find a more wanton act of tyranny than the removal of these Indians from their homes. They would have saluted a Gesler's hat without a murmur; they would have paid a tax on tea without much remonstrance; a foreign lord might have lived in their Dublin Castle without making them desperate. It is almost questionable whether Nero would have been capable of treating his friends and allies as the humane gentlemen treated these unfortunate bands, and yet men ask why the Apaches cannot be made peaceable. No war resulted in this case, because the soldiers could not be induced to compel the removal of the three obdurate bands. But it came finally. There are some Indians into whose necks it will not do to grind your heels too far.

The next victims of humanity were the Chiricahuas. There were, on the Chiricahua reservation, in Southeastern Arizona, the Northern Chiricahuas, under Tah-za, a son of old Cochise, who had died in peace on the reservation some eighteen months before, the Southern Chiricahuas, whose head chief was Juh (Hoo, Who), and a mixed band of Mogollons, Mimbres, and Coyoteros. The management of these warlike bands by the Indian Bureau had been criminally inefficient, and its faults had been pointed out repeatedly. To begin with, their reservation had been made to join the Mexican line, giving every opportunity for raiding from either side. It will be remembered that there were large bands of predatory Apaches in Northern Mexico, and that the Mexicans were still pursuing the old, treacherous system of warfare. The authorities of Sonora complained that the Chiricahuas committed depredations within their borders, which was true in a number of cases. The agency people did not keep count of their Apaches, as General Crook was doing, and there were no restrictions imposed upon them that were sufficient to keep them on their reservation. On the other hand, the Mexicans were constantly coming on the reservation to sell whiskey, or in search of scalps. On July 23, 1875, a party of Chiricahuas who were gathering acorns on the reservation, fifteen miles north of the Mexican line, were fired upon by a party of Mexican soldiers. Notwithstanding these acts of lawlessness, there were no troubles with the whites, on our side of the line, during the four years, from 1872 to 1876, that the Indians were located there. In April of the latter year two white men were killed by two Indians at Sulphur Springs, a mail station on the reservation. The killing was not justifiable, and yet the victims were not entitled to the slightest sympathy. Their death resulted from a violation of the laws of the United States. The Indians were hunting in the Dragoon Mountains, about thirty-five miles from the agency, owing to the fact that their supply of food was exhausted, and the agent had sent them out to procure some for themselves. They obtained whiskey from Mr. Rogers, the station-keeper at Sulphur Springs, who had several times been warned against selling it to them. They got drunk and had a fight among themselves, in which two men and a child were killed; a part of the band then returned to the agency, leaving a chief named Eskina (Skinya), with a dozen warriors and their families. Two of these, a sub-chief named Pi-hon-se-nay and his nephew, went to Sulphur Springs for more whiskey. Rogers sold them small quantities two or three times, and then refused to let them have more, they being drunk. They watched their opportunity, killed Rogers and an employé named Spence, stole the whiskey, ammunition, and horses at the place, and returned to camp. Eskina's entire party got drunk and decided to go on the warpath, which they did, with the result of an American killed, another wounded, and four horses stolen on the next day. A company of cavalry was sent after them, but failed to capture them. Early in June, after committing other depredations, Eskina and his men came to Tahza's camp and tried to induce

47

him to join them.   Tahza and his people refused, and a fight
ensued, in which six men were killed and three wounded.
Pi-hon-se-nay was shot in the shoulder by Tahza, and Eskina
was killed by Tahza's youngest brother.

In the mean time Governor Safford had been consulted by
the Indian Bureau, and had recommended the removal of all
the Chiricahuas, either to Ojo Caliente, in New Mexico, or to
San Carlos.   Removal to Ojo Caliente had been proposed to
them the year before, and they had replied that they " would
sooner die than live there."   The department, instead of cutting off the southern part of the reservation and asking for
troops to guard the Mexican line and punish the guilty Indians, decided to send the innocent ones to San Carlos, the
guilty being at large.   Tahza reluctantly agreed to go, but said
he could not answer for the other bands.   On June 7, Juh,
Geronimo (Heronemo—Jerome), and Nolgee, who had sided
with Eskina in the fight, agreed to go also, but on the same
afternoon they fled with all their people and went into Sonora.
320 of the Chiricahuas went with Tahza to San Carlos, in June;
a small band, under Gordo, had gone to Ojo Caliente just after
Rogers and Spence were killed; the remainder of the 965 Indians reported to be on the reservation, which was three or
four hundred more than were in fact there, went to war.   By
October the hostiles had stolen 170 head of stock and killed
20 persons—probably more; because a number of prospectors
who were known to be in the mountains were never accounted
for.

The evil did not stop there.   In the spring of 1877 Mr.
E. A. Hayt, the man of many removals, became Commissioner
of Indian Affairs under Secretary Schurz.   His policy was " a
steady concentration of the smaller bands of Indians upon the
larger reservations."   It was found that about 250 of the
Chiricahua renegades had taken refuge on the Ojo Caliente
reservation, and made raids from there, assisted by some of the
Hot Springs Indians; hence the Hot Springs reservation must
be broken up, and the Indians removed to San Carlos.   A force
of 103 Indian police was sent over from San Carlos, and the
available troops stationed in New Mexico were concentrated
about the reservation.   Geronimo and other renegades were

found there and arrested. None of the Indians wished to leave Ojo Caliente, but there was no chance for resistance. Very few escaped, the principal party being some 40 warriors led by Victorio, a chief who made himself unpleasantly notorious later on. 453 of them arrived at San Carlos in May. There had been reported 2100 Indians at this place in 1875, and 1600 in 1876, but it was evident that no such number had been there. On September 2, 300 of these Hot Springs and Chiricahua Apaches escaped from San Carlos. They were pursued by the agency Indians, but only 30 women and children were brought back. The remainder made their way to New Mexico, attacked a settlement there, killed 8 persons, and ravaged the neighboring country. Troops were hurried after them, and on September 10 a fight occurred, in which 12 of the hostiles were killed and 13 captured. On October 13, 190 of them surrendered at Fort Wingate, and 50 came in afterwards. All these were taken to Ojo Caliente to await orders for their final disposition. It was decided to take them all back to San Carlos, against which they protested, saying they were willing to go anywhere else, and a number took their chances on a break for the mountains rather than go; 80 of them got safely away. In December 67 of these came to the Mescalero reservation and asked leave to stay there, which was granted.

In February, 1878, Victorio and his band, who had been in Mexico, surrendered at Ojo Caliente, but announced their intention to resist any attempt to take them to San Carlos. In April it was decided to remove them to the Mescalero reservation, but they refused to go, and fled to the mountains. Towards the last of June they went to the Mescalero agency, of their own accord, and promised to remain there. Their wives and children, who were at San Carlos, were sent for, and there appeared to be a prospect of their final settlement, when, most inopportunely, the judge, prosecuting attorney, and other officials of Grant County appeared at the Mescalero reservation on a hunting excursion. Victorio and others of his band were under indictment in Grant County, and they took this to be a move for their arrest. They left the reservation, taking with them all the Chiricahuas who had taken refuge there, and made a most destructive raid through Southwestern New Mexico and Southeastern Arizona, until they were chased into Mexico by the soldiers a few weeks later.

Victorio's stay in Mexico was short. On September 4, 1879, he suddenly appeared near Ojo Caliente with 60 warriors; they killed the post herders, and captured all the horses of the cavalry stationed there. Major Morrow, with the 9th Cavalry, was sent after them, but was able to accomplish but little. Victorio roamed the mountains of Southern New Mexico, depredating in all directions, and spreading terror everywhere. About 200 Mescaleros were induced to join him, and he was further reinforced by at least 100 renegade Comanches and other warriors from Mexico. When dislodged in one mountain range they would fall back to another which afforded a position of equal strength, and if too hard pressed they would scatter in small bands, to unite at some well-known rendezvous. In April, 1880, Colonel Hatch, who had returned from his labors with the Colorado Utes, disarmed all the Indians remaining on the Mescalero reservation and then took up the chase of Victorio. The hostile bands were driven back through the San Mateo, the Mimbres, and the Mogollon mountains. The Arizona forces, under Colonel Carr, turned them to the south, and they were soon driven into Mexico. This outbreak occasioned an unusual loss of life to the scattered herders of New Mexico. These people, mostly Mexicans, had formerly been left unharmed by the Apaches, who secured provisions from the herds and frequently obtained arms and ammunition from the herders. The Mescaleros, Comanches, and other renegades, who had joined Victorio, abandoned his shrewd policy of maintaining friendly relations with these convenient commissaries, and killed them at every opportunity. The result, as nearly as could be ascertained, was that of 73 persons killed during the outbreak 53 were Mexicans, of whom a large percentage were herders. It was claimed that the number of persons killed was in excess of this, and it is probable that a correct list would reach 100.

The bitterness of this warfare, against such desperate odds, set the people of Arizona and New Mexico to thinking of the cause of it all. Said General Willcox, commanding the Department of Arizona: "It is believed by many that Victorio was unjustly dealt with in the first instance, by the abrupt removal of his people from Ojo Caliente, New Mexico, to San Carlos; and that such removal, if not a breach of faith, was a harsh and cruel measure, from which the people of New Mexico have reaped bitter consequences." General Pope, of the Division of the Missouri, was even more pointed in his remarks, and his opinion in this case is the more weighty as he was never an admirer of the Apaches; he had unreservedly expressed his opinion that they were "idle vagabonds, utterly worthless and hopeless," and again, that they were "a squalid, untrustworthy people, robbers and thieves by nature." He said: "This outbreak of Victorio, and the severe campaign against him, still in progress, involving the loss of many of our men, and the murder by Indians of about seventy persons, mainly Mexican herders, were due to the determined purpose of the Interior

GENERAL POPE.

Department to effect the removal of the band to the San Carlos agency in Arizona. There is already a large number of Indians collected at that agency, mainly Indians of Arizona. Victorio and his band have always bitterly objected to being placed there, one of the reasons given by him being the hostility of many of the Indians of the agency. He always asserted his willingness to live peaceably with his people at the Warm Springs (Ojo Caliente) agency, and, so far as I am informed, gave no trouble to any one while there. I do not know the reasons of the Interior Department for in-

742   MASSACRES OF THE MOUNTAINS.

sisting upon the removal to San Carlos agency, but certainly
they should be cogent to justify the great trouble and severe
losses occasioned by the attempts to coerce the removal. The
present is the fourth time within five years that Victorio's
band has broken out. Three times they have been brought
in and turned over by the military to the Indian Bureau
authorities. Both Victorio and his band are resolved to die
rather than go to the San Carlos agency, and there is no
doubt it will be necessary to kill or capture the whole tribe
before present military operations can be closed successfully.
The capture is not very probable, but the killing (cruel as it
will be) can, I suppose, be done in time. I am trying to separate the Mescaleros from Victorio, and yet hope to do so, but
there is not the slightest prospect that Victorio or his band
will ever surrender under any circumstances. He and others
of his band are understood to be indicted for murder in the
courts in New Mexico, and they are well aware of it, and prefer being shot in battle to being hung. It is proper to represent this state of facts, that the work still before the troops in
New Mexico may be clearly understood, and prosecuted to the
end if the authorities in Washington so desire and direct.
Although I entertain strong convictions on the merits of the
controversy which has resulted in this Indian war, I do not
consider it my duty to express them in this report, but I think
it would be well for the Secretary of the Interior to ascertain
what were the engagements entered into and the promises
made by the agents of that department from the time of
General Howard's mission to this band of Apaches down to
the late outbreak. It is probable that much would be developed by such investigation to extenuate, at least, the feeling, if not the conduct, of the tribe."

It will be observed that neither of these officers goes back
to the original source of the trouble—the removal of the
Chiricahuas. Two drunken Indians killed two whiskey smugglers, and forthwith the Indians who happened to live on the
same reservation, who had no connection with the killing,
were ordered to be removed from their homes; fugitives from
this reservation took refuge at Ojo Caliente, and forthwith the
Indians there, guilty and innocent alike, were ordered to be

removed ; fugitives from Ojo Caliente invaded the Mescalero reservation and induced half of that tribe to go to war ; New Mexico and Arizona reaped a harvest of five years of savage murdering and plundering—nay, more, for this war was not stopped until 1882, and the dissatisfaction caused by these re- movals has had its weight in every outbreak since then. In this connection it may be well to look at other parts of the country, where the success of the concentration policy was being demonstrated in 1879. In the spring the much-abused Poncas were snatched by writ of *habeas corpus* from the hands of the military, who, in accordance with the wishes of the Indian Bureau, were dragging them back to Indian Territory, from their homes in Dakota. Later in the year the Northern Cheyennes were fighting with a desperation that was blood- curdling—fighting soldiers, with knives made of pieces of stove-pipe, and slungshots made of fragments of the stove in their prison—to escape being taken back to Indian Territory. In the Indian Territory were Joseph's Nez Percés, sickening and dying in their rotten teepees. In Arizona the Hualapais would have starved to death, or into hostility, if the War De- partment had not relieved them. South of these, the Papagos were relapsing into barbarism for want of proper teachers ; their school-houses were stripped of windows and doors, and the grand old cathedral of San Xavier del Bac was robbed of its consecrated vessels. And yet the Commissioner of Indian Affairs was on hand, with the annual recommendation for more concentration. If concentration were beneficial, why were not some of its good effects shown on the tribes that had been concentrated at the cost of life, treasure, and broken faith ? It is a perversion of the English language to call such a system a peace policy.

In January, 1880, Juh and Geronimo came voluntarily to the White Mountain reservation, with 108 Chiricahua rene- gades. They were induced to leave the fastnesses of the Sierra Madre, in Northern Mexico, by Lieutenant Haskell and Interpreter Jeffords, who went to their haunts and reasoned them into returning. Victorio depredated and fought Mexican troops for a few months, and in August crossed into Texas, one hundred miles below El Paso del

Norte. He was twice driven across the Rio Grande by Colonel Grierson, and then remained in Mexico, at war with the people there. He was killed by the Mexican troops some weeks later. In July, 1881, Nané, with 15 warriors, who had been with Victorio, crossed the Rio Grande and made his way into New Mexico, when he was joined by some 25 Mescaleros. He then made a rapid and bloody raid across Southern New Mexico, falling upon herders and prospectors, who had no warning of his coming, and murdering them without mercy. He was chased back into Mexico by the troops, in the latter part of August. In Arizona there were two outbreaks during the year: one, among the White Mountain Indians, was caused by the arrest of a medicine-man, named Nockay-Delklinne, who was holding dances for the purpose of bringing dead warriors to life, with the ultimate design of repeopling the country and driving out the whites. It was considered advisable to suppress him, although it did not appear that he had succeeded in reviving any of the departed—it would have been a splendid time to tell the Indians he was a humbug, and let him prove it; his arrest only made them think the whites were afraid of his powers. While removing him, the Indian scouts with the command took up his cause, and a fight ensued, in which the medicine-man and five soldiers were killed. The Indians then killed all the whites they could find, and attacked Camp Apache, to which Colonel Carr's party had retired. They killed in all ten soldiers and eight citizens. On the approach of reinforcements they fled, but, with the exception of about a dozen, who escaped and became outlaws, they were driven back to the reservation without any fighting. Five of the scouts were tried by court-martial; three were hung, and two were sent to prison on Alcatraz Island. On the night of September 30, a number of Chiricahuas, under Juh and Nachez, broke away from the reservation. The reasons given for this were that the agency authorities would not help them make an irrigating ditch, and treated them worse than the other Indians in various respects. They were driven into Mexico early in October, after a sharp fight at Cedar Springs.

In April, 1882, a number of the hostiles from Mexico made

SAN XAVIER DEL BAC.

their way quietly to the San Carlos agency, and induced all the remaining original renegade Chiricahuas, and also Loco's band of Ojo Caliente Indians, to leave the reservation and run for Mexico. They were pursued by the troops from several posts, and struck by two detachments; Lieutenant-colonel Forsythe attacked them at Horse Shoe Cañon, in New Mexico, and Major Tupper followed them into Mexico and whipped them badly in the Hatchet Mountains. They fled, leaving five dead warriors and two squaws, but carrying off others; and two days later were ambushed by Lieutenant-colonel Garcia, of the Mexican army, who inflicted severe punishment upon them. On July 6, a part of the White Mountain Indians at San Carlos, under Nan-tia-tish and Ar-shay, known as the Cibicu Indians, from their former location on Cibicu Creek, killed four of the Indian police and escaped from the reservation. They committed several robberies and killed six people within ten days. On the 17th they were overtaken and terribly punished at the "Big Dry Wash," on the old Moqui trail, a wild, desolate cañon, two hundred feet deep, with rocky side cañons and forbidding surroundings. They left sixteen dead, including Nan-tia-tish, and lost all their property. They scattered in the night, and, under cover of a heavy hail-storm, which obliterated their trails, straggled into the reservation completely destitute, and sated with war.

Some important changes in the affairs of the Arizona Indians were made in 1882. One of the most noticeable was the treaty effected with Mexico, on July 29, by which troops of both countries were authorized to pursue fleeing savages across the line in "unpopulated or desert parts." This made the punishment of the hostiles a possibility for the first time. Before that they had only to reach the Mexican line to be safe; our troops could pursue them no farther. Another important change was the return of General Crook to the command of the department. No dereliction can fairly be charged against Colonel Kautz or General Willcox, who had commanded there since Crook left; but nature has made a difference in men, and General Crook is one whose character has made him phenomenally successful in the management of Indians. Most important of his qualifications is his habit of keeping strict faith with the Indians; they are never contented under the control of a man whom they cannot trust. Next to this is the possession of common-sense, a qualification in which some people who have held responsible positions have been sadly lacking. Consider this statement, made by him in 1879: "During the twenty-seven years of my experience with the Indian question I have never known a band of Indians to make peace with our government and then break it, or leave their reservation, without some ground of complaint; but until their complaints are examined and adjusted, they will constantly give annoyance and trouble." He does not say that the Indians are always right nor that they are always wrong; but he does not leave room for a single case of their making war from "pure deviltry." This language was not called forth, however, by the mistreatment of Indians at the hands of lawless whites, or by the dishonesty of Indian agents; it was used in regard to the attempted removal of the Northern Cheyennes to the Indian Territory. Concerning this he further says: "In the present case, the Cheyennes claimed that they had been wronged, and had become desperate as a pack of wolves. The army had orders to take them back to the Indian Territory, and had no option in the matter. It seems to me to have been, to say the least, a very unnecessary exercise of power to insist upon this particular portion of the band going back to their former reservation, while the other fragments of the same band, which surrendered to the troops on the Yellowstone, or escaped to the Red Cloud and Spotted Tail reservations, had been allowed to remain North unmolested." And who were these Cheyennes that must be hounded back to the chills, fever, and starvation that they had run away from? He says: "Among these Cheyenne Indians were some of the bravest and most efficient of the auxiliaries who had acted under General Mackenzie and myself in the campaign against the hostile Sioux in 1876 and 1877, and I still preserve a grateful remembrance of their distinguished services, which the government seems to have forgotten." Do you think that any of the concentration humanitarians will ever rank with this stern Indian-fighter in the lists of humane men?

Immediately after General Crook's return there came about a reasonable harmony between the representatives of the Indian Bureau and the War Department in Arizona, which had not existed during his absence. Just how this was effected has not been made public, but the fact was soon notorious. He then talked to the Indians, publicly and privately, until he learned the state of their feelings. He found them sullen, distrustful, and, as they confessed, on the verge of going to war. Conflicting statements had been made to them till they had lost confidence in every·one; they had been told that they were to be disarmed, attacked by troops, and removed from Arizona. He explained to them that their enemies, who wanted their reservation, were trying to get them to make war; and that they would certainly lose their reservation and everything else if they did. He showed them that their well-being must depend mainly on themselves, and secured their co-operation in reinstating all the old measures he had used so successfully ten years before, but which had since been discontinued. Every male Indian capable of bearing arms was required to wear constantly a metal tag with his number and the designation of his band. The police were reorganized, and frequent roll-calls were required. He next obtained permission for six or seven hundred of the White Mountain Indians to leave the hot valleys of the Gila and San Carlos rivers, and return to their old homes in the northern part of the reservation. To obtain this privilege he became personally responsible for their good behavior; and the Indians agreed to be self-supporting after they got their first year's crop. Both of these promises have been kept, notwithstanding that the Indians had to use sharpened sticks for planting and caseknives for harvesting implements. The lot of these Indians was so much more pleasing to many of the red men than that of the "fed savages" at the agency, that over one third of the forty-five hundred Indians there (not counting the Chiricahuas) have gathered in the northern part of the reservation, and are supporting themselves with very little assistance. To the officers explicit orders were given to give and require "justice to all—Indians as well as white men." There were to be no wrongs and no mistakes. The orders were: "There must be

no division of responsibility in this matter; each officer will
be held to a strict accountability that his actions have been
fully authorized by law and justice, and that Indians evincing
a desire to enter upon a career of peace shall have no cause of
complaint through hasty or injudicious acts of the military."

Having adopted these means for the preservation of peace
on and about the reservation—means which have proven completely successful, without any exception — General Crook
next turned his attention to the hostiles in Mexico. They
were the worst product of the bad faith and bad policy of
the past six years, and the most difficult to dispose of. Their
native homes could not be restored to them. There was nothing that could be offered them except fair treatment on the
White Mountain reservation, and that had little attraction to
savages whose tastes led them to piratical lives, and who had
experienced our fair treatment. He tried to open negotiations
with them, but succeeded only in learning that a raid was imminent. All that could be done was to prepare for it as well
as possible, for which purpose pack-trains were put in readiness and the troops stationed at the most available points. In
March the Chiricahuas began operations. A party of fifty
warriors, under Geronimo, swept through Sonora to obtain
stock, while Chato (Flat Nose—a mule had kicked him in the
face and flattened his nose), with twenty-six men, dashed
through Arizona and New Mexico, chiefly to obtain ammunition. The latter party killed about a dozen persons in Arizona, circled through Mexico, and crossed back near the Hatchet Mountains. The atrocity committed by them that attracted the greatest attention was the murder of Judge McComas
and wife, and the capture of Charley McComas, on March 28.

On the day previous to this terrible tragedy an event occurred which led to the final overthrow and capture of the
renegades. It was the desertion from Chato's party of a warrior named Pe-nal-tishn, commonly called "Peaches." He
made his way to San Carlos, was there arrested, and was induced by General Crook to guide the troops to the stronghold
of the Chiricahuas. General Crook made hasty visits to Sonora and Chihuahua, and secured promises of co-operation
there. He stationed troops along the line to watch for any

future raiders, and, with 193 Apache scouts, 42 men, and 9
officers, started for the hiding-place of the Chiricahuas. It
was situated in the Sierra Madre, the range that separates Sonora from Chihuahua, one of the roughest mountain countries
in America, but covered with forests of pine and oak, and furnished with an abundance of good water. Here were a series
of natural and almost impregnable fortresses which the Mexican troops had never been able to reach, and which Crook
might not have penetrated if the Chiricahuas had not been

CROOK'S BATTLE-FIELD IN THE SIERRA MADRE.

wholly unsuspicious of his approach. As it was, his forces
moved quietly into the mountains; his scouts located Chato's
camp; and the party would have surrounded it but for the
haste of some scouts, who fired on two Indians. The camp
was at once attacked, and the Indians were defeated, with a
loss of about a dozen killed and five captured. There was
now no hope of securing the Indians by pursuing them, for
they scattered, as usual, and the pursuing force could not scatter to follow them. The only chance of getting them was to

induce them to surrender, if possible. Communication was obtained, through the captives, and they were soon satisfied that they had better surrender on the terms offered, which were substantially an agreement to overlook the past and start with a clean page on the White Mountain reservation. Almost all the renegades came in under this arrangement, among them Geronimo, Nachez (a son of Cochise), Chato, and Bonito. Juh had fallen out with the band and gone away to the South, with one man and two or three squaws, before Crook arrived.

By an agreement made between the War and Interior departments, in July, 1883, the Chiricahuas were placed under the exclusive control of General Crook; and the police authority of the entire reservation was put in his hands. By his permission the renegades selected lands for themselves on Turkey Creek, near Camp Apache, and, with the aid of the soldiers, began cultivation. In 1884, Geronimo and Chato had farms which were among the most creditable on the reservation. The prejudice of the Apache men against labor was never so strong as that of the average Indian, and on the reservation no disgrace attached to a man who worked. In 1884 more than one half of all the labor was performed by men and boys. The results of the Indian work on the reservation for that year were 3,850,000 pounds of corn, 550,000 pounds of barley, 540,000 pounds of beans, 20,000 pounds of potatoes, 50,000 pounds of wheat, 200,000 pumpkins, and 90,000 melons, besides garden stuff; and this, notwithstanding that the Apaches on the Gila lost nearly all their crops by freshets, and those in the northern part of the reservation lost about one third of theirs by late rains and early frosts. They also supplied large quantities of wood and hay, made ditches, and performed other labor. There was only one appearance of trouble during the year, and this was occasioned by Ka-e-te-na (The Looking-glass), a young chief of a Mexican tribe, who was with the renegades at the time of their surrender. At one of their dances he made a speech which was calculated to raise hostile feeling; for which offence he was arrested by Chiricahua police, convicted by an Apache jury, and sentenced to three years' imprisonment, in irons, at Alcatraz Island, in San Francisco Bay.

With such a record, continued till the recent outbreak of Geronimo, that outbreak was naturally unexpected. Theories of its cause should not be hastily formed; and yet the only one thus far announced—detection in the manufacture of tiswin, and flight from fear of punishment—is not improbable. Tiswin, or p'tis wing, is a fermented drink of native manufacture, somewhat resembling beer. Its basis is usually corn, but other materials are sometimes used. It had long been a favorite drink with some of the tribes; and on the reservation, owing to the enforcement of the intercourse laws, it was the

ALCATRAZ ISLAND.

popular intoxicant. Es-kim-en-zin, the unfortunate Camp Grant chief, was a large manufacturer of it, and had grown quite wealthy from selling it to the other Indians. The results of its use were practically as deplorable as those resulting from liquors sold by the whites, in consequence of which determined efforts have been made of late years to break up the manufacture. Through the aid of the Indian police these efforts have been very successful, and but few who have made it have escaped punishment. If this were the cause of the outbreak, the escaped Indians apparently deserve severe punishment for their crimes; but in any event, General Crook is

entitled to the confidence of the people that he will do what
is just.

It is hardly to be supposed that there will never be any
more troubles with the Apaches, for there are causes which
will produce trouble, if not removed, and our government is
slow of motion.   There are coal mines on the southern part
of the reservation, that are very valuable, on account of the
scarcity of fuel in Arizona, which certain white men have
been trying to secure.   It has been thought possible by some
that difficulty in regard to these might best be avoided by
leasing them.   A proposed law for that purpose was submitted to Congress in 1882, and bills to cut off the parts of the
reservation containing them have since been introduced ; but
no action has been taken on any of them.   Possibly a good
solution would be to make miners of the Apaches.   They are
industrious and quick to learn, and could dig coal as well as
plant corn.   The whites would then be supplied with coal and
the Indians would have the benefit of the mines, besides being
initiated in a new field of industry.   The Apaches are anxious
to obtain the release of their people now held in Mexico, some
of whom were captured within the past five years.   The Mexican captives, held as hostages for the return of these, were
released by General Crook in 1883 ; but the Apache captives
are still slaves.   The government cannot neglect this matter
and retain the respect of civilized men.   There were indications of a rupture between the military and Indian authorities in Arizona under the late administration ; but the firm
stand of Commissioner Atkins against disarming the Apaches
indicates that he is in harmony with General Crook.   It would
be folly to disarm them, even if it could be accomplished.
They would be left subject to the outrages of the Arizona
outlaws, who prey on every one, and also at the mercy of the
rabid exterminationists.   In 1883 a company of "rangers"
was organized, to attack the peaceable Indians at San Carlos,
and marched nearly to the reservation.   No time was wasted
in begging these men to be law-abiding.   The Indians were
notified that they would be expected to defend themselves ;
and the rangers, on learning this, concluded that they had not
lost any Indians.   They marched back to Tombstone without

making an attack.   There has been much talk of removing the Apaches from Arizona, which, if it were attempted, would produce war; it would be a terrible war too.   The Apaches cannot be driven about like cattle.   On the other hand, if the policy of the past three years is followed to its proper limits—if the Apaches are treated fairly, and all disturbing causes are removed, as far as possible—there is no reason why these demons of the past should not continue to develop into a quiet, self-sustaining people.

LIST OF AUTHORITIES.

OWING to the great extent of territory covered in this book, it has been thought best to classify the authorities, in order that those who desire to investigate any subject herein discussed may be directed at once to the evidence relating to it. It is hoped that those who are interested in Indian affairs, or in local history, will thus be relieved of needless search through irrelevant documents. In furtherance of this object, many authorities consulted by the author are omitted altogether, only those being mentioned which are considered of material value. The Executive Documents referred to are documents of the House of Representatives. Up to 1861 the same documents will usually be found in the Senate Documents for the same years, as also Senate Documents referred to, prior to 1861, will usually be found in the Executive Documents. Some authorities have been used in almost every chapter; and these, to avoid repetition, will, except as to matters of unusual importance, be mentioned but once, and

IN GENERAL:

Historical and Statistical Information respecting the History, Condition, and Prospects of the Indian Tribes of the United States, etc. Henry R. Schoolcraft. In 5 vols. Philadelphia, 1851–55; also a sixth volume of same, under title Archives of Aboriginal Knowledge, etc. Philadelphia, 1860.

Reports of Generals of the Army, and accompanying documents: 1846–84.

Reports of Commissioners of Indian Affairs, and accompanying documents: 1849–84.

Reports of Pacific Railroad Surveys, Ex. Docs. 1854–55, vol. xi. (in 11 parts); same in Sen. Docs., vol. xiii.; also Supplemental Report, Ex. Docs. 1859–60, vol. xi. (in 2 parts); same in Sen. Docs. 1858–59, vol. xviii.

The Native Races of the Pacific States of North America. Hubert Howe Bancroft. In 5 vols. New York, 1875.

All Ratified Treaties, prior to 1843, are in U. S. Stats. at Large, vol. vii. For those of later date, see vol. ix. U. S. Stats. at Large, and subsequent volumes.

CHAPTER I.

INTRODUCTORY.

Report of Joint Special Committee on Condition of Indian Tribes, under Joint Resolution of March 3, 1865.   Washington, 1867.

Report of Special Commission appointed to Investigate the Affairs of Red Cloud Indian Agency.   Washington, 1875.

Report of Committee on Indian Affairs on Indian Frauds, House Rep., No. 98, 1872–73.

The Legal Position of the Indian.   G. F. Canfield, in *Am. Law Rev.*, vol. xv., p. 21.

The Red Man and White Man in North America, etc.   G. E. Ellis. Boston, 1882.

Indian Titles to Land; in Commentaries on American Law, vol. iii., pp. 379–400.   James Kent.

CHAPTER II.

THE ACQUISITION OF THE MOUNTAINS.

Thirty Years' View of the American Government.   Thos. Benton. New York, 1871.

Commerce of the Prairies, etc.   Josiah Gregg.   New York, 1844.

Oregon.   W. Barrows.   Boston and New York, 1884.

A History of Oregon, etc.   W. H. Gray.   New York, 1870.

Oregon and California in 1848.   J. Quinn Thornton.   New York, 1849.

The American Statesman: A Political History, etc.   Andrew W. Young. New York, 1855.

Discussion of the Oregon Question; in *Congressional Globe*, First Sess. 29th Congress, pp. 44–692, and Appendix.

CHAPTER III.

THE ONE OFFENCE OF THE PUEBLOS.

The History of Mexico and its Wars, etc.   John Frost, LL.D.   New Orleans, 1882.

The Conquest of New Mexico and California, etc.   Gen. P. St. G. Cooke. New York, 1878.

El Gringo ; or, New Mexico and her People.   W. W. H. Davis.   New York, 1857.

Adventures in Mexico and the Rocky Mountains.   Geo. F. Ruxton. New York, 1848.

Report of Colonel Price.   Ex. Doc. No. 8, 1847–48, pp. 520–538.

CHAPTER IV.

MURDER OF THE MISSIONARIES.

Gray's Oregon (*supra* ch. ii.).

Barrow's Oregon (*supra* ch. ii.).

Protestantism in Oregon : Account of the Murder of Dr. Whitman, etc.

Rev. J. B. A. Brouillet, S. J. New York, 1853. Reprinted in Ex. Doc. No. 38, 1857–58.

Portraits of North American Indians (with biographical notes). J. M. Stanley. In Smithsonian Mis. Coll., vol. ii.

The Ely Volume. T. Laurie, D.D. Boston, 1881.

Recollections and Opinions of an Old Pioneer. P. H. Burnett. New York, 1880.

Papers and Correspondence relating to Indian Affairs on the Pacific, from War and Interior Depts. Ex. Doc. No. 76, 1856–57, vol. ix.

CHAPTER V.

THE CURSE OF GOLD.

Mormon Discovery of Gold. Geo. M. Evans. In *Hunt's Merchants' Magazine*, vol. xxxi., p. 385.

Memoirs of Gen. Wm. T. Sherman, by himself. New York, 1875.

Thornton's Oregon and California (*supra* ch. ii.). Appendix.

American Adventure. *Blackwood's Magazine*, vol. lxvii., p. 34.

Discovery of the Yosemite, and the Indian War of 1851, etc. L. H. Bunnell. Chicago, 1880.

Ex. Doc. No. 76, 1856–57 (*supra* ch. iv.).

Correspondence on California Indian Affairs. Sen. Doc. No. 4, Special Sess., 1853.

Correspondence and Reports on California Agencies. Sen. Doc. No. 46, 1859–60 (vol. xi.); also Ex. Docs., 1856–57, vol. ix., pp. 136–145.

Report of Special Agent Bailey. Ex. Docs. 1858–59, vol. ii., pt. 1, pp. 649–657.

The Coast Rangers. J. Ross Browne. In *Harper's Magazine*, vol. xxiii., p. 306.

Mission Indians. Report of J. G. Ames. Ex. Docs. 1873–74, vol. iv., pt. 1, p. 397.

Mission Indians. Report of B. C. Whiting. Ex. Docs. 1871–72, vol. iii., pt. 1, p. 1107.

Mission Indians. Helen Hunt Jackson. In *Century*, vol. xxvi., pp. 1, 199, 511.

CHAPTER VI.

OATMAN FLAT.

Captivity of the Oatman Girls, etc. R. B. Stratton. New York, 1858.

Adventures in the Apache Country. J. Ross Browne. New York, 1874.

Recovery of Miss Oatman. Sen. Doc. No. 66, 1855–56, p. 67.

Personal Narrative of Explorations, etc. J. R. Bartlett. Vol. ii., p. 203. New York, 1854.

Lieutenant Sitgreave's Expedition. Sen. Docs., 1852–53, vol. x.

Notes on the Tonto Apaches. Capt. Charles Smart. In Smithsonian Report for 1867.

Ex. Doc. No. 76, 1856–57 (*supra* ch. iv.).

CHAPTER VII.

THE ROGUE RIVER, YAKIMA, AND KLICKITAT WARS.

Gray's Oregon (*supra* ch. ii.).

Ex. Doc. No. 76, 1856–57 (*supra* ch. iv.).

Military Reports. Sen. Docs. 1856–57, vol. iii., pp. 147–203.

Papers and Correspondence, with affidavits. House Mis. Doc. No. 47, 1858–59, vol. i.

Local Legislative Action. House Mis. Docs. Nos. 64, 77, and 78, 1855–56; also House Mis. Docs. Nos. 71 and 116, 1857–58.

Report of J. Ross Browne on Indian Wars of Oregon. Ex. Doc. No. 38, 1857–58, vol. ix.

Report of J. Ross Browne on Indian Reservations of the Northwest. Ex. Doc. No. 39, 1857–58, vol. ix.

CHAPTER VIII.

ASH HOLLOW AND THE CHEYENNE EXPEDITION.

Correspondence and Evidence concerning Grattan Affair. Sen. Doc. No. 91, 1855–56, vol. xiv.

Harney's Report. Ex. Docs. 1855–56, vol. i., pt. 2, p. 49.

Cooke's Report. Sen. Doc. No. 58, 1856–57, vol. viii.

Sign Language. In First Annual Report of Bureau of Ethnology. Washington, 1881.

Grammar and Dictionary of the Dakota Language. Rev. S. R. Riggs. In Smithsonian Contributions to Knowledge, vol. iv.

Cheyenne Troubles of 1856. Sen. Docs. 1856–57, vol. iii., pp. 106–112.

Sumner's Expedition. Sen. Docs. 1857–58, vol. iii., pp. 96–99.

The Oregon Trail, etc. Francis Parkman. Boston, 1866.

The Plains of the Great West and their Inhabitants. R. I. Dodge. New York, 1877.

City of the Saints, etc. R. F. Burton. New York, 1862.

CHAPTER IX.

LOS NABAJOS.

Report of 1867 on Condition of Indian Affairs (*supra* ch. i.). Appendix.

El Gringo (*supra* ch. iii.).

Historical Sketch. Sen. Docs. 1858–59, vol. i., pp. 540–543.

An Account of the Navajoes of New Mexico. Major Backus. In Schoolcraft's Hist. and Stat. Inf. (*supra*), vol. iv., p. 209.

Military Reports. Sen. Docs. 1858–59, vol. ii., pp. 278–329; also, Sen. Docs. 1859–60, vol. ii., pp. 256–354.

Lieutenant Simpson's Memoir of Washington's Expedition. Sen. Doc. No. 64, 1849–50, vol. xiv.

The Undeveloped West. J. H. Beadle. Cincinnati, 1873.

CHAPTER X.

MOUNTAIN MEADOWS.

Correspondence and Evidence from War and Interior Departments. Sen. Doc. No. 42, 1859–60, vol. xi.

Military Reports. Sen. Docs. 1859–60, vol. ii., pp. 121–255.

Trial of Gunnison Murderers. Ex. Docs. 1855–56, vol. i., pt. 2, p. 167.

Emissaries to Indians. Ex. Doc. No. 38, 1857–58.

Emissaries to Indians. Ex. Doc. No. 76, 1856–57.

Emissaries to Indians. Sen. Docs. 1859–60, vol. ii., p. 339.

Judge Cradlebaugh's Account. *Congressional Globe*, 1862–63. Appendix, p. 119.

Mormonism Unveiled, etc. (Autobiography, trials, and confessions of John D. Lee.) W. W. Bishop. St. Louis and Cleveland, 1882.

Life in Utah. J. H. Beadle. Philadelphia, 1870.

Western Wilds and the Men who Redeem Them. J. H. Beadle. Cincinnati, 1878.

CHAPTER XI.

WAR WITH THE SPOKANES, ETC.

Lieutenant Mullan's Topographical Memoir. Ex. Doc. No. 32, 1858–59, vol. x.

Father Hoecken's Account of the Attack on Steptoe. Sen. Docs. 1858–59, vol. ii., p. 127.

Military Reports and Papers. Sen. Docs. 1858–59, vol. ii., pp. 330–415.

Indian Bureau Reports and Papers. Sen. Docs. 1858–59, vol. i., pp. 566–635.

CHAPTER XII.

DEATH TO THE APACHE.

Cooke's Conquest of New Mexico (*supra* ch. iii.).

Gregg's Commerce of the Prairies (*supra* ch. ii.).

Bartlett's Narrative (*supra* ch. vi.).

Report of 1867 on Condition of Indian Tribes (*supra* ch. i.). Appendix.

Life Among the Apaches. John C. Cremony. San Francisco, 1868.

Across America and Asia. Raphael Pumpelly. New York, 1870.

Colyer's Report. Ex. Docs. 1871–72, vol. iii., p. 454.

El Gringo (*supra* ch. iii.).

CHAPTER XIII.

SAND CREEK.

Evidence. Report on Conduct of the War, 1864–65, pt. 3.

Evidence. Report of 1867 on Condition of Indian Tribes (*supra* ch. i.). Appendix.

Evidence. Sen. Doc. No. 26, 1866–67.

Documents from Interior Department concerning Custer's Fight on the Washita. Sen. Doc. No. 13, 1868–69.

Documents from War Department concerning Custer's Fight on the Washita. Sen. Doc. No. 18, 1868–69.

My Life on the Plains. G. A. Custer. New York, 1874.

Sheridan's Troopers on the Border. De B. R. Keim. Philadelphia, 1870.

New Colorado and the Santa Fé Trail. A. A. Hayes. New York, 1880.

A Century of Dishonor. Helen Hunt Jackson. New York, 1881.

The Indian and White Man. Rev. D. W. Risher. Indianapolis, 1880.

CHAPTER XIV.

CAÑON DE CHELLY AND BOSQUE REDONDO.

Lieutenant Simpson's Memoir (*supra* ch. ix.).

Beadle's Undeveloped West (*supra* ch. ix.).

Report of 1867 on Condition of Indian Tribes (*supra* ch. i.). Appendix.

Carson's Report. MS., War Department.

Pioneer Life and Frontier Adventure. D. C. Peters. Boston, 1881.

Report of Captain Walker. Sen. Docs. 1859–60, vol. ii., p. 316.

CHAPTER XV.

FORT PHIL KEARNEY.

Papers and Correspondence from War and Interior Departments, including Report of Special Commissioners. Sen. Doc. No. 13, 1867.

Military Reports: Report of Sec. of War, 1867, pp. 31–61.

Dodge's Plains of the Great West (*supra* ch. viii.).

Absaraka, Home of the Crows. Mrs. M. I. Carrington. Philadelphia, 1869.

Absaraka, Land of Massacre. Col. H. B. Carrington. Philadelphia, 1878.

CHAPTER XVI.

PUNISHING THE PIEGANS.

Historical Sketch. Schoolcraft's Hist. and Stat. Inf. (*supra*), vol. v., p. 179.

Early Relations to U. S. Sen. Docs. 1858–59, vol. xviii.

Papers and Evidence from War Department. Ex. Doc. No. 269, 1869–70, vol. xii.; also, Sen. Doc. No. 49, 1869–70.

Baker's Report. Ex. Doc. No. 197, 1869–70, vol. vii.

Papers and Correspondence from Interior Department. Ex. Doc. No. 185, 1869–70, vol. vii.

Congressional Globe, 1869–70, pt. 2, pp. 1575–1599.

Adventures of Captain Bonneville, etc. Washington Irving. New York, 1864.

CHAPTER XVII.

THE TRAGEDY OF THE LAVA BEDS.

Papers and Correspondence from War and Interior Departments, including Proceedings of Military Commission. Ex. Doc. No. 122, 1873–74, vol. ix.

Meacham's Report. Ex. Docs. 1873–74, vol. iv., p. 442.

Gillem's Report. Sen. Doc. No. 1, 1877 (bound with Docs. of 1876–77).
Cost of War. Ex. Doc. No. 131, 1874–75, vol. xv.
The Modocs. Stephen Powers. In *Overland Monthly*, vol. x., p. 535.

CHAPTER XVIII.
THE LITTLE BIG HORN.

Custer's Expedition to the Black Hills. Sen. Doc. No. 32, 1874–75.
Jenney's Expedition to the Black Hills. Sen. Doc. No. 51, 1875–76.
Disturbances leading to the War. Sen. Doc. No. 52, 1875–76.
Invasions by Miners. Sen. Doc. No. 2, 1875 (bound with Docs. of 1874–75).
Report of Commission to Treat for Black Hills. Ex. Docs. 1875–76, vol. iv., pt. 1, p. 686.
Report of Commission to Treat with Sitting Bull in Canada. Ex. Docs. 1877–78, vol. viii., p. 719.
Terry's Report. Sen. Doc. No. 81, 1875–76.
Sheridan's Report. Ex. Docs. 1876–77, vol. ii., pt. 1, p. 439.
Movements of Troops. Reports of General of the Army for 1876 and 1877.
Autobiography of Sitting Bull. *Harper's Weekly*, July 29, 1876.
Record of Engagements with Hostile Indians, etc. Lt.-gen. P. H. Sheridan. Chicago, 1882.
A Popular Life of Gen. George A. Custer. F. Whittaker. New York, 1877.
Dodge's Plains of the Great West (*supra* ch. viii.). Introduction.

CHAPTER XIX.
JOSEPH'S NEZ PERCÉS.

Origin of the War. Report Sec. of War for 1875, vol. i., pp. 124–131 ; also, Report Sec. of Interior for 1875, vol. i., p. 762; also Report Sec. of War for 1876, vol. i., pp. 91, 92 ; also Report Sec. of Interior for 1876, vol. i., p. 449.
Report of Commission to Treat with Joseph. Ex. Docs. 1877–78, vol. viii., p. 607.
Report of General Howard. Report Sec. of War, 1877, vol. i., pp. 119–133.
Reports of Gibbon, Sturgis, and Miles. Report Sec. of War, 1877, vol. i., pp. 68–77.
Report of General Sherman. Report Sec. of War, 1877, vol. i., pp. 7–15.
Joseph's Statement. *North American Review*, vol. cxxviii., p. 412.
Howard's Reply. *North American Review*, vol. cxxix., p. 53.
Nez Percé Joseph, etc. Gen. O. O. Howard. Boston, 1881.
The Return of the Nez Percés. Rev. G. L. Deffenbaugh. In *The Foreign Missionary*, July, 1885, p. 71.
Lindsley's Report. In Minutes of Eighth Annual Session of the Synod of the Columbia, p. 71. Seattle, W. T., 1884.

CHAPTER XX.
WHITE RIVER AGENCY.

Historical Sketch. Major Powell. House Mis. Doc. No. 86, 1873–74.

Fight near Poncha Pass. Ex. Docs. 1855–56, vol. i., pt. 2, p. 49.

Brunot's Council. Ex. Docs. 1873–74, vol. iv., pt. 1, pp. 451–481.

Ute Affairs, 1873–79. Sen. Doc. No. 29, 1879–80, vol. i.

Papers and Correspondence from Interior Department. Sen. Doc. No. 31, 1879–80, vol. i.

Report of Special Commissioners Hatch and Adams. Ex. Doc. No. 83, 1879–80, vol. xxiv.

Evidence before Committee on Indian Affairs. House Mis. Doc. No. 38, 1879–80, vol. iv.

CHAPTER XXI.
CRUELTY, PITY, AND JUSTICE.

Colyer's Report (*supra* ch. xii.).

Howard's Report. Ex. Docs. 1873–74, vol. iii., p. 533.

Reports from Department Commanders of Arizona and New Mexico, accompanying Reports of Generals of the Army, 1872–84.

Reports from Agencies of New Mexico and Arizona, accompanying Reports of Commissioners of Indian Affairs, 1872–84.

Message of Governor Safford for 1875. Journal of Eighth Legislature of Arizona.

INDEX.

ABBOTT, J. B., withdraws troops from Uncompahgré Park, 687.

Absaroka, same as Crows, 479.

Adams, Gen. Charles, goes to Utes to release captives, 710; brings in captives, 713; statement as to urging withdrawal of troops, 713, 714.

Ahnahaways, who are, 379.

Ahuutupuwit, Ute warrior, captures Mrs. Price, 705; surrender of, demanded, 714.

Albert, Indian boy, witnesses Mountain Meadow massacre, 298; induced to lie about it, 319.

Alcatraz Island, Modocs sent to, 582; Apaches sent to, 744, 752.

Alcedo, Antonio, estimate of population of California, 131.

Alder Gulch, mines of, 478.

Alexander, Colonel, ordered from Utah by Brigham Young, 288, 289.

Allakaweah, who are, 379.

Allen, Lieut. J. K., death of, 352; mentioned, 354.

Allen, Agent R. A., reports starvation of Piegans, 537, 538.

Almy, Lieutenant, killed, 732.

Alvord, Major, quoted, 105.

Always Ready. See Giannahtah.

American Horse, Sioux chief, killed, 625.

American Indian Aid Association, intercedes for Modocs, 581.

Ames, John G., reports on Mission Indians, 149.

Amoroko, Snake chief, band of, 276.

Ankatosh, Ute chief, mentioned, 689.

Antelope, Ute warrior, aids in murder of Eskridge, 703; aids in massacre, 704; surrender of, demanded, 714.

Anthony, Major, opinion of Indians at Sand Creek, 416, 417; takes command at Fort Lyon, 418; official report of, 419; sends Cheyennes away, 420; Cheyennes defy, 421; advice to Chivington, 422.

Antonio Garra, Yuma chief, conspiracy of, 180.

Apache Cañon, Kearny at, 49, 50; fight at, 407.

Apache Mohaves, same as Yampais, 358.

Apache Pass, fight at, 380; resistance to Carleton at, 382.

Apache Yumas, same as Hualapais, 358.

Apaches, location and origin of, 82, 245; damage by, to Mexican settlements, 159; common opinions of, 356; divisions of, 357; names of, 358; troubles of, with Mexicans, 359; troubles of, with traders and trappers, 360; massacres of, 361; scalp-bounty for, 362; meet General Kearny, 365; meet Bartlett's party, 366; slavery among, 367, 368, 372, 373; troubles with Bartlett's party, 373; try to drive out miners, 374; massacre White's party, 377; Mexicans attack, 378; not protected by intercourse laws, 379; hostilities of, at beginning of rebellion, 380;

381; Californians defeat, 382; operations against, 383; at Bosque Redondo, 384; Carleton's campaign against, 385, 386; extermination theory tried on, 389, 391; effect of extermination policy, 390; troubles at Bosque Redondo, 392; failure of extermination policy, 395; extermination policy continued, 717, 718; establishment at Camp Grant, 719, 720; massacre of, at Camp Grant, 721–725; peace policy tried, 726, 727; failure of peace policy, 728, 729; Crook's policy inaugurated, 729, 730; features of Crook's policy, 731; success of same, 732; removal policy inaugurated, 733, 734; effects of removals, 735–743; hostilities in 1880–82, 743–747; Crook returns to, 747, 748; renews his policy, 749; renegades brought in, 750–752; success of Crook's policy, 753, 754; causes of trouble remaining, 754, 755.

Applegate, Jesse, appointed on Modoc commission, 559; removed, 560.

Applegate, Oliver, appointed on Modoc commission, 559; removed, 560.

Arapahoes. See Cheyennes and Arapahoes.

Archuleta, Col. Diego, bought up by Magoffin, 50; conspiracy of, 61.

Arivapas, Apaches, who are, 357; location of, 358; capture Inez Gonzales, 366; come to Camp Grant, 719, 720; Camp Grant massacre, 721–725; attack on, 725; reservation made for, 727; sent to San Carlos, 730.

Arizona, description of southwestern part, 151, 152; established as a territory, 157, 158; description of northeastern part, 244, 245; Apache warfare in, 356; a refuge for criminals, 362; Indian slavery in, 372, 373; overrun by Apaches, 380, 381; gold discoveries in, 385; operations against Apaches in, 385, 386; put in Department of California, 391; progress of, 392, 395; press of, defends Camp Grant massacre, 724, 725; threatens Colyer, 726; Crook's policy inaugurated in, 729; success of same, 732; removal policy tried in, 733; results of removals, 734–743; changes of 1882 in, 747, 748; Crook's policy renewed, 749, 750; Apache renegades brought in, 752; Geronimo's outbreak, 753; remaining sources of Apache troubles, 754, 755.

Armijo, General, commands Mexican troops in New Mexico, 49; bought up by Magoffin, 50; retires to Mexico, 51.

Arrow, the. See Ouray.

Arroyo Hondo, massacre at, 66–68.

Arshay, Apache chief, revolt of, 747.

Ashburton treaty, mention of, 41.

Ash Hollow, location of, 234; fight at, 235; criticism of fight at, 236; fight at, praised on frontier, 433, 434.

Assinaboines, location of, 81.

Astoria, sketch of history of, 32, 33.

Athabascans, related to Navahos, Apaches, and Umpquas, 82, 245, 246.

Atsina, same as Arapahoes, 221.

Augur, General, succeeds General Cooke, 503; member Board of Peace Commissioners, 716.

BABBITT, A. W., Secretary of Utah, killed by Indians, 239.

Babcock, Lieutenant, defeats Tontos, 730.

Backus, Major, quoted, 254, 255.

Bacon, Lieutenant, sent to cut off Nez Percés, 655.

Bacon, Special Agent, reports on California reservations, 137, 138.

Baillie-Grohman, quoted, 226.

Baker, Col. E. M., sent against Piegans, 528; recovers horses from Bloods, 529; report of, 530; probable facts of fight, 531; criticism of fight, 532; Sheridan's orders to, 533; supported by army officers, 534.

Bald Head. See Hushhushcute.

Baldwin, Lieutenant, defeats Sitting Bull, 626.

Baliran, Sutler, killed, 615; murderer of, detected, 616.

Bannocks, who are, 275, 276.

Barncho, Modoc warrior, takes part in murder of commissioners, 569; tried, 580; convicted, 581; sentence of, commuted, 582.

Barstow, A. C., member of Nez Percés commission, 646; responsibility of, 672.

Bartlett, J. R., releases slaves of Mimbreños, 366; hostilities to, 373; leaves Copper Mines, 374.

Bateman, William, aids John D. Lee at Mountain Meadows, 295.

"Baylor's Babes," fight of, with Colorado troops, 407.

Beale, Superintendent, estimate of Indians in California, 130, 131.

Bear, the, Sioux chief. See Mahto Iowa.

Bear Chief, Piegan chief, becomes hostile, 524; camp of, attacked, 528.

Bear Rivers, Utes, same as Yampas, 681.

Bear Spring, treaty at, 256; fight at, 263.

Beaubien, Narcissus, murdered by Pueblos, 65.

Beckwith, Jim, guides Colorado troops, 396; a chief of the Crows, 479.

Belknap investigation, Custer's connection with, 601, 602.

Bell, Lieutenant, defeats Jicarillas, 377.

Benedict, ——, shoots at Nez Percés Indians, 636.

Bennett, Captain, recommends native police for Navahos, 472.

Bennett, Ute warrior, Douglas refuses to surrender, 696.

Bent, Charles, Governor of New Mexico, character of, 152; murdered by Pueblos, 62, 63; buried at Santa Fé, 78.

Bent, George, writes letter for Cheyenne chiefs, 411; believed to be a rebel emissary, 425.

Bent's Fort, described, 52.

Benteen, Captain, sent ahead by Custer, 608; report of, 609; besieged, 610; estimate of number of Indians, 620; not in fault, 624; cuts off Nez Percés herd, 657.

Benton, Thomas, calls attention to value of Oregon, 46; regrets discovery of gold in California, 124, 125; mention of, 241.

Beswick, Nate, representations of, to Modocs, 559.

Bewley, Lorinda, captured by Cayuses, 96; given to Five Crows, 99; deposition of, 113–115.

Big Bill, Pi-ede chief, at Mountain Meadow massacre, 293.

Big Thunder, Nez Percé chief, orders Joseph away, 631.

Bingham, Lieutenant, killed by Sioux, 491.

Birtsell, Dr. C. S., testimony of, concerning Sand Creek, 416.

Blackfeet, location of, 81; who are, 509; tribal organization of, 510; reputation of, 511; cause of reputation, 512; torture of, by Flatheads, 513; generosity of, 514; location of, in 1853, 515; treat with Stevens, 516; peaceful relations of, 517, 518; location in 1869, 528; neglect of, 536; sufferings of, 537; starvation of, 538; right of, to aid, 541; helplessness of, 542; harassed by Sioux, 593. See also Piegans and Bloods.

Black Foot, Sioux warrior, mistreats Mrs. Ewbanks, 428.

Blackfoot Sioux, who are, 231; treaty of 1866 with, 481; on the war-path, 500; not related to Blackfoot nation, 510 (note); location of, in 1876, 591; at war, 618; make peace, 628.

Black Hills, held sacred by Indians, 585; gold believed to exist in, 586; gold discovered, 587; invasion of, 588; Indians refuse to sell, 589, 590; Indian title to, extinguished, 628.

Black Jim, Modoc warrior, refuses to surrender, 553; meets commissioners, 567; shoots at Meacham, 569; arraigned, 579; tried, 580; sentenced, 581; executed, 582.

Black Kettle, Cheyenne chief, commands Cheyennes at Sand Creek, 408; admits hostility, 411; considered friendly, 416; escapes from Sand Creek, 417; band of, confused with Little Raven's Arapahoes, 418–420, 430; display of flag by, 422; claims authority over Dog Soldiers, 431; surprised by Custer, 440.

Black Knife, Apache chief, meets Bartlett's party, 366.

Black Tigers, Sioux, who were, 591.

Blair, Sam, representations of, to Modocs, 559.

Blanchet, Jesuit bishop, arrives in Oregon, 93; baptizes Wailatpu murderers, 102; treatment of Miss Bewley, 113–116.

Blood atonement, Mormon doctrine of, 284, 285, 290, 298, 313.

Bloods, who are, 509; treat with Stevens, 516; hostilities by, 518; steal horses, 522; encouraged by Hudson's Bay Company, 523; location in 1869, 528; surrender stolen horses, 529. See also Blackfeet and Piegans.

Bloody Point, fight at, 192; massacre of Modocs at, 193.

Bloody Tanks, massacre of Apaches at, 389.

Bluewater, fight on. See Ash Hollow.

Blunt, General, ambushed by Cheyennes and Arapahoes, 412, 444; co-operates with Carleton, 423, 424.

Board of Indian Commissioners, importance of, 15; should call for aid for destitute tribes, 538; organization of, 716.

Bogus Charley, Modoc warrior, carries message to commissioners, 565; accompanies Riddle to council, 567; assaults Dr. Thomas, 569; betrays Captain Jack, 576; witness at trial, 580; becomes chief, 583.

Bogy, Indian commissioner, did not believe in hostile Indians, 480; ignorance of Indian affairs, 485; explanation of Fetterman massacre, 501, 502.

Bolen, Indian agent, murdered by Yakimas, 204; murderers of, remain at large, 333; murderers punished, 352.

Bonito, Apache chief, returns to reservation, 752.

Bordeaux, trader, declines to accept submission of Cheyennes and Arapahoes, 230.

Boreman, Judge, sentences John D. Lee, 319.

Bosque Redondo, Mescaleros sent to, 383, 384; troubles at, 392; selected as a reservation

by General Carleton, 452 ; Navahos depredate at, 453; Navahos sent to, 464; Indians
quarrel at, 465; agriculture fails at, 466;
description of, 467; suffering at, 468, 469;
Carleton's mistake, 470; decided a failure,
471; Navahos removed from, 472.
Boston Charley, Modoc warrior, at council,
567; shoots Dr. Thomas, 569; surrenders,
577; tried, 580; convicted, 581; executed,
582.
"Bostons," Indian name for Americans, 102.
Bowpiths, Sioux, same as Sans Arcs, 231.
Bozeman, Montana, settlement of, 478.
Bozeman Route, desirability of road by, 478,
479 ; Indians oppose road, 482; right to
road, 484, 485, 507; road abandoned, 508.
Bracito, battle at, 51.
Brady, Joseph, carries message for Ouray, 706;
opinion as to the pictures, 712.
Brannan, Samuel, Mormon bishop of California,
119; reports receipts of gold, 121.
Brewer, Dr. Charles, quoted, 290, 307–309.
Briesly, Dr., testimony concerning Camp Grant
massacre, 721, 722.
Brooks, Major, negro servant of, killed by a
Navaho, 262; demands murderer, 262, 263;
expedition of, 268.
Brouillet, Father, quoted, 93; arrives at Wailatpu, 99; objects to Indian testimony, 109;
statement of, 109 - 113; Miss Bewley's account of, 113–115.
Brown, Capt. F. H., volunteers with Fetterman's party, 491; body found, 495; probable suicide of, 496, 499.
Browne, J. Ross, quoted, 107; action of, criticised, 333; opinion of Stevens's treaties, 334.
Brulés, Sioux, designation of, in sign language,
225; who are, 231; part of, in Grattan massacre, 232; go to war, 233; defeated at Ash
Hollow, 235; submission of, 236; treaty of
1866 with, 481; remain friendly, 483, 484;
some hostile, 500; location in 1876, 591; at
war, 618; make peace, 628.
Brunot, Felix, treats with Utes, 683; Ouray's
statement to, 684.
Buchanan, President, promotes General Harney, 238; quoted, 286.
Buffalo, destruction of, 2, 3, 4; belief of Indians
as to permanence of, 243; extermination of,
537, 538.
Buffalo eaters, who are, 275.
Bull Bear, Cheyenne chief, desires to treat, 408;
friendliness of, 411; in council at Denver,
412; a sub-chief to Black Kettle, 431.
Bunnell, Dr., account of Yosemite war, 133,
134; quoted, 135.
Burgwin, Captain, killed at Pueblo de Taos, 77.
Burke, Col. Martin, furnishes goods to Francis-
co, 181; letter to Olive Oatman, 183; reports
her recovery, 184.
Burns, Captain, captures Yampais, 730.
Burnt Thighs. See Brulés.
Byers, W. N., Meeker's letter to, 698, 699.

CABALLO EN PELO, Yuma chief, massacres Gal-
latin party, 362.
Cabanisse, Dr., negotiates with Modocs, 577.
Cache Valley Indians, who are, 277.
Cadété. See Giannahtah.
Cajuenches, same as Cuchans, 358.
Calhoun, Captain, killed at Little Big Horn,
611; a brother-in-law of General Custer, 623.
Calhoun, Governor, treats with Navahos, 257,
258; releases slaves, 368; treats with Jica-
rillas, 377.
California, conquered, 47; discovery of gold in,
118–125; early settlers of, 125–127; Indians

of, 127–129; first Indian troubles of, 129,
133–135; native population of, 130–133; reservations of, 135–137; Indian ring in, 137,
138; barbarous treatment of Indians of, 138–
142; Mission Indians of, 142–150; Indians in
northern part of, 190, 191; sends troops
against Modocs, 192; Indian titles in, 194;
Mormons incite Indians of, 281; Mormons
recalled from, 286; criminals from, in Arizona, 362; slavery in, 371; volunteers from,
in New Mexico, 382, 383; Southern sympathy in, 404; pay to militia of, in Modoc war,
578.
Calispels. See Pend d'Oreilles.
Campbell, Captain, quoted, 293.
Camp Grant, establishment of Apaches at, 719,
720; massacre at, 721–723; attempted defence of, 724; evil effects of, 725, 726, 729.
Camp Yuma, location of, 158; Lorenzo Oatman,
at, 179.
Canby, Gen. E. R. S., drives back Texans, 382,
407; relieved by Carleton, 383; fight at Valverde, 404; campaign against Navahos, 451;
sketch of, 550; recommends separate reser-
vation for Modocs, 552; made a member of
Modoc commission, 560; opinion as to last
council, 565; refuses to deceive Modocs, 566;
goes to council, 567; speech at council, 568;
killed, 569; body recovered, 570 ; indignation at murder of, 571.
Cannon, George Q., denies guilt of Mormons at
Mountain Meadows, 314.
Cannon, Lieutenant, testimony of, concerning
Sand Creek, 434.
Cañon Alsada described, 455, 456; entered by
Colonel Miles, 458.
Cañoncito Bonito described, 258.
Cañon Creek, fight at, 657.
Cañon de Chelly reached by troops, 256; par-
tially explored, 257; explored, 265; expedi-
tion against Navahos in, 454; extent of, 455;
description of, 456; cliff-houses in, 457; ex-
plorations of, 458; Carson marches to, 461;
operations at, 462; misstatement concern-
ing, 463; results of operations at, 464, 465.
Cañon del Trigo, location of, 456; entered by
Lieutenant Simpson, 458.
Capotes, Utes, who are, 277; included in Southern Utes, 681.
Captain Billy, Tabequache chief, mentioned,
689.
Captain Jack, Modoc chief, troubles of, at Klamath reservation, 545; leaves reservation,
546; conduct of, 549; attacked by Captain
Jackson, 552 ; takes no part in murder of
settlers, 553; goes to Lava Beds, 554; joined
by Hot Creek Indians, 559; message of, to
commissioners, 562; desires peace, 563; decides for war, 564; saves Judge Steele's life,
565 , meets commissioners, 567; speech at
council, 568; kills General Canby, 569; leaves
Lava Beds, 576; captured, 577; Indians call
him insane, 578; arraigned, 579; tried, 580,
581; executed, 582.
Carasco, General, attack of, on Apaches, 359
Carey, Captain, accompanies Carson at Cañon
de Chelly, 461; sent through the cañon, 462.
Carleton, General, quoted, 125; erects monument at Mountain Meadows, 309; advances
to New Mexico, 382 ; operations against
Mescaleros, 383; sends Mescaleros to Bosque
Redondo, 384; protects Arizona miners, 385;
result of operations in Arizona, 386; infatuated with Bosque reservation project, 392;
instructs Carson not to make peace, 423;
decides to remove Navahos to Bosque Redondo, 452 ; operations against Navahos,

453, 454; quoted, 458; mistake of, in number of Navahos, 465; objects to interference of Steck, 467, 468 ; comforts the Navahos, 469 ; persists in Bosque Redondo project, 470.

Carr, Colonel, attacked by Apaches, 744.

Carrington, Col. H. B., sent to Powder River country, 483 ; locates Fort Phil Kearney, 486; constructs fort, 487; neglects scouting, 489; asks for reinforcements, 490; orders of, disobeyed, 499; removed, 500; misrepresented, 501; exonerated, 502; faults of, 503, 504.

Carson, Kit, saves Fremont's party, 191; guides dragoons against Jicarillas, 377 ; accepts surrender of Mescaleros, 383; commands at Fort Canby, 454; expedition of, to Cañon de Chelly, 461; immediate results of expedition, 462; misstatement concerning, 463; ulterior results of expedition, 464 ; sent against Comanches, 465; treats with Utes, 681.

Casas Grandas, what are, 54–57; no tradition of occupancy by Navahos, 245.

Cascades, the, described, 211; massacre at, 212.

Casino, Klickitat chief, splendor of, 201, 202, 371.

Catlin, George, meets Nez Percés messengers, 36, 37.

Cayuses, location of, 86; derivation of name, 86 (note); religious dissensions of, 90–93; massacre by, at Wailatpu, 93–100; punishment of, 101; treaty with, 217; treaty ratified, 355; removal of, recommended, 645.

Chan-Deisi, Apache chief, attacks Agent Larrabee, 731; killed, 732.

Chandler, Special Agent, statement concerning Sioux treaty of 1876, 483.

Chapitone, Navaho chief, makes treaty, 257; murdered, 258.

Chase, Samuel, appointed on Modoc commission, 559; removed, 560.

Chato, Apache chief, raid of, 750; returns to reservation, 752.

Chavanaugh. See Shavano.

Cheis. See Cochise.

Chemakane Mission, location of, 87; abandonment of, 341.

Chemehueves, location of, 157; present state of, 187.

Cherokees, in Confederate army, 424.

Cherry, Lieutenant, at Milk Creek, 700.

Chesterfield House, whiskey sold to Indians at, 515.

Cheyennes and Arapahoes, fraudulent estimates of, 16; location of, 81; treaty of 1851 with, 220; early history of, 221, 222; separations of, 222; language of, 223; designations of, in sign language, 225; government and police of, 227; first troubles with, 229, 230; hostilities of 1856, 238, 239; Sumner's expedition against, 239, 240; become peaceable, 240; treatment of, by Colorado settlers, 241, 242, 429; treaty with, 423; attack on, at Sand Creek, 396–401; sketch of hostilities, 408 ; effect of hostilities on whites, 409, 410; admit hostilities, 411–416; proofs of hostilities, 416, 417; not promised protection, 417–422; instructions to punish, 423; sympathy with rebels, 424, 425; treachery of, 426; brutality of, 427–430; report of Congressional committee, 430–433; misrepresentations of Sand Creek affair, 433–437; treaty of 1865 with, 437; go to war, 438; supplies issued to, 439; defeated by Custer, 440; defended by Wynkoop, 443; Chivington's opinion of, 444, 445; aid Sioux against

Crows, 479; aid in Fetterman massacre, 500; location of northern band in 1876, 591; at Rawlin's Springs massacre, 595; removal of northern band, 743; Crook's opinion of the removal, 748.

Chickasaws, in Confederate army, 424.

Chief Joseph. See Joseph, Young.

Chihuahua, policy of, to Apaches, 359; offers scalp-bounty, 360; results of scalp-bounty, 361–363; joins United States in fighting Apaches, 385, 386; slaves from, sold in New Mexico, 447.

Chimoneth, Cascade chief, hanged, 212.

Chinaman, Ute warrior, Douglas refuses to surrender, 696.

Chinooks, location of, 82; sacrifice of slaves by, 372.

Chiricahuas, Apaches, who are, 357; treachery to, 380; go to war, 381; fight Carleton, 382; operations against, 385, 386, 391; failure of extermination policy with, 395; refuse to be removed, 727 ; Coyoteros take refuge with, 735; removal of, attempted, 736, 738; cause of attempt, 737; war results, 738; effects of attempt, 742, 743; come to White Mountain reservation, 743; leave reservation, 747; raids of, 750, 751; brought in by General Crook, 752; Geronimo's outbreak, 753.

Chivington, Col. J. M., attack on Cheyennes at Sand Creek, 396–401; statement of number killed, 401; early life of, 402; enters army, 403; fight at Apache Cañon, 407; not fairly tried, 417; did not promise Cheyennes protection, 420; justification of, 422; instructions to, 423; considers Indians allies of the South, 425; report of Congressional committee on, 430–433; misrepresentation of Sand Creek, 433–437; attacked in treaty, 437; moves to Ohio, 443; address of, in Denver, 444, 445; returns to Colorado, 445.

Choate, Senator, opposes Oregon land donation bill, 42.

Choctaws, in Confederate army, 424.

Chowchillas, conquered, 131.

Chuntz, Apache chief, killed, 732.

Cibicu Indians, outbreak of, 747.

Claiborne, Capt. Thomas, report of, on Bosque Redondo, 466, 467.

Clarke, Gen. N. S., objects to Mormon influence, 332; opposes Stevens's treaties, 332; Indian messages to, 335; sends messengers to Indians, 341.

Clarke, Gen. William, Indian Superintendent at St. Louis, 36. See also Lewis and Clarke.

Clarke, M., murder of, 524, 527.

Clay, Henry, defeated by Polk, 47.

Clearwater, fight on, 649, 650.

Cliff-houses described, 58; in Cañon de Chelly, 457.

Clymer, Heister, involves Custer in Belknap investigation, 601.

Cochees. See Chiricahuas.

Cochinay, Apache chief, killed, 732.

Cochise, Apache chief, who was, 357; relation to Mangas Colorado, 374; escape of, 380; resists Carleton, 382; leaves Cañada Alamosa, 727; death of, 736.

Cocopahs, description of, 155; attacked by Mohaves, 177.

Cœur d'Alène Mission described, 348; treaty at, 351.

Cœur d'Alènes, location of, 81; friendly before 1858, 324; menace Steptoe's command, 325; attack it, 326; fight with, 328; admissions of wrong, 330; causes of discontent, 331–336; defiance of, 342; Colonel

Wright marches against, 343; defeated at Four Lakes, 344; sue for peace, 348; country of, 348, 351; make treaty, 351.

Cok. *See* Slolox.

Colley, Major, Cheyenne chiefs' letter to, 411.

Collins, Superintendent, treats with Navahos, 451.

Colorado, early settlement of, 219, 220; discovery of gold in, 240–242; treatment of Indians by settlers, 241, 242; Indian slavery in, 371, 372; volunteers from, in New Mexico, 382, 404–407; at Sand Creek, 403; Indian troubles during the Rebellion, 408–411; Cheyenne and Arapahoe hostilities in, 411–416; loyal feeling in, 424, 425; cause of bitterness of people to Indians, 426–430; reunion of old settlers, 443–445; stands by Sand Creek, 445; desire in, for removal of Utes, 675–680; early Ute troubles in, 680, 681; San Juan excitement, 682–684; invasion of Uncompahgré Park, 685–687; conduct of Utes, 692, 693; conduct of whites, 694, 695; Utes removed from, 714, 715.

Colorado River Indians, who are, 187.

Colorow, White River chief, mentioned, 690; meets Thornburgh, 699.

Colville mines discovered, 204; trouble near, 324.

Colwell, ——, settles on Lapwai reservation, 641.

Colyer, Vincent, misrepresents Lieutenant Pease and General Sully, 531, 532; sent to Arizona, 726; establishes Apaches, 727; failure of plans of, 729.

Comanches, location of, 81; in Confederate army, 424.

Concentration. *See* Removal and Concentration.

Condé, General, forwards released slaves to Mexico, 367.

Congiato, Father, Joset's letter to, 329; goes to Indians as mediator, 341.

Connelly, Governor, treats with Navahos, 451; calls out militia, 452.

Cook, Colonel, killed at Little Big Horn, 612; probably survived others, 615.

Cooke, Gen. P. St. G., accompanies Magoffin, 49; commands Mormon battalion, 51; at Ash Hollow, 234, 235; quoted, 236; Carrington asks reinforcements from, 486; blamed for Fetterman massacre, 502; relieved, 503; fault of, 504.

"Cooper's Indian" not purely mythical, 24.

Copper Mine Apaches, same as Mimbreños, 357.

Coupes-Gorges, same as Sioux, 225.

Cowan's party attacked by Nez Percés, 655.

Cow Island, fight at, 658.

Cox, Ross, quoted, 512, 513.

Coyoteros, Apaches, threaten the Oatmans, 160; who are, 357; location of, 358; permitted to leave Bosque Redondo, 470; settled at White Mountain reservation, 719; assist troops, 731; removal of, to San Carlos, 734; effects of removal, 735, 736; return to White Mountain reservation, 749; good conduct of, 752.

Cradlebaugh, Judge John, gives date of Mountain Meadow massacre, 299; investigates massacre, 312; Hamlin's story to, 319.

Cramer, Lieutenant, testimony of, concerning Sand Creek, 434.

Cranston, Lieutenant, killed in Lava Beds, 573.

Crazy Horse, Ogallalla chief, who was, 591; fight with Reynolds, 597; controversy concerning fight, 598; fight with Crook, 604; number of Indians supposed to be with, 617; at Little Big Horn, 618; leaves Sitting Bull, 625; invites Sitting Bull to join him, 626; killed, 627.

Cremony, Colonel, statement as to Apache burials, 356, 357; Apache slaves take refuge with, 366; services of, 384.

Crittenden, Lieutenant, killed at Little Big Horn, 611.

Crook, General, opposed to Ponca removal, 21; expedition against Sioux, 596, 598; second expedition, 601; fight with Sioux, 603, 604; mistake as to number of Sioux hostiles, 617, 618; further operations against Sioux, 625, 626; opinion of Apaches, 728; inaugurates his policy, 729, 730; features of policy, 731; success of policy, 732, 733; goes to Department of the Platte, 734; returns to Arizona, 747; opinion of Cheyenne removal, 748; restores harmony in Arizona, 749; brings in renegades, 750–752; success of policy, 752; Geronimo's outbreak, 753; difficulties to be encountered, 754, 755.

Crow Creek agency, fare of Indians at, 17.

Crow Dog, Sioux chief, trial of, for murder, 10.

Crow Feather, Sioux chief, opinion of Black Hills, 589, 590.

Crows, location of, 81; designation of, in sign language, 225; description of, 479; harass Gros Ventres of the North, 510; harassed by Sioux, 593, 594; complaints of, 595, 596.

Crucifixion by Indians, case of, 178.

Cuchans. *See* Yumas.

Cuchillo Negro. *See* Black Knife.

Cullen, Special Commissioner, attempts to enforce law at Fort Benton, 522.

Cummings, Governor, reception of, in Utah, 315.

Curly, Crow scout, escape of, at Little Big Horn, 612; statement of, 615.

Curly-headed Doctor, Modoc chief, band of, 546; accused of lawlessness, 549; depredations by, 553.

Curtis, General, sends troops against Cheyennes, 412; instructions to Chivington, 422, 423; opinion of hostiles, 424; statement as to effect of fight at Sand Creek, 433, 434.

Curtis, Judge-Advocate, exculpates Captain Jack, 553; conducts trial of Modocs, 581; reports on Barncho and Slolox, 581, 582.

Custer, Boston, killed at Little Big Horn, 612, 623.

Custer, Capt. T., killed at Little Big Horn, 612, 623.

Custer, General, estimate of Indian population, 1; campaign of 1867, 438; surprises Black Kettle's camp, 440; writes up Cheyenne affairs, 443; expedition to Black Hills, 587, 588; testifies in Belknap investigation, 601; Grant's treatment of, 602; marches against Sioux, 603; starts to Little Big Horn, 607; fight on Little Big Horn, 608–615; arrest of Rain-in-the-Face, 616; mistake as to force of Sioux, 617, 618; drawn into a trap, 619–622; not in fault, 623, 624.

Cut-arms, same as Cheyennes, 225.

DAKOTAS. *See* Sioux.

Dame, Colonel, orders Mountain Meadow massacre, 295; retains standing in Mormon Church, 315.

Davidson, Lieutenant, defeated by Jicarillas, 377.

Davis, Gen. J. C., takes command against Modocs, 574; decides to execute Modocs, 578, 579.

Davis, Inspector-general, holds council with Apaches, 390, 391.

Davis, Superintendent, reports on condition of Navahos, 471.

Deaf mutes, communicate with Indians by signs, 223.

Deffenbaugh, Rev. G. L., quoted, 671.

Delano, Secretary, definition of peace policy, 19.

Delgadito, Apache chief, treachery of, 373, 374.

Delgado, Felipe, reports on condition of Navahos, 470.

Del Shay, Tonto chief, captured, 730; killed, 732.

Democratic party, favors annexation of Texas, 29; favors occupation of Oregon, 42; diversity of sentiment in, 43.

Denver, treatment of Indians by people of, 242.

De Rudio, Lieutenant, escapes at Little Big Horn, 611.

De Smet, Father, fears conversion of Indians to Protestantism, 90.

De Trobriand, General, quoted, 524; report of Baker's fight, 531, 534; opinion of Piegan hostility, 535.

Des Chutes, location of, 86; defeated by Captain Lee, 100; Stevens's treaty with, 217; treaty ratified, 355.

Devine, ——, killed by Nez Percés, 647.

Diablo. See Eskyinlaw.

Diggers. See Pah-Utes and California Indians.

Digues de pitié. See Tookarikas.

Disease, effect of, on Indian population, 5, 6; among Cayuses, 102; among Navahos, 253; among Nez Percés in Indian Territory, 664–666, 669, 670; among Hualapais, 730.

Doane, Lieutenant, destroys Piegan camp, 529.

Doctors. See Medicine-men.

Dodge, Captain, Meeker sends for, 702; relieves Payne's command, 706.

Dodge, General, quoted, 228, 243.

Dog Cañon, fight at, 383.

Dog-eaters, same as Cheyennes, 225.

Dog Soldiers, what are, 227; duties of, 228; powers of, 229; refuse to let their leader treat, 408; not an independent band, 431; do not accept treaty of 1865, 437; hostilities by, 438.

Doña Ana, massacre of Mescaleros at, 378.

Doniphan, Colonel, expedition to Chihuahua, 50, 51; expedition against Navahos, 256.

Doolittle, Senator, bias in Chivington investigation, 431; investigates Indian affairs of New Mexico, 470.

Douglas, Stephen A., views on extension of United States boundaries, 47.

Douglas, White River chief, leader of a faction, 690; Meeker makes friend of, 691; refuses to surrender offenders, 696; opposes Meeker, 698; proposes to accompany Meeker, 702; war-dance at camp of, 703; takes part in massacre, 704; takes Mrs. Meeker, 706; surrender of, demanded, 714.

Dresser, Frank, escapes from Utes, 704; separates from women, 705; body found, 710.

Dresser, Henry, body of, found, 709.

Drew, Lieutenant, visited by scalp-hunters, 362; quoted, 365.

Dudley, L. E., removes White Mountain Apaches, 735.

Dull Knife, Cheyenne chief, camp of, destroyed, 626.

Dundy, Judge, opinion of Ponca removal, 21.

Dunn, Lieut. Clark, fight with Cheyennes, 411; Indian account of fight, 415.

Dyer, L. S., appointed on Modoc commission, 560; opposes last council, 565; goes to council, 567; pursued by Hooker Jim, 569; escapes, 560; witness at trial, 580.

Eaton, George, killed by Utes, 710.

Ebenezer, Ute warrior, aids in murder of Eskridge, 703; aids in massacre, 704; surrender of, demanded, 714.

Edmonton House. illicit traffic at, 523.

Ellen's Man, Modoc warrior, at council, 567; shoots Dr. Thomas, 569; killed, 580.

Ellis, Nez Percé chief, made head-chief, 631.

Embudo, fight near, 70, 73.

Eskimenzin, Arivapa chief, comes to Camp Grant, 719; conduct of band of, 720; attack on, 721–724; second attack on, 725; manufactures tiswin, 753.

Eskina, Chiricahua chief, revolt of, 737; killed, 738.

Eskridge, Wilmer, murdered, 703; body found, 709.

Eskyinlaw, Apache chief, refuses to remove, 736.

Evans, George M., claim to discovery of gold in California, 118–121.

Evans, Governor, goes to treat with Cheyennes, 408; calls for troops, 409, 410; talk with Cheyenne and Arapahoe chiefs, 412–416; did not promise Cheyennes protection, 420, 432; did not wish to treat, 422.

Ewbanks, Mrs. Lucinda, captured by Cheyennes, 412; deposition of, 427–429; daughter and nephew die of injuries, 429.

Ewell, Captain, defeats Mescaleros, 378.

Ewtaws. See Utes.

Exkinoya, defined, 510.

Extermination policy, not possible of accomplishment, 7; failure of, in Oregon, 205–207, 217; tried in Arizona, 386, 389; effects of, 391, 392; failure of, 395; continued in Arizona, 717, 718; result of, 719; at Camp Grant, 721–724; evils of, 725, 729; not believed in by General Crook, 728, 733.

Fairchild, John, Meacham desires to accompany commission, 565; receives valuables of Meacham and Dyer, 567.

Fall River Indians, same as Arapahoes, 221.

Fancher's train, described, 289; treatment of, by Mormons, 290; reaches Mountain Meadows, 291; attacked, 292; defence of, 293, 294; entrapped, 295, 296; massacred, 297–299; value of property of, 300; Brigham Young's account of, 302; innocence of, 306, 307, 317; survivors of, 309, 310; heirs of, should be compensated, 311.

Faraones, same as Navahos, 358.

Fauntleroy, Colonel, fight near Poncha Pass, 680, 681.

"Fed Savages" described, 16, 17.

Fernandez de Taos. See Taos.

Fetterman, Lieutenant-colonel, pursues Sioux, 490; commands troops at Fort Phil Kearney massacre, 491; crosses Lodge Trail Ridge, 492; body found, 495; probable suicide of, 496, 499; disobeyed orders, 499.

Fetterman massacre. See Fort Phil Kearney.

Fillmore, President, quoted, 194.

Finley, ——, kills Nez Percé Indian, 636; Indians refuse to prosecute, 639.

Finney, ——, settles on Lapwai reservation, 641.

Fire arrows, use of, in signalling, 226.

Fitzpatrick, Agent, quoted, 219.

Five Crows, Cayuse chief, how named by whites, 99; ravishes Miss Bewley, 113–115.

Flatheads, location of, 83; custom of flattening head discontinued, 83 (note); Stevens's treaty with, 217, 516; treaty ratified, 355; treachery by, 512; torture Blackfeet, 513.

Forney, Dr., gives date of Mountain Meadow massacre, 299; instructed to investigate massacre, 305; first report of, 306; makes new discoveries, 306, 307; returns survivors, 309; Albert's story to, 319.

Forsythe, Lieutenant-colonel, defeats Apaches, 747.

Fort Benton, relations of Indians at, 514; hostilities at, 518; lawlessness at, 522–524.

Fort Bridger, burned by Mormons, 286.

Fort Buchanan, trouble with Chiricahuas near, 380.

Fort Buford, attack on, 504; Sitting Bull's autobiography brought to, 591; Sitting Bull surrenders at, 628.

Fort Canby, operations from, 453, 454; Carson's expedition from, 461; Navahos surrender at, 464; abandoned, 465.

Fort C. F. Smith, located, 487; abandoned and burned, 508.

Fort Craig, action near, 404; operation from, 453.

Fort Defiance established, 258; described, 259; soldier killed at, 261; negro boy Jim killed at, 262, 271; preparations for war at, 263–265; operations from, 265–272, 453.

Fort Fauntleroy, massacre of Navahos at, 448.

Fort Fillmore, taken by rebels, 404.

Fort Klamath, Modocs tried at, 579–581; executed at, 582.

Fort Laramie, treaty with Sioux at, 507.

Fort Larned, treachery of Indians at, 421, 422.

Fort Phil Kearney, location of, 486; orthography of name, 486 (note); description of, 487; country surrounding, 488; depredations near, 489, 490; massacre near, 491–500; misrepresentations concerning massacre, 501, 502; responsibility for massacre, 503, 504; action near, 504, 505; abandoned and burned, 508.

Fort Reno, horses driven off from, 486; General Wessels commands at, 500.

Fort Thorne, massacre of Mescaleros at, 379.

Fort Union, location of, 404; Colorado troops supplied at, 405.

Fort Vancouver, described, 87.

Fort Walla-Walla, described, 87; plundered, 206; fight near, 207; new fort built, 324.

Fort Wingate, Apaches surrender at, 739.

Fort Wise, treaty at, 242; treaty repudiated by Indians, 408, 416.

Fort Yuma, location of, 158; Grinnell at, 180; Olive Oatman arrives at, 184.

Foster, Vice-President, investigates Indian affairs in New Mexico, 470.

Foul Hand, Tookarika chief, mentioned, 276.

Four Lakes, battle at, 343, 344.

Francisco, Yuma Indian, goes to release Olive Oatman, 181; speech to the Mohaves, 182; brings Olive to Fort Yuma, 183; is made a chief, 184; killed, 187.

Fremont, John C., crosses San Juan mountains, 41; aids in conquering California, 47; attacked by Klamaths, 191; trouble with Cheyennes and Arapahoes, 229; description of Salt Lake Basin, 275.

Fresno reservation, established, 137; abandoned, 138.

Fur trade, effect of, on settlement of Rocky Mountains, 31–34.

Gadsden Purchase, what was, 48; caused by Southern influence, 51.

Gall, Sioux chief, flees to British America, 627.

Gallantin, John, villainy of, 362.

Gallatin, Albert, favors separate government for Pacific slope, 47.

Gallaudet, Professor, wonderful use of facial expression by, 223.

Gambler's Gourd. See Washikie.

Ganado Blanco, Navaho chief, leaves Bosque Redondo, 470.

Garcia, Lieutenant - colonel, defeats Apaches, 747.

Garland, General, subdues Jicarillas, 377, 378; protects Mescaleros, 379.

Garnett, Major, campaign against Yakimas, 352, 354.

Garrotéros, probably same as Coyotéros, 358.

Garry, Spokane chief, opinion of Stevens's treaties, 335; sketch of, 338, 341; message to General Clarke, 342; interview with Colonel Wright, 347; treats with Colonel Wright, 351, 352.

Gaston, Lieutenant, killed at Ingossomen Creek, 327; buried at Fort Walla-Walla, 353.

Gay, Lieutenant, ambushed by Mormons and Indians, 313.

Gazzous, Louis, murdered by Sioux, 486.

George, Modoc warrior, taunts Captain Jack, 564.

Geronimo, Apache chief, refuses to be removed, 738; comes to White Mountain reservation, 743; raid of, 750; surrenders, 752; last outbreak of, 753.

Gerry, Elbridge, sent to bring in Cheyennes and Arapahoes, 408.

Giannahtah, Mescalero chief, submission of, 383, 384; quoted, 467.

Gibbon, General, leads detachment against Sioux, 601; communicates with Terry, 604; directions to, 607; reaches scene of Custer massacre, 611; fight with Nez Percés, 652.

Gibbs, George, quoted, 331.

Gibson, Captain, murder of, 233.

Gileños, Apaches, who are, 357; hostilities by, 381; reservation for, 727.

Gillem, General, quoted, 559; warned by Riddle, 566; does not believe Modocs will attempt treachery, 567.

Gilpin, Lieutenant-colonel and Governor, winters among Cheyennes and Arapahoes, 230; expedition against Navahos, 256; recruits troops in Colorado, 404.

Gold, discovered in California, 118–125; effect of, on Indians, 125; discovered in Colorado, 240–242, 675; discovered in Arizona, 385; discovered in Idaho and Montana, 477, 478; believed to exist in Black Hills, 585, 586; discovered in Black Hills, 587–589; search for in Nez Percés country, 636; believed to exist in Elk Mountains, 679.

Goldstein, Carl, killed by Utes, 709.

Good Hearts, same as Arapahoes, 221.

Gordo, Apache chief, leaves Chiricahua reservation, 738.

Gosi-Utes, who are, 277.

Grand Coquin, Bannock chief, mentioned, 276.

Grand Lake, assassination of commissioners at, 694.

Grand Rivers, Utes, who are, 277; included in White Rivers, 681.

Grant, General, orders investigation of Fetterman massacre, 500; influence on, to pardon Modocs, 581; commutes sentence of Barncho and Slolox, 582; cause of feeling towards Custer, 601; refuses to see Custer, 602; permits Custer to accompany his regiment, 603; effect on Custer's action, 623; withdraws Uncompahgré Park from public domain, 685; peace policy of, 716.

Grattan massacre, occasion of, 232; result of, 233.

Gray, W. H., emigrates to Oregon, 37; custodian of funds for Whitman monument, 117 (note).

Great American Desert, extent of, 34.

Great Basin described, 81, 275. See also Utah.

Greenhow, Robert, estimate of the West, 44, 45.

Gregg, General, gives name Apache Yumas to Hualapais, 358.

Gregory, John, discovery of gold by, in Colorado, 241.

Grierson, Colonel, drives Victorio into Mexico, 744.

Grinnell, ——, search for Oatman girls, 180; sends out Francisco, 181; announces return of Olive Oatman, 183.

Gros Ventres of the North, who are, 510; troubles with Blackfeet, 514; location of, in 1853, 515; treat with Stevens, 516; remain peaceful, 517, 518; troubles with Piegans, 521; separated from Blackfoot nation, 522.

Gros Ventres of the South, same as Arapahoes, 221.

Grover, Governor, demands surrender of Modocs, 559, 578; claims Nez Percés have no title to Wallowa valley, 634; puts his theory before Congress, 637.

Grummond, Lieutenant, accompanies Fetterman party, 491; body found, 496.

Guadalupe Hidalgo, treaty of, 47; Mission Indians citizens under, 148; effect of, on Apaches, 365.

Guero, Tabequache chief, mentioned, 689.

Guerrier, Edmond, writes letter for Cheyenne chiefs, 411.

Gunnison, Lieutenant, murder of, 278, 279.

HAIGHT, Mormon bishop, orders Mountain Meadow massacre, 295; elected senator, 315.

Hairy Man. See Poemacheeah.

Hale, C. H., makes treaty with Nez Percés, 633.

Halleck, General, opinion of Apaches, 391.

Haller, Major, campaign against Yakimas, 204.

Hamlin, Jacob, Fancher's train passes house of, 291; survivors of massacre taken to house of, 299; reports to Brigham Young, 300; gives information to Dr. Forney, 306; testimony of, 318; deceit of, 319.

Hamockhaves. See Mohaves.

Hancock, General, expedition of, in 1867, 438; representations of Major Wynkoop concerning, 443; attempt to blame, for attack on Piegans, 533.

Hardie, General, quoted, 524; investigates Piegan troubles, 527; instructions to, 533; opinion of Piegan hostility, 535.

Hardscrabble, Colorado, in 1847, 219, 220.

Hare, Bishop, opinion of Indian laws, 10.

Harney, General, marches against Sioux, 234; defeats them at Ash Hollow, 235; establishes first Indian police, 236; criticism of, 236; summoned before court-martial, 237; promoted and sent to Oregon, 238; Mormon poetry on, 287; action of, admired on frontier, 433; member Board Peace Commissioners, 716.

Harris, E. R., aids in releasing Indian slaves, 371.

Hasbrouck's cavalry, capture Modocs, 576.

Haskell, Lieutenant, induces return of Apache renegades, 743.

Hastings, Agent, report on Sioux in 1876, 598, 619.

Hatch, Capt. John P., expedition against Navahos, 265, 266.

Hatch, General, treats with Utes, 687, 688; demands surrender of hostiles, 714; operations against Apaches, 740.

Hatch, Ira, takes part in Mountain Meadow massacre, 298, 299.

Hawalcoes. See Hualapais.

Hawonjetah, Minneconjou chief, death of, 24.

Hayt, E. A., favors removals, 23; treatment of Nez Percés, 660, 663; misstatements of, exposed, 664–668; enforces removal policy in Arizona, 738.

Hazen, General, inspects Fort Phil Kearney, 487.

Head, Agent, quoted, 371, 372.

Heintzelman, Colonel, sends force to rescue Oatman girls, 179; chastises Yumas, 180.

Helena, Montana, settlement of, 478.

Henderson, J. B., member Board Peace Commissioners, 716.

Herrara, Sergeant, fight at Cañon de Chelly, 461.

Hickland, Hudson's Bay factor, encourages horse-stealing, 523.

Hickman, Bill, cut off from Mormon Church, 316.

Hickorias. See Jicarillas.

Higbee, Major, commands at Mountain Meadow massacre, 295; gives signal for massacre, 297; robs bodies, 299.

High Back Bone, Minneconjou chief, commands at Fetterman massacre, 499.

Higher law of Mormons, 274, 295, 320.

Hines, Surgeon, sent to look for Fetterman party, 492.

Hitchcock, General, quoted, 194, 195.

Hodt, Captain, testimony of, 448.

Hoecken, Father, Joset's letter to, 329.

Hogans, what are, 245; superstitions concerning, 246, 249.

Hokandika. See Cache Valley Indians.

Homily, love of native home, 23.

Honzinger, Dr., killed, 615; murderer detected, 616.

Hooker Jim, Modoc warrior, who was, 553; joins Captain Jack, 554; opposes peace, 561, 563; taunts Captain Jack, 564; in council, 567; action at council, 568; pursues Dyer, 569; betrays Captain Jack, 576; witness at trial, 580.

Hooper, William H., denies guilt of Mormons, 314; buys plundered property, 315.

Hosta, Pueblo chief, accompanies Colonel Washington, 257.

Hot Creek Indians, who were, 546; scattered by settlers, 559.

Hottentot Venus, case of, 14.

Hovey, Eugene, killed by Modocs, 571.

Howard, Agent, report on Sioux in 1876, 598, 617.

Howard, Gen. O. O., commissioner to treat with Joseph, 638; recommends removal, 642, 643; first opinion of case, 645; ordered to effect removal, 646; marches against Nez Percés, 649; fight on the Clearwater, 650; pursues Nez Percés, 651, 652; horses of, run off, 655; quoted, 656; present at surrender, 660; responsibility of, 672, 673; establishes Chiricahua reservation, 727.

Howe, Lieutenant, killed in Lava Beds, 573.

Howe, S. D., makes treaty with Nez Percés, 633.

Howland, Lieutenant, expedition against Navahos, 268.

Hualapais, belong to Yuma nation, 156; go to war, 391; attempted removal to Colorado River, 730; assist troops, 731; starvation of, 743.

Hudson's Bay Company, possession of Astoria by, 33; attempts to prevent emigration to Oregon, 38; post at Wallula, 87; receives Whitman kindly, 87; action and motives of, 88, 89; ransoms American prisoners, 100; responsibility for Wailatpu massacre, 102, 108; claim against United States, 116; incite Yakimas, 202; distrust of, in Oregon, 328, 329; action in Spokane war, 333; encourages slavery, 370, 371; sells whiskey to Indians, 515; buys stolen horses, 522; encourages horse-stealing, 523.

Hugus, W. B., tried for cattle-stealing, 695.
Humboldt Bay, massacre at, 141, 143.
Humme, captain of scouts, killed, 709.
Hungate family murdered by Indians, 412, 413.
Hunt, Governor, treats with Utes, 681.
Hunter state, what is, 1, 2.
Hurt, Agent, flees from Utah, 285, 286.
Hushhushcute, Nez Percés chief, at treaty council, 638; given time to remove cattle, 647.
Hutchins, Charles, treats with Nez Percés, 633.

Idaho, settlement and organization of, 477; feeling against Nez Percés in, 667, 668, 672.
Ignacio, Muache chief, made head-chief of southern Utes, 688; does not recognize Ouray's authority, 689.
Ilges, Major, pursues Nez Percés, 658.
Indian Bureau, should have control of Indians, 18; responsible for Apache troubles, 733, 742, 743.
Indian Commissioners. See Board of Indian Commissioners.
Indian lands purchased by all the colonies, 8; none in Mexican cession, 8, 133, 148, 379; legal status of, 8; right of appropriation, 484, 485; taken without compensation, 541.
Indian police, first established by General Harney, 236; established among Navahos, 472.
Indians, number of, in the United States, 1; legal status of, 8-14; laws governing, 9-11, 14; status of treaties with, 11; citizenship of, 11-13, 148; no provision for naturalizing, 13; frauds on, 15-19, 133-135, 147; transfer to War Department, 18; habits of, 23-25; diversity of, 24, 25; civilization of, 12, 25, 26; schools for, 26; first school for in Oregon, 35; of Rocky Mountains, 81-86; effect of gold discoveries on, 125-127; of California, 127-129, 132, 135, 143; sign language of, 223-227; of Utah, 275-277; relative standing of Apaches, 356; slavery among, 367-373, 447, 725, 754; estimate of, at close of Rebellion, 480, 481; roads through lands of, 484, 485; torture by plains tribes, 489; Bogy's statements, 502; ignorance of suffering of, 538; helplessness of Piegans, 541; neglect of Piegans, 542; expense of subduing Modocs, 578; frontier representations of evil-doing, 694.
Inez Gonzales, capture and release of, 366.
Ingossomen Creek, fight at, 325-328.
Inmuttooyahlatlat. See Joseph.
Iron Dog, Sioux chief, escapes with band, 626; surrenders, 627.
Iturbide, revolution of, in Mexico, 30.

Jack, White River chief, leader of a faction, 690; opposes work at agency, 691; goes to Denver, 696, 697; Meeker appeals to, 698; meets Thornburgh, 699; at Milk Creek, 700.
Jackson, Andrew, advises limitation of United States boundaries, 46.
Jackson, Captain, attacks Modocs, 552, 553; exculpated by Curtis, 581.
Jackson, Helen Hunt, recommends attorneys for mission Indians, 147, 150; reports on mission Indians, 149; death of, 147 (note).
Jamajabs. See Mohaves.
Jane, Ute squaw, assists captives, 711.
Janos, massacre of Apaches at, 359; Mangas Colorado taken to, 382.
Jefferson, Thomas, estimate of Indian population, 4; originates idea of settling Pacific slope, 35, 36; favors separate government for West, 46, 47.
Jeffords, Interpreter, induces return of Apache renegades, 743.

Jemaspie, Hualapais chief, captured, 730.
Jenney, Professor, expedition to Black Hills, 588.
Jerome, D. H., member of Nez Percés commission, 646; responsibility of, 672.
Jesuits, come into Oregon, 89; controversy with Protestants, 90; meet Whitman, 93; responsibility in Whitman massacre, 108-116; suppressed in Spain, 144; establish mission of San Xavier del Bac, 155; distrust of, in Oregon, 328.
Jesus Lopez, murders an Apache, 373.
Jicarillas, Apaches, who are, 357; massacre White's party, 374, 377; part of, take refuge with Utes, 378; drunkenness of, 379; friendliness of, during rebellion, 381; fight near Poncha Pass, 680, 681.
Jim, negro boy, murder of, 262, 271; war on account of, 263-272.
John, Rogue River chief, hostilities by, 206; surrenders, 216.
Johnson, ——, murders Apaches, 361.
Johnson, White River chief, mentioned, 690; civilization of, 697; assaults Meeker, 698; brother of, shot, 704; outrages Mrs. Price, 706; surrender of, demanded, 714.
Johnson, Captain, quoted, 367.
Johnson, Nephi, leads Indians at Mountain Meadows, 293; testimony of, 318.
Johnston, Agent, quoted, 145.
Johnston, Col. A. S., commands expedition to Utah, 287; ordered to use troops as posse comitatus, 312.
Jones, Agent, report on Nez Percés, 664.
Jordan, Agent, report on Nez Percés, 665, 666.
José Rey, Chowchilla chief, mortally wounded, 133.
José Trinfan released from Apaches, 366.
Joseph, Old, Nez Percés chief, speech to Oregon troops, 101; aids Colonel Wright, 343; sketch of, 630, 631; character of, 632; refuses to sell his country, 633, 634; death of, 635.
Joseph, Young, Nez Percés chief, love of native home, 23; character of, 24; name of, 635; sketch of, 636; grief of, 637; meets commission, 638, 639; objects to churches, 640; statement of his case, 642, 645; agrees to leave his country, 646; opposes fighting, 647; takes command of hostiles, 648; defeats Perry, 649; fights Howard, 650; retreats over Lolo trail, 651; defeats Gibbon, 652; runs off Howard's horses, 655; treatment of Cowan's party, 657; fights Sturgis, 657; Miles marches against, 658; surrenders, 659; sent to Indian Territory, 660; quoted, 662; sufferings of band of, 664-666; feeling against in Idaho, 667, 668; Price's statement concerning, 669; band of, returned to Lapwai, 670, 671; statement of Howard's motives, 672.
Joset, Father, meets Steptoe, 325; tries to pacify Indians, 326; accusations against, 328; puts blame on Nez Percés, 329, 330; services of, 331; quoted, 337, 338; goes to Indians as mediator, 341; reports Indians subdued, 348.
Juan José, Mimbreños chief, murder of, 361.
Juan Ortega, attacks Mescaleros, 379.
Juh, Apache chief, band of, 736; flees to Mexico, 738; goes to White Mountain reservation, 743; leaves reservation, 744; leaves renegades, 752.

Kaetena, Apache chief, offence and punishment of, 752.
Kalispels. See Pend d'Oreilles.

Kamiakin, Yakima chief, repudiates treaty with Stevens, 202; leads in Cascade massacre, 212; causes discontent among Spokanes, 338; flees across the mountains, 353.

Kanarrah, Pi-ede chief, at Mountain Meadow massacre, 293.

Kane, Colonel, negotiates with Mormons, 315.

Kaniache, Southern Ute chief, mentioned, 689; struck by lightning, 714.

Kanosh, Pah Vant chief, not implicated in Mountain Meadow massacre, 306, 307.

Katihotes, Yakima chief, camp of, surprised, 352.

Kautz, Colonel, opposes removals, 734; intercedes for Indians, 736.

Kaws, in Union army, 425.

Kayatana, Navaho chief, expedition against, 267, 268.

Kearny, Gen. S. W., sent to occupy New Mexico and California, 47; conquest of New Mexico, 49, 52; establishes provisional government, 52; terrifies Cheyennes and Arapahoes, 229; assumes protection of Mexicans, 256; meets Mimbreños, 365; orthography of name, 486 (note).

Kearny, Maj. Philip, defeats Rogue Rivers, 191; turns prisoners over to General Lane, 192; orthography of name, 486 (note).

Kelly, Hall J., efforts to colonize Oregon, 34, 35.

Kena. See Bloods.

Kendrick, Major, dealings with Navahos. 261.

Kennon, Dr. Louis, statement concerning Indian slavery, 447.

Kensler Toussaint, discovers gold in Black Hills, 587.

Kikatsa, same as Mountain Crows, 479.

Kings River farm, established, 137; Indians driven from, 138.

Kiowas, location of, 81; supposed to have originated sign language, 225.

Kirkham, Captain, quoted, 331.

Klamaths, divisions of, 190; sign for insanity, 224; slavery among, 371; treaty of 1864 with, 544; harass the Modocs, 545, 546; accused of lawlessness, 549, 559, 580; witness execution of Modocs, 582.

Klickitats, location of, 86; title to Wallamet valley, 195; conquests by, 201; power of, 202; Stevens's treaty with, 217; treaty ratified, 355; slavery among, 371.

Klingensmith, Philip, at Mountain Meadow massacre, 299; reports to Brigham Young, 300; testifies, 317.

Knapp, Agent, selects location for Modocs, 546.

Knight, Samuel, at Mountain Meadow massacre, 297; testimony of, 318.

Koolsatikara, who are, 275.

Kootenais, Stevens's treaty with, 217, 516; treaty ratified, 355; harass the Gros Ventres of the north, 510.

Krentpoos. See Captain Jack.

La Cañada, fight at, 70.

La Lakes, who are, 545.

Lamanites, what are, 278.

Lame Deer, Minneconjou chief, killed, 627.

Lane, Gen. Joe, first governor of Oregon, 189; marches against Rogue Rivers, 199; treats with them, 200.

Langford, ——, settles on Lapwai reservation, 641.

Lapwai Mission established, 38; location of, 87.

"Laramie Loafers," who were. 484.

Larkin, T. O., announces discovery of gold in California. 121.

Larrabee, Agent, attack on, 731.

Lava Beds, described, 554; Modocs retire to, 555; troops advance into, 556; Hot Creek Indians go to, 559; Modocs offer to take for reservation, 563; fight of April 14th in, 571; fight of April 26th, 572-574; Modocs leave, 576.

Lawson, Captain, at Milk Creek, 701.

Lawyer, Nez Percés chief, Milkapsi's charge against, 330; friendship of, 331; assurances to, 333; Indian name of, 335; aids Colonel Wright, 343; asks ratification of Stevens's treaties, 354; made head-chief by Stevens, 631.

Lawyer, James, Nez Percés preacher, welcomes exiles, 671.

Leadville, mining excitement of. 675-679.

Leal, J. W., murdered by Pueblos, 65; buried at Santa Fé, 78.

Le Conte, Dr., meets Oatman family, 161; robbed by Tontos, 162.

Lee, Gen. Elliott, escapes from Taos, 65.

Lee, John D., leads Indians at Mountain Meadows, 293; betrays emigrants, 295, 296; takes part in massacre, 297; ravishes and murders girl, 298; charges Government for stolen property, 299; reports to Brigham Young, 300; quoted, 302, 312; honored by Young, 315; captured, 316; tried, 316-319; confessions of, 319; executed, 320.

Lee, Stephen, murdered by Pueblos, 62.

Left Hand, Arapahoe chief, band of, at Sand Creek, 408; not connected with Little Raven, 416; joins Black Kettle, 419; mortally wounded, 417.

Leland, Judge, opinion as to feeling against Nez Percés, 667.

Lennon, Cyrus, killed by Apaches, 389.

Leschi, Nasqualla chief, eloquence of, 203; attacks settlements. 207.

Lewis and Clarke, expedition of, 32; sent out by Jefferson, 36; treatment of, by Nez Percés, 629.

Lindsay, Captain, expedition against Navahos, 267; bold charge of, 268.

Lindsley, Rev. A. L., recommends Nez Percés commission, 637; investigates feeling in Idaho, 667.

Lipans, who are, 358.

Little Arkansas, treaty with Cheyennes at, 437.

Little Bear, Sioux chief, on invasion of Black Hills, 590.

Little Big Horn, Custer's fight on, 607-615; number of Indians at, 617, 618; number of Indians not suspected, 619, 620, 623, 624.

Little Dog. Piegan chief, killed, 521.

Little Eagle, Piegan warrior, accused of murdering James Quail, 527.

Little Raven, Arapahoe chief, hostility of, 416; surrenders to Wynkoop, 418; sent away from Fort Lyon, 419; confused with Black Kettle's band, 430.

Little Thunder, Sioux chief, head-chief of Brulés, 233; defeated at Ash Hollow, 235.

Little Wolf, Cheyenne chief, opinion of Black Hills, 589.

Llaneros, same as Lipans, 358.

Lolo trail, Nez Percés retreat to, 650; described, 651.

Lolocksalt. See Slolox.

Lone Horn, Sioux chief, on invasion of Black Hills, 590.

Long Beard, Snake chief, band of, 277.

Long Sioux, who were, 591.

Looking Glass, Nez Percés chief, band of, 638; troops sent to arrest, 649; talks to soldiers, 651; killed. 652.

Lookout Station, massacre at, 438.

Lorey, Agent, reports Cheyennes discontented, 408; goes to make treaty, 444.

Lost Cabin, probable origin of story of, 587; reputed location of, 658.

Lost River, Modocs wish reservation on, 550, 551; fight at, 552, 553; objections to reservation on, 561.

Louderback, ——, testimony of, 434.

Loughridge, Representative, quoted, 239; erroneous statement concerning Sand Creek, 434, 437.

MACKENZIE, COLONEL, defeats Dull Knife, 626.

Magoffin, James, services in conquest of New Mexico, 49, 50.

Mahaos, belong to Yuma nation, 156.

Mahto Iowa, Sioux chief, connection with Grattan massacre, 232; meaning of name, 232 (note); death of, 233.

Mahtotopa, character of, 24.

Man-Afraid-of-his-Horses, Ogallalla chief, opposes treaty of 1866, 482; withdraws from council, 483; makes treaty, 504; chief of Sioux police, son of. 589.

Mandans, location of, 81; supposed remnant of Madoc's Welsh colony, 81.

Mangas Colorado, Mimbreños chief, meets Kearny, 365; cause of hostility, 374; activity of, 381; killed, 382.

Manuelita, Navaho chief, made head-chief, 261; attack on, 268; cattle of, shot, 269; chief of Navaho police, 472.

Mariano Martinez, Navaho chief, makes treaty, 257; treaty repudiated, 258.

Maricopas, location of, 152; join the Pimas, 155; attacked by Yumas, 184; defeat them, 187; aid United States against Apaches, 385, 386, 389.

Mariposa battalion, services of, 133.

Marsh, Professor, charges against Red Cloud agency, 16.

Martin, Captain, defeats Apaches, 381.

Martin, Mrs., captured by Cheyennes, 412; surrendered, 429.

Martin, trumpeter, quoted, 620.

Mason, General, put in command in Arizona, 391.

Mason, Harry, whips Nez Percés Indians, 636; killed, 648.

Mattole Valley farm, established, 137; abandoned, 138; Indians murdered at, 141.

McBeth, Miss, labors of, among Nez Percés, 670.

McCleave, Captain, defeats Apaches, 383.

McComas family, massacre of, 750.

McCormick, Representative from Arizona, classifies Indians, 25.

McCulloch, Benjamin, treats with Mormons, 315.

McDougal, Captain, with Custer's expedition, 608; message to, 609.

McDougal, Governor, estimate of California Indians, 129, 130, 132.

McDowell, General, commands Department of California, 391.

McDuffie, Senator, opinion of plains, 34; opposes occupation of Oregon, 46.

McGregor, Captain, captures Hualapais, 730.

McIntyre, C. H., on Uncompahgré Park invasion, 686.

McKay, Donald, leads Warm Spring Indians, 571; accompanies Captain Thomas, 572; separated from troops, 573.

McMurdy, ——, aids in Mountain Meadow massacre, 297.

McNeil, Inspector, reports on Nez Percés, 664.

Meacham, A. B., induces Captain Jack to return to reservation, 546; urges separate reservation for Modocs, 551; on Modoc Commission, 559; opposes last council, 565; proposes deception in case of treachery, 566; goes to council, 567; speech at council, 568; shot, 569; saved by Toby, 570; testifies, 580.

Medicine Cow, Sioux Chief, opinion of Dr. Burleigh, 15.

Medicine-men, murdered when unsuccessful in treatment, 105–108, 546.

Medina, Governor, objects to massacre of Apaches at Janos, 359.

Meeker, Josie, opinion as to time of plot, 703; takes refuge in milk-house, 704; captured, 705; treatment of, 706; Persune infatuated with, 712; death of, 713; statement of treatment, 714.

Meeker, Mrs., opinion as to time of plot, 703; takes refuge in milk-house, 704; wounded, 705; taken by Douglas, 706; treatment of Jane, 711; statement of treatment, 714.

Meeker, N. C., character of, 690; management of Utes, 691; complains of Utes, 696; Indians distrust, 697, 703; assaulted by Johnson, 698; applies for protection, 699; correspondence with Thornburgh, 700, 702, 703; massacre at agency, 704, 705; mutilation of, 710.

Mendocino reservation, character of, 136; cost of, 137.

Meriwether, Governor, treats with Navahos, 261; dismisses Jicarillas, 377.

Merritt, Colonel, defeats Cheyennes, 625; arrives at Milk Creek, 706; advances to White River, 709; captives reach camp of, 713.

Mescaleros, Apaches, who are, 357; defeated by California troops, 378; assailed by Mexicans, 379; go to war, 381; conquered by Carleton, 383; sent to Bosque Redondo, 384; leave same, 392, 466; quarrel with Navahos, 465; Victorio settles with, 739; renegades join Victorio, 740.

Mesquite, described, 175, 176.

Messila Guard, attacks Mescaleros, 378; punished by troops, 379.

Methodist missions, first in Oregon, 37; sold to American Board, 87; none among Piegans, 536.

Mexican Boundary Commission, bury remains of Oatmans, 188; release Apache slaves, 366, 367; troubles with Mimbreños, 373, 374.

Mexican Cession, Indian titles in, extinguished, 8, 379; extent of, 27; Indians of, made citizens, 144.

Mexicans, character of, 53, 61; lead in Pueblo insurrection, 77, 78; wars with Apaches, 358–365; slavery among, 368–373; attack Mescaleros, 378, 379; supposed disloyalty of, 404; invade our reservations, 737.

Miguel, Coyotéro chief, peaceful, 719; assists troops, 731.

Miles, Col. D. S., commands in Navaho country, 262; arrives at Fort Defiance, 263; expeditions of, 265, 267, 268; explores Cañon de Chelly, 458.

Miles, Gen. N. A., defeats Sitting Bull, 626; defeats Crazy Horse, 627; marches against Nez Percés, 658; defeats them, 659; promises them return to Idaho, 660; Indians claim fulfilment of promise, 669.

Milk Creek, fight at, 700, 701, 706–709.

Milkapsi, Cœur d'Alène chief, begins attack on Steptoe, 326; message to General Clarke, 330, 331; blamed by the Indians, 338; quoted, 342; humiliated, 352.

Miller, J. W., conduct of, in survey of Ute lands, 685.

Mills, Captain, defeats American Horse, 625.

Miltimore's train, attack on, 313.

Mimbreños, Apaches, who are, 357; treachery to, 361; meet Kearny, 365; meet Bartlett, 366; release of slaves of, 366, 367; troubles with Bartlett's party, 373, 374; hostilities by, 374, 381; refuse to be removed, 390, 391; failure of extermination policy against, 395; attempted removal to Tularosa, 726, 727; attempted removal to Arizona, 738–740; official opinions of treatment of, 741, 742; raids of, 744–747.

" Mina maska," defined, 510.

Minneconjous, Sioux, who are, 231; in Grattan massacre, 232; treaty of 1866 with, 481; in Fetterman massacre, 499; numbers and loss of, at massacre, 500; location in 1876, 591; at war, 618; defeated by Miles, 627; make peace, 628.

Minnetarees, location of, 81.

Mission Indians, converted by Franciscans, 143; citizens of Mexico, 144; stupidity of, 145; no provision for, 146; homes taken from, 147; denied all rights, 148; no title to lands, 149; attorneys employed for, 150.

Mitchell, W. C., loss of relatives at Mountain Meadows, 305; meets surviving children, 309.

Mockpeahlutah. See Red Cloud.

Modocs, location of, 190; meaning of name, 191; hostilities by, 192; massacre at Bloody Point, 193; attack emigrants, 200; defeated by Captain Walker, 201; slavery among, 371; character of, 543; treaty of 1864 with, 544; annoyed by Klamaths, 545; leave reservation, 546; conduct of, 549; desire separate reservation, 550; misrepresented by Odeneal, 551; attacked by Captain Jackson, 552; murder settlers, 553; go to Lava Beds, 554; troops sent against, 555; fight of January 17th, 556; conduct of whites towards, 559; commission sent to, 560; afraid to surrender, 561; causes of fear, 562, 563; Captain Jack becomes hostile, 564; preparations for last council, 565–567; the council, 568; murder of commissioners, 569–570; advance of troops, 571; battle of April 26th, 572, 573; General Davis takes command, 574; fight at dry lake, 575; leave Lava Beds, 576; capture of, 577; cost of war, 578; trial of, 580, 581; execution, 582; subsequent history, 583.

Mofras, Duflot de, estimates population California, 131.

Mogollons, Apaches, who are, 357; location of, 358; mixed with Chiricahuas, 736.

Mohaves, belong to Yuma nation, 156; names of, 157; character of, 174; tattoo Oatman girls, 175; famine among, 176; war with Cocopahs, 177; crucify Cocopah woman, 178; surrender of Olive Oatman, 181–183; attack Maricopas, 184; present condition of, 187.

Mohuaches, or Muaches, Utes, who are, 277; included in Southern Utes, 681.

Moketaveto. See Black Kettle.

Moleles, location of, 86; treaty with, ratified, 355.

Monos. See Pah Utes.

Montana, gold discovered in, 477; settlement of, 478; need of road to, 479; right to make road, 484, 485, 507; road abandoned, 508; organized, 518; lawlessness in, 521–524; state of war in, 534, 535.

Moore, Julius, killed by Utes, 709.

Mopeah, Snake chief, band of, 277.

Moquetas, Pah Ute chief, at Mountain Meadow massacre, 293.

Moquis, Pueblos, location of, 53; name of, 54; consolidation of agency of, 475.

Mora, fight at, 66.

Morgan brothers, charged with cattle-stealing, 695.

Mormons, send battalion to Mexican war, 49; winter at Pueblo, 51, 219; at Salt Lake, 81; claim to discovery of gold, 118–121; incite Oregon Indians, 203, 331; furnish arms to Navahos, 266, 267; treatment of, in the East, 273; higher law of, 274, 295, 320; treatment of Indians, 277–281; disloyalty of, 281, 282; doctrine of polygamy, 283; reformation of, 283, 284; blood atonement, 284, 285, 290, 298, 313; lawlessness of, 286; resist United States authorities, 287–289; treatment of Fancher's train, 282–291; attack train, 292; murder Aden, 294; treachery of, 295, 296; Mountain Meadow massacre, 297–299; divide property of emigrants, 299, 300; guilt of, 300–303; guilt exposed, 306; claim for ransoming children, 307; survivors recovered, 309, 310; slander of survivors, 311, 314; concealment of criminals, 312; crimes of, 313; terrors of, 314; receive Governor Cummings, 315; change in position of, 316; abandon Lee, 317; convict him, 318, 319; American hatred of, 320–323; sell arms to Nez Percés, 332; law concerning Indian slavery, 369, 370; pleased with the rebellion, 404; encourage Ute war, 710, 711.

Morrow, Major, pursues Apaches, 740.

Mountain Chief, Piegan chief, assaulted, 522; retaliates, 524; expedition against, 528; escapes, 529, 535.

Mountain Crows, who are, 479.

Mountain House, illicit traffic at, 523.

Mountain Meadows, description of, 291; massacre at, 295–300; date of massacre, 299; appearance after massacre, 302, 307, 308; monument erected at, 309; survivors of massacre recovered, 309, 310; heirs of victims should be compensated, 311; becomes barren, 314; trial of Lee, 316–319; results on American people, 320, 323; Lee executed at, 319.

Mountain-sheep Eaters, who are, 276.

Mowry, Lieutenant, goes in search of Oatman girls, 179.

Muckalucks, who are, 545.

Mullan, Lieutenant, opinion of Stevens's treaties, 334; urges their ratification, 354.

Mungen, Representative, criticises attack on Piegans, 532.

Nachez, Chiricahua chief, leaves reservation, 744; returns, 752.

Naked Horse. See Caballo en Pelo.

Nané, Apache chief, raid of, 744.

Nantiatish, Apache chief, revolt of, 747.

Napea, a Blackfoot divinity, 511.

Naqui naquis, Tonto chief, surrenders, 730.

Narbona, Navaho chief, killed, 257.

Nasquallas, location of, 82.

Natatotel, Tonto chief, surrenders, 730.

National Association to Promote Universal Peace, intercedes for Modocs, 581.

Navahos, location of, 82, 244; names of, 244; country of, 245; customs of, 246; industries of, 249; women of, 250–253; religion of, 253, 254; government of, 254; source of hostilities with, 255; Doniphan's expedition against, 256; Washington's expedition, 257; Sumner's expedition, 258; treaty of 1855, 261; murder of negro Jim, 262; fight at Bear Spring, 263; duplicity of, 264; Colonel Miles's expedition, 265; Hatch's expedition, 266; aided by Mormons, 267; operations against, 268; treaty of 1858, 271; name of. 358; slavery of, 447; attack on Fort Fauntleroy, 448;

Canby's campaign against, 451; Carleton's plan for, 452; operations against, 453, 454; Carson marches against, 461–463; removed to Bosque Redondo, 464; expense of subsistence there, 466; prefer their old country, 467; sufferings of, 468–471; returned to old home, 471; advance of, 472–475; present condition of, 475, 476.

Na-watk. *See* Left Hand.

Nesmith, Superintendent, opinion of Stevens's treaties, 333; changes his opinion, 354, 355.

Nevada, part of Arizona ceded to, 158.

Newby, Colonel, expedition against Navahos, 256.

New Mexico, conquest of, 49; people of, in 1846, 52, 53; Arizona set off from, 158; description of northwest part, 244, 245; losses in, by Indians, 255, 256; Apache warfare in, 356; slavery in, 368, 369, 373; put in Department of Missouri, 391; Texan invasion of, 381, 382, 402–407; troubles with Mimbreños, 738–743.

Nez Percé Joseph. *See* Joseph, Young.

Nez Percés, superiority of, 25; deputation visit St. Louis, 36; meet missionaries, 37; offer to protect Spalding, 100; protect Stevens, 203; sign for, 225; not Pueblos, 245; aid Steptoe's command, 328; blamed by Joset, 329; innocence of, 330; Mormons sell arms to, 331, 332; want Stevens's treaty ratified, 335; aid Colonel Wright, 343, 347; treaty ratified, 355; making of treaty, 516; friendliness of, 629; tribal organization of, 630, 631; country of Lower, 632; treaty of 1863, 633; Lower do not sell country, 634, 635; growth of trouble with, 636, 637; effort to induce removal, 638–642; removal ordered, 645, 646; prepare to resist, 647; kill settlers, 648; defeat Perry, 649; fight Howard, 650; retreat to Montana, 651; defeat Gibbon, 652; run off Howard's horses, 655; treatment of women captives, 656; fight Sturgis, 657; Miles marches against, 658; surrender, 659; sent to Indian Territory, 660; Hayt's statement, 663; sufferings of, 664–666; feeling against in Idaho, 667, 668; Price's statement, 669; part return, 670; remainder return, 670; responsibility for, 672, 673; compared with other wrongs, 674.

"Noble red man" not wholly a myth, 24.

Nobows. *See* Sans Arcs.

Nockay-Delklinne, Apache Medicine-man, killed, 744.

Nolgee, Apache chief, flees to Mexico, 738.

Nome Cult reservation, established, 135; whites settle on, 136; massacre at, 138.

Nome Lackee reservation, established, 135; cost of, 137; abandoned, 138.

Norton, A. B., reports on Navahos, 470.

Oatman Flat, description of, 162, 163; Oatman family buried in, 188.

Oatman, Lorenzo, statement of, 161; attacked by Tontos, 165; escape of, 166–171; efforts to release his sisters, 179, 180; subsequent history of, 184.

Oatman, Mary, taken by Tontos, 166; fright of, 171; treatment of, 173; sold to Mohaves, 174; tattooed, 175; becomes helpless, 176; dies, 177.

Oatman, Olive, determines not to be captured, 163; taken by Tontos, 166; carried away, 171; assailed, 172; enslaved, 173; sold to Mohaves, 174; tattooed, 175; labor of, 176; terrors of, 177, 178; Mohaves try to prevent release of, 181; released, 183; subsequent history of, 184.

Oatman Royse, sketch of, 158; starts West, 159; forebodings of, 163; meets Tontos, 164; killed, 165.

Odeneal, F. B., succeeds Meacham, 551; advises placing Modocs on reservation, 552; blamed by Colonel Wheaton, 554.

Ogallallas, Sioux, who are, 231; police of, 227; in Grattan massacre, 232; treaty of 1866 with, 481; opposition to treaty, 482; efforts to conciliate, 483; in Fetterman massacre, 500; location in 1876, 591; at war, 618; make peace, 628.

Ogden, P. S., ransoms prisoners, 100; quoted, 105.

Ohhastee. *See* Little Raven.

Ojo Blanco, Mescalero chief, leaves Bosque Redondo, 392.

Ojo del Oso. *See* Bear Spring.

Okkowish. *See* Modocs.

Old Snag, Snake chief, band of, 276.

Ollacut, Nez Percé warrior, a brother of Joseph, 636; not in first hostilities, 648; killed, 659.

Oncpapas, Sioux, who are, 231; treaty of 1866 with, 481; at war, 500; location in 1876, 591; at war, 618; make peace, 628.

One Eye, Cheyenne chief, killed at Sand Creek, 417.

Oohenonpa. *See* Two Kettles.

Ord, General, policy to Apaches, 717, 718; results of, 719.

Oregon, first visitors to, 32, 33; Kelly's efforts to colonize, 34, 35; efforts of Benton and Floyd, 36; the Nez Percé messengers, 36–42; first Indian school in, 35; first missionaries, 37; early emigrants, 38; English colonization frustrated by Whitman, 38–42; Ashburton treaty, 41; boundary settled, 41–43; Greenhow's estimate of, 45; differing views of, 46, 47; Indians of, 83, 84; action of Hudson's Bay Company, 88, 89; Cayuse war, 100; Indians of, kill medicine-men, 105–108; organized as a territory, 189; Indians of southern part of, 190, 191; Indian titles in, 194; aggressions by settlers, 195, 196; behavior of Indians, 196; conduct of volunteers, 205–207, 211; removal of Governor Palmer, 208; General Harney sent to, 238; the Stevens treaties, 333, 336; slavery in, 370, 372; pay of militia of, in Modoc war, 578.

Ortiz, Lieutenant, conduct at Fort Fauntleroy, 448.

Ortiz, Tomas, leads conspiracy in New Mexico, 61.

Osages, in Confederate army, 424; in Union army, 425.

Otis, Colonel, defeats Sitting Bull, 625.

Otis, Major, investigates charges against Modocs, 549.

Otoahnacco. *See* Bull Bear.

Ott, Larry, kills Nez Percé Indian, 636.

Ouray, Ute chief, meaning of name, 683; on encroachments of whites, 684; on sale of Uncompahgré Park, 688; under pay from government, 689; stops hostilities, 706; orders surrender of women, 711; death of, 714.

Owahi, or Owhi, Yakima chief, repudiates treaty with Stevens, 202; causes discontent among Spokanes, 338; comes to Colonel Wright's camp, 352; put in irons, 353.

Owen, Agent, quoted, 342.

Pachico, Bannock chief, band of, 276.

Pageah, Snake chief, band of, 277.

Pahsappa. *See* Black Hills.

Pah-Utes, who are, 277; in Mountain Meadow

massacre, 293, 295, 298; took no captives there, 307; captured for slaves, 369; Mormon effort to relieve, 370.

Pah Vants, said to be poisoned by Fancher's train, 290; deny they were poisoned, 306; not at Mountain Meadow massacre, 307; poison story disproved, 317.

Pal, Piegan warrior, shoots Mr. Clarke, 527.

Pala reservation, Indian title to, 147; taken by settlers, 149.

Palmer, Governor, controversy with Oregon Legislature, 208.

Palmer, Sergeant, testimony as to Sand Creek, 434, 437.

Papagos, location of, 152, 153; reservation for, 187; aid United States against Apaches, 385, 386; neglect of, 743.

Paramucka, Apache chief, killed, 389.

Parkman, Francis, quoted, 27, 585, 586.

Pawnee Killer, Sioux chief, commands hostiles, 438.

Pawnees, in Union army, 425; Cheyennes go to attack, 439, 440.

Payne, Captain, at Milk Creek, 701; explanation of pictures, 712.

Peace Policy, definition of, 19; not successful as practised, 25; neglect of Navahos under, 475, 476; tried on Modocs, 556; effect on Nez Percés, 674; defects of, 716, 717, 743.

Pease, Lieutenant, reports on Piegan surprise, 530; misrepresented, 531, 532.

Pedro, Apache chief, refuses to remove, 736.

Pelouses, location of, 86; Stevens's treaty with, 217; Steptoe marches against, 324; attack on Steptoe, 325–327; bands of, 338; fight Colonel Wright, 344; property of, destroyed, 347; punishment of, 353; treaty with, ratified, 355.

Penaltishn, Apache warrior, guides General Crook, 750.

Pend d'Oreilles, location of, 83; Stevens's treaty with, 217, 516; probable origin of name, 351, 352; treaty ratified, 355.

Penn, Captain, warns Whitman of attack, 721.

Penn, William, not only purchaser of Indian lands, 8; quoted, 250.

Peonage, what is, 368.

Perry's cavalry, capture Modocs, 577.

Perry, Colonel, sent against Nez Percés, 648; defeated, 649.

Persune, Yampa warrior, captures Josie Meeker, 705; takes her for wife, 706; infatuation of, 712; Utes amused at, 713; surrender of, demanded, 714.

Petalesharro, Pawnee chief, character of, 24.

Peter, Piegan warrior, kills Mr. Clarke, 527.

"Pet Lambs," sobriquet of Colorado troops, 407.

Pfeiffer, Captain, sent through Cañon de Chelly, 461; results of expedition, 462.

Phillips, Wendell, on Indians, 23; letter to Sherman mentioned, 717.

Piah, White River chief, mentioned, 690.

Pi-Edes, Utes, at Mountain Meadow massacre, 293; sacrificed, 372.

Piegans, starvation of, 17, 538; origin of, 509; now include Blackfoot nation, 510; religion of, 511; reputation of, 512; location in 1853, 515; treat with Stevens, 516; remain peaceful, 517; rise of troubles with, 520; depredations by, 521; bad treatment of, 522; encouraged by Hudson's Bay Company, 523; conduct of whites, 524; increase of depredations, 527; Baker sent against, 528; result of expedition, 529; Indian account of fight, 530; probable truth, 531; criticism of fight, 532; result of criticism, 533; officers defend ac-

tion, 534; opinions of officers, 535; neglect of, 536; sufferings of, 537; right to aid, 541; helplessness of, 542; reported depredations by, 542 (note). See also Blackfeet and Bloods.

Pigeon's ranche. See Apache Cañon.

Pihonsenay, Apache warrior, kills Rogers and Spence, 737; wounded, 738.

Pike, Lieut. Z., expedition to Red River, 29; opinion of American desert, 34.

Pike's Peak mining excitement, 241.

Pimas, location of, 152; joined by Maricopas, 155; Oatmans at village of, 160; relieve Lorenzo Oatman, 168; defeat Yumas, 187; aid United States against Apaches, 385, 386, 389.

Pinal treaty, described, 389.

Pinaleños. See Arivapas.

Pinaquana. See Washikee.

Pindah Lickoyee, Apache name for white men, 392 (note).

Pino Alto mines, settlement at, 374; attack on, 381; Fort West established near, 384.

Piopiomoxmox, Walla-Walla chief, conduct of, 206; killed, 207.

Pitkin, Governor, Jack appeals to, 697; Meeker appeals to, 698.

Pitone, Apache chief, refuses to remove, 736.

Pitt River Indians, hostilities by, 192; slavery among, 371.

Pi-Utes same as Pah-Utes, 277.

Plumbe, John, efforts for Pacific railroad, 44.

Pocatara. See White Plume.

Poemacheeah, Bannock chief, band of, 276.

Polakly Illeha, Leschi's description of, 203.

Polk, J. K., advises occupation of Oregon, 42; accepts compromise line, 43; causes occupation of New Mexico and California, 47.

Pollock, Inspector, quoted, 714.

Polotkin, Spokane chief, message to General Clarke, 341, 342; held as prisoner, 347; treats with Colonel Wright, 351, 352.

Polygamy, Mormon doctrine of, 283, 284.

Poncas, release of, 13; removal of, 21.

Poncha Pass, fight near, 680, 681; meaning of name, 680 (note).

Pony Express, how conducted, 238.

Pope, General, commands Department of Missouri, 391; memorial to, 694; statement as to Apache war, 741, 742.

Population, Indian, in United States, 1–3; in Virginia, 4; in Kentucky, 5; in Texas and Mexican cession, 6; present increase of, 6, 7; in California, 130, 133.

Poston, C. D., buries remains of Oatman family, 188.

Pottawattamies, in Confederate army, 424.

Powder River country described, 480; Indians oppose road through, 481, 482; troops sent to, 483; right to road, 484, 485; forts built in, 486–488; hostilities by Indians, 489, 490; Fetterman massacre, 491–500; no prospectors in, 502; our claim to, surrendered, 507; abandoned, 508; Sioux title confirmed, 584, 585; Sioux refuse to sell, 589; Sioux ordered out of, 596; Sioux title released, 628.

Powell, L. W., treats with Mormons, 315.

Powell, Major, attacked by Sioux, 504; defeats them, 507.

Pratt, Captain, reforms Modocs, 583.

Price, Commissioner, recommends return of Nez Percés, 669.

Price, Gen. S., commands in New Mexico, 51; marches against Pueblos, 70; conquers them, 74–77.

Price, Mrs., at White River agency, 704; statement of, 705; treatment of, 706.

Price, Shaduck, killed by Utes, 704.

Princess Mary. *See* Queen Mary.
Prophecy of war by Joseph Smith, 281, 282.
Pueblo, Colorado, Mormons winter at, 51; settlement at, 81; in 1847, 219.
Pueblo de Taos described, 73; battle at. 74–77.
Pueblos, invasion of lands of, 11, 12; described, 53–61; origin unknown, 54; houses of, 58; join conspiracy, 61; begin insurrection, 62; massacre at Fernandez de Taos, 62–66; massacre at Arroyo Hondo, 66–69; Price marches against, 70; fight at Pueblo de Taos, 74–77; beg for mercy, 77; subsequent good behavior, 78; religious troubles. 79; object to taxation, 79 (*note*); Navahos not descended from, 245; of Zuñi assist troops, 268.
QUAIL, JAMES, murder of, 527.
Qualchian. Yakima warrior, excites discontent among Spokanes, 338; hanged, 353.
Quapaws, in Confederate army, 424.
Queen Mary, Modoc squaw, carries message for Captain Jack, 562; captured, 577.
Quelaptip, Pelouse chief, band of, 338.
Quinaielts, treaty with, ratified, 355.
Quitaniwa. *See* Foul Hand.

RAILROAD, first, to Mississippi River, 43; early proposals for Pacific, 44; proposals for Southern Pacific, 51; Cheyennes object to Kansas Pacific, 243, 408; effect of Pacific, on West, 585; effect in Leadville excitement, 676, 677.
Rain-in-the-Face, Sioux warrior, said to have killed Custer, 615; cause of hatred of Custer, 616.
Rains, Lieutenant, killed, 649.
Rains, Major, campaign against Yakimas, 204.
Randall, Captain, attack on, 649; captures Tontos, 730.
Ravalli, Father, builds Cœur d'Alêne church, 348.
Rawlins Springs, massacre at, 595.
Rawn, Captain, tries to stop Nez Percés, 651.
Red Cloud, Ogallalla chief, sketch of, 481; opposes treaty of 1866, 482; goes to war, 483; Sioux gather to, 484; attacks Fort Phil Kearney, 490, 491; not in Fetterman massacre, 500; attacks Major Powell, 504; defeated, 507; makes treaty, 507, 508; willing to sell Black Hills, 588; deposed, 626.
Red Cloud agency, fraud at, 16.
Red Horn, Piegan chief, becomes hostile, 524; camp of, attacked, 528; killed, 529.
Red Sleeves. *See* Mangas Colorado.
Reed, Autie, killed at Little Big Horn, 612.
Removal and Concentration Policy, cause of Indian wars, 19–22; unreasonable, 22, 23, 25; Spokanes object to, 335, 336, 355; Apaches object to. 390, 391; failure of, in Arizona, 395; tried with Navahos, 452, 464; evils of, 464–466; opposed by Dr. Steck, 467, 468; failure of, 468–471; tried with Modocs. 545, 546, 551, 552; Modocs object to, 568; no reason for, 642; tried on Nez Percés, 646; they go to war, 647, 648; sent to Indian Territory, 660; returned to Idaho, 670, 671; failure with Mimbreños, 726, 727; inaugurated in Arizona,733,734; failure with White Mountain Apaches, 735, 736; tried on Chiricahuas, 736–738; tried on Mimbreños, 738–740; official statements of results, 741, 742; effects of, 743.
Reno, Major, scouts on Rosebud River, 604; report of, 603, 609; tries to reach Custer, 609; besieged, 610; estimate of number of hostiles, 618; number of hostiles, 620; in action at same time as Custer, 621; not in fault, 624.

Reservations, food at, 17; of California, 135, 138, 147, 149; need of better title in Indians, 142, 150; lessened without compensation, 538, 541.
Reuben, James, Nez Percé preacher, works among exiles, 670.
Reynolds, Charley, detects Rain-in-the-Face, 616.
Reynolds, Colonel, fight with Sioux, 597; criticism of fight, 598.
Rickarees, location of, 81.
Riddle, Interpreter, warns Modoc commissioners, 565; warns Gillem, 566; goes to council, 567; pursued, 569; escapes, 570; testifies. 580.
Ridgely, ——, statement concerning Custer massacre, 621.
Riley, Lieutenant, killed at Little Big Horn, 612.
River Crows, who are, 479; Gros Ventres of the North consolidated with, 522.
Rocky Mountain Fur Company, organized, 33.
Rogers. ——, killed by Apaches, 737.
Rogue River Indians, description of, 190; hostilities by, 191; make peace, 192; kill Capt. Ben Wright, 193, 211; go to war, 196, 199; treat with General Lane, 200; massacre of, 205; fight at Big Bend, 216; go to Grande Ronde reservation, 216; treaty with, 218; slavery among, 371.
Roper, Miss, captured by Cheyennes, 412; treatment of, 429.
Roseborough. Judge, legal adviser of Modocs, 549; member of Modoc Commission, 560.
Ross, John, commands Oregon volunteers with Ben Wright. 193; commands militia in Modoc war, 562.
Ross, Representative, investigates Indian affairs in New Mexico, 470.
Russell, Green, discovers gold in Colorado, 240.
Russell, W. H., intercedes for General Harney, 237; power of, 238.

SAFFORD, GOVERNOR, on Indian affairs of Arizona in 1875, 732.
Sahaptins, location and divisions of. 86.
Sah-patch, White River chief, mentioned, 690.
Sakitapix, same as Blackfoot nation, 509.
Saline River, outrages on, 439, 440.
Salmon River. discovery of mines on, 477; settlers on. killed, 647, 648.
Sanborn, J. B., member Board Peace Commissioners, 716.
Sand Creek, attack on Cheyennes and Arapahoes at, 396–401; troops at, 403; Indians at, 408; hostilities leading to, 408–411; Indians admit hostility, 411–416; proofs of hostility, 416; Indians not promised protection, 417–421; attack justified, 422; desire of officers to punish Indians, 423; feelings of loyal people, 424, 425; why women and children were killed, 426–429; Congressional report on, 430–433; misrepresentations of, 433–437; used against Chivington politically, 443; Chivington's account of, 444, 445; compared with other massacres, 446.
Sandoval, Navaho chief, accompanies Colonel Washington, 257; efforts at neutrality, 263; privileged in treaty of 1858, 271.
San Francisco, full name of, 52 (*note*).
San Juan country, mining excitement in, 682, 683.
San Pasqual reservation, title to, 147; taken by settlers, 149.
Sanpitches, who are, 277.
Sans Arcs, Sioux. who are, 231; treaty of 1866 with, 481; at war, 500; location in 1876, 591; at war, 618; make peace, 628.

Santa Anna, treatment of Texans, 27, 28.
Santa Fé, trade to, 29–31; full name of, 52 (note); excitement at, during Pueblo insurrection, 70.
Santa Rita del Cobré, home of Mimbreños, 357; massacre at, 361; Kearny meets Apaches near, 365; Bartlett's party at, 366; hostilities at, 373,374.
Santees, Sioux, who are, 231.
San Xavier del Bac, cathedral of, built, 155; despoiled, 743.
Sapavanari, Uncompahgré chief, accompanies surveying party, 685; quoted, 688; meaning of name, 689 (note); accompanies Brady, 703.
Sarap, White River chief, mentioned, 690.
Sarcillo Largo, Navaho chief, resigns office, 261; summoned to Fort Defiance, 262; reports arrest of murderer, 263, 264; attacked and defeated, 266.
Saskatchewan, meaning of, 509.
Satsika. See Blackfeet.
Saulotken. See Polotkin.
Saverro Aredia released from ·Apaches, 366.
Scalp-bounty, given by Mexican States, 360; results of, 361, 362; causes murder of our Indians, 362, 363.
Scar-faced Charlie, Modoc warrior, refuses to surrender, 553; favors war, 563; who was, 564; stands·guard over Steele, 565; shoots Lieutenant Sherwood, 570; surrenders, 577; testifies, 580.
Schonchin John, Modoc warrior, favors war, 563; at council, 567; speech at council, 568; assaults Meacham, 569; surrenders, 577; arraigned, 579; tried, 580; sentenced, 581; executed, 582.
Schonchin, Modoc chief, authority of, contested by Captain Jack, 545.
Schoolcraft, H. R., estimate of land needed to support Indians, 2; estimate of population of California, 131.
Schurz, Secretary, gives time to settlers in Uncompahgré Park, 687.
Scott, Agent, report on Nez Percés, 670.
Scott, General, supports General Wool, 211; quarrels with General Harney, 236–238.
Seattle attacked by Indians, 207.
Selish. See Flatheads.
Semig, Dr., wounded in Lava Beds, 573, 574.
Seminoles, in Confederate army, 424.
Senecas, in Confederate army, 424.
Shacknasty Jim, Modoc warrior, at council, 567; pursues Riddle, 569; betrays Captain Jack, 576; testifies, 580.
Shampoag, treaty at, 202.
Shanks, General, Joseph's argument to, 640; quoted, 647.
Shastas, include Rogue Rivers, 190; divisions of, 191; troubles with, 200; slavery among, 371.
Shavano, Tabequache chief, mentioned, 689; son of, killed, 715.
Shawawai, Yakima chief, excites discontent among Spokanes, 338.
Shawnees, in Confederate army, 424.
Shepherd's train, attack on, 313.
Sheridan, Gen. P. H., commands at Cascades, 212; in Yakima country, 217; orders to Colonel Baker, 533; quoted, 534.
Sherman, General, tests first gold in California, 121; commands Division of the Mississippi, 391; orders Cheyennes to their reservation, 440; advises extermination of Sioux, 446; treats with Navahos, 471; stops sale of arms and ammunition, 501, 502; quoted, 530; justifies Colonel Baker, 534; statement concerning Custer massacre, 617; opinion of Lolo trail, 651; report of Nez Percé war, 660; member Board Peace Commissioners, 716; Phillips's letter to, 717.
Sherwood, Lieutenant, assassination of, 570.
Shirland, Captain, captures Mangas Colorado, 382.
Shis Inday, same as Apaches, 357.
Shooters, who were, 591.
Shoshokos, who are, 276.
Shoshonees, or Snakes, location and divisions of, 83; murder emigrants, 200; sign for, 225; bands of, 275–277; aided by Mormons, 331; attack Nez Percés, 332.
Shumahiccie, Cayuse warrior, enamoured of a white girl, 99, 100.
Sibley, General, invades New Mexico, 381, 382, 403–407.
Sicangu. See Brulés.
Sign language, universality of, 223; theories of, 224; tribal designations in, 225; for long distances, 226; mirrors used in, 227.
Sihasapa. See Blackfoot Sioux.
Sinta Gallessca. See Spotted Tail.
Sioux, location of, 81; war with Cheyennes, 221; sign for, 225; soldiers or police of, 227; tribal divisions of, 231; massacre Grattan's party, 232; go to war, 233; General Harney defeats, 234, 235; submission of, 236; rise of hostilities of 1864, 424, 425; hostilities of 1867, 438; acquire Powder River country, 479; treaty of 1866 with, 481; disagreement as to treaty, 482; repudiate treaty, 483; go to war, 484; depredations of, 486, 487; torture by, 489; harass Fort Phil Kearney, 490; Fetterman massacre, 491–500; misrepresentations of massacre, 501, 502; continue hostilities, 504; defeated by Major Powell, 507; burn forts, 508; rights of, under treaty of 1868, 584, 585; object to invasion of Black Hills, 589, 590; divisions of, in 1876, 591; depredations by, 593, 594; ordered to leave Powder River country, 596; Reynolds's fight with, 596–598; expedition against, 598–601; Crook's fight with, 603, 604; Custer massacre, 605–624; operations against, 625–627; treaty of 1876, 628.
Sitting Bull, Sioux chief, sketch of, 591; autobiography of, 592, 593; refuses to leave Powder River country, 596; expedition against, 598–601; Custer massacre, 605–624; operations against, 625, 626; goes to British America, 627; returns, 628.
Skinarwan, Yakima chief, assists troops, 352.
Skitsuish. See Cœur d'Alênes.
Skloom, Yakima chief, excites discontent among Spokanes, 338.
Slavery, women slaves of their husbands, 250; among Apaches, 367; among Mexicans, 368; Diggers enslaved, 369; Mormon law concerning, 370; in Oregon, 371; in Colorado, 372; evil effects of, 373; in New Mexico, 447; Camp Grant captives sold into, 725.
Slolox, Modoc warrior, aids at massacre of commissioners, 569; arraigned, 580; convicted, 581; sentence commuted, 582.
Slough, Colonel, leads Colorado volunteers, 404; joins Canby, 405.
Smellers, same as Arapahoes, 225.
Smith, E. P., opposes removal policy, 20.
Smith, George A., Mormon apostle, connection with Mountain Meadow massacre, 294; deposition at Lee's trial, 318.
Smith, Jack, murdered at Sand Creek, 398; attacks stage-coach, 432.
Smith, Joseph, Mormon prophet, murder of, 273; war prophecy of, 281, 282; deceit of,

283; responsibility for death of, put on Fancher train, 290.

Smith, J. Q., favors removals, 20.

Smith, J. S., at Sand Creek, 397; son of, killed, 398; testimony as to Dog Soldiers, 431; aids in treaty, 437.

Smith, Lot, destroys United States trains, 289.

Smith, Gen. P. E., quoted, 239.

Smohallie. religion of, 640.

Snake Creek, fight at, 658, 659.

Snakes. See Shoshonees.

Snyder, Mrs., suicide of, 429.

Soie, Pelouse chief, band of, 338.

Solomon's Fork, action on, 239, 240.

Sonora, policy towards Apaches, 359; pays scalp-bounty, 360, 362; results of scalp-bounty, 361; slaves sold into, 369, 726.

Southern Snakes. See Cache Valley Indians.

Southern Utes, who are, 681; mistreatment of, 682; cede San Juan country, 683; lands of, surveyed out, 685; make cession, 687; chiefs of, 688, 689; established in Colorado, 715.

Spalding, Rev. H. H., goes to Oregon as missionary, 37; located at Lapwai, 87; controversy with Jesuits, 90; escape of, 99, 110; quoted, 102; with Nez Percés, 116.

Spencer, Cascade chief, murder of family of, 212.

Spokanes, friendly before 1858, 324; menace Steptoe, 325; attack him, 326; pursue him, 327; causes of hostility uncertain, 328–333; probable cause, Stevens's treaties, 333–338; who are, 338, 339; refuse to surrender offenders, 341, 342; Colonel Wright marches against, 342, 343; defeated at Four Lakes, 344; property of, destroyed, 347; treaty with, 351, 352.

Spotted Tail, Brulé chief, murder of, 10; surrenders as a hostage, 236; sketch of, 482; Indians desert, 484; willing to sell Black Hills, 588; made head-chief, 626.

Squaws. See Women.

Stanley, J. M., quoted, 371.

Stanley, J. Q. A., intercedes for Mission Indians, 148, 149.

Stanwood, Captain, ratifies Lieutenant Whitman's actions, 721.

Steamboat Frank, Modoc warrior, aids in massacre of commissioners, 569; betrays Captain Jack, 576; witness at trial, 5s0; becomes preacher. 583.

Steck, Dr. Matthew, treats with Mescaleros, 378; opposes Bosque Redondo reservation, 467; Carleton complains of, 468; succeeded by Felipe Delgado. 470.

Steele, Judge, legal adviser of Modocs. 549; acts as messenger to them, 564; saved by Captain Jack, 565.

Steptoe, Colonel, captures Gunnison murderers, 279; expedition to Fort Colville, 324; menaced by Indians, 325; attacked. 326; fight on Ingossomen Creek, 327; retreats, 328; quoted, 333; recovery of guns abandoned by, 353.

Stevens. Gen. I. I., first governor of Washington Territory, 196; treaties of, repudiated, 202; protected by Nez Percés, 203; controversy with General Wool, 208; quoted, 215; treaties of, 217, 218; trouble over treaties, 333–336; treaties favored. 354; treaties ratified, 355; among Blackfeet, 514; makes treaties, 516; appoints head-chief of Nez Percés, 631.

Stickney, William, member Nez Percé commission. 646; responsibility of, 672.

Stockton, Commodore, aids in conquest of California, 47.

Stokes, William, arrests John D. Lee, 316.

Strong Hearts, a Sioux fraternity, 592.

Sturgis, General, attacks Nez Percés, 657; Nez Percés escape, 658.

St. Vrain. Felix, leads volunteers against Pueblos, 70; position at Pueblo de Taos, 74; services at same, 77.

Sully, General, Blackfeet offer to aid, 518; quoted, 523, 524; misrepresented by Colyer, 531, 532; opinion of Piegan hostility, 534, 535.

Sumner, Col. E. V., quoted, 236, 237, 240; sent against Cheyennes and Arapahoes, 239; defeats them, 240.

Sun dance, what is, 616 (note).

Sunflower-seed Eaters, who are, 276.

Sun River farm, provision for, 516; a humbug, 517; abandoned, 518; buildings at, burned, 521.

Susan, Ute squaw, assists captives, 711.

Sutter, John A., connection of, with gold discovery in California, 118–121.

Sweet Root. See Pachico.

Tabby, Uintah chief, mentioned, 690.

Tabequaches, Utes, who are, 271; location of, 681; arable lands of, 683; chiefs of, 689; removed to Utah, 715.

Table Rock, treaty at, 200.

Tahza, Chiricahua chief, band of, 736; consents to remove, 738.

Talsi-Gobbeth, Pi-ede chief, at Mountain Meadow massacre, 293.

Tamatabs. See Mohaves.

Tamsuky, Cayuse warrior, murders Dr. Whitman, 94; betrays the fugitives, 96; convicted and hanged, 101, 102.

Taos, settlers at, 52; massacre at, 62–66.

Tappan, Colonel, presides over Sand Creek commission, 417; treats with Navahos, 471; member Board Peace Commissioners, 716.

Taracones, same as Navahos. 358.

Tashunkah-Kokepah. See Man-Afraid-of-his-Horses.

Tatankahyotankah. See Sitting Bull.

Tatkannais, who were, 591.

Tawaitu, Cayuse chief, confers with Jesuits, 93.

Taylor, Captain, killed, 327; buried at Fort Walla-Walla, 353.

Taylor, Commissioner, conduct at Sioux treaty of 1866, 483.

Taylor, John, Mormon President, veracity of, 283; quoted, 287.

Taylor, N. G., treats with Utes, 681; member Board Peace Commissioners, 716.

Tejon reservation, character of, 136; cost of, 137; abandoned, 138.

Teller, H. M., intercedes for settlers in Uncompahgré Park, 686, 687; Meeker's letter to, 690.

Ten Eyck, Captain, sent to reinforce Fetterman, 492; finds bodies of command, 495; brings them in. 496.

Terribio, Navaho chief, captured, 268.

Terry, General, Sitting Bull's message to, 596; connection with Custer-Grant quarrel, 601; intercedes for Custer, 603; reaches Powder River, 604; instructions to Custer, 607; reaches scene of massacre, 611; mistake as to number of Sioux, 617, 618, 623; member Board Peace Commissioners, 716.

Tetons, Sioux, who are, 231; location of, 232; possible derivation of name, 516; location in 1876, 591; at war, 618; make peace. 628.

Texan invasion of New Mexico, history of, 381, 382, 403–407.

Texas, American settlement of, 27; annexation question, 28, 29; reputed value of, 44, 47.

Theller, Lieutenant, cut off at White Bird Cañon, 649.

Thomas, Captain, enters Lava Beds, 572; killed, 573.

Thomas, Rev. E., appointed on Modoc commission, 560; opinion as to last council, 565; refuses to deceive Indians, 566; goes to council, 567; speech at council. 568; killed, 569; body recovered, 570; indignation at murder of, 571; statement of son of, 582, 583.

Thompson, Arthur, killed by Utes, 704.

Thornburgh, Maj. T. T., investigates conduct of Utes, 692; advances to White River, 699; fight at Milk Creek, 700; killed, 701; picture on body of, 712.

Thunder Hawk, Sioux warrior, murder of, 10.

Tierra Blanco, Ute chief, attacks settlements, 680; defeated, 681.

Tilcoax, Pelouse chief, band of, 338; hostilities of, 347, 348.

Tilokaikt, Cayuse chief, meaning of name, 86; in council with Jesuits, 93; mangles Dr. Whitman's body, 96; convicted and hanged, 101, 102.

Timothy, Nez Percé chief, aids Steptoe, 328; aids Wright, 343.

Timpanagas, who are, 277.

Tinnéh. See Athabascans.

Tinney, Mormon bishop, incites California Indians, 281.

Tiswin, what is, 753.

Tlickitacks. See Klickitats.

Toby Riddle, Modoc squaw, warned of treachery, 565; goes to council, 567; assaulted by Slolox, 569; saves Meacham, 570; testifies, 580.

Tomas, Pueblo chief, brutal treatment of Governor Bent, 65; shot, 78.

Tontos, Apaches, location and description of, 157, 358; rob Doctor Le Conte, 162; meet Oatman family, 164; murder them, 165, 166; carry off Oatman girls, 171, 172; treatment of captives, 173; sell girls to Mohaves, 174; subsequent history of, 187; enslaved, 369; located at Camp Verde, 730; hostiles punished, 732; removal of, 733, 734.

Toohulhulsute, Nez Percé chief, at treaty council, 638; removal from council, 646; resentment of, 647; killed, 659.

Tookarikas, who are, 275, 276.

Travis, Wes, in Ute agency cattle robbery, 695.

Triggs, Lieutenant, takes Mrs. Ewbank's deposition, 427.

Tubac, deserted, 381; reoccupied, 392.

Tucson, antiquity of, 159; effect of Apache war on, 381; recovers its population, 392, 395.

Tularosa Valley reservation, established, 726; abandoned, 727.

Tulé River, farm established, 137.

Tumwater, Oregon, settled, 190.

Tupper, Major, defeats Apaches, 747.

Turley, Simeon, character of, 67; defence of mill, 68; killed, 69.

Two Face, Sioux warrior, treatment of Mrs. Ewbanks, 428; refuses to sell her to Cheyennes, 429.

Two Kettles, Sioux, who are, 231; treaty of 1866 with, 481; at war, 500; location in 1876, 591; at war, 618; make peace. 628.

Tyler, President, favors annexation of Texas, 29.

Uintahs, Utes, location of. 690.

Umatillas. Stevens's treaty with, 217; treaty ratified, 355; removal of, recommended, 645.

Umpquas related to Athabascans, 82; hostilities by, 191; slavery among, 371.

Uncommute, Uncompahgré chief, mentioned, 689.

Uncompaghré Park, title to, in Utes, 683; reserved by treaty, 684; cut off by surveyor, 685; settled, 686; settlers remain, 687; sold by Utes, 688.

Uncompahgrés, Utes, location of. 681; arable land of, 683; chiefs of, 689; among hostiles, 705, 712; influence of peaceful portion, 714; removed to Utah, 715.

Unkpahpahs. See Oncpapas.

Upsaroka. See Crows.

Upson, Agent, treats with Blackfeet, 518.

Uré. See Ouray.

Utah. Ashley in Salt Lake Basin, 33; Harney relieved from command of expedition, 237, 238; secretary of, killed, 239; Fremont's description, 275; Indians of, 275-277; Indian troubles in, 278-281; reformation in, 283, 284; lawlessness in, 285, 286; expedition to, 287; martial law proclaimed in. 288; Fancher's train in, 289-292; Mountain Meadow massacre, 292-300; investigation of massacre, 305-310, 312-315; duty of Gentiles, 311; trial of John D. Lee, 316-319; execution of Lee, 320; situation in, 322, 323; slavery in, 369, 370.

Utes, relations to Colorado settlers, 241, 242; divisions of, 277; Jicarillas take refuge with, 378; assist United States, 465; removal of, desired in Colorado, 675-6.80; fight near Poncha Pass, 680, 681; treaty of 1868 with, 681; objections to treaty, 682; treaty of 1872, 683; treaty not kept by United States, 684, 685; Uncompahgré Park trouble, 686-688; organization of, 689, 690; Meeker's troubles, 690, 691; charges against, 692-694; bad white neighbors, 695; refuse to surrender offenders, 696; troubles increase, 697; Meeker assaulted, 698; Thornburgh marches against, 699; fight at Milk Creek, 700, 701; conduct at the agency, 702, 703; attack on agency, 704, 705; close of hostilities, 706-710; surrender of captives, 711-713; the pictures, 712; councils with, 714; removal of, 715.

Vallé, Alexandre, quoted, 407.

Valverde, fight at. 404.

Van Buren, Martin, opposes annexation of Texas, 29; defeated, 47.

Van Vliet, Captain, sent to Salt Lake City, 287; returns to army, 288.

Victor, Pend d'Oreille chief, attacked by Milkapsi, 326.

Victorio, Mimbreños chief, refuses to be removed, 739; raids of, 740; official opinions of his case, 741, 742; killed. 744.

Vincent, Cœur d'Alène chief. talks with Steptoe. 326; recalls messengers, 328; statement to Joset, 329; charge of insult to, 330; quoted, 337; band of, 341.

Virginia City, Montana, settlement of. 478.

Voorhees, Representative, criticises attack on Piegans, 532; quoted, 535, 542.

Waba Yuma, Hualapais chief, murdered, 391.

Wagoner massacre, described. 206.

Wailatpu Mission established, 38; meaning of name, 86; described, 86, 87; massacre at, 93-100; Fort Waters established at, 101; present appearance of, 102.

Wailatpus, location and divisions of, 86.

Walker, Capt. Jesse, defeats Modocs, 200, 201.

Walker, Capt. J. G., quoted, 267.

Walker, Major, expedition against Navahos, 256.

Walker, Ute chief, sacrifices at burial of, 372.
Wallammutekint Indians, who were, 630.
Walla-Walla. *See* Fort Walla-Walla.
Walla-Wallas, location of. 86; Stevens's treaty with, 217; treaty ratified, 355; removal of, recommended, 645.
Wallowa Valley described, 632; Nez Percés retain title to, 633–635; proposed for reservation, 637; wishes of Nez Percés for, 639, 640; Nez Percés ordered from, 646.
Walnut Creek, massacre at, 412, 444, 445.
War Bonnet, Arapahoe chief, in attack on General Blunt, 416.
War Department, should have inspection of agencies, 18.
Warm Springs Indians, aid against Modocs, 571; accompany Captain Thomas. 572; separated from troops, 573; scout in Lava Beds, 574; follow Modocs, 577.
Warner, Dr., testimony of, 467.
Warrarikas, who are, 276.
Warren, Lieutenant, attempts to enter Black Hills, 585.
Washikee, Snake chief, sketch of, 275.
Washington, Col. J. M., expedition against Navahos, 257; treaty of, not ratified, 258.
Washington Territory organized, 189; first settlement in, 190; discovery of Colville mines, 204; rise of Spokane war, 324–328; causes of war, 328–337, Indians of eastern part of. 338, 341; Wright's campaign, 341–354; Garnett's campaign, 352; ratification of treaties, 355; discovery of Salmon River mines, 477.
Watkins, Inspector, reports on Sioux, 596.
Webster, Daniel, negotiates Ashburton treaty, 41; opposes annexation of Texas, 46, 47.
Weeminuches, included in Southern Utes, 681.
Weir, Captain, attempts to reach Custer, 609.
Weir, Lieutenant, killed by Utes, 709.
Wells, D. H., commands Mormon forces. 289.
Wells, Fargo & Co., horses stolen from, 523.
Wessels, General, succeeds Carrington, 500; attempts campaign. 504.
Wheat Cañon. *See* Cañon del Trigo.
Wheaton, Colonel, instructions to, 552; blames Odeneal, 554; proceeds against Modocs, 555; asks reinforcements, 556.
Whipple, Captain, describes Wallowa Valley, 632; statement as to Old Joseph, 634; tells Nez Percés they must move, 634.
White Antelope, Cheyenne chief, in council, 412; quoted, 415. 416, 420, 421.
White Bird, Nez Percé chief, band of, 638; joins hostiles, 648; escape of, 659, 660.
White Bird Cañon, fight at, 648, 649.
White Cattle. *See* Ganado Blanco.
White Eagles, who were. 591.
White, Elijah, appoints head-chief of Nez Percés, 631.
White Eyes, Apache name for Americans, 392.
White family, murdered by Jicarillas, 374–377.
White Knives. *See* Shoshokos.
White Plume, Snake chief, band of, 276; quoted, 280.
White River agency, location of, 691; massacre at, 703–706; appearance after massacre, 709, 710.
White Rivers, Utes, who were, 681; chiefs of, 690; Meeker's troubles with, 691, 697, 698; behavior of, 692–694; white neighbors of. 695; refuse to surrender offenders, 696; troops sent against, 699; attack troops. 700, 701; destroy agency, 703–705; suspend hostilities, 706; removed to Utah, 715.
White Thunder, Sioux chief. murder of. 10.
White Wolf, Arapahoe warrior, warns whites, 425.

Whiteman, Agent, reports on Nez Percés, 665.
Whiting, Agent, reports on Nez Percés, 665.
Whiting, Superintendent, recommends reservations for Mission Indians, 147; quoted, 149.
Whitman, Dr. M., goes to Oregon, 37; takes first wagon, 38; rides to the States, 38, 39; secures emigration, 41, 42; mission at Waiilatpu, 86, 87; controversy with Jesuits. 93; murder of, 94; accused of poisoning Indians, 113; proposed monument to, 117 (*note*).
Whitman, Lieutenant, receives Apaches at Camp Grant, 719; reports to head-quarters, 720; action of, approved, 721; account of massacre, 722, 723; charges against, unfounded, 724.
Whitman, Silas, Nez Percé preacher, welcomes exiles, 671.
Whittaker, Captain, criticism of Reno and Benteen, 624.
Wilbur, Father, recommends removal of Nez Percés, 640.
Wilkes, Captain, estimate of population of California, 131.
Willcox, General, opinion of Victorio's treatment, 741.
William, or Whim, Modoc warrior, warns Toby, 565; testifies, 580.
Wilson, B. D., reports on Mission Indians, 146.
Winnebago reservation, lesson of, 150.
Winthrop, Congressman, opposes occupation of Oregon. 46.
Wohlpape Snakes, placed on Klamath reservation, 544.
Women, Indian, fight at Ash Hollow, 236; treatment of, 250; among Navahos, 253, 254, 262; treatment by Mexicans. 368–370; generally. 372, 373; fight at Sand Creek, 398; behavior of, 426; fight at the Washita, 440; difference in, 465; torture by, 513; killed in attack on Piegans, 530, 531; criticism in Congress, 532; statements of officers, 534; treatment at Camp Grant, 721–723.
Women, white, treatment by Apaches. 367: by Mexicans, 368–370; generally, 372, 373; treatment by plains Indians, 427, 428; by Nez Percés, 656; by Utes, 706, 711, 713.
Wood, Lieutenant-colonel, opposes forcible removal of Nez Percés, 646, 672.
Wool, General, controversy with Stevens, 208; supported by General Scott, 211.
Woolsey. King S., massacres Apaches, 389.
Wright, Capt. Benjamin, defeats Modocs, 192; massacres Modocs, 193; killed, 211; effect of massacre in Modoc war, 561, 562, 564; should have been punished, 582.
Wright, Colonel, marches against Indians. 211; fight at Cascades, 212; treats with Indians, 216; sent against Spokanes and others. 342; battle at Four Lakes, 343, 344; destroys Indian supplies, 347; treats with Cœur d'Alènes, 351; treats with Spokanes, 352; punishes Pelouses, 353; results of campaign, 354.
Wright, Lieutenant, killed in Lava Beds, 573.
Wyeth, N. J., expedition of, 33; quoted, 45; fight with Blackfeet, 512.
Wynkoop, Major, estimate of killed at Sand Creek, 401; sent to Cheyennes and Arapahoes, 412; concedes Little Raven hostile, 416, 418; investigates Sand Creek, 417; subsists Little Raven's Arapahoes, 418; no authority to treat, 421; statement as to Governor Evans, 422; as to Dog Soldiers, 431; Cheyennes did not surrender to, 432; at treaty of 1865, 437; reports of, 439.

XICARILLAS. *See* Jicarillas.

INDEX.

YAHOOSKIN SNAKES, treaty with, 544.
Yainax agency, established, 545; Modocs leave, 546.
Yakimas, location of, 86; discontent of, 202; go to war, 204; massacre by, at Cascades, 212; Colonel Wright marches against, 215; Stevens's treaty with, 217; attack Steptoe, 325; malcontents of, 338; campaign against, 352; renegades from, hung, 353; treaty ratified, 355.
Yampais, location of, 157; placed at Camp Verde, 727; hostiles brought in, 730; scheme to remove, 733; removal of, 734.
Yampas, Utes, included in White Rivers, 681.
Yanktonnais, Sioux, who are, 231; location of, 232.
Yanktons, Sioux, who are, 231; location of, 232; intimidated by hostiles, 424, 425.
Yates, Captain, killed at Little Big Horn, 612.
Yavapais. See Yampais.
Yellow Livers, who were, 591.
Yellow Serpent. See Piopiomoxmox.

Yomas, Apache warrior, saves life of Agent Larrabee, 731.
Yosemites, reputation of, 133; hostilities of, 134; beg for peace, 135.
Young, Brigham, Indian policy of, 280, 281; said to have introduced polygamy, 283; preaches blood-atonement, 285; resists United States troops, 286, 287; proclaims martial law, 288, 289; connection with Mountain Meadow massacre, 300, 301; report of, 302; accused of moving monument, 309; conceals criminals, 312; abandons Lee, 318, 319; dies, 320; visit to Oregon, 331.
Young, Ewing, brought to Oregon by Kelly, 35; estate escheats, 35; brings cattle to Oregon, 88.
Yumas, division and location of, 156; take Camp Yuma, 179; subdued, 180; massacre Gallantin's party, 362.

ZABRISKIE, JUDGE ADVOCATE, takes Mrs. Ewbanks's deposition, 427.

THE END.